W9-ALN-925

Glencoe Communication Applications

Virginia Hunter Myers
June Hubbell Smith
Marcia Myers Swanson

Maridell Fisher Fryar
Major Consultant

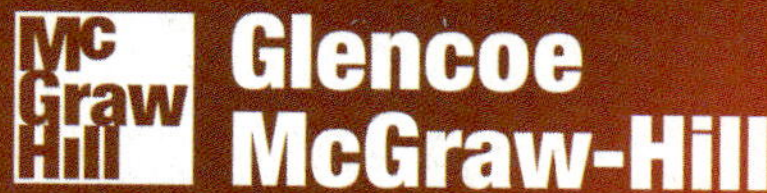

New York, New York   Columbus, Ohio   Woodland Hills, California   Peoria, Illinois

Authors

Virginia Hunter Myers is an Associate Professor and Coordinator of Speech in the Division of Communication Arts at Wayland Baptist University in Plainview, Texas. Mrs. Myers has had a distinguished career teaching English, Speech, and Theatre in secondary and postsecondary schools in Texas. She has served as president of the Texas Speech Communication Association and vice president of the Texas Forensic Association. She has served on a variety of committees and task forces for state and national speech associations. She has authored two previous textbooks and presented numerous papers, programs, and seminars for professional communication associations as well as other organizations.

June Hubbell Smith is an Associate Professor of Communication at Angelo State University. Dr. Smith's research includes small group communication issues, communication methods, and organizational communication. She has presented at state and national communication conventions, is published in communication journals, and has served in various offices in the Texas Speech Communication Association.

Marcia Myers Swanson is an adjunct faculty member in the Career Education Division at Bryant and Stratton College in Virginia Beach, Virginia. Mrs. Swanson has taught professional communication courses at the secondary and postsecondary level in New York, Maryland, and Virginia. She has also served as a communication consultant for various corporations.

Major Consultant

Maridell Fisher Fryar taught speech communication and English and coached debate and competitive speech in both California and Texas at the middle, secondary, and postsecondary levels. She retired in 1993 from the Midland Independent School District, where she served as the Executive Director of Instruction, K–12. Ms. Fryar has served as president of the Texas Speech Communication Association, the West Texas Forensic Association, and the American Forensic Association. She has authored six textbooks, presented numerous workshops, and served in advisory capacities to the Texas Education Agency.

The Standardized Test Practice pages in this book were written by The Princeton Review, the nation's leader in test preparation. Through its association with McGraw-Hill, The Princeton Review offers the best way to help students excel on standardized assessments.

Glencoe/McGraw-Hill

A Division of The ***McGraw·Hill*** *Companies*

Send all inquiries to:

Glencoe/McGraw-Hill, 8787 Orion Place, Columbus, Ohio 43240

Printed in the United States of America.

ISBN 0-02-817244-2

9 10 071 10 09 08

Business Advisory Board

John Breed
Director of Media and Government Relations
Cooper Industries, Inc.
Texas Business and Education Coalition
Houston, Texas

Bob Digneo
Division Manager
Southwestern Bell
Texas Business and Education Coalition
Austin, Texas

Vickie M. Hall
Senior Manager of Business Travel
American Express
Houston, Texas

Dan McCormack
Education Technology Consultant
Apple Computer, Inc.
Austin, Texas

Hillary Pennington
President
Jobs for the Future
Boston, Massachusetts

Susan L. Traiman
Director of Education Initiative
The Business Roundtable
Washington, D.C.

Andrea M. Watros
Vice President
Bank One Corporation
Chicago, Illinois

Program Contributors and Reviewers

Ronald B. Adler
Instructor
Santa Barbara City College
Santa Barbara, California

R. Scott Allen
Director of Speech and Theatre
Humble High School
Humble, Texas ISD

James P. Barnes
Communication Instructor
Irvin High School
El Paso, Texas ISD

Mary Bozik, Ph.D.
Professor of Communication Studies
University of Northern Iowa
Cedar Falls, Iowa

Linda Brown
Instructor
University of Texas at El Paso
El Paso, Texas

Paul Bryne
Speech Teacher
Humble High School
Humble, Texas ISD

Barbara L. Clinton, Ph.D.
Chair, Department of Speech
Highline Community College
Des Moines, Washington

Aleisha Force
Speech Teacher
Humble High School
Humble, Texas ISD

Darin L. Garard, Ph.D.
Instructor
Santa Barbara City College
Santa Barbara, California

Georgene Gallagher
Educational Consultant
Morton Grove, Illinois

Kathryn S. Harr
Educational Consultant
Pickerington, Ohio

Stephanie Herman
English Teacher
Pickerington Local School District
Pickerington, Ohio

Shona Huffman
Speech Teacher
Colleyville Heritage High School
Grapevine-Colleyville, Texas ISD

Richard Jeffery
Speech Teacher/Drama Sponsor
Canutillo High School
Canutillo, Texas

Sandra Jowers
Assistant Principal for Instruction
Pelion High School
Pelion, South Carolina

Kathleen Kain
Educational Consultant
Houston, Texas

Margaret Kendrick
Speech Teacher/Debate Coach
Sharpstown High School
Houston, Texas ISD

Carolyn Kiesewetter
Speech and Debate Instructor
Fossil Ridge High School
Keller, Texas ISD

James May
Educational Consultant
Communities Creating Connections
Kooskia, Idaho

Shawn Mena
Instructor
University of Texas at El Paso
El Paso, Texas

Lisa Morefield
English Teacher
Southwestern City Schools
Grove City, Ohio

Sherwyn P. Morreale, Ph.D.
Associate Director
National Communication Association
Washington, D.C.

Joe Old
Instructor
El Paso Community College
El Paso, Texas

Claire Paccione
Assistant Principal-English
Richmond Hill High School
Queens, New York

Carolyn D. Perry
K–12 Project Assistant
National Communication Association
Washington, D.C.

Jana Riggins
Assistant Academic Director
University Interscholastic League
University of Texas at Austin

Susan Seld
Instructor
El Paso Community College
El Paso, Texas

James Russell Smith Jr.
Education Consultant
North Carolina Department of Public Instruction
Raleigh, North Carolina

Susan Kauth Sharkey
Business Instructor
Ripon High School
Ripon, Wisconsin

David Watros
English Teacher
Pickerington Local School District
Pickerington, Ohio

Denise Wardlow
PAR Consultant
Columbus City Schools
Columbus, Ohio

Table of Contents

CHAPTER 4
Discovering the Power of Oral Language

CHAPTER 8
Developing Effective Interpersonal Skills

CHAPTER 9
Exploring the Interview Process

UNIT 3 Group Communication

CHAPTER 10
Understanding the Nature of Groups

CHAPTER 11
Making Groups Work

CHAPTER 15
Organizing Presentations

CHAPTER 16
Supporting Presentations

CHAPTER 17
Preparing for Presentations

CHAPTER 18

Making and Evaluating Group Presentations

Appendix

Features

Communication Self-Assessments

Critical Thinking Skills

Applying Reading Skills

Technology Skills

Communication Through Writing

Communication Practice Labs

Practice for the Workplace

Internet Activities

Technology Activities

Global Communication

UNIT 1

The Communication Process

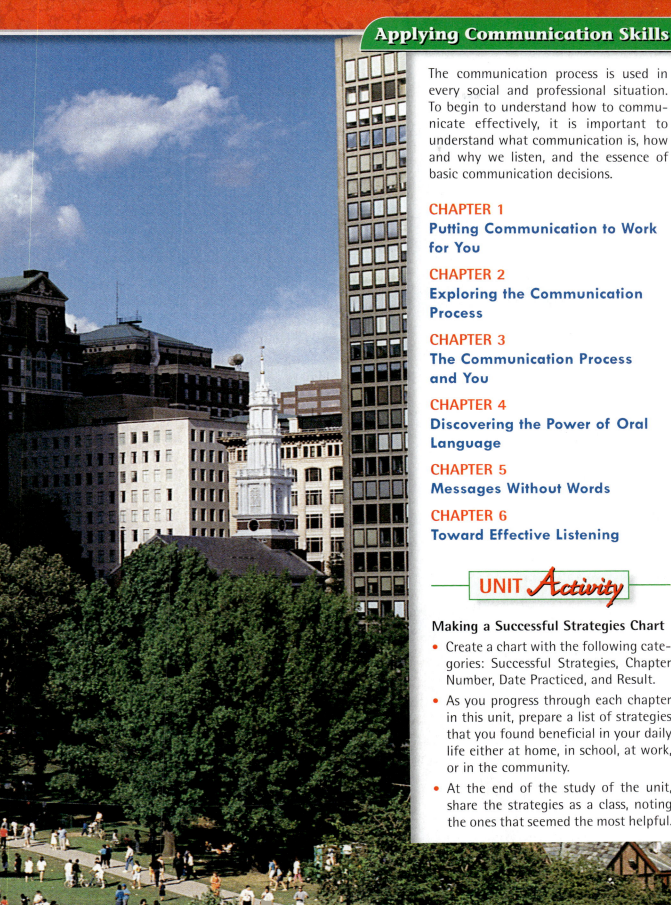

Applying Communication Skills

The communication process is used in every social and professional situation. To begin to understand how to communicate effectively, it is important to understand what communication is, how and why we listen, and the essence of basic communication decisions.

Making a Successful Strategies Chart

- Create a chart with the following categories: Successful Strategies, Chapter Number, Date Practiced, and Result.
- As you progress through each chapter in this unit, prepare a list of strategies that you found beneficial in your daily life either at home, in school, at work, or in the community.
- At the end of the study of the unit, share the strategies as a class, noting the ones that seemed the most helpful.

CHAPTER 1

Putting Communication to Work for You

WHY IT'S IMPORTANT

Choosing your words carefully can make a big difference in the messages you send. Making the appropriate choices in your actions and attitude, too, will help you be the most competent communicator you can be.

To better understand the importance of making appropriate communication choices, view the **Communication in Action** Chapter 1 video lesson.

Visit the *Glencoe Communication Applications* Web site at **communicationapplications.glencoe.com** and click on **Overview–Chapter 1** to preview information about communication choices.

"The difference between the almost right word and the right word 'tis the difference between the lightning bug and the lightning."

—Mark Twain, American author and humorist

Section 1

Communication Choices

GUIDE TO READING

Objectives

1. Use context as a basis to judge the appropriateness of a communication choice.
2. Identify how context determines roles and norms and sets standards for making appropriate choices.
3. Explain the importance of making communication choices that are appropriate for self, listener, occasion, and task of a situation.
4. Explain the importance of effective communication skills in professional and social contexts.
5. Identify the tools needed to develop the mind-set of a competent communicator.

Terms to Learn

communication
context
appropriateness
role
norm
standard
competent communicator
task skill
relationship skill

Look around you. You're just starting a new class on communication. How will it affect your school work? Your job? Your relationships? You may even be wondering, "Why should I study communication? I already know how to talk."

Communication involves much, much more than just the spoken word. The way you dress, the way you walk, and the way you act all speak volumes about who you are.

UNDERSTANDING COMMUNICATION CHOICES

Communication is the process of creating and exchanging meaning through symbolic interaction. These symbols may be verbal, which means in the form of spoken or written words, or nonverbal, perhaps in the form of gestures, eye contact, or tone of voice. In any interaction between people, the message is more than the actual words. It is the sum of all the parts of that interaction: words, gestures, attire, posture, and more.

When researching possible careers, remember that in every career choice, verbal and nonverbal communication are necessary to doing an effective job. Identify several forms of nonverbal communication.

Dressing in business attire like the attire in the photograph is appropriate for the context of an interview. What is the importance of context in communication?

Therefore, whether you are talking or not, you are constantly communicating messages to others about yourself.

Being aware of the messages you're sending will help you present an accurate picture of who you are and what you want to convey. For example, imagine that you have an opportunity to try for a summer internship at a local television station. In preparation for the job interview, you have researched the station's history, ratings, and broadcast market. However, you arrive at the interview wearing a swimsuit, a T-shirt, and sandals. Even if you impress the interviewer with your knowledge, you probably won't get the job. The message you've presented through your casual attire—you'd rather be at the beach than working—speaks much louder than your knowledge about the station.

Making Choices

When we have to make choices, our options usually aren't simply right or wrong. What may be acceptable for one occasion may be completely inappropriate for another. Dressing in a swimsuit, a T-shirt, and sandals isn't always a poor choice; that's what you'd expect to find at the beach. For the job interview, however, it was the wrong choice of attire.

Know the Context

What makes one communication choice better than another? As in the case of the swimsuit, it all depends upon the context. **Context** is the situation in which communication occurs. A beach is the perfect context for wearing a swimsuit.

Context includes the people present, the occasion, and the task. Context is important in communication because it provides a framework for communication and is the basis for making appropriate communication choices.

Appropriateness is what is suitable for a specific situation. The volume of your speaking voice, for example, varies according to what's appropriate in a given context. Shouting may be appropriate at a soccer game; however, it may get you into trouble during an exam. When you understand the specific contexts in which you are communicating, you can make the best choices for your behavior because you have a basis to decide if your communication choices are appropriate. In order to make these decisions, it is important to understand how roles and norms operate in a context.

Context Determines Roles and Norms

Each context has roles and norms. The communication behaviors appropriate to that context depend on both the roles you play and the norms for communication behavior in that context. Understanding the roles and norms within professional and social contexts gives you a basis to decide if your communication choices are appropriate.

Context Determines Roles A **role** is a part played in a specific setting or situation. Your role will vary depending on the context you're in. Being aware of the roles you play and being flexible enough to change them as you change contexts will help you make the most appropriate communication choices possible.

For example, you often play the role of a student. However, carrying that role into your home or your circle of friends would be very awkward. Can you imagine raising your hand to get a friend's permission to speak? Or addressing your mom in the same way you do a teacher?

While those examples may make it seem simple enough to understand roles, in reality the line between roles can blur. Suppose your older sister is your boss at your after-school job. While she may tease you as your sibling at home, it would be inappropriate for her to do so as your boss. The context of the workplace determines the roles you will play.

When faced with complicated situations, it often is difficult to play the roles that have been set for you. Imagine that the grocery store where you and your sister work has to cut back on its number of employees. As a supervisor, your sister is forced to lay off an employee. Since you were the last to be hired, you may be the first to be released. Making choices expected of a boss probably will be difficult for your sister, since as a sister she may resist having to lay you off. However, if she can distinguish between her roles as boss and sister, she can make the appropriate choice to help ensure her success at her job.

Context Determines Norms Each context in which you find yourself brings with it its own norms too. A **norm** is a stated or implied expectation. In other words, a norm is a guideline of what's appropriate for a given context.

Dress code policies in a school or workplace can be considered norms. Many schools and offices have stated policies; they may be written in the school code of conduct or workplace employee manual. Your school's policies may state that certain types of clothing may not be worn during classes or some school activities. Having that norm written down leaves little room for interpretation or error.

The role one plays as an employee in a fast food restaurant differs from the role one plays at home. Identify two factors that will help you make the most appropriate choices in the roles you play.

COMMUNICATION Strategies
MAKING APPROPRIATE COMMUNICATION CHOICES
Understand the context.
Define your role.
Discover the communication norms.
Set the standards based on self, listener, occasion, and task.

However, having a norm that is implied or understood is as binding as one that is written or stated. You can sometimes determine implied norms by observing others' behavior. Staying in tune with those implied norms is a key to being successful in both the social and professional worlds. For example, there are no written rules for dating. It's clear, though, that if you ask someone out for a dinner date, it's inappropriate to arrive late to meet him or her and ignore the person once you show up. Knowing what's expected of you on a date will make your time more enjoyable and increase the chances of a second invitation!

Imagine that you have just accepted a job as a sales clerk at your local pharmacy. During your interview, the supervisor didn't mention the store's dress code. You're due to arrive for your first day on the job in an hour. What should you wear? Would jeans and a T-shirt be appropriate? How do you know?

You can't err on the side of being overdressed. If you go to your job in slacks and a dress shirt and, once there, find out that khakis are acceptable, you've still made a positive first impression. Over time, you can relax your dress according to the norms of that workplace. On the other hand, if you had arrived the first day wearing jeans, your supervisor might have questioned your judgment. Customers also might have had difficulty taking you seriously. You'd be faced with overcoming a negative first impression plus the other new job pressures.

Consider another example. Imagine that one of your main responsibilities at the pharmacy is taking telephone calls from customers and physicians. If no one tells you exactly what to say when you answer the phone, what should you do? Is the way you answer the phone at home appropriate for the context of the pharmacy? Until you have a chance to ask your boss, use the most professional and polite greeting you can. You should assume that the accepted norm is as high as any standard you can imagine; once you have confirmed the actual norm, you can adjust your behavior.

Context Sets the Standards

Part of making appropriate communication choices depends on the standards you've set. A standard is an established level of requirement or excellence. Your standards are important because they are the foundation on which you make your communication decisions. They also guide you to make the best communication choices for yourself.

There are no absolute rules in oral communication. You, as a communicator, have the responsibility to establish your own standards

Figure 1–1 Context Sets the Standards

for the situations in which you find yourself. You want to be satisfied with each communication choice you make. As Figure 1–1 shows, to get the most satisfaction, you should make your choices based on four standards—what is appropriate for yourself, your listener, the occasion, and the task.

Appropriate for Self As you send and receive messages, your first standard for making a communication choice should be what is appropriate for you. This means knowing who you are, what you want to achieve, and how you want others to perceive you.

For example, if you want others to see you as serious about your job, you will want to make communication choices that give that impression. If you work a part-time job after school, you might want to make sure you arrive on time, wear the appropriate attire, and communicate courtesy to customers.

Appropriate for Your Listener Part of choosing what is appropriate for a situation depends on the people involved. If you want others to respond to your messages, you consider their needs, desires, and limitations. This often requires you to be flexible and patient. It may mean making careful language choices, being aware of your own and others' nonverbal behaviors, and listening carefully to others.

Making appropriate communication choices that are true to yourself and your listeners can be difficult. It also may take courage to reach beyond your normal capabilities. For instance, the image you have of yourself may include being somewhat shy and serious. However, your pep squad coach might need you to communicate in a very animated and excited manner during a performance on the field. In order to be a successful pep squad member, you make a communication choice that meets the coach's needs in that context.

Practice for the Workplace

Appropriate Choices Communication situations in the workplace can be informal conversations or formal meetings; can be held in an office, on a factory floor, or in an auditorium; and can involve customers, coworkers, or supervisors. In any situation, your communication choice should be appropriate for the context.

BUSINESS PRACTICE *Activity*

In groups of four to six students, list the tasks that employees of a small retail clothing store would have to accomplish during a particular time period. Under each task, list appropriate communication choices for each. For example, one task might be to greet customers as they walk through the door. It would not be appropriate to ignore a customer, but it would be appropriate to ask if the customer needs any help. Once each group has completed its list, prepare a skit that acts out the appropriate communication choices. As a class, discuss the effects the choices would have on the success of the business.

Appropriate for the Occasion Your coach may not need you to be completely full of energy at every practice—the occasion doesn't require it. The minute the half-time show begins, though, your enthusiastic self needs to shine through! The occasion, or time, place, and purpose, of an event makes specific demands on your communication.

The behavior you display during the half-time show won't be necessary for other occasions. Hanging out with friends after school, going to a student council meeting, and attending a tutoring session are occasions where you'll act differently than you would during the show. Each occasion brings with it different expectations of appropriate behavior.

Appropriate for the Task Imagine that, in your attempt to better understand algebra through a tutoring session, you clap your hands, shout, and jump up and down. While your tutor may appreciate your enthusiasm, she'll probably give you a funny look. The task, or job, at hand didn't require the kind of behavior you displayed. Listening and taking notes would be more appropriate for the task of trying to make sense of algebra.

Getting your classmates pumped up about the big homecoming basketball game, on the other hand, calls for some shouting and jumping. The task you're trying to accomplish in that context is very different from that of the tutoring session. Being flexible enough to make the right choices, based on what's appropriate for the context, will prove to be important for your success.

Throughout your life, you will be faced with situations in which your idea about what's appropriate for a situation collides with the actual demands of the context. Others may expect more from you than you expect of yourself. The occasion or task of the situation may require certain behavior from you that is not your norm. The role you must play or norms you must obey might challenge you. In order to be successful, you'll need to put aside your preferences, wants, or needs and rise to that challenge!

A friend is one who chooses to help you, even when it is inconvenient for him or her. A granddaughter who chooses polite and respectful language in her grandfather's presence is a valued family member. A nurse who chooses soothing words and a pat on the arm when trying to calm a nervous patient will be a success. Being aware of the demands of certain contexts can help make appropriate choices seem obvious. Making these choices can help you become a more successful person in any context.

Figure 1–2 Skills Most Looked for in Potential Employees

Rank	Skill
1	Oral communication
2	Self-motivation
3	Problem solving
4	Decision making
5	Leadership
6	Human relations
7	Teamwork
8	Work experience

Global Communication

Norms During Negotiations

The norm during business negotiations in Denmark is for business people to avoid making any personal comments to each other. Even complimenting someone on his or her attire can be considered inappropriate. Research the norms of other countries with respect to discussing personal issues during business meetings and share your findings with the remainder of the class.

The Importance of Communication Skills

Every time that you interact with another human being you are communicating. As you just read, communicating includes the entire set of messages that you send, from the words you speak to the way you walk. In addition to the constant nonverbal communication you're involved in, you probably also spend a fair amount of time engaged in oral and written communication. While the skills needed to be effective in your oral and written communication are already important in your school and social worlds, they will grow in importance as you develop relationships in your adult life and as you move into the professional world.

A business study based on responses from 1,000 employees shows staggering results. Those workers received an average of 178 messages each day via telephone, e-mail, fax, pager, and face-to-face communication. That's more than 22 messages every hour in a typical eight-hour work day. It also has been estimated that, on any given day, the average business executive spends about 45 minutes of each hour communicating!

Everyone communicates at work in a variety of ways. Depending upon your chosen field, specialized knowledge may play an important part in your job. When communicating with the maintenance crew, an airline pilot must be able to explain in detail any faults in the aircraft. Similarly, a legal assistant must be aware of the technical language used in legal briefs and rulings. More importantly, he or she must be able to communicate in that language. The assistant who can define thousands of legal terms but cannot speak clearly, put together complete thoughts, or write cohesive paragraphs will be of little use to any legal firm.

As **Figure 1–2** shows, oral and written communication skills are vital in any profession. A survey of 500 managers in retail, manufacturing, service, and finance industries revealed the priority they place on oral communication: They ranked it first in importance above other skills. In another study, 1,000 managers ranked the ability to communicate well higher than work-related experience and academic achievement. Communication skills even have an impact on other important employee qualities, such as problem solving, leadership, and teamwork.

COMMUNICATION Strategies
COMPETENT COMMUNICATORS KNOW ABOUT
Communication
Themselves
Others (listeners, readers, and observers)
The world around them
Reason and logic

Competent Communicator

Once you've made the choice about what your actions say about you, you need to be sure your words also say what you mean. This helps you become a competent communicator. A **competent communicator** is someone who incorporates knowledge, attitude, and skills into his or her communication to communicate effectively and appropriately. This course will provide you with knowledge about effective and appropriate communication. Before you get into these vital details, though, it's important to get into the mind-set of a competent communicator. Being willing to acquire new knowledge and skills and having the right attitude will help you do just that!

Knowledge

Competent communicators recognize the need to be informed. It is important to have complete, accurate, and recent information in order to support ideas and to process messages from others. Knowledge also includes

Figure 1–3 Attitude Rating Scale

the ability to analyze and interpret information and to reason and think logically to reach decisions and make sound judgments. Knowledge also implies the ability to use information effectively. Finally, it includes having valid information and using "good common sense." For example, a knowledgeable voter tries to find out about candidates and issues before voting.

Attitudes

Attitudes influence the way you see yourself and other people. These views influence your choices, and in doing so, also impact your communication. As shown in **Figure 1–3,** attitudes generally are positive or negative. Your behavior in a situation tends to reflect the positive or negative tone of your attitude. As a result, your attitude greatly affects your communication choices. If you have a negative attitude in a class, you may not listen or participate effectively in that class, resulting in your being a less than competent communicator. On the other hand, if your attitude is positive and enthusiastic, you probably look forward to the class and exert extra effort to do well. Your positive attitude enhances your communication competence.

How Attitudes Impact Others

Have you ever heard the expression "One bad apple spoils the bunch"? This describes how attitudes impact others. Employees with negative attitudes about their jobs may criticize coworkers and complain about conditions in the workplace. Their negative thoughts, words, and behaviors can quickly impact other workers, who begin to respond and talk negatively as well. Employers generally appreciate employees who demonstrate positive attitudes and enthusiasm. This does not mean that employees with positive attitudes do not have concerns or issues at work. It only means that they have learned to deal with and reduce negative feelings so they—and others—aren't overwhelmed by them. They also have learned to communicate their concerns in a positive way. There is a strong link between employee attitudes, morale, productivity, communication, and positive human

Figure 1–4 Are Students Ready for Work?

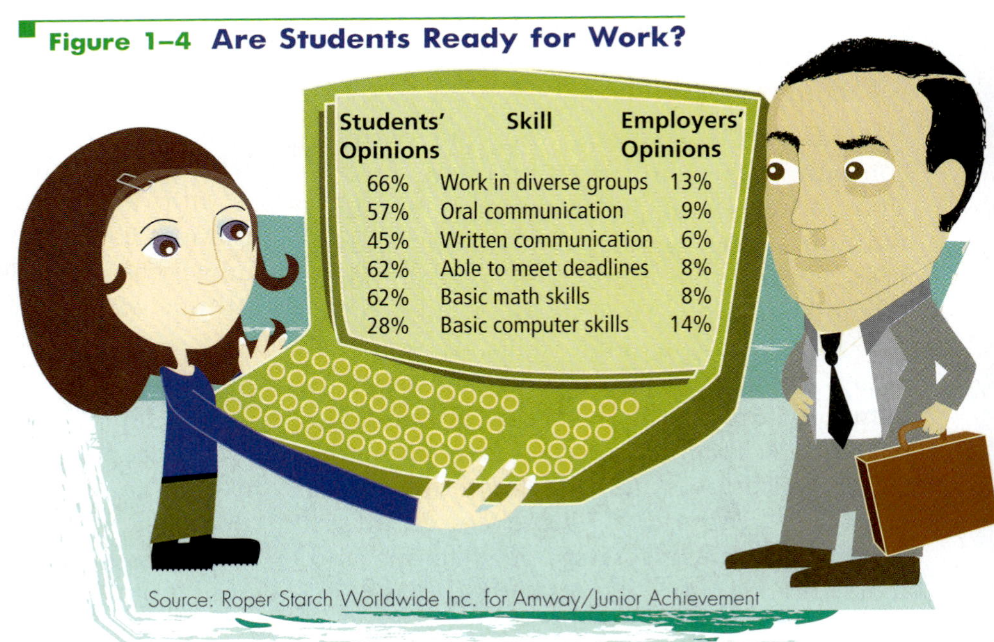

Students' Opinions	Skill	Employers' Opinions
66%	Work in diverse groups	13%
57%	Oral communication	9%
45%	Written communication	6%
62%	Able to meet deadlines	8%
62%	Basic math skills	8%
28%	Basic computer skills	14%

Source: Roper Starch Worldwide Inc. for Amway/Junior Achievement interactions at work. Positive attitudes tend to reap positive results in professional and social contexts.

Managing Your Attitude Can you manage and control your attitudes? Yes, you can—and you probably should. The first step is to recognize how attitudes are formed. Your attitudes basically are the result of related experiences. For example, if you have had positive experiences in school, you probably have a positive attitude toward school. If you think of most of your experiences as negative, your attitude toward school may be negative.

Changing Your Attitude Can you change your attitudes from negative to positive? Yes. However, attitude adjustment may mean a change in your experiences. People sometimes change their environment, friends, interests, or perhaps even their jobs to "make a fresh start." This helps them bring about positive changes in attitudes that have gone sour. For example, to change a negative attitude to a positive one, you might choose to spend more time with positive people. You have the choice!

Skills

As Figure 1–4 shows, the gap between students' and employers' views on students' workplace skill levels varies. Employers often are aware that competent communicators need a wide range and variety of communication skills. The skills necessary for making appropriate communication choices and for using communication strategies effectively can be divided into two categories: task skills and relationship skills.

Task Skills **Task skills** are the communication skills needed to do a job, complete a task, or reach a goal effectively. Task skills include logically thinking through problems at work or giving clear instructions for someone to complete a task. They might also include making the choice to listen in a particular situation so you can understand someone else's message. Task skills also include effectively using nonverbal behaviors such as gestures and eye contact to make your communication clear and meaningful to others.

Relationship Skills **Relationship skills** are the communication skills needed to nurture and maintain goodwill with people. They

COMMUNICATION PRACTICE LAB

Analyzing Your Task Skills

To analyze your task skills, follow these steps:

Step 1 As a class, brainstorm a list of communication tasks you perform in school or at home each day.

Step 2 Select one of the tasks that you think you do well.

Step 3 List all the communication skills you possess that help you perform that task. For example, being a good listener and knowing teaching strategies can help you with the task of tutoring younger children.

Step 4 Which of these skills should you work on to make better? What other skills could you develop to help you perform the task?

include the ability to give and receive suggestions and praise. Tact, courtesy, and respect for others also are good relationship skills. They include listening carefully to others so you can understand the meanings and feelings they are attempting to convey. Relationship skills promote communication that allows you to interact successfully in any situation.

Realizing the importance of communication in the business world and understanding how your communication choices impact your social world can help you to develop the communication skills—verbal, nonverbal, and listening—that you need to be a competent communicator. Communication applications will help you to develop the professional and social identity you desire.

Section 1 Assessment

Visit the *Glencoe Communication Applications* Web site at **communicationapplications.glencoe.com** and click on **Self-Check and Study Guide 1.1** to review your understanding of making communication choices.

Review Key Terms

1. Define each term and write it in a sentence: communication, context, appropriateness, role, norm, standard, competent communicator, task skill, relationship skill.

Check Understanding

2. Would yelling with an angry tone be appropriate at your school's awards banquet? Explain why or why not, based on your understanding of context.
3. What four standards are important for you to use when making communication choices?
4. How might poor communication skills affect whether or not a person gets hired for a job?
5. Identify and describe the three tools needed to begin to become a competent communicator.
6. **Apply** Imagine that you are a salesclerk at an electronics store. An angry customer confronts you about a faulty CD player. What specific task skills and relationship skills would you need to handle this situation?

APPLICATION *Activity*

Playing the Role of a Competent Communicator Imagine that you have been asked to coach tee ball for a team of first graders. In order to be an effective coach, there are some things you'll need to do to be prepared. Divide a piece of paper into three rows. Label them *Knowledge*, *Attitudes*, and *Skills.* Then divide each row into two columns, labeling them *Have* and *Need.* Think about the knowledge that you already possess to be a good tee ball coach. Fill in your charts. As a class, discuss your charts. Brainstorm ways to acquire the knowledge, attitudes, and skills you still need to be prepared to coach.

Critical Thinking Skill

Analyzing Information

To become a competent communicator, you must understand what is and what is not appropriate in a given context. Part of knowing what's appropriate is to analyze any information that is part of a communication exchange or part of preparing to communicate. Analyzing information involves breaking it into meaningful parts so that the speaker, reader, or listener can form an opinion about it.

Learning the Skill

To analyze information, use the steps that are listed below.

STEPS TO ANALYZE INFORMATION

Step 1	Identify the general topic of the information being relayed.
Step 2	Identify the main points of the piece of information.
Step 3	Summarize the information in your own words based on your understanding.

Practicing the Skill

Read the following passage and answer the questions that follow.

You probably won't be asked to write research papers on the job, but most likely you will have to research products and new ideas and write business letters, memos, and reports—all of which need to be organized and presented clearly. And though you might not have to give a formal speech before a large group, you may have to preside at a meeting or present ideas to a small group—and those ideas must be presented clearly, concisely, and with an effective style.

Writing papers and preparing speeches prepares you for on-the-job reports and correspondence. These assignments give you a chance to show initiative, use judgment, apply and interpret information, research resources, organize ideas, and polish your style. Public speaking skills also help you inform and persuade others at informal meetings and presentations. Good writers and speakers are not born, nor is there a secret to their success. Like any other skills, speaking and writing can be learned with practice and effort.

1. What is the main topic of the passage?
2. What are the main points of the passage?
3. Write a summary statement about the passage.

APPLICATION *Activity*

To help you analyze your interests with respect to a possible future career, do the following:

1. Find the description of a particular job you might want to pursue by researching jobs on the Internet, in newspapers, magazines, or books.
2. Analyze the job description by listing the main qualifications and responsibilities of the job.
3. Write a summary paragraph about your qualifications for the job in light of the tasks you have mastered and those you still need to learn to function effectively in that position.
4. Share your summary paragraph with other members of your class.

Section 2

Communication in Organizations

GUIDE TO READING

Objectives

1. Explain the importance of organizations as contexts for communication.
2. Describe three functions of organizations.
3. Explain the concepts of personal and organizational culture.
4. Analyze the seven elements of organizational culture and their influence on members of the organization.
5. Identify appropriate strategies for communicating across diversity.

Terms to Learn

organization
culture
organizational culture
culture shock
social responsibility
conflict

Would you rather build a house by yourself or with a group of workers? Even with all the latest power tools, building it on your own would be a huge job.

Most people would agree that building a house with a team of people would be much more efficient than one person working alone. This also holds true for communication tasks. Every day, groups of people come together in professional and social situations to work, learn, and have fun. Communicating in these groups requires special skills. It's important to be prepared for the challenges that accompany being part of a diverse organization of people.

THE INFLUENCE OF ORGANIZATIONS

Given its importance to communication, being aware of context will be an essential part of your study in this course. You will focus mainly on acquiring knowledge and building skills to apply in two specific areas: professional and social organizations. In other words, your energy will focus on two worlds that have a great effect on your life—the world of work and the community in which you live.

Working alone on a task such as a large masonry job can be challenging. Identify some of the benefits of membership in an organization.

In these two worlds, you'll be faced with many contexts. You may be a member of the ecology club at school or work part-time at a local construction company. In many contexts you'll find that you are not only a part of the group, club, team, or staff that seems most obvious but also a member of a larger organization. An organization is a number of people with specific responsibilities who are united for some purpose. Your school organization, for example, is composed of its teachers, students, and staff members, as well as the variety of groups they form. The organization's chief purpose is educating the youth of your community.

Organizations can be professional, relating directly to the workplace, or social, relating to a society's values, beliefs, interests, and the talents of its people. Professional organizations are set up to serve customers, clients, or stockholders. Social organizations are set up to complete the tasks of the society, community, and even the nation.

To be able to fully participate in the organizations that you're a part of requires understanding the context of each organization. Getting to know the people in your group, the setting for meetings, and the purpose of the organization are important. In addition, knowing your role within the organization as well as any written or implied norms will help you make choices that are appropriate to that organization. It also will help you become a valued organizational member.

Functions of Organizations

People develop interests, pursue various goals and ambitions, and meet many of their needs through their involvement in groups and organizations. Having a positive experience as a member of an organization will depend upon whether you receive benefits equal to or greater than the effort you must put into being a member. Membership can offer many benefits: a place to spend time with friends, a way to learn new skills, or an opportunity to earn academic credit, to name a few. In addition to specific benefits like these, the function of organizations is to fulfill three broader needs: identity, unity, and preservation.

Communication Practice Lab

Evaluating Organizations

To evaluate the organization of your school, follow these steps:

Step 1 As a class, make a list of groups within the organization of your school.

Step 2 From the list, select one of the groups to which you do not belong.

Step 3 Identify the teachers or staff members involved in the group you chose. You may wish to use a school directory to help you.

Step 4 Talk with one of these individuals about the specific responsibilities the group provides to the school or community. Ask the person about how the group contributes to the goal of the organization as a whole. Also ask him or her to share with you the kinds of communication skills that are most needed in that group.

Step 5 At your next class meeting, share your findings. Discuss the purposes groups provide in your school or community. Analyze how each of the chosen groups come together to form the organization of your school.

Identity

The first reason why organizations are important is that they provide a chance for you to define who you are. If you were to list different ways to introduce yourself to others, you might say, "I am a student." You might also give more detail by saying, "I am a member of the junior class, an employee at the grocery store, a member of the National Honor Society, and the goalie for the Rockets hockey team." Regardless of the descriptions you choose, you probably identify yourself in relation to some group or organization to which you belong.

Unity

People throughout history have united to form colonies, governments, and corporations to meet mutual needs and to accomplish common goals. By joining together, people often can accomplish feats that no single individual can accomplish alone. In addition, working with others can build an individual's self-confidence, providing him or her with feelings of camaraderie and belonging. When people unite to achieve a common goal, individual differences are diminished and common ground can be established.

Preservation

Finally, organizations are important because they preserve the things we believe in and find important. Just as churches preserve religion, choirs, choruses, and orchestras preserve our musical heritage. Historical societies maintain our awareness of history and renew interest in historical issues, people, and events. Corporations and other professional organizations in our country help preserve our economic system. Some social organizations even contribute to our sense of charity and volunteerism.

interNET ACTIVITY

Investigating Organizations Online With classmates, generate a list of professional or social organizations that directly touch your lives. Limit your list to the five organizations in which you and your classmates are most interested. Log on to the Internet to find information about one of these five organizations. You might investigate the services it provides, benefits for individual members, and communication skills needed for successful participation. At your next class meeting, discuss your findings with the other students who investigated the same organization. As a group, organize your findings and then discuss them as a class.

Culture in Organizations

An important aspect of every organization is its culture. **Culture** is the set of life patterns passed down from one generation to the next in a group of people. You may be most familiar with culture as a group's specific language, food, and dress. However, your family's holiday celebrations or its definitions of family roles are also examples of your family's culture. If family members say, "This is how we've done this since we were children," they have adopted a particular behavior as part of their culture.

Culture is learned behavior. You learn about your culture from members of your family, other students and teachers at school, and people in your community and nation.

Understanding Organizational Culture

You may gain a better understanding of organizational culture if you look at your personal culture. Your personal culture is a pattern of behaviors that includes the languages you speak, foods you eat, sports you play, activities you enjoy, clothes you wear, music you like, and holidays and traditions you observe. Your personal culture is the way you think and the way you do things.

Organizational culture follows the same principles. **Organizational culture** is how an organization thinks, what it finds important, and how it conducts business. Organizational culture is evident when a member talks about "the way we do things around here." Understanding the culture of an organization helps you know the role that you have in the organization. Understanding the culture of an organization also helps you determine the expected norms for your behavior.

Success in Organizations What does this mean to you? If you are to succeed in an organization, you need to be aware of as many aspects of that organization's culture as possible. Understanding an organization's culture can help you get a job when you prepare for and answer questions in an interview. It can help you keep a job because your attitudes and behavior support the beliefs and policies of the organization. It can help you make choices and build communication skills that can lead to promotion and recognition. Just as understanding your school's policies on dress codes, grading standards, and attendance can help you be a better student, understanding a professional organization's expectations about telephone etiquette, travel, and sick days can help you be a better employee.

Think about a time when you changed schools, tried out for a team, or joined a new club. Perhaps you have also had the experience of getting a job and entering the workplace. If you have done any or all of these things, you have encountered organizational culture. You may have made a smooth transition, adapting easily to the culture of the organization. On the other hand, you may have been overwhelmed by many of the different expectations you had to meet. People often refer to the type of reaction that you experienced as culture shock. **Culture shock** is the confusion or anxiety that sometimes results when people come into contact with a culture different from their own. Culture shock can happen in any organizational context.

"I don't know how it started, either. All I know is that it's part of our corporate culture."

Figure 1–5 Elements of Organizational Culture

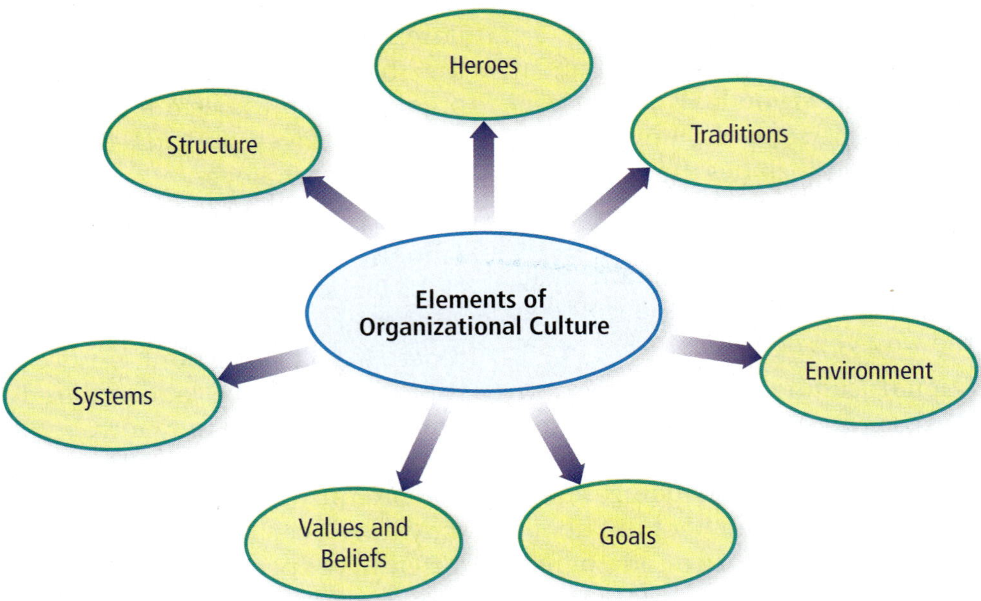

Elements of Culture

Even though all organizations are unique, they have several elements in common. As Figure 1–5 shows, they include structure, systems, values and beliefs, goals, environment, traditions, and heroes. How each organization approaches and implements these elements makes up the organization's culture.

It is wise to find out the specifics of these elements in each organization you want to join. Whether you're considering becoming a member of the staff at a large hospital or of the Habitat for Humanity team at your school, gathering information about the organization's culture can help you know what to expect from the organization. It also can help you understand what the organization expects from you.

Structure Professional and social organizations have a specific structure. Structure includes the parts of an organization as well as the relationship between those parts. The structure also reveals the functions and purposes of each part of the organization, as well as its place in the organization's hierarchy. This hierarchy, or chain of command, shows the relationship between parts of the organization from the top down. Hierarchy answers questions about who is responsible to whom for what.

Your school district follows a specific structure and hierarchy. It probably has a board of education with officers and committees who have specific responsibilities. The school also has a superintendent who oversees a staff of assistant superintendents, directors, coordinators, principals, supervisors, teachers, staff members, and you, the student. The hierarchy of your school also defines the functions of each of its parts. Who makes what decisions? Which person or department is responsible for what areas?

Systems Communicating in an organization, no matter its size, requires order and coordination. This coordination can be achieved through systems, or networks of channels for orderly interaction. Otherwise, members would spend or waste all their time trying to communicate simple messages. Imagine that the 17 employees of a small company receive every communication of every person in the company. If you do the math for that 17-person company, can you imagine the communication conflicts that many messages might create?

While communication must be orderly, it also must be simple to achieve. Systems energize organizations by allowing information to flow easily within the structure. Systems also provide channels of communication to the community outside of the organization.

Again, your school can be used as an example of how systems operate within the structure of an organization. Think first of the methods that are used to inform students about events at your school. There may be morning announcements over the public address system, a school newspaper, or colorful posters in the hall to boost school spirit or to advertise upcoming plays, concerts, or athletic events.

Other Communication Systems in Organizations Some organizations also utilize other communication systems to keep the public informed. They may host open meetings to invite public participation and input on certain matters. Some organizations also hold hearings, town meetings, and focus groups to encourage members of the public to air their views, discuss issues, and solve problems.

Values and Beliefs At the core of every organization is a set of values and beliefs that governs its policies and actions. A value is a priority or an idea that is prized or cherished. It is what you or your organization considers important. A belief is an idea that someone holds to be true.

Personal Values Analyzing your own values and beliefs and how they provide a basis for your behavior can help you understand organizational values. As an individual, you may value good grades. You may believe that hard work in school will bring rewards in the future in the form of scholarships or a good job. This set of values and beliefs probably influences your behavior. You may spend much of your free time studying and researching, working ahead on school projects, or organizing class notes. By influencing the behavior choices you make, your values help define the image other students have of you. The same is true of the values and beliefs of an organization.

Organizational Values Professional organizations such as companies usually value making a profit. Some businesses also place a high priority on the productivity and efficiency of employees. A company that recognizes the relationship between employee morale and productivity may provide a number of benefits for employees, such as insurance, profit sharing, or investment opportunities. It also may recognize and reward employees for loyalty,

These individuals work on a newspaper that helps inform and maintain open communication within their organization. Identify some of the ways your school informs students about events taking place within the school.

commitment, and leadership. Most companies strive to reach a balance between the profits needed to stay in business and the need to promote morale among employees.

Social Responsibility To reinforce this trend, many organizations are beginning to recognize the value of social responsibility. **Social responsibility** is an obligation or willingness to work toward the well-being of others. This may include placing a priority on environmental concerns and community issues. Many business executives believe that a healthy company cannot survive in an unhealthy society for long. That belief is echoed by others who consider it their social responsibility to support their workers, their workers' lives, and their communities.

Successful employees try to understand company values and beliefs in order to anticipate what their employer will look for in their performance. Employees then have a basis for making their own choices and can more accurately estimate the rewards and consequences of their behavior.

Goals Organizations set and try to achieve goals. A goal is an end result or outcome that someone strives to attain. Organizational goals stem from the organization's values and beliefs. Goals often are stated in mission statements. To be most effective, goals should be laid out in detail with specific plans within a set time.

A school district that values academic achievement may have a goal to raise test scores. A company that values diversity may set a goal of hiring more minorities. Service organizations often set goals for fund-raising. Employees are expected to share in efforts to reach company goals. Rewards and prizes often are offered as incentives to those who make outstanding contributions toward those goals.

Environment Environment refers to your physical surroundings. Your culture is reflected in your home, your school building, local architectural styles, and the condition of buildings or streets in your community. An organization's environment often reveals its values and culture. For example, a company with brightly colored walls and comfortable chairs may place importance on the energy level, comfort, and productivity of its employees. A school whose walls are covered with posters advertising an a cappella choir concert shows that its music program is a priority.

City Year is an organization that promotes social responsibility by encouraging young people to participate in community service projects such as restoring homes. How do businesses promote social responsibility?

Environment can influence relationships, morale, and even productivity. **What does the photo suggest about this school's environment?**

Look around and evaluate the environment of your classroom. Is the room crowded or spacious? Colorful or drab? Does it present a bright, safe, and comfortable environment? Does it have a climate that invites participation, curiosity, and creativity? How do these conditions affect your feelings, your attitude, or your communication? Environment affects the quality of interaction. This, in turn, influences the relationships, morale, and productivity of individuals within that environment.

Traditions Organizations usually have traditions. A tradition is a practice or ceremony that is carried out and celebrated in the same manner year after year. Your school may have an annual homecoming celebration with traditional activities such as a pep rally, a football game, the crowning of the homecoming king and queen, and an after-game dance. Special ways of doing things set your school apart from other schools and provide an opportunity to celebrate your school.

Traditions in social and professional organizations usually are aimed at promoting higher morale and positive relations among members. Some businesses host holiday parties, awards banquets, and annual seminars. They may recognize an employee of the month or sponsor employee sports teams. Such traditions provide a social dimension to organizations.

Heroes A hero is an individual who is respected and admired for the contributions he or she has made to an organization or to society as a whole. Heroes often serve as role models. Think for a moment about the heroes in your school. Perhaps a school hero is the star of the school play, the president of the National Honor Society, or a student with a physical challenge who has overcome overwhelming odds. Whether the school hero is a student body leader, an academic leader, a courageous student, an athlete, or simply a person who always smiles and offers encouragement to others, the hero represents the values of your school.

TECHNOLOGY *Activity*

Electronic Research and Reporting As a class, generate a list of heroes. Include people of different time periods to reflect a range of interests and organizations. Try to include people of different genders, ethnic groups, and ages. Do not neglect heroes from your own community or school. Divide the list so that each person in the class has one hero.

Use the Internet or an electronic encyclopedia to gather information about your hero. Analyze what characteristics and contributions might account for the hero's status. Using word-processing software, write a brief essay explaining whether or not you think your assigned hero would be a good role model. Share your essays as a class. Discuss whether each hero on your class list reflects the values or priorities of a group or organization.

Professional and social organizations have heroes whose values and behaviors have won the respect of others. Mary Kay Ash, for example, is considered a hero by many business women because of her innovation, dedication, and hard work. Michael Jordan became a hero not only because of his skill in basketball but also because of his good nature and his positive attitude. John Glenn became a hero twice. He was acclaimed a hero as a young man with his first venture into space and became a hero again at age seventy-seven with his return to space after a long career in the United States Senate.

Not all heroes become famous, however, nor do they all serve as positive role models. A class clown may be a hero to unmotivated students because his or her disruptions provide comic relief. In the same manner, a dishonest or rebellious employee may become a hero to workers who feel victimized by management.

Whether positive or negative, heroes reflect the values of a segment of an organization's members. Heroes also influence the behavior of those individuals and ultimately affect the culture of the organization.

Just as heroes enrich our world, organizations enrich many aspects of your life. They provide you with outlets for your energy and creativity, teach you new skills, and help you help others. Additionally, as organizations add to your life, you also give something back. You provide fresh ideas, new solutions, and broader perspectives with the individual culture you bring to an organization.

Diversity in Organizations

As people join together to form companies, countries, churches, and communities, they form a rich mix of cultures. Today, many of the cultural barriers between people have been lowered—even erased in some cases. People of every race, gender, and any legal age work side by side. Segregation is becoming a trend of the past. Peace throughout much of the world has expanded markets and communication among nations, and technology allows us to instantly connect with almost anyone anywhere at any time. As shown in Figure 1–6, this trend toward a more diverse population will continue.

Michael Jordan, Mary Kay Ash, and John Glenn became heroes because of their accomplishments within their respective organizations. How can a hero affect the culture of an organization?

Figure 1–6 Projected Population Characteristics in the United States

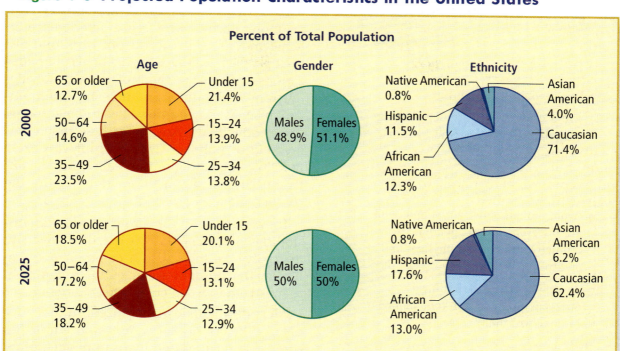

Percent of Total Population

Year	Age	Gender	Ethnicity
2000	65 or older 12.7%; Under 15 21.4%; 50–64 14.6%; 15–24 13.9%; 35–49 23.5%; 25–34 13.8%	Males 48.9%; Females 51.1%	Native American 0.8%; Asian American 4.0%; Hispanic 11.5%; Caucasian 71.4%; African American 12.3%
2025	65 or older 18.5%; Under 15 20.1%; 50–64 17.2%; 15–24 13.1%; 35–49 18.2%; 25–34 12.9%	Males 50%; Females 50%	Native American 0.8%; Asian American 6.2%; Hispanic 17.6%; Caucasian 62.4%; African American 13.0%

It is important to remember, however, that this trend also may pose challenges. It is likely that in many of the organizations you join, you'll encounter people of different cultures, races, ages, religions, abilities, and genders. This is known as diversity, or variety, and it has become the norm in today's United States. Improved access for the physically challenged, increased immigration, longer life spans, and more opportunities for women all have added to diversity in organizations.

The United States and the organizations that are a part of it have become a sort of "salad bowl" of diversity. This salad bowl analogy, a term popular in multicultural studies today, suggests that each individual can retain and value his or her own personal culture while working cooperatively with others in an organization.

Because no two people are exactly alike, you encounter people of different ages and ethnic and religious backgrounds every day. Since you also are unique, you add to the diversity of groups in which you participate. As a result, you may be aware of the demands on communication that result from people's differences. For instance, if a student from another state or country comes to your school, it may be a challenge for you to find a common interest that you can use as a basis for friendship. If you volunteer to visit residents of an assisted living facility, you probably will learn that you cannot use your school slang to communicate.

Effects of Diversity

The effects of diversity can be either positive or negative. Diversity can provide enrichment and interest and promote people's appreciation of cultural differences as they get to know one another. It can also cause conflict.

Enrichment Enrichment is a positive effect of diversity. Diversity can provide new interests, ideas, understandings, and appreciation for individuals. For example, sharing

COMMUNICATION *Strategies*

DEALING WITH DIVERSITY

- Learn about other cultures.
- Avoid using language such as slang or dialect that is specific to your individual culture.
- See your differences as an opportunity to learn and grow.
- Avoid looking down on people who are different in age, gender, ethnicity, religion, or physical and mental abilities.
- Be willing to discuss cultural differences and adapt your behavior to minimize them.

experiences with a new student from another country might expand your knowledge about geography, history, or language. Talking with a parent or grandparent can help you to understand different times, different places, or different ways of life.

The expression "If two people think exactly alike, one of them is dispensable" can help explain the effect diversity can have on an organization. People from differing backgrounds often tend to view things differently, have different ideas about solving problems, and take different stands on issues. In organizations where people can express openly their ideas and where people listen to one another, both the organization and individuals can benefit, often leading to better ideas and better solutions to problems. In addition, diversity within an organization can help meet the needs of a diversity of customers and community members. As a result, the organization can anticipate many of the demands it will face in the world market.

Conflict Conflict is often a negative result of diversity. **Conflict** is the struggle between two or more parties who sense interference in achieving goals. It can disrupt work and distract people from reaching the goals of organizations. Different methods of problem solving, different work habits, and different communication styles may be viewed as threatening by some individuals. Any time these differences are judged "right" or "wrong," conflict is likely to follow. It is important to realize that the different ways of doing things don't create the conflict; the responses to the difference do.

Individuals who cooperate to share responsibilities and benefits can use their diversity to resolve conflicts. Using common goals to bridge the gaps between cultures can help them avoid judging each other's differences.

Most people today recognize that individuals of different ages, genders, and ethnicities can work together and learn from each other in professional and social organizations. As a result, they can increase the collective knowledge and experience of any organization.

Cultural Challenges

As you enter into organizations in the world around you, you often may encounter cultural challenges. As a result, real conflicts can occur. Think about the types of conflicts that might result in each of the following examples:

- A school strictly enforces its hair and dress codes. As a result, a young Native American student is required to cut his long hair before he may attend classes.
- A school club has a strict policy against students wearing jewelry that indicates religious preferences or cultural affiliation.
- A company's work schedule conflicts with the celebration of a particular culture's special holiday or observance.

These students are required to wear school uniforms. Organizational policies, such as dress codes, sometimes conflict with personal beliefs. What choices do you have if your beliefs conflict with policy?

- A factory's new uniforms are designed for safety and mobility, but they conflict with some employees' traditional cultural attire.
- An organizational policy appears to award promotions based on age, gender, or ethnic identity.

If you are faced with an organizational culture that threatens your personal culture, you have some important choices to make. Will you join the organization? If you already are a member, will you leave? One way to avoid getting involved in an incompatible organizational culture is to research it before you join. Although many areas of professional and social life may require some amount of compromise on your part, you may decide to keep looking for an organization that is a better cultural match for you.

Challenges of Policies and Procedures If, after becoming involved in an organization, you become aware of policies or procedures that present you with personal conflict, you have a more difficult choice. You may choose to leave the organization, try to change conflicting policies, or you may simply choose to make the best of your situation.

For example, if you enter a school that has dress and hair codes that are not to your liking, you may have no choice other than to conform. You might attempt to have these policies changed, but in the meantime you must be prepared to abide by the existing rules. In a work setting, your employer may not allow time off for a religious holiday that you observe. In this case, you might choose to negotiate for the time off—perhaps by working on a different holiday to make up the time. Basically, when you face a conflict with

an organization's culture, your choices are to adapt, look elsewhere for an organization whose culture better matches your own, or negotiate and compromise.

Changing Organizational Culture

Can organizational culture change? Yes, but change in the business world usually is gradual. Fortunately, most successful corporations listen to their employees, clients, and customers and typically change their practices especially if this means an increase in profits and productivity. In the past, employee groups have been successful in persuading businesses to make changes such as more casual dress codes on Fridays, job sharing, and on-site child care at many companies.

As you move from the organization of your school into professional and social contexts, you'll want to be ready to be a competent communicator. Knowing the special challenges that communicating in organizations presents can only help you be prepared for the situations you'll face. Communication applications will get you ready for the wide world ahead of you!

Section 2 Assessment

Visit the *Glencoe Communication Applications* Web site at **communicationapplications.glencoe.com** and click on **Self-Check and Study Guide 1.2** to review your understanding of the challenges to communicating in organizations.

Review Key Terms

1. Define each term and write it in a sentence: organization, culture, organizational culture, culture shock, social responsibility, conflict.

Check Understanding

2. Why is understanding the contexts of different organizations important?
3. Explain the three primary functions of organizations.
4. Why should you investigate the culture of a professional organization before you seek a job there?
5. How could information about an organization's goals, traditions, or heroes be used to predict the kind of skills needed by its members?
6. **Solve** Imagine that you work only with people of the opposite gender or who belong to a different age group or ethnic group. Explain your strategies to communicate effectively with them in the face of diversity.

APPLICATION Activity

Designing an Organization Think about the organizations of which you enjoy being a member or would like to become a member. What is it about their organizational cultures that appeals to you? How do they complement your personal culture? Using the seven elements of culture, design the organization of your ideal workplace. Make any changes to your organization's culture necessary for the profitability of your business.

Communication Self-Assessment

Analyzing How You Communicate

How Do You Rate?

On a separate sheet of paper, answer the following questions. Put a check mark beside each skill you would like to improve.

KEY: **A** Always, **U** Usually, **S** Sometimes, **R** Rarely, **N** Never

1. I consider the context of a situation when I make communication choices.

2. I think about my listener when I choose language to explain something.

3. I think about what is appropriate or inappropriate to wear to a special occasion.

4. I stay informed on current events.

5. I generally have a positive attitude.

6. I participate in many organizations.

7. I benefit from my participation in organizations.

8. I have a firm grasp of the culture of my school.

9. I often experience a sense of community between my culture and the culture of the organization.

10. I change my behavior to meet the needs of a variety of populations.

How Do You Score?

Review your responses. Give yourself 5 points for every A, 4 for every U, 3 for every S, 2 for every R, and 1 for every N. Total your points and evaluate your score.

41–50 Excellent You may be surprised to find out how much you can improve your skills.

31–40 Good In this course, you can learn ways to make your skills better.

21–30 Fair Practice applying the skills taught in this course.

1–20 Needs Improvement Carefully monitor your improvement as you work through this course.

Setting Communication Goals

If you scored Excellent or Good, complete Part A. If your score was Fair or Needs Improvement, complete Part B.

Part A

1. I plan to put the following ideas into practice:

2. I plan to share the following information about communication with the following people:

Part B

1. The behaviors I need to change most are:

2. To bring about these changes I will take these steps:

The Writing Process

There are certain steps to follow when writing a report, an article for the company newsletter, a memorandum, a letter, or any other type of written information. These steps are recursive; that is, they do not always follow one another in order and you may repeat steps until you end up with the result you want.

Whether you will give the information to a supervisor or other individual, share with other team members, or present to a large audience, you need to put your ideas into a logical and useful form. Using the steps in the writing process will help you do just that.

Writing tasks are completed in five steps:

Step 1 prewriting

Step 2 drafting

Step 3 revising

Step 4 editing/proofreading

Step 5 publishing/presenting

Step 1 Prewriting In general, the pre-writing process is the way you approach a given writing project. During prewriting you decide on your topic, establish your purpose and audience, and research and plan your writing. Your purpose is what you want to accomplish through your writing or presentation. Your audience is whoever will read or hear your words. You planning includes developing an outline.

Step 2 Writing a Draft After you have defined your topic and audience and have organized your ideas, you can begin to write a draft of your report. As you write, make sure your report has an introduction, the body, or main part, and a conclusion.

Step 3 Revising A first draft is the first version of a written work. Professional writers know that they must never turn in a first draft to a publisher because it is not a final, finished product. After finishing the first draft, writers know that they must take a critical look at their ideas and find ways to improve them.

Some effective ways to review your writing are to read the work carefully as if you were seeing it for the first time. You might choose to read it aloud, listen to a tape-recording of yourself reading it aloud, or have someone else read it and give you feedback. At this point you have the opportunity to move sentences or paragraphs around, improve paragraphs, and check the content and structure of your writing.

During the revision process, you can adjust the tone and style of your writing. Ask yourself if the writing reflects the purpose that you originally intended. Is the

For additional information about the writing process, see the *Language Handbook* in the Communication Survival Kit found in the Appendix.

Communication Through Writing

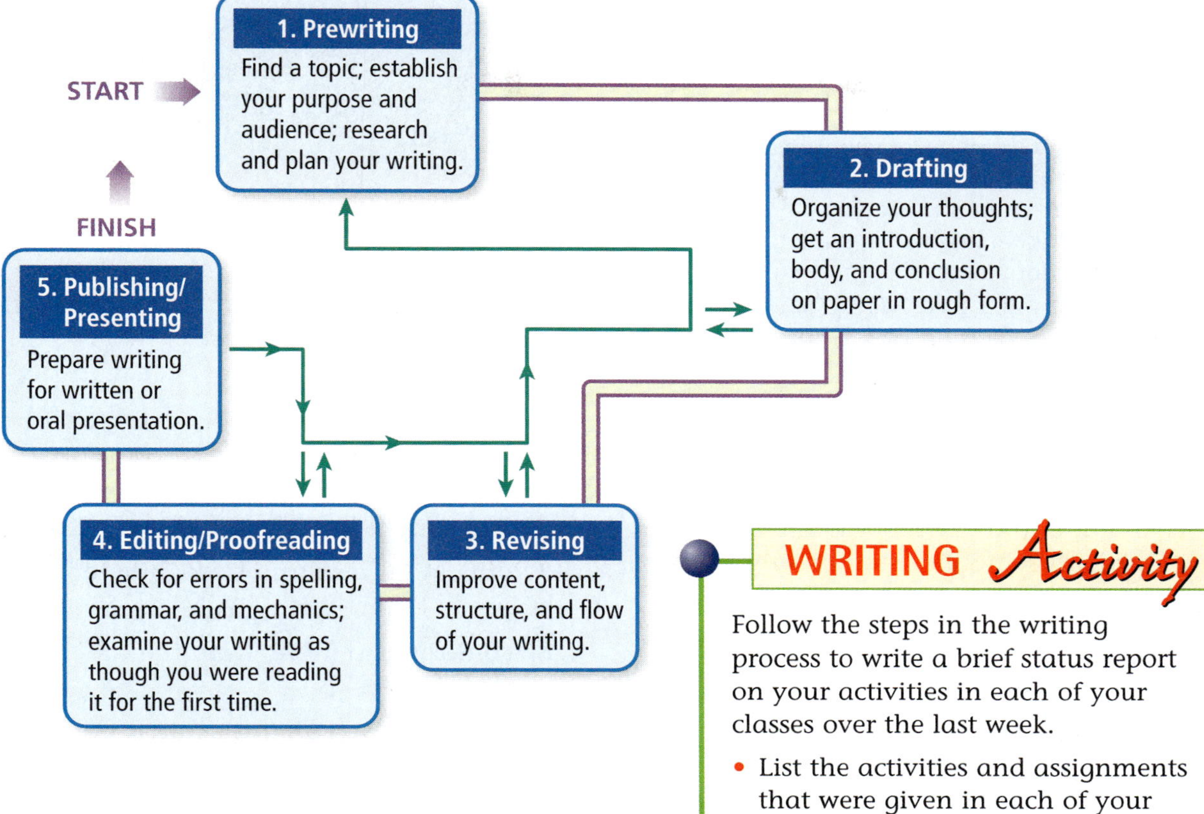

language specific, descriptive, and non-sexist? Are the words and ideas clear?

START
FINISH
1. Prewriting
Find a topic; establish your purpose and audience; research and plan your writing.
2. Drafting
Organize your thoughts; get an introduction, body, and conclusion on paper in rough form.
3. Revising
Improve content, structure, and flow of your writing.
4. Editing/Proofreading
Check for errors in spelling, grammar, and mechanics; examine your writing as though you were reading it for the first time.
5. Publishing/Presenting
Prepare writing for written or oral presentation.

Step 4 Editing/Proofreading Once you have revised your draft, you still need to refine your work. Check for errors in sentence structure, capitalization, spelling, punctuation, and grammar. If you have used word-processing software, run a spelling check on your work.

Step 5 Publishing/Presenting You now are ready to send or present your work to your audience. Often, someone else, such as your teacher, a supervisor or manager, or a member of an organization, will define the method of delivery.

WRITING *Activity*

Follow the steps in the writing process to write a brief status report on your activities in each of your classes over the last week.

- List the activities and assignments that were given in each of your classes.
- List your progress in meeting those assignments.
- Write a first draft of your status report. Make sure you have an introduction, body, and a conclusion. Your audience will be your teacher.
- Revise the content, structure, or flow of your report where necessary.
- Edit and proofread your work for errors in grammar, sentence structure, spelling, punctuation, and capitalization.
- Prepare the final draft of your status report.

CHAPTER 1 Assessment and Activities

GLENCOE Online

Visit the *Glencoe Communication Applications* Web site at **communicationapplications.glencoe.com** and click on **Chapter 1 Activity** for additional practice in putting communication to work for you.

Reviewing Key Terms

On a separate sheet of paper, write the communication term defined in each item.

1. creating and exchanging meaning through symbolic interaction
2. specific situation in which communication occurs
3. what is suitable in a particular instance
4. guideline to use as a basis for making appropriate communication choices
5. people who have specific duties united for a particular purpose
6. "the way things are done around here"
7. difficulties resulting from individual or group differences
8. confusion resulting from the clash of two cultures
9. uses effective communication skills
10. willingness to help others

Reviewing Key Concepts

On a separate sheet of paper, answer the following questions in complete sentences.

1. Why is it critical to understand and analyze context when making communication choices?
2. Why is appropriateness an important consideration in communication?
3. What can be used as a guide to determine appropriateness?
4. What is the function of a standard in your communication choices?
5. What three criteria can be used to determine if someone is a competent communicator?
6. Name and describe the three needs fulfilled by membership in organizations.
7. Analyze and respond to the statement "Culture influences every aspect of an organization."
8. What are two possible effects of diversity within an organization?

Assessment and Activities

Reading and Critical Thinking Skill

1. **Making Predictions** Describe five communication tasks that you might be required to do as a worker in a business of your choice.
2. **Analysis** Why is the hierarchy of a corporation important to the organization's culture?

Skill Practice Activity

Analyzing Information Read the excerpt below and write a summary sentence of the passage.

Whenever you make an important decision in your life, you first "weigh the consequences." A consequence is the result of an action or series of events. For example, if you were deciding whether to buy or rent a house, you might think about the advantages and disadvantages of both actions. In other words, you examine the various results of each action. By analyzing the possible outcomes or consequences, you arrive at a better understanding of the situation.

Cooperative Learning Activity

Communication Challenge Break up into groups of three to five students. One group of three will act as judges. The other groups will write a scenario of a communication situation they find challenging and make recommendations to remedy, solve, or avoid the situation. Each group will then act out its situation for the other class members and present its recommendations. After each presentation, other groups will list communication strategies they believe will remedy, solve, or avoid the situation. After all groups have presented, the three-judge panel will confer briefly to choose the group that generated the most appropriate list of suggestions. The panel will justify their choices to the class.

Chapter Project

Planning Choose a career or profession in which you are interested. Investigate your chosen profession. Consult a variety of sources for the information you need. Find the answers to these questions: What is the employment potential in this field? What kind of educational and vocational training is most needed for employment? Are there any special requirements for entering the field, such as qualifying exams, special fees, or licenses? What communication skills are especially helpful for getting a job, keeping a job, and getting promotions in this field? Record your findings and prioritize your ideas.

Presenting Use your findings to develop and give a three-minute presentation on your chosen career.

CHAPTER 2

Exploring the Communication Process

WHY IT'S IMPORTANT

Communication is a powerful tool that we use to meet our needs, accomplish goals, and get results. Communication is the key to success in many professional and social contexts.

To better understand how important the communication process is in your social and professional lives, view the **Communication in Action** Chapter 2 video lesson.

"If all my possessions were taken from me with one exception, I would hope to keep my power of communication—for by it I would regain all the rest."
—Daniel Webster, American jurist

GLENCOE Online

Visit the *Glencoe Communication Applications* Web site at **communicationapplications.glencoe.com** and click on **Overview–Chapter 2** to preview information about the communication process.

Section 1

The Nature of the Communication Process

GUIDE TO READING

Objectives

1. Explain the five principles of communication.
2. Identify the components of the communication process.
3. Identify the basic functions of the components of the communication process.
4. Analyze the processes used by sender-receivers and receiver-senders.

Terms to Learn

transactional
sender-receiver
receiver-sender
message
channel
noise
barrier
feedback
data
sensory perception
encoding
transmitting
acquiring
decoding

What do playing baseball and communicating have in common? Both are a series of actions that work together to produce a result. In other words, they are both processes.

Think about baseball. There are separate processes for each action, such as pitching, batting, or fielding. All of these elements work together in a process that results in a game. Communication also has separate processes. All of the elements of communication work together in a process that results in people creating and exchanging meaning.

The Communication Process

When you understand the processes involved in communicating, you have some powerful tools under your control. These tools can help you make appropriate communication choices for the results you want to achieve. They will also help you to develop the knowledge, attitude, and skills to become a competent communicator.

Baseball players must work through all of the separate processes of baseball in order to play the game. What is the result of the process of communication?

Elements of Communication

In Chapter 1, communication is described as the process of human beings creating and exchanging meaning through symbolic interaction. You can break this definition down to further reveal that communication has three distinct elements: process, meaning, and symbols.

Communication as a Process As shown in Figure 2–1, communication is an interactive process—the parts and actions work together to achieve results. As individuals talk with one another, listen to one another, and use nonverbal behaviors to communicate their meanings and feelings, they are interacting. Energy and meaning are being exchanged between participants in the process.

Because it is a process, communication constantly moves, shifts, and changes; it does not stand still. The communication process is made up of individual components, and these components occur in a specific sequence: action, energy, and results. The components and actions involved in communication change from one situation to another, but the circular nature of communication and continuity of the process remain the same.

Just as any process involves energy, the communication process uses the mental and physical energy of people who speak, listen, use nonverbal behaviors, and interpret the verbal and nonverbal behaviors of others. As a result, communicators seek to use their energy wisely, as in building productive relationships and solving problems in groups.

Meaning in Communication Meaning is an important part of the definition of communication. It includes the thoughts, ideas, and understandings that are created, exchanged, and shared by communicators. We

Figure 2–1 Parts and Actions of a Process

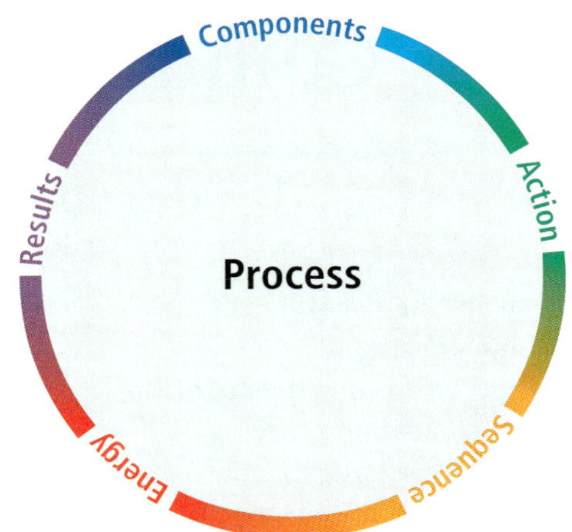

constantly create meanings as our brains try to make sense of the world around us. We, as communicators, also seek to share those meanings and understandings with others. Each time we communicate with another person, we create new meanings and understandings.

For example, imagine that you are confused by an assignment for a history class. You decide to talk to your teacher. As a result of the conversation, both of you gain new understandings or new meanings. Later you discuss the project with another classmate. You communicate with one another to interpret information, talk about issues, solve problems, and make plans. Through the give-and-take of your interactions you develop still more understandings and ideas. In this way, exchanging and creating new meanings may result in a better project.

Symbols in Communication A symbol stands for an idea or a feeling. For example, a trophy is a symbol for a team's victory. We cannot communicate meanings and feelings by reading each other's minds. Symbolic interaction means that we rely on words (written and oral) and nonverbal behaviors such as gestures, eye contact, and facial expressions to communicate meanings and feelings.

Principles of Communication

As a communicator, it is important to understand what communication is before you can understand how to apply it to your life. To help you understand, consider the five basic principles, or understandings, of communication that are given below:

- transactional
- complex
- unavoidable
- continuous
- learned

Communication Is Transactional

Communication is a transactional process. A transactional process is one that involves an exchange. Communicators exchange messages, sending and receiving them at the same time. Each communicator is both a sender and a receiver of messages, often juggling several different messages at the same time.

In communication, participants also perform other transactions. They bargain and negotiate with one another to create and exchange meanings. Communicators involved in a conversation may be bargaining for acceptance as persons, for understanding of a particular behavior or action, for attention, or to persuade a listener to accept a particular point of view.

Another transactional characteristic of the action of communication is that all components and processes are interactive. In other words, each part and each action affect the others.

Communication Is Complex

Communication consists of a number of components and a series of interrelated processes. As shown in the chart below, communication is complex.

COMMUNICATION IS COMPLEX BECAUSE IT IS . . .

Interactive	Communication involves a series of complicated and interrelated processes. Each of these processes affects each of the others and becomes interactive as we communicate.
Symbolic	Meaning is communicated through the use of symbols. Because these symbols stand for meaning, they are always open to interpretation.
Personal and Cultural	Because words and gestures are symbols for meaning and feeling, they are very personal. A person's culture can also add a new or different meaning to a phrase or gesture.
Irreversible	Once you have sent a message, you cannot take it back. It is forever. You can only send additional messages to try to correct any mistakes or misunderstandings that may have been communicated along with your original message.
Impossible to Duplicate	Each interaction between a sender and a receiver is unique and happens only once in exactly the same way. The conditions of the communication will never again be exactly the same.
Circular	Communication involves original messages and feedback to those messages. Feedback is necessary to confirm that communication has occurred.
Purposeful	There is always a reason behind an intentional message. It has a stimulus and a purpose. Communication helps us meet needs such as the need to secure food and shelter, get and give information, belong, and be respected and valued as a person.

Communication Is Unavoidable

Even though most of us have heard someone say, "We're not communicating," the truth is that it is impossible not to communicate. Even a refusal to communicate is a type of communication.

Think about the last time you were alone on an elevator and then another person got on. You may have felt uncomfortable with a stranger in your personal space. To avoid communication, you might have looked straight ahead, stared at the floor, or casually examined the elevator's floor and ceiling. The stranger may have stood in the farthest corner of the elevator and stared straight ahead at the door. Were you communicating with one another? Believe it or not, the answer is yes. A great deal of energy was exchanged between the two of you even though you did not say a word to each other. You were telling each other "I'm uncomfortable communicating with you." Attempting to avoid communication is communication in itself.

Communication Is Continuous

Communication is ongoing. Once you have had an interaction with an individual, future communication with him or her is forever impacted by your initial communication and your memories of it. Even the business or social activity that was the context for the interaction is affected. For example, your communication with the salesperson at the music store will affect your feelings and behavior toward him or her, possibly the store, and perhaps even salespeople in general. Communication continues to influence future interactions and shape our relationships.

Skillful Communication Can Be Learned

Communication skills are mainly learned behaviors. Although you were taught how to read and write, you likely learned to speak and listen in your native language much more indirectly: by observing and mimicking the verbal and nonverbal behaviors of the people around you.

Fortunately, it is possible to improve your communication skills. No matter how effective you may believe them to be, listening, speaking, reading, and writing skills are all improved through practice.

Components of the Communication Process

Communication has a specific set of interactive components. Each has a unique function in the process and affects the communication that takes place. The components of the communication process and their functions are shown in the chart on page 39.

Context

In Chapter 1, you learned that context includes people who are playing specific roles. It also includes the occasion and the task. The function of context in communication is found in that definition. It includes the place and time when the communication occurs and the relationship between the communicators. Context helps us make appropriate communication choices in a given situation. For example, it may not be considered appropriate for a student to get up and walk around during a class lecture. However, it is perfectly acceptable to do so while you are watching television at home.

COMPONENTS OF THE COMMUNICATION PROCESS AND THEIR BASIC FUNCTIONS

Component	Basic Functions
Context	Provides the people, the occasion, and the task
Physical Environment	Influences the quality of interaction within the physical space
Climate	Influences the emotional, attitudinal, and intellectual tone of the communication
Communicator	Creates meaning, sends and receives messages, and exchanges meaning
Message	Conveys meaning, feeling, and various kinds of energy from sender-receiver to receiver-sender
Channel	Provides the space through which the message must pass; determines the method used to send the message
Noise	Interferes with or disrupts communication
Barrier	Blocks communication
Feedback	• Assures the sender-receiver that communication has occurred • Allows the receiver-sender to adjust or modify a message • Provides insight into the sender-receiver's communication

Physical Environment

The second component in the communication process is physical environment. The physical environment in communication functions to provide the surroundings or the space in which communication takes place. The physical environment affects the quality of interaction. A positive environment leads to better communication. Likewise, a negative environment can lead to communication problems. For example, think about how you feel and behave when your classroom is either too hot or too cold. The temperature of the room may become a distraction that affects your communication. If you are too hot, you may become irritable or sleepy. If you are too cold, you may become withdrawn, devoting all your energy to trying to stay warm.

Just as teachers understand the effects of physical environment on their students, business people recognize that environment can affect productivity. They understand that most people work best in environments that are safe, comfortable, clean, well lit, orderly, and cheerful.

Climate

A third component of the communication process is climate. You may ask what the function of climate is in communication. It is the emotional atmosphere—the tone in which interaction takes place. Emotions and attitudes create the climate. Also, the content of the communication and the history of the participants affect climate.

Negative Climate For example, upon entering a room full of people, you may sense an overall feeling of tension. The communicators' tones, facial expressions, and gestures may shout "We're stressed out!" whether the conversation communicates stress or not. In this case, the emotions and attitudes of the communicators are overriding the intellectual content of the conversation.

This classroom is set up to encourage various types of student and teacher interaction. **What kind of classroom arrangement might be set up for small group interaction?**

Positive Climate Even just one or two people can affect the climate of an entire room. They can charge the climate with stress and tension, or they can provide a calming, soothing climate. Have you ever walked into a room where you sensed an overall relaxed feeling? People were smiling. The discussion was interesting and interactive. The climate in that room could be described as warm (emotions), positive (attitudes), and interesting (intellectual content).

Environment and Climate Architects often study the relationship between communication and climate when designing the spaces in which people live, learn, and work. A successful design considers the kind of interaction that is intended to take place within a particular environment. This, in

Global Communication

Communication Climate

Americans are sometimes considered to be individualistic. This may become evident in meetings when individuals express their personal opinions openly and directly. In some cultures, such as Chinese, Korean, or Japanese, group goals and decisions often are valued more than individual efforts. The emphasis there is more on the group in workplace communication. Keeping this in mind, why might Americans and Japanese describe the climate of the same meeting differently?

turn, helps create a desirable climate. For instance, teachers create an environment and influence the climate of a classroom when they design seating arrangements. For lectures, a teacher wants students to pay attention. He or she also will want to limit interaction between students. Therefore, students' desks or chairs may be arranged in rows facing the teacher. To invite a climate of active participation and discussion, the teacher may arrange chairs in small circles or seat students around tables so they can work together.

Climate and physical environment affect the communication that takes place in a meeting. **How does the seating arrangement in the photograph encourage the audience to pay attention to the speaker?**

Communicator

The people involved in an interaction make up the fourth component in the communication process. The basic function of communicators is to create and exchange meaning. Because communicators send and receive messages at the same time, they are both sender-receivers and receiver-senders.

Sender-Receiver The **sender-receiver** is the person who sends a message to someone. At the same time the message is being sent, the sender-receiver is receiving and processing feedback from the receiver-sender.

Imagine that you have applied for a summer job at a local business. You approach the receptionist, give your name, and state that you have an appointment with the manager. Because you are the person beginning the give-and-take of the interaction, you assume the role of sender-receiver. As you send your message by speaking, you also are noting the receptionist's smile and listening to the suggestion that you sit in a nearby chair to wait for the manager. You have sent and received messages at the same time.

Receiver-Sender The **receiver-sender** is the person who receives, or believes he or she has received, a message. Like the sender-receiver, a receiver-sender obtains and provides feedback at the same time. The receptionist in this example is the receiver-sender. This person watches as

Figure 2–2 Building the Communication Process Model

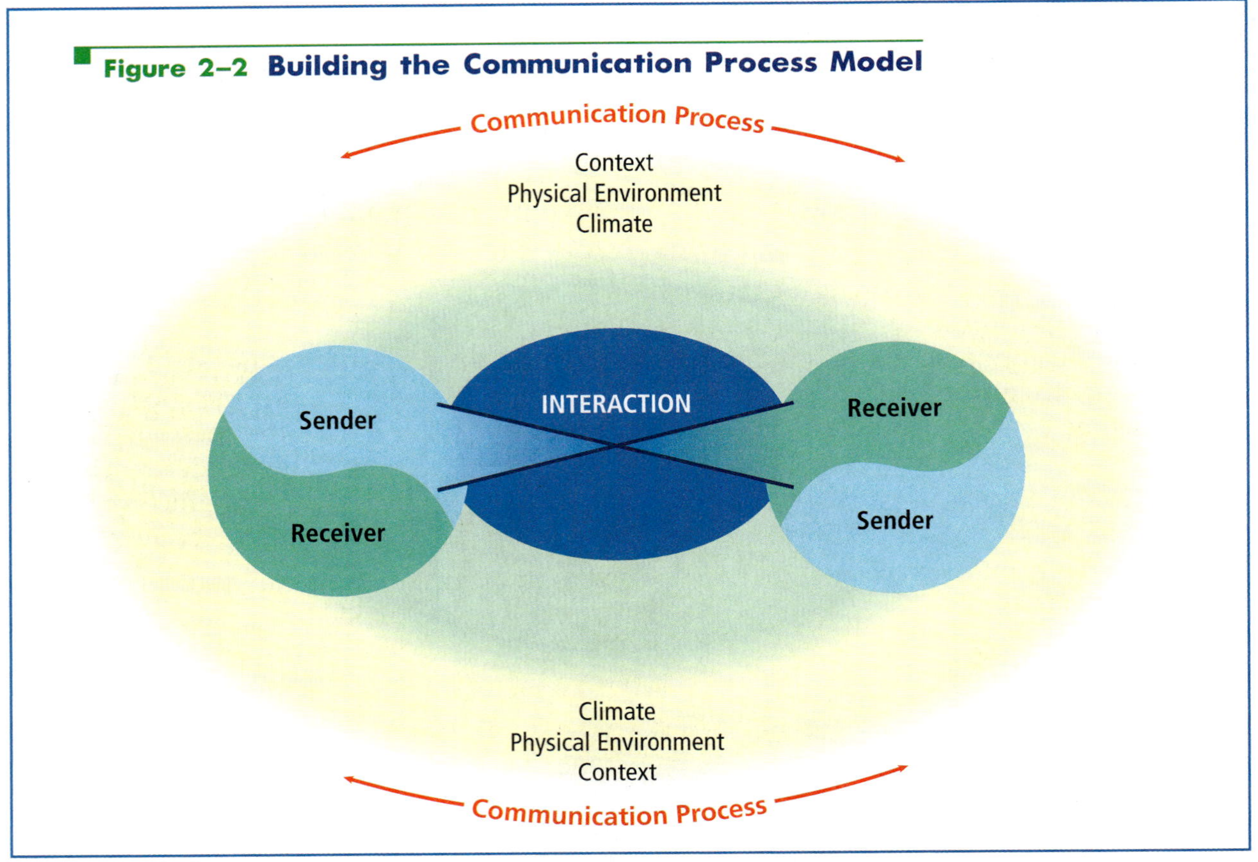

you—the sender-receiver—approach and listens to your explanation. The receptionist's feedback indicates that your message has been received. By smiling and initiating a new message, "If you'll wait over there for a moment, I'll try to find the manager," the receptionist has exchanged roles with you to become the sender-receiver. This person may make a mental note of your confident manner and think, "The manager probably will like this applicant." The receptionist also is receiving and sending messages at the same time.

You can see in **Figure 2–2** that communication requires lots of interaction—all at the same time—between communicators. In addition, the roles of these communicators change continually from sender-receiver to receiver-sender.

Message

Message probably is the most difficult component of the communication process to define. You might think that messages usually are clear and easy to understand. You also may assume that if a receiver-sender can hear your message, he or she can understand it. Finally, it is easy to believe that feedback is a sign that your message has been heard and understood.

Defining Message Interestingly, all of these assumptions can be false. A **message** is the information that is exchanged between communicators. What is the function of a message? Its purpose is to convey meanings and feelings between senders and receivers.

Interpreting a Message Every message is open to interpretation—or misinterpretation. Just because someone sends a message doesn't mean that the exact message was understood by the receiver. In fact, messages can be misunderstood, or they might not be received at all. The Amelia Bedelia stories, by Peggy Parish, illustrate how messages can be misinterpreted. In the series, Amelia constantly misinterprets messages; for example, when asked to "dress," or stuff the turkey, she puts clothes on it.

Receiving a Message Receiver-senders at work also do not always receive a message as it was intended. Studies on the differences between male and female managers have uncovered differences in how men and women communicate, and these differences affect how messages are received by their staffs. For example, imagine that your manager says to you, "Would you do me a favor and back me up at tomorrow's meeting?" How might you, as the receiver-sender, interpret this request? Is the message a request you can refuse?

Does "back me up" mean take your boss's place? Be prepared to explain all the research behind your department's request for more technology funds? Or, does it mean that, if you're free, you should show up and sit quietly during the meeting?

Female managers tend to soften work-related directions with words like "do me a favor," "if you could," and "would you mind," while male managers, according to studies, are more direct in phrasing their requirements. Nevertheless, if messages are unclear to the receiver, misinterpretation and misunderstandings are bound to occur. Understanding more about messages can help you make your meanings clear.

The receptionist and applicant are communicating; therefore, they are sending and receiving messages. What is the function of message in the communication process?

Receiver–Sender
Sender–Receiver
"Hello, I'm Joe Martin. I have an appointment at 3:00 with David Smith."
Watches. Listens.

Receiver–Sender
Sender–Receiver
"3:00. I spoke with him last Thursday."
Listens. Dials on intercom.

Sender–Receiver
Receiver–Sender
"What time?"
Waits. Listens.

Sender–Receiver
Receiver–Sender
"If you'll wait over there for a moment, I'll try to find him."
Listens. Moves to a chair.

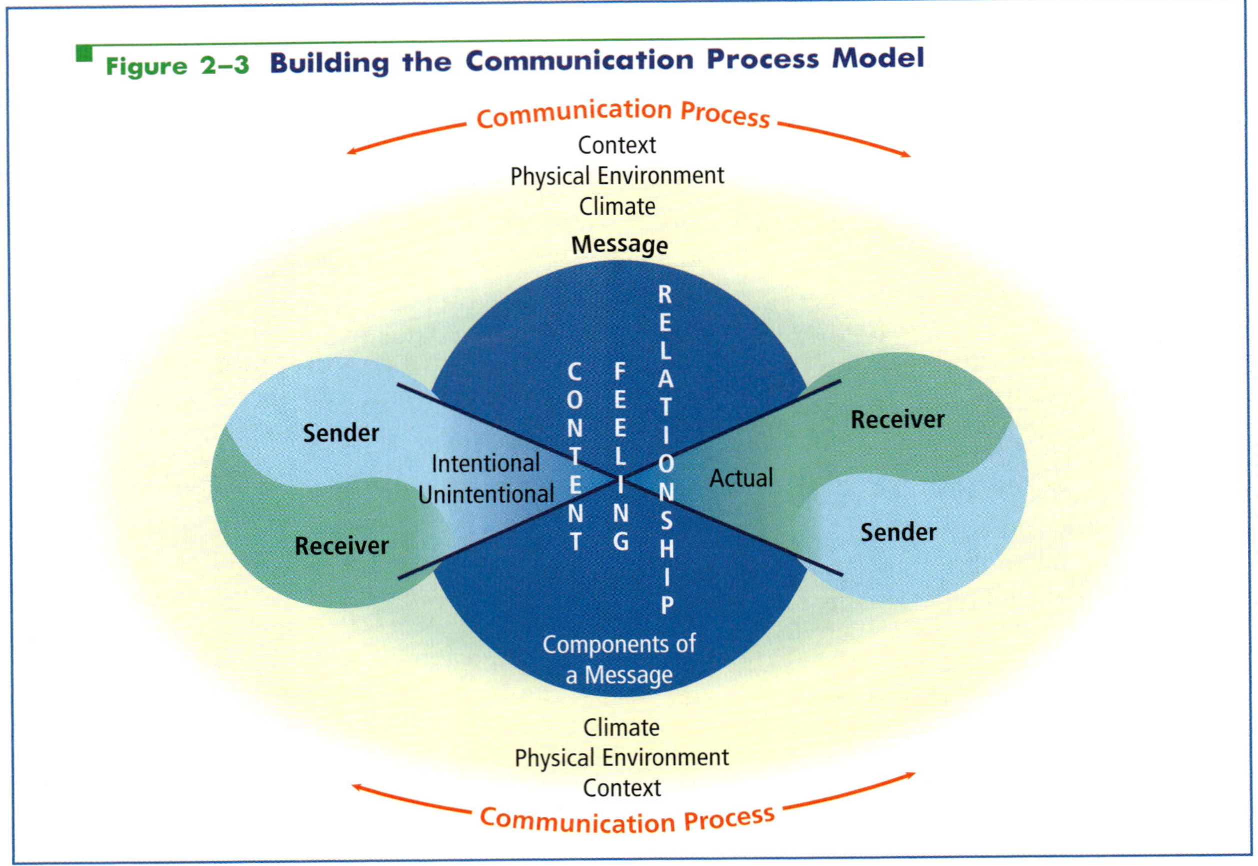

Figure 2–3 Building the Communication Process Model

Classifying a Message Messages can be classified by both the intentions of the person who sends the message and the interpretation of the person who receives it. There are three kinds of messages: intentional, unintentional, and actual. Notice how these have been added to the model in **Figure 2–3** above.

Intentional Message An intentional message is made up of the meanings and feelings one person wishes to send to another. When you open a conversation, you usually have a message you intend to send. You might say, "May I borrow your pencil?" "I'm here to apply for a job," or "Sorry I'm late for class."

Most of the time, you probably assume that your meaning is clear, whether or not it is. For example, when you ask "May I borrow your pencil?" your question appears to be a clearly worded message conveying your intent: You need a pencil. Typically, senders use their best language skills to send intentional messages that express specific meanings and feelings.

Unintentional Message An unintentional message is one that the sender-receiver either does not mean to send or is unaware of sending. An unintentional message can lead to communication problems if it contradicts or clouds a receiver-sender's interpretation of an intended message.

Unintentional messages can be tricky. In fact, the sender-receiver may be completely unaware of some meaning the receiver-sender has assigned to an intended message. For example, "May I borrow your pencil?" may unintentionally send the message as "I'm careless and can't keep track of my things" or "I'm never prepared for class." The receiver-sender may perceive you as making a habit of borrowing pencils in class.

Intentions stated in words may be contradicted altogether by your choice of language. For instance, you might not be aware of using poor grammar or of overusing some slang term. The same effect can be caused by nonverbal behaviors of which you are not even aware. Avoiding eye contact may send an unintended message that you are uninterested or have something to hide.

However, all these behaviors may unintentionally change the meaning of your intended message. Individuals constantly send unintentional messages that can cloud the meanings and feelings they intend to convey.

Actual Message An actual message is the message the receiver-sender receives. It is what he or she thinks the speaker is actually saying. What happens if the sender's intended message and the receiver's actual message differ? Misunderstandings occur when the meaning a receiver assigns to a sender's message does not relate to the meaning the sender attempted to convey.

Components of a Message Regardless of whether a message is intentional or unintentional, it is made up of three specific components: the content of the message, the communicators' feelings, and the relationship between the communicators.

Content When two or more people communicate, the main purpose of the interaction is to exchange information. At home, you may tell your parents what time you'll be home from practice. At school, your teacher may give you a formula to solve math problems. At work, you and your coworkers may discuss how to improve customer service to build up your client base. In all these examples, specific content, or information, is communicated between the sender-receivers and the receiver-senders.

Feeling When you talk, you not only send messages about what you are thinking but also how you feel about the topic. In addition, you convey how you feel about the situation in which you are involved. Sometimes, you may express your feelings in other ways besides simply stating them. For instance, you might not always state "I'm terribly bored with this meeting" or "I really enjoy your company." Instead, you may convey these messages through your attitudes or actions.

Relationship Another aspect of a message involves an equally important component: relationship. The relationship that exists between the communicators—from how much they like each other to the roles they

This student is saying one thing in words while communicating something entirely different through his body language. What communication problems result from unintentional messages?

play—affects the message. For example, you might speak casually with a friend about a pair of gym shoes you want to buy. However, the same conversation with a shoe store clerk might be more business-like. Relationship, therefore, is an important factor in both sending and receiving messages. At work, a suggestion from a well-liked coworker probably will be received more positively than a suggestion from a coworker you dislike or do not trust. Whether you are the sender-receiver or the receiver-sender, you can't always know for sure how the other person interprets your message. Because of these variables, messages can be misunderstood.

Channel

So far, you have learned that the context, physical environment, climate, communicator, and message all are components of the communication process. Another important component is the channel. **Channel** is the space in which the message is transmitted. In one sense channel is the method, or medium, by which the sender conveys the message. Examples of a channel of communication include face-to-face dialogue, a phone call, an e-mail, or a letter. Even voice-mail or answering-machine messages are channels. The basic function of the channel is to provide the means of transmitting a message.

Choosing the channel or medium of communication appropriate to the context is an important decision in professional and social situations. If you wish to communicate news of an upcoming sale to your preferred customers, you might want to consider making personal telephone calls or sending personal notes to these special customers. If you have less time to devote to the project, you might choose a less personal method such as a flyer. Each method conveys a different perception of the relationship between you and your customer. Different channels may yield different results.

The telephone represents a channel of communication.
What are other channels of communication?

Noise

Another component of the communication process is noise. **Noise** is anything that interferes with a message and is usually temporary. Noise has a negative function in communication. Both internal noise and external noise can be sources of communication difficulty.

Internal Noise Sometimes, communicators create their own noise. Interference that originates from and resides within a communicator is known as internal noise. For example, if you are sleepy, cold, or ill, you may find it difficult to concentrate on messages from others. Anger, preoccupation, and moodiness are other examples of internal noise. Internal noise—whether physical or emotional—can disrupt communication.

TECHNOLOGY *Activity*

Communication Channels For one week, keep a journal that includes how much time you spend using various types of technology to send and receive messages. These may include such channels as television, telephone, e-mail, the World Wide Web, radio, and fax. Based on your journal, discuss the advantages and disadvantages of each channel. Then, select one channel and prepare a one-minute presentation about it. In your presentation, explain why you prefer that channel to convey your message to your receiver-senders.

External Noise External noise is a distraction in the channel or in the physical environment. The smell of rolls baking in the cafeteria may distract you as you try to take notes during class. The constant talking of a coworker may interfere with your ability to do your job efficiently. A speaker's sloppy appearance or unclear speech may create external noise in the communication channel that interferes with listeners' clear reception of the message.

Internal and external noise can exist in any part of the communication process. Trained communicators learn to overcome the obstacles noise presents. They work to develop concentration skills that help them neutralize noise, limit its effects, and improve their ability to focus on the task at hand. The following Communication Strategies can be used when trying to overcome noise.

Barrier

The eighth component of the communication process is barrier. The basic function of barrier is found in its definition. In communication, a **barrier** is any obstacle that blocks communication. Like noise, barriers can be internal or external. Unlike noise, they tend to be long-term problems.

Internal Barriers An internal barrier is a barrier that originates from or resides within a communicator. Some of the common barriers to communication are ignorance, prejudice, defensiveness, and competitiveness. These conditions may block a communicator's desire to communicate with others. They also can affect a communicator's interpretation of the messages of others.

If you and a coworker were to compete for the same promotion, competitiveness could destroy the trust needed for productive day-to-day communication. This lack of trust could negatively affect your job performance and even destroy the relationship between you and the coworker. This, in turn, could influence whether or not either of you is awarded the job.

Barriers can be extremely destructive in the communication process. They can cause communicators to tune out or seriously misinterpret the messages of others. Because barriers tend to run deep within communicators' thinking processes, they can be difficult to overcome.

COMMUNICATION *Strategies*

OVERCOMING NOISE

- **Prepare, if possible, for the communication situation.**
- **Develop concentration skills.**
- **Neutralize internal distractions where possible.**
- **Focus on the task at hand.**
- **Speak clearly.**
- **Be aware of the listener's response.**

Airplane passengers sometimes have difficulty hearing messages relayed over the public address system due to external barriers within an airport. Identify other external barriers to communication.

External Barriers Like external noise, an external barrier exists in the channel or in other parts of the communication process. Two people who don't speak the same language may experience barriers to their communication. Unclear speech also can pose a barrier. Information mumbled unclearly over an airport's public address system may result in confused passengers who are put in danger of missing their flights.

Different interpretations of nonverbal signals often present barriers to communication. For example, the well-known thumbs-up gesture is open to many different interpretations around the world. In the United States, the gesture conveys a message of strong approval, such as "Well done," "You're doing great," or "Go for it." However, the same gesture can have very different meanings elsewhere. In Germany, for example, thumbs up means "one." So, you might use the thumbs-up sign to order one glass of lemonade. However, if you used the same symbol in Japan, you probably would be surprised when your server returned with five full glasses. In Japan, thumbs up means "five." Interestingly, thumbs down seems to be bad news no matter in what country you are. It typically means something is wrong or bad.

Like spoken language, nonverbal language varies from country to country. Paying close attention to their own nonverbal cues can help travelers avoid barriers to communication.

In addition to nonverbal barriers, time and distance also may create barriers. Much of the technology of the twentieth century has been devoted to removing and neutralizing barriers created by time and distance. Telephones, fax machines, computer networks, e-mail, airplanes, subways, and freeways all help to minimize these common communication barriers.

Feedback

The final component of the communication process is feedback. **Feedback** is one person's observable response to another's message. When you acknowledge a friend's greeting with a smile and a wave, you send nonverbal feedback that says, "Thanks for that warm hello! Hello to you too!" Some feedback is oral, as when the taxi driver acknowledges the street address a rider asks to be taken to. Finally, no response, too, is feed back. Even without words or gestures, this type of silent feedback is very powerful and can indicate how one person feels about another.

Feedback has three basic functions in the communication process:

- It assures the sender-receiver that communication has occurred.
- It allows the sender-receiver to adjust or modify a message for greater clarity and understanding by the receiver-sender.
- It provides insight into the communicator's message.

Assurance It is unsafe to assume that communication has occurred until there is feedback. If you do not return your friend's greeting, your friend may draw the wrong conclusion about your lack of an obvious response to the message. While it is possible that you saw and heard the greeting and just chose not to respond, your friend cannot even be sure you received the message until he or she receives some kind of feedback.

Adjustment Feedback completes the circular pattern of communication. It allows a sender-receiver to adjust a message when the feedback indicates that there is a lack of understanding by the receiver-sender. The sender-receiver may restate the idea, provide an example, or give a definition.

Insight Feedback from others can give communicators valuable insights into their own communication skills and styles. What kinds of results do you get when you communicate with others? How can you use feedback to adapt and build your verbal, nonverbal, and listening skills? Can feedback help you achieve better relationships or more effective results from your communication interactions? Learning to use feedback to adapt your communication can yield positive results.

Each of the nine components of the communication process has a powerful effect on understanding. By learning more about context, physical environment, climate, communicators, message, channel, noise, barriers, and feedback, you improve your ability to convey precise meanings and achieve results.

COMMUNICATION PRACTICE LAB

Identifying Components of the Communication Process

Follow these steps to identify components of a communication interaction.

Step 1 As a class, make a list of familiar places in your school or community where professional or social activities are carried out on a daily basis. For example, you might list the main office of your school, the local post office, or a local business.

Step 2 If possible, observe a communication interaction in a particular location. If you cannot observe one, describe a situation that might take place in such a location.

Step 3 Identify each component of the communication process that was evident in the interaction.

Step 4 List the positive and negative effects of each component of the interaction.

Step 5 Present your communication situation to the class. Make sure you also give them your observations.

Analyzing the Action

Picture a Hollywood movie set. The actors, sets, lights, and cameras are all in place. However, one element is still missing. The process of making a movie doesn't start until someone yells "Action!" As with movie making, communication needs action. The different parts of the communication process are all in place. Now it needs the energy of the participants to drive the process and make interaction possible.

At this point, the study of communication shifts to the action of the process. What purposes do each of the components of communication serve in the overall process? How does the function of each part affect the functions of other parts?

interNET ACTIVITY

Sensory Perception Log on to the Internet and access a dependable World Wide Web search engine to search for sites that include audio and video clips with a lot of sensory appeal. You might search for art museums like the Louvre in Paris at **mistral.culture.fr/louvre** or other museums like The Cooper-Hewitt National Design Museum at **www.si.edu/ndm.** You might also search for zoos, astronomy sites, aquariums, movies, and music sites. Analyze the sensory data provided at the site. What sensory data seems to be missing?

Processes Used by Sender-Receivers

In a car's engine, fuel provides the energy. What provides the energy in the communication process? As a sender-receiver, your ideas, feelings, needs, and goals fuel the process. In order to send message about them, you use a sequence of processes. As shown in Figure 2–4, sender-receivers use the following three processes:

Figure 2–4 Processes Used by Sender-Receivers

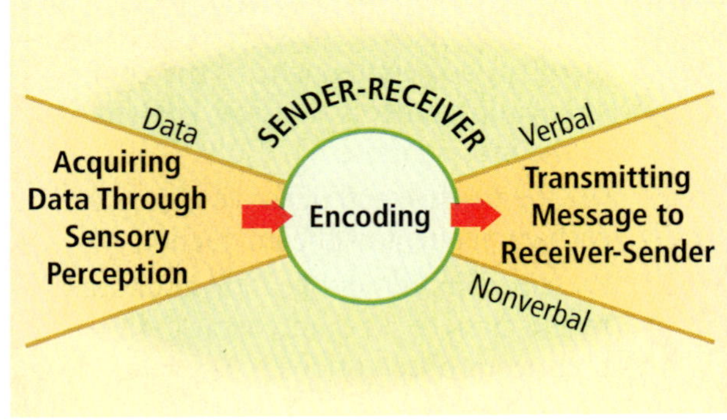

- sensory perception
- encoding
- transmitting

Sensory Perception Think about all the data that your brain processes every day. **Data** is made up of those things that catch a communicator's attention, such as objects, people, sounds, thoughts, memories, and the messages sent by others. You take in this data through your senses. **Sensory perception** is the complex physical process of taking in data through the five senses. Seeing, hearing, smelling, tasting, and touching all are important sensory processes. How does a chef know something is burning on the stove? How does he or she know whether a pot of soup needs additional seasoning? The chef relies on the senses of smell and taste to acquire the information used in cooking.

Data by itself has no meaning until a person discovers it and assigns meaning to it.

Our knowledge of the world around us is driven by a variety of stimuli. Sometimes, a stimulus is external, driven by our senses. Other times, a fleeting memory, a thought, or other internal stimulus moves us to communicate. As the first step in the series of actions, sensory perception motivates the sender-receiver to communicate.

Encoding Once a stimulus from one of the senses is relayed to the brain, the brain immediately begins organizing the data and trying to assign meaning to it. This sorting and filtering process is called encoding. **Encoding** is the mental process of assigning meaning and language to data.

To encode a message, your brain performs two functions. First, it connects meaning to the data by filtering it through your previous knowledge and experience. Second, it filters the meaning through the brain's language center to assign a word symbol or language to the data.

What happens if there is no knowledge or experience to which your brain can relate the data? What happens if you have no specific word stored in your language memory to assign to the concept? In such instances, your brain will struggle through the encoding process. It will use what information it does have as best as it can to build upon similar or existing connections and relationships it stores away just for occasions like the one just described.

Transmitting Once you have encoded a message, you can transmit, or convey, it to someone else. **Transmitting** is the physical process of sending verbal and nonverbal messages. After encoding information, sender-receivers transmit it to receiver-senders. Together, verbal and nonverbal communication allow us to express what we mean and what we feel.

Figure 2–5 Processes Used by Receiver-Senders

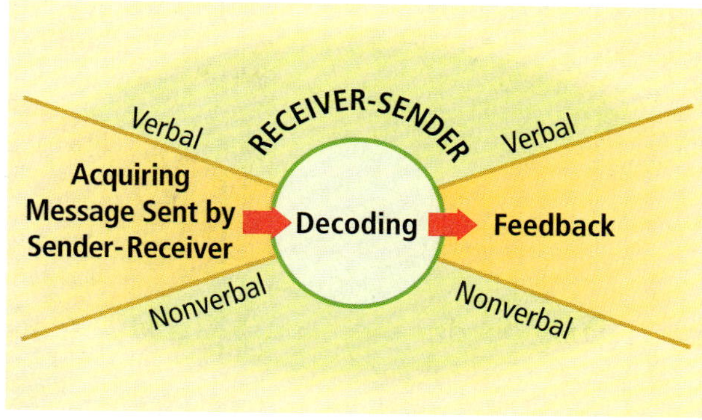

Processes Used by Receiver-Senders

How do receiver-senders fit into the communication process? As shown in Figure 2–5, receiver-senders also go through three processes:

- acquiring the message
- decoding the message
- providing feedback to the message

Acquiring the Message The receiver-sender tunes in to the sender's message and acquires it through the senses. **Acquiring** is the physical process receiver-senders use to take in the sender's message. Acquiring can involve many senses all at once. You may smell the fragrance a friend is wearing, see the friend's smile, and shake hands. You also may hear the friend's voice and the words it conveys. Your senses are bombarded with verbal and nonverbal cues that you acquire at the same time and sort out as the sender's message.

Decoding the Message Once the acquired data is relayed to the receiver's brain, decoding begins. **Decoding** is the mental process receiver-senders use to create meaning from language. It is the opposite of

Figure 2–6 The Communication Process Model

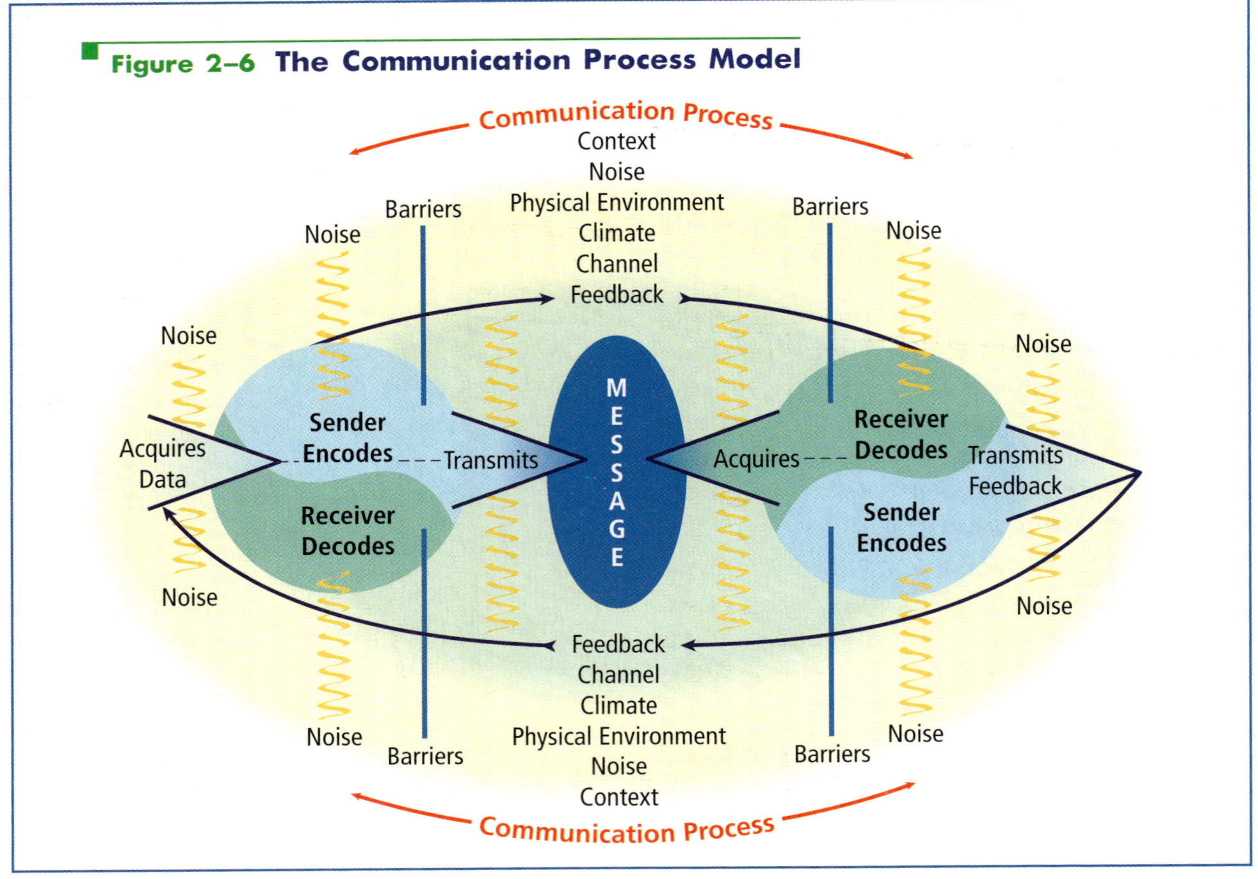

encoding. The decoding process takes symbols such as words and gives them meaning. For example, a receiver hears a speaker's words and observes a variety of nonverbal cues. The receiver's brain goes to work, deciding what those words and other cues mean. The receiver's brain filters this information through its own bank of language skills and life experiences to determine what message the sender is trying to convey.

Providing Feedback When a receiver-sender takes in a sender-receiver's message, he or she responds by providing feedback. As you learned, feedback is the receiver-sender's observable response to what he or she has decoded as the message. Feedback includes both verbal and nonverbal responses to a message. Even if a receiver-sender does not respond to a message, he or she still sends feedback to the sender-receiver.

By sending feedback to a message, the receiver-sender completes the cycle of action in the communication process. After acquiring the data of the original message, the receiver-sender decodes, or assigns meaning to, the words. He or she then creates feedback by encoding his or her own message and transmitting it to the original sender. This circular process requires sender-receivers and receiver-senders to continually switch roles and to do so, sometimes, at the same time. Together, the sender-receiver and the receiver-sender are jointly responsible for sending and receiving messages, and encoding and decoding meaning in the communication process.

How the Process Meets Needs

Once the processes used by sender-receivers and receiver-senders have been added to the model of the communication process, the model is complete, as shown in Figure 2–6 on page 50. As the model indicates, communication is a complex process that you use to meet your goals and needs in social and professional contexts.

At some point in your day, you probably have used your communication skills to meet your own need to be respected and valued. Communication also helps you address your need to be included, interact with others, and form strong relationships. In addition, it helps you in practical ways when you need to get basic information about day-to-day living. Whether you are trying to make a good impression, win acceptance of an idea, understand others, or get others to understand you, you now have a chance to make the most appropriate and effective communication choices for yourself.

Section 1 Assessment

Visit the *Glencoe Communication Applications* Web site at **communicationapplications.glencoe.com** and click on **Self-Check and Study Guide 2.1** to review your understanding of the communication process.

Review Key Terms

1. Define each term and write it in a sentence: transactional, sender-receiver, receiver-sender, message, channel, noise, barrier, feedback, data, sensory perception, encoding, transmitting, acquiring, decoding.

Check Understanding

2. Define the five principles of communication.
3. What are the nine components of the communication process?
4. Describe the function of channel in the communication process.
5. What are the processes a sender-receiver follows to send a message and a receiver-sender follows once the original message has been sent? Explain each step.
6. **Hypothesize** Give one example of how a communicator's feedback might help you solve problems with a chosen channel of communication.

APPLICATION Activity

Creating a Model Think about what you have learned about communication. What does the word *communication* mean to you? Define it in your own words. Create a model of your concept of communication. Share your model with the class. Be prepared to answer questions about your definition and your model. Use feedback from your classmates to make any necessary improvements to your work. Display the completed model in your classroom.

Technology Skill

Using E-Mail

E-mail is messages or data sent electronically from one computer to another via a network. Some e-mail networks are limited to a single building or group of buildings while others can connect e-mail users anywhere in the world. To send e-mail, you need a computer equipped with a modem and telecommunications software. A modem allows computers to communicate over telephone lines.

Learning the Skill

After accessing a computer's e-mail application, you may either compose a message or select an existing file to send. Then, simply enter the destination's e-mail address and click the *Send* button. The computer sends the message through the modem to a local network server or an Internet Service Provider (ISP) where it is stored in an electronic "mailbox." The recipient is notified that he or she has received a message and can retrieve it at any time.

Practicing the Skill

Use e-mail to share information about an upcoming event at your school.

1. Select the e-mail application on your computer.
2. Choose the command to create a new message and then enter "Upcoming Event" in the Subject line of the header.
3. In the To line of the header, enter the e-mail address of a friend.
4. Write a brief summary of an event at school. Ask your friend to reply with any further information about the event and whether he or she plans to attend.
5. Proofread your message.
6. Select the Send button.
7. Periodically check for your friend's reply. Share your responses as a class.

APPLICATION *Activity*

Create a new e-mail message that lists your name, e-mail address, and the type of job or volunteer work you would like to find. Next, send the list to a friend, asking if he or she knows of any opportunities in that area. Have the friend respond, adding his or her own e-mail address and work interests to the list. Keep forwarding the message to friends and acquaintances until you have created your own job-finder's network.

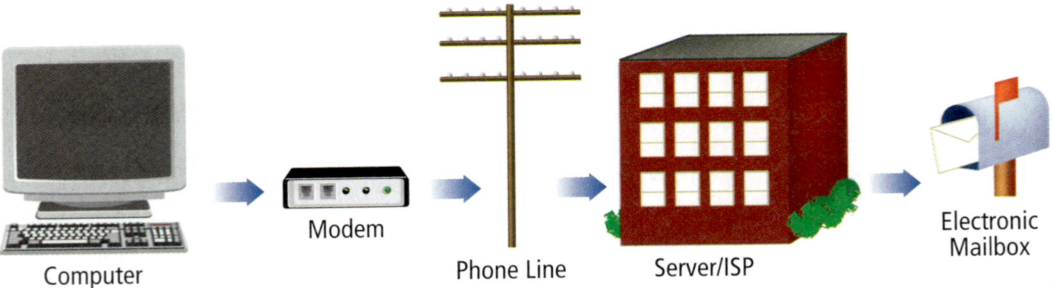

Section 2

Communicating for Success

GUIDE TO READING

Objectives

1. Identify the five levels of communication.
2. List the characteristics of a competent communicator.
3. Analyze the behaviors of a competent communicator.

Terms to Learn

intrapersonal communication
self-talk
interpersonal communication
small-group communication
one-to-group communication
mass communication
mass media

How would you complete the sentence "I spend most of my waking time . . ."? Would you answer that you spend most of your time with your family? Watching television? Going to class? Working at a part-time job?

Research shows that 75 percent of our waking time is spent communicating. Whether it is through oral language, written communication, or nonverbal cues, we are continually sending and receiving messages. For this process to occupy so much of our time, it must be fairly important. What makes communication such a vital part of our lives?

CHARACTERISTICS OF COMMUNICATION

You communicate for a reason, and that reason is to successfully achieve a goal. The stronger your communication skills, whether you are at home, at school, or at work, the better you will be able to meet your communication goals and respond to those of others with whom you interact. Knowing the characteristics of oral communication will help you organize your own communication goals.

In order to succeed at a part-time job, such as at a garden center, you must develop effective communication skills. How much time during the day do we spend communicating?

FIVE LEVELS OF COMMUNICATION

Level of Communication	Business Example	Social Example
Intrapersonal	Should I tell my manager that her plan has a flaw?	Do I agree with the way this club plans to spend its money?
Interpersonal	Did you go to the meeting?	May I sit here?
Small Group	Who will volunteer to research the personnel needs for this project?	Who will make the signs for the fund-raiser?
One-to-Group	Over the next half hour, I intend to show our sales potential among 15- to 25-year-old consumers.	Remember, everyone needs to bring a dish for next week's potluck dinner.
Mass	The public is invited to attend a free financial workshop this weekend, sponsored by Fidelity Trust Enterprises, Inc.	As the weather gets warmer, remember to provide plenty of fresh water for your pets. For more tips on pet care, contact your local chapter of People for Pets.

Five Levels of Communication

Although many communication skills are important, oral communication skills are essential for success in all types of organizations. Whether you are interacting with your family, with your community, in your school, or at your place of work, communication occurs on five different levels. Each new level builds upon the previous, requiring specific skills in oral communication, nonverbal communication, and listening.

Five Levels of Communication

- intrapersonal
- interpersonal
- small group
- one-to-group
- mass

Intrapersonal Communication

The prefix *intra-* means *within.* Therefore, **intrapersonal communication** is the communication that occurs in your own mind. This sometimes is known as self-talk. **Self-talk** is the inner speech or mental conversations that we carry on with ourselves. You use this type of communication to think about something, reason it out, and decide what it means. You also use it to interpret the world around you as you make choices and interpret messages from others. Your self-talk determines what you like or dislike and what you hold to be important. In this way, it becomes the basis for all your feelings, biases, prejudices, and beliefs.

All communication begins on the intrapersonal communication level. After all, it's what you tell yourself to do before you do it and what to say before you say it. Making wise communication decisions on the intrapersonal level is crucial to successful communication on other levels. You will learn more about intrapersonal communication in Chapter 3.

Interpersonal Communication

The prefix *inter-* means *between* or *among.* Therefore, **interpersonal communication** is communication between two people. The term interpersonal communication, however, is sometimes used for communication between three or more people in certain informal conversations. It can take the form of small talk, impromptu conversation, or planned conversation begun for a specific purpose.

Next to intrapersonal communication, you probably use the interpersonal level of communication most often each day. When you say, "Hello, how are you?" "See you later," or anything in-between to another person, you are communicating on an interpersonal level. You also communicate interpersonally when you use technology to communicate, such as in a phone message or e-mail. Through interpersonal communication you maintain relationships with others. Your ability to cooperate with others, get others to cooperate, lead others, and help others solve problems relates directly to your skills in interpersonal communication.

Small-Group Communication

Small-group communication is communication within formal or informal groups or teams. This may include group interactions that result in decision making, problem solving, and discussions within an organization. In the organizational context, groups and teams have become increasingly important for making plans and recommendations, solving problems, and managing conflicts. Because of this, practicing effective small-group communication skills can make you a valuable asset to any organization.

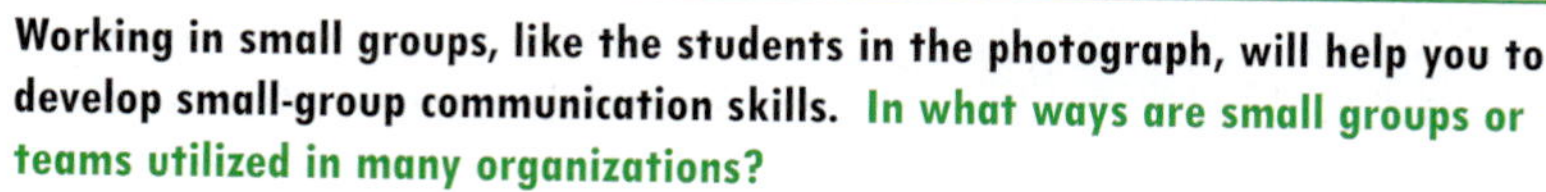

Working in small groups, like the students in the photograph, will help you to develop small-group communication skills. In what ways are small groups or teams utilized in many organizations?

One-to-Group Communication

One-to-group communication involves a speaker who seeks to inform, persuade, or motivate an audience. It also includes the role of a listener as an evaluator of the presenter's message. Members of professional and social organizations often make formal and informal presentations for a variety of purposes.

One-to-group presentations often involve giving reports or speeches to groups or leading group discussions. If you give a report to your student council or make an introduction or announcement in a club meeting, you are using one-to-group communication. Similarly, people involved in professional and social organizations may find themselves giving fund-raising speeches, making informative reports to management, or giving pep talks and sales presentations. Individuals with strong presentation skills often find themselves in leadership or management positions because of their ability to communicate clearly and to influence others. They also tend to assume active roles in professional associations and social organizations.

The ability to listen to presentations and analyze and evaluate their content is equally important. Being able to follow a speaker's points, understand his or her claims and supporting information, and remember what has been said are vital communication skills. Responsible communicators recognize that listening skills are the basis for making wise choices and decisions.

Mass Communication

Mass communication is the electronic or print transmission of messages to the general public. Although mass communication is not conducted face to face, it still is considered a level of communication. In mass communication, individuals and groups use mass media to transmit messages. **Mass media** are outlets of communication, such as radio, television, film, and print, that are designed to reach large audiences.

Professional and social organizations often use mass media to disperse information on a broad scale. They also use various forms of mass media extensively for advertising purposes. In addition, some organizations such as police departments, health departments, and the National Weather Service use mass media to alert citizens to emergencies and disasters.

Recently, the wide use of mass communication has prompted citizens to analyze and evaluate the quality, content, and influence of media messages. We've learned that more information does not always mean better information. Users of mass media often compete for audiences by trying to be first with a breaking story. Other users may compete for your purchasing dollars by making sensational but unfounded claims. Often, sources and claims are not adequately confirmed, resulting in errors and, sometimes, outright falsehoods. Similarly, the lack of control over information posted on the Internet means that anyone can put information on the World Wide Web without taking personal responsibility for its truth. For these reasons, producers and consumers alike have a tremendous responsibility when they use the mass communication process.

Becoming a Competent Communicator

As you learned in Chapter 1, if you are a competent communicator you are capable and well qualified to communicate. You build a base of knowledge and a positive attitude. You also work to acquire skills that allow you to deal with a variety of communication situations. Competent communicators use two specific sets of communication skills. They use certain skills to accomplish their goals and tasks, and other skills to build productive relationships. As **Figure 2–7** shows, learning to balance these different skills can be a challenge.

For example, suppose a friend stops you as you leave school to talk about a problem he or she is

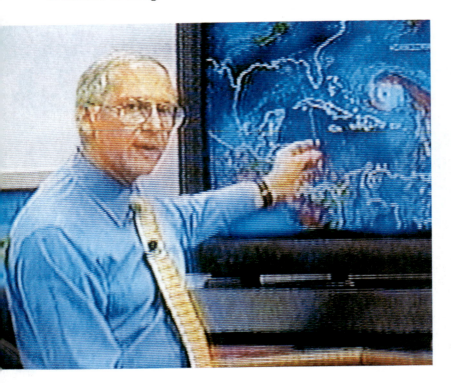

The National Weather Service uses television to alert citizens of disastrous weather situations. Identify other outlets of mass media communications.

Figure 2–7 Competent Communicator

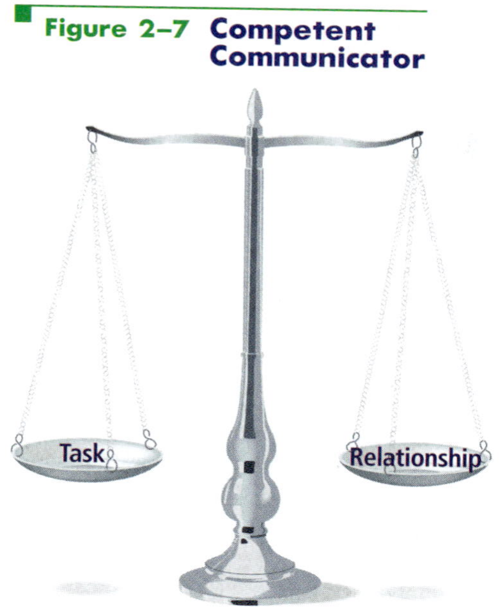

having. The friend is feeling a need to confide in you. You have an urgent practical need—you need to get to work on time. You also care about the relationship with your friend. At this point, you are caught in a dilemma.

Conflict between person and task is not unusual in professional and social contexts. Teachers sometimes have to explain failing grades to their students. Bosses sometimes have to lay off valued employees. Competent communicators strive to polish communication skills so they can deal with difficult situations to accomplish tasks and to preserve relationships.

Value of Good Business Communication

Some companies recognize that one way to improve customer service and increase business is to meet more of their clients' needs. To do so, they train employees to communicate with customers in a manner that makes the clients feel valued and important.

Businesses that specialize in meeting customers' needs value employees who treat clients with dignity, courtesy, and respect. They also recognize that, generally, everyone in a company has the responsibility of communicating with clients effectively and appropriately. This helps create a personal relationship between employees and customers. It also makes customers and employees alike feel important as individuals. By concentrating on individuals' communication needs as well as their need for a certain product or service, the company creates satisfied customers.

Characteristics of Competent Communicators

Competent communicators develop effective communication strategies and skills to achieve their goals. Sometimes we refer to

Practice for the Workplace

Evaluating Business Communication Meeting the needs of customers is a priority for many businesses. Without quality communication with customers, businesses can project a negative image and may even lose customers.

BUSINESS PRACTICE *Activity*

As a class, choose two students to act as a customer and a salesperson at a music store. Imagine that the customer needs help, but the store's only salesperson is on the phone and ringing up another customer's purchase. Act out the scenario by first having one student play the role of a distracted, uncooperative salesperson. Then have him or her portray a helpful salesperson. Make a list of appropriate communication choices for a salesperson and a customer in each situation. Make a second list of inappropriate communication choices for these types of business situations.

Figure 2–8 Competent Communicator Characteristics

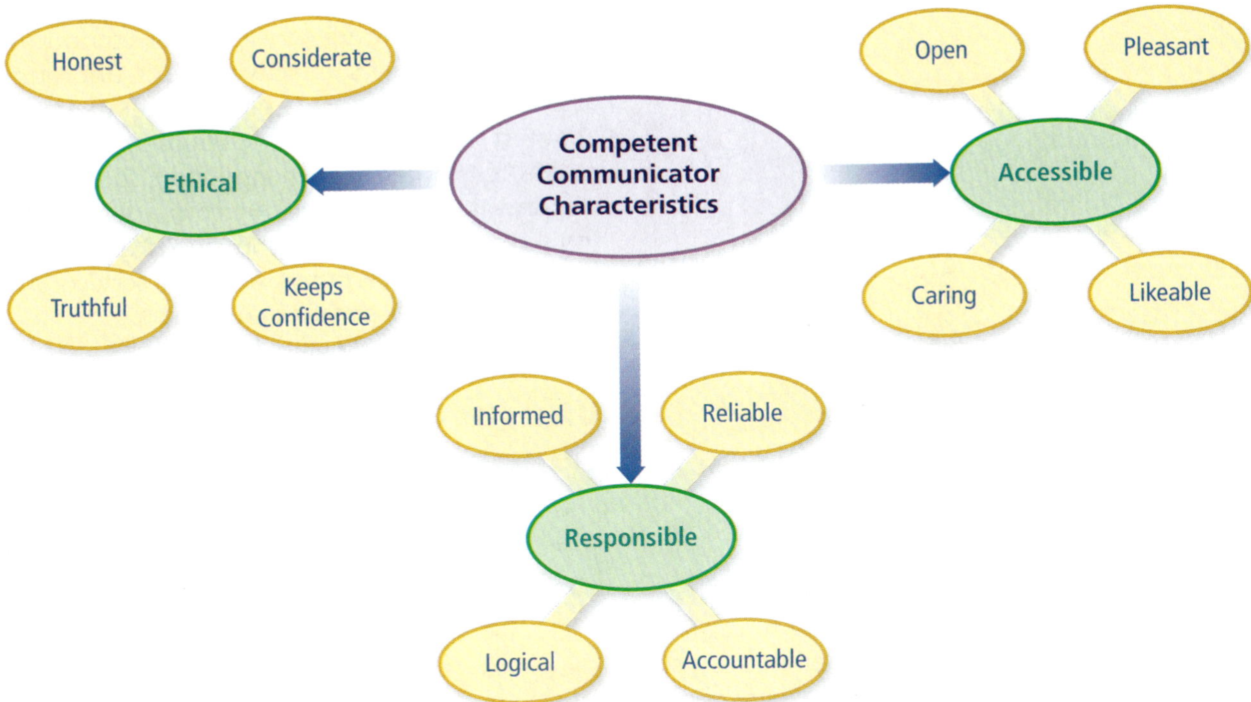

a person as an effective, or competent, speaker or a competent, or effective, teacher. By this, we mean the person has shown the characteristics of the competent communicator and made appropriate communication choices.

Even though there is no one perfect way to communicate and there are no written rules to ensure success, competent communicators, including people successful in the business world, tend to share certain characteristics. As shown in **Figure 2–8** above, they are

- ethical
- responsible
- accessible

Ethical Competent communicators are ethical. Ethics is the study of the general nature of morals, or a society's codes of conduct. Ethics also refers to the specific moral choices made by an individual in relationship to others. In communication, ethics has to do with how we, personally, behave and how we treat others. In the world of work, ethics includes the standards governing the conduct of the members of a profession. In our personal lives, societies help establish standards for the actions and behaviors of its members.

According to some communication experts, there are five questions you can ask yourself to check whether you are acting ethically. You can find these questions on the Communication Strategies list.

Ethical communicators try to treat others as they, themselves, would like to be treated. They are honest and truthful. Ethical communicators also keep confidences and are cautious about spreading gossip or unfounded rumors. They consider the needs, rights, and feelings of other people.

Sacrificing ethics for other potential rewards can cause problems. A teen who lies to a parent to get his or her way may win a

COMMUNICATION Strategies

ACTING ETHICALLY

- The Golden Rule: Would I want to be treated this way by others?
- The Professional Ethic: How would a jury of my peers view this action?
- The Global View: Could our society continue to function if everyone acted like this?
- The Utilitarian Rule: Does this action do the most good for the most people over the longest period of time?
- The TV Test: Would I be comfortable explaining this action on a national TV show?

small battle but suffer greater consequences, such as a lack of trust and a loss of future privileges. A receptionist who doesn't forward a client's calls because of a personal vendetta may feel some sense of vengeance but lose his or her job if the unethical behavior is discovered.

For example, assume that a salesperson who fails to tell a customer that the used car he or she is considering buying is due for some expensive repairs. By not telling, the salesperson denies the customer the right to purchase the best car the customer can find for his or her money. Even though the salesperson may make a sale, he or she would be acting unethically and, possibly, illegally. An ethical communicator avoids giving false information or withholding information that would deny others their right to make informed choices.

Responsible

Competent communicators are responsible for their own communication choices and behavior. Responsible communicators are informed, make logical decisions on their own, account for their own actions, and are dependable.

Informed Responsible communicators are well informed and able to support what they say with facts or examples. They understand the need to be well versed on many topics in order to make sound communication choices. They act after first considering the most complete, accurate, reliable, and recent information available to them.

Imagine that you have been chosen to represent your school's views on a proposed teen center. You have been asked to attend your town's next community planning meeting.

In order to act as an ethical communicator, this salesperson should be honest about the product he is selling. **Describe an ethical communicator.**

COMMUNICATION PRACTICE LAB

Identifying a Competent Communicator

To understand the characteristics of a competent communicator, follow these steps.

Step 1 On your own, choose a well-known person you regard as a competent communicator.

Step 2 In your school library, online (with supervision) or using resources at home, research supporting information about the individual and his or her effectiveness as a communicator.

Step 3 Make a list of the characteristics of a competent communicator found in this section. For each, give one example of the individual's competent communication behaviors.

Step 4 As a class, review the choices and communication behaviors each reflects.

You will want to know all the facts and issues that are involved in your project so that you can speak effectively about them and gain support for your proposal. If you are planning a professional presentation, you need to be well informed about your topic in order to support your information and to answer questions from the audience.

Logical Responsible communicators also develop reasoning skills and use logical reasoning to draw conclusions and reach decisions. They avoid faulty judgment and poor decision making. If your boss at your weekend job at the bagel shop asks why you think sales are dropping, you may need to draw conclusions based on your observations. Perhaps the dough lately has been of lesser quality. Customers may gripe about an increase in price, a change in the hours of operation, or poor service. Competent communicators apply logic to their interactions to solve problems.

Accountable Responsible communicators take personal responsibility for their information, their decisions, and their actions. This is sometimes called "owning" or "owning up" to your words, behaviors, and actions.

Competent communicators own up to, or admit and take responsibility for, their actions and decisions, whether or not these are appropriate or inappropriate, effective or ineffective. Responsible communicators are up front about being late or making a mistake in counting a day's receipts and take responsibility for the consequences.

Owning your own communication eliminates statements like "It's her fault" or "He made me do it." It leads to comments like "I'm sorry. This won't happen again" or "I learned my lesson this time. I'll try to do a better job next time."

Owning communication can also include being open with feelings, ideas, or suggestions when asked. "You know, I really feel we're on the wrong path here" may be the remark of a group member willing to risk owning and sharing ideas with others.

Reliable Responsible communicators are reliable, or dependable. They can be trusted to keep their word even if a decision may not be to their benefit. They establish consistent patterns of behavior that make their actions predictable to others.

At home, school, and work, reliable individuals have more responsibility, more freedom, and more trust. A supervisor who believes an employee to be reliable will assign that employee a task with confidence. The supervisor knows that the employee's past performance indicates that he or she does the task well, will do exactly what is being asked, and will do the work on time. Your principal may ask you to arrive early in the day to set up the materials for a school assembly. The principal knows you are reliable and can be depended upon to do what is asked. Your parents may impose fewer curfews and give you more freedom if your previous actions confirm that you act reliably. Reliability is a valued characteristic in relationships.

Accessible Competent communicators tend to value positive relationships with peers, supervisors, and clients. They are open and approachable, and others see them as accessible. Accessible communicators are seen as caring, likable, and pleasant to be around.

Think for a moment about someone you would describe as easy to talk to and open to ideas from others. Which characteristics account for how you view that person as a communicator? You probably view the person as friendly, someone who likes people. Other traits might include being a good listener, having a good sense of humor, and being courteous and considerate of others. People who are seen as open, sincere, genuine, and pleasant to be around tend to be very accessible.

Competent communicators make appropriate choices and use effective communication strategies to accomplish tasks and maintain relationships. You could say, for example, that a speaker's use of visual aids was effective in his or her presentation. You would mean that the visual aids supported the points the speaker made. You would also mean that the speaker used the visual aids skillfully. You might also remark that a friend's pep talk at a critical moment worked effectively to reassure your lack of confidence.

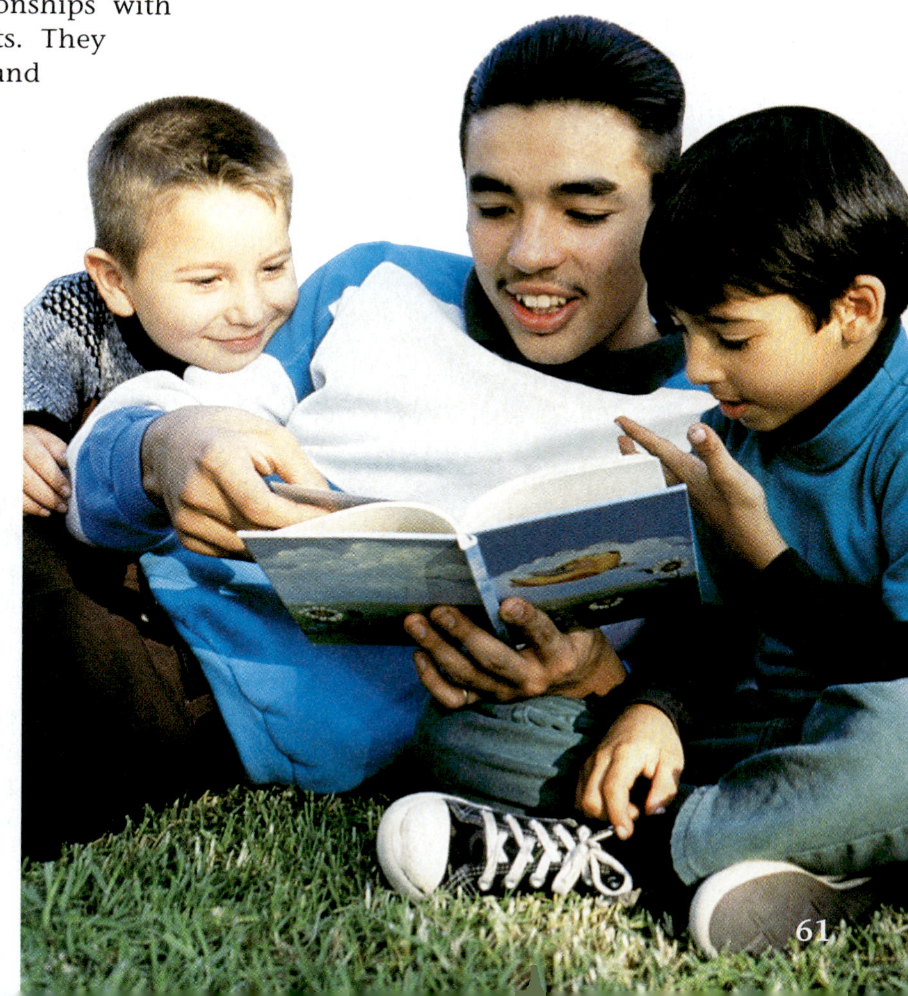

Parents must have confidence that the person providing care for their child, such as the young man shown here, is reliable and responsible. How can a person establish a reputation of being reliable?

Is it possible to make ethical and responsible communication choices, be accessible, and use effective communication strategies and still not get desired results? Yes, even the most-skilled communicators do not always get the results they seek. However, the odds are strong enough for you to make the effort to develop effective skills.

While on your road to becoming a competent communicator, you may stumble. Rest assured, however, that each setback will get you closer to your goal of effective communication. As American author Elbert Hubbard once observed, "Constant effort and frequent mistakes are the stepping stones to genius."

Section 2 Assessment

Visit the *Glencoe Communication Applications* Web site at **communicationapplications.glencoe.com** and click on **Self-Check and Study Guide 2.2** to review your analysis of the action of the communication process.

Review Key Terms

1. Define each term and write it in a sentence: intrapersonal communication, self-talk, interpersonal communication, small-group communication, one-to-group communication, mass communication, mass media.

Check Understanding

2. What are the five levels of communication, and how do you use them to communicate?
3. What are the characteristics of competent communicators, and how do they impact the quality of the communication?
4. **Analyze** How do competent communicators display responsibility?

APPLICATION *Activity*

Presenting an Argument Choose one of the following sentences and list three reasons why you think the statement is true or false.

- There always is a reason behind communication.
- Communication is irreversible.
- Communication cannot be duplicated.
- It is impossible not to communicate.
- For communication to occur, it must have feedback.

Using your list, prepare a two-minute argument to convince your classmates to agree with your position. Include examples to support each of your claims and answer questions from the class.

Present your argument to the class. Then vote to see who agrees and who disagrees with you. What might you do to make your communication more effective and to convince more listeners of your position?

Communication Self-Assessment

Analyzing Your Ability to Transmit Meaningful Messages

How Do You Rate?

On a separate sheet of paper, use the key to answer the following questions. Put a check mark at the end of each skill you would like to improve.

KEY: **A** Always **U** Usually **S** Sometimes **R** Rarely **N** Never

1. When I have difficulty understanding, or decoding information, I ask questions.
2. I use reason and logic, as opposed to emotion, as I reach decisions.
3. When I disagree with others or try to persuade them of my viewpoint, I consider what matters to them as well as what I would like to accomplish.
4. I use respectful language.
5. I avoid making false or misleading statements.
6. When I give information to others I take responsibility for accuracy and completeness.
7. I can be trusted to share my ideas and stand behind what I say, taking on accountability for what I say.
8. When I give a presentation or a talk, I try to use all possible means to reach my audience.
9. I try to be accessible to other people.
10. I communicate without defensiveness or competitiveness.

How Do You Score?

Review your responses. Give yourself 5 points for every A, 4 for every U, 3 for every S, 2 for every R, and 1 for every N. Total your points and evaluate your score.

41–50 Excellent You may be surprised to find out how much you can improve your skills.

31–40 Good In this course, you can learn ways to make your skills better.

21–30 Fair Practice applying the skills taught in this course.

1–20 Needs Improvement Carefully monitor your improvement as you work through this course.

Setting Communication Goals

If you scored Excellent or Good, complete Part A. If your score was Fair or Needs Improvement, complete Part B.

Part A

1. I plan to put the following ideas into practice:
2. I plan to share the following information about communication with the following people:

Part B

1. The behaviors I need to change most are:
2. To bring about these changes, I will take these steps:

Using Correctness in Writing

Have you ever read something that you felt was confusing or insensitive? Have you ever written something that was misinterpreted? If you answered yes to either question, you know that written communication sometimes can have unintended results.

The Importance of Correctness Because your writing is a reflection of yourself and your organization, it is important to state your message clearly, effectively, and with sensitivity. The best way to accomplish this is by following the rules of correctness. Correctness in writing means accurately presenting information for the intended reader(s) and for the desired result.

To write with correctness, remember to follow these four basic steps.

1. **Define the Purpose of the Writing** What is the main reason for your written communication? Are you writing a document to inform? Persuade? Motivate? Entertain? Try to keep this purpose in mind as you write to help you stay on task.
2. **Determine the Style and Format for the Writing** Businesses and other organizations typically have a preferred format and style for most types of writing, including e-mail, letters, faxes, and reports. Be sure to use the framework appropriate to your specific task. A memo, for example, may need to be written on company letterhead and sent to a certain group of individuals.
3. **Target the Writing to the Audience** Depending on attitudes, cultures, and experiences, people sometimes have different perceptions of the same words and phrases. Your writing should use language that is appropriate for the specific audience. This includes avoiding stereotypes such as gender bias. For example, rather than referring to a mailman, a better choice would be letter carrier.

For additional information about business writing, see the Language Handbook section of the Communication Survival Kit in the Appendix.

4. Use Correct Grammar and Mechanics
Always proofread your work carefully. Check for typographical errors and mistakes in spelling and grammar. Finally, make sure your message is complete and easy to understand.

Imagine that you are writing a letter to persuade someone to donate to the cancer research fund where you work. Your letter might look something like this.

Helping People Cancer Research Foundation
P.O. Box 1234
Dallas, TX 75225

July 5, 2002

Ms. Opal Wells
359 Magnolia Boulevard
Macon, GA 31201

Dear Ms. Wells:

This month marks the beginning of Helping People Cancer Research Foundation's tenth annual funding drive. This year, we hope to raise $50,000 for cancer research. Your past donations have helped us in many ways, including the development of a new drug that may help prevent some types of cancer.

The enclosed brochure describes some of our ongoing research, such as finding a better way to detect cancer in its early stages. We also are continuing to develop more effective and patient-friendly surgeries and treatments.

We truly appreciate your past contributions and hope we can count on your gift again this year. Whatever amount you choose to give will be greatly appreciated. Thank you for playing such a vital role in the ongoing battle against cancer.

Sincerely,

Your Signature

Your Typewritten Name
Public Relations Assistant

WRITING *Activity*

Imagine that you work for a travel agency, and a customer has asked one of your coworkers for information about traveling to Rome, Italy. The coworker has written a response and wants you to edit it. Rewrite the letter to make it more correct.

Hi, Mr. Wu,

In response to your letter, here are some tips regarding your upcomming trip to italy. First, the official language in Rome is Italian. While most shop, hotel, and restaraunt folks speak some English, romans are delighted when visitors try to speak a few words or phrases in Italian.

While your there, I figure you'll want to visit some old churches. Italian churches are definitely the most beautiful things you've ever seen. When touring a church, just dress like you normaly would at your own church. To show respect, though, it's important that your and your wife's shoulders are covered. Tank tops, sleeveless shirts, and sleevelessdresses are not acceptable.

Finally—and you'll hate this—tipping is customary everwhere in Rome. In hotels, tips of 20 percent of the cost of services may be added to you're bill. In most restaurants, a 15 percent tipp is added to your bill. And if you liked the service, an additional 10 percent is expected.

Hope this information helps. Let me know if their is anything else I can do. Have a great vacation in Rome!

Sincerely,

Arlene Bettis

CHAPTER 2 Assessment and Activities

GLENCOE Online

Visit the *Glencoe Communication Applications* Web site at **communicationapplications.glencoe.com** and click on **Chapter 2 Activity** for additional practice in becoming a more competent communicator.

Reviewing Key Terms

Read each statement. On a separate sheet of paper, answer True or False. If the statement is false, rewrite the sentence to make it true.

1. Communication is a never-changing process between two people.
2. The receiver-sender initiates communication and sends the message to the sender-receiver.
3. The sender-receiver is unaware of the fact that he or she is sending an unintentional message.
4. A printed brochure would be a preferred channel of communication between a salesperson and a special customer.
5. Hunger is an example of internal noise that can interfere with communication.
6. It is unsafe to assume that communication has occurred until there is some kind of nonverbal cue.
7. You acquire a message through the encoding process.
8. One reason communication is transactional is that communicators bargain and negotiate with one another.

Reviewing Key Concepts

1. Explain why communication is a continuous process.
2. What are the five principles of communication?
3. What are the components of the communication process and what is the function of each?
4. What are the three basic functions of feedback in the communication process?
5. How do the content, feelings, and relationship between communicators affect a message?
6. What does channel do to a message?
7. Name three barriers to communication; are they internal or external?
8. Describe the process sender-receivers and receiver-senders typically follow to send and receive a message.
9. What factors influence a well-communicated message?
10. What are the characteristics of a competent communicator?

Assessment and Activities

Reading and Critical Thinking Skill

1. **Applying** You are dissatisfied with the way your boss schedules teenagers to work on holidays. Which channel would be an effective one to use to challenge your schedule? Explain your answer.

2. **Synthesizing** You are trying to decide how to convince your boss to give you next Saturday off so you can attend a concert with friends. On which level of communication are you focusing?

Skill Practice Activity

Researching Online Research the e-mail addresses of companies or groups dedicated to supplying information about a hobby or interest you have. Draft an e-mail message that lists your name, e-mail address, and the type of information you would like to find out about your chosen hobby. Ask each company or group to provide you with information and the dates of events dedicated to people who have the same hobby or interest. With your teacher's permission, send your e-mail message.

Cooperative Learning Activity

Creating a Gestures Chart As a class, brainstorm a list of socially acceptable gestures used by teens in everyday communication. Display the list on the chalkboard or on an overhead transparency and add a sketch of each gesture. In groups of four to six people, choose a country such as France, Japan, Brazil, or Saudi Arabia and look for the meanings for the same gestures in that country. You may wish to consult travel guides, books on cultural etiquette, or geography texts to search for this information. Create a chart showing how each gesture is used in your chosen country and present the chart to the class.

Chapter Project

Planning On a sheet of paper, list the objectives found at the beginning of the two sections of this chapter. Cut the list into strips so that there is only one objective on each strip. Fold each strip and place it into a container or on a desk. Form groups of four or five students. Have a group member select one objective for the group. Together write a skit including characters, dialogue, and stage directions that communicates the information needed to meet your chosen objective.

Presenting Present your group skit to the class. After the skit, analyze as a class the messages conveyed by individual actors in each skit. Categorize each message as intentional or unintentional.

CHAPTER 3

The Communication Process and You

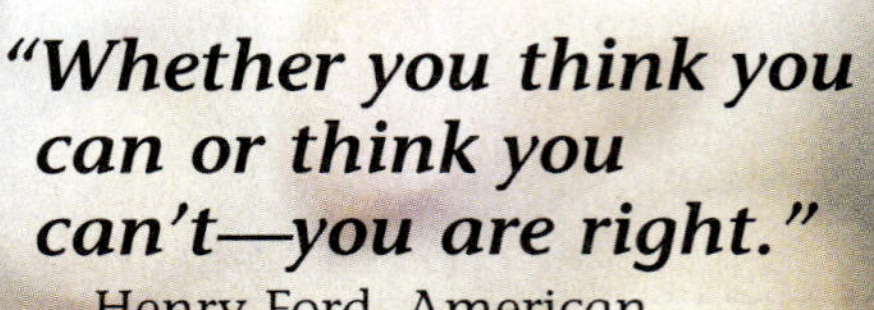

"Whether you think you can or think you can't—you are right."

—Henry Ford, American automobile manufacturer

WHY IT'S IMPORTANT

Communication begins within you. How you perceive yourself, your experiences, and the world around you lays a foundation for social and professional communication.

To better understand yourself as a communicator, view the **Communication in Action** Chapter 3 video lesson.

GLENCOE *Online*

Visit the *Glencoe Communication Applications* Web site at **communicationapplications.glencoe.com** and click on **Overview–Chapter 3** to preview information about how you fit into the communication process.

Section 1

Understanding Intrapersonal Communication

GUIDE TO READING

Objectives

1. Identify and explain the three steps of the perception process.
2. Describe the factors that influence selective perception.
3. Describe the factors that influence personal perception.
4. Use perception checks to clarify and confirm understanding.
5. Explain the importance of gathering and using accurate and complete information as a basis for perception choices.

Terms to Learn

perception
selective perception
personal perception
perception check
feed-forward

I am the voice. I will lead, not follow. I will believe, not doubt. I will create, not destroy. I am a force for good. I am a leader. Defy the odds. Set a new standard. Step up!"

Did you know that you communicate messages to yourself all the time? Author and speaker Anthony Robbins recommends including positive messages like the one above in your communication with yourself about yourself. Telling yourself that you can succeed could help you create a more positive self-image. This, in turn, could give you the confidence and motivation you need to succeed. Your own self-image, along with the way you perceive others, plays a large role in shaping your communication choices and influences your effectiveness as a communicator.

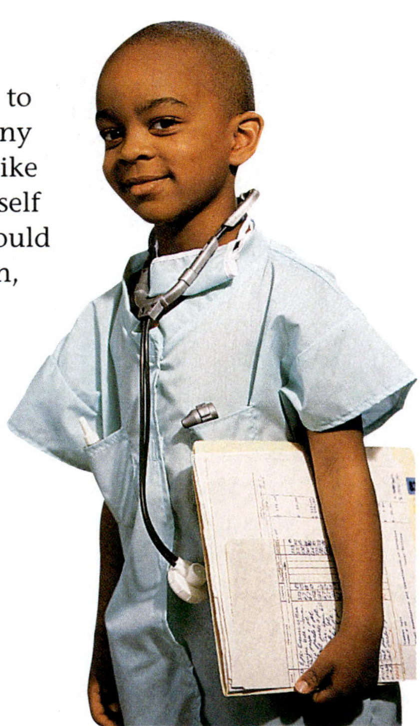

Most children, like the one shown here, dream of their future careers. How can communicating positive messages to yourself help you succeed?

Communication Begins with You

When you were younger, you may have been asked what you wanted to be when you grew up. Over time, you probably learned that this question actually meant, "What kind of job or profession do you hope to have?" Regardless of your answer, you probably pictured yourself as a grown-up in some sort of professional capacity.

Today, if you were asked what you hope to become, you might answer differently. In addition to answering with a career choice, you might also picture yourself assuming social roles in your church, community, or other organizations. Envisioning yourself with a fulfilling job and in positive social roles can help you pinpoint the type of person you might like to become.

However, to define who you are and establish what identities you would like to assume requires more than just wishful thinking. Start by asking yourself some important questions. "Who am I?" "What do I want to do with my life?" "What knowledge and skills do I need to reach my professional and social goals?" Answering these questions can help you determine the types of technical and communication skills you will need to establish a successful identity in the social and professional world.

Intrapersonal Communication

Effective communication skills are critical to achieving professional and social success. You might think that communication is interaction between two or more people. However, have you ever considered that, in addition to being able to communicate successfully with others, you need to learn to communicate effectively with yourself? This type of communication is known as intrapersonal communication, the first, or basic, level of communication. It begins with an understanding of who you are and what you think of yourself.

Self-Talk

Intrapersonal communication is a form of self-talk, or inner speech. It includes the questions and comments you make to yourself. "Should I look for a ride to school or catch the bus?" "Wow! I did that really well!" "Is my presentation for work good enough to impress my boss, or should I practice one more time?" Because these types of thoughts are stated only to yourself, they are examples of self-talk.

Self-talk is a powerful influence in your life. How you view things in your mind very much affects your attitude and your ability to reach your goal. If, for example, you believe that you cannot run that last lap, your brain

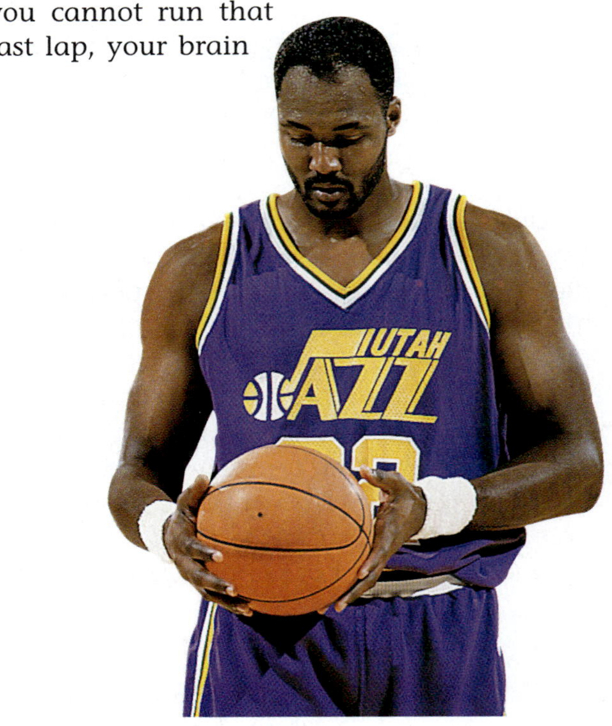

Athletes like Karl Malone may use positive self-talk to achieve greater success. What is the source of self-talk?

probably will convince your body that you can't do it. If, on the other hand, you give yourself a personal pep talk, your brain may help your body respond more positively.

Even though you may be unaware of it, you use self-talk all the time. This includes when you

- think things through
- interpret events
- interpret the messages of others
- respond to your own experiences
- respond to your interactions with others

Researchers are convinced that, whether spoken aloud or processed mentally, more positive self-talk can increase your focus, concentration, and performance. Sports psychologists note that athletes who talk positively to themselves—during practice, in competitions, or even during injury rehabilitation—experience greater success than those who do not.

Similarly, people who are afraid or under intense pressure often are able to reduce their stress by repeating calming words to themselves. Why? This type of positive self-talk helps them focus on achieving the task at hand and helps block out distracting internal and external noise.

Self-Talk Whether positive or negative, self-talk can have a powerful influence on your behavior and others' responses to you. Log on to the Internet and access a dependable World Wide Web search engine to search for sites related to self-talk. Then think about the type of self-talk that was helpful to you during your first week as a high school student. Use your own experience and the information from the Web to develop a one-page guide for incoming freshmen. Include a definition of self-talk and give examples and advice for using self-talk effectively.

"It's all according to your point of view. To me, you're a monster."

Modern Maturity

The Perception Process

The process you use to assign meaning to data about yourself or the world around you is called **perception**. Much of self-talk is based on your perceptions. People seldom share precisely the same perceptions. Since each person is unique, his or her perceptions are highly personal and individualized.

You form your perceptions by acquiring data, focusing on specific parts of that data, and deciding how to organize and interpret the data you selected. These three steps of the perception process are

- sensory perception
- selective perception
- personal perception

Sensory Perception

As you learned in Chapter 2, sensory perception is the physical process of taking in data through the senses. Seeing, hearing, smelling, tasting, and touching all are physical senses that provide links between you and the world. They allow you to take in information and to learn. They allow you to respond to the data—to communicate with yourself and others about what you experience. Think about how you know when it is time to go to school or to work. You probably look at a clock and interpret the time, communicating to yourself your interpretation of the data you collected. You may feel a chill in the air or listen to a weather report forecasting cool conditions that day. You may then use your sensory perceptions to decide that you should wear a jacket when you go outside. Every day our senses send us hundreds of cues that guide our behaviors. Our senses also guide our communication choices.

Selective Perception

The second step of the perception process is selective perception. **Selective perception** is the mental process of choosing which data or stimuli to focus on from all that are available to you at any given time. We are constantly bombarded with information—far more than we are able to take in. So, we constantly are making decisions about which information to focus on and which to ignore. Our selective perception, then, influences what we notice.

Imagine that a mowing crew is cutting the grass outside your classroom window. The noise of the mower and the voices of the crew catch your attention so you focus on them for a moment. During this short sensory vacation away from the classroom, you acquire literally dozens of different stimuli.

However, what classroom data did you tune out when you turned your attention outside? Did you miss a communication opportunity by not hearing your name as your teacher called on you to answer a question? The important things to remember about selective perception are that you have a choice about what you tune in or tune out and that the choices you make influence your communication. Every time you choose to focus your attention on a particular stimulus, you screen out dozens of other cues to which you might have paid attention.

The stimuli people create around you in a movie theater sometimes make it hard to concentrate on the movie itself. What communication decisions must be made in regard to all the stimuli we receive?

Figure 3–1 Factors That Influence Selective Perception

data may not always be the most important.

Repetition People also tend to notice repetitious stimuli. The ticking of a clock or the constant drip of water from a faucet may become so distracting that you cannot seem to hear anything else. Advertisers and politicians know that the messages most often repeated are the ones people tend to believe. By saturating the media with memorable images, phrases, and slogans, they constantly bombard consumers with their message. The idea is that the more we hear—and, in turn, are influenced by—a message, the more likely we are to buy the product or vote for the candidate.

Making Perception Choices From the example on the previous page, you can see that you make conscious choices hundreds of times a day about what you perceive. You also make perception choices subconsciously. In other words, you make many choices that you do not even realize you are making.

It takes focused communication energy to select and concentrate on the most important stimuli. Understanding what influences your selections can help you make appropriate communication choices for yourself, the occasion, and the task.

Factors That Influence Selections As shown in Figure 3–1, there are several factors that influence your selection of stimuli. Four important ones are intensity, repetition, uniqueness, and relevance to our individual needs, interests, and motivations. Stimuli that display these characteristics tend to have a greater influence on our perception choices than other stimuli.

Intensity As a rule, the more intense or dramatic the stimulus, the more likely we are to notice it. For example, you are more likely to notice someone screaming than someone talking quietly in the corner of a room. Unfortunately, the most intense or noticeable

Uniqueness People usually notice things that are new, unusual, unexpected, or unique. This can have either a positive or negative effect. Performers often rely on a new look or gimmick to catch the public's attention and to boost their popularity. This may be necessary to remain noticed in the constantly changing world of entertainment. However, in the business world, many companies frown on employees who draw attention to themselves through their appearance.

Many companies want to present a specific company image and may require employees to wear uniforms or a specific style of clothing anytime they are working or representing the company. Many schools also have dress codes, and some social situations call for a specific look or image. In each situation, eliminating unusual data or stimuli is designed to focus people's attention on what is more important—the company's product or the task of learning.

Relevance We often notice things that mirror our own interests, needs, and motivations. This can influence data selections. If you are in the market to buy a car, you probably will begin noticing cars similar to the one you want. You may see this model more often as you travel to school or work, and you may begin noticing more advertisements for that type of car. You have subconsciously begun focusing on data that meet your specific needs at that time.

Not only do we tend to notice things that are relevant to our interests and needs, but we also tend to tune out stimuli that we think do not pertain to us. For instance, a coach may notice certain details about a ball game that spectators are likely to miss. However, he or she may be totally unaware that threatening storm clouds are moving in overhead. By focusing his or her attention on the game, the coach overlooks information that may be necessary to keep the team safe.

Sometimes, the most important data is not the data that is the most intense, repeated, unusual, or related to your needs and interests. By studying your own perception patterns and analyzing what types of data are most important in a given situation, you can learn how to focus your communication energy for maximum effectiveness.

Managing Selective Perception

Think about how air traffic controllers, truck drivers, machinists, or surgeons must focus their attention on the job. Allowing themselves to become distracted for even an instant could lead to tragedy. While the consequences might not be quite as extreme, the same rule applies to most people, whether they are on the job or at school. In order to perform more effectively, individuals can learn to screen out distractions and focus on the task at hand by using the following suggestions.

COMMUNICATION *Strategies*

Developing Selective Perception Skills

- ✓ Stay alert.
- ✓ Make conscious choices about what is and what is not important data.
- ✓ Screen out distractions and noise that may interfere with concentration.
- ✓ Monitor your selection patterns and choices and set goals for improvement.

The first step in making more effective perception selections is to stay alert. It can be easy, at times, to let your mind wander. For example, have you ever watched the news so you could find out what the weather would be like the next day and yet still miss it? Staying alert can help you avoid this type of oversight.

The second step is to ask yourself what you need to focus your attention on. Obviously, if you are in class, you should focus on the class and avoid daydreaming. Similarly, if you are driving a car, you should make a conscious decision to keep your attention on the road. Talking and choosing what music to play can be entertaining but should not draw your attention from driving safely to your destination.

Third, screen out distractions and noise. This means taking control of your mental processes. Much of your effectiveness as a competent communicator is related to your ability to concentrate and hold your focus on whatever needs your attention at the moment. This may take practice, but it is an important and valuable skill.

Figure 3–2 What Do You See?

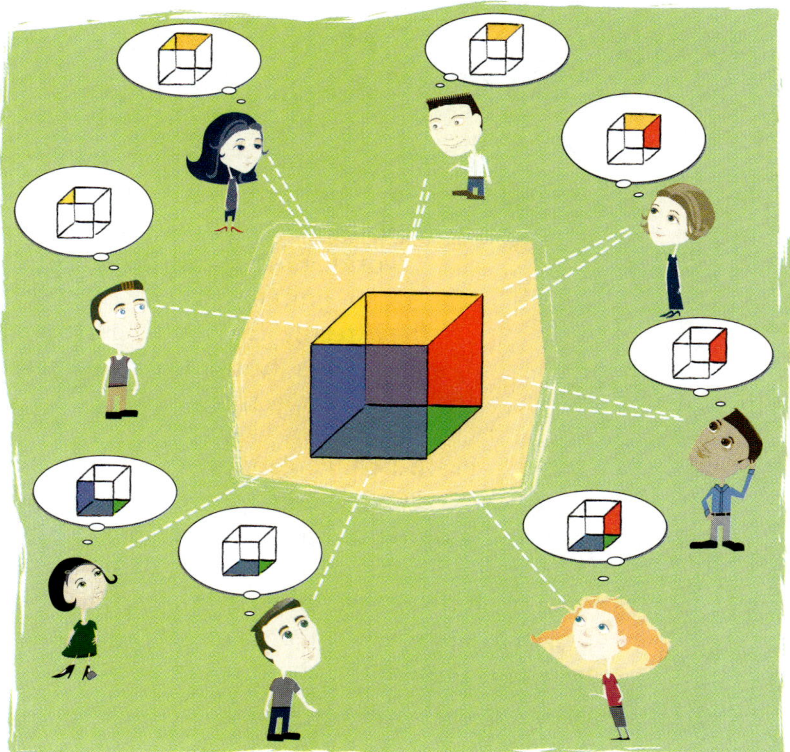

The product of this part of the process is your personal perception. **Personal perception** is your own understanding of reality. As shown in **Figure 3–2,** it is the reality you construct for yourself as you organize and interpret data and as you create and assign meaning to events, people, and objects around you. Your personal perceptions become the basis for the judgments and decisions you make. They also determine the appropriateness of your communication choices.

Factors That Influence Personal Perception Your perceptions are as personal and unique as you are. As shown in **Figure 3–3** on the next page, a number of different factors affect your personal perceptions.

Finally, monitor the way you select data. If you realize that you have some weak patterns, correct them. Use self-talk to raise your level of awareness and to tune out distractions. Then set goals to make more effective choices in specific professional and social situations. Developing better skills in selective perception will help you become a more competent communicator.

Personal Perception

The third step of the perception process involves organizing and sorting the data to which to pay attention. During this filtering process, you create meanings for the events, people, and objects around you. You tell yourself what is happening, interpret what the data means to you, and decide how to respond to each set of data.

Global Communication

Making Assumptions

It is important to remember that one individual's behavior does not necessarily represent the values, beliefs, or practices of an entire culture. Consider how you might feel if one student from your school were chosen at random to represent all American high school students. What is one cultural assumption you made in your selection? Did you base this assumption on fact or opinion? How might you avoid making this type of assumption in the future?

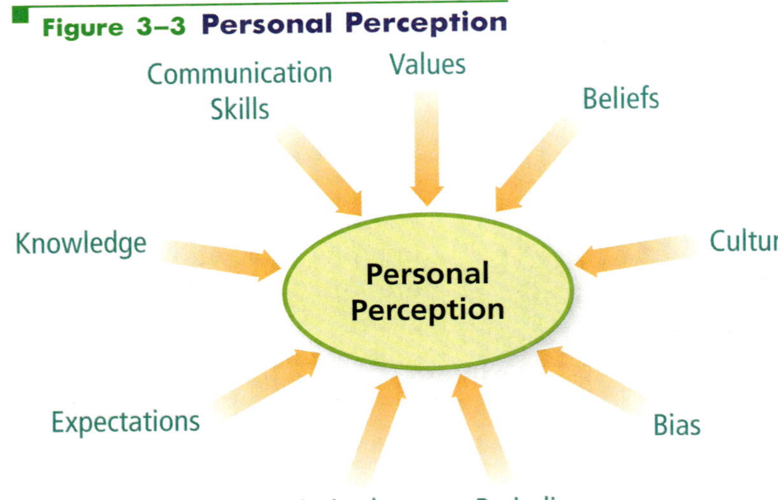

Figure 3–3 Personal Perception

Values Values reflect your priorities. They help you answer the questions "What do you think is important?" and "How important do you think it is?" For example, you may value strong family relationships, friendship, and honesty. When you select specific data to focus on, you filter it through these values. This helps you determine how information applies to you and what judgments or decisions you will make in order to use it.

Beliefs People often feel so strongly about their beliefs—thoughts and ideas they accept as true—that they will fiercely defend them. Your beliefs are a part of the system through which you filter incoming information. They help you decide whether to accept or reject information. They also help you determine how the information affects your decisions and communication choices.

Culture You can be part of a family culture, a community culture, or even an organizational culture. Different parts of the country and the world, different religions, and different ethnicities form and practice their own cultures. Culture affects virtually every aspect of your life and your communication. It is a strong influence on how you view, organize, and interpret the information and messages you receive.

Bias Another influence on perception is bias. Bias is a consistent attitude, viewpoint, or pattern of perception through which we view the world. Biases can be positive or negative. In either case, they result from our personal experiences and also from our cultural perspectives.

Prejudice Perception also can be influenced by prejudice. Prejudice is a preconceived judgment. Broken down into its syllables, prejudice literally means to *pre-judge.* It means to judge based only on opinion, not on fact. Facts can be verified or proven; opinions are beliefs that cannot be proven.

Prejudices usually stem from negative emotions such as fear, hate, suspicion, and distrust. They are based on opinion, on a lack of information rather than on fact. When prejudices are not acknowledged and eliminated, they can present barriers to logical judgment and effective communication.

Attitudes A person's attitude generally is classified as either positive or negative. It is the way we choose to respond to various situations. Attitude is a powerful force in influencing our perceptions, our decisions, and our communication with others.

Expectations What you expect something to be like and what you expect from others also influences your perceptions. For example, if a movie does not meet the promises made in its advertisements, you may be disappointed. If a friend's actions exceed your expectations, you may be delighted. In either case, you are basing a judgment on what you expected rather than on what actually happened. The fact that your expectations were or were not met is a questionable basis for making judgments or communication choices. Your expectations may not reflect what an acceptable outcome might be.

Knowledge Knowledge also influences your perceptions. What you know and what you do not know influence how you organize and interpret information. If you have studied music, acting, dance, athletics, or painting, you are likely to view a performance or work of art differently from someone who has not had training in that field. The expression "Knowledge is power" relates to the fact that the more knowledge you have, the better you can understand information, process and filter ideas, make decisions and judgments, and communicate with others.

Communication Skills Your communication skills also affect how you view the world. If you do not understand the words others use, you cannot decode or interpret their messages as effectively. If you have not learned how to listen effectively, you may have difficulty acquiring the messages of others and organizing and interpreting them.

To understand ourselves, it is vital to understand the different factors that influence our perceptions. Of course, the amount of influence each factor has on your filter system can vary. However, by monitoring these factors closely, you can ensure that your self-talk, decisions, and communication choices are as effective as possible.

Analyzing Perceptions

Everyone sees himself or herself, others, events, and the world in general from a different viewpoint. Therefore, it is easy to understand why each person's perceptions are unique. Our communication is influenced by our perceptions of ourselves and others, what we talk about, and the setting in which the communication takes place. This explains why two people in the same room can have completely different perceptions of the same event. As a communicator, it is important to understand not only our own perception process, but to recognize that others can experience the same event but interpret it differently.

Examine Figures 3–4 and 3–5. Do you and your classmates all perceive the same information about these drawings?

Think about the class you are in right now. No two people in your classroom are experiencing the exact same class. One person may view the class as interesting while another perceives it as dull. One student may feel uncomfortable participating in classroom

Figure 3–4 Face or Vase?

Figure 3–5 Which Line Appears Longer?

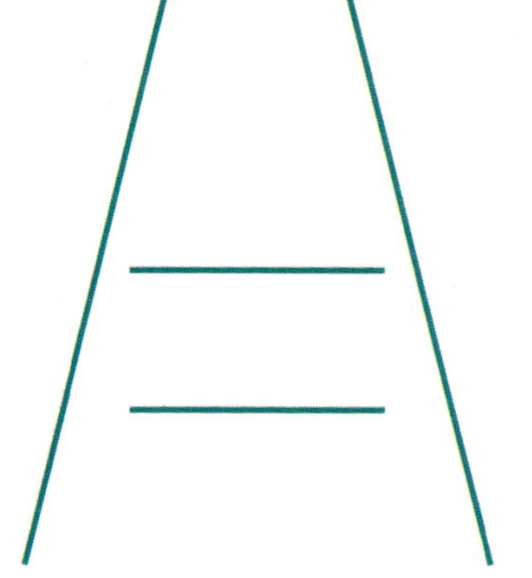

COMMUNICATION PRACTICE LAB

Examining Different Perceptions

To understand how people can have different perceptions of the same event, follow these steps:

Step 1 As a class, act out the following scenario: While moving a cash register from one counter to another, two workers accidentally drop it, damaging it severely. Several coworkers and customers observe the incident.

Step 2 Take turns describing what each student observed. Was everyone's perception of the event exactly the same? Discuss why or why not.

Step 3 On the chalkboard, list factors that may have influenced people's perceptions.

Step 4 Using this list, arrive at a group consensus about what actually occurred. How did the class reach agreement?

discussions while another enjoys the opportunity to interact with classmates. The perceptions and attitudes that each student forms are unique and will affect his or her performance and communication in class.

If perceptions can vary among students in the same classroom, you can imagine how much they can vary among people of different backgrounds and cultures. This can lead to some barriers to communication. People with different perceptions tend to make different kinds of communication choices, draw different conclusions, and make different judgments.

It is these types of differences that account for many of the conflicts and misunderstandings people encounter in personal, professional, and social situations. One way to overcome these problems is to continually check your own perceptions to make sure they are as accurate as possible. This can help you function more effectively as a competent communicator.

Using Perception Checks

How do you know you really saw what you think you saw or heard what you think you heard? In many cases, you can't. However, you can learn to use perception checks to improve your accuracy in gathering and using information as a basis for making your communication decisions.

A **perception check** is a question that helps you determine the accuracy and validity of your perceptions. The secret to checking perceptions is never to assume that what you perceived as the truth is the actual, absolute truth.

You need to base your communication choices on accurate perceptions. To do this, you can use two kinds of perception checks: intrapersonal and interpersonal.

Intrapersonal Perception Checks

Like your communication, your perception checks begin within you. Start the process by checking the accuracy of your self-talk. To do this, ask yourself questions based on the steps of the perception process.

Begin by questioning your sensory perception. If you were a witness to a car accident, you might ask yourself the same types of questions a police officer or attorney might ask. "Could I actually see the accident well?" "Was the sun in my eyes" "Was it dark, making details hard to see?"

After checking appropriate details of your sensory perception, question your selective perception. Ask yourself, "Was I actually looking at the accident at the moment of the crash, or did I hear the screech of brakes or the cars colliding and then change my focus to look at the cars? Was my attention distracted, even for a split second? Did I actually see all of what happened?"

Finally, question your personal perception. You might ask, "What influenced my interpretation of the accident? Have my conclusions been influenced by a similar experience I had? Was I influenced by any biases or prejudices about the circumstances of the accident?"

How, then, do sensory perception, selective perception, and personal perception relate to communication? Using perception checks helps you safeguard the accuracy of your self-talk and avoid making wrong assumptions about the things that you observe. Perception checks help you check for accuracy before taking action or communicating your perceptions to others. To help you understand how perception checks can help you become a more competent communicator, think about the sayings "Think before you speak" and "Look before you leap."

Intrapersonal perception checks do not always provide firm proof that your perceptions are accurate. In fact, they may raise additional questions that make you say, "I'm still not sure." When you can't clear up your perceptions yourself, your next step is to perform some interpersonal perception checks.

COMMUNICATION *Strategies*

QUESTIONS FOR CHECKING PERCEPTION

- **Do I stay alert?**
- **Do I strive for sensory awareness?**
- **Am I making conscious choices about what to tune in and what to tune out?**
- **Do my choices focus on what is most important rather than what is most obvious?**
- **Am I easily distracted?**
- **Am I aware of factors that influence my self-talk?**
- **Do I ask myself "Is this really what I saw or heard or merely what I told myself I saw or heard?"**
- **Do I compare my perceptions to the perceptions of others to check for accuracy?**

Interpersonal Perception Checks

One of the basic guidelines you can use to check perceptions is to clarify meanings so you will not misunderstand someone else's messages. Other guidelines are to analyze others' points of view and to take responsibility for your own communication. Developing skills in these areas can give you real power in professional and social situations where accurate perceptions are vital.

Clarifying Your Perceptions of Others' Messages Interpersonal perception checks involve asking others about their perceptions of an event. For instance, you might ask someone else who witnessed the same car accident you did to explain his or her perception of what occurred. Comparing your perceptions to the other person's can help you both get a clearer picture of what actually occurred.

Similarly, after hearing your boss explain a new project during a staff meeting, you feel you may have misunderstood some of the

THE INVESTIGATION
HE WAS A REAL TALL GUY DRESSED NORMALLY, WITH LIGHT, DRY HAIR.
HE WAS A HEALTHY, GOOD LOOKING YOUNG KID... BUT DRESSED RATHER SHABBILY.
HE WAS REAL BIG AND REAL OLD.
HE WAS A WELL-DRESSED SORT, A LITTLE OVERWEIGHT AND WITH A LOT OF HAIR.
16
I REMEMBER HE HAD A LARGE HEAD AND HE SMELLED FUNNY.
HE WAS SURELY A WESTERNER.
HE WAS A SCRAWNY LITTLE SHORT-HAIRED TWERP FROM BACK EAST.
HE HAD DARK HAIR AND A CUTE NOSE. A REAL DOLL.
HE WAS A ROUGH, FURRY GUY WITH LITTLE BEADY EYES. PROBABLY INEDIBLE.
JONIK

(Reprinted by permission of John Jonik from Psychology Today.*)*

details. You might ask a coworker about his or her perceptions of the information. This can help you clear up any misunderstandings and proceed more effectively.

Whether clarifying your own perceptions or the perceptions of others, it is important to be as accurate and easy to understand as possible. In other words, make clear requests, give accurate directions, ask appropriate and purposeful questions, and respond appropriately to the requests, directions, and questions of others.

Analyzing Others' Points of View

A second method of interpersonal perception checking is to try to analyze the other person's point of view. Asking someone else how he or she feels about an event can provide you with valuable insight. In some cases, it can make you aware of issues or special circumstances that you might not have considered before. After analyzing the other person's point of view, you can confirm, clarify, or you might even decide to change your own perceptions as necessary.

Taking Responsibility for Your Own Communication

A third basic method of interpersonal perception checking is to take responsibility for your own communication. When you feel someone else has not fully understood your message, it is your responsibility to check that person's perceptions. By asking questions, you can confirm what the person does or does not understand.

Also, if you're not sure you fully understand someone else's message, use questions to clarify your own understanding. Making a "feed-forward" statement shows that you take responsibility for needing more information. To **feed-forward** is to offer an explanation that you want to make or a reason or explanation for a question, request, or offer.

For instance, if you need clarification in a meeting, you might make a feed-forward statement such as "Let me see if I understand this recommendation correctly." Then you could ask "Is this what we're recommending?" and restate the recommendation as you understand it.

You might also use a feed-forward method to clarify perceptions related to your own memory. If, for example, you are uncertain about the time and place of a prom committee meeting, you might call a friend and say, "I'm sorry. I forgot today's announcement. Can you tell me when and where the meeting will be held?" Again, you are taking responsibility for your perception and asking a question to clear up your confusion.

By taking responsibility for a potential misunderstanding, asking a question, and restating the issue as you understand it, you create a climate for clarification. Your purpose is obvious: You wish to clarify understanding, not start a dispute or argument.

Perception checking is just one more skill that can help make your intrapersonal communication more effective. It is your intrapersonal communication skills that form the basis for your interpersonal, group, and one-to-group interactions. In other words, how you view yourself and the world around you has a great impact on how you communicate with others.

Section 1 Assessment

Visit the *Glencoe Communication Applications* Web site at **communicationapplications.glencoe.com** and click on **Self-Check and Study Guide 3.1** to review your understanding of intrapersonal communication.

Review Key Terms

1. Define each term and write it in a sentence: perception, selective perception, personal perception, perception check, feed-forward.

Check Understanding

2. Explain perception as a process.
3. Describe the four factors that influence selective perception and give an example of each.
4. Identify the nine factors that influence personal perception. Choose one factor and describe how it affected your personal perception of a past event or issue.
5. Imagine that, while shopping at the mall, you saw someone snatch a woman's purse. How might you check your perception of the event? Why?
6. **Drawing Conclusions** Why is it important to make sure your perceptions are as accurate and complete as possible before acting on them?

APPLICATION *Activity*

Checking Perceptions Imagine that your boss just walked into your office and said, "I know the project you're working on is important. This report is important too. Finish it as soon as possible." Write a list of questions you might ask yourself to clarify your perception of what he or she said. Next, write a list of questions you might ask your boss. Be sure to use feed-forward statements when appropriate. Finally, share your questions as a class and discuss how to tactfully question unclear communication.

Applying Reading Skill

Monitoring Comprehension

When you comprehend something, you understand it completely. Monitoring your reading comprehension can help you get the most out of everything you read.

Learning the Skill

Step 1 Look for the Main Idea. After reading a few paragraphs, start thinking about the main idea of a selection. You can gather clues about the main idea by examining the main title and subheads and any introductory or background material. After you have determined the main idea, think about what it means. You may even wish to write it down as a reminder.

Step 2 Underline Important Ideas. If you are allowed to write on what you are reading, use a highlighter to mark important information. As you read, underline any ideas, facts, and supporting details you will want to remember. Highlighting allows you to quickly review material. This can be especially helpful when studying for tests, writing papers, or preparing presentations.

Step 3 Take Brief Notes. When a sentence or idea is complex or confusing, rewrite it in a way that makes sense to you. Also, take notes on the main ideas and supporting details of what you are reading. Writing information in your own words boosts comprehension and helps you remember what you have read.

Step 4 Make Lists. Sometimes it is important to remember instructions or other information in a specific sequence. Rewriting the information in list form can help you remember the proper sequence. Lists also are helpful for remembering a series of dates, places, names, or events.

Practicing the Skill

Read the following selection from a recent economics text. Rewrite the main topic, or idea, in your own words. Then, take notes on the most important information. Create lists as necessary.

Government at every level—local, state, and federal—is closely tied to the U.S. economy. Over the past 50 years or so, that government has grown significantly larger. In 1929, the U.S. government at all levels employed just over 3 million civilian workers. During the Depression, however, more government services were needed. As a result, the government grew. In 1999, about 2.7 million people worked for the federal government alone. With state and local employees added in, the government employed a total of 19.6 million workers by the end of the twentieth century. The U.S. government had increased to six times its size while the population had only doubled. This has had a great impact on our nation's economy.

APPLICATION *Activity*

Close your book and ask yourself what you remember about the four steps for monitoring comprehension. On a separate sheet of paper, make a list of these steps. Rely on your memory to explain each step in your own words.

Section 2

Understanding Self as a Communicator

GUIDE TO READING

Objectives

1. Identify and analyze common influences on self-concept.
2. Analyze the relationship between self-concept and interpersonal communication.
3. Explain the effects of self-fulfilling prophecy on communication and personal performance.
4. Analyze and use the Johari window to evaluate personal interaction with others.

Terms to Learn

self-concept
self-fulfilling prophecy
self-disclosure

Imagine you are prepared for an important job interview. You have studied the company's background, possess the right skills for the position, and look and feel your best. You are confident that the job is yours. On the way into the interviewer's office, however, you realize that you are wearing two different shoes. Now you feel very self-conscious. Does this change the situation? How?

One step to building better communication skills with others is to take a close look at your own self-concept. **Self-concept,** also known as self-perception, is the view you have of yourself. It is the person you think you are, formed from your beliefs and attitudes. Your self-concept also is influenced by other factors, such as how you think others see you and the person you were in the past, are today, and would like to be in the future.

Displaying your work with confidence indicates positive self-concept. Self-concept plays an important role in developing communication skills. What factors influence self-concept?

Understanding Self-Concept

You are a unique person, made up of many different dimensions that form a kind of "core" self. In addition, other influences impact who you are. How you feel about each of these different parts of yourself makes up your self-concept. The list on this page explains some of the different dimensions of your self-concept.

As your experiences and relationships with others change, your self-concept can change in specific areas. For example, your concept of your social self may change as you mature and are involved in a wider variety of social situations. Your perception of your artistic self may change dramatically after writing a poem, drawing a cartoon, singing for an audience, or demonstrating your creativity in some other way.

In addition, one part of your self-concept can become more important than the others at any given time. If you make a perfect score on a test, your concept of your academic ability may soar. If you find yourself feeling awkward around a group of people you don't know, your social self may influence you to believe that you are miserable and you want to leave.

Your self-concept is responsible for that little voice that tells you, "You're doing great" or "You're not doing so well right now." The important thing to remember is that you control that little voice. In fact, in the words of Anthony Robbins, "You are the voice!" How you perceive yourself—positively or negatively—impacts your life in many ways, including how you communicate with others.

Factors That Influence Self-Concept

Your self-concept is influenced by many factors, such as your own experiences and relationships. However, the following three factors tend to have the greatest influence on self-concept:

SELF-CONCEPT

Dimension of Self	Defined by . . .
Real Self	Your "core" self; who you really are
Perceived Self	Who you see yourself to be
Ideal Self	Who you want to be now or in the future
Public Self	The self you freely disclose to others; who you are in public situations
Private Self	The self you do not share with others; who you are in private
Professional Self	Who you are in your job or profession
Social Self	Who you are when you interact with other individuals, in groups, in society, or in social situations
Intellectual Self	Who you are as a student and a learner; the part of you that acquires and uses knowledge
Emotional Self	The part of you that uses and processes feelings
Physical Self	Who you are physically, including your concept of your own body, athletic ability, gracefulness and coordination, level of attractiveness, and physical health and well-being
Artistic Self	The part of you that is creative or artistic

COMMUNICATION PRACTICE LAB

Analyzing Your Self-Concept

To better understand your self-concept, follow these steps:

Step 1 On a sheet of paper, draw a large circle. Label this circle **Self.**

Step 2 Review the chart of different selves on page 80 and choose all the selves that represent you.

Step 3 Within the large circle, draw smaller circles and label them as the different selves that make up you. The size of each circle should reflect that self's importance to you.

Step 4 Indicate how you perceive each part of yourself by marking a plus for a positive feeling or a minus for a negative feeling within each circle.

Step 5 Analyze your drawing to gain insight about your self-concept. In what areas do you feel really good about yourself? Which areas do you feel need improvement?

Step 6 Make a personal improvement plan for those areas you would like to make more positive. Try to list behaviors that you can practice; set goals for yourself to master the positive behaviors. Making a plan and acting on it will improve your self-concept and your ability to communicate effectively with others.

- How you perceive that you are seen and treated by others
- Your own expectations and the standards that you set for yourself
- How you compare yourself to others

As you can see, two of the three main influences on self-concept focus on your relationships with others. This is why it is important to develop effective skills for communicating with others.

The messages you perceive as positive or negative from other people, especially those whom you admire and respect, impact your self-concept and your self-esteem. In turn, your self-concept and self-esteem greatly affect the messages you send.

Importance of Self-Concept

Your self-concept lays the foundation for your communication with others on a one-to-one basis, in groups, and in one-to-group situations. You are likely to repeat certain patterns of communication in specific situations. For example, your concept of your social self affects how you communicate when you are with friends. If you have a positive concept of yourself in that situation, your communication is likely to be very effective. You may tend to fall into a relaxed pattern of communication that makes your interactions predictable and enjoyable.

On the other hand, if you frequently seem to clash with another student or a coworker, your communication behavior may be following a different sort of "script." Each time you meet, your communication may become defensive or hostile, based not only on a specific interaction but on your previous negative interactions that have influenced your self-concept. Because of this, your interactions are less successful than they would be if you were to identify and break the cycle of your behavior.

The chart on the next page describes four specific scripts people tend to follow when interacting with others. Which script you

INTERACTION SCRIPTS

Script	Roles	Outcome of Interaction
I'm OK, you're OK.	I see us both as positive influences on the interaction	Positive; A win-win script
I'm OK, you're not OK.	I see myself as positive, you as negative	Possibly negative; A win-lose script
I'm not OK, you're OK.	I see myself as negative, you as positive	Possibly negative; A lose-win script
I'm not OK, you're not OK.	I see us both as negative influences on the interaction	Negative; A lose-lose script

follow depends largely on how you see yourself in relationship to the other person. The roles you both assume then influence the outcome of your interaction with that person.

Building a Positive Self-Concept

Having a positive self-concept can give you the confidence you need to communicate effectively. This kind of confidence is a key to success in personal, professional, and social situations.

Most of us are pleased with at least some aspects of ourselves. In those areas that we view positively, we tend to have confidence in ourselves. This can help develop assertiveness and a sense of accomplishment. Negative views of self, on the other hand, may be expressed as a lack of confidence or a sense of inadequacy or ineffectiveness.

How do you accentuate your positive perceptions about yourself and minimize the negative ones? The secret lies in identifying your strengths. Learning to draw from your strongest communication skills can help you improve upon the less effective ones. It also can help you build confidence and develop assertiveness, tact, and courtesy with others.

First, think about the parts of yourself in which your self-concept is the strongest. If you have completed the Communication Practice Lab on page 85, look at the circles containing pluses. Are you particularly confident of your communication skills in social situations? Are you proud of your intellectual ability?

Next, focus on the areas in which you feel you need improvement. In the activity on page 85, these are the circles containing minuses. Do you wish you could speak more confidently around your peers? Would you like to improve your decision-making ability? You can use your strengths in other areas to improve these skills.

If, for example, you feel that your emotional self influences too many of your decisions and actions, you might use your strengths in another area to make changes. You might make the conscious decision to rationally consider the facts surrounding any future decision or action. In this way, you use

TECHNOLOGY *Activity*

Graphing Self-Concept Choose five different dimensions of yourself, such as artistic self and public self. Assign points to rank these five selves in order of personal importance to you. Total points should equal 100. Using charting or graphing software, create a pie graph to show this ranking. Next, create a graph that shows how you rank your abilities in the same five areas. Does your current self-concept reflect what you think is most important? How might you make these two rankings as similar as possible?

your strong intellectual self-concept to offset "minuses" in your emotional self-concept.

The physical self is sometimes the easiest self to change. To boost your concept of how attractive you are, draw on your creative strengths. You might simply decide to smile more often. Or, you might experiment with changes to your clothing or hair to project a more stylish or positive image. Once you change a behavior to influence your self-concept, it is important to validate or confirm the effectiveness of the change. What kind of feedback, if any, did you receive? Have you addressed the real issue or does another area deserve more attention?

Setting Goals for Change Moving from negatives to positives is not always easy. You can begin by picturing yourself with strong skills in the areas where you currently

The poem suggests that an adult's self-concept in large part is the result of the relationships and experiences of childhood. Describe the effect of a positive self-concept on the communication process.

Children Learn What They Live

by Dorothy Law Nolte

If children live with criticism,
They learn to condemn.

If children live with hostility,
They learn to fight.

If children live with fear,
They learn to be apprehensive.

If children live with pity,
They learn to feel sorry for themselves.

If children live with ridicule,
They learn to feel shy.

If children live with jealousy,
They learn to feel envy.

If children live with shame,
They learn to feel guilty.

If children live with encouragement,
They learn confidence.

If children live with tolerance,
They learn patience.

If children live with praise,
They learn appreciation.

If children live with acceptance,
They learn to love.

If children live with approval,
They learn to like themselves.

If children live with recognition,
They learn it is good to have a goal.

If children live with sharing,
They learn generosity.

If children live with honesty,
They learn truthfulness.

If children live with fairness,
They learn justice.

If children live with kindness and consideration,
They learn respect.

If children live with security,
They learn to have faith in themselves and in
those about them.

If children live with friendliness,
They learn the world is a nice place in which
to live.

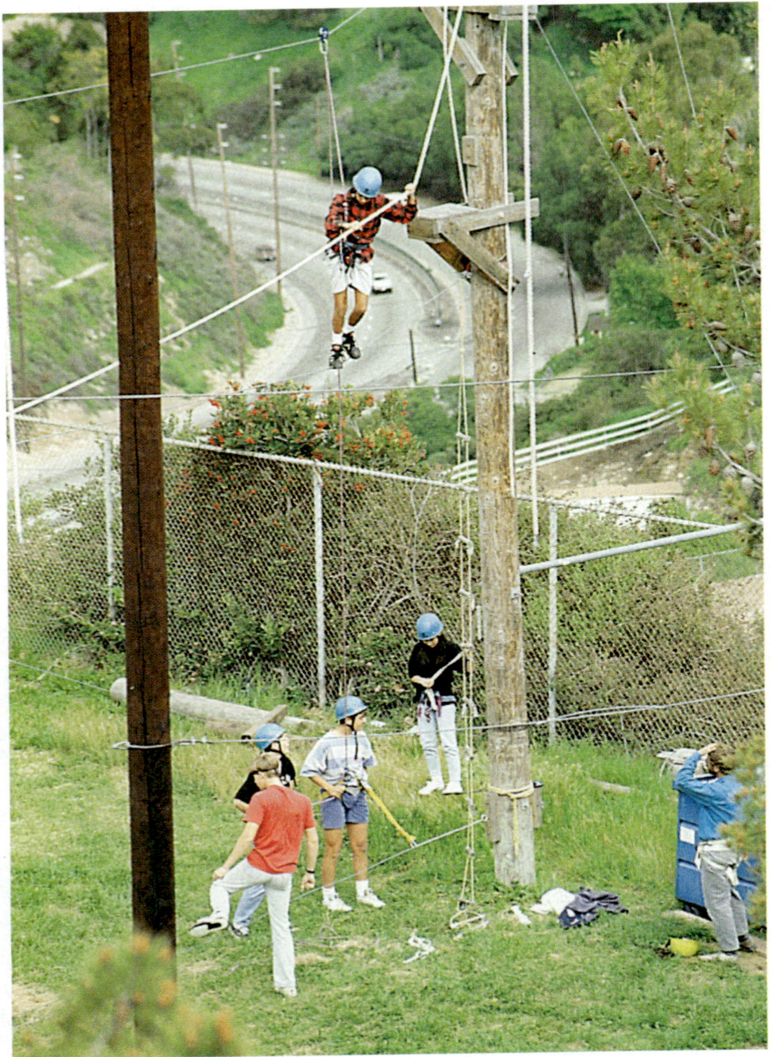

Challenges like rope climbing require setting goals and believing in yourself to achieve success. **Identify some of the guidelines for goals.**

To make sure you are moving in the right direction, you sometimes may need feedback, assistance, or support from others. The key is to believe that you can achieve anything you set your mind to. Picturing yourself as a success is a strong first step toward achieving your goal.

need improvement. Think about what it will take for you to get to that point. Once you have determined what actions you need to take, set specific goals and write them down. Then post your goals someplace where you will see them every day. Remember, writing down your goals and using positive self-talk can go a long way toward improving your self-concept.

In addition to setting goals, change also requires self-monitoring and reflection. Do your methods of improvement seem effective? Are you consistently making an effort to improve?

Self-Fulfilling Prophecy

You may have heard it said that we create our own destiny. Carefully checking our perceptions and correcting false assumptions, as outlined in **Figure 3–6**, allow us to make appropriate communication choices. Sometimes we fail to use our communication skills to improve our perception of the world. Instead, we decide what our viewpoint is, collect data to support that viewpoint, and discard any data that disagrees with it. Once we have formed perceptions based on this very subjective process, we then communicate with others as if our viewpoint were the absolute truth, not simply our own perspective.

A **self-fulfilling prophecy** is a prediction or expectation of an event that shapes your behavior, making the outcome more likely to occur. There are two kinds of self-fulfilling prophecies. The first comes from your own self-concept and the expectations you establish for yourself. We tend to behave as consistently as

Figure 3–6 Self-Fulfilling Prophecy

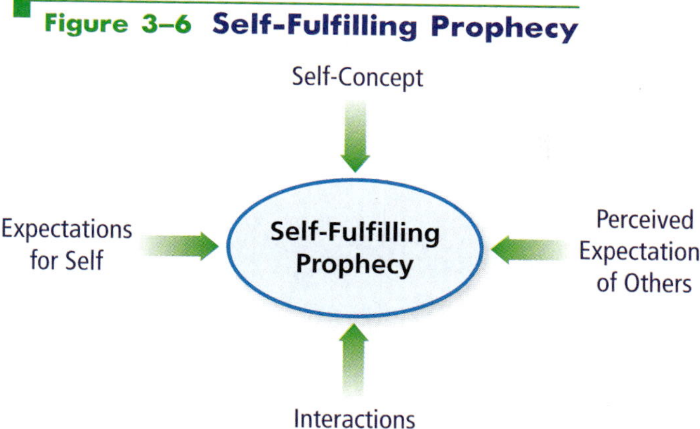

possible with the person we see ourselves to be. The second kind of self-fulfilling prophecy comes from what you think others expect of you. We tend to be especially sensitive to the expectations of people we admire and respect.

Fulfilling Your Own Expectations

Imagine that you are going to audition for a role in the upcoming school theatrical production. As you study the lines and prepare for the audition, your own self-concept will play an important role in how well you do. If you see yourself as capable and able to perform the role, you will enter the audition with a positive outlook. You will expect success. On the other hand, if you have doubts about your ability to perform the role, you will probably approach the tryout without confidence. Either of these expectations could construct a self-fulfilling prophecy.

Fulfilling the Expectations of Others

Just as we tend to live up to our own expectations of ourselves, we also are influenced by the expectations others have for us. Avery Johnson, the point guard for the 1999 National Basketball Association Champion San Antonio Spurs, was not seen by many fans as a great point guard. A former teammate from another team had commented that no team could win a championship with Avery Johnson at point guard. Even so, Avery Johnson became the hero of the final game when he made a jump shot in the closing seconds of the game to win the game for the team. Later, Avery Johnson talked about his not too successful career in basketball. He said that he always believed in himself. He tried and worked hard. More important, Coach Popovich believed in him more than he believed in himself. Avery Johnson had confidence in himself. Moreover, he was boosted to success by a coach who believed he could play

Practice for the Workplace

Using Skills in the Workplace Sometimes, a strength or skill in one area can help you succeed in a seemingly unrelated area. For example, skills that allow you to write or draw creatively also may help you think of creative solutions. When interviewing for a job, be prepared to point out how all your strengths and skills can be useful in the workplace.

BUSINESS PRACTICE *Activity*

What skills, talents, or personality traits do you possess that might benefit you in the workplace? List your top five strengths and the possible workplace benefits of each. Then, with a partner, take turns acting out a job interview. When it is your turn to be interviewed, point out all the relevant on-the-job uses for your skills. When you are the interviewer, ask questions that require your partner to back up his or her claims.

basketball. He fulfilled a coach's expectations by playing like the player he thought the coach believed him to be.

Believing in yourself does not always guarantee success, but it is very difficult to succeed without having the confidence needed to do well. We look for ways to reinforce our own perceptions and expectations, and we look for ways to reinforce what we perceive to be the perceptions and expectations of others.

Visualizing Success

How can you begin to manage outcomes and predict your own success? Successful people often visualize their success. They picture themselves succeeding in whatever they do. Once they "see" themselves winning an award, becoming a faster runner, or making a new friend, the path between where they are and where they want to be becomes clearer. This can make the individual more focused and the goal more attainable.

Public speakers often are advised to think ahead of time how they want to behave as a speaker. Perhaps they want to have a good command of information, to appear confident and poised, and to relate to the audience in a relaxed and sincere manner. Visualizing themselves acting in this way can give speakers the confidence they need to make their vision a reality.

Mentally "seeing" yourself as a success in a professional or social situation can build positive expectations for you to fulfill. Setting realistic goals and continually building skills can help put you on the path to success.

SELF AS AN INTERACTOR

The level to which you express yourself to others is your level of self-disclosure. **Self-disclosure** is the deliberate revelation of significant information about yourself that is not readily apparent to others. Self-disclosure can be tricky, however, because it can be either appropriate or inappropriate for a particular time, place, or circumstance.

Understanding Self-Disclosure

To make self-disclosure a positive element of communication requires analysis. You need to know what facts, opinions, or feelings are appropriate to reveal under the circumstances. Why and how you disclose information about yourself that most people don't know is important.

A graduate realizes the success she had visualized during her school years. **What can a speaker accomplish by visualizing success?**

Figure 3–7 The Johari Window

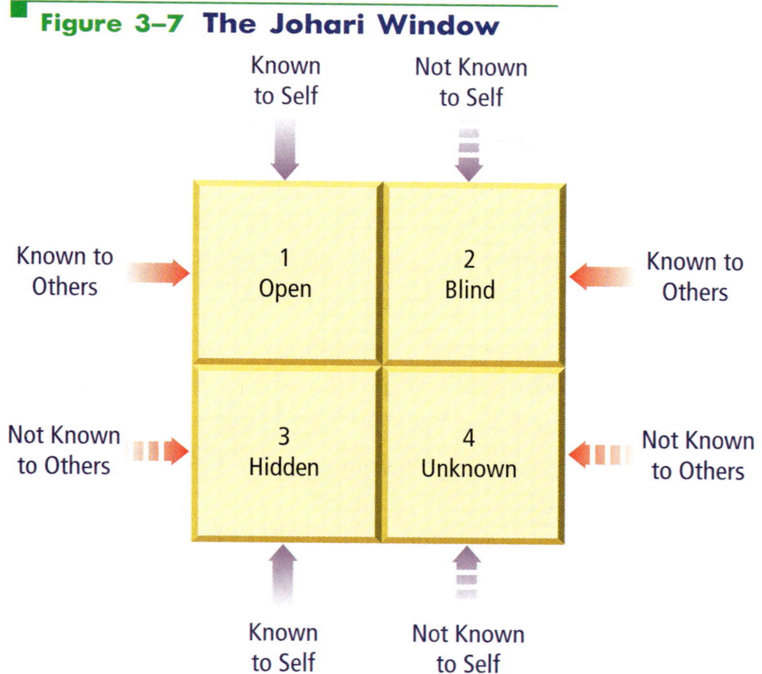

Imagine that you've just started an after-school part-time job at a preschool. The lead teacher in your classroom praises how well you interact with the youngsters in your care. You reveal that you have several younger brothers and sisters and always have enjoyed playing with them. This example of self-disclosure is positive and appropriate. Insight into your background and work-related experiences will give others confidence in your ability. It may also open doors to other opportunities that otherwise may not have been offered to you.

It is important to carefully consider the purpose of any self-disclosure, its appropriateness, and the communication goals you hope to reach when deciding what and how much to disclose. The goal of self-disclosure should be to enhance your interpersonal relationships, improve your communication, and strengthen your communication bonds. Wise choices for self-disclosure will help you achieve this.

Analyzing Your Interaction Style

As you interact with others in a variety of situations, you make different choices about what to disclose. These choices are based on what information is already known and what is not known. The Johari window, shown in Figure 3–7, is a four-part diagram communicators use to identify what they know about themselves and others. It is helpful for analyzing and evaluating the effectiveness of your communication.

The diagram looks like a window with four panes. The panes help you analyze your communication with yourself and your interaction with others.

The Johari Window

The Johari window is particularly helpful for analyzing your communication with others, including what you are willing to disclose. First, consider what you know about yourself and what types of things you may not know completely. Then, think about what others know and do not know about you.

Area 1: Open The things that you know about yourself and that you allow others to know about you are included in this area. Area 1 is called the open area because many of a person's behaviors, motivations, feelings, likes, and dislikes are openly communicated to others.

Area 2: Blind This is known as the blind area. It includes information known to others but not to you. For example, you may not notice that you tend to cut off other speakers before they have finished talking. In this area, you also are blind to what others perceive about you.

Feedback from others may make you aware of this information. When this happens, it moves out of the blind area into the open area because everyone knows it. You may or may not decide to adapt or change your behavior based on this information.

Area 3: Hidden This is the area of hidden information. It represents the things you know or believe about yourself but that you do not choose to share with others. For example, some people don't share certain information about their background or family. Others may not disclose personal information such as age, hobbies, or accomplishments.

Should you disclose everything you know about yourself? Probably not, especially if you think others are not willing to accept your disclosures or if you feel that too much risk is involved. However, your willingness to disclose and deal openly and honestly with information about yourself can be an important asset to communication.

Area 4: Unknown This is the area of unknown information—things that neither you nor others know or acknowledge. A subconscious fear or a yearning would be placed in this area. In addition to complete unknowns, this area may include things that you simply do not remember. Even though old memories may be forgotten, they can still affect your communication with others.

Your Own Johari Window Practice creating your own Johari window. Start by making a list of things that relate to you. Your list might include your goals, strengths, weaknesses, ideas, beliefs, fears, insecurities, perceived needs, values, personal facts, such as your age and height—anything you think is important about you. Then draw a blank Johari window on a sheet of paper. Number the window panes from 1 to 4 and label them **Open**, **Blind**, **Hidden**, and **Unknown**.

Next, sort the items from your list into their proper areas. For example, if your goal is to be a photographer and you often talk about that goal, you would list "want to be a photographer" in the Open area (1). If you do not want people to know you made a failing grade on your algebra test, you would write "algebra test" in the Hidden area (3).

Evaluating Interaction Styles

When you have finished plotting your Johari window, analyze the information you have generated. This will help you see just how willing you are to disclose information and learn from others' feedback.

What does it mean if you have few open items but a great deal of hidden information? What if your blind area contains more items than any of the other areas? Analyzing your Johari window can help you understand your approach to interaction and, if necessary, take steps to change it.

First, examine which areas of your window contain the most items. Based on that information, you can use the following guidelines to get a general idea of your interaction style. Keep in mind that your personal style may combine the characteristics of two or more areas.

A large number of items listed in this area may mean:

Open You are willing to disclose a great deal of information about yourself. You also know much about yourself through personal insight and feedback from others.

Blind You may be reluctant to seek feedback from others or learn from it. You also may not be using self-reflection to know more about yourself.

Hidden You have a great deal of personal information that you are not willing to disclose. You also may be providing little feedback to others.

Unknown A low interaction level may be keeping you and others "in the dark" about certain valuable information about yourself. Through reflection and self-analysis you can discover more about yourself.

The chart below contains descriptions of four common types of communicators. Compare the information to your own Johari window. While these models may not exactly match your interaction style, they can give you some insight into how others may perceive you and into the effects of your self-disclosure and feedback habits. The models of the common interaction styles also can help you analyze the effectiveness of others' communication styles.

Changing Interaction Style

If you wish to change your interaction style, it is important to set goals. To begin, make a list of items you would like to move from one area of your Johari window to another. For example, if you need to tell your parents about your failing grade on the algebra test before report cards are sent home, you might set a goal to move your algebra test from the Hidden area (3) to the Open area (1). If you don't understand why you failed the test, you could write algebra test in the Unknown area (4). You might set a goal to move it to Open (1), and make an appointment with your teacher to discuss the test.

In each case, meeting your goal depends on your communication. You may need to open up in your interactions with others. On the other hand, you may need to talk less about yourself and pay closer attention to the messages and feedback you receive from others. You may also need to practice new ways to seek additional information and reduce the number of unknowns in your Johari window.

Whatever your interaction style, it is important to remember that you are in control. The more information you have in your open area, the better chances you have of interacting successfully with others.

COMMON INTERACTION STYLES

Interaction Style	Disclosure/Feedback	Possible Results
Spend little time disclosing information or giving and receiving feedback; much information in Hidden area; often perceived as quiet, shy, introspective, or withdrawn	They know little about others; others know little about them	Close relationships may be difficult due to a lack of shared information
Spend much time receiving feedback from others, but disclose little about themselves; may be perceived as mysterious, secretive, or unapproachable	They know a great deal about others; others know little about them	Close relationships may be difficult because communication is so one-sided
Spend much time disclosing information and giving feedback, but not open to feedback from others; may be perceived as great talkers or as uncaring people	They know little about others; others know a great deal about them	Close relationships may be difficult because communication is so one-sided
Disclose information openly and appropriately; freely give and accept feedback; may be perceived as friendly, open, and sensitive to others	They know a great deal about others; others know a great deal about them	Openness of both parties make conditions excellent for close relationships

Now that you have an understanding of intrapersonal communication, you can begin to analyze your perception and the perception of others in communication situations. Making continual perception checks and clarifying the meaning of your messages and those of others will guide you to make appropriate communication choices.

Building a positive self-image, setting goals for yourself, and visualizing yourself as a success in meeting those goals will also help assure that you act as an effective communicator. The more you know and analyze your self as an interactor in social and professional contexts, the closer you will be to becoming a more competent communicator.

Section 2 Assessment

Visit the *Glencoe Communication Applications* Web site at **communicationapplications.glencoe.com** and click on **Self-Check and Study Guide 3.2** to review your understanding of yourself as a communicator.

Review Key Terms

1. Define each term and write it in a sentence: self-concept, self-fulfilling prophecy, self-disclosure.

Check Understanding

2. Identify three factors that tend to influence self-concept. Give an example of each.
3. Explain how self-concept influences our choice of "script" when interacting with others.
4. Differentiate between the two kinds of self-fulfilling prophecy. What is the effect of each on communication and personal performance?
5. **Predicting** Imagine that you currently have many items listed in the Hidden area of your Johari window. How are others likely to perceive you? How might their perceptions change if you move items from the Hidden area to the Open area?

APPLICATION *Activity*

Using Feedback to Improve Self-Concept Divide into groups of four or five students. Cut a sheet of paper into smaller squares so that you have one square for each member of your group. Other group members should do the same. On the squares, write something positive about each member of your group, fold the paper, and write the person's name on the outside. Finally, exchange papers. Were you previously "blind" to some of these positive perceptions of you? Discuss as a class how you might use this feedback to improve your self-concept.

Communication Self-Assessment

Analyzing Your Communication Style

How Do You Rate?

On a separate sheet of paper, use the key to answer the following questions. Put a check mark beside each skill you would like to improve.

KEY: **A** Always, **U** Usually, **S** Sometimes, **R** Rarely, **N** Never

1. I use positive self-talk to build my confidence and my performance.
2. I listen wisely by staying alert and tuning out distractions.
3. I understand that people can perceive the same situation differently. I use this information to avoid misunderstandings.
4. I try to use methods that will help me to improve my communication style.
5. I am aware of my own biases and prejudices.
6. I regularly check and evaluate my perceptions before I take action.
7. I use feed-forward statements and take responsibility for my need for clarification.
8. My positive self-concept helps me build good working relationships.
9. I visualize myself as a success in areas where I need improvement.
10. I deal honestly and openly with others but avoid taking too much risk in what I disclose to others.

How Do You Score?

Review your responses. Give yourself 5 points for every A, 4 for every U, 3 for every S, 2 for every R, and 1 for every N. Total your points and evaluate your score.

41–50 Excellent You may be surprised to find out how much you can improve your skills.

31–40 Good In this course, you can learn ways to make your skills better.

21–30 Fair Practice applying the skills taught in this course.

1–20 Needs Improvement Carefully monitor your improvement as you work through this course.

Setting Communication Goals

If you scored Excellent or Good, complete Part A. If your score was Fair or Needs Improvement, complete Part B.

Part A

1. I plan to put the following ideas into practice:
2. I plan to share the following information about communication with the following people:

Part B

1. The behaviors I need to change most are:
2. To bring about these changes, I will take these steps:

Clarity and Conciseness in Writing

Clarity and conciseness make your writing easier to read. In writing, clarity means simplicity. Similarly, conciseness means writing something in the fewest possible words. You can perfect writing clearly and concisely by following the tips below.

Use Action Verbs Action verbs show the subject engaging in some form of mental or physical activity. They are direct and straightforward. Passive verbs make sentences wordy and more difficult to read. Consider the differences in the following sentences:

- My friends and I enjoyed the concert.
- The concert was enjoyed by many people, including four of my friends and me.

Which of these sentences is more concise? Clearer? More direct? In the first example, the people are taking direct action. In the second example, they are no longer the subject. The new subject, concert, passively receives the action.

Use Colorful Adjectives and Adverbs Adjectives tell more about a noun or pronoun and help turn a bland sentence into one that paints a vivid mental picture. Adverbs tell more about a verb, verb phrase, adjective, or another adverb. You can use them to add detail to a sentence.

Read the following sentences. Which one provides more precise information?

- I need a person to help me carry a box.
- I need a strong person to help me carry this heavy computer box into my office down the hall.

Using adjectives and adverbs in the second sentence made the meaning much clearer.

Combine Sentences to Avoid Redundancy When parts of two sentences are similar or very closely related, you may be able to combine them. This eliminates unnecessary words. Which of the following examples seems more concise?

- The man who came into the room was handsome. When he stormed into the room, he was angry.
- The handsome man angrily stormed into the room.

For additional information about business writing, see the *Language Handbook* section of the Communication Survival Kit in the Appendix.

Communication Through Writing

Use Basic Editing Skills To make sure your writing is clear and concise, be sure to give it a thorough edit. For example, is all the information in the correct sequence? Have you eliminated highly technical language and slang? Can you make long sentences shorter or replace long words with words of fewer syllables? Use a thesaurus to avoid overusing certain words, and always check your spelling, punctuation, and grammar for errors.

The following letter is an example of clear and concise business writing.

ACCU-COMP COMPUTER SERVICE
1212 Sprocket Drive
Fort Worth, Texas 76133

May 2, 2002

Mr. Mark McCovey
693 Morningside Ave.
Lakewood, NJ 08701

Dear Mr. McCovey:

I would be happy to answer your question about increasing your computer's speed. If I understand correctly, your main goal is to gain faster access to Internet information.

Basically, three elements of your computer system help determine this speed. They are the

1. speed (in megahertz) of the computer
2. speed (in kilobytes per second) of the computer's modem
3. amount (in megabytes) of Random Access Memory, or RAM, available for use

I have enclosed a brochure explaining more about computer speed. Don't let the technical language confuse you. In short, the higher the number, the faster the computer.

If I can answer any other questions or assist in upgrading your system, please let me know.

Sincerely,

Richard Clemons

Richard Clemons,
Account Representative

WRITING 

Use the following steps to write clear and concise instructions to a classmate:

- Choose a partner in your class. Write a letter to him or her explaining how to use a computer printer, photocopier, video camera, or other device.
- Use a business-style format for your letter. Make the steps of your instructions as clear and concise as possible.
- Use action verbs whenever possible.
- Use adverbs and adjectives to make your instructions more descriptive.
- Be sure the steps of your instructions are in the correct sequence.
- Consider the reader. Avoid using slang or highly technical language that may be difficult to understand.
- Combine sentences as necessary to avoid redundancy.
- Avoid vague language and long, complex sentences.
- Proofread your letter and correct any errors in spelling, punctuation, and grammar.
- Exchange papers with your partner and read the instructions. Circle any language that seems unclear to you. Discuss with your partner how you might make your letters clearer and more concise.

CHAPTER 3 Assessment and Activities

Visit the *Glencoe Communication Applications* Web site at **communicationapplications.glencoe.com** and click on **Chapter 3 Activity** for additional practice in understanding your part in the communication process.

Reviewing Key Terms

On a separate sheet of paper, write the vocabulary term that fits each description. The number of spaces indicates the number of letters in each answer (hyphens do not count).

1. How you see yourself
   \- - - - – - - - - - - -
2. A type of statement that offers a reason for a question you want to ask
   \- - - - – - - - - - - -
3. Your own version of reality
   \- - - - - - -   - - - - - - - - - - -
4. A positive or negative view that shapes the outcome of an event
   \- - - - – - - - - - - - - - - -   - - - - - - - - -
5. The basic process of assigning meaning to the things you experience
   \- - - - - - - - - - -
6. Sharing information about yourself that people would not otherwise know
   \- - - - – - - - - - - - - - -
7. A question to help determine whether things happened exactly the way you think they did
   \- - - - - - - - - - -   - - - - -
8. Choosing what to focus on and what to ignore
   \- - - - - - - - - -   - - - - - - - - - - -

Reviewing Key Concepts

On a separate sheet of paper, answer the following questions in complete sentences.

1. What is another name for intrapersonal communication, and what does this process involve?
2. What is the first step in the perception process? Give three examples of this type of perception.
3. What negative consequence may occur when you focus on a specific set of data? How can you avoid this problem?
4. Why is it important to visualize success when setting personal goals?
5. What effect can too little self-disclosure have on your relationships? Too much self-disclosure?

Assessment and Activities

Reading and Critical Thinking Skills

1. **Synthesizing** Reread the information on the factors that influence personal perception. Using all nine factors, create a brief description of a competent communicator.
2. **Drawing Conclusions** Explain why it is important to keep an open mind when using perception checks.
3. **Analyzing** Imagine that you are not confident of your public speaking ability. Write one goal for improving your self-concept in this area. Analyze and briefly describe a plan for reaching this goal.
4. **Applying** Imagine you are a team leader who has assigned projects to two team members. Later, one of them tells you, "That's not fair!" Use the concepts from this chapter to respond as a competent communicator.

Skill Practice Activity

Writing Clearly and Concisely On a sheet of paper, rewrite the following paragraph to make it clear and concise.

One way to improve your interaction style is by moving items around in your Johari window. Items can be moved from the Blind area to the Open area. To do this, you really ought to be willing to (a) recognize feedback from others and (b) accept feedback from others. Either verbal or nonverbal is the way this feedback may be. Both verbal and nonverbal feedback can help a competent communicator.

Cooperative Learning Activity

Using Sensory Stimuli On the chalkboard, create a chart of the five senses. Then, in groups of three or four students, write a short script that uses as many of these senses as possible to convey messages. As two or three group members perform the script for the class, have another member place a check mark in the chart each time a sensory stimulus is used. As a class, analyze ways to use sensory stimuli to convey messages.

Chapter Project

Planning Choose one person with whom you would like to improve your communication. List any negative perceptions or communication patterns influencing your interactions with that person. For each negative one, list a positive perception, behavior, or communication skill you could use to improve your interactions. Before this class meets again, use these skills in an interaction with the chosen person. Afterward, note how he or she responded.

Presenting Describe to the class the problems you were experiencing as a result of negative communication patterns. Then, describe the positive communication skills you substituted and the reaction to each. Predict how you think these new patterns might affect your future communication.

CHAPTER 

Discovering the Power of Oral Language

WHY IT'S IMPORTANT

As you approach adulthood, the language choices you make have an increasing impact on your power as a communicator. Learning to use language appropriately in a variety of situations can be your key to success in today's world.

To better understand the nature of oral language, view the **Communication in Action** Chapter 4 video lesson.

Visit the *Glencoe Communication Applications* Web site at **communicationapplications.glencoe.com** and click on **Overview–Chapter 4** to preview information about oral language.

"He who hasn't hacked [apart] language as a youth has no heart. He who does so as an adult has no brain."

—John Moore, American jurist

Section 1

The Nature of Oral Language

GUIDE TO READING

Objectives

1. Define oral language and identify its characteristics.
2. Describe the characteristics of speech sound.
3. Compare and contrast pronunciation, articulation, and enunciation.
4. Analyze communication challenges presented by dialect.
5. Explain how oral language choices can affect individuals on a personal level and on a cultural level.

Terms to Learn

oral language
vocabulary
structure
grammar
diction
pronunciation
articulation
enunciation
dialect

Speech is learned, purposeful behavior. Think about all the ways you use speech and oral language in a single day. You may talk with friends, have a serious conversation with a coworker, or ask and answer questions in a class discussion.

While each of these situations is different, they all incorporate spoken language. Have you ever given serious thought to how you talk? Speech is something you depend on every day to reach out to friends, express your ideas and feelings, accomplish your goals, and meet your needs. Are you taking it for granted? Looking carefully at language from a new perspective can give you new insight and a new appreciation for the potential power of language.

Oral language provides the means for a supervisor to effectively explain a process to another employee. **What does the spoken language allow you to do?**

Figure 4–1 Characteristics of Oral Language

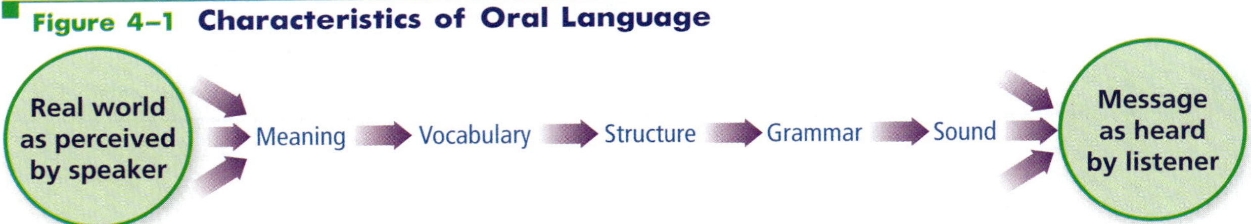

Defining Language

Language is a system used for human communication. Like other systems, language consists of specific interrelated components and processes that interact to achieve a desired result or purpose. **Oral language** is language that is spoken and heard rather than written and read.

Language Has Rules

Like other systems, language is governed by rules that make the system work and give it order. The rules also make it possible for us to understand one another. In the case of oral language, the conventions or rules may be different from the rules you have learned to use for writing. The conventions for oral language are seldom taught directly, such as by saying, "This is how we talk." Rather, new speakers learn rules for oral language as they listen to others and learn to speak and use the language. No one explains to a child learning to talk, "Every sentence must have a subject and verb." Yet the child learns to understand and use words and put them together to form complete thoughts that are consistent with the ways language is used in the child's culture.

Language Is Like a Code

Each language system has its own set of agreed-upon conventions and rules that regulate the system and make it different from other languages. A language system is often referred to as a code. Each code has its unique system of sounds, symbols, and structures as determined by the rules that govern the use of the particular language. Think of English, French, Spanish, and other languages as different codes because each has its own set of sounds, word symbols, and structures that make the language unique.

Encode and Decode Understanding language as code can further your understanding of the terms *encode* and *decode.* *Encode,* if you remember, means to assign meaning and language to data. In other words, it means putting data into code or into language. *Decode* means to assign meaning to someone else's words. Literally, *decode* means to take meaning from language.

Differences Between Oral and Written Language It may be helpful to think about oral language and written language as two separate codes. Oral language is sometimes considered the primary code because it is the language you learned first, the one you use every day, and the language you use most often. Writing is a secondary code because it is based on an attempt to describe speech sounds. Writing preserves thought and speech. In addition, it provides a code to substitute for speech when speech is not possible.

The two systems—oral language and written language—are interdependent and interrelated. Sometimes they overlap because they have the same set of rules. However, there are differences in the way they approach language. Standards for oral communication are based on appropriateness, while standards for writing are based on correctness. Speech choices should be appropriate for the specific situation or context. Writing should be correct according to rules for the specific form.

The Characteristics of Oral Language

At the beginning of your study of communication, you learned that systems have specific components and processes that interrelate and work together to make the system work. In order to understand language as a system, you need to look at the specific series of characteristics and processes that interact to make the language system work. As shown in Figure 4-1, the characteristics of the oral language system are meaning, vocabulary, structure, grammar, and sound.

Meaning

The first characteristic of language is meaning. You learned earlier that the data we observe in the world around us has no meaning of its own except that which we assign. In addition, the word symbols we use to talk about or describe the data have no meaning other than those we give them. We communicate with others based on the meanings we assign to things around us and the symbols we use to communicate those meanings.

When people share knowledge and understanding of language, they are able to communicate effectively. Think, for example, about how hard it can be for a patient and a doctor to communicate with each other. The doctor may ask specific questions about symptoms in order to diagnose the illness. The doctor's questions and language will reflect the doctor's knowledge as a medical expert. The patient, on the other hand, may have difficulty interpreting and responding meaningfully to the doctor's questions because of lack of knowledge about medicine and lack of familiarity with the words the doctor uses. A broad base of knowledge and meaning on a wide range and variety of subjects, along with knowledge about language, provides a base for effective communication.

Vocabulary

The second characteristic of language, vocabulary, is closely associated with meaning. **Vocabulary** is all the word symbols that make up a particular code or language. Your personal vocabulary is the total collection of word symbols you know and use to think, to express yourself, and to listen and respond to others. Having a large and flexible vocabulary is important because language

- is symbolic
- has standards for appropriateness
- adds interest to communication

Symbolic Nature of Language

Word symbols have no meanings of their own; instead, the meaning of a symbol resides within individuals. Symbols are always open to

Just as the American flag symbolizes the United States of America, word symbols represent ideas and meaning used in communication. What is the relationship between word symbols and vocabulary?

Singers use artistic language to compose and perform their music. Identify another type of artist who uses artistic language.

interpretation. If you asked ten people what a symbol such as the American flag means, you would probably get ten different answers.

Similarly, if you were to ask ten English speakers what the word symbol "low" means, you may hear it defined as a measurement of depth, a level of sound, a state of depression, or even the sound a cow makes. The uncertain and fragile nature of words as symbols for conveying meaning is echoed in Humpty Dumpty's words, "When *I* use a word, it means just what I choose it to mean; neither more nor less."

The problem with words as symbols for communicating meanings is that we cannot know what a particular word symbol means to someone else. The arbitrary nature of symbols means that the more symbols we have at our disposal to express a specific concept or meaning, the more apt we are to choose symbols that are understood by listeners. If you want to communicate your meanings clearly to others, a large collection of word symbols will assist you.

Standards for Appropriateness A second reason for building a large and flexible vocabulary is to communicate appropriately in a variety of situations. For this purpose you will need a large collection of word symbols that are appropriate for expressing who you are, what you mean and feel, and what you are really like. You will also need a wide variety of word symbols to meet the needs of your listener, your occasion, and your task. In this sense, your vocabulary can be compared to your wardrobe. You know that you need a variety of clothing to meet the demands of your lifestyle. You may need casual clothes for casual occasions, special clothes for work or school, clothes for attending or participating in public or social events, and perhaps more formal clothes for formal occasions. Occasionally, you may choose to wear something unusual or "artsy" to express your creative side.

The same is true of language. You need different kinds of language and a large collection of word symbols to communicate appropriately in different contexts and situations. You might speak casually with friends and family, use special terminology at work or school, and use more standard language for formal situations. On some occasions, you may even use artistic language such as poetry or song to express your creativity.

Adds Interest to Communication A large and flexible vocabulary can add interest, originality, vitality, and clarity to your communication. What did you have for lunch yesterday? Was it broth, soup, or stew? It might not matter to you now, but knowing the

WHY IT'S IMPORTANT TO BUILD YOUR VOCABULARY

Your language makes an impression on others and influences their perceptions of who you are and what you are like.
Language depends heavily on context and is subject to standards for appropriateness. Meeting standards shows skilled use of language.
A large vocabulary allows you to express yourself clearly and effectively in a wide range of situations with a wide variety of people.
The ability to express yourself clearly and interpret and respond to the messages of others appropriately and accurately is vital in professional and social contexts.
Building a large vocabulary is an easy way to add interest and personality to your image as a communicator.

difference and using the most appropriate word would matter when you order from a menu. Certainly, distinguishing the three dishes and knowing the appropriate word symbol for each are important to the server and the chef. As your lifestyle expands into professional and social contexts, you will discover a need to expand your vocabulary along with your wardrobe to meet the norms of new situations. Several major reasons for making a serious effort to build and increase your vocabulary are found in the chart above.

Structure

Structure, the third characteristic of language, is the way the different parts of a language are arranged. Both words and sentences must follow an accepted structure in order to carry meaning from a speaker to a listener.

Words have syllables that go in a particular order and influence the function and meaning of the word. For example, in English the word symbol *form* can be used to describe an outward shape or appearance. If you add the syllable *al* to the end, however, you create the new word *formal.* In so doing you change both the function and the suggested meaning of the word to describe something that follows an established custom. Add the syllable *in* to the beginning of the word, and you create *informal,* a word that means the exact opposite of *formal.* Each syllable must be added at the correct place to carry a specific meaning. *Alformin* makes no sense and cannot be recognized as an English word. The parts must be in the right order. The conclusion you can draw is that the way to build words in a language is regulated by the particular code or structure of the language.

Structure is also important in making statements and asking questions. Speakers learn to arrange words in sentences so that

Practice for the Workplace

Communication Tools Just as the words we choose can affect our communication, the channel of delivery also can affect the way we communicate. Choosing the most appropriate channel of communication for a specific situation can greatly influence the effectiveness of a message.

BUSINESS PRACTICE *Activity*

Read the following list of communication channels found in most schools. Then, speak to a businessperson in your community and identify channels in the business world that might parallel these channels.

- school newspaper
- school announcements
- student handbook
- club meetings
- state conferences
- distance learning classes
- e-mail
- flyers

their thoughts are stated clearly for audiences to understand and remember. People who interview others learn to structure questions clearly so they can get the answers they desire. People who are being interviewed learn to structure answers to questions clearly so they can give appropriate responses to the specific questions asked. In the workplace, in the classroom, and in interpersonal situations, clear and appropriate language structures are important to clear communication.

Grammar

Grammar, the fourth characteristic of language, is the basic understandings and rules that regulate the use of a language. These rules identify all the different components of a language, explain their functions, and dictate the way they are used in communication.

Not all languages observe the same rules of grammar. For example, in Spanish, nouns precede adjectives. A Spanish speaker would say *la mesa grande,* "the table large." In English, adjectives precede nouns. English speakers would therefore say "the large table." Learning the rules that regulate a particular code is important to using a language appropriately and skillfully.

Grammar, meaning, vocabulary, and structure are interrelated parts of a language system. If you could watch your encoding process in slow motion, you would realize that you first assign meaning to data and then choose language symbols or vocabulary to express what you want to say. After that, you have to structure your ideas into the complete thought you want to express. Finally, you formulate the statement to incorporate the grammar of the code so you can make a literate, articulate statement. All four steps tend to occur subconsciously and simultaneously as you speak and express your ideas.

"GOT IDEA. TALK BETTER. COMBINE WORDS. MAKE SENTENCES."

Reprinted by permission of Sidney Harris.

Sound

Sound is central to the very idea of oral language. In fact, *oral* means uttered or spoken. Speech sound is the observable characteristics of oral language. Every oral language has its own sounds that represent its unique set of word symbols. Without sound, the words cannot convey meaning orally.

Importance of Sound Sounds not only are vital for understanding the words of a language, they also affect the interpretation of messages. That is, the way you sound affects the messages you send to others. What your spoken words convey to others is an important part of your image and effectiveness as a communicator.

Sound and Image Fair or not, individuals often are judged and labeled according to the way their speech sounds. Speakers, for example, can gain or lose credibility because of the way they sound. A speaker who is articulate and clear can give a speech that has little or no worthwhile content and still be perceived as credible by listeners. This theory has been demonstrated in a number of experiments and often is referred to as the Dr. Fox Hypothesis.

During a convention, a group of highly respected psychiatrists, psychologists, social workers, and educators attended a speech by Dr. Myron Fox. Dr. Fox delivered a stirring half-hour discussion on "Mathematical Game Theory Applied to Physical Education." At the conclusion of Dr. Fox's speech, questionnaires were distributed, allowing the audience to evaluate the presentation they had just heard. The completed questionnaires revealed an overwhelmingly positive response to the session. Listeners indicated that they found the lecture to be informative and interesting.

What's so unusual about that? Dr. Fox was a fraud. He had been portrayed by a professional actor coached in the art of intelligent-sounding language and double-talk. His lecture was a series of jokes, contradictory statements, and references to unrelated topics. Yet he spoke with enough eloquence and style to convince listeners of his credibility.

The message of this story is that how you sound is an important part of the message you convey. It takes focused thought, appropriate language, and clear, articulate speech to communicate effectively with others.

Characteristics of Speech Sound

Everyone who speaks shapes the sounds of his or her speech in a unique way. However, although everyone's speech sounds different, there are some general guidelines we all should try to follow when it comes to forming words.

The way your words sound can affect the messages you send. For instance, if you sloppily run together the words of a formal introduction, you may be perceived as lazy or disrespectful. If you continually mispronounce words during a job interview, you could be perceived as uneducated or careless. If you speak with a heavy regional accent, people may have trouble understanding you.

By following some important guidelines, you can make sure that your speech sounds are as clear and correct as possible. As shown in **Figure 4–2** below, these guidelines relate to diction—which includes pronunciation, articulation, and enunciation—and also to dialect.

Figure 4–2 Characteristics of Speech Sound

Diction

At some point in your life, you probably have heard a speaker who pronounced words incorrectly, did not complete words, or changed the sound so much that he or she seemed to be saying another word entirely. If so, you might say that the person had poor diction.

Diction is the degree of clarity and distinctness in a person's speech. It is the way his or her words are spoken. A person with good diction speaks clearly and uses appropriate and effective speech sounds to get his or her meanings across. Your own diction is determined by the choices you make in pronunciation, articulation, and enunciation.

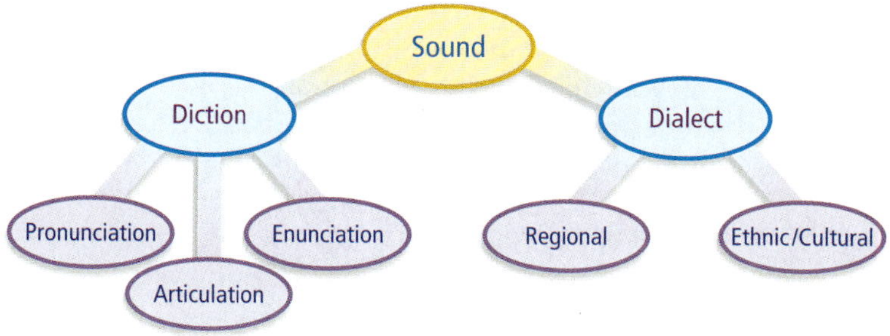

Pronunciation **Pronunciation** is the standard set for the overall sound of a word. The pronunciations of most words are listed in the dictionary. Often, the preferred or most-used pronunciations are listed first, followed by other ways people might pronounce the word. For example, the preferred pronunciation of *often* is "ah' • fun." However, so many people say "ahf' • tun" that many dictionaries list this as a second or alternative pronunciation. When a dictionary lists multiple pronunciations of a word, it is a good idea to use the one that is listed first.

Other words have only one correct pronunciation. Consider the word *athlete,* for instance. The dictionary lists its pronunciation as "ath' • leet" with no alternatives. Therefore, if you have a habit of saying "a' • thuh • leet," you are mispronouncing the word. It is important to know that a mispronounced word can confuse the meaning of a message and reflect poorly on a speaker's credibility or image. On the other hand, clear, appropriate word pronunciation is the mark of a knowledgeable and literate communicator.

Articulation It is not enough to simply pronounce a word. It also is important to articulate it. **Articulation** is the act of clearly and distinctly uttering the consonant sounds of a word. There are four kinds of articulation problems that can interfere with speech. They are omission, addition, substitution, and slurring.

Omission Sometimes, people omit, or leave out, certain consonant sounds within a word. For example, a person who says "bi'ness" instead of "business" is omitting the *s* from the middle of the word. Similarly, saying "he'p" instead of "help," "dolla'" instead of "dollar," or "'Uston" instead of "Houston" is an articulation problem related to the omission of a consonant sound.

Addition The opposite of omission is addition. This type of problem occurs when a person adds extra consonant sounds to a word. For example, if you say "warsh" instead of "wash" or "Florider" instead of "Florida," you have added an inappropriate *r* sound that does not belong.

Substitution Another common articulation problem is substitution. This occurs when a speaker substitutes one consonant sound for another. If you say "idn't" instead of "isn't," you are substituting a *d* for an *s* sound. Saying

COMMUNICATION PRACTICE LAB

Eliminating Pronunciation Errors

To eliminate mispronunciations in your speech, follow these steps:

Step 1 As a class, brainstorm a list of words that are commonly mispronounced. Ask your teacher for additional suggesions. Write each term on the chalkboard or an overhead transparency. Explain the meaning of each term as it is listed.

Step 2 Discuss as a class how you think each word should be pronounced correctly.

Step 3 Use a dictionary to look up the correct pronunciation of each word. Were your predictions on target?

Step 4 As a class, discuss how mispronouncing words might affect your image as a communicator in different situations.

"mirrow" rather than "mirror" substitutes a *w* for an *r* sound, and saying "liddle" rather than "little" substitutes a *d* for a *t* sound. Substitution sometimes is described as "lazy speech" because instead of the correct sound, the speaker has used a consonant sound which requires less effort to produce than the originally intended sound.

Slurring A fourth type of articulation problem occurs when consonant sounds are slurred, or run together. This occurs when speakers simply slide over a group of sounds, pronouncing some but failing to give proper emphasis to others. Slurring results in unclear speech that listeners may find difficult to understand. An example of slurring is shown in the center column of the chart below. The clear articulation of each sentence is shown in the right column.

One entertaining way to test your articulation skills is by repeating tongue twisters. If you can rapidly repeat "rubber baby buggy bumpers" or "She sells sea shells by the seashore" without substituting or omitting sounds, you have great articulation skills! However, if you're like most people, you may occasionally get your tongue tangled. When that happens, just keep trying. With enough practice, you may be able to sharpen your skills and become a more articulate speaker.

DICTION

	Slurred Diction	Clear Diction
Speaker 1	"Jeet?"	"Did you eat?"
Speaker 2	"Novyu?"	"No. Have you?"
Speaker 1	"Nopedyuwanna?"	"Nope. Do you want to?"
Speaker 2	"Surefyurgonna."	"Sure, if you're going to."

The gentleman in the photograph appears to be having a difficult time understanding the speaker. If a person has poor diction, he or she will not be an effective communicator. What four articulation problems can interfere with speech?

Enunciation

Just as articulation relates to consonant sounds, enunciation refers to vowel sounds. **Enunciation** is the act of clearly and distinctly uttering the vowel sounds of a word.

Sometimes, vowel sounds can become distorted. This may be the result of faulty placement of the teeth, tongue, or lips as a vowel sound is formed. For example, if you say "git" instead of "get," it may be because the jaw and lips are not properly opened to shape the short *e* sound. A closed jaw or flattened lip opening will instead form a short *i* sound. If you look in a mirror while you repeat "git, get, git, get, git, get" you can see the different mouth shapes for both vowel sounds. Failing to shape your mouth to form the short *e* sound also may cause you to say "pin" rather than "pen," "jist" rather than "just," and "inyone" rather than "anyone." Most of the time, poor enunciation is subconscious. By paying attention to vowel sounds, you can learn to enunciate clearly and effectively.

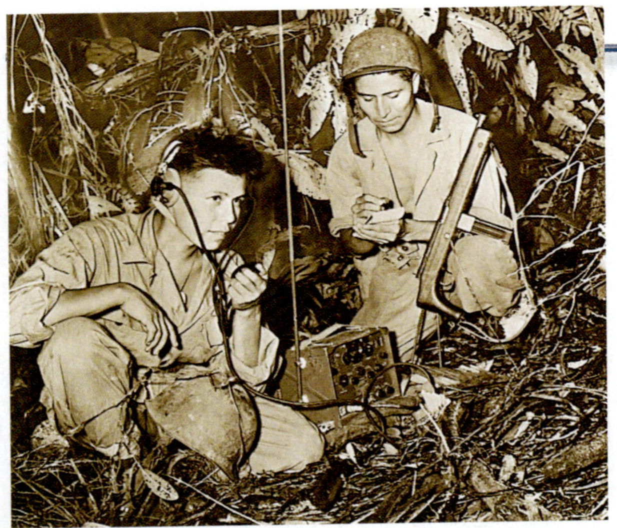

During World War II, young Navajo Indians, or "code talkers," used their native language to transmit intelligence messages for the Allies. Why was this practice successful in preventing enemies from breaking the codes?

Dialect

Dialect can be used to describe two different aspects of speech. First, dialect can refer to a language that exists only in oral form. During World War II, for example, the Navajo language was exclusively oral. Also, very few people outside the Navajo nation spoke the language. Because of this, young Navajo Indians used their native language as a code for transmitting intelligence messages for the Allied Forces. The "Code Talkers," as they were called, successfully prevented enemy intelligence from breaking Allied codes. Because there was no print representation of the Navajo language, the messages were virtually impossible for the enemy to translate.

The second aspect of dialect probably is the most common and is the focus of this study. **Dialect** is a unique combination of speech sounds that identify speech with a particular group of people. The dialect of a specific region may have different vocabulary, grammar, and pronunciations from dialects of other regions. Some dialects—such as Mandarin and Cantonese, both of which are versions of Chinese—can be so distinctive that speakers of one may not be able to speak or understand the other. On the other hand, some dialects are similar enough that they simply are referred to as accents.

Regional Dialect The so-called "southern drawl" is a regional dialect characterized by prolonged vowel sounds, soft consonant sounds, and some unique vocabulary such as *y'all* or *fixin'*. A person who speaks this dialect generally is easily identified as being from the southern United States. By the same token, a person may be usually identified as a New Yorker if he or she tends to drop hard consonant sounds within some words, drops *r*'s from the ends of some words, and uses unique vocabulary such as *youse* or *wit'*.

Ethnic and Cultural Dialect Dialect also can relate to the speech characteristics of various ethnic or cultural groups. Sometimes, these groups may continue to use some of the characteristics of their first or native language when speaking another language. For example, a native speaker of Japanese who has not yet mastered the sounds of Spanish may continue to use some characteristics of his or her own language and perhaps even inject Japanese words when speaking Spanish. This creates a personal dialect that, at times, may be difficult for the native speaker of Spanish to understand.

In today's global society, people from all regions of the world communicate with each other across all sorts of language, ethnic, and cultural lines. Because all these variations can work against the effectiveness of communication, it is important for your speech to be as clear as possible. For English speakers in the United States, speech educators generally recommend developing a general American dialect that is relatively free of regional or ethnic influence.

Although strong regional, ethnic, or cultural dialects may be perfectly acceptable for informal communication within the culture,

COMMUNICATION *Strategies*

SPEAKING CLEARLY AND EFFECTIVELY

- Make appropriate language choices that reflect knowledge and understanding of the topic.
- Draw from a large and flexible vocabulary.
- Apply conventions and rules of language appropriately.
- Practice clear diction, including appropriate pronunciation, clear articulation of consonant sounds, and distinct enunciation of vowel sounds.
- Strive to eliminate distracting elements of dialect.

they may be less appropriate for more general contexts. For example, if you listen to a national news cast, you will seldom find the anchor using a regional dialect.

To function effectively in most professional and social contexts, individuals need to develop diction that is clear and easy to understand by a variety of listeners. Generally speaking, this kind of speech reflects appropriate use of language and diction that is relatively free of diverse dialects.

PUTTING LANGUAGE INTO PERSPECTIVE

Now that you have defined oral language and explored its components and characteristics, you may be wondering, "How does all this affect me?" It helps to understand that speech is highly personal and cultural in nature.

Personal Implications of Oral Language

Now that you understand some of the ways your speech influences how you are perceived by others, you may want to give some thought to the image you want your language to project.

Projecting Image The first step toward determining your image is to ask yourself, "Who am I, really?" Of course, the answer will not be simple. You are made up of many different aspects, each of which may have its own language needs. So, you might want to begin by considering what type of language is most appropriate for the "personal you" in interpersonal relationships and academic settings. You also may want to start developing language skills for the "professional you" and the you who is involved in social projects and organizations.

All of these aspects of you, your activities and pursuits, require different sets of language skills. To equip yourself, it is a good idea to become a collector of words, improving your personal vocabulary and speaking skills.

The girl's style of dress distinguishes her "personal image" from her "professional image." Language is also instrumental in creating your image. Give an example of when it is appropriate to use "personal you" language.

Conveying Attitudes As you begin thinking about language skills, remember that your speech conveys powerful messages about your attitudes and feelings toward your listener. Therefore, it is important to remind yourself of the interpersonal signals you are sending. As a competent communicator, you not only need to develop language skills that help you clearly and efficiently complete tasks such as asking and answering questions, giving directions, and explaining information. You also need to complete these tasks with courtesy, civility, and respect for others.

Determining Success It would be difficult to overestimate the role of language in determining your success in professional contexts. In fact, studies have shown that many employers value strong verbal skills more than any other communication skill in their employees. In addition, as you have been involved in interpersonal relationships, you probably have experienced some of the effects of language skills in social contexts. Most of us realize that there are times when saying the right thing in the right way can make a world of difference.

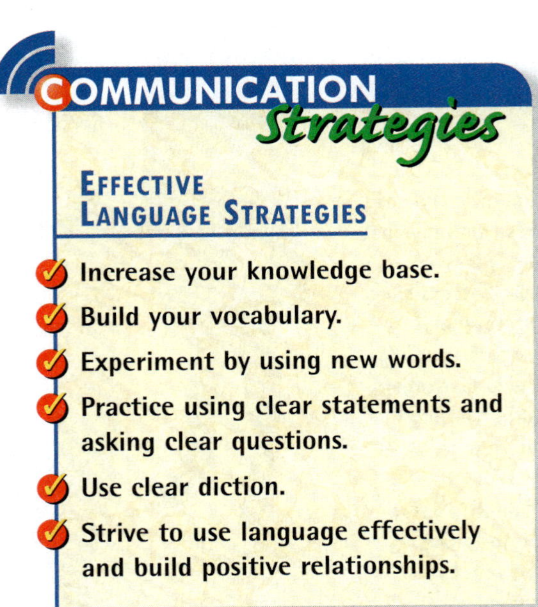

COMMUNICATION Strategies
EFFECTIVE LANGUAGE STRATEGIES
Increase your knowledge base.
Build your vocabulary.
Experiment by using new words.
Practice using clear statements and asking clear questions.
Use clear diction.
Strive to use language effectively and build positive relationships.

Global Communication

Gender Differences

Researchers claim that American women engage in more supportive, tentative, and emotionally expressive communication than males, who are more direct, assertive, and fact-oriented. Remember this when you interact with people from other countries or cultures. There are not only culturally determined differences in communication styles, but also gender differences within cultures. How do men and women you encounter communicate their attitudes differently?

One way to begin building language skills is to increase your knowledge base in the personal, professional, and social arenas of your life. As you expand your knowledge, you also expand your vocabulary by learning new terms, words, and expressions related to the subjects you are studying. In addition, it is helpful to continually build your general vocabulary. The goal is to develop an interesting, precise, and flexible word bank that will energize your language and serve you well in personal, professional, and social contexts.

Whenever possible, experiment with using new words. You also might practice different ways to structure statements and explanations and ask and answer questions to get the results you want. Remember to incorporate and practice the language of courtesy to demonstrate respect for others. You might enjoy experimenting with different language tactics to see what kinds of results you get. One obvious reward of new language skills is likely to be a new appreciation for and enjoyment of language itself.

Cultural Implications of Oral Language

Language is so closely related to culture that some scholars insist that language *is* culture. This theory is based on the notion that culture affects how we think and, therefore, how we use language. Given the complexities of today's multicultural society, this idea has some special implications.

Historical Research In the early 1800s, German scholars Jakob and Wilhelm Grimm began gathering the stories that would eventually become the well-known *Grimm's Fairy Tales.* The brothers Grimm traveled from province to province and community to community throughout Germany listening to people as they told the stories of their culture. What the brothers Grimm discovered was that, although many of the stories' minor details changed from region to region, the tales were essentially the same. Names and details changed, perhaps, but the wolves, witches, dwarves, lost children, maidens, and princes all seemed to share common adventures from version to version of the famous stories.

As they gathered their stories, the Grimms became fascinated with the differences in language that they encountered. They began to record not only the stories but also how people spoke in different cultures and regions. The brothers wrote detailed phonetic descriptions of different storytellers' speech patterns and language choices throughout the land. The Grimms' comparative study of speech is still used today as a basic study in oral language.

Grimm's Law The Grimms' study resulted in what is known as Grimm's law, which has some important implications in today's society. First, the Grimms refuted the notion that one speech pattern was superior to another. They concluded instead that the oral language used in each area of Germany best served the needs of the people within that culture. Each was effective in allowing the people to verbally communicate with one another.

Expanding upon this idea, they also suggested that there are no grammatical errors within an oral culture. Remember that grammar relates to the agreed-upon conventions for using language. So if the people's established rules are not being violated, no error has occurred. However, before you celebrate the idea that you can talk any way you want, think carefully about the last four words of the Grimms' rule: "within an oral culture." A literal translation of the Grimms' conclusion suggests that the agreed-upon language is appropriate only as long as you remain in the culture. The translation also suggests that once you cross a cultural line, the language choice may not be appropriate.

Jakob and Wilhelm Grimm, authors of *Grimm's Fairy Tales,* studied different cultures and language throughout Germany. What did Grimm's law imply about oral language?

Diversity The implications of Grimm's law are significant. How many times do you cross cultural lines each day? How can you anticipate your future involvement with diverse cultures in the future? Of course, some of us are more affected by cultural crossovers than others. However, almost everyone encounters cultures different from their own on a regular basis.

In many cases, an individual may experience vastly different language cultures at home and at school. For instance, if Spanish is the primary language spoken at home and English is the primary language spoken at school, a person may have to make several major language transitions each day. Along the same line, street language or school slang probably will not be appropriate in the culture of most organizations or workplaces. Casual language used with your friends might not cross cultural lines and work effectively with some adults. Moreover, your regional language and dialect may not be acceptable in certain professional, public, or social situations. As with any other aspect of communication, the standards for your language choices should be appropriate for yourself, the listener, the occasion, and the task.

Section 1 Assessment

Visit the *Glencoe Communication Applications* Web site at **communicationapplications.glencoe.com** and click on **Self-Check and Study Guide 4.1** to review your understanding of the nature of oral language.

Review Key Terms

1. Define each term and write it in a sentence: oral language, vocabulary, structure, grammar, diction, pronunciation, articulation, enunciation, dialect.

Check Understanding

2. Define oral language and briefly explain each of its characteristics.
3. Describe the two main characteristics of speech sound.
4. How are pronunciation, articulation, and enunciation alike? How are they different?
5. Describe one communication problem that might result from using a strong dialect. What is one possible solution to this problem?
6. **Apply** Explain one way your oral language choices might affect you on a personal level and on a cultural level in your future.

APPLICATION *Activity*

Analyzing Dialect Working in groups of three or four, select a dialect and brainstorm a list of common words that might be considered part of that dialect. As a class, list your words in a chart and classify each as regional, ethnic, or cultural. Brainstorm how you might replace each word with more standardized language. Were there any words you had difficulty replacing? Why?

Critical Thinking Skill

Recognizing Bias

Just as there is a need to send clear messages in social and professional contexts, there also is a need to be aware of the messages being sent by others. Sometimes those messages contain bias statements. A bias is a prejudice. It prevents you from looking at a situation in a reasonable or truthful way.

Learning the Skill

To recognize bias, follow these steps:

- Analyze the sender's message in terms of his or her views and possible reasons for making the statement.
- Try to notice language in the message that reflects an emotion or opinion. This may include words such as *all, never, best, worst, might,* or *should.*
- Look for imbalances in the message. Does it give only one viewpoint and fail to provide equal coverage of other possible viewpoints?
- Identify statements of fact. Factual statements usually answer who, what, where, and when.
- Identify the bias in the message.

Practicing the Skill

Read the advertisement in the next column and answer the questions that follow.

1. Who is the sender of the message?
2. What are the sender's reasons for sending this message?
3. List any words or phrases that indicate emotion or opinion.
4. List any factual statements.
5. Identify the bias in the message.

Best Desks, Incorporated makes only the very highest quality office furniture. Once you have used a Best Desks ergonomically designed chair, you will never want to use any other furniture. Our desks are made of solid wood and always are attractive and comfortable. Our padded chairs can be adjusted to your size and to the height of your desktop. Our prices are among the lowest in the industry. In addition, when you buy from Best Desks, you receive two free gifts: an attractive desk clock and a useful desk calendar.

APPLICATION *Activity*

Choose an editorial from a newspaper. In groups, read your chosen editorials aloud. As you read, emphasize any emotional or opinionated words through tone or expression you use. As a group, go through the steps to identify the bias in each editorial.

Section 2

Developing Skills for Power Language

GUIDE TO READING

Objectives

1. Analyze the characteristics of power language.
2. Analyze and apply standards for using formal, technical, standard, and informal language appropriately.
3. Compare and contrast the functions of oral language.
4. Identify and describe the types of language to avoid in oral communication.

Terms to Learn

formal language
technical language
jargon
standard language
informal language
colloquialism
slang
ungrammatical language
social ritual
denotation
connotation
filler
tag

Think about the world of nature. What is the most sophisticated communication you can think of in the animal kingdom? How does that compare to the communication skills of a typical human of kindergarten age?

Through language, human beings have the power to communicate as no other animal can. True, some animals are capable of communicating a wide variety of messages—"Watch me," "Go away," "I'm hungry," "I'm sad," or "Run!" to name a few. However, these types of messages are on a level of communication that most humans achieve early in their language development. Even Koko, a much-studied primate who not only speaks "Gorilla" but also some human sign language, is only able to communicate a limited range of ideas through her "speech."

It is through sophisticated thought and language that human beings are set apart from other animals. Language has allowed us to communicate specific, complex messages; preserve and study others' ideas; and use tools such as persuasion, manipulation, honesty, and conviction to influence those around us. In other words, language is power. Certainly, if this idea is true, we all need to learn how to use that power to help meet our personal needs and goals.

Koko, the well-known gorilla, developed language skills through the use of human sign language. What sets humans apart from animals?

UNDERSTANDING AND USING POWER LANGUAGE

Why do people communicate? We all communicate to meet specific needs and goals. As you learn more about communication, you will discover ways to use "power language" to efficiently meet these needs and goals. Power language is a valuable tool for enhancing your image as a communicator. Power language is also valuable for achieving positive results and promoting effective relationships.

Characteristics of Power Language

Think about the most effective communicator you know. Whether this person is a teacher, parent, businessperson, or celebrity of some sort doesn't matter. What is important is his or her ability to get to the point, meet the listener's needs, and achieve positive results from communication. In other words, this person is skilled in using power language.

You too can learn to use power language in your day-to-day communication. The following chart describes the traits displayed in power language.

CHARACTERISTICS OF POWER LANGUAGE

Language Displays . . .	How	Effect on Communication
Clarity	Speech is precise, clearly organized, and grammatical. Speech is easy to understand.	Speaker may develop an image as a knowledgeable, efficient communicator. Understanding may be enhanced by ability to speak effectively.
Courtesy and Tact	Speaker listens empathically, negotiates with respect, disagrees without being disagreeable, and focuses discussions on issues rather than on people.	Showing respect and consideration to others promotes positive relationships. Speaker is considered a real "pro" in social and professional interactions.
Ownership of Thoughts and Feelings	Speaker takes responsibility for thoughts and feelings. Speaker uses "I" messages to express opinions, ideas, and feelings: "I was bored" rather than "That was boring."	When the speaker is seen as responsible, self-confident, and nonjudgmental, clarity and understanding are promoted. Speaker is viewed as someone who gets things done rather than a "blamer."
Inclusion of Others	Speaker listens empathically and personalizes speech with direct references to others: "What do you think about this issue?" "I'd really like to hear your opinion."	Including others helps establish a common ground and paves the way for cooperation and understanding. Speaker is seen as open-minded and interested in others.
Vividness and Imagery	Speaker expresses ordinary ideas in new and imaginative ways. Imagery is used to help people visualize complex ideas.	Speech is interesting and memorable. People look forward to hearing what the speaker has to say.
Appropriate Usage	Speaker uses a level of language that is appropriate for the specific context.	Speaker is often viewed as reasonable, thoughtful, and with a strong command of the language. Others trust him or her to communicate appropriately.

Most governmental proceedings, such as the council meeting shown, involve aspects of formal language. **What is formal language?**

Power language is not as mysterious as it sounds. In short, it is clear, interesting, effective language. You already are familiar with much of what it takes to use power language. It involves mastering the components of language you read about in Section 1. It also emphasizes the diction and dialect habits you read about earlier and the easy-to-understand concepts of courtesy, ownership, inclusion, and vividness. Still, there is something more to power language. It also requires a thorough understanding of when to use different types of language.

Understanding Levels of Usage

Skilled communicators learn early on that certain types of language strategies are appropriate for different situations. They also learn to avoid language that is inappropriate for a particular context. For example, you wouldn't use highly technical computer jargon to talk to most four-year-olds, nor would you use street slang to communicate in a job interview.

Speech has five basic levels of usage, each with its own type of language. These levels of language and usage are

- formal
- technical
- standard
- informal
- ungrammatical

Standards for Using Formal Language

Formal language is language that conforms to a highly structured set of rules; that is, there are strict standards dictating its use. Formal language typically is reserved for situations that require rigid protocol and form. Most legal proceedings and many religious services use some type of formal language. Certain social club meetings and political ceremonies also may adhere to a strict set of language rules.

Perhaps the clearest example of formal language is parliamentary procedure, which applies strict rules to all group communication. The formality involved in parliamentary procedure is really quite extensive. First, it requires a working knowledge of *Robert's Rules of Order,* which lists all the necessary guidelines for parliamentary-style meetings. In these meetings, participants address the presiding officer by his or her formal title and ask to be recognized before speaking to the group. They also structure each statement formally. For instance, you might say "I move that we . . ." before making a suggestion or motion.

interNET ACTIVITY

Etymology The etymology of a word is a history of the uses of the word and how its definition or usage has changed over the years. The meaning of many words, including names, slang, technical language, and greetings, can be traced back hundreds of years. Do an Internet search using the word *etymology* to find the meaning of words you use on a daily basis.

Standards for Using Technical Language

Technical language is language associated with a particular profession, activity, or field of study. Another name for technical language is **jargon.** Medicine, law, finance, technology, and sports are just a few fields that depend heavily on jargon. You probably also have encountered various types of technical language in the classes, clubs, and organizations to which you belong. Any time you take a course in a new area of study, enter a new activity, or take a new job, you probably will encounter a new technical vocabulary.

Videoconferencing is an effective channel often used by members of the medical profession. Medical professionals utilize technical language frequently. What are some other fields that rely on technical language?

Technical language often can be misunderstood by those outside the profession or group. In addition, the same term can mean something quite different when used in a different context. The term *pound,* for example, can stand for a specific thickness of fishing line in a sporting goods store, a measurement of weight in math class, or a unit of currency at a bank.

The Changing Nature of Technical Language Even if you have a background in a specific field, you still are likely to encounter new vocabulary from time to time within that setting. Technical language tends to change rapidly and continually. Sometimes, things change so quickly that communicators simply make up new terms to meet specific needs. If these temporary terms remain useful over a period of time, they may become incorporated into the group's standard jargon. Eventually, they may even find their way into the public's vocabulary.

Applying Technical Language

Knowing and using technical language can be vital to your success in many specialized activities or in the workplace. As you become more accustomed to using technical language in various contexts, you will realize that certain standards govern its use. For instance, technical language generally should be avoided when you are speaking with people outside your field. For example, use technical language sparingly when speaking with customers, clients, patients, audience members, or others whom it might confuse. If certain forms of jargon are unavoidable, be sure to explain the term carefully so the listener can understand.

Standards for Using Standard Language

Standard language is the language used by the majority of knowledgeable communicators within a specific language. It is what most people refer to as "correct" speech. The standards for using standard speech include a precise vocabulary, appropriate use of language structures, adherence to the rules of the language, and clarity of diction. Standard language is the level of usage recommended for most professional and social contexts. It is often called "power language" because it is the level of usage that most directly affects your success in most situations.

One colloquialism used in the agricultural community is "till the cows come home." What is important to remember when utilizing colloquialisms?

Standards for Using Informal Language

Informal language is the type of language most often used in casual situations and close interpersonal relationships. It would be incorrect to assume that because language is informal, it has no rules. The standards for using the two most common types of oral language–colloquialisms and slang–are analyzed here.

Colloquialisms

A **colloquialism** is a term associated with a specific regional culture. Most regional dialects contain a number of individual colloquialisms, which often are firmly entrenched in the speech traditions of the people. For example, many colloquialisms in the United States stem from the nation's agricultural roots. You may have heard someone speak of "going to bed with the chickens" to describe going to bed early or staying somewhere "till the cows come home" to describe staying a long time. Both are widely used examples of informal language.

Limitations of Colloquialisms Almost every culture has a number of colloquialisms rooted in its speech. These terms, phrases, and sentences usually are familiar to most people within a culture and may even be prized for adding a local flavor to the language. It is important to remember, however, that colloquialisms often do not translate well outside of their original culture. They can be easily misinterpreted or completely meaningless to anyone from a different regional culture.

Using Colloquialisms For this reason, colloquialisms are best reserved for informal communication with close friends or casual relationships within the culture. Generally speaking, they are not appropriate for use in interviews, conversations related to professional or social business, or public presentations. Although some situations may allow a "folksy" or "homespun" communication style, it is important not to overuse these informal terms. Heavy reliance on colloquial language may give others the impression that a communicator has limited language skills or education.

Slang

Slang is a second type of informal language. It can be described as temporary language because it typically is used for only a brief period of time by a limited group of people.

Slang can be compared to a fad in clothing. Both stem from popular culture, and neither tends to last for very long. A slang term used in a movie or popular song may become popular for two or three years but eventually fades away as enthusiasm for that movie or song declines. Slang often results from a need to make language more fun or interesting or to find new ways to express ideas and feelings. It often is associated with young people who invent new language terms to communicate within their own groups.

Limitations of Slang Slang presents some definite limitations to communication. While it often is used to help define who belongs to the "in" crowd, it also excludes outsiders from understanding or participating in conversations. Also, like certain items of fad clothing, it can be unbecoming when used by people who obviously do not belong to the intended user group. For example, an adult speaker who tries to use teen slang in a speech to a high school audience may appear to be insincere or out of touch. His or her use of slang may unintentionally have the opposite effect of what was desired.

A third limitation of slang is its temporary nature. What is "cool" one year may be "bad" the next, "hot" six months later, and "phat" before the end of the school term. So, by the time you work a slang term into your everyday speech, it may no longer be popular. Allowing a slang term to linger too long in your vocabulary can result in tired, lackluster language. Terms such as "Awesome!" "No way!" and "Chill out!" have become overused and boring over the years. So, remember, choosing to use slang can make you appear out of date and out of touch very quickly.

Using Slang Even though slang can be fun to use at times, it should be used sparingly. As informal language, it often does not measure up to the standards of appropriate communication. As a general rule, try to limit that use of slang to communication with

TECHNOLOGY Activity

Language Choices Context is a major factor in determining the level of language chosen by the sender. For one week, keep a log of the language levels you observe and look for patterns in how technical, formal, or colloquial the messages are. Do you observe a difference between local and national newscasters? Between e-mail messages from friends and form letters or business correspondence your family may receive through the mail? Between communication among friends in a sitcom and how information is presented in a documentary? Between disc jockeys on a top-forty radio station and an easy-listening station? Are the language choices made in each context appropriate? Why or why not?

friends in informal situations. Over time, relying too heavily on slang can have a crippling effect on your ability to express yourself effectively. It can begin to creep into other areas of your speech where it is inappropriate. Slang always should be avoided in business-related situations and usually is unacceptable for discussions and public presentations.

Ungrammatical Language

Ungrammatical language is language that does not use expected standards of grammar or mechanics. Ungrammatical phrases such as "I seen" or "they was" can detract from a communicator's credibility. It is important to try to eliminate this type of language from your speech because it can detract from your message and tarnish your credibility as a speaker.

Choosing Your Speaking Style

In Section 1, your vocabulary choices were compared to the choices you make about what to wear in different situations. Earlier in this section, slang was compared to fad clothing. However, the comparison doesn't end there.

Just as you may be known for wearing a particular style of clothing, you probably are known for your style of speech. While both of these reveal information about you to others, your language probably tells more about you than your clothes.

The level of usage that you choose for most situations helps define your overall image as a communicator. If you follow the rules of usage for standard language in most situations, use formal and technical language when appropriate, limit your use of informal language to casual settings, and eliminate ungrammatical language from your speech, you will build an image as a competent communicator.

Functions of Oral Language

Once a communicator has mastered the components of language, refined the characteristics of his or her speech, and determined appropriate levels of usage for different contexts, the power language process is almost complete. The remaining step is to understand the true functions of language that are shown in Figure 4–3 and use them to their fullest extent.

Expressing and Responding to Feelings

An important aspect of gaining power through language is the ability to put your feelings into words. Equally important is your ability to respond to others' feelings.

Expressing Feelings Sometimes, perhaps due to cultural upbringing or lack of confidence, individuals have trouble expressing their feelings to others. As a result, they may go to great lengths to avoid letting others know how they feel. Learning to state and label feelings in a rational way, however, can be very empowering.

For example, knowing how to calmly and effectively express your feelings can help change a frustrating situation. Instead of simply enduring the situation until you are completely fed up, you might say, "I was

Figure 4–3 The Five Functions of Oral Language

- Expressing and responding to feelings
- Informing
- Controlling or persuading
- Participating in social rituals
- Creating and imagining

The child in the center is clearly experiencing frustration. An important part of oral language is finding an effective way of expressing one's feelings. **How can you deal with a frustrating situation effectively?**

frustrated by his lack of cooperation," or "I was angry about the interruption." No one can fault you for calmly and honestly stating your feelings. Rather, your words may open the door to discussion and prevent irrational outbursts of emotion.

Responding to Feelings A certain amount of power also lies in listening and responding appropriately to the feelings of others. For example, if you have learned to say, "I'm sorry you were disappointed" rather than "You shouldn't be disappointed," you are more likely to gain people's trust and respect. Both statements express concern over someone's disappointment, but each sends a different message about your attitude toward both the person and the situation.

Giving and Seeking Information

In professional and social contexts, a major function of language is giving and seeking information. Students and teachers, supervisors and employees, group leaders and group members all need to be able to ask questions and provide answers that are clear and effective. The key to providing information to others is using clear language that is appropriate for the speaker, listener, occasion, and task. Instructions, reports, and other types of spoken information are most effective when they are tailored to the specific context. Clarity also is the key to seeking information from others. The ability to phrase questions so that they focus directly on the information needed is a mark of a skilled communicator.

Controlling and Persuading

A great deal of personal power lies in your ability to influence others. Whether you are serving customers, talking your boss into giving you a raise, or convincing a friend to see a particular movie, you are attempting to persuade or influence others. Much of your effectiveness in making suggestions or requests depends on the language you use. Also, giving commands or making demands of others requires special skills. It takes competent communication skills and knowledge to get others to achieve the results you want while still preserving the relationship. This balancing act requires not only clarity, directness, and self-confidence but also courtesy, tact, and integrity. As you continue to work though this text, you will have an opportunity to practice some of these skills.

Participating in Social Rituals

Believe it or not, much of your personal power lies in the way you interact in everyday social rituals. A **social ritual** is a communication situation that is frequently repeated in

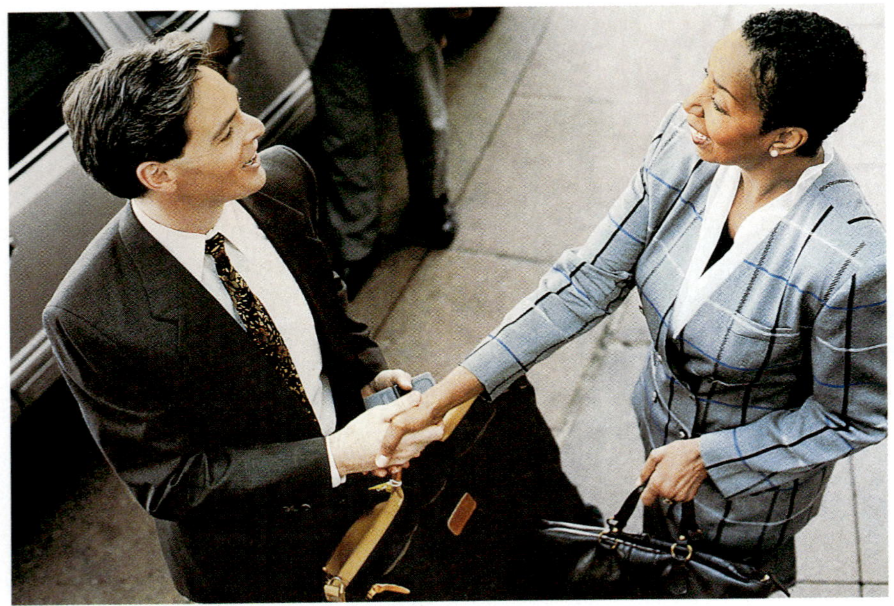

The two individuals are practicing the social ritual of shaking hands. Explain how social rituals help one to become a competent communicator.

daily social interaction. For example, if you exchange a friendly "good morning" with the same people as you arrive at school or work every day, you are taking part in a social ritual. Making and acknowledging introductions, giving and accepting compliments, engaging in short personal conversations with coworkers, and giving and responding to praise and suggestions all are forms of social rituals.

Social rituals usually follow a pattern and sometimes call for using social etiquette. They provide the basis for interpersonal communication in the workplace and group situations. They also are the first stepping stone to developing relationships with others. Social rituals usually are characterized by courtesy, tact, good manners, and civility—all of which are keys to success as a competent communicator.

Creating and Imagining

The ability to imagine and create is vital to success in almost any area of life. Creativity gives you the ability to find new solutions, generate new ideas, and envision new alternatives—some of the most valuable skills in professional and social contexts. However, all the imagination and creativity in the world is fairly useless if you cannot adequately express your ideas.

So, how do you describe an idea that is new and different? How do you persuade others to share your vision? Expressing ideas or describing products that have not yet taken form requires an imaginative and creative use of language. You may find yourself searching for new descriptive terms, learning to ask thought-provoking questions, or using language that reflects imagery, energy, and conviction.

Language to Avoid

As a skilled communicator, you not only need to know what language is appropriate for a specific context but also what language to avoid. Language plays an important role in establishing the climate for communication, determining the impact of communication, and defining the quality of relationships. Therefore, as shown in the chart on the next page, it is important to avoid words and strategies that can result in negative or defensive responses from listeners.

Understanding Denotations and Connotations

One thing to remember as you begin to fine-tune your language skills are that words have denotations and connotations. A denotation is a word's objective description or meaning. A word's connotation, on the other hand, is the emotions or feelings with which it is associated. A word's denotation is found in the dictionary, its connotation is not. If, for example, you are talking about a particular dwelling, you might

STRATEGIES FOR AVOIDING TROUBLESOME LANGUAGE

Language	Description	Alternative Language Strategy
Sexist	Sexist language implies that something is more suited to a specific gender. It groups men or women into a category and perpetuates gender-based stereotypes.	Use descriptive language that replaces gender related terms with general terms. Examples of sexist/nonsexist language include: mankind/humankind, chairman/chair, fireman/firefighter, housewife/homemaker, congressman/representative
Racist	Racist language applies labels or behavioral characteristics to an entire race of individuals. It is the language of prejudice and stereotypes and is extremely offensive.	Racist language is never appropriate. Use personal names and descriptions that do not refer to ethnic identity.
Profane or Obscene	Profane language is vulgar, irreverent, or abusive language that can be considered offensive in social and professional contexts. Dependence on profanity or obscenity can damage a speaker's credibility.	This type of language is never appropriate. Learn to express and assume ownership for feelings. Say, "I am angry" or "I am frustrated" when these feelings arise.
Judgmental	Judgmental language implies an inappropriate evaluation or critique of someone or something. Qualitative words such as *good, bad, worthwhile*, or *worthless* may imply that you are sitting in judgment of someone or their behavior. *Why* questions are sometimes seen as defensive and can convey judgment on the speaker's part.	Try to assume ownership of your remarks and use descriptive, supportive words that give information in an objective way. For example, instead of saying, "That was a good introduction," the critic would say, "Your introduction really caught my attention" (giving information focused on a specific criterion for an effective introduction). Also, ask information seeking questions that begin with *how, what, when, where*, and *who* whenever possible.
Accusatory	Using "you" messages improperly can make a speaker sound bossy or judgmental. The listener may feel as if he or she is being accused or attacked.	Instead of saying sentences like "You need to clean this up," try saying, "I'm uncomfortable with the way this place looks."
Assumptive	Assumptive language implies that everyone shares your views, opinions, or concerns. Overusing words such as *we, everyone, everybody* and forms of the verb *to be* can trigger the response "No, I don't," and quickly put listeners on the defensive.	Try using qualifiers such as *may be, can be*, or *appears to be.*
Absolute	Absolutes assume that there are no exceptions. Absolute language is risky for two reasons: few things stay the same forever, and there are exceptions to every rule.	Avoid words such as *every, always, never*, or *will.* Instead, use less-rigid terms such as *most, usually, seldom*, or *may.*

refer to it as either a "house" or a "home." The word *house* denotes a particular kind of structure but does not imply any particular feeling about that structure. On the other hand, the connotations of the word *home* tap into images and feelings that may have little to do with the structure itself.

Using words that have strong emotional associations often requires careful analysis of the listener and the occasion. For instance, if you are describing a dog to a veterinarian, he or she probably will understand that your use of the word *mutt* simply denotes a mixed-breed dog. However, if you are speaking to the dog's owner, calling the dog a "mutt" may result in hurt feelings. The owner may focus on the negative connotations of *mutt* as a lowly or worthless animal and may become defensive. Developing your vocabulary so that you better understand the connotations of various words will help you communicate your intentions more clearly to others and avoid unintentionally offending them.

A connotation of the word home could bring to mind a scene like the one shown. Why is it important to understand connotations?

Avoiding Troublesome Language

Understanding possible negative connotations in your speech is a good way to start avoiding troublesome language. There are other steps you can take as well. As you found out from the chart on page 125, problematic language can negatively affect communication. Some of the most troublesome words are short, simple ones that we use frequently without giving thought to the effect these terms have on our listeners.

Avoiding Powerless Language

You've gained knowledge about how to speak and use language appropriately for each situation, apply the functions of language to your advantage, and avoid offending your listeners. You're well on your way to mastering power language. However, there is still one important adjustment to make. Now it is time to eliminate powerless language from your speech patterns.

Powerless language tends to be vague and accomplishes very little. It does nothing to enhance others' perceptions of a speaker, and therefore does not contribute to powerful speech. In fact, it actually can erode a speaker's power by making him or her seem indecisive or lacking in confidence.

Fillers You probably already are familiar with the form of powerless language known as fillers. A **filler** is a word or phrase used to cover up hesitancy in speech. Some common fillers are "uh," "um," "like," "so," "you know," and "totally." When these words are used to fill gaps in speech, they not only add no value to the message, but they also detract from the speaker's image as a competent communicator.

POWERLESS LANGUAGE FILLERS

Message With Fillers	Message Without Fillers
"Well, I, uh, want to, you know, graduate with, uh, honors, you know, because I, like, want to, uh, get a good job or, uh, maybe even, like, go to, uh, college."	"I really want to graduate with honors because I want to get a good job or perhaps even go to college."

Tags A tag is a statement or question added to the end of a statement to invite approval or cooperation from others. Like fillers, tags can make speakers appear as if they lack confidence or knowledge. When concluding a presentation, you probably would not want to say, "It's time to go, don't you think?" This might make you sound as if you lack self-assurance or as if you are uninformed about when to end. Saying "It's time to go," or "I think it's time to go," or even asking "Don't you think it is time to go?" projects a much more powerful image than does a statement with a tag.

Vague Wording Vague, unproductive sentences often rely heavily on words such as *it*, *they*, or *but*. These sentences tend to be "throw-aways," providing little information and detracting from your power as a communicator.

For example, overusing the words *it* and *they* tends to make communication impersonal, abstract, and without detail. The result is that communicators may lose interest. For instance, consider which sentence might mean more to you on the job: "They need you to sign it," or "Our office manager and the people in accounting need you to sign this purchase order." By including relevant details, you can make your speech more valuable to listeners.

COMMUNICATION PRACTICE LAB

Avoiding Fillers

To practice ridding your speech of meaningless fillers, follow these steps:

Step 1 Form a group with two or three other students and brainstorm several questions on a topic with which you are all familiar.

Step 2 Have one group member ask another a question from your list.

Step 3 The second person must give a thirty-second response that does not contain the words "uh," "like," or "you know." Pauses can be no longer than one second.

Step 4 Have the third group member time the response, stopping immediately if a filler or long pause is used.

Step 5 Take turns timing and trying to respond without using fillers. Who had the best time in your group? In the class?

Another hallmark of vague language is the repeated use of the word *but*. Frequently placing the word *but* between statements results in a message "wipeout" that can be time-consuming and frustrating to listeners. For example, if you say "I'll try to be there, but don't wait for me," or "She's a hard worker, but she doesn't get along with her coworkers," the second statement confuses or contradicts the meaning of the first. Consequently, this type of language can make you seem like an indecisive or confused speaker.

The words and expressions you use can be your best ally or your worst enemy. Choosing and using power language is a real asset to everyday communication. It not only can help you get the results you want from your interactions with others, but it also can help you achieve the goal of becoming a competent communicator.

Section 2 Assessment

Visit the *Glencoe Communication Applications* Web site at **communicationapplications.glencoe.com** and click on **Self-Check and Study Guide 4.2** to review your understanding of using power language.

Review Key Terms

1. Define each term and write it in a sentence: formal language, technical language, jargon, standard language, informal language, colloquialism, slang, ungrammatical language, social ritual, denotation, connotation, filler, tag.

Check Understanding

2. Writing one sentence for each characteristic, describe how you might use each characteristic of power language in your daily communication at school.
3. Which type or types of language might be most appropriate to use in a job interview? Which might be least appropriate? Why?
4. Which function of oral language serves mainly the interests of the speaker rather than the listener? Explain your answer.
5. **Evaluating** Which types of troublesome language do you consider the worst? Why?

APPLICATION *Activity*

Becoming a Powerful Speaker On a sheet of paper, write the one characteristic of power language that most needs improvement in your current speaking style and why. Then, write a three-step plan detailing how you might improve this speaking skill over the next week. Share your plans as a class and discuss real-world opportunities for testing your skills.

Communication Self-Assessment

Analyzing Your Oral Communication Skills

How Do You Rate?

On a separate sheet of paper, use the key to respond to the following statements and assess your communication style. Put a check mark beside each skill you would like to improve.

Key: **A** Always **U** Usually **S** Sometimes **R** Rarely **N** Never

1. I choose my words carefully when I communicate with others.

2. When I don't know how to pronounce a word, I ask someone to pronounce it for me or I look it up in the dictionary.

3. I clearly articulate my consonants.

4. I seldom slur my words.

5. I regularly try to add new words to my vocabulary.

6. When I disagree with someone, I carefully select my words when I respond.

7. I use the word "I" to express my opinions, ideas, and feelings.

8. I try to be imaginative when I explain something.

9. I avoid sexist, racist, and profane language.

10. I try not to speak in absolutes.

How Do You Score?

Review your responses. Give yourself 5 points for every A, 4 for every U, 3 for every S, 2 for every R, and 1 for every N. Total your points and evaluate your score.

41–50 Excellent You may be surprised to find out how much you can improve your skills.

31–40 Good In this course, you can learn ways to make your skills better.

21–30 Fair Practice applying the skills taught in this course.

1–20 Needs Improvement Carefully monitor your improvement as you work through this course.

Setting Communication Goals

If you scored Excellent or Good, complete Part A. If your score was Fair or Needs Improvement, complete Part B.

Part A

1. I plan to put the following ideas into practice:

2. I plan to share the following information about communication with the following people:

Part B

1. The behaviors I need to change most are:

2. To bring about these changes, I will take these steps:

Formatting Business Messages

Every day, millions of business messages are written throughout the world. These include letters, e-mail messages, faxes, brief notes, and memorandums, or memos. The format of these messages can vary from handwritten notes to memos to published reports and legal correspondence. Although the ways in which these messages are relayed can vary, all identify the date, sender, and recipient and provide some sort of address along with the content of the message.

Format of a Letter One effective format for a business letter is shown here.

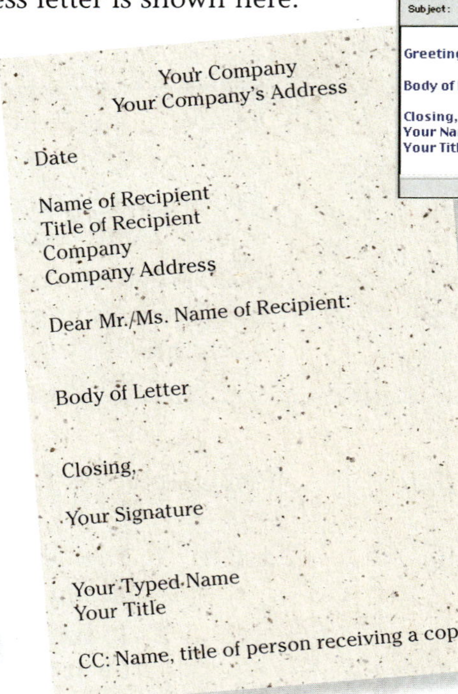

Your Company
Your Company's Address

Date

Name of Recipient
Title of Recipient
Company
Company Address

Dear Mr./Ms. Name of Recipient:

Body of Letter

Closing,

Your Signature

Your Typed Name
Your Title

CC: Name, title of person receiving a copy

Format of an E-Mail Message An e-mail message is sent from one computer to another through an internal network or through an e-mail provider. Usually, the date and the sender's e-mail address are automatically shown at the top of each message. Also, a greeting is optional if the recipient is clearly identified in the "To" field. One effective format for an e-mail message is shown here.

Charcoal 12

To... Recipient's E-mail Address
Cc... E-mail Addresses of Those Who Will Receive Copies
Subject: Main Topic of the Message

Greeting (if necessary):

Body of E-Mail Message

Closing,
Your Name
Your Title

For additional information about business writing, see the *Guide to Business Communication* section of the Communication Survival Kit in the Appendix.

Format of a Fax Cover Sheet Each facsimile, or fax, you send should have a cover sheet that provides important information about the attachment, sender, and recipient. One effective format for a fax cover sheet is shown here.

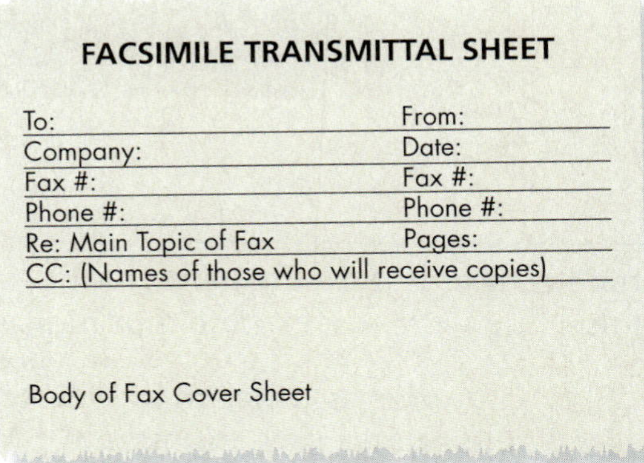

FACSIMILE TRANSMITTAL SHEET

To:	From:
Company:	Date:
Fax #:	Fax #:
Phone #:	Phone #:
Re: Main Topic of Fax	Pages:

CC: (Names of those who will receive copies)

Body of Fax Cover Sheet

Below is an example of an effectively formatted memorandum.

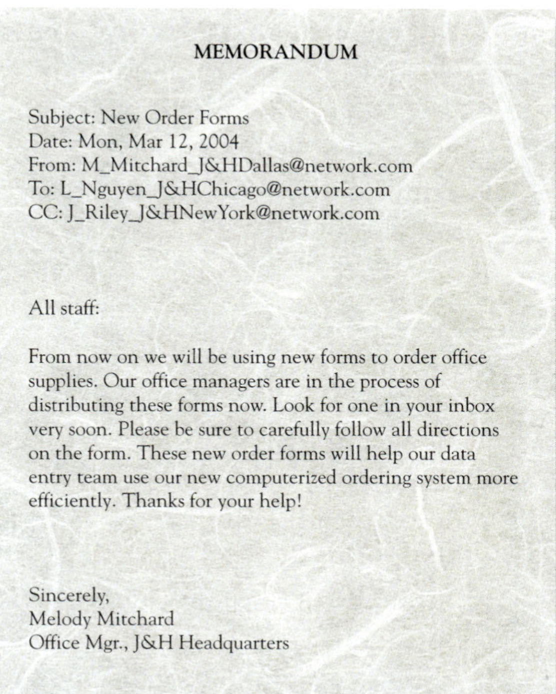

MEMORANDUM

Subject: New Order Forms
Date: Mon, Mar 12, 2004
From: M_Mitchard_J&HDallas@network.com
To: L_Nguyen_J&HChicago@network.com
CC: J_Riley_J&HNewYork@network.com

All staff:

From now on we will be using new forms to order office supplies. Our office managers are in the process of distributing these forms now. Look for one in your inbox very soon. Please be sure to carefully follow all directions on the form. These new order forms will help our data entry team use our new computerized ordering system more efficiently. Thanks for your help!

Sincerely,
Melody Mitchard
Office Mgr., J&H Headquarters

WRITING *Activity*

Take the following ideas into consideration as you unscramble the e-mail message below. Write the message in the correct format on a separate sheet of paper.

- You are in charge of filling orders for a company that sells outboard motors over the Internet.
- Customers typically order products through an e-mail link on your Web site.
- Payment must be received in full before items will be shipped.
- Due to a computer malfunction, you receive the following scrambled e-mail order.

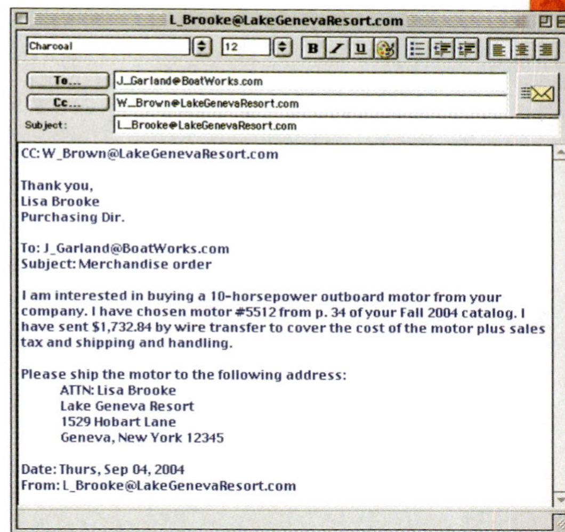

L_Brooke@LakeGenevaResort.com

To... J_Garland@BoatWorks.com
Cc... W_Brown@LakeGenevaResort.com
Subject: L_Brooke@LakeGenevaResort.com

CC: W_Brown@LakeGenevaResort.com

Thank you,
Lisa Brooke
Purchasing Dir.

To: J_Garland@BoatWorks.com
Subject: Merchandise order

I am interested in buying a 10-horsepower outboard motor from your company. I have chosen motor #5512 from p. 34 of your Fall 2004 catalog. I have sent $1,732.84 by wire transfer to cover the cost of the motor plus sales tax and shipping and handling.

Please ship the motor to the following address:
ATTN: Lisa Brooke
Lake Geneva Resort
1529 Hobart Lane
Geneva, New York 12345

Date: Thurs, Sep 04, 2004
From: L_Brooke@LakeGenevaResort.com

CHAPTER 4 Assessment and Activities

GLENCOE Online

Visit the *Glencoe Communication Applications* Web site at **communicationapplications.glencoe.com** and click on **Chapter 4 Activity** for additional practice in developing powerful oral language.

Reviewing Key Terms

On paper, write whether each statement is true or false. If the statement is false, copy the statement, underline the word that makes it false, and write a substitute that makes it true.

1. Connotation is the degree of clarity and distinctness in a person's speech.
2. All the sounds in a language make up its vocabulary.
3. The most basic rules of a language relate to the structure of words and sentences.
4. Pronunciation is the general understandings and rules that regulate the use of a language.
5. Medicine, law, finance, technology, and sports are just a few fields that depend heavily on specialized language or slang.
6. Grammar is a system of symbols, rules, and sounds used for human communication.
7. Articulation is the act of leaving out certain consonant sounds within a word.
8. Pronunciation is the act of clearly and distinctly uttering the vowel sounds of a word.
9. The "southern drawl" is an example of a regional diction.
10. Enunciation is the way that a specific word sounds.

Reviewing Key Concepts

1. How are all oral languages similar?
2. What is a major difference between oral language and written language?
3. Give examples of two situations for which you would use different kinds of language.
4. Why is it important to build strong vocabulary?
5. What allows you to add interest and personality to your messages?
6. List the three functions of grammar.
7. What are two drawbacks of mispronouncing words?
8. What is the level of language usage recommended for most professional and social contexts?
9. What are the five functions of oral language?
10. How do denotations and connotations differ?

Assessment and Activities

Reading and Critical Thinking Skill

1. **Applying Information** How do you determine which pronunciation to use for the word *harass* when a dictionary lists two pronunciations?
2. **Cause-Effect** What are the results when a speaker expresses ordinary ideas in imaginative ways and uses imagery to help people visualize complex ideas?
3. **Making Contrasts** How do the articulation errors of addition and substitution differ?
4. **Summarization** Sum up five guidelines for speaking clearly and effectively.
5. **Classifying Information** At what level of language does a speaker use *Robert's Rules of Order*?

Skill Practice Activity

Recognizing Bias Identify the bias in the following quotes. On a separate sheet of paper, rewrite the quotes avoiding troublesome words.

"The republican is the only form of government which is not eternally at open or secret war with the rights of mankind." Thomas Jefferson

"The trade of critic, in literature, music, and the drama, is the most degraded of all trades." Mark Twain

Cooperative Learning Activity

Powerful Language With a partner, hold a ten-minute discussion about language usage in your school. List some of the powerful and troublesome language that you hear from students. Prepare a list of suggestions for making students' language more powerful. Share your list with other members of the class.

Chapter Project

Planning Throughout one school day, record on audiotape everything you say. Transcribe your words and then evaluate your diction according to the following criteria: Which words did I mispronounce? In which words did I omit consonant sounds? In which words did I add consonant sounds? In which words did I substitute one consonant for another? In which words did I slur consonant sounds? In which words did I fail to enunciate?

Make a list of words that show poor diction. Practice saying them correctly.

Presenting Try to use all the words on your list during the course of one school day. Be conscious of your pronunciations, articulations, and enunciations. Congratulate yourself if you get through the day saying all the words on your list correctly.

CHAPTER 5

Understanding Nonverbal Communication

WHY IT'S IMPORTANT

Not all communication is accomplished with words. What you do, how you look, and the sound of your voice can send nonverbal messages even more powerful than words.

To better understand nonverbal communication, view the **Communication in Action** Chapter 5 video lesson.

"The most important thing in communication is to hear what isn't being said."
—Peter F. Drucker, Austrian writer and educator

GLENCOE Online

Visit the *Glencoe Communication Applications* Web site at **communicationapplications.glencoe.com** and click on **Overview–Chapter 5** to preview information about nonverbal communication.

Section 1

Principles of Nonverbal Communication

GUIDE TO READING

Objectives

1. Describe nonverbal communication.
2. Explain the functions of nonverbal communication.
3. Describe the characteristics of nonverbal communication.

Terms to Learn

nonverbal communication
ambiguous

Have you ever felt as if you weren't in the mood to talk? Maybe you were tired or upset or just in a quiet mood. Regardless of your reason, you may have taken a break from talking to your family or friends. What did your lack of speech communicate to them? Think about the statement "You cannot not communicate." Do you agree or disagree? Why?

What was your first reaction to the statement above? If you are like many people, you may have thought, "Of course I can avoid communicating. All I have to do is keep my mouth shut!"

However, that's not exactly true. Even if you don't talk to anyone around you—don't say hello, ask questions, or even answer questions—you still are communicating. Your facial expressions, body language, and even the way you use distance and space all send messages to others. Surprisingly, these messages often speak louder than words.

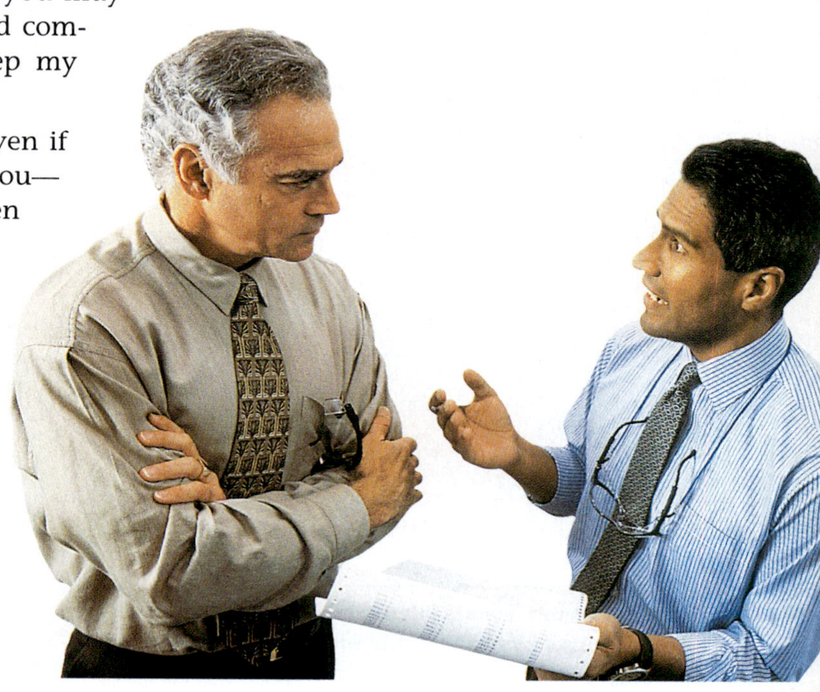

Body language is an example of nonverbal communication. Identify the ways in which the two men shown are using nonverbal communication.

What Is Nonverbal Communication?

Nonverbal communication is a system of symbolic behaviors that includes all forms of communication except words. A symbolic wave of the hand, for example, can mean "Hello," "Good-bye," "Go ahead," "I'm over here," or a number of other things, depending on the context or situation. A laugh can symbolize such emotions as humor, nervousness, or sarcasm, just as a sigh can symbolize sadness, wishfulness, anger, or impatience.

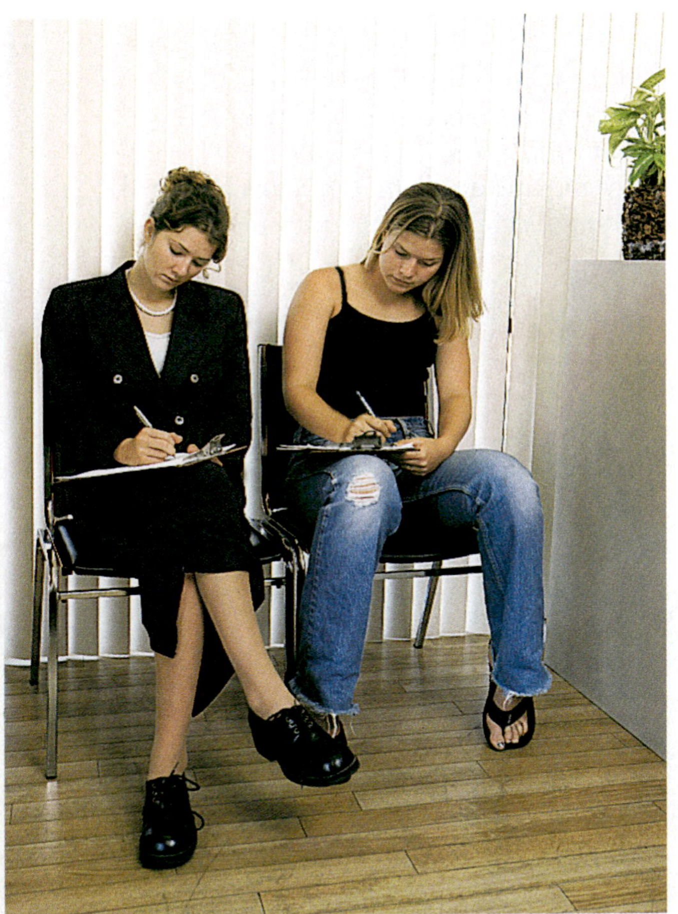

Two young women indicate interest in a job position by filling out an application. Identify what their nonverbal clues suggest about their interest in the job.

Think about all the ways you convey messages and feelings without words. These are your nonverbal behaviors. Nonverbal behaviors can be organized into three categories:

- sounds, including the voice and vocalizations that substitute for speech
- body language
- environmental factors such as time, touch, distance, and objects and artifacts

Studies in nonverbal communication have concluded that anywhere from 65 to 93 percent of meaning communicated from one person to another is communicated nonverbally. Although these numbers vary, they all point to one important fact: Most of the meaning in messages is conveyed nonverbally rather than through words.

Nonverbal communication can be a powerful tool or a real hindrance to a communicator. That is why it is important to understand it and learn how to use it effectively.

Functions of Nonverbal Communication

Nonverbal communication represents a wide range of behaviors and is a vast area of study. However, we can identify two main functions of nonverbal communication:

- It relates to verbal communication.
- It conveys emotional and relationship dimensions of a message.

Relates to Verbal Communication

Nonverbal cues may exist on their own, or they may accompany a person's words. As mentioned earlier, waving hello is a form of

Global Communication

Nonverbal Messages

Look around your classroom. Is someone sitting with the arms crossed over the chest? How many people are slouching or have their feet resting on another chair? Have you ever pointed to objects in a room or waved your hand to get someone's attention? Do you expect others to maintain eye contact with you when you are speaking to them? What messages do each of these nonverbal actions convey? Find someone in your community who works with international clients. Ask that person what these nonverbal behaviors suggest to people who are not from the United States.

nonverbal communication. In addition, your voice, the facial expressions you use, and your accompanying hand gestures and body movements also are forms of nonverbal cues.

Reinforces a Verbal Message Nonverbal behaviors often support, or reinforce, verbal messages. For example, imagine that a job applicant tells an interviewer, "I really want this job. I also believe that I have the qualifications you're looking for." As she speaks, she seems relaxed, but she still sits up straight in her chair. Her speech is clear and firm, and her voice is businesslike and sincere. She makes direct eye contact with the interviewer. Her dress and grooming also convey a businesslike appearance.

In this situation, all the applicant's nonverbal cues clearly support her words. They reinforce her message, making it seem more believable to the interviewer.

Contradicts Verbal Messages On the other hand, some nonverbal cues can make verbal messages less believable. Suppose another job applicant meets with the interviewer. She also says that she wants the job and thinks she is qualified. However, as she speaks, she fidgets uncomfortably in the chair. She hesitates in her answers, and her voice often is so soft it is difficult for the interviewer to hear. In addition, the applicant keeps looking around the room, avoiding direct eye contact with the interviewer.

In this case, the person's words—taken alone—would convey confidence and a desire to get the job. Her nonverbal behaviors, however, seem to contradict her stated message. They suggest that the applicant may not be as confident of her abilities as her words imply. Her actions may even imply that she is being dishonest about how well suited she is for the job.

It is important to note that, when a nonverbal message contradicts a verbal message, the receiver usually will believe the nonverbal message. At best, the receiver will be confused about the meaning that is being conveyed.

Acts as a Substitute for a Verbal Message Nonverbal messages often are used as a substitute for verbal messages. For instance, a highway worker may stand at an intersection wearing a hard hat and waving a red flag to slow traffic. This person does not need to tell individual drivers to slow down for construction because his or her dress and actions convey that information.

Similarly, if a new student asks you, "Where is the principal's office?" you may simply smile and point to the second door on the left. You may use a quick handshake to say hello or a pat on the back to express approval. If you think about your day-to-day communication, you probably use a variety of nonverbal behaviors as a substitute for spoken messages.

A police officer directs traffic by using nonverbal communication. **What is the risk involved when using nonverbal communication?**

Unfortunately, there is some risk in using nonverbal messages as a substitute for words. Nonverbal messages can be open to many different interpretations. Because nonverbal cues are received on the subconscious level, are highly personal, are highly cultural, and often are fleeting, they can be confusing and difficult to interpret.

Conveys Emotional and Relationship Dimensions of Message

In Chapter 2 you learned that there are three dimensions, or components, of a message. Most messages have an intellectual component, an emotional component, and a relationship component.

Communicators usually use their best available verbal skills to express what they mean. The remaining two dimensions of a message that relate to feelings, however, almost always are communicated nonverbally.

Messages About Feelings Imagine that the school board has called a meeting to discuss making your school a closed campus. Under this policy, students would not be allowed to leave the school grounds for lunch or free periods. Individuals who oppose the plan and those who support it are both registered to speak.

As the meeting progresses, speakers for both sides begin to shout at one another. One listener sneers and laughs as someone with an opposing view speaks. Even if these individuals' verbal messages remain fair and reasonable, their meanings are overshadowed by strong feelings of hostility implied in the nonverbal behavior. In the end, the meeting becomes disruptive and must be adjourned.

During this meeting, no one actually said, "I'm angry." However, the speakers' sharp voices and other nonverbal cues conveyed that message loudly and clearly. The feeling component of a message is most often conveyed and read by others in terms of nonverbal behaviors.

Messages About Relationships

Individuals seldom speak openly about their feelings or their relationships with others. For example, a teacher might find it difficult to tell students, "I enjoy having you in my class." Similarly, you might hesitate to tell a coworker, "I really don't like working with you."

We often reveal how we feel about others and our relationships with them through nonverbal messages. We may depend on a touch, a glance, or a smile to convey "I really like you" or "I really appreciate your friendship." On the other hand, we may avoid eye contact, frown, or fold our arms to convey "I don't want to talk to you" or "I don't enjoy your company. You really annoy me."

Characteristics of Nonverbal Communication

Imagine this situation. As you and a friend step into the checkout line at the grocery store, you suddenly realize that you've cut in front of a gentleman with a cart full of groceries. When you start to apologize, he says, "No. By all means, you go first." Now you feel bad because you think his tone was sarcastic. Your friend, on the other hand, thinks the man was sincere and that he let you go first because you had only an item or two to purchase.

Figure 5–1 Characteristics of Nonverbal Communication

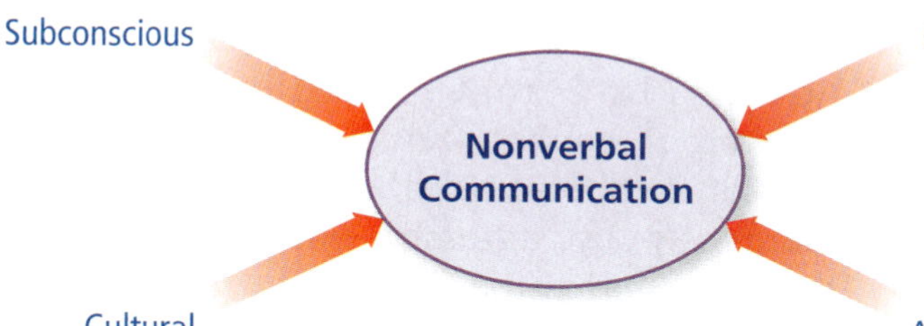

What actually happened? Only the message sender knows for sure. Nonverbal communication can be open to a variety of interpretations, any of which may or may not be valid. This is because nonverbal communication has some unusual characteristics. As illustrated in Figure 5–1, it is by nature subconscious, contextual, ambiguous, and cultural.

Subconscious

Nonverbal communication is most often sent and received on a subconscious level. In other words, we are usually not aware of the messages we send nonverbally. In addition, we tend to process, interpret, and respond to the nonverbal messages of others on the subconscious level.

For instance, think about the Academy Awards. The camera zooms in on the nominees' faces as the winner's name is announced, but only one jumps up and rushes to the stage. The others smile politely and applaud, but their disappointment is painfully clear to millions of viewers. The expression in their eyes, the slump of their shoulders, or the looks exchanged with friends send subconscious messages to others.

The same is true of most people. While you may pay great attention to how you look for a certain occasion, you may not always think about your tone of voice, posture, facial expressions, or gestures. However, if a receiver observes the behavior, he or she will assign meaning to it. All of the nonverbal messages, conscious or subconscious, send messages about you, your attitude, and your feelings. The impression you wanted to convey with your careful grooming may be completely shattered by a hurt look or a slumped posture of which you are not even aware.

Students raising their hands to ask questions in a classroom represent contextual nonverbal communication. **What affects how we interpret nonverbal communication?**

Not only are most nonverbals and the messages they send transmitted on a subconscious level, but they also tend to be interpreted on the subconscious level by the receiver. Imagine that you see a man push in front of a person in a wheelchair as they both are entering a building. You may later relate the incident to someone else and remark that you do not like the man—without realizing the source of your dislike. You probably did not stop to analyze the reason for your feelings or to question whether you interpreted his behavior appropriately. You simply made your judgment subconsciously.

Contextual

Like other forms of communication, nonverbal communication is highly contextual. In other words, it depends on the situation in which it occurs.

Think again of the man who pushed his way into the building. What if you learned that he was a doctor rushing to the aid of a heart-attack victim? Would this change your interpretation of his behavior? Now you might not consider him rude or inconsiderate. In fact, you might think of him as considerate for successfully dodging the wheelchair when he was in such a hurry.

The roles, norms, and standards of every context vary. These, in turn, affect how we interpret nonverbal communication. A competent communicator works to take into account the special circumstances surrounding another's actions before interpreting the behavior and making a snap judgment based on those interpretations.

Ambiguous

In Chapter 4 you learned that meanings lie in people rather than in language. Nonverbal symbols have no specific meanings of their own. They may be interpreted differently by different people. Therefore, they are said to be ambiguous. **Ambiguous** means they are open to interpretation and often confusing. For example, if you are talking to someone whose arms are folded, you may get the impression that he or she is angry. Another person may think the person is bored. What if that individual is simply feeling chilly and is trying to get warm?

Not only are nonverbal cues ambiguous and open to interpretation, but they also tend to happen very quickly. Studies show that facial expressions usually last only a split second. A flick of a wrist, a stamp of the foot, or a shrug of the shoulders also happens quickly and may be difficult to catch. A sigh or a pause may go unnoticed or be misinterpreted.

The best advice for interpreting and assigning meaning to nonverbal messages is to strive to increase your awareness and sensitivity to the nonverbal messages of others. In other words, try to process messages on the conscious rather than the subconscious level. If you find yourself feeling confused or uncertain about the cues you receive, you can use intrapersonal and interpersonal perception checks to try to clarify your interpretations and check your responses.

Cultural

Nonverbal communication also has a distinctly cultural nature. A particular nonverbal message commonly used in one culture may send a completely different message in another culture. For instance, a loud tone of voice is much more acceptable in some cultures than it is in others. Other cues such as direct or indirect eye contact; greeting someone with a handshake, hug, or kiss; or what are considered acceptable or unacceptable styles of dress also vary among different cultures.

Cultural differences in nonverbal communication are so important in international relations that the U.S. State Department has specially trained experts in the field. Their task is to counsel ambassadors and other diplomats who travel to other countries about specific nonverbal cultural differences.

The impact of culture on nonverbal communication was clearly illustrated in 1995 when a U.S. congressman accidentally offended Iraqi leader Saddam Hussein while attempting to negotiate the release of two American hostages. After shaking hands

COMMUNICATION PRACTICE LAB

Considering Context

To practice interpreting nonverbal communication according to its context, follow these steps:

Step 1 Divide the following contexts among five equal groups of students:

- A cubicle in an office
- A hospital waiting room
- A car
- A witness stand in a courtroom
- A first date

Step 2 Have one member of each group act out the following nonverbal behavior for his or her group: fidgeting, glancing around the room, tapping one foot, sighing repeatedly.

Step 3 Have each group discuss its interpretation of these behaviors and arrive at a consensus.

Step 4 As a class, share your interpretations. How did they differ? Why? Discuss the effect of context on nonverbal communication.

with the Iraqi leader, the congressman sat down and crossed his legs. At this point, Hussein immediately stood up and walked out of the room.

The congressman had unwittingly insulted Hussein by showing him the sole of his foot. In some Arab cultures, the bottom of the foot is considered to be the lowest, dirtiest part of the body. As one writer stated, the congressman unfortunately started the negotiations off "on the wrong foot."

Culture is just another factor that influences the way nonverbal communication is interpreted. Remember, nonverbal cues can mean different things to different people. They also can change meanings in different contexts and happen so fast you may miss part or all of them. Therefore, the best advice for interpreting or assigning meanings to nonverbal messages is to be careful and consider the context, the relationship, and the communication.

Section 1 Assessment

Visit the *Glencoe Communication Applications* Web site at **communicationapplications.glencoe.com** and click on **Self-Check and Study Guide 5.1** to review your understanding of the principles of nonverbal communication.

Review Key Terms

1. Define each term and write it in a sentence: nonverbal communication, ambiguous.

Check Understanding

2. Compare and contrast verbal and nonverbal communication.
3. What are the two main functions of nonverbal communication? Explain each function.
4. Describe the four characteristics of nonverbal communication.
5. **Analyze** Imagine that you missed your bus and are late for class. As you are explaining your reason for being late to the principal, she begins slowly shaking her head back and forth. Name two ways you might interpret this nonverbal cue. What characteristic of nonverbal communication does this example illustrate?

APPLICATION *Activity*

Interpreting Nonverbal Behaviors Choose one student to act out a ten- to fifteen-second scenario for the class. The scenario should nonverbally convey some emotion or attitude. Individually, write your interpretation of the student's actions. Then, share your ideas as a class. Were most students' interpretations similar? What cues led you to your specific interpretation? What did the student intend to convey with his or her actions? Were you close?

Technology Skill

Using a Word-Processing Program

Word-processing software can be used to create, edit, print, and store electronic documents.

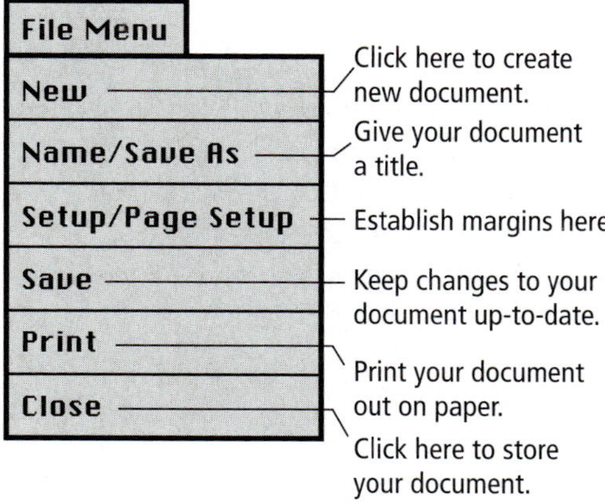

Learning the Skill

- Open your word-processing program, then click on the *File* pull-down menu in the top left-hand corner of your screen.
- Click on the word *New* from the *File* menu. This brings up a screen that allows you to create a new document.
- Label the document by selecting *Save As* or *Name* from the *File* menu. Enter the new name of the document when you are prompted.
- Establish margins for your new document by clicking on *File* and selecting *Setup* or *Page Setup* and responding to the prompts.
- You are now ready to begin entering information into your new document. Find the cursor and start typing.
- Proofread, correct, and then save the document by clicking on *File,* then *Save.*
- Print the document by clicking on *Print* from the *File* menu. Store the document by selecting *Close* from the *File* menu.

Practicing the Skill

Read the steps below to sharpen your word-processing skills.

Step 1 Open your word-processing program and create a new document in which you will summarize the characteristics of nonverbal communication.

Step 2 Label the new document.

Step 3 Establish margins for your document.

Step 4 Type the information into the document.

Step 5 Proofread and save your work.

Step 6 Print the document, then store it.

APPLICATION *Activity*

Assume that you have been asked to give the introduction at a banquet honoring your favorite teacher, who has been recognized as the teacher of the year in your district. Use a word-processing program to write and edit the introduction, print the document, and save it as a file on a computer.

Section 2

Using Nonverbal Communication to Create a Professional Image

GUIDE TO READING

Objectives

1. Explain how nonverbal skills can convey the confidence, poise, assertiveness, and immediacy needed for a positive image in professional and social contexts.
2. Describe the types of nonverbal communication and their possible effects.
3. Describe the four characteristics of voice.
4. Recognize the importance of effective nonverbal strategies such as a firm handshake, direct eye contact, and appropriate use of space and distance.

Terms to Learn

pitch	tone	kinesics
range	rate	artifacts
inflection	tempo	

Imagine that you are a restaurant manager. At staff meetings, you notice that one server always seems to complain loudly and often leaves angry. Another server typically sits silently near the back of the group. A third server can be counted on to participate with enthusiasm and offer helpful suggestions. Which of these waiters is projecting a professional image?

As you develop competence and effectiveness as a communicator, you will face many challenges. Some of these challenges will take place in your school, community, or possibly in a business context. One of the most important challenges will be participating effectively with coworkers, supervisors, or customers in business conversations, discussions, and presentations. To make your communication in these situations as effective as possible, you will want to convey a professional image.

Barbara Walters exhibits a professional image. **How can you create a positive professional image through nonverbal communication?**

Characteristics of a Positive Professional Image

A positive professional image and presence can be important to your success in professional and social contexts. It means that others see you as poised and confident. It also means that you consistently conduct yourself in a businesslike manner in the workplace. Finally, a professional image means that you can be depended on to communicate appropriately and effectively in any situation that may arise.

Through nonverbal communication, you can project certain messages about yourself and your abilities as a communicator. With enough practice and skill, you can create a professional image that projects all of the following characteristics:

- confidence
- poise
- assertiveness
- immediacy

Image That Projects Confidence

A strong voice and an attentive and positive attitude project an image of confidence. These nonverbal cues show that you believe in yourself and your communication skills. Confidence conveys to others that you believe you can accomplish tasks successfully and that you can build and maintain positive relationships.

Image That Projects Poise

People who are known for their poise generally have an ability to "read" any situation and act appropriately. They don't hesitate in their speech and are seldom uncertain about how to act in a given context. They also tend to keep their cool in a stressful situation.

Poise stems from an understanding of communication situations and a strong sense of appropriateness and correctness. Poise sends the nonverbal message that you are in control of your communication and the situation.

These young ladies are projecting a positive professional image. What does an image that projects confidence convey to others?

Image That Projects Assertiveness

Assertiveness suggests a strong sense of purpose. It means that you are confident of yourself and your opinions or beliefs and are not afraid to take a stand when necessary. An assertive individual will not allow a pushy salesperson, a bullying coworker, or an inconsiderate friend to treat him or her unfairly. Instead, that person will project verbal and nonverbal messages that convey logical reasoning and command respect.

Unlike an aggressive person, an assertive individual does not try to impose his or her ideas on others, forcing them to change or take action against their will. Rather, an assertive person uses tact and persuasiveness to take a stand and, if necessary, win others over to his or her way of thinking.

Image That Projects Immediacy

A competent communicator has a sense of immediacy in interacting with others. A communicator who has the quality of immediacy is perceived by others as approachable, friendly, and open. When you bring a problem to this person, you usually feel satisfied that you have his or her full attention. Immediacy—especially when used in combination with confidence, poise, and assertiveness—is a valuable aspect of projecting a professional image.

As these characteristics illustrate, image depends on more than just strong verbal skills. It also relies heavily on effective nonverbal communication. In the following pages, you will learn more about the role nonverbal communication plays in creating and maintaining a positive professional image.

Types of Nonverbal Communication

Have you thought about how the way you laugh, the way you dress, how you use space, and how you protect your territory convey nonverbal messages about you? Perhaps you have not considered how your use of time sends messages about your priorities, your attitudes, and your feelings about relationships. All of these are ways you communicate nonverbally.

There are three main types of nonverbal communication: voice, body talk, and environmental cues. Within each of these broad categories are a number of subcategories. The following table lists a wide variety of nonverbal cues that people use in everyday communication.

TYPES OF NONVERBAL COMMUNICATION

Voice	Body Talk	Environmental Cues
Pitch	Dress and grooming	Space and distance
Range and inflection	Posture	Territory
Volume	Muscular tone and tension	Touch
Quality and tone	Movement and gesture	Time
Duration: Rate and tempo	Facial communication	Artifacts
Pause and silence	Eye communication	Color
Laughter		Fragrance and odor
Vocalizations		

Voice as Nonverbal Communication

Voice, as shown in Figure 5–2, is the human sound that is used to transmit oral language from sender to receiver. The speaking voice that carries words is often accompanied or replaced by other vocal cues, such as a sigh or a laugh.

Voice is an important aspect of your overall communication. Studies generally agree that when voice is involved in communication, it accounts for 38 percent of the message received by the receiver. When voice is involved in communication, it is one of the most influential kinds of nonverbal cues. For this reason, a pleasant speaking voice can be very important to creating a professional image.

Characteristics of Voice

Imagine that a supervisor called to say, "You need to get your report in on time." The meaning of the words probably would be clear. However, you would need to pay attention to the supervisor's voice to decide whether the call was a gentle reminder, a brief scolding, or a stern warning. Your response would be influenced not only by the meaning of the person's words but also by the characteristics of his or her voice.

Figure 5–2 From Voice to Speech

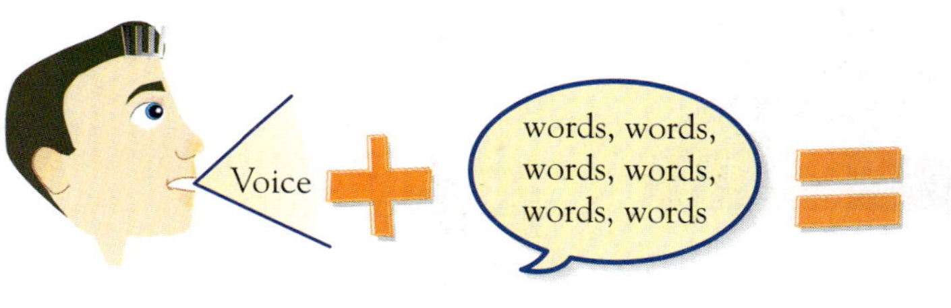

Figure 5–3 Characteristics of Voice

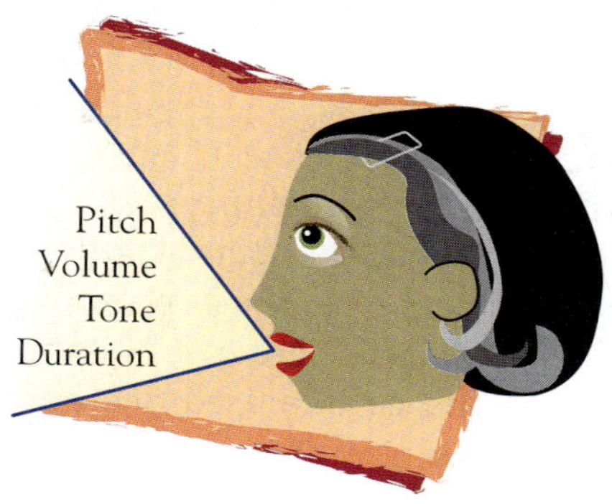

As sound, your voice has the same four characteristics, illustrated in Figure 5–3, as all other sounds. They are the following:

- pitch
- volume
- tone
- duration

The way these characteristics blend in your speaking makes your voice unique and different from all other voices.

Pitch

Pitch is one of the most important characteristics of voice because it is so closely tied to the emotion of a message. **Pitch** is the highness or lowness of sound on a musical scale. Think about how you respond to the pitch of a musical instrument or singing voice. Whether the music energizes you, makes you feel peaceful and calm, or makes you feel sad or happy and "upbeat" probably depends to a large extent on the use of high and low pitch. Similarly, the pitch of your voice affects others' interpretation and emotional response.

High Pitch People often associate a high-pitched voice with external factors such as stress, fear, tension, excitement, frustration, or uncertainty.

High pitch can also indicate fatigue, youth, uncertainty, or a low energy level. Occasional use of high pitch can add variety, humor, and enthusiasm.

Medium Pitch Medium pitch is the pitch you use when you speak normally in conversations, discussions, and presentations. A medium pitch usually conveys calmness and confidence and can be used to emphasize the intellectual content of a message.

Low Pitch Low-pitched voices often are described as rich, deep, or resonant. Low pitch can express a wide range of emotions from sadness to uncertainty and from tenderness to concern. Because they are usually pleasant to listen to, low-pitched voices can be a real asset in professional and social conversations, discussions, and presentations. However, consistent use of low pitch in long discussions and presentations can lull listeners to sleep and cause them to lose interest in what the speaker has to say.

Range and Inflection Vocal range and inflection are both associated with pitch. **Range** relates to the variations possible for a speaker to reach—from the highest pitch possible to the lowest pitch possible. **Inflection** is the rising and falling of pitch that adds variety to speaking. A person's inflection often reveals the meaning and feeling underlying his or her message.

Individuals who speak consistently at the same pitch without variety in range and inflection are said to speak in a monotone. Unfortunately, few things kill the impact and effectiveness of a message like a monotonous voice that lacks animation and inflection.

Volume

It is the speaker's responsibility to be clearly heard and understood by listeners in conversations, discussions, and presentations. Being understood depends on clear, articulate sounding of words. Being heard depends on using appropriate volume for the situation.

Listeners tend to be sensitive to the volume of the messages they receive. For instance, you may view a loud, boisterous speaker as rude or overbearing. On the other hand, if a speaker consistently talks too softly, you may view him or her as incompetent, inconsiderate, shy, or lacking confidence.

As a general rule of thumb, use listener feedback to judge the appropriateness of your volume. If you notice listeners leaning

Mexican President Carlos Salinas and Canadian Prime Minister Brian Mulroney lean in to hear one another better. How does volume affect communication?

forward or turning one ear toward you to hear better, speak a little louder. You also might use perception checks to help you find the right volume and ensure that your message is heard.

Tone The human voice is unique because of its tone. **Tone** is a specific vocal quality. Think of how you would describe the tone of a bell, a siren, or an alarm. Some bells produce rich, mellow sounds, but others sound weak and small. Sirens often are shrill. An alarm may be harsh and grating. Like these sounds, voices often are thought of as pleasant or unpleasant depending upon their tone.

The good news is that almost everyone can develop a pleasant speaking voice. Competent communicators usually want to develop voices that are rich, melodic, resonant, and full. One tip for developing the full resonant voice is to breathe deeply for speech and speak from the diaphragm like actors and singers.

Duration Almost everyone has encountered a speaker who raced through his or her words so quickly a listener could hardly keep up. You probably also have heard speakers plod along so slowly you wondered if they would ever finish a sentence. Duration has two related components: rate and tempo. **Rate** refers to how fast or how slowly an individual speaks. **Tempo** refers to the rhythmic quality of a person's speech. Tempo results from variations in an individual's rate of speech.

The rate of a person's speech can have a significant effect on listeners. For example, if a speaker talks too fast, listeners may have difficulty following and understanding the message. If a speaker goes too slowly, listeners may tire of the slow pace and lose interest. The key is variety. Speeding up and slowing down the rate of speech appropriately can help you create a tempo that holds listeners' interest and helps them understand your message.

How do you know whether or not your rate and tempo are suitable in a given situation? The answer once again is to analyze the feedback from your audience. If you have a question, use perception checks and adapt your rate to meet the needs of your listeners.

TECHNOLOGY *Activity*

Hearing Yourself Speak How you say something is just as important as the words that you use to say it. Assume that you have just won a free dinner with your favorite media celebrity or athlete. The famous person wants to know why you are such a big fan. With a classmate, develop a series of questions that the celebrity might ask. Using an audio recorder, tape your answers to the questions. Listen to the recordings of yourself and your partner. Analyze each voice's pitch, range, tone, and rate. Are your answers convincing? Record your responses again while concentrating more on the sound of your voice and compare the results.

Cues That Accompany Speech

Speech is often accompanied by a variety of attributes or vocalizations, such as pause and silence, laughter, sighs, sobs, or other sounds. Such vocal cues may be intentional or unintentional messages about meanings and feelings.

Pauses and Silence When you pause in your speech, it typically is only for a brief period of time. Silence usually refers to a longer

Laughter is an effective nonverbal cue. **How does laughter contribute to communication?**

period of suspended sound. Pauses punctuate speech by setting off specific units of thought. They can also be used deliberately to provoke thought, develop curiosity or suspense, create a dramatic effect, or raise questions.

You may have heard the expression "Speech is silver; silence is golden." In other words, you often can communicate more with silence than you can with sound. Silence, including pauses, can indicate a willingness to listen. It also can communicate a willingness to defer to another speaker or to consider a matter carefully before speaking. Silence can be used to express approval, disapproval, or total apathy. It also can be used to demonstrate courtesy, respect, or profound emotion.

Laughter Laughter can be an extremely effective nonverbal cue. It can clearly convey humor, friendliness, acceptance, and good feelings. Depending on the context, however, it also can convey cruelty or sarcasm. Either way, laughter can add a wealth of meaning to a conversation, discussion, or presentation. The key to using laughter is appropriateness and a few simple rules that are shown in the Communication Strategies checklist.

Vocalizations When you make sounds without forming words with meaning, you are vocalizing. Sounds such as sighs, whines, or throat clearing are all examples of vocalizations. Vocalizations send messages about a sender's feelings. A sigh, for example, may be interpreted as wishfulness, boredom, or fatigue. It also could indicate pleasure or complete relaxation. Random or overused vocalizations such as "um" or "ah" tend to clutter speech and interrupt a smooth and meaningful transfer of information from sender to receiver.

COMMUNICATION *Strategies*

Sending Positive Messages with Laughter

- ✓ Analyze the context. Is it appropriate to laugh in a particular situation?
- ✓ Listen to your laugh. Is it pleasant and controlled? Generally avoid overly loud, raucous laughter.
- ✓ Laugh *with* others, not at them.
- ✓ Learn to laugh at yourself. Lighten up and take little mistakes, miscues, and failures in stride.
- ✓ Use laughter to promote good-natured humor and goodwill.

To communicate more clearly, become aware of the vocalizations you tend to use. Analyze them and evaluate their effect on your communication. If you find that ineffective vocalizations clutter your speech, you can develop your awareness and try to eliminate them from your speech.

Voice Production

Voice can be a determining factor in a job interview, making a sale, or persuading a group to adopt your point of view and take action. It can project an image on the telephone, and it can determine whether others enjoy being around you or not. Remember that with analysis, work, and practice, almost everyone can have an effective voice that is easy to listen to. Some tips for improving the quality of your voice are found in the Communication Strategies checklist.

COMMUNICATION *Strategies*

Improving Voice

- Breathe deeply using the diaphragm to control exhaling air.
- Stand and sit tall when you speak to allow your sound waves to resonate, but be sure not to draw your shoulders upward to your neck. Let your shoulders remain relaxed and unmoving while you breathe.
- Speak from the diaphragm instead of the chest or head.
- Become aware of how sounds are properly shaped in the oral cavity.
- Create clear speech sounds by using the hard and soft palate.

Members of a choir must be aware of voice production. **How can voice production impact one's communication success?**

Body Talk as Nonverbal Communication

In addition to voice, another type of nonverbal communication is body talk. If voice is the nonverbal language of sound, body talk is the nonverbal language of silence. Body talk is the visual messages we send with our physical presence. It includes the following factors:

- personal appearance
- kinesics
- movement and gesture
- facial communication

Personal Appearance

What do you first notice when you are introduced to someone new? Studies indicate that most people respond first to what they see (body talk and environmental cues); second, to what they hear (voice); and third, to what they understand (words and other nonverbal cues we process as messages).

Because we base so much of our first impressions on what we see, personal appearance can have a great impact on communication. In fact, some aspects of appearance can tend to block out other messages. For instance, an interviewer might be so distracted by an applicant's inappropriate attire that he or she cannot concentrate on the applicant's answers.

For this reason, remember to "watch your nonverbals" when interacting in professional and social contexts. In these situations, making a good impression and conveying a professional image can be vital to your success.

Dress Your choices about how you dress can substantially influence the way others view and respond to you. Because of this, your attire can add to or detract from the image you want to project in social and professional contexts.

A major factor to keep in mind is that appropriate dress for professional and social situations depends to a large extent on an organization's culture. Organizational expectations for attire may be carefully laid out in employee policy manuals or may be part of your employee orientation and training. On the other hand, clothing choices may be left up to your own best judgment. In either case, you will want to project a positive, professional image to others at all times.

It is important to note that clothing need not be brand-new or expensive to be appropriate and professional. Rather, it should be well maintained and in good taste. Three concepts to keep in mind when dressing professionally are *classic, clean,* and *conservative.*

Of course, not all workplaces require a classic or conservative style. Many creative fields allow or even encourage more expressive forms of dress. For instance, an advertising agency, a contemporary art gallery, or any fashion-related business may set different standards for personal appearance on the job. Keep in mind that appropriate dress depends to a large extent on organizational culture and protocol.

Grooming Grooming, as shown in **Figure 5–4,** can be very important to your professional image. It shows others whether or not you take pride in your appearance. It also implies that you want to look and be your best—and, therefore, are likely to be a conscientious, responsible worker.

Hair Hair should always be clean and, in most cases, conservatively styled. The classic hairstyle for men typically is a short haircut with short sideburns. For women, classic hairstyles are typically neatly trimmed and well styled or pulled away from the face. Fad

Figure 5–4 **Personal Appearance: Grooming**

haircuts and unnatural hair colors should be avoided in all but the most unconventional organizations.

If you are in doubt about the norms for hairstyle or hair color for a job that you want, it may be wise to investigate the organizational culture as part of your interview preparation. Ignoring organizational or community norms can lead to negative stereotyping, which may ultimately keep you from getting a job or may cause you problems at work. The general rule is to choose a neat, simple hairstyle that is becoming to you and does not get in your way as you work.

Face Facial grooming should follow the same guidelines. If you are a male, observe whether sideburns, mustaches, and beards are worn in your workplace. If they aren't, they may be inappropriate even if they are not officially forbidden. In many workplaces, the less facial hair the better.

If you are a female, facial grooming should consist of conservative makeup styles and colors. If you are in doubt, observe the makeup choices of the most successful employees in the organization. Then, use these standards as a basis for making choices of your own.

For either gender, multiple piercings or visible tattoos may be unacceptable in a workplace. As a general rule, females should wear only one earring per ear. For males, earrings may or may not be appropriate, depending on the company. For both genders, any other piercings should be left unadorned while at work. Many businesses require that tattoos remain covered while employees are on the job.

All of these guidelines relate to conveying a professional appearance to employers, coworkers, and the public. However, body talk goes far beyond hair, face, and clothing. It also includes the physical presence you command. How you sit, stand, and move also has an impact on the image you project.

Kinesics

Kinesics refers to the use of the body in communication. It typically is the first thing people think of when they hear the term "body language" or "body talk." It is the nonverbal messages we send with our bodies.

The speaker above draws the audience's attention with a gesture. **What is a gesture?**

Posture

Generally, a straight but relaxed posture sends a message of confidence and purpose. Standing tall as you enter a room, speak to a client or coworker, or make a point in a discussion can help you create an image that says, "I have everything under control." Good posture not only makes your clothes fit better, but it also gives you an air of confidence, poise, and immediacy.

Sitting tall creates much the same effect. The receptionist who sits tall at his or her desk can easily use direct eye and facial communication with customers and clients. Such direct contact is more difficult when a seated person stays slumped over his or her work. Good sitting posture also helps prevent much of the fatigue tension in the shoulders and back that often accompanies desk jobs.

Muscular Tone and Tension

Your comfort level in a given situation generally is revealed through your muscular tone and tension. These nonverbal signals send a variety of messages about your feelings, emotional state, and level of well-being.

Have you ever been advised to "settle down" or "loosen up" when you were feeling tense about something? Maybe you have commented that a friend was "uptight" about an upcoming interview or test. Such expressions illustrate how body tone and tension reveal our emotions. Taut muscles, a stiff neck, and jerky movements may indicate that you are stressed or ill at ease. Muscles that are more relaxed may indicate that you are comfortable and in control of the situation, confident and poised.

Analyzing Your Own Signals You can learn to be more aware of your own muscular tone and tension. Pain at the base of your neck or between your shoulders can indicate that you need to take a break and relax. In addition, feedback from others may give you clues about whether or not you are sending messages about being open and friendly.

If you think you tend to send messages of anger, tension, or fatigue, you can learn some simple relaxation techniques to help you convey a more positive image. You can use these at your desk or before a presentation to eliminate tension. If tension or anxiety is a chronic problem, you will need to investigate more complex techniques.

Movement and Gestures

Imagine participating in a meeting at work. You are professionally dressed and groomed, relaxed, standing tall, and projecting a confident professional image. However, you can shatter this image in an instant with uncontrolled, overly aggressive, or hesitant movement and gestures.

Movement

Movement generally refers to gait. Gait describes the way you walk or move from one place to another. Studies show that gait can reveal a great deal of information about an individual's mood and attitude. Practicing a confident gait can help you project a positive image. You can begin by standing tall and moving with assurance and poise. Try not to make overly aggressive and long strides, shuffle or drag your feet, or make many hesitant movements.

Gestures

A gesture is a movement of any part of the body that reinforces another message or acts as a substitute for speech. For instance, tapping the foot may suggest nervousness or impatience. Holding both hands palm-up at shoulder level can mean "Who knows?" or "I don't get it." A wink, a nod, a wave, or any other of a wide variety of movements can send intentional or unintentional messages that affect communication.

It is important to note that gestures tend to be highly cultural in nature. For example, in the United States, a nod of the head usually indicates agreement or consent. In parts of Greece, Turkey, and some other countries, however, nodding the head means "no."

One problem with gestures is that they often develop into personal mannerisms that can become distracting or annoying to others. You may know someone who repeatedly points his or her index finger to emphasize a point or continually nods his or her head in agreement while listening to others speak.

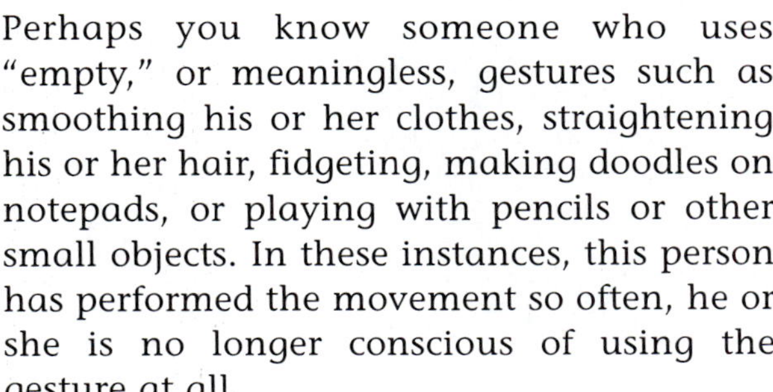

Perhaps you know someone who uses "empty," or meaningless, gestures such as smoothing his or her clothes, straightening his or her hair, fidgeting, making doodles on notepads, or playing with pencils or other small objects. In these instances, this person has performed the movement so often, he or she is no longer conscious of using the gesture at all.

To become more aware of any gestures you may be overusing, carry on a conversation with a friend in front of a mirror. Watch your reflection to see if there are any mannerisms you would like to eliminate. Then, practice speaking without them. Eventually, you can break old habits and eliminate unnecessary gestures from your communication. You also may want to add certain gestures to bring interest and clarity to your communication.

interNET ACTIVITY

Nonverbal Communication Online Computer-mediated communication is considered an impersonal channel of communication because so few nonverbal cues are available. As a result, many conventions and symbols have been developed by computer users to illustrate the emotions that accompany their writing. Typing in capital letters, for example, is considered shouting. Symbols added to the written text such as ;-), a wink, are called *emoticons.* Do an online search using the term *emoticons.* Compile a list of at least ten of these symbols and their meanings and share them with the rest of the class.

Facial Communication

Next to vocal characteristics, facial expression may be the most noticeable and important aspect of nonverbal communication. Certainly, it can display a wider range of emotions more accurately and immediately than any other form of body talk. Expressions such as "I never forget a face," "You should have seen the look on your face," or "Put on your game face," all emphasize the fact that people tend to be very aware of faces and their important role in communication.

Many times, facial expressions may last only a split second. Yet, even in that short period of time, they can communicate some of our most subtle and complex feelings. Like other aspects of nonverbal communication, facial expressions are highly personal and cultural. However, in the United States, many of the more obvious facial expressions tend to be interpreted in a similar manner.

Eye Communication In communication, the eyes are capable of sending powerful nonverbal messages. People use the eyes to make contact with others, to maintain and regulate interaction, and to provide space or distance when others get too close or a situation becomes overly emotional or intense.

Eye communication is strongly influenced by culture. In the United States, many communicators value direct, personal eye contact. You may have been told by an adult, "Look at me when I talk to you." You may have heard someone say, "I don't think he was telling the truth. He wouldn't even look me in the eye." However, children of Native American,

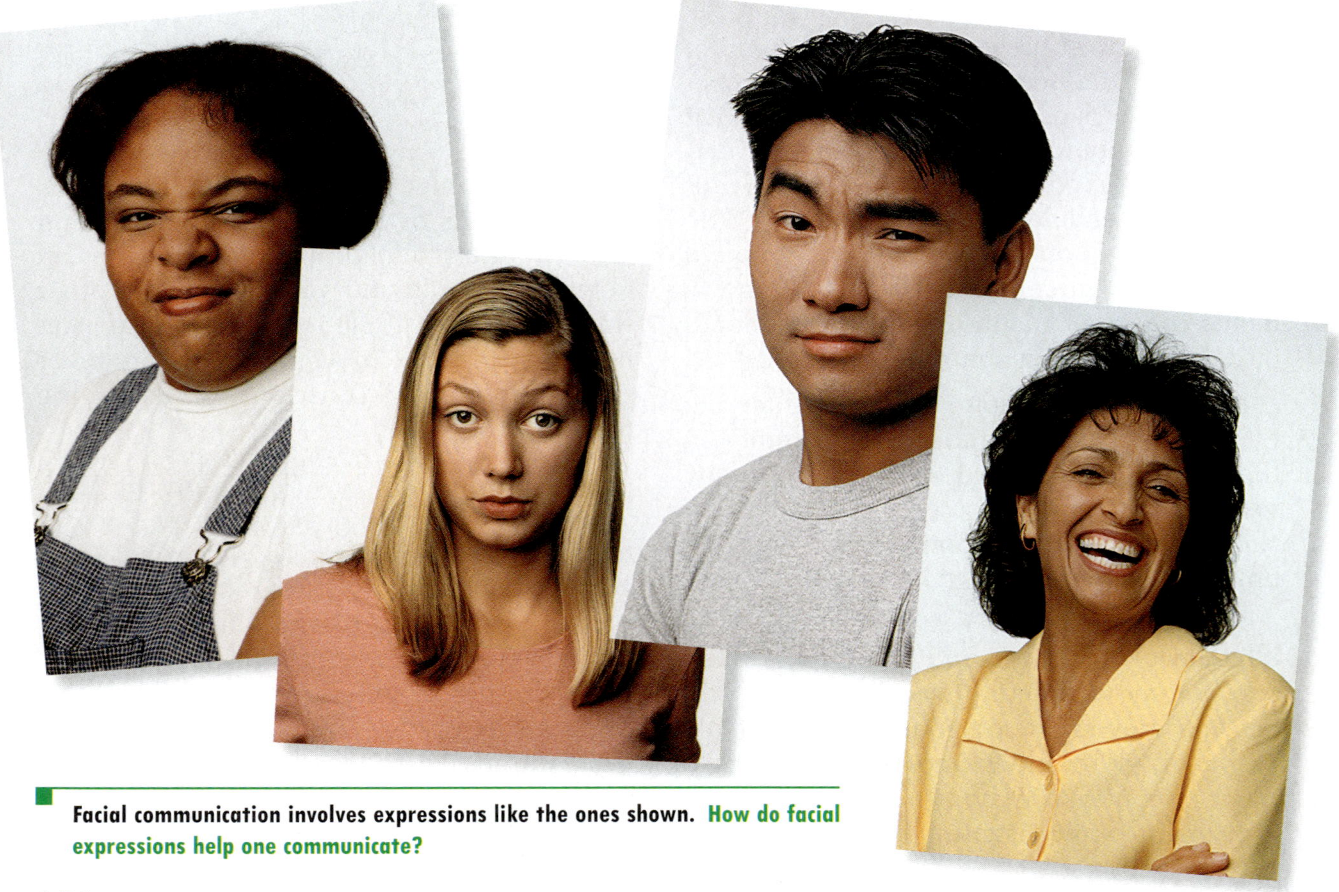

Facial communication involves expressions like the ones shown. How do facial expressions help one communicate?

African, Asian, or Hispanic descent may have been taught to look down when addressing elders to demonstrate respect.

Many people believe that the eyes are a form of "window" to a person's inner intentions and feelings. Therefore, great importance is often placed on eye communication. The messages you send with your eyes most certainly will be interpreted as your "true" feelings about yourself and your interpersonal relationships.

Eye Communication Importance

Eye communication tends to be very important in professional and social contexts. Making direct eye contact often will be viewed as a sign of honesty and credibility. Avoiding eye contact may be seen as a sign of dishonesty or an effort to hide certain feelings. Because these assumptions are so widespread, learning to use eye communication appropriately can be the difference between success and failure in some situations.

Eye communication is an important aspect of body talk. However, body talk—and voice, as you learned earlier—are not the only ways people send nonverbal messages. The way we alter or work within our surroundings also says something about us.

Environmental Cues as Nonverbal Communication

Environmental cues can reveal much about a person's feelings and relationships and can be vital to projecting a positive professional image. Some of the environmental aspects of nonverbal communication may surprise you. For example, the way you use space, distance, and territoriality communicates messages about you and your relationships. How you manage time and allocate time to others also sends nonverbal messages. Similarly, touch, color, and fragrance communicate much about your feelings and relationships.

Spatial Communication

Spatial communication refers to your perception and use of space. Using space appropriately in professional and social contexts involves balancing personal and interpersonal needs with efficiency. Individual perceptions and needs related to space and territory can vary widely.

In addition, the kind of space you need to do your work well may vary from the needs of other people. Regardless of the situation, human beings tend to have definite spatial perceptions, needs, and preferences. How we use space and observe and respect the spatial needs of others is an important factor in working with other people. It can be a source of conflict or, if used appropriately, can help to promote positive relationships.

Space and Distance

Like other aspects of nonverbal communication, the way you use space and distance is highly personal and strongly influenced by your cultural background. Generally speaking, however, there are four types of distances that describe spatial communication, as illustrated in Figure 5–5 on the next page.

Intimate Distance Intimate distance is up to eighteen inches from your body. You might use this space when you make a quiet or confidential comment to someone or when you carry on a private conversation. You also may work within your intimate distance when sharing a book, working closely with one of your friends, or giving someone a hug.

Because intimate distance is the area closest to the body, communication within this range tends to be very personal. Most people feel uncomfortable with someone in their intimate distance unless they have invited him or her into that space.

Personal Distance Personal distance extends from eighteen inches to four feet from the body. This area is your own space in which to move freely.

Whom do you allow to enter your personal space and under what circumstances? Typically, people allow friends, family members, and some coworkers to enter their personal space comfortably. However, if someone else gets too close, you may feel that he or she is "invading your space." If, for example, you begin to feel uncomfortable when a salesperson or other stranger approaches, it may be because he or she has come into your personal space.

Social Distance Social distance extends from about four feet to twelve feet from the body. This distance still allows communicators to see and hear one another easily, while maintaining enough distance to avoid highly personal interaction. Social distance is logically the most appropriate distance for interpersonal and small group interactions in professional and social contexts.

Social distance shows respect for a person's individual space when a close relationship has not yet been established. Therefore, it often is used for making and acknowledging interpersonal introductions, business conversations, and informal presentations.

Public Distance Public distance extends from about twelve feet to twenty-five feet or more. It is far less interpersonal than any of the

Figure 5–5 Spatial Communication

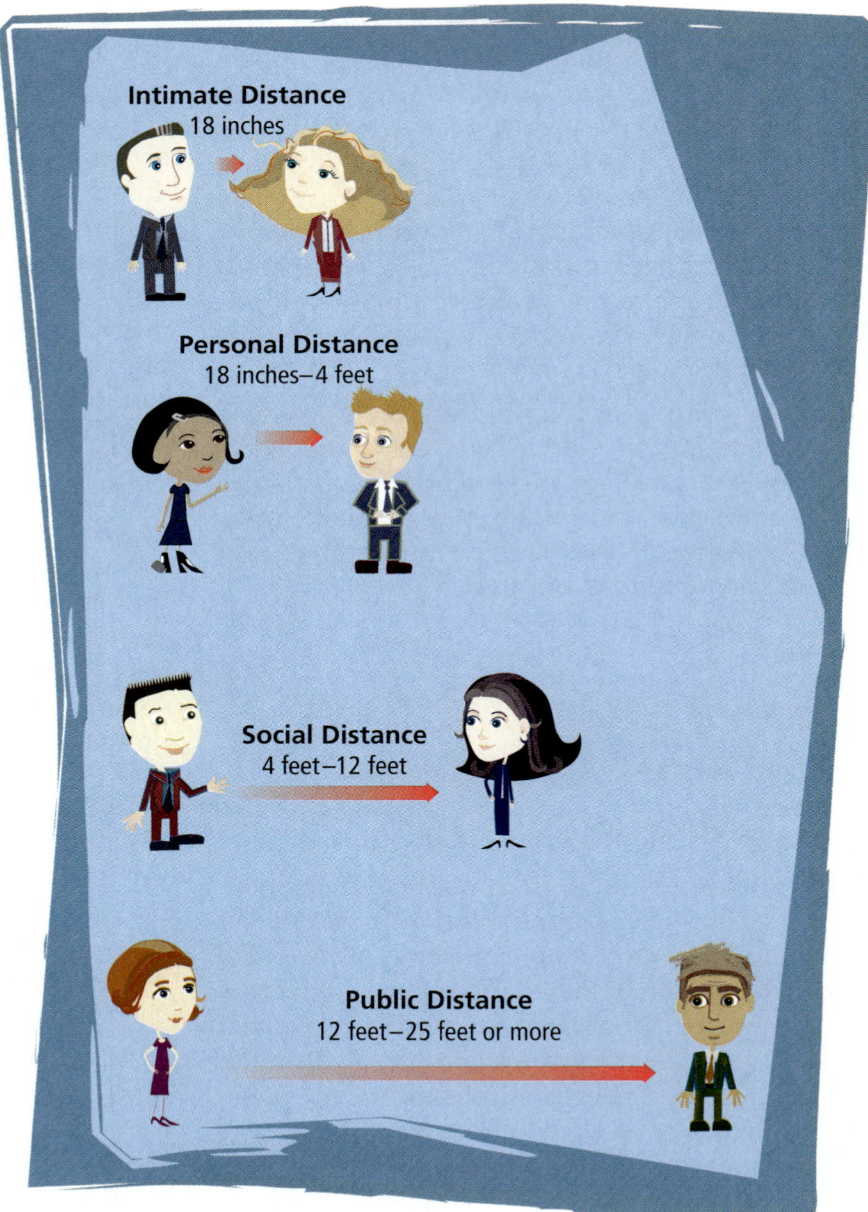

other types of distances. Public distance is most often used for formal presentations. At a public distance, special lighting and sound-projection equipment may be needed to allow the presenter and audience to see and hear one another clearly.

Presenters sometimes choose to come out from behind a podium or down off a stage to achieve more personal interaction with an audience. However, depending on the kind of meeting or program and the size of the audience, public distance may be most appropriate for a formal presentation.

Violating Distance Norms Using distance inappropriately can create embarrassment, discomfort, and conflict. For instance, asking a personal question at a public distance and expecting a public answer containing private information can cause everyone in the area to feel uncomfortable. By the same token, invading a stranger's personal or intimate space may make him or her uncomfortable, defensive, or afraid. As a general rule, fit your use of space to the context of the situation.

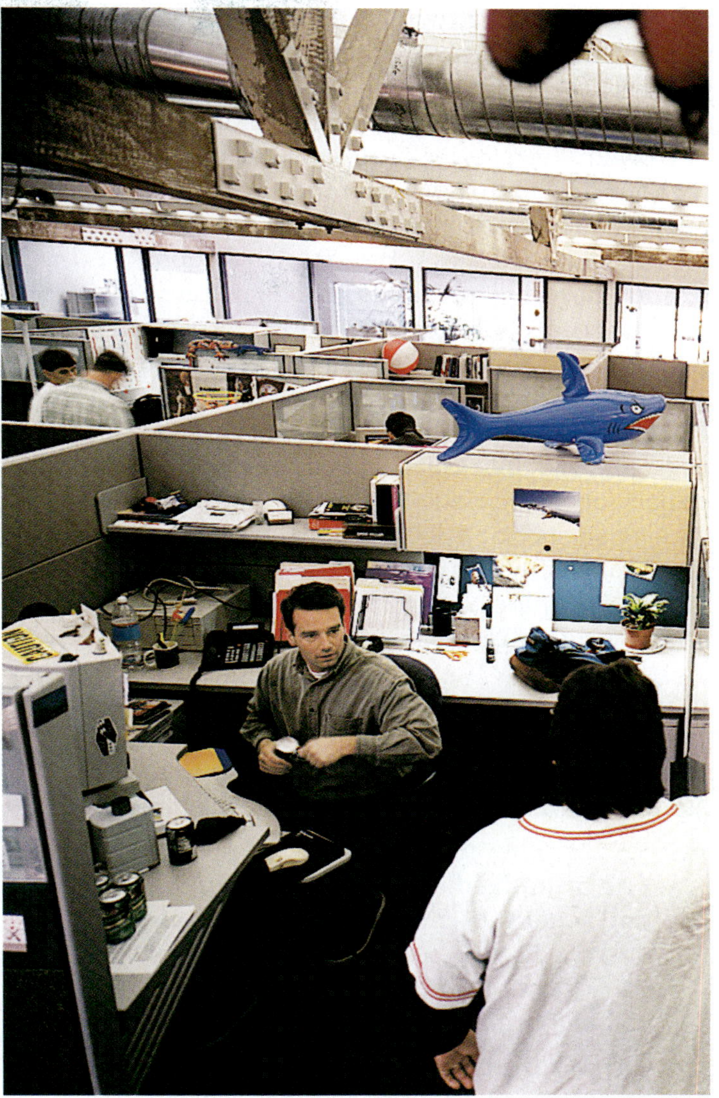

Employees in an office setting usually personalize their office space. Why?

Territory Sometimes, people will identify a space or territory, claim it, and protect it as their own. You probably have done this yourself at some point. Have you ever entered a classroom to find someone sitting in "your" chair? Even though there may have been no prescribed seating plan, you might have selected a space and then occupied the same place every day. Therefore, you felt it was your territory.

Workers often personalize their cubicles or office spaces by arranging them a certain way, decorating them with art or photos from home, and otherwise adding their own special touches. This nonverbal behavior makes it very clear that "This space is mine." They may also claim a certain chair for staff meetings or a certain coffee mug in the break room and may become offended if someone intrudes on their territory.

Violating Territory Norms Sometimes, real hostilities over territory can develop among coworkers. Imagine how a secretary might feel, for example, if coworkers often borrowed the stapler from his or her desk without asking first. What if they periodically opened the secretary's desk drawers to look for needed supplies? He or she probably would become annoyed or even angry because the coworkers were not respecting the secretary's space. In fact, when you are visiting coworkers' workspaces, it is considered good manners even to keep your gaze averted from their computer screen and from papers on their desk unless the purpose of your visit is to discuss those matters. To develop positive interpersonal relationships in the workplace, it is important to respect others' privacy and personal territory.

Sending Nonverbal Messages How you use and maintain your territory or workspace sends a variety of messages about you. Your use and control of space can give others any of the following messages:

- **I'm organized.** When books, papers, and other materials are systematically arranged, you send a message that you are in control of your space and are well organized.
- **I'm disorganized.** A messy desk or workspace filled with random papers, trash, and other clutter sends a message that you may be struggling with work and are not well organized.
- **I take pride in my space.** Keeping your office or workspace neat and personalizing it show that you want your space to reflect all your best qualities. In some organizations, there may be policies about what may or may not be displayed in a work area; however, within the available limits, you can nearly always make your mark.
- **I don't like it here.** A messy office or one that looks exactly as it did the day you moved in tells others that you don't value that space and don't care to make it your own.
- **You're welcome in my space.** Often, a person will use a bowl of candy, a comfortable chair, or some novelty item to make people want to spend time in his or her workspace.

Touch

To touch or not to touch has become a critical question for people in the workplace and social organizations. In recent years, rules and norms have taken a definite shift toward "Don't touch." Touching can be considered harassment and intimidation and can cause serious emotional and legal issues.

However, this does not exclude all forms of touch. Certainly, a firm handshake can be considered an appropriate gesture for both men and women. The handshake has become a standard gesture used in professional and social contexts for making and acknowledging introductions and for extending congratulations or recognition. In many professional and social situations, a handshake is usually considered more appropriate than hugs, pats, and other forms of contact.

Time Communication

In today's busy world, the excuse "I just didn't have time!" has become commonplace in professional and social contexts. When people fail to appear at meetings, carry out responsibilities, meet deadlines, or return calls, they often claim that they just didn't have enough time to do what was expected. In reality, these people may actually have had enough time, but they just managed it inappropriately.

Sending Messages with Time

How you manage time is a form of nonverbal communication. If you have a friend who is consistently late for dates or meetings, you may begin to wonder if that person cares about you very much. Similarly, if your employer pays you late every month, you probably will conclude that salary issues don't mean that much to him or her, and you may even look for another job.

How you use time sends strong messages about you, your perceptions of others, your relationships with them, and your attitude about responsibilities. Therefore, learning how to manage time can be vital to building a professional image and succeeding in professional and social contexts.

Time Management As you begin learning to manage your time, consider this: Not everyone has the same amount of money, talent, or physical ability, but everyone has the same amount of time. We all have exactly twenty-four hours every day. How you use your time reflects your priorities and sends messages about your effectiveness as a student, an employee, and a communicator.

Second, try not to think of time as something that is constantly moving. Instead, think of it as an object that stays in one place. You can arrange its parts however you wish.

Arranging "Slices" of Time If you begin to think of time as a kind of circle graph reflecting one twenty-four-hour day, as illustrated in Figure 5–6, you can start thinking of different activities as individual slices of the total pie. For instance, you probably need eight hours of sleep each day. So, one-third of your pie is already filled in, leaving you with sixteen hours. You probably also need about eight hours for work or school. That leaves eight hours for recreation, homework, household responsibilities, meals, and relationships.

Suddenly, managing your time sounds a lot like budgeting your money, doesn't it? The idea is the same for both. You have a limited amount of something, and you must arrange it carefully to get the most from it.

Noting Special Time Commitments Once you have learned to arrange your time, it is important to make a note of special commitments such as meetings, appointments, and deadlines so you won't forget them. In professional and social contexts, it is vital not only to remember your commitments but also to be prompt and punctual.

Learning to Say "No" If, after learning to manage your time, you still find yourself running behind schedule, you may need to make some changes. Consider whether you have too many time commitments. You might need to learn how to decline politely when others ask you to take on extra responsibilities. Alternatively, if you feel you must participate, you might say "I can do that, but I won't be able to get it done until next week." Knowing how to divide your time and stay within your limits is a major part of being a responsible friend, group member, or employee.

Figure 5–6 Slices of Time

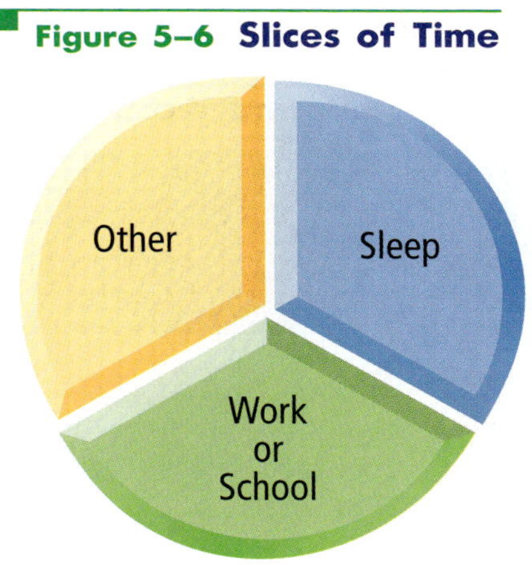

Other Types of Environmental Cues

Besides distance, territory, touch, and time, you also send messages with other aspects of your surroundings. Think about how you personalize your room at home, your locker or backpack, even your own appearance. These environmental cues all say something special about you.

Artifacts and Objects Most people surround themselves with artifacts and objects that communicate a variety of messages. **Artifacts** are articles of adornment you use to decorate yourself or your surroundings. Jewelry and accessories are artifacts. Clothing may be considered an artifact. Pictures on walls, visual themes or motifs, trophies, favorite books, and posters all are artifacts people use to decorate their rooms and offices.

Objects include all the materials that you keep in your space or take with you to classes, meetings, presentations, or other events. A backpack and a notebook may be objects that stay with you all day at school. The way you maintain or personalize each of these sends messages about your personality, likes, and dislikes. A briefcase and date book may communicate that an employee is highly organized and professional. The personal photos on a person's desk may indicate that he or she has a strong sense of home and family.

In social and professional contexts, objects and artifacts generally should be kept in good repair. They also should be attractively arranged and logically organized. As with dress, three key words to remember are *classic, clean,* and *conservative.* Keeping these things in mind will help you project the best possible image of the professional you.

Color What is your favorite color? Do you tend to buy clothes, artifacts, and objects in

Practice for the Workplace

Subtle Clues The artifacts that you surround yourself with are nonverbal clues to your interests and values. Other people assign meaning to the artifacts you display. The items in your backpack, your locker, your car, or your home reflect your interests and values. Professionals know that others will interpret the artifacts observed in their offices. For example, you would expect to find different artifacts in a dentist's office than you would in a travel agent's office.

BUSINESS PRACTICE Activity

Visit your school's main office, the gymnasium's office area, the cafeteria, the library, a science classroom, an art room, and the instrumental or vocal music room. Observe the artifacts found in each location. Report your observations and the interpretations of your findings to the class.

Figure 5–7 Cool and Warm Colors

that color? Have you ever been attracted to a color because it was associated with a certain meaning or feeling?

Advertisers and manufacturers fully understand the nonverbal messages sent by color. Advertisers use color to grab your attention or to convey an overall feeling about a product. Fashion designers use color to attract attention and to create a specific effect with clothing. Decorators, lighting consultants, and others often use color to create a specific mood and atmosphere.

For example, interior designers sometimes use light blue walls or room accessories to create a calming effect. Soft, gold-toned lights may be used to evoke a warm feeling of home. Navy, gray, brown, and black tend to project a formal mood and, therefore, are most often chosen for formal professional attire. See **Figure 5–7** for a visual description of cool and warm colors in a spectrum.

Fragrance and Odor Of all the senses, the sense of smell is believed to provide the most direct link to the emotion center of the brain. It has great power to instantly evoke memories, feelings, and permanent impressions. In short, fragrance and odor can send powerful nonverbal messages.

In recent years, an entire industry has developed around so-called "aroma therapy." This is the intentional use of certain smells to promote relaxation, energy, comfort, or other emotional states. For instance, realtors often recommend that homeowners bake bread or an apple pie when a potential buyer is scheduled to visit because most people have fond memories of the smell of warm apple pie or freshly baked bread. The theory is that the aroma will provoke warm images of family and home and make the individual want to buy the house. In many cases, the theory seems to be effective.

Today, many businesses and meeting places deodorize the premises to avoid inappropriate or unpleasant responses. Unless you're in the food or fragrance business where smell could attract customers, business environments should, for the most part, be kept odor free. The same advice as that given for clothing and artifacts applies to the appropriate use of

COMMUNICATION PRACTICE LAB

Interpreting Messages from Color

To practice recognizing the nonverbal messages sent by different colors, follow these steps:

Step 1 Working in groups of three or four, choose one of the following objects and draw it five times on a sheet of white paper:

- an expressionless face
- a mid-length jacket
- a square sign on a signpost

Step 2 Color the first four objects on the sheet of paper these colors: red, blue, green, and yellow. Leave the last object white.

Step 3 As a group, discuss the nonverbal messages sent by each object. Below each, write what you think that color of object represents. For example, if you had drawn a red flower, you might have said it represents romance.

Step 4 As a class, discuss your interpretations of each object. How did color influence your interpretations? How might you use colors in other ways to communicate nonverbal messages?

fragrance by individuals in professional and social contexts. Fragrance should be light, conservative, and sparingly used. Cleanliness and personal hygiene can prevent unpleasant odors. Remember that you don't want to project any smell that might cause you to alienate a client, lose a sale, or offend a boss or coworker.

Nonverbals: voice, body talk, and the use of environmental cues are powerful influences on the professional image you project. Remember, nonverbal cues represent about 90 percent of what you communicate. Using that 90 percent to convey positive, appropriate messages will help establish you as a competent communicator.

Section 2 Assessment

Visit the *Glencoe Communication Applications* Web site at **communicationapplications.glencoe.com** and click on **Self-Check and Study Guide 5.2** to review your understanding of creating a professional image through nonverbal communication.

Review Key Terms

1. Define each term and write it in a sentence: pitch, range, inflection, tone, rate, tempo, kinesics, artifacts.

Check Understanding

2. What are the characteristics of a positive professional image? Explain how you might demonstrate one of these characteristics using nonverbal skills.
3. What are the three main categories of nonverbal communication? Choose one category and describe how those types of nonverbal signals might affect communication between an interviewer and a job applicant.
4. Using the four characteristics of voice, describe how a person might contradict a spoken message with his or her nonverbal vocal cues.
5. **Synthesize** Describe an appropriate use of handshake, eye contact, space, and distance when meeting your new boss for the first time. What might be the overall effect of this behavior?

APPLICATION Activity

Enhancing Relationships Working with a partner, brainstorm a list of nonverbal cues and behaviors that put you at ease and make you feel closely bonded with another individual. Then, brainstorm a list of cues and behaviors that have the opposite effect. Finally, choose a topic and conduct a one-minute interaction that employs only those nonverbal behaviors that help enhance an interpersonal relationship. Share your conclusions as a class.

Communication Self-Assessment

Evaluating Your Nonverbal Communication Skills

How Do You Rate?

On a separate sheet of paper, use the key to respond to the following statements. Put a check mark at the end of each skill you would like to improve.

KEY: **A** Always **U** Usually **S** Sometimes **R** Rarely **N** Never

1. I know how to use body language and the sound of my voice to support what I say.
2. I try not to use nonverbal communication as a substitute for verbal communication.
3. When I am with people of a different culture, I try to learn all I can about their nonverbal communication customs.
4. I use confidence, poise, assertiveness, and immediacy to manage situations.
5. I use a variety of pitches, tones, and tempos when I speak.
6. In business settings, my dress and grooming are appropriate to the norms of the organization.
7. In tense situations, I use feed-forward statements or humor.
8. When I want to convey honesty and credibility, I use eye contact.
9. To avoid making other people feel uncomfortable, I respect their social, personal, and public space.
10. I manage my time commitments promptly and on schedule.

How Do You Score?

Review your responses. Give yourself 5 points for every A, 4 for every U, 3 for every S, 2 for every R, and 1 for every N. Total your points and evaluate your score.

41–50 Excellent You may be surprised to find out how much you can improve your skills.

31–40 Good In this course, you can learn ways to make your skills better.

21–30 Fair Practice applying the skills taught in this course.

1–20 Needs Improvement Carefully monitor your improvement as you work through this course.

Setting Communication Goals

If you scored Excellent or Good, complete Part A. If your score was Fair or Needs Improvement, complete Part B.

Part A

1. I plan to put the following ideas into practice:
2. I plan to share the following information about communication with the following people:

Part B

1. The behaviors I need to change most are:
2. To bring about these changes, I will take these steps:

Writing a Business Letter

No matter what career path you follow, you will almost certainly be required to write a business letter at some point. A business letter is a tool that is used universally because it has many applications. A business letter can request information, serve as an introduction, resolve problems, or clarify issues. Use a business letter when the contents are too formal or detailed for an e-mail or telephone call. Refer to the sample on the next page as you read about the parts of a business letter described below.

The Heading The heading is the first element of a letter. It includes a date line, which usually follows the sender's name and mailing address. Put the heading at the top of the letter, even with the left margin. The lines within the heading should be single-spaced. Double-space only after the last line. Many companies have personalized stationery that shows the company name and address at the top of the page. If this is the case, you need only include the date after the address.

The Opening The opening includes the inside address, which is the address of the person or business designated to receive the letter, and the salutation, or greeting, which begins the letter. This information, like the heading, should be even with the left margin of the paper. The opening should be spaced in the same way as the header.

The Body The most important part of the business letter is contained in the body. This is where the reader gets your message. The body is sometimes preceded by a subject line, which tells the recipient what the letter is about before he or she begins to read. Identify the purpose of the letter, then decide how you will proceed. If the purpose of your letter is to solve a problem, for example, you would first describe the problem, then provide a solution. The lines within each paragraph should be single-spaced, but you should double-space between paragraphs. Many business letters use a block style. This means that the paragraphs within the body are not indented. While the block style is very popular, indenting the paragraphs is also acceptable as a style choice.

The Closing The closing signals the end of the letter. It first shows respect for the recipient, then it gives the writer's name and title. The most commonly used closing is *Sincerely.* Other closings are *Regards* and *Very truly yours.* Triple-space after the closing and type the signature block. The person whose name is typed here will sign the letter. If you are enclosing additional material, write the word

For additional information about business writing, see the *Guide to Business Communication* section of the Communication Survival Kit in the Appendix.

enclosures followed by the number of items to be sent. List the names of any persons who will receive copies of the letter. Make sure the appropriate person signs the letter.

Proofreading the Letter Check your letter for spelling and grammar mistakes. Make sure the format of the letter is correct. Make changes only if they are necessary to improve the appearance of the letter.

City Landscaping
2500 Majestic Street
Dayton, Ohio 45454 — HEADING

February 17, 2004 — DATE

Mr. John Ellis
Tree and Shrub Company — INSIDE ADDRESS
1705 Wetland Drive
Albany, New York 12222

Dear Mr. Ellis: — SALUTATION

We purchased 5 trees and 25 low-growing evergreen shrubs from your company last year on March 28. We used them for a landscaping project here in Dayton, Ohio. This year we are planning to do a similar job in Mobile, Alabama, and would like to purchase similar trees and shrubs that are appropriate for the different climate there. The trees that we purchased last year were item 500759 in your 2003 catalog. The shrubs were item 406928 in last year's catalog. — BODY

Please send us a copy of your 2004 catalog. If possible, please indicate which trees and shrubs have a similar appearance to those purchased last year and can withstand Mobile's climate. We will also need to know how the items can be shipped to Alabama.

Sincerely, — CLOSING

Jeremy Focus — SIGNATURE BLOCK
Jeremy Focus
City Landscaping

Enclosures — ENCLOSURES
1. Receipt from last year's order

Copies: Juanita Baez — COPIES
Jim O'Brien

WRITING Activity

Assume that you are a work-study student with an automotive firm and your supervisor asks you to write a letter that he will sign. The letter is about an automobile recall. Be sure to include all of the points listed below.

- Your supervisor is John Anders, Assistant Vice President.
- The company for which you work is Detroit Motor Company, 99 Automobile Lane, Detroit, Michigan 48222.
- A problem has been discovered regarding the black, maroon, and navy paint used on all models.
- The defective paint was used on vehicles manufactured between March 1 and November 22, 2000. The paint may seriously crack, which could cause the cars to rust.
- Apologize to the customer for any inconveniences caused by the problem.
- Offer a free repainting job to all owners of these cars. Ask them to return their cars to the nearest Detroit Motor Company Service Center.
- The letter should be ready to send on December 15 of this year.

CHAPTER 5 Assessment and Activities

GLENCOE Online

Visit the *Glencoe Communication Applications* Web site at **communicationapplications.glencoe.com** and click on **Chapter 5 Activity** for additional practice in nonverbal communication.

Reviewing Key Terms

Read each definition. On a separate sheet of paper, write the number of the description and the letter of the term that fits the description best.

1. Articles of adornment used to decorate oneself or one's surroundings
2. The use of the body in communication
3. A system of symbolic behaviors that includes all forms of communication except words
4. The distance between the highest and lowest pitch someone can produce
5. Something that has more than one meaning
6. The rhythmic quality of someone's speech
7. A specific vocal sound or quality
8. Rising and falling speech

a. nonverbal communication
b. ambiguous
c. range
d. inflection
e. tone
f. tempo
g. kinesics
h. artifacts

Reviewing Key Concepts

1. List the three major categories of nonverbal behaviors.
2. What are three main functions of nonverbal communication?
3. List four qualities that describe the nature of nonverbal communication.
4. What four qualities project a professional image?
5. How can a speaker with a monotone voice increase the effectiveness of his or her message?
6. Give four examples of vocal cues that accompany speech.
7. What six factors does body talk include?
8. What three adjectives should you keep in mind when dressing for a job interview?

Assessment and Activities

Reading and Critical Thinking Skill

1. **Classifying Information** Into which major category of nonverbal behavior does a frown fall?
2. **Synthesis** How might you use nonverbal behavior to communicate the idea of a bird to someone who speaks a different language?
3. **Applying Information** A fire starts in the cafeteria, and a student runs from room to room shouting, "Fire!" Would the student's voice most likely be high-pitched, medium-pitched, or low-pitched? Explain your answer.
4. **Cause-Effect** What may be the result of ignoring a company's norms in dressing for a job interview?
5. **Making Comparisons** Research the use of eye communication in two cultures. You might make your choice from one of the following: Native American, African, Asian, Hispanic.

Skill Practice Activity

Recalling Information On a sheet of paper, draw a four-column chart. Label the four columns Intimate Distance, Personal Distance, Social Distance, and Public Distance. Then write each description below in the correct column: a teacher lecturing the class, a principal speaking at an assembly, a gossiping friend, a waving neighbor, a hugging parent, an angry parent, and a salesperson giving a pitch.

Cooperative Learning Activity

Nonverbal Communication and Culture With a partner, choose a country and research its culture. List significant nonverbal messages and their meanings in that culture. For example, white is the color of mourning in Japan. Write the name of the country at the top of a poster. Then, illustrate the nonverbal messages on the poster and display the poster in class.

Chapter Project

Planning Think of a career that you would like to pursue. Compile a list or find photographs of at least five artifacts that represent that occupation. Do not reveal your career choice or the artifacts that represent it to your classmates.

Presenting Reveal your photographs or the artifacts on your list to your classmates one item at a time. After each item is revealed, let the rest of the class guess what career you have chosen. If the class guesses your occupation, let them try to identify the remaining items.

CHAPTER 6 Toward Effective Listening

WHY IT'S IMPORTANT

Effective listening skills not only are the key to knowledge and understanding, but they also increase our own creativity and our value to others.

To better understand how to listen effectively, view the **Communication in Action** Chapter 6 video lesson.

GLENCOE *Online*

Visit the *Glencoe Communication Applications* Web site at **communicationapplications. glencoe.com** and click on **Overview–Chapter 6** to preview information about listening effectively.

"The key to success is to get out into the store and listen to what the associates have to say. . . ."
—Sam Walton, founder of Wal-Mart

Section 1

Understanding the Listening Process

GUIDE TO READING

Objectives

1. Explain the importance of listening in professional and social contexts.
2. Identify the four steps of the listening process and describe their related functions.
3. Analyze the factors that can affect listening.
4. Apply specific suggestions to improve listening in each step of the process.
5. Describe the importance of feedback in the listening process.

Terms to Learn

listening
hearing
attending
understanding
interpreting
responding

During a typical day, we communicate in many different ways, including through writing, reading, speaking, and listening. Which of these activities do you think takes up the largest part of your communication time? You may be surprised by the answer.

You may think you spend the largest portion of your communication time speaking. However, if you are at all typical, your answer should be *listening*. Listening is our most-used communication skill. In fact, a study of people from various occupational backgrounds showed that 70 percent of their waking time was spent in communication. Of that time, as shown in **Figure 6–1** on the next page, writing consumed 9 percent, reading absorbed 16 percent, talking accounted for 30 percent, and listening occupied 45 percent. That means we spend much more time listening than we do speaking!

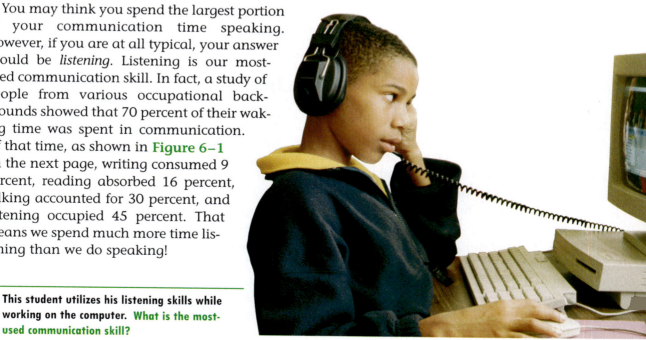

This student utilizes his listening skills while working on the computer. What is the most-used communication skill?

Figure 6–1 Waking Time Activities

Why Learn About Listening

Because we spend so much of our time listening, it is important that we learn to listen well. Unfortunately, effective listening tends to be the least taught and least understood communication skill. Parents and teachers often assume that if a child can hear well, he or she can listen well too. Listening skills are assumed to develop naturally. Therefore, little attention is given to training children to listen effectively.

Generally, the little training we do receive is negative and often the result of trial and error. For instance, if you have ever allowed your attention to wander in class, you may have been instructed to "Sit up and pay attention!" If you "tuned out" while a parent was speaking, you may have been told "Look at me when I talk to you." In both situations, you may have been jolted into paying attention, but you probably learned little about avoiding the problem again in the future.

A recognized authority in listening, Dr. Ralph Nichols, once conducted tests to see just how effectively most people listen. His tests revealed that immediately after the average person listens to someone speak, he or she remembers only half of what was said—no matter how carefully the person thought he or she was listening. The tests further indicated that after only eight hours, the average listener tends to forget an additional one-half to one-third of what he or she originally grasped of a speaker's message. Unfortunately, remembering only about twenty-five percent of a test review or a supervisor's instructions can cause a great deal of trouble in the real world.

Defining Listening

A first step toward understanding listening is to realize that listening, like other aspects of communication, is a process. It consists of specific sets of skills that can be identified and learned. Your understanding of this process begins with an examination of the meaning of listening. Listening as a process includes much more than just hearing sounds and understanding language. Rather, **listening** is a physical and psychological process that involves acquiring, assigning meaning, and responding to symbolic messages from others.

Importance of Listening

The primary reason for listening is to acquire oral messages from others. These messages are vital to the way we function in our everyday lives. Many of the most important aspects of your life are influenced by your skills—or lack of skills—in listening. For instance, the quality of your friendships depends, in large measure, on your ability to listen well. Making appropriate listening choices also affects the strength of family bonds. Following are just a few of the areas in life that are directly affected by your effectiveness as a listener, as shown in **Figure 6–2.**

School You probably are well aware of the importance of listening in school. Your ability to participate in class discussions, ask meaningful questions, give relevant answers, carry out detailed homework instructions, and score well on tests relates directly to your ability to listen. One recent study of college students stresses the importance of listening in school. According to the report, faulty listening, more than any other factor, determines student failure in colleges and universities.

Relationships Listening skills also play a vital role in interpersonal relationships. For example, good listeners tend to be valued as friends because they are perceived as sensitive and caring. When someone listens closely to the message another is sending, he or she conveys a sense of acknowledgment, concern, and respect for the other person. As a result, effective listeners tend to be trusted and may be sought out as leaders. In their own lives, the ability to listen well may help them avoid certain conflicts and form close, productive interpersonal relationships.

Social Groups and Organizations Listening skills also play a vital role when participating in social contexts. Making and acknowledging introductions and asking for and following directions all require special listening skills. Listening skills also play a vital role in your ability to participate effectively in social and community organizations. Your own personal effectiveness and how you are perceived by others in these groups may be influenced by your listening ability. Whether participating in a youth group, a city council meeting, or a legislative body, members who listen effectively tend to make better decisions and are more likely to influence the outcome of individual or group goals.

Figure 6–2 Areas of Life Affected by Listening

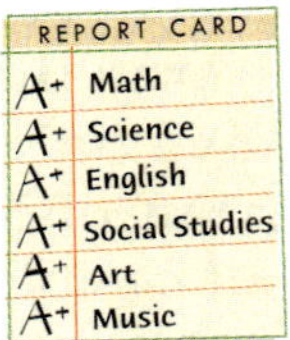

Public Dialogue Another level of social interaction involves listening to speeches and other forms of public messages. Effective listening skills allow you to better understand and remember what you hear, which helps you make better decisions. They also help you participate more effectively in public dialogues both as a citizen and as a consumer.

The Workplace Being able to listen well can be vital to your success on the job. Listening skills are important to businesses because they help employees be more productive. This, in turn, can create greater profits for the company. Reports from the Department of Labor as well as from several major corporations all underscore a direct relationship between listening ability, productivity, and job performance.

Costs to Business There are an estimated one hundred million workers on the job in the United States today. One report points out that if each worker were to make a simple ten-dollar mistake as a result of poor listening, the overall cost would add up to a billion dollars. Sound hard to believe? Actually, that estimate may be low. Faulty listening is estimated to cost American industry approximately eighty-six billion dollars per year.

We all make inappropriate listening choices from time to time. As a result of poor listening skills, you may find yourself redoing homework or asking a teacher or another student to repeat instructions. On the job, faulty listening can lead to revising letters or reports, rescheduling appointments, researching incorrect information, and rerouting shipments, among other errors. Each of these mistakes not only costs a company money but also trickles down as costs to the consumer.

Cost to Consumers Any time business suffers a consistent loss, it is likely to pass the cost along to consumers through higher prices and extra charges. One recent report suggests that at least 10 percent of the cost of consumer goods is added on by businesses to absorb the cost of faulty listening in the workplace.

Inconvenience Faulty listening leads not only to more expensive products but also to inadequate services. At one time or another, you probably have been inconvenienced by an inefficient worker who made a mistake because he or she just wasn't listening. Perhaps a server at your favorite lunch spot brought you a hamburger with mayonnaise and pickles when you clearly ordered a cheeseburger with mustard and no pickles. As a result, there was an extra cost. Either you suffered the "cost" of eating a meal that was not to your liking, or the restaurant management suffered the cost of replacing part or all of the first burger.

Safety Issues However, not all costs are so easily absorbed. Sometimes, the faulty listening skills of highly trained professionals can lead to tragedy. One such incident occurred in 1982 as a commercial airliner was taking off from Washington International Airport. In this instance, the pilot failed to heed a message from his copilot that the jet's engines were not delivering enough take-off power. As a result, seventy-eight people died when the plane left the runway and plunged into the icy Potomac River.

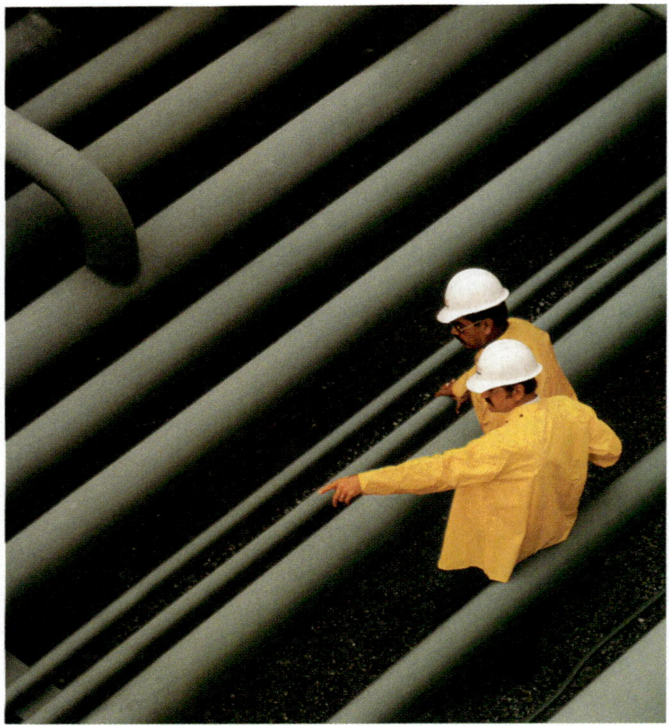

Listening on the job is important to the safety of you and other employees especially in environments such as the one shown. Identify benefits of effective listening.

Benefits of Effective Listening

Just as faulty listening can have costly results, effective listening skills can produce great rewards. Individuals who have reputations as effective listeners tend to build successful relationships. In school, effective listeners tend to find classes more interesting, become more actively involved, and make better grades. Businesses with employers who are effective listeners are usually rewarded not only with increased sales and more satisfied customers but also with increased productivity and overall profits. Employees who are good listeners are usually valued by coworkers. They also tend to get better jobs, receive more promotions, and have more satisfactory work experiences than their coworkers with poor listening skills.

Effective communication between airplane pilot and copilot is imperative for a safe flight. What is the first step to becoming an effective listener?

Misconceptions About Listening

Listening well can benefit you in many ways throughout your life. However, as important as these skills may be, they still tend to be underappreciated and misunderstood. Understanding exactly what listening is—and is not—can help you analyze your skills and develop better listening habits. Some of the common misconceptions known about listening are listed in the table below.

Analyzing the Listening Process

The invisible, complex phenomenon we know as listening is more than merely hearing sounds or understanding language. Rather, listening is a process that involves making sense of verbal and nonverbal messages. Study Figure 6–3 on page 176, which displays a model of the listening process. As a process, listening involves four active steps that build upon one another. These include

- acquiring
- attending
- understanding
- responding to messages from others

LISTENING MISCONCEPTIONS

Misconceptions	Fact
Listening and hearing are the same thing.	Hearing is the physical first step in the listening process and does not imply understanding.
Listening is easy or automatic.	Listening is a complex process that requires energy, effort, and skills.
Listening develops naturally.	Listening consists of learned skills and behaviors that can be learned, relearned, improved, and refined.
Anyone can listen well if he or she really tries.	You can exert effort in the listening process, but if you don't have the needed skills, you may not be able to listen effectively.
The speaker is primarily responsible for the message and for the success of the interaction.	In effective communication, the speaker and the listener share responsibility. For communication to be successful, listeners may have to compensate for a sender's lack of ability in transmitting messages.
If that's what I heard, then that's what you said!	Listeners cannot assume they have understood messages correctly and should use perception checks to clarify messages.
Attitude and listening are unrelated.	Attitude is a very important factor in listening and retaining information.
People remember most of what they hear.	Listening and memory are related, but failure to remember may or may not indicate faulty listening.

Figure 6–3 The Listening Process

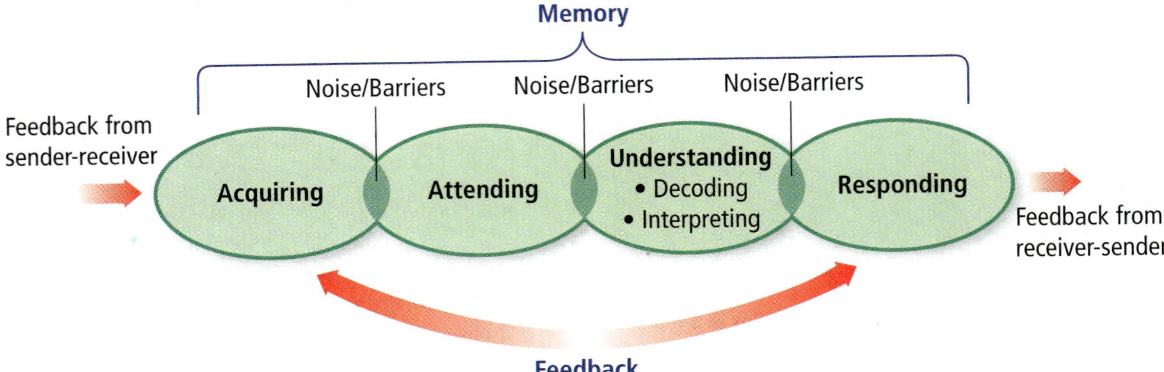

Acquiring

The listening process begins with acquiring. As you learned in Chapter 2, acquiring is the act of picking up some type of stimulus through the senses. Usually, the first sense involved in listening is **hearing,** or the physical process of receiving sound. Sound can come from someone's voice or from some nonverbal cue, such as a knock on the door. As shown in Figure 6–4, the outer ear, which serves as an antenna to aid sound reception, first picks up sound waves. These waves are then relayed to the middle ear, where they are amplified and passed to the inner ear. The inner ear transforms this acoustical energy into electrical impulses and relays the impulses to the brain for processing.

Hearing Ability It was once thought that all people hear in exactly the same way. Today, we know that the physical ability to receive sound waves varies from one person to another. Not everyone can distinguish different sounds, levels of volume, or high and low pitches.

Noise and Barriers to Hearing In addition to our individual hearing ability, many other factors affect our ability to acquire sounds in specific situations. Loud noises, such as traffic, blaring music, jet engines, sirens, and ringing telephones, also can interfere with hearing and sometimes cause hearing loss. Even chronic ear infections and repeated doses of certain kinds of antibiotics can damage hearing.

Other factors can also interfere with hearing. Visual and auditory messages can conflict, causing listeners to question what they hear. A speaker can use inappropriate or distracting physical movements that overshadow his or her spoken message. A speaker's voice can be harsh or irritating and cause listeners to lose concentration.

Figure 6–4 Model of the Human Ear

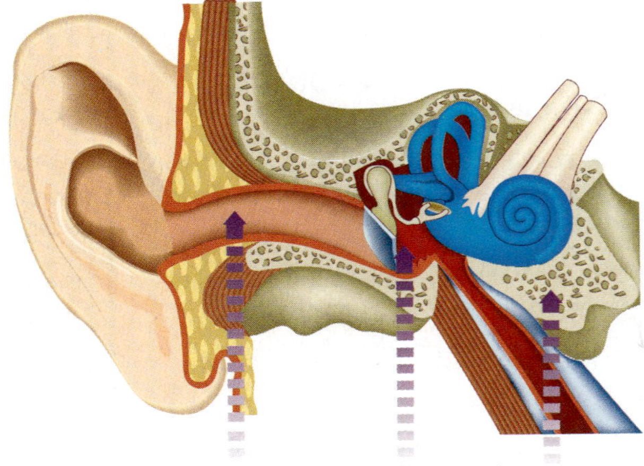

Even the attitude or emotions that a receiver is feeling can interfere with the hearing process. You can, for example, become so angry that you literally do not hear the words someone speaks. Despite an individual's physical ability to hear, when other factors create noise or barriers that keep a person from hearing the message, listening will be blocked in this initial step of the process.

Attending

Are you interested in entering a particular field of business someday? If so, you are likely to listen more intently to discussions about that line of work. You also are more likely to participate in those discussions. On the other hand, if you consider a topic to be boring, irrelevant, or unimportant, you are more likely to "tune out" the speaker. Both of these situations involve a choice on your part. You are choosing which information you will attend and which you will not. **Attending** is the act of choosing—consciously or subconsciously—to focus your attention on verbal or nonverbal stimuli.

Choosing to Attend Many people assume that paying attention is automatic. If that were the case, however, you would never daydream or allow your mind to wander. Instead, you can learn to play an active role in focusing your attention on a message. When you decide to attend to a message, you use selective perception. You focus on specific stimuli that are being received at a particular time. If you choose not to attend to a message, you may give in to distractions or simply ignore those stimuli.

What are some of the elements that affect your ability to attend? Your own needs, interests, attitudes, and knowledge at a given time affect your choice of whether you will attend to or ignore a message. For example, if you have chosen and been accepted to a particular college, you probably will pay little attention to a speaker who is a recruiter from another university. Your lack of interest in this information affects your attending choices.

Specific needs also affect these choices. Imagine that a supervisor at work tells you to present a report on your project in a meeting as soon as she finishes her opening remarks. How much attention do you think you will give to the supervisor's opening remarks? Probably very little. Instead, you may feel it is more important to mentally review what you want to say in your report. Just the stress of being called on to give an impromptu speech can be an extreme barrier to attending to other messages. Barriers to attending can, however, be overcome. You can use the points listed in the Communication Strategies checklist on this page to help you become a more attentive listener.

Communication Strategies

Improving Attending Skills

- Evaluate the communication situation by determining what is important and what should be attended.
- Adjust your attitude to expect the message to be interesting or rewarding.
- Turn off other thoughts and focus your energy on the sender's message.
- Determine what you have to gain from focusing your attention and listening.
- Ignore outside distractions. Bring your attention back to the speaker when you realize that your mind is wandering.
- Stay focused and maintain your concentration.

TECHNOLOGY *Activity*

How Do I Sound? Radio and TV broadcasters are hired, in part, based on several vocal variables. Have you ever changed a TV or radio station or psychologically tuned out a presentation because the speaker's voice was irritating? Find out how your voice sounds to others by making an audio recording of yourself. Recite a nursery rhyme, read a paragraph out of a book, and tell a joke. Play the recording and listen critically. Would others find you easy to listen to? Do you have a monotonous sound? Do you talk too fast? Do you speak clearly? How can your presentation be improved? Record the same readings again and listen for improvements.

Understanding

Why do you talk to others? You probably want them to understand the messages you send and who you are as a person. Why do you listen? You listen because you want to comprehend what others are saying, form relationships, and build mutual trust and understanding. **Understanding** is a complex mental process that involves decoding the symbolic message received from others and then interpreting and assigning a personal meaning to that message.

Decoding To understand what someone says, you must first decode it. Decoding was defined earlier as a listener's assigning meaning to a sender's words and nonverbal cues. Decoding involves listening carefully to a speaker's words to try to understand the meaning the speaker intends to convey. Next, you interpret or filter the message based on your own experiences. Decoding is essential to effective listening because without it you cannot understand the language of the speaker.

Such factors as knowledge, culture, and language skills affect your ability to decode messages. Remember that language is code, and different languages have different codes or word symbols for the same meaning. If someone were to speak to you in a language that you had never learned, you probably would have trouble decoding the message.

Even words of the same language can be unfamiliar or mean different things to different people. If you are in a class and the teacher uses a term you don't recognize, you may be facing a decoding gap in your listening process. It can be extremely difficult to understand a concept if you don't know the meaning of the terms used to describe it.

Interpreting Decoding the words and nonverbal cues is only the initial step in understanding a sender's message. The receiver also has to interpret the meanings or feelings the speaker is expressing. **Interpreting** is a process in which you personalize the sender's message to determine meaning for you. It relates to the process of perception, or self-talk, in which you tell yourself what the speaker is saying.

COMMUNICATION *Strategies*

IMPROVING DECODING SKILLS

- **Build your speaking and listening vocabularies to help with listening.**
- **Use perception checks to clarify a sender's use of words and nonverbal behaviors.**
- **Assume responsibility for your own listening and language skills rather than always expecting others to adjust their messages for you.**

COMMUNICATION *Strategies*

CHECKING INTERPRETATIONS

- ✓ Check factors in your "filter system" that influence your interpretation of messages. Remember, factors like feelings and needs can change momentarily.
- ✓ Make a habit of asking yourself, "Is this what the sender is really saying or is this merely what I am hearing?" and "Are there other interpretations that I am overlooking?"
- ✓ Ask questions to gain more information and increase your understanding before finalizing your interpretation.
- ✓ Take responsibility for your personal interpretations and remain open and flexible to adapt and adjust.

It has been said that the message lies in the receiver. It is the receiver who determines the meaning of the actual message. Your knowledge or lack of knowledge, attitudes, values and needs, culture, language, beliefs, biases, prejudices, expectations, and self-concept all are important elements that influence your personal interpretation of the sender's message. How can you know if your interpretation and understanding are correct? Often, you can't be sure. You can, however, be reasonably sure that it is unlikely that any two people will interpret a particular message in exactly the same way.

Students interpret the teacher's message by personalizing the message to determine its meaning. Identify factors that influence personal interpretation of a message.

Word symbols used by speakers are inexact and depend on the context in which they are given. Each listener's interpretative "filter system" is unique. The guidelines in the Communication Strategies checklist will help you interpret messages to prevent future misunderstandings.

Responding

Once you have arrived at your own personal understanding—or misunderstanding—of a message, you will respond to it. **Responding** is the listener's internal emotional and intellectual reaction to a message. The verbal and nonverbal feedback is the listener's external response to the message. Generally, when you respond to a message, you go through the following processes:

- You first respond emotionally to the message. At this point, you determine how you feel about it.
- You respond intellectually to the message. You decide what you think about your feelings and the message.
- You analyze and evaluate your response to the message.
- You encode choices about what to say or do in response to your understanding of the message and your reaction to it.

Reacting to Messages To help understand the responding process, imagine the scenario outlined in Figure 6–5. You have just learned that you failed a history test even though you had studied hard for it. Your first emotional reaction is shock and disbelief. Then you react intellectually and tell yourself, "There must be something wrong." You scan the paper and the comments made by the teacher. You decide to remain after class to ask the teacher about your grade and if you can do some extra work to raise the grade. You have just gone through the entire responding process. You reacted emotionally to the grade. Then you thought about the grade and decided to talk to your teacher to ask for extra work.

Communication Strategies

Improving Responding Skills

- Monitor, analyze, and evaluate your emotional and intellectual reaction.
- Consider possible alternative reactions.
- Consider basic standards of appropriateness and balance the rewards and consequences of alternative responses.
- Take responsibility for your chosen response.
- Consider all responses before giving feedback.
- Adapt and adjust your messages according to the feedback you receive.
- Choose words that are clear to the listener.

Practice for the Workplace

Responding Options It is important to analyze the messages of others and remember that you have several options when responding to them. Interpretation and analysis are especially important in the workplace.

BUSINESS PRACTICE Activity

Consider how you would use effective listening skills to respond to each of the following scenarios. In groups of three, take turns responding. Focus on how effectively listening would help you respond appropriately in each situation.

1. A couple calls and orders a pizza. You take the call. They do not know exactly what they want and change their order several times.
2. A shopper asks to exchange a suit that was already damaged when purchased. The style is no longer available.
3. A coworker complains to you about another employee who is always late.

Analyzing Reactions You have reacted emotionally to the situation and intellectually decided what kind of action you want to take and what message or feedback you want to send. Now, suppose the scenario continues. Your teacher scans your paper and responds with feedback, "I don't think extra work is the answer. However, you can take another version of the test." The cycle begins again. This time your emotional reaction to the teacher's feedback may be one of real frustration, perhaps even anger. You may then think to yourself one of the following: "Oh well, it's not that important. It's just one grade, after all;" "She doesn't like me anyway, and that's why she won't let me do extra work;" or "Even though I don't want to retake the test, it looks like my only option. I'll just have to study more." The choice is yours. Which are the most appropriate emotional and intellectual responses for you? Which responses probably are inappropriate? Why? What kind of feedback would accompany your response?

If you look at the first reaction, your mental self-talk may be saying, "Forget it, it doesn't matter." The second reaction might mean, "What difference does it make? She doesn't like me and I'll make a bad grade in this class anyway." The third response still reflects your feelings of anger, but your self-talk says, "I don't want to retake this test. It may not even help my grade, but it looks like my only option. I'll have to study more and try." In each case the scenario features the same feeling but results in a different intellectual response to those feelings.

In order to analyze the three reactions, this student would need to pause to weigh and consider the most appropriate response, he or she could make—the one in keeping with the goals for the course. Which response would send the most positive message about his or her attitudes about self, school, or the class?

Figure 6–5 Reacting to Messages

This audience is responding and providing feedback to the speaker. How?

To help you learn to respond and provide feedback appropriately, you can use the same standards you learned in Chapter 1. Which choice is more appropriate and productive for me, for my listener and our relationship, for the occasion (history class) and the task (passing the test)? Before giving feedback, competent communicators analyze and evaluate their responses and the situation before deciding what to do and say about their responses.

Providing Feedback Despite your emotional and intellectual reaction or response, you still have a choice about the feedback you give. You've heard, "Think before you speak," and "Look before you leap." That advice could be important at this point in the responding process. The saga of the history class has not ended. The disappointed student has not provided feedback to the teacher.

COMMUNICATION PRACTICE LAB

Training Your Memory

To practice improving your memory, follow the steps below:

Step 1 On a sheet of paper, create three lists of ten objects each. Try to make the objects as unrelated as possible, such as *chalkboard, bicycle, dog,* and so on.

Step 2 With a partner, take turns completing the following test. Begin by slowly reading your first list to your partner. When you have finished, ask your partner to repeat as many objects as possible from the list. Put a check mark beside each item recalled.

Step 3 Repeat Step 2, using your second list.

Step 4 Now, ask your partner to go back and name the items from the first list. How many can he or she remember?

Step 5 Finally, read your third list to your partner. After reading each item, allow your partner to repeat the word three times before moving on.

Step 6 At the end of the third list, have your partner repeat every word he or she can remember. Did repeating the word increase his or her memory? Discuss your results as a class.

To provide a happier ending, we might assume that the student chose the third response. The student still must make choices about giving feedback. Should the student say, "Okay, I'll take the test," or merely ask, "When can I take the test?" Remembering that competent communicators need to use both task and interpersonal skills, the student might say, "I'm really disappointed in my grade. I really did study. I appreciate your giving me another chance. May I have a few days before I retake the test to look over my notes?" Carefully choosing the verbal and nonverbal feedback you want to give is a vital last step in the responding process.

Importance of Giving Appropriate Feedback Feedback is one person's observable response to a message. A speaker generally cannot be certain that oral communication has occurred until he or she receives some kind of observable feedback from the listener. As an effective listener, you have the responsibility to provide appropriate feedback. Feedback gives the speaker some idea about whether or not the message was received. Finally, feedback also gives the speaker clues about how the listener decoded, interpreted, and reacted to the message the speaker sent.

Benefits of Appropriate Responses and Feedback Carefully considering all responses and providing constructive, realistic feedback are hallmarks of a competent communicator. They not only show your skill as a listener but also may determine your success in social and professional interactions. For example, if you discuss politics at a social gathering, you should consciously stay calm if you want to make your point. Getting angry or lashing out at a guest who does not share your opinion may only make you look like an ineffective communicator.

Responding and Providing Feedback Appropriately in the Workplace One airline company recognizes the importance of careful response choices in the workplace. This company stresses the value of humor in the workplace and routinely tests applicants to see how they might respond to an unpleasant stimulus. First, job applicants are given a typical scenario involving an unhappy passenger. They then are asked how they might resolve the conflict using humor. Again, responding appropriately to the unpleasant stimulus reveals an applicant's communication skill level. Making carefully crafted decisions to keep cool or to use humor appropriately in difficult situations can be a valuable asset to any effective communicator.

Global Communication

Cultural Distinctions

People sometimes are distracted by internal listening barriers when communicating with people from other cultures. These barriers often exist because the listener has had few opportunities to observe people from different regions or cultures. Look for opportunities to learn about the cultures of other people. Watch a national news broadcast for one week, search the Internet for photos, scan your textbooks, recall movies you have seen, and cut out newspaper photos that show different cultures. Identify five visible regional or cultural characteristics and tell how they could affect your ability to listen when in conversation with someone from another culture.

Figure 6–6 **Barriers to Listening**

Factors That Affect the Listening Process

Imagine that a coworker walks up to you in a hallway and says, "You won't believe what happened in the management meeting today." What type of reaction would you have? What types of listening behaviors would you show? What kind of listening do you think your friend expects? How you react to your coworker's statement depends on your listening skills.

What factors cause us to listen poorly at times? Why do we listen effectively at other times? The listening process is influenced by three key factors. They are as follows:

- noise
- barriers
- memory

Noise

The first critical factor that affects the listening process is noise—the internal and external distractions that interfere with listening and concentration. Noise can exist in every step of the listening process—hearing, acquiring, attending, and responding. The truck driver who is having a stressful day or the store clerk who is eager to meet friends after work may experience internal noise that can result in mistakes and difficulty in listening. Internal noise such as confusion, impatience, or annoyance may drown out valuable incoming messages.

Similarly, external noise can distract you and keep you from fully understanding a message. Trying to listen to a lecture when a room is too warm or too cold can create noise that makes it difficult to concentrate. Static on a telephone line or people talking loudly nearby are examples of external noise that may reduce listening efficiency.

MEMORY

Category	Explanation	Example
Immediate	Recalling information for a brief period of time	"Yes, Joe called a few minutes ago."
Short Term	Recalling information for carrying out a routine of daily task	"The homework assignment is to practice giving the presentation in front of a mirror."
Long Term	Recalling information from past experience	"I was very nervous my first day on the job."

COMMUNICATION *Strategies*

IMPROVING MEMORY SKILLS

- Concentrate on each message as you are receiving it.
- Use calendars, lists, or notes as reminders.
- Summarize, rehearse, repeat, or write information to seal it in your memory.
- Form mental associations and organize elements of information into related memory clusters.
- Try to learn new information in small portions rather than all at once, as in cramming for a test.

Barriers

Barriers to the listening process, like barriers to other aspects of communication, can prevent or block effective communication. Some of these barriers are shown in Figure 6–6. Speech problems, incompatible language, and reduced hearing ability are some of the external barriers that block message reception. External barriers tend to be harder to eliminate than noise because they involve more complex or long-term problems.

You also might experience internal barriers in the listening process. Internal barriers often result from ignorance, intolerance, fear, or traumatic experiences. They tend to be deeply rooted attitudes, biases, prejudices, and beliefs that interfere with listening.

Memory

Memory, or the process of retaining or recalling information, affects all aspects of the listening process. Without memory, there would be no knowledge and no learning. In addition, memory often is an incentive for listening. You may listen closely to an introduction to remember someone's name. You may listen to a lecture to remember facts that will show up on your next quiz. You may listen to a trainer to remember how to operate a new piece of machinery.

Memory is not always so straightforward, however. Like other aspects of listening, memory can be selective. For instance, you may choose what you wish to remember, remember an incident only as you wish to remember it, or eliminate or suppress certain memories if you do not wish to be reminded of them.

Three Types of Memory As shown in the Memory chart, memory can be classified into three categories: immediate memory, short-term memory, and long-term memory. Your ability to remember can be affected by many different factors, including not paying attention or being easily distracted. Others include mental or physical health problems, denial or suppression of memories, fatigue and stress, and communication overload. The tips in the Communication Strategies checklist are designed to help you improve your memory skills.

Using Feedback to Analyze Listening

One way to analyze your and others' listening is to look at the feedback. If the feedback does not appear appropriate, it might be because of one of the following situations.

- The receiver cannot or did not hear the message.
- The receiver may lack appropriate verbal or vocabulary decoding skills.
- The receiver may interpret the message as unrelated to him or her, or as uninteresting, offensive, or irrelevant.

- The listener's knowledge, attitude, feelings, or culture may be the source of unique or inaccurate interpretations of the intended message.
- The listener's response may reflect unique elements of personality, personal bias, or past experiences with which the sender is unfamiliar.
- Internal or external noise or barriers may interfere with listening and cause a discrepancy between expectations and responses.
- The listener may not remember the message.
- For any number of reasons, the listener may choose to give feedback that the speaker considers inappropriate.

You can use these checks to help you create an atmosphere of understanding. As you put these concepts to work in your life, remember that effective listening is a win-win situation. Not only does the speaker succeed in getting the message across, but you also have the opportunity to grow and learn.

Section 1 Assessment

Visit the *Glencoe Communication Applications* Web site at communicationapplications.glencoe.com and click on **Self-Check and Study Guide 6.1** to review your understanding of the listening process.

Review Key Terms

1. Define each term and write it in a sentence: listening, hearing, attending, understanding, interpreting, responding.

Check Understanding

2. Relate the following to the importance of listening in professional and social contexts.

   Courage is what it takes to stand up and speak; courage is also what it takes to sit down and listen.

   —Winston Churchill

3. Identify the four steps of the listening process and describe their related functions.
4. Of the factors that affect listening, which do you think is the hardest to change? Why?
5. Give one specific suggestion for improving effectiveness in each step of the listening process.
6. **Cause–Effect** How might communication be different if no one ever provided feedback? Explain your answer.

APPLICATION *Activity*

Creating a Chart Talk with a parent or friend about the importance of listening effectively at his or her work or school. Ask how much total time he or she spends listening each day. Next, ask the person to describe effective and ineffective listening experiences he or she has had. Create a chart that lists the person's answers for both of these categories and share your findings as a class.

Critical Thinking Skill

Recalling Information

Listening is useful only if you can recall what you heard. Recall is the ability to remember. It helps you put new information to use.

Learning the Skill

Follow these guidelines when you listen to a lecture or speech.

- **Focus your attention on the speaker.**
- **Be prepared to take notes.**
- **Listen for concepts.** Concentrate on the main points or concepts of the presentation. Concepts are different from facts. For example, a blueprint for building a skyscraper is a concept. The number of floors that will be in the skyscraper is a fact.
- **Ask questions.** If something is unclear to you, ask questions. If you don't have a chance to do this during the presentation, write your question down so you can ask it at a later time.
- **Listen critically.** Even if you think you already agree or disagree with a speaker's message, you should listen to the entire presentation. You can't be critical of a presentation if you haven't listened to it completely. To better understand the concepts being presented, pay close attention to the graphics and visual aids. Try to determine how this information might be useful.
- **Listen for emphasis and repetition.** Speakers use special voice tones and physical gestures when they want to emphasize an important idea. Watch and listen for these variations. Also, listen for ideas that are repeated. Speakers often repeat important aspects of a presentation.

Practicing the Skill

Read the sample presentation, then answer the questions that follow.

If we do not vote to build a subway system, we will be making the biggest mistake of our lives. We need a subway system because our roads are too crowded. Over 90 percent of us depend on our roads for transportation. We need a subway system because almost 60 percent of us sit in traffic jams at least once a week. Our roads are getting more crowded every day. We need a new means of transportation. We need a subway system.

1. Read the first sentence again. What is your initial reaction to this statement? Do you think what the speaker says is true?
2. What is the main concept of this presentation? How do you know?
3. What are some facts that the speaker uses in the presentation?
4. What questions would you ask if you were at this presentation?

APPLICATION *Activity*

With three or four other students, create a list of the ways you study for tests. Describe how you use class notes, homework, quizzes, and readings from the text. Have your group share its list with the rest of the class. Then, listen to the ideas presented by the other groups. Combine all the lists into one master list explaining how to study for a test.

Developing Listening Skills

GUIDE TO READING

Objectives

1. Compare and contrast the characteristics of active, passive, and impatient listening.
2. Evaluate the results of active, passive, and impatient listening.
3. Describe the four kinds of listening.
4. Determine the most appropriate kind of listening for a given situation.

Terms to Learn

active listening
passive listening
impatient listening
critical listening
deliberative listening
empathic listening
appreciative listening

As you are searching frantically for a pen, one of your friends begins telling you about a movie he saw last night. You continue to rummage through your locker, occasionally mumbling "Uh-huh" or "Nope" when asked a question. After a few minutes, your friend says "Forget it. You're not even listening." You're sure you were acquiring, attending, understanding, and responding. So what's the problem?

Listening is listening, isn't it? If you can recall what your friend said about the movie, then weren't you listening effectively? The truth is, while your listening style may have been effective, your friend may not have seen it as appropriate. He probably wanted to participate in an interactive conversation with you. However, your lack of participation made the conversation too one-sided for his purposes.

In this section, you will learn that, although the listening process always is the same, it can have different purposes and characteristics from one situation to the next. Each purpose requires a different kind of listening. Each kind, in turn, requires its own set of communication skills.

Close friendships are built on effective listening. **Why does the listening process change from one situation to the next?**

Characteristics of Listening

Imagine you and a friend disagree about who is the best singer of all time. What types of listening behaviors do you use as you debate the issue? Now think about your listening behaviors as you sit through a long meeting. In both cases, you are listening, but you probably take a more active role in one situation than in the other.

The listening process usually uses the same steps in the same sequence. However, the way that you listen varies according to the context and what you want to get out of the communication. You can listen three ways: actively, passively, or impatiently.

Active listening is important to a child's education. Identify three ways to listen.

Active Listening

In **active listening,** the listener participates fully in the communication process. When you listen attentively, provide feedback, and strive to understand and remember messages, you are being an active listener.

Active listeners view communication as a dynamic, transactional process of sending and receiving messages. They see themselves as active participants in conversations, group discussions, and group decision-making processes. Generally, active listeners expect listening to be rewarding and enjoyable. They demonstrate their enthusiasm by asking questions and giving positive, supportive feedback.

Competent communicators tell themselves, "There's something in this message for me. How can I gain the most from this interaction?" They realize that active listening results in certain valuable rewards. For example, active listeners typically make better grades than those who take more passive roles. They also tend to get more enjoyment and useful

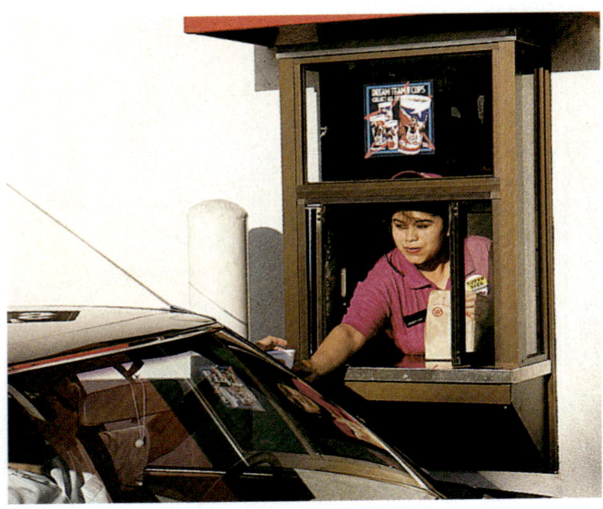

The fast-food employee shown must practice active listening skills in order to do the job effectively. Identify ways in which active listening makes a productive employee.

information from conversations and group discussions. On the job, active listeners tend to make fewer mistakes, resulting in better performance, higher productivity, and increased value as employees.

Passive Listening

In passive listening, the listener does not actively participate in interactions. Passive listeners think they can absorb information even when they do not contribute to the interaction. They tend to view communication as a one-way process and place the responsibility for successful communication on the speaker.

Passive listening is sometimes called "lazy" listening. Passive listeners often perceive themselves as message receivers rather than as interactors. The communication context is viewed as a one-way process rather than as a give-and-take. Passive listeners often view listening as easy or automatic and see little need to invest energy or effort in the process. They may easily become bored or distracted, ask few questions, or give negative nonverbal feedback.

There are generally no rewards for passive listening. The results most often are boredom, apathy, and a general lack of interest in the people or topics involved in the communication.

Impatient Listening

In impatient listening, short bursts of active listening are interrupted by noise and other distractions. Impatient listeners usually intend to pay attention—and may even be successful for short periods of time—but then they allow their mind to wander in some way. Types of impatient listening are described in the following chart.

Impatient listeners fail to assume responsibility for promoting understanding in communication. They often make mistakes or forget details or instructions because they have "tuned out" the speaker and "tuned in" to some distraction or other interest. Impatient listeners may shift their gaze, nod, or give verbal comments such as "Right," or "Uh-huh" at inappropriate times. This "fake listening"

TYPES OF IMPATIENT LISTENING

Type	Description
Anticipatory Listening	Listener anticipates what the speaker will say and then rushes ahead in his or her mind to plan a response
Defensive Listening	Listener's main goal in listening is to argue or disagree
Combative Listening	Listener's main goal in listening is to "win" or to put down a speaker
Distracted Listening	Listener pays attention to the first part of a statement, assumes what the speaker will continue to say, then stops listening and starts thinking about something else

COMMUNICATION PRACTICE LAB

Demonstrating Listening Characteristics

To understand the advantages and disadvantages of listening actively, passively, and impatiently, follow these steps:

Step 1 As a class, brainstorm a list of listening occasions at home, at school, with friends, in organizations, and on the job. Ideas might include listening to a homework assignment or conversing with friends about what movie to see. List your ideas in a single column on the chalkboard.

Step 2 In a second column, list whether you would typically listen actively, passively, or impatiently in each situation.

Step 3 As a class, discuss the advantages and disadvantages of your usual listening choices.

Step 4 In a third column, list the most appropriate listening choice for each listening occasion. Discuss the reasons for your answers. Do you notice any patterns in this column?

effort is intended to mask a lack of concentration or interest. Instead, it is a dead giveaway that the listener is not paying attention.

Listening Flaws

Competent communicators avoid relying heavily on passive listening or using it inappropriately. They also avoid impatient listening whenever possible. Generally speaking, both of these characteristics can be classified as faulty listening habits.

On the other hand, effective listening skills include focusing attention on the message, clarifying meanings, and actively promoting understanding. Your challenge is to become an active listener whenever possible, participating fully in the communication process.

Kinds of Listening

Just as you may listen in different ways—actively, passively, or impatiently—you also may have different goals for listening. Depending on your goal and the context of the communication, you may choose a different kind of listening.

The four major kinds of listening include critical listening, deliberative listening, empathic listening, and appreciative listening. Each has

The listener shown above is exhibiting signs of impatience. Describe an impatient listener.

These future chefs are listening critically to a lecture. **What is the main purpose of listening critically?**

a unique purpose, requires a specialized application of listening skills, and has its own rewards. When used effectively, each kind of listening can help you communicate successfully in social and professional contexts.

Critical Listening

The first kind of listening is probably very familiar to you. You use critical listening every day in school as well as in other areas of your life. **Critical listening** is listening to comprehend ideas and information in order to achieve a specific purpose or goal. Critical listening is sometimes referred to as "comprehensive listening" because your reason for listening is to comprehend or understand the sender's message.

Critical listening skills are particularly useful when you listen actively to understand and act upon an informative message. For example, when you listen to a lecture in class, you use critical listening because your goal is to acquire and understand information. You also use critical listening when you listen to announcements that inform you about upcoming school or social events. Critical listening skills also are important when listening to directions to a location or instructions for a new task.

Deliberative Listening

Deliberative listening is listening to understand, analyze, and evaluate messages so you can accept or reject a point of view, make a

Communication Strategies

Tips for Critical Listening

- Identify the goal or purpose for listening.
- If possible, gather information about the topic before the listening experience to build a vocabulary and have background information available.
- Focus your attention on the sender's verbal and nonverbal messages.
- Organize the information to grasp the speaker's main idea and supporting details.
- Use perception checks to form appropriate responses.
- Consciously store the information in your memory bank.
- Ask questions, give appropriate feedback, and take appropriate action.

decision, or take action. This kind of listening sometimes is referred to as "evaluative listening" because the listener's purpose is to analyze and evaluate information as a basis for future action.

You use deliberative listening skills when receiving and evaluating persuasive messages. Persuasive messages may range from a friend's plea of "I need help!" to a customer's request or complaint. In each case, you need to analyze and evaluate the message because you are expected to take some kind of action. What kind of help are you being asked to provide? Are you actually capable of helping your friend or should you refer him or her to someone else? What does the customer expect you to do to solve the problem? Would it be ethical or wise to do what the customer is asking? Listening to persuasive messages requires the listener to evaluate the message and deliberate, or think over, the position or action he or she is being asked to take.

Empathic Listening

Have you ever listened to a friend tell a story and felt that you could completely understand what the friend was going through? If so, you had empathy for that person. In other words, you understood and appreciated his or her situation. As you listened to the friend's story, you probably used empathic listening. **Empathic listening** is listening to understand, participate in, and enhance a relationship.

Even though empathic listening frequently is used in interactions between two people or in a small group, it can be used appropriately in larger group, social, professional, and public contexts. Regardless of the setting, the goal of empathic listening is to develop understanding and appreciation of the meanings and feelings expressed by a message sender.

COMMUNICATION Strategies

TIPS FOR DELIBERATIVE LISTENING

- ✓ Identify your goal or purpose for listening.
- ✓ If possible, gather information before the listening experience to provide a basis for evaluation, deliberation, and judgment.
- ✓ Listen specifically to understand, analyze, and evaluate the message.
- ✓ Organize your listening to grasp the speaker's claim or idea, the use of supporting information, the reasons to support the speaker's claim, and the use of emotional appeals and persuasive strategies.
- ✓ Observe the speaker's use of language and nonverbal cues to identify, analyze, and evaluate his or her attitudes or feelings. Then, determine whether these behaviors support or counteract the speaker's message.
- ✓ Analyze the speaker's motivation or intent.
- ✓ Reflect on your own responses and reasons for accepting or rejecting the speaker's message.
- ✓ Form reasoned responses and give appropriate feedback. Delay action if necessary.
- ✓ Reserve judgment if you are unsure of all the facts.
- ✓ When you feel you have enough information, make responsible decisions and take prudent action.

COMMUNICATION *Strategies*

TIPS FOR EMPATHIC LISTENING

- Listen carefully to the speaker's words to understand the meaning of the speaker's message and the feelings he or she is expressing.
- Observe the speaker's nonverbal behaviors to analyze his or her feelings about the listener or the relationship involved and the context or situation.
- Monitor your understanding of the speaker, the message, and the situation.
- Analyze your own responses, feelings, biases, or prejudices toward the speaker, the message, or the situation.
- Use personal perception checks such as, "Is this what the speaker really is saying, or is this just what I am hearing and telling myself about the speaker's message?"
- Try to paraphrase the sender's message.
- Ask questions to help the sender clarify his or her meanings and feelings.

When you listen empathically, you try to put yourself in another person's place or see the world through his or her eyes. Empathic listening does not, however, mean listening to agree or to sympathize with those meanings and feelings. As an empathic listener you may find yourself saying, "I think I understand what you are saying, and I appreciate your concern, but I'm not sure I share your position on this issue."

Skills in empathic listening are essential for full participation in communication. They also are the key to developing productive personal relationships.

Appreciative Listening

Appreciative listening is listening to enjoy, or appreciate, a speaker's message or a performance on an artistic level. It is listening for fun—to laugh, cry, use your imagination, or extend your creativity. You most likely use appreciative listening skills in social situations, such as when you attend concerts, plays, dance presentations, or even sporting events. You also use appreciative listening or viewing when you attend movies or watch television, listen to music, or go to the theater.

The main goal of appreciative listening is enjoyment. Not only can appreciative listening help a person relax or escape from everyday stress, but it also can inspire and provide an outlet for personal growth and fulfillment.

The audience is practicing appreciative listening while being entertained by the musicians. What is the goal of appreciative listening?

Using the Four Kinds of Listening

Why do you need to know about the four major kinds of listening? It's no secret that people pay the most attention to what is interesting or important to them. When you understand the goal of listening in a specific situation, you can pay attention to the things that are most important for reaching that goal. For instance, the goal of listening to a sales presentation is to evaluate the information so you can make a decision. Understanding this goal can help you concentrate on the information that is most important to making that decision.

Identifying the appropriate kind of listening for each situation is a valuable life skill. It not only helps you achieve the results you want but also helps others see you as an effective listener. Listening skills are highly valued in personal relationships, in school, in organizations, and on the job. Most importantly, they help you function effectively as a competent communicator. As a communicator, keep in mind the following when you are listening to the messages of others.

TIPS FOR APPRECIATIVE LISTENING

- Listen with the goal of enjoying and appreciating.
- Consider selecting some listening experiences especially to expand your knowledge and understanding of art, philosophy, nature, or a particular sport.
- Before the listening experience, investigate the style and format of the performance and the techniques and skills used by the performers. Understanding the form, rules, or conventions of what is being performed may enhance your understanding, enjoyment, and appreciation.
- Become familiar with background information and critiques of the players or actors themselves to get the maximum results from your listening investment.
- Avoid distractions and keep your focus on the performance.
- Avoid making judgments about the performance until it is over.
- Respond appropriately to the ideas, feelings, and skills of the performers.
- Give appropriate and considerate feedback.

interNET ACTIVITY

Classical to Current You have probably heard someone say, "I don't like classical music!" How do you know if you have not tried it? You can find sample sound clips on the Internet by entering any of these words or phrases in your Internet search engine: music, jazz, German music, country music, classical music, dance music, reggae, blues, folk music, opera. Find and listen to any two types of music you have never heard before. Can you identify the different instruments? Does music ever have an impact on your mood? Why do you appreciate one type of music more than another? Why do you listen to music?

- Try to identify the kind of listening needed in a given situation and then adapt to it.
- Set a goal for listening. Decide what you can gain from your listening experience. What is your specific listening task?
- As a part of your goal, consider the relationship with others involved in the interaction. Plan how you can use listening to protect or enhance the relationship.
- Use memory techniques to remember useful parts of the sender's message.
- Keep an open mind. Avoid prejudging what the sender is saying until you have heard everything he or she has to say.
- Be an interactive listener by paying attention, responding appropriately, and giving useful feedback.

Section 2 Assessment

Visit the *Glencoe Communication Applications* Web site at **communicationapplications.glencoe.com** and click on **Self-Check and Study Guide 6.2** to review your understanding of the characteristics and kinds of listening.

Review Key Terms

1. Define each term and write it in a sentence: active listening, passive listening, impatient listening, critical listening, deliberative listening, empathic listening, appreciative listening.

Check Understanding

2. Describe the characteristics of active, passive, and impatient listening. How are these characteristics similar to each other? How are they different?
3. Imagine that a friend is giving you complex directions to a shopping mall in another city. How should you listen—actively, passively, or impatiently? Why?
4. Consider critical, deliberative, empathic, and appreciative listening. Describe the main goal of each kind of listening.
5. **Apply** Imagine that you are a teacher listening to a student explain why she did not complete her report on time. The student wants an extra day to finish the report. What kind of listening would you use and why?

APPLICATION Activity

Listening with Purpose Working in four groups, listen to a volunteer read a short magazine article or, if a television is available, observe a single report from a newscast. Each group should listen to the performance using a different kind of listening—critical, deliberative, empathic, or appreciative. Discuss what types of information each group listened for and your resulting impressions of the performance. Did each group get something from the experience?

Communication Self-Assessment

Evaluating Your Listening Skills

How Do You Rate?

On a separate sheet of paper, use the key to respond to the following statements. Put a check mark at the end of each skill you would like to improve.

Key: **A** Always
U Usually
S Sometimes
R Rarely
N Never

1. I listen carefully to others in order to be a more successful communicator.
2. When I hear words that I don't know, I try to find out their meanings.
3. I realize that as a listener I share the responsibility for understanding the person speaking.
4. When a speaker presents a viewpoint different from mine, I work at understanding what is said rather than "tuning out" or becoming defensive.
5. To improve my listening skills, I maintain eye contact with the speaker and ignore outside distractions.
6. I choose my responses by evaluating the situation and weighing the consequences of my feedback.
7. I use memory skills like concentrating, taking notes, and organizing ideas when I listen to a presentation.
8. To help me listen more actively, I tell myself, "There's something in this message for me."

How Do You Score?

Review your responses. Give yourself 5 points for every A, 4 for every U, 3 for every S, 2 for every R, and 1 for every N. Total your points and evaluate your score.

31–40 Excellent You may be surprised to find out how much you can improve your skills.

21–30 Good In this course, you can learn ways to make your skills better.

11–20 Fair Practice applying the skills taught in this course.

1–10 Needs Improvement Carefully monitor your improvement as you work through this course.

Setting Communication Goals

If you scored Excellent or Good, complete Part A. If your score was Fair or Needs Improvement, complete Part B.

Part A

1. I plan to put the following ideas into practice:
2. I plan to share the following information about communication with the following people:

Part B

1. The behaviors I need to change most are:
2. To bring about these changes, I will take these steps:

Note Taking

Note taking is a way of recording the important parts of a speech or presentation. Taking notes also helps you recall information. You should take notes

- in class
- during an interview
- at business presentations
- in press briefings
- when learning a new skill
- when doing research

The guidelines explained below will help you get the most out of your notes.

Survey the situation. When you begin, write down the date, time, and place of the presentation. Record the topic of the lecture, and list the names of the people presenting the information.

Listen carefully. Follow the speech as closely as possible. Presenters usually tell the audience which parts of their speech are the most important. Write down the main ideas as they are introduced. Leave space between the main points to add supporting information as it is given.

Know what to write. How you take notes will mainly be determined by the kind of information being presented. If you are taking notes on a history lecture, your focus will probably be on important people, events, and dates. At a business meeting, you might find it useful to record information shown in graphs or charts. When learning a new skill, you'll want to record all of the steps necessary to complete that process. Most of the time, your notes will resemble an informal outline. There will be main points and subpoints, mostly written in a very brief style.

Keep your notes short and to the point. Don't try to write down every word the speaker says. Instead, try to write as little as possible while still getting the main ideas. You can do this in many different ways. One method is abbreviating long words or phrases. If you are at a lecture about the United States Department of Agriculture, for example, you could use the initials *USDA*. Also, common words like *a*, *an*, and *the* can be left out of your notes. When possible, use symbols to represent numbers, money, and percentages. Use a plus sign instead of the word *and*. Another way to take shorter notes is to paraphrase what is being said. When you paraphrase information, you are putting it into your own words. Use short sentences when you paraphrase.

Stay alert. Keep your attention focused on the speaker. If there are loud noises or

For additional information about business writing, see the *Guide to Business Communication* section of the Communication Survival Kit in the Appendix.

other distractions, you will have to listen more carefully. You may have to ask the presenter to speak louder or pause until the disturbance stops. Ask questions if you do not understand the information being presented.

Taking Notes at a Business Seminar Suppose you attend a seminar on documenting Internet research sources. Your notes might look something like the ones shown below. Which suggestions for taking notes have been followed in this example?

Documenting Internet Research Sources
July 28, 2004
Rosemont Convention Center, Chicago, Illinois
Presenters: Carl Bibson and Cindy Peters
Source: "Guide to Using the Internet and Other Electronic Resources." Glencoe/McGraw-Hill, 2000.

*Set up page for citations at end of paper
-Number as last page of report (if report ends on p. 5, make citations p. 6)
-Title "Works Cited" should be centered one inch from top of page
-Double-space page

*Alphabetize entries
-Use author's last name when possible
-If author's name is not given, use name of editor, compiler, translator, or publisher of site

*When citing books, articles, poems, + other written works that are available in print but quoted online, follow rules in grammar book

*Give the URL (Web address) of site + list page numbers used

*Reference last date of electronic posting

*Print out source to use in case it's changed when updated

WRITING *Activity*

Turn back to the section titled "Critical Listening" on page 190, then follow these instructions with a classmate. Use this activity to improve your note-taking skills.

- Assume that this information is being presented in a seminar or workshop. Read this selection aloud while your partner takes notes, then switch roles (your partner reads the same information while you take notes).
- After you have both taken notes, switch papers.
- Read your partner's notes. Find the date, time, and location of the presentation and circle this information. If this information is not in your partner's notes, write it at the top of the page.
- Locate the main idea and put a star to the left of it. If you cannot find the main idea, write it in.
- Look for abbreviated words or symbols. Circle any examples that you find.
- Underline any paraphrased information.
- Return the notes to your classmate.
- Discuss any shortcuts or abbreviations you learned from the activity.

CHAPTER 6 Assessment and Activities

GLENCOE Online

Visit the *Glencoe Communication Applications* Web site at **communicationapplications.glencoe.com** and click on **Chapter 6 Activity** for additional practice in listening effectively.

Reviewing Key Terms

On a separate sheet of paper, write the communication term that completes each statement.

1. _______ is a physical and psychological process involving acquiring messages, assigning meaning to them, and responding.
2. The act of choosing to pay attention to verbal or nonverbal stimuli is called _______ .
3. _______ is a filtering process that begins when sound is relayed to your brain.
4. When you personalize a sender's message to determine meaning, you are _______ .
5. The listener's intellectual and emotional reaction to a message is called _______ .
6. _______ listening includes listening attentively, providing feedback, and trying to understand and remember.
7. Listening only to argue or disagree is a type of _______ listening.
8. The goal of _______ listening is to comprehend the listener's message.
9. The purpose of _______ listening is to analyze and evaluate information as a basis for future action.
10. An important goal of _______ listening is to enhance a relationship.

Reviewing Key Concepts

1. Are listening and hearing the same thing? Why or why not?
2. What are the four active components of listening?
3. Explain the roles of the outer ear, middle ear, and inner ear in the process of hearing.
4. List six ways to improve your attending skills.
5. What other process must come first before you can interpret a message?
6. What are usually the consequences of passive listening?
7. List the four factors that influence listening.
8. What style of listening would you choose when a sales person is trying to sell you a product?

Assessment and Activities

Reading and Critical Thinking Skill

1. **Synthesis** Imagine you are a flight attendant. A passenger complains that the airplane's aisle is too narrow. How would you respond to resolve the conflict with humor?
2. **Cause-Effect** What results when a listener fails to give appropriate feedback?
3. **Classifying Information** Under which key factor that influences the listening process would you classify an intolerance for bluegrass music?
4. **Applying Information** Which style of listening should a student choose during a lecture given in class?

Skill Practice Activity

Recalling Information Adapt the tips suggested for improving memory to prepare for your next exam.

- Concentrate on the teacher's words as he or she lectures.
- Jot down the important points in notes.
- After the lecture, paraphrase, rehearse, repeat, or write the information to seal it in your memory.
- Form mental associations and organize elements of information into related memory clusters.
- Memorize facts in small portions, rather than cramming for the exam the night before.

After you receive your graded exam, compare the grade to one you received before you tried to improve your memory skills.

Cooperative Learning Activity

Graphing the Effects of Noise Make three lists, each including ten simple words. Have the rest of the class prepare sheets of paper for a spelling test. Choose a music CD that your teacher has previewed, then read the list of the words for the class to spell while the CD is playing. Turn off the CD and present the second list of words to the class. Say the words on the third list quickly in succession. Grade the tests and analyze the scores. Then draw a conclusion about oral tests and noise based on the analysis.

Chapter Project

Planning Test the theory that many people's longest-lasting memories are formed between the ages of seventeen and twenty-five. Interview an adult from your parents' or grandparents' generation. Ask him or her to describe the ten most memorable events of his or her life. Then, note the age of the speaker at the time of each event.

Presenting As a class, combine the data from the interviews. Plot the number of events remembered for each age between one and fifty on a large graph displayed in the classroom and use this graph to reach a conclusion about the validity of the experts' theory.

Standardized Test Practice

Read each passage. Some sections are underlined. The underlined sections may be one of the following:

- **Incomplete sentences**
- **Run-on sentences**
- **Correctly written sentences that should be combined**
- **Correctly written sentences that do not need to be rewritten**

Choose the best way to write each underlined section and mark the letter for your answer. If the underlined section needs no change, mark the choice "Correct as is."

Thomas Edison was a masterful inventor, Edison was also very skilled at improving existing inventions. (1) His first invention was a gadget that made communication easier, and believe it or not, it nearly cost him his job.

Invented by Samuel Morse in 1838. The telegraph allowed the first reliable form of long-distance communication. (2) As a young boy, Edison was fascinated by the telegraph. At the age of sixteen. Edison moved to Canada to become a telegraph assistant. (3) His job was to report to Toronto every hour by telegraph signal. Young Edison came up with a better idea. He converted the telegraph's mechanism so that it would transmit and receive automatically. Edison's boss discovered him asleep at his station. Edison was almost fired. (4) Edison's invention was later used as part of the automatic telegraph, improving worldwide communication.

1 **A** Thomas Edison was a masterful inventor, and he was also very skilled at improving existing inventions.

B Thomas Edison was a masterful inventor. And Edison was also very skilled at improving existing inventions.

C Thomas Edison was a masterful inventor, he was also very skilled at improving existing inventions.

D Correct as is

2 **F** Invented by Samuel Morse in 1838, the telegraph allowing the first reliable form of long-distance communication.

G Invented by Samuel Morse in 1838, the telegraph allowed the first reliable form of long-distance communication.

H Invented by Samuel Morse in 1838, the telegraph. It allowed the first reliable form of long-distance communication.

J Correct as is

3 **A** At the age of sixteen, Edison moved to Canada, it was to become a telegraph assistant.

B At the age of sixteen, Edison moved to Canada. To become a telegraph assistant.

C At the age of sixteen, Edison moved to Canada to become a telegraph assistant.

D Correct as is

4 **F** Edison's boss discovered him asleep at his station, but Edison was almost fired.

G Edison's boss, who discovered him asleep at his station, was almost fired.

H When Edison's boss discovered him asleep at his station, Edison was almost fired.

J Correct as is

UNIT 2

Interpersonal Communication

Applying Communication Skills

Effective interpersonal communication is based on learned skills that, when applied effectively, build credibility and enhance self-esteem. Whether you most often participate in informal social conversations or respond formally to customers at work, learning how and when to use appropriate verbal, nonverbal, and listening skills will build up your image as a competent communicator.

UNIT Activity

Making a Successful Strategies Chart

- Create a chart with the following categories: Successful Strategies, Chapter Number, Date Practiced, and Result.
- As you progress through each chapter in this unit, prepare a list of strategies that you found beneficial in your daily life either at home, in school, at work, or in the community.
- At the end of the study of the unit, share the strategies as a class, noting the ones that seemed the most helpful.

CHAPTER 7 Building Effective Interpersonal Relationships

WHY IT'S IMPORTANT

The secret to "getting along" with others is to learn how to interact productively with them on an interpersonal basis. To do this, you'll need to learn some special skills in communication.

To better understand interpersonal relationships, view the **Communication in Action** Chapter 7 video lesson.

GLENCOE Online

Visit the *Glencoe Communication Applications* Web site at **communicationapplications.glencoe.com** and click on **Overview–Chapter 7** to preview information about interpersonal relationships.

"The most important single ingredient in the formula of success is knowing how to get along with people."
—Theodore Roosevelt, U.S. President

Section 1

Understanding Interpersonal Relationships

Objectives

1. Identify the types of interpersonal relationships in professional and social contexts.
2. Explain the importance and purpose of each type of interpersonal relationship.
3. Describe the five characteristics of productive interpersonal communication.

Terms to Learn

integrating

Picture the beginning of a typical day. You get up, get dressed, and say good morning to someone in your family. Perhaps you discuss the day's plans as you eat breakfast. Then, it's off to school, where you communicate with various friends, classmates, and teachers all day. However, what if you never were allowed to speak with others on a one-to-one basis?

It's hard to imagine not communicating with others on a one-to-one basis—or at least in very small groups. How many times a day do you interact with teachers, coworkers, or fellow students? As you learned in Chapter 2, this level of one-to-one communication is called interpersonal communication. While most interpersonal communication occurs between only two individuals, it sometimes may refer to interaction among three family members, friends, or coworkers. It also includes one-to-one talk in formal interviews and professional conversations. It is through these types of interpersonal interactions that we build relationships and carry on the meaningful business of the day in professional and social contexts.

Interpersonal communication occurs between coworkers. What is the purpose of interpersonal communication in social and professional contexts?

The Role of Interpersonal Communication

In Chapter 1, you learned that communication skills are vital to your success in professional and social contexts. However, of all your communication skills, interpersonal skills may be the most important to your employability, productivity, and career success. Interpersonal skills also play a significant role in the relationships that you develop.

Applicants who demonstrate strong interpersonal skills in interviews have a definite advantage over less-skilled communicators. Similarly, individuals who work and relate well with coworkers help promote goodwill and positive morale in the workplace. They also are more likely to keep their jobs or be promoted than peers who lack interpersonal skills.

On the other hand, poor human-relations and interpersonal skills can actually cause a person to lose his or her job. Employers and social organizations usually seek individuals who can form productive interpersonal relationships. The bottom line in workplace and social contexts is that harmonious, positive interactions produce a climate of cooperation. Cooperative relationships help improve morale, enhance success, and increase productivity.

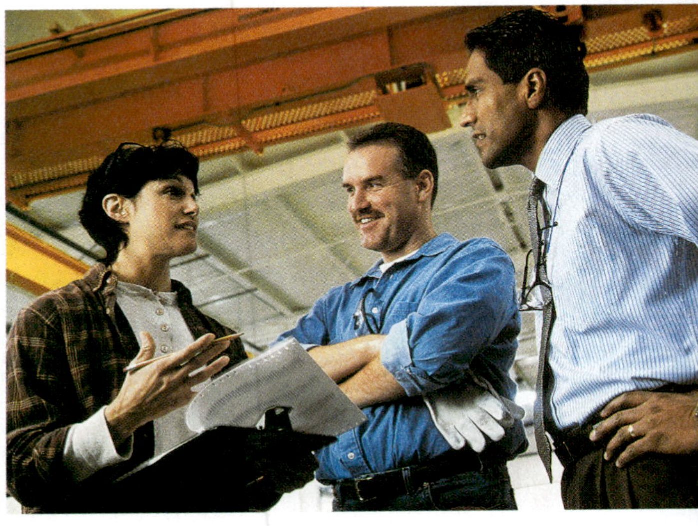

Interpersonal communication skills can determine career success. **What type of applicants do employers and social organizations look for?**

Relationships in Professional and Social Contexts

Relationships are formed and nurtured through interpersonal interactions. In fact, the quality of your interpersonal communication determines the quality and nature of your relationships. In other words, if your communication is positive, the relationship that results is likely to be positive and productive. If your communication is hostile, rude, or otherwise perceived as negative, the relationship most likely will be negative, strained, or even hostile.

There are two important considerations regarding relationships in professional and social contexts. First, why are relationships important? Second, what kinds of relationships are necessary and appropriate at work and in various social contexts?

Importance of Relationships

Relationships at work and in social organizations are important because the people who work together in these settings are interdependent. That is, they must depend on one another and combine their tasks and skills to see that work is done efficiently.

For example, a supervisor may depend on his or her administrative assistant to send out a memo to employees about a change in policy on the job. The employees then work together to adapt their individual tasks and functions to conform to the new policy. Similarly, in a social organization, a committee may establish procedures and goals for a community fund-raiser. The members of the organization then work together to see that the goals are reached.

Individuals in professional and social contexts not only are interdependent in their tasks and functions, but they also share resources and supplies. This means they must cooperate to keep budgets in line. As an employee or member of an organization, you may find yourself sharing a workroom, a locker, a fax machine, office supplies, tools, lunch room, and secretarial and accounting services with others. You also will need to share your time and have others share their time with you in order to meet the goals of the company, conduct daily business, meet deadlines, and work cooperatively.

Types of Professional Relationships

Relationships in professional contexts typically are determined by a company's culture and by the different roles individuals fill in the company's hierarchy. In other words, your day-to-day communication with others at work probably will be shaped by your role or function within the company. Professionals usually communicate role to role, depending on their job or function within the organization. There generally are three types of relationships necessary for getting work done in a professional context. These are relationships between

- management and employees
- employees and other employees
- employees and clients or the public

As you study each of these professional relationships, pay particular attention to the importance of each and to the purpose each serves to help the organization achieve its goals.

COMMUNICATION PRACTICE LAB

Practicing Interdependent Communication

To practice communicating effectively in an interdependent relationship, follow these steps:

Step 1 Choose a partner.

Step 2 Have one partner describe an object in as much detail as possible. The partner should not name the object or hint at its identity through his or her clues and descriptions.

Step 3 The second partner should then attempt to draw the described object on a clean sheet of paper. Use a pencil to erase any mistakes.

Step 4 Exchange as much information and feedback as necessary to create an accurate drawing of the described object. Remember, the describer cannot reveal the identity of the object or assist in the drawing.

Step 5 When you have completed your drawing, share it with the class and reveal what the object is supposed to be.

Step 6 As a class, discuss the types of communication skills you used when working interdependently with your partner. Which skills were most effective and which created problems?

Management and Employees The culture, philosophy, and size of an organization usually determines the norms and protocol for communication between management and employees. In large companies, communication between upper-level management and employees may be indirect. This communication takes the form of written company policies, salaries, or benefits that establish the tone of the workplace.

For example, a chief executive officer for a large company may communicate concern for employees by providing generous sick-leave and health benefits, on-site child care, and extra vacation time as compensation for working overtime. His or her employees might then perceive the CEO as being generous and considerate. Therefore, the relationship between employees and upper-level management at that company is likely to be warm and mutually rewarding.

Communication between lower- or mid-level managers and employees tends to be more direct, immediate, and ongoing. It is more of a give-and-take type of relationship. For instance, it is the duty of all employees and managers to see that the company runs smoothly, work is carried out efficiently, and the clients' and customers' needs are met. Managers and employees must be able to communicate clearly on a day-to-day basis and cooperate as a team to accomplish all of these goals.

Importance Positive relationships between managers and employees are important for a variety of reasons. As in any other interpersonal situation, the way individuals interact and form relationships establishes a climate for communication. When this climate is positive, morale is boosted, and the mood and tone of the workplace are improved. This typically results in increased productivity and higher job satisfaction.

Purpose The purpose of positive relationships between managers and employees is to keep open the lines of communication in the workplace. Open and direct communication helps clarify expectations, procedures, policies, and deadlines. It also invites participation, suggestions, and constructive feedback. Finally, it promotes a general sense of understanding and well-being on the job and generates a climate of mutual ownership in company decisions. In short, positive relationships between various levels of management and employees make businesses operate more efficiently and successfully.

DILBERT reprinted by permission of United Feature Syndicate, Inc.

Employees and Other Employees

The everyday work of a company is most often carried out by its rank-and-file employees. Even though these individuals are not members of management, they fill different roles and command different amounts of authority depending on their job functions.

Your school, for example, probably has teachers, a secretarial staff, a maintenance staff, a food-service staff, and other employee personnel. Each has a designated role within the school's overall hierarchy. Each has his or her area of expertise or authority. In order to carry out the business of your school, all these different employees need to work in cooperation with each other.

Most of the time, employees work productively together to accomplish the goals of a company. They form positive relationships that allow them to communicate with each other and function more productively in their jobs. Sometimes, however, differing levels of authority and responsibility can lead to problems among fellow employees. Tensions and competitiveness can create barriers to effective communication.

To avoid these problems, employees need to view themselves as valued members of a team. In a team, each person has a different role that is equally vital to the team's success. Therefore, it is expected that other team members will have different responsibilities and areas of authority. Once employees learn to understand and appreciate each other's contributions in the workplace, they may find it easier to form positive and productive employee-to-employee relationships.

Importance Positive employee relationships can be so important that some companies sponsor special events to encourage employees from all divisions to get to know one another better. These events may include company softball or basketball tournaments, parties, picnics, or other social gatherings. The hope is that, through these events, employees will develop closer, more positive interpersonal relationships.

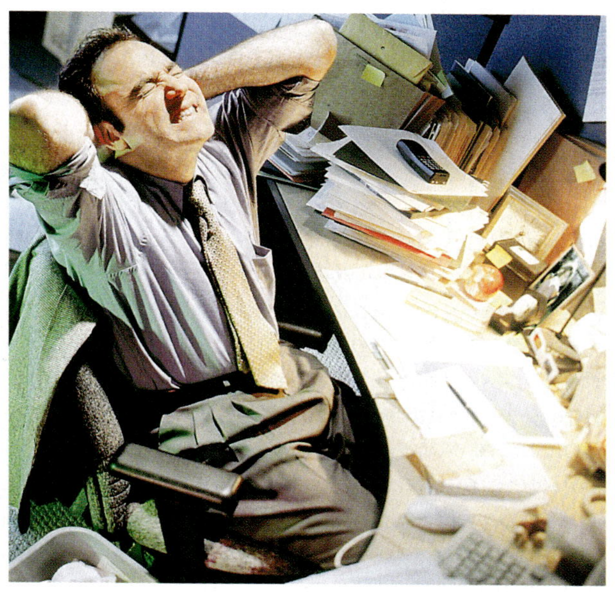

Tension and competitiveness in the workplace can create barriers to effective communication between employees. How can tension and competitiveness be avoided?

Purpose Employees who form positive relationships with coworkers have a better understanding of their interdependence with others on the job. This makes them more likely to cooperate and communicate productively in the workplace. It also adds to employees' enjoyment of their jobs. As a result, they tend to do better work. In general, employees—and the company as a whole—benefit from positive productive relationships in the workplace.

Employees and Clients or the Public

One-to-one communication between the employee and the individual customer can have a great influence on a company's success. Most companies realize that their overall image is a reflection of these interpersonal relationships. Because this is so important, businesses often train employees to interact with customers in a way that projects certain positive attributes.

One way employees send positive messages to customers or the public is by the way they dress on the job. Dress codes project an organization's philosophy about its relationship with customers. It may reflect a very professional level of communication, or it may convey a message of informality and friendliness, inviting a more casual relationship with customers. Similarly, employees usually are trained to use a pleasant voice on the telephone and handle troublesome phone calls with courtesy and efficiency. Sales associates also are trained to listen carefully and to deal with clients in a professional manner.

Importance Positive interpersonal relationships between employees and clients or the public are important because of their effect on business. If customers perceive that they have a positive relationship with a certain employee, they may be more likely to take their business to him or her.

A nurse builds an interpersonal relationship with her patient. **How does a client benefit from an interpersonal relationship with a business?**

Practice for the Workplace

Word-of-Mouth Advertising Have you ever been unhappy with the food or service at a restaurant? If you were like most customers, you probably told all of your friends about your negative experience. If that restaurant is suggested to your friends in the future, they will probably recall that you did not enjoy it. With that in mind, they will probably go to another restaurant. This is a powerful form of advertising known as word-of-mouth. Word-of-mouth is just that—words, usually in the form of an assessment, from the mouths of others. This type of information affects many of the decisions we make as consumers each day.

BUSINESS PRACTICE *Activity*

Why do you choose one store or business over another? Visit three different local businesses in the next week. Observe the actions of the employees in these businesses. Were you greeted when you entered the store? Were the employees eager to assist you? Did the sales people answer your questions correctly the first time? Did you get exactly what you wanted? How were the employees dressed? Write down examples of why you would or would not recommend these businesses to others. What areas need the most improvement and why? Share your evaluations with the rest of the class.

However, businesses aren't the only ones who benefit from these positive relationships. Forming interpersonal relationships with clients can make an employee's job more enjoyable. Customers usually benefit from better, more personalized service. Finally, open lines of communication reduce misunderstandings and lead to faster solutions when problems arise.

Purpose The main purpose of positive employee-customer relationships is to create goodwill and a feeling of loyalty. Employees who feel a sense of loyalty to their company and customers are likely to do better work and may stay with the company longer. When individual customers or the public in general feel loyal to a company, they are more likely to choose its products over a competitor's. They also tend to spread good news about the firm, generating new business. Finally, a loyal customer is more likely to be a repeat customer—which results in a better bottom line for any company.

Joan Baez works with others in a social organization. Identify why it is important for a leader to establish open lines of communication with members in a social organization.

Types of Social Relationships

When you talk with a friend or play a game of basketball with someone you just met, you are interacting on an interpersonal level in a social context. You probably have a lot of social relationships in your life. However, one type of social relationship that you may be less familiar with is your interaction with other members of an organized group or club.

These social relationships are special because they often include people of different ages, ethnicities, and backgrounds who have come together to accomplish a common goal. They also may share certain interests that they want to support in some public way. The interpersonal relationships between members of an organization can have a great impact on achievement of the group's goals. Three important relationships in this context are between

- leadership and members
- members and other members
- members and the public

Leadership and Members

Much like in the workplace, most social organizations have leaders who make sure work stays on track and goals are accomplished. Open lines of communication between leaders and members make it easier to convey information, share ideas, and solve problems. They also allow leaders to communicate their commitment and enthusiasm for a project to build group cohesiveness.

Individual members of organizations also form interpersonal relationships with their leaders. This allows members to clarify information, share ideas, and work interdependently to achieve the organization's goals. Positive relationships also serve as a motivator, keeping group members' interest and enthusiasm high and making members more productive.

Importance Effective interpersonal relationships between leaders and members are essential for the success of any organization. Without these close ties, it can be much more difficult to work as a cohesive unit to achieve onal goals. For example, when a ...rd member makes a decision that is unpopular with teachers, the quality of the teachers' work may be affected and students' education can suffer.

Problems also can occur if members do not build productive relationships with their leaders. A lack of positive one-to-one interaction between members and leaders can disrupt the communication within the organization. This can result in a lack of interest or direction, low morale, and ineffectiveness.

Purpose All of these potential problems relate directly to the need for open, supportive channels of communication between leaders and members in social organizations. The purpose of positive interpersonal relationships on this level is to build a sense of interdependence and to facilitate the achievement of goals. If the goal is to plan a special event, respect for a leader's direction may be essential to get everything ready in time.

Members and Other Members

Many times, members of social organizations may represent similar interests, ethnic groups, ages, and socio-economic levels. These common qualities provide a basis for communication and interpersonal relationships. In some social organizations, on the other hand, members may represent a wide variety of cultures and interests. Whether their interests are similar or different, members may have varying levels of communication skills.

Importance Reaching organizational goals and advancing specific causes depends on the interpersonal relationships of group members. Social organizations often sponsor events specifically to promote personal relationships and goodwill between group members. A church may have a pie supper or potluck dinner to bring members together. A team or committee may have a picnic. A large organization may hold a banquet to encourage interaction.

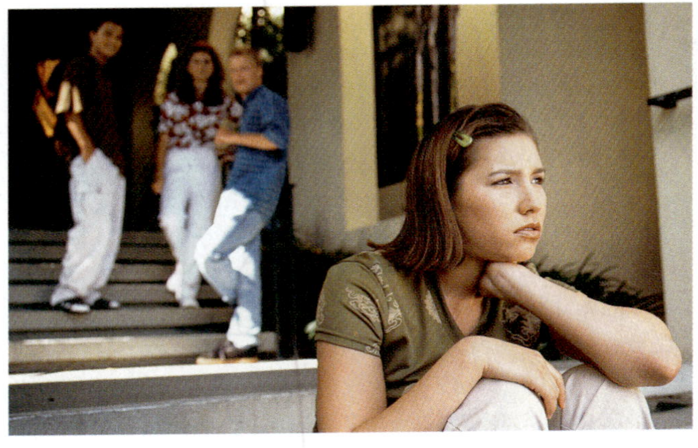

Individuals are diverse and therefore may have different interests than other group members. Why must an individual set aside his or her own personal interests when working with a group?

Most of these occasions are intended as icebreakers to allow people to get to know one another outside of the context of group work.

Purpose The first guideline for any organizational member is to set aside his or her own personal interests and focus on the group goal. Therefore, the main purpose of member-to-member relationships is not to benefit the individual—even though this is a common side effect. Rather, the main purpose in this context is group cohesiveness. When individual members use skills in assertiveness, confidence, tact, courtesy, respect, and ethics to build cooperative relationships, they create a positive environment for reaching group goals and operating a successful organization.

Members and the Public You don't have to be a specialist in advertising or public relations to understand that public image plays a large role in the success of an organization. Each member of an organization serves as the group's ambassador. Each member affects public perception of the organization through his or her relationships within the community. In turn, this public perception can influence the success of the organization.

For example, if a committee member gossips with a friend about internal conflicts in an organization, the friend may decide not to make a donation to the group's cause. A team member who constantly complains to outsiders about group members' lack of interest may unwittingly discourage someone else from joining the team.

For this reason, leaders and individual members of social organizations should communicate positively with the public. They should consistently promote the organization throughout the community. In other words, the motto "Say something good, or say nothing at all" is good advice for members who want their organization to be a success.

Importance Positive relationships between organization members and the public are important for two reasons. First, creating a sense of goodwill with the public can generate much-needed funding or support or both for the group's cause. It also can promote a sense of cooperation in the community that helps eliminate certain barriers to the group goal.

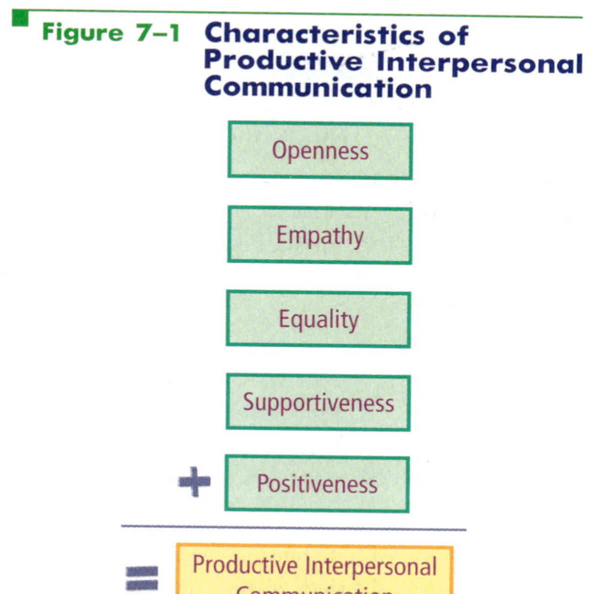

Figure 7–1 Characteristics of Productive Interpersonal Communication

Second, interpersonal relationships between group members and outsiders benefit the public. Open lines of communication allow members of the community to contribute ideas regarding the organization's work. Also, many organizations repay supportive communities by building parks, contributing money or volunteers to local events, or providing special services for the public.

Purpose The purpose of productive relationships between organizational members and the public is to create goodwill for the group and support for the group's goals. That is why it is important to always keep in mind that others view you as a representative of your organization. The image you project with your behavior and communication skills is likely to shape others' overall opinion of the organization. In short, your relationships with the public can play a large part in the success or failure of your organization.

Characteristics of Productive Interpersonal Communication

The communication choices you make every day have a great impact on your interpersonal relationships. Typically, negative, unproductive communication leads to unproductive relationships. On the other hand, positive, productive communication tends to lead to productive relationships. Thus, the question becomes, "What kind of communication skills do I need to develop to build productive relationships?"

Communication in most productive relationships seems to share some basic characteristics. These characteristics help the individuals involved feel valued and understood. If any characteristic is missing, the relationship tends

COMMUNICATION *Strategies*

KEEPING COMMUNICATION OPEN IN RELATIONSHIPS

- Use "I" messages to demonstrate ownership of all your thoughts and ideas.
- Use active listening skills and provide appropriate feedback to show your interest in others' ideas.
- Use intrapersonal and interpersonal perception checks to make sure you clearly understand others' messages.
- Carefully reflect on the messages that have been communicated so you can adapt and make appropriate decisions.

COMMUNICATING EMPATHICALLY IN RELATIONSHIPS

- Use appropriate facial expressions, eye contact, and an attentive posture to demonstrate interest in the other's messages.
- Respect the other person's feelings about personal space and physical contact.
- Use tentative but supportive language to show that you don't necessarily know all the answers but are willing to help find them.
- Use perception checks and descriptive language to help the other person express exactly what he or she is feeling.
- Listen without judging the other person's feelings or actions as right or wrong.

to suffer. Once you learn about these characteristics, you can use your knowledge to evaluate your own interpersonal communication. As Figure 7–1 on page 215 shows, the five characteristics most needed for effective interpersonal relationships are as follows:

- openness
- empathy
- equality
- supportiveness
- positiveness

Openness

In productive social and professional relationships, communication tends to be open. Open communication typically displays the following traits:

- willingness to share ideas and feelings and to disclose appropriately to others
- willingness to listen carefully and to consider the ideas and feelings of others
- willingness to reflect on the effectiveness of communication and adapt it to be more productive

Effective communicators recognize equality in communication. What does it mean to have equality in communication?

Empathy and supportiveness are characteristics for building a social relationship. **How does empathy strengthen an interpersonal relationship?**

Analyzing the Johari window in Chapter 3 provided some insight into the need for openness in communication. As you examined the various degrees of openness reflected by the four windows, you discovered that open communication leads to productive interpersonal relationships. On the other hand, closed communication—which is characterized by hesitancy to disclose, unwillingness to listen to others, and being closed to change and information about self—can seriously damage relationships.

Empathy

In addition to openness, productive relationships require empathy. Empathy, or the ability to understand and appreciate, involves feeling *with* someone rather than feeling *for* someone. In other words, you are putting yourself in someone else's position and seeing the world through his or her eyes.

Empathy does not demand that you agree or disagree with the other person's views. It simply allows you to say, "I think I understand how you're feeling." When you are able to understand and appreciate another's position, ideas, and opinions, your relationship is likely to be more harmonious and productive. The Communication Strategies checklist describes what you can do to make your communication empathic.

Equality

Competent communicators tend to view one another as equals. In professional and social contexts, individuals often have different jobs, responsibilities, status, and authority. They may have unique talents, abilities, strengths, and weaknesses, and represent a blend of different genders, ethnicities, and ages. However, equality in communication does not imply sameness. Rather, it embraces personal and cultural differences.

Equality in communication means all participating individuals have equal respect, rights, and opportunity. It asserts that individuals, regardless of their status or ability, have equal dignity as human beings. Communicators who value equality in relationships often have a general attitude of "I'm OK, and you're OK too." An underlying sense of equality lays a firm foundation for win-win communication and relationships. The following checklist provides tips for communicating with an attitude of equality.

Supportiveness

In productive relationships, the individuals involved are supportive of one another. That is, they care about and respect one another. They also encourage and help each other reach their personal and organizational goals.

As with empathy, you do not always have to agree with the other person or approve of his or her behavior to be supportive. For instance, a supportive teacher may care deeply about a student and do everything possible to help that student reach his or her goals. Still, the teacher may disapprove of that student's disruptive behavior and failure to complete assignments. The teacher may encourage the student to reach his or her potential by offering after-school tutoring or counseling.

A supportive employee will find ways to help coworkers do their jobs effectively. For instance, he or she may volunteer to help out when a coworker is given the responsibility of hosting a company picnic. He or she may offer to help prepare the food, provide transportation, or do some other task to make the coworker's job easier and ensure the picnic's success.

Supportiveness in professional and social relationships can work wonders in building trust and loyalty. It also tends to be contagious. When you are consistently supportive of others, you are more likely to be supported in your own endeavors. The Communication Strategies checklist offers some tips for being supportive in your social and professional relationships.

Global Communication

Status, Respect, and Courtesy

Some people from Japan customarily bow when greeting one another as a formal sign of respect and courtesy. Bowing is also a way to recognize the status of the other person. Identify five verbal or nonverbal actions that people in other cultures, including your own, use to show respect and to acknowledge the status of others.

Communication Strategies

Being Supportive in Relationships

- Whenever possible, use descriptive rather than evaluative language.
- Try to speak in terms of possibilities, not certainties.
- Avoid "preaching" and using negative communication strategies such as "you" statements, "why" questions, labels, and names.
- Be an active, attentive listener.
- Give appropriate nonverbal feedback.
- Use perception checks to show interest and to clarify understanding.

Establishing Equality in Relationships

- Make sure your verbal and nonverbal messages demonstrate respect, courtesy, and tact.
- Avoid evaluative, judgmental language or language that may put the other person on the defensive. This includes terms such as "should," "ought," "must," "right," and "wrong," as well as "you" statements and "why" questions.
- Demonstrate a willingness to listen carefully to others without interrupting or responding with judgmental statements.
- Use "feed forward" statements to personalize messages.
- Use perception checks to show interest and clarify understanding.

Positiveness

Positive interpersonal interactions tend to build productive relationships. Positiveness can be described several ways. First, positiveness is based on positive attitudes and communication that moves relationships and tasks toward mutually rewarding results. Positiveness is often marked by optimism, confidence that you and other individuals will be able to accomplish goals, and a general sense of well-being.

Individuals who demonstrate positiveness often encourage others through their own enthusiasm and tend to see some element of hope or humor in even the most difficult situations. Positive communication focuses more on the solution than the problem. It also provides constructive suggestions and well-deserved praise to help others reach their goals. The checklist on the right describes some ways you can encourage positiveness in your own relationships. Try to follow these strategies to become a more positive communicator.

COMMUNICATION *Strategies*

BEING POSITIVE IN RELATIONSHIPS

- ✓ Adjust your attitudes so that you consistently look on the bright side of things.
- ✓ Always expect the best from yourself and others.
- ✓ Be generous with sincere compliments and praise.
- ✓ Be an active listener, demonstrating true concern for others.
- ✓ Use nonverbal signals that show you are interested and in a pleasant frame of mind.
- ✓ Provide feedback that encourages others and gives them a sense of hope or accomplishment.

TECHNOLOGY *Activity*

Sending Copies of E-Mails To show support for a person, you can write a letter of recommendation to his or her supervisor. A letter of recommendation acknowledges accomplishments or recognizes good deeds. Copies of the letter are usually sent to the person for whom you wrote the recommendation and their other supervisors. Write a letter of recommendation for a teacher, friend, coach, or volunteer at your school. Create the letter as an e-mail message and have your teacher check the content and the format. With your teacher's approval, send a copy of the document to the subject of the letter and at least three people to whom that person reports.

INTEGRATING INTERPERSONAL SKILLS WITH TASK SKILLS

As a competent communicator in the workplace or in social settings, you will face many challenges. One of these will be balancing the communication skills necessary to carry out tasks effectively with the interpersonal skills necessary to build productive relationships. While clarity, efficiency, and accuracy may be useful for carrying out tasks, people skills such as empathy, supportiveness, and equality are more useful for strengthening relationships.

The most successful communicators learn to integrate their interpersonal skills with task skills. **Integrating** means to blend things so that they function together as a whole. Most communicators find that using a balance of skills often provides more personal satisfaction than continually focusing on task skills alone. That is, you might achieve your goals through the use of task-oriented skills. However, you can enjoy working with others and develop satisfying relationships along the way through the use of interpersonal skills.

As the previous chapters have shown, the hallmark of a competent communicator is an ability to use skills with versatility and appropriateness. Learning to size up a specific situation and use the most appropriate skills helps you grow as a communicator and build a reputation as a valued friend and colleague.

Section 1 Assessment

Visit the *Glencoe Communication Applications* Web site at **communicationapplications.glencoe.com** and click on **Self-Check and Study Guide 7.1** to review your understanding of interpersonal relationships.

Review Key Terms

1. Define this term and write it in a sentence: integrating.

Check Understanding

2. Name three types of interpersonal relationships that occur in professional contexts and three types that occur in social contexts.
3. Give a real-life example of one type of social or professional relationship. Then, explain the importance and purpose of your example relationship.
4. Imagine that you and your best friend are both hired by the same company. Compare and contrast appropriate interpersonal interaction on the job and away from the workplace.
5. **Predict** Imagine that a coworker—with whom you have a positive interpersonal relationship—has been denied a promotion because he frequently misses work. He is upset and asks for your input on the situation. Explain how you might use all five characteristics of productive communication in your discussion.

APPLICATION *Activity*

Identifying Types of Relationships Divide the class into two equal groups: one focusing on professional relationships, the other on social. With your group, brainstorm a list of job titles in a chosen company or position titles in a chosen social organization. Write your group's ideas on the chalkboard in two equal columns. Then, draw lines to randomly match up the titles in the two columns. Finally, label each match with one of the types of relationships you studied in this section. Which type of relationship was most common? Do you think that is accurate in most cases?

Applying Reading Skill

Using the Context to Define Words

Everyone has seen or heard words that they do not recognize. When you encounter a word that you have not seen or heard before, there are strategies you can use to determine that word's meaning. These strategies are based on the use of the context, or words and sentences positioned near the unfamiliar term. The information below explains how to use the context to determine the meaning of a word.

Learning the Skill

Context clues are the hints that we gather from the words surrounding an unknown term. These clues enable you, as a reader or listener, to make an "educated guess" at the meaning of the undefined word.

One context clue is the word itself. To find the meaning of an unfamiliar word, first determine its part of speech. Then, look for other uses of these parts of speech within the context. Sometimes, a similar word will be used in the same sentence. Try one of those words in place of the one you don't know. If the sentence makes sense and is still grammatically correct, you likely have found the meaning of the unknown word.

If you are still uncertain of the word's meaning, use the other parts of speech near or next to the word in the sentence. Other parts of speech can help you determine the meaning of a word. Nouns and verbs can provide clues for each other. In turn, adjectives and adverbs provide clues for nouns and verbs.

Unfortunately, you will not be able to guess the correct meaning of every word, even when you use context clues. If you are still unsure about an undefined term, you have two options. First, you can look up the meaning of the word in a dictionary. This may be necessary for words that are exceptionally technical, outdated, or rarely used. Your other option is to skip the word and hope that you will find its meaning within some later context. This technique is unreliable, so it should be used only when absolutely necessary.

Practicing the Skill

This chapter focuses on building interpersonal relationships. Some words that characterize good interpersonal relationships are used in the following sentences. Use the context clues to determine the meaning of the underlined word in each sentence.

1. The senator, proud of his reputation for honesty, is a veracious communicator.
2. Donating those coats was a very altruistic deed.
3. Our supervisor sets a good example because she is always affable when talking to customers.
4. Friends who are supportive embolden each other to try new things.
5. Effective interpersonal communicators participate fervently in lively conversations.

APPLICATION *Activity*

Reread the paragraphs on page 210 that describe relationships between management and employees. Using the context within these paragraphs, provide definitions for the following terms: *compensation, morale, perceive, mutually,* and *tone.*

Section 2

Personal Style in Interpersonal Relationships

GUIDE TO READING

Objectives

1. Identify and describe four types of personal style.
2. Determine your own current personal style.
3. Explain how differences in personal style can affect interpersonal relationships.

Terms to Learn

personal style
dominant style
influencing style
steady style
conscientious style

You probably have heard statements like "She always wears the latest style!" or "That's an interesting style of architecture," or "This author has a great writing style"—but have you ever thought of style as the way someone communicates with others?

In the first section of this chapter you learned that a competent communicator faces the challenge of integrating task skills with interpersonal skills in professional and social contexts. To communicate effectively and appropriately within these contexts, it is helpful to try to understand how you generally speak and listen to others and how others can communicate most effectively with you. Both of these situations are based on your personal style.

Personal style is a pattern of clear and consistent communication choices that reflects a person's individuality and distinguish him or her from other individuals. Your personal communication style describes how you relate to others and the world around you. It refers to your attitudes, your use of language, your nonverbal expressions, and your use of listening skills. In short, your personal style is a blueprint of who you are.

Oprah Winfrey exhibits her personal style while interacting with guests on her television show. What is personal style?

Identifying Personal Style

The first and most important rule about personal style is that no single style is better than any other. They are just different. Once you understand that, you can learn to analyze your own and others' styles and adapt your communication to be more effective. You also can learn to integrate personal styles to accomplish goals more efficiently.

Finally, understanding people's personal communication styles can help you predict and avoid many different kinds of conflict. For instance, it can help you learn not to take certain types of communication personally. It also can help you avoid finding fault or blame when you encounter someone with a different personal style.

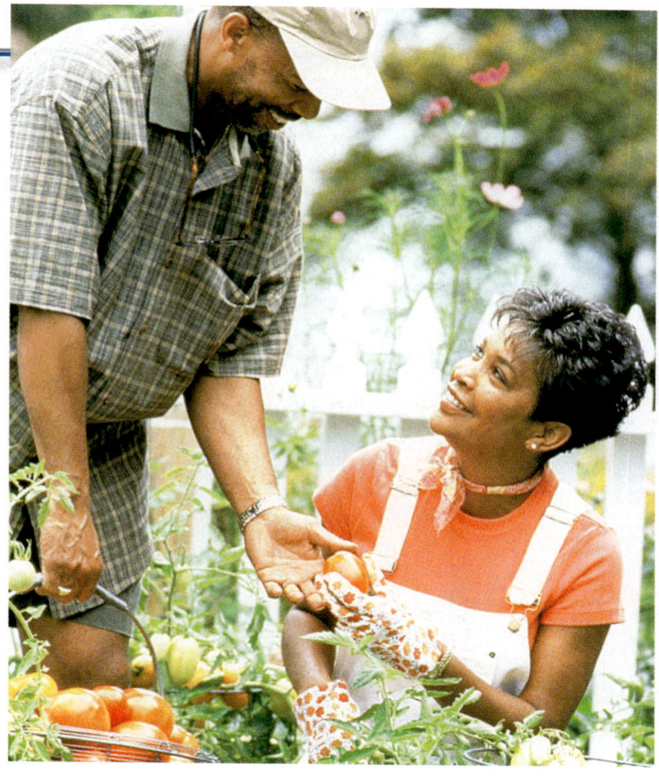

One's personal communication style describes how that person communicates with others. What is included in one's personal communication style?

Four Types of Personal Style

Have you ever taken a "personality test" just for fun? If so, you may have been surprised to find that, for the most part, you fit the profile of a general personality category.

Of course everyone is unique. Therefore, no behavioral category will describe you perfectly. However, in most cases, your basic traits can identify you as a particular personality type. The same is true for communication types.

The following information about personal communication style is widely used by businesses for making decisions about hiring, promotions, assignments, training, and counseling. It often is used by social organizations to organize teams and assign persons to groups where their style will complement the style of others and strengthen the effectiveness of a group. Individuals also tend to make day-to-day communication choices based on a basic understanding of personal style—even if they are unfamiliar with the study of personal style.

As you read the description of each style, you probably will recognize yourself and other people you know. It may be helpful to note that most people tend to have one predominant style. This is referred to as your "high" style, which describes your usual approach to conducting business and dealing with others. It also is important to note, however, that most people also exhibit characteristics from other styles. In fact, we probably all exhibit some degree of each of the four types of personal style shown in the following list:

- dominant
- influencing
- steady
- conscientious

"HIGH D" CHARACTERISTICS

How the High D Speaks	• Direct and to the point • Can be blunt and critical • Can be sarcastic • Gives instructions for the big picture but often omits details that must be accomplished before the project can get under way • Inspires others but can be overly optimistic in the actual carrying out of the plan • Does not hide accomplishments and can be self-centered in his or her talk • Will escalate conflict • Can be manipulative in order to get desired results • Will close off all communication except through a messenger when highly stressed • Sometimes needs to be confronted to get his or her attention—you may have to push back to gain respect
How the High D Listens	• Not a patient listener; seldom seeks others' opinions • Wants brief answers • Wants the bottom line first and reasons or contingencies second • Will ask questions if he or she wants more detail • Is more interested in task-oriented information than in people issues
How to Speak to a High D	• Provide direct answers; be brief and to the point. • Ask "what" questions, never "how" questions. • Stick to business; outline the possibilities for the person to get results, solve problems, or be in charge. • Stress the logic of specific ideas or approaches. • Agree with the facts and ideas, not the person. • Provide facts and figures about the probability of success or the effectiveness of options. • Show how the person will reach his or her goals.

Dominant ("High D") Style

According to research, about 15 percent of all people have a highly dominant personal style. A **dominant style** of communication is one that is fast-paced and more task-oriented than people-oriented. Highly dominant communicators, or "High D's," often appear very businesslike and want others to quickly get to the point of their messages. High D's generally like others to be efficient and decisive. They want to get things done but may have little patience for details. For this reason, they often delegate detail work to others who they feel are competent.

High D's typically are "movers and shakers"—outgoing risk-takers whose goal is to get results. If something gets in the way of reaching a desired result, a High D will do whatever is necessary to overcome the obstacle. High D's typically are skilled at providing direction to others. Therefore, they often are sought out as leaders.

This drill sergeant exemplifies a dominant style of communication. Describe how High D's generally appear to others and how they want others to communicate.

"HIGH I" CHARACTERISTICS

How the High I Speaks	• Friendly initiator of communication • Spontaneous and often humorous • Makes positive and enthusiastic remarks • Physically expressive with face, tone of voice, and gestures • Often promises more than he or she can deliver • Uses excuses liberally • Influences and persuades others through verbal praise • Makes judgments intuitively rather than by analyzing the data • A physical communicator, shaking hands, giving hugs, patting shoulders • Has a real need to express himself or herself verbally and at length
How the High I Listens	• Responsive • Encourages speakers verbally and nonverbally • May interrupt in order to compare experiences, not to dominate • Very empathic because of his or her high degree of emotionality • May hear only what he or she wants to hear • May not hear negatives • May react too quickly to a speaker's first few words and then inappropriately offer comments out of context
How to Speak to a High I	• Be a good listener. • Provide a chance for him or her to verbalize about ideas, people, and his or her intuitions. • Speak in democratic terms such as "we" or "the team," rather than "I'm the boss. You do what I say." • Give the big picture without getting bogged down in details. However, be sure you put the details in writing. • Provide testimonials from people he or she sees as important and prominent. • Provide extra incentives, since he or she enjoys being recognized as a leader. • Lead the High I step-by-step to conclusions. He or she may tend to jump to conclusions and not be analytical. • Be willing to converse about items of mutual interest before getting down to business. • Be very realistic. High I optimism does not need support from you. • Give clear instructions, then get a firm commitment through a handshake or in writing. • Confront the High I only as a last resort. Persuasion and encouragement work better. • Accept his or her failures and encourage rather than punish.

Influencing ("High I") Style The influencing style is sometimes referred to as the "interactor" style. Another 15 percent of the population falls into this category. An **influencing style** of communication is one that is fast-paced and more people-oriented than task-oriented. Highly influencing communicators, or "High I's," tend to be extroverted, enthusiastic, outgoing, spontaneous, and optimistic. High I's often appear very stylish and like stimulating conversation. They sometimes have difficulty with boring or routine tasks. They get results by influencing and persuading others.

High I's often are valued and sought out by others because of their fun-loving, optimistic nature. Yet, they also enjoy having others recognize their achievements with compliments and other methods of recognition. For example, because a High I is often a friendly initiator, he or she might walk into a team, committee, or other type of group meeting, smile, introduce himself or herself to new people, and welcome the newcomers to the meeting. A High I might then make a comment about one of the positive accomplishments the group or an individual had recently made.

"HIGH S" CHARACTERISTICS

How the High S Speaks	• Usually not the initiator of conversation or new ideas; likes the stability of a group, so he or she often refers to work situations as "we" or "our" business • Gives practical advice • Prefers to ask "how" questions rather than "if" or "when" questions because he or she is not comfortable initiating decisions • Always takes time to think things over • Is very faithful and loyal—sometimes to a fault—when it comes to people in institutions • May not communicate well under stress, keeping thoughts and feelings to self and becoming silent or noninvolved • Will not attack, suppressing own anger; however, will hold a grudge • Stores up a list of grievances, ultimately making him or her suspicious of others • Can overuse kindness when assertiveness would have been more effective • Often will not say "no" when it needs to be said • Presents well-thought-out, logical, orderly, step-by-step plans • Can be blunt when disagreeing with others or defending self • Withholds expression of true feelings and rarely expresses much enthusiasm • Tends to think in terms of either/or rather than compromise
How the High S Listens	• Patient, empathic listener because of his or her people involvement • Prefers honesty and openness • Tends to withhold evaluative feedback; has excellent insights—although he or she won't share unless asked • Often creates an open-door atmosphere in which sharing thoughts about work as well as family and personal issues is acceptable • Controls emotional expression so the speaker feels accepted • Can be a wonderful conversationalist because he or she is a wonderful listener
How to Speak to a High S	• Provide a sincere, personable, and agreeable environment. • Show sincere interest in the person and, particularly, in his or her family. • Ask "how" questions to get his or her opinions. • Draw out his or her goals systematically. • Present new ideas or departures from the status quo in a non-threatening manner and show the benefits to the High S. • Clearly define goals in any new plans and point out how the High S fits into those plans. • Provide personal assurance and reassurance. • Give the High S constant, specific appreciation. • Refrain from aggression, ultimatums, and conflict. • Always use logical, systematic, rational systems when explaining or asking for cooperation. • Give him or her time to process information and make decisions. • Be loyal and supportive.

Steady ("High S") Style About 35 percent of the population has a personal communication style known as the steady, or "High S," style. The **steady style** tends to be slow-paced and both people- and task-oriented. As a result, these communicators typically are cooperative and efficient and can be counted on to get the job done. High S's are fairly reserved, pay attention to detail, love structure, and are very stable. They also are good team players, even though they may appear somewhat pessimistic. High S's tend to appear casual and conforming. Because High S's reach their objectives by cooperating, they tend to have warm personalities and a calming effect on others.

Conscientious ("High C") Style About 35 percent of the population falls into the conscientious, or "High C," category of personal style. The **conscientious style** tends to be slow-paced and task-oriented. High C's are highly analytical perfectionists who love detail. They also tend to be introverts, guarded in their

"HIGH C" CHARACTERISTICS

How the High C Speaks	• May pass the buck if you go to him or her for answers • May yield a position in order to avoid controversy • Becomes defensive when threatened • Exact about details; feels quality is extremely important; may talk at great length about details that don't seem important to other styles of communicators • Asks many, many detailed questions to clarify the other person's position • Slow to respond because he or she must process all the information • Extremely critical of own work and, often, highly critical of others who do not meet his or her expectations • Influences others by collecting and organizing factual data and logical presentations • Seldom admits to true emotional reactions and will withhold insights and opinions until he or she feels it is safe to share them • Seldom gives positive feedback of appreciation to others • Has a special talent for organizing and communicating instructions correctly • Follows life's rules and fulfills commitments • As a method of analysis, he or she often will seek someone's opinion only to argue with it or move on to seek someone else's opinion • Very cautious about expressing opinions or making recommendations until all data have been checked and rechecked • Enjoys intellectual argument as a way of exercising his or her reasoning abilities • May seem to take little initiative or contribute few ideas; fears criticism and may keep to self to feel protected
How the High C Listens	• Attentive, intuitive listener; sensitive to the feelings of the speaker • May miss the main point and get off on tangents • Will ask many, many questions—which, at times, may begin to feel like an attack • Will need to hear the same things repeatedly, reprocess the same information, and ask the same questions • Will take criticism or comments personally although they were not aimed directly at the High C
How to Speak to a High C	• Take time to prepare your case logically in advance. • Provide straight pros and cons of the ideas and support ideas with accurate data. • Provide exact job descriptions with precise explanations of how each fits into the big picture. • Provide reassurance that no surprises will occur. • Provide a step-by-step approach to the goal. • Be specific if agreeing; if disagreeing, disagree with the facts, not the person. • Be prepared to provide many explanations and answer "how" and "if" questions in a patient, persistent manner. • Encourage verbal independence as well as job independence. • Provide many assurances that you value quality and accuracy. • Refrain from antagonistic responses that breed withdrawal and avoidance. • Offer as much reassurance and support as possible; assure the High C that everything will be all right.

relationships and avoiding risk at all costs. Because of this, High C's tend to seek the safety of rules and regulations and appear very formal and conservative. They follow rules and meet deadlines conscientiously and expect others to do the same. They get results by working within the guidelines or prescribed structure to ensure quality and accuracy. High C's sometimes prefer to work alone rather than in groups, but often they are sought out for advice about routine and details.

Interpersonal conflict occurs between a referee and coach. How can one avoid interpersonal conflict?

Analyzing Style to Prevent Interpersonal Conflict

You may have heard people talk about personality conflicts. Many times, these problems reflect a conflict in personal communication style.

Consider, for example, the pace at which each style works. This factor alone can cause different styles to come into conflict in the workplace. For instance, the fast-paced High D who cares little about details and thinks only about results may come into direct conflict with the slower-paced High S who is detail-oriented. The fast-paced, outgoing High I and the slow-paced, structure-oriented High C may annoy one another when working together.

Determining Your Personal Style

You may have characteristics of all the personal styles described. However, you can try to get an idea of which style best describes you by completing the Communication Practice Lab on the next page. Once you do this, you may have a better idea of how to handle conflicts in communication situations with others who have a style different from yours.

Avoiding Conflict If you examine the tables provided for each personal style, you probably will see a number of areas in which conflicts are likely to occur. These may include pace, attention or lack of attention to details, openness, willingness to change, and people versus task orientation.

To avoid conflict, you may find it helpful to adapt your own communication behavior slightly from relationship to relationship. For example, if you are a High I and your boss is a High C, you can use your knowledge of the two styles to avoid problems. You might make a special effort to get your reports done quickly and efficiently. You also might have a coworker check your work for accuracy before you give it to the boss.

If you are a High D, you might try to be more aware of your tendency to be overly aggressive in pursuit of results. You might make a point of developing empathic listening skills and work toward developing sensitivity and empathy for your slower-paced counterparts who, after all, are really responsible for getting the work done.

Another thing that can help you avoid conflict is realizing that a person's communication style is his or her natural orientation toward getting work done. It really has nothing to do

*inter*NET ACTIVITY

Analyzing Your Personality To understand yourself better, you can analyze your personality. Conduct an Internet search using *personality tests* as your search term. You will find several surveys, questionnaires, and personality profiles. These tests are scientifically designed to try to pinpoint your personality type. They are usually in a multiple-choice format. Review at least three different personality assessment tests or surveys. What do the tests have in common? What is different about each test? Ask your guidance counselor which tests are used the most. For what purposes are the results of personality tests used?

COMMUNICATION PRACTICE LAB

Personal Style

To practice determining your own personal style, follow these steps:

Step 1 Divide the class into four groups.

Step 2 Work with your group to develop a list of fifteen adjectives that describe one specific personal style. (Be sure each of the four groups describes a different style.) Describe how a person of that style might be perceived by coworkers, bosses, or other group members.

Step 3 Present your group's list of adjectives to the class and write them on the chalkboard. Discuss all the lists as a class and make any necessary changes.

Step 4 On a separate sheet of paper, copy the Personal Style Profile and Scoring Sheet found on pages 647 and 648 of the Appendix. Take the profile and determine which style best describes you. Write that style on a sheet of paper. Then, below that style, write the remaining three styles in the order that they describe you.

Step 5 Choose four adjectives that describe you and your personal style. Compare these adjectives to the ones the class listed under that style.

Step 6 Compare personal styles as a class. Discuss how all four styles work interdependently to help your class function and get work done.

with that person's perception of you. This realization can help you depersonalize the individual's actions and better understand him or her.

Finally, you may be less likely to clash with others if you realize that all four styles are necessary to get work done in professional and social contexts. We need High D's to get us going and keep us on task. We need the optimism, energy, and humor of High I's to establish a positive and creative atmosphere on the job. We need High S's to calm us down—and sometimes slow us down—so we can do the job right. We need High C's to keep us on task and in line with the rules. Regardless of which style you identify with, you are a valuable force in the workplace.

Section 2 Assessment

Visit the *Glencoe Communication Applications* Web site at **communicationapplications.glencoe.com** and click on **Self-Check and Study Guide 7.2** to review your understanding of personal style in interpersonal relationships.

Review Key Terms

1. Define each term and write it in a sentence: personal style, dominant style, influencing style, steady style, conscientious style.

Check Understanding

2. Name each type of personal style and describe its main characteristics.

3. Which style most closely describes you? Explain how you might use that communication style effectively in the workplace.

4. **Predict** Imagine that you are a High C and your partner on a class project is a High I. How do you think these different styles might affect your working relationship? How might you both adapt your communication behavior to work together productively?

APPLICATION *Activity*

Integrating Personal Styles Choose a partner with a personal style that is different from your own. (If none is available, choose someone whose secondary styles are in a different order.) Next, imagine the two of you must work together as boss and employee. Discuss how you each might adapt your behaviors to avoid conflict and better meet each other's communication needs. Then, switch roles. Share your conclusions with the class.

Communication Self-Assessment

Interpersonal Communication Skills

How Do You Rate?

On a separate sheet of paper, use the key to respond to the following statements. Put a check mark at the end of each skill you would like to improve.

KEY: **A** Always, **U** Usually, **S** Sometimes, **R** Rarely, **N** Never

1. I try to maintain a positive attitude in my relationships with others.
2. I use "I" messages in my interpersonal communication to show ownership of my thoughts and ideas.
3. I use active listening skills and provide appropriate verbal and nonverbal feedback in my interpersonal communication.
4. I use supportive language to show my willingness to help find answers to questions.
5. I use perception checks to make sure I clearly understand others' messages.
6. I try to listen without being judgmental, and I try to avoid preaching.
7. I avoid evaluative language.
8. I use feed-forward statements to personalize messages.
9. I give frequent and specific compliments and praise.
10. I try to understand each person's interpersonal style and adapt my communication to it.

How Do You Score?

Review your responses. Give yourself 5 points for every A, 4 for every U, 3 for every S, 2 for every R, and 1 for every N. Total your points and evaluate your score.

41–50 Excellent You may be surprised to find out how much you can improve your skills.

31–40 Good In this course, you can learn ways to make your skills better.

21–30 Fair Practice applying the skills taught in this course.

1–20 Needs Improvement Carefully monitor your improvement as you work through this course.

Setting Communication Goals

If you scored Excellent or Good, complete Part A. If your score was Fair or Needs Improvement, complete Part B.

Part A

1. I plan to put the following ideas into practice:
2. I plan to share the following information about communication with the following people:

Part B

1. The behaviors I need to change most are:
2. To bring about these changes, I will take these steps:

Writing a Letter of Complaint

A letter of complaint is a way of expressing unhappiness with the quality of a product or service. You might write a letter of complaint to ask that a damaged product be replaced, request compensation for inferior goods, or avoid a similar problem in the future. Some suggestions for writing a letter of complaint are provided below.

Be Specific. Explain the problem you are writing about in as much detail as possible. State the problem clearly and specifically so that the recipient understands all of the important details. For example, a manufacturer would not know where to look for a problem if you wrote only, "Your products don't work!" Provide the make and model number of the product, where and when it was purchased, and then carefully describe the problem you're having with it.

Be Objective and Polite. Maintain a friendly, positive tone in your letter. Avoid threats, insults, and strong emotional responses. Don't make an enemy of the person who reads your letter. He or she needs clear, logical information in order to solve your problem. Do not blame a specific person or group of people. If you can suggest that a simple misunderstanding is at fault, you are more likely to receive a prompt, courteous, and satisfying reply.

Use Proper Procedure. Manufacturers often have specific procedures for returning merchandise. Make sure that you abide by these policies. If you are asked to send an item back in its original package, be sure to do so. If you are asked to send proof of purchase, do this as well.

Ask for the Compensation You Want. Most companies want to change your unfavorable opinion of them before you tell others about your negative experience. Let companies know what actions you expect them to take. If you would like a replacement for a defective product, say so. If you received poor or unfriendly service, ask that the sales staff be spoken to about their professional etiquette. If you would like your money back for an inferior product, make this clear. If an item has been repaired but still does not work, let the company know if you want a proper repair job or if you would prefer to get your money back.

Keep a Copy of Your Letter. If you need to write to the same company again, attach copies of all previous correspondence.

For additional information about business writing, see the *Guide to Business Communication* section of the Communication Survival Kit in the Appendix.

Communication Through Writing

The following is a letter of complaint about a defective part in an automobile. Note how the customer is specific, objective, politely goes through the proper procedures, and asks for compensation.

575 Olympic Street
Seattle, WA 98060
January 28, 2003

United Motors, Inc.
8415 Sandhill Road
Lafayette, IN 47901

Dear United Motors, Inc.:

I am writing to inform you that your new Pacesetters may have a design flaw in the steering column assembly. According to the mechanic who repaired mine, the wiring is bundled so tightly that it is no wonder a cable frayed and parted after only a few weeks of wear.

On the morning of January 22, 2003, with all four members of my family aboard, I was turning our new Pacesetter from southbound Orion onto Burlington Boulevard in Seattle. All of a sudden, I was trying to steer a car that had no power steering. If traffic had not been unusually light, I might not have been able to guide the car safely to the berm. My family and I were lucky to escape harm.

I bought the car new at your dealership last November 19. At the time of the incident, the odometer read 1,455 miles.

Westgate Automotive, Inc., repaired the steering column assembly and promised that the car would be safe to drive, but I am not satisfied. I want to have the car thoroughly examined by your own experts because neither my wife nor I trust it as we used to. We also think you should reimburse us for the repairs.

Yours truly,
Drew Brooks
Drew Brooks

Use the steps outlined earlier and the following facts to write an effective letter of complaint.

- You bought a toy truck from Land of Toys at 1771 West Elm Street in your town last week.
- You are enclosing a copy of the receipt.
- The first time the child played with it, both front tires fell off.
- You want either a refund or a new toy truck.

Write your letter of complaint and then share it with a classmate. Read your classmate's letter, and suggest improvements if you can. If you were an employee of Land of Toys, how would you respond to the complaint letter you wrote? Why

CHAPTER 7 Assessment and Activities

GLENCOE Online

Visit the *Glencoe Communication Applications* Web site at **communicationapplications.glencoe.com** and click on **Chapter 7 Activity** for additional information about interpersonal communication.

Reviewing Key Terms

Read each statement. On a separate sheet of paper, write whether the statement is true or false. If the statement is false, rewrite it so that it reads true. Underline the words that you substitute to make statements true.

1. The dominant style of communication is slow-paced and more task-oriented than people-oriented.
2. A person with a steady style of communication tends to be critical and sarcastic.
3. A person with a conscientious style of communication is generally both people- and task-oriented.
4. Integrating means to blend things so they function as a whole.
5. The conscientious style of communication often includes spontaneity and humor.
6. Personal style is a pattern of clear and consistent choices that reflects a person's individuality.

Reviewing Key Concepts

1. What are the three types of relationships in a professional context?
2. Give three purposes for open and direct communication in the workplace.
3. How do some companies encourage employees to get to know one another better?
4. A receptionist at a doctor's office dresses in jeans and T-shirts and uses a pleasant phone voice. What kinds of messages is this worker sending to clients who visit the office or call on the phone?
5. What is the main purpose of trying to maintain a positive employee-customer relationship?
6. How do positive relationships with leaders in a social organization motivate members?
7. List the five characteristics of an effective interpersonal relationship.
8. Identify and briefly describe the dominant characteristics of each type of personal style.

Assessment and Activities

Reading and Critical Thinking Skill

1. **Cause-Effect** What is often the effect when one person's communication with another is rude?
2. **Making Comparisons** How is communication between upper-level managers and employees different from that between lower- or mid-level managers and employees?
3. **Synthesis** A student brings home a report card with five Cs and one D. Formulate a question or comment that this student's parent might make that avoids evaluative, judgmental language.
4. **Classifying Information** Which style of communicator wants brief, direct answers?

Skill Practice Activity

Using Word Context Clues A reader can often guess the meaning of an unfamiliar word based on the context, or the passage in which the word is used. Write your definition of the underlined word based on its context:

Because High S's <u>attain</u> their objectives by cooperating with others, they tend to have warm personalities and a calming effect on the group.

Cooperative Learning Activity

Evaluating Communication Styles With a partner, create a survey that determines a person's communication style. Write multiple-choice items for which each answer represents a different style. Base the items on the charts in Section 2. Work on the item stems with your partner. Share the task of writing the answers by writing the options for two styles and letting your partner write the options for the others. Use the following item as a model.

When carrying out a plan, you tend to be

A. overly optimistic (High D)

B. spontaneous and humorous (High I)

C. thoughtful, orderly, and logical (High S)

D. exact about details (High C)

Chapter Project

Planning Share with the class the survey that you created for the Cooperative Learning Activity. As a class, select the best questions from each pair of students and combine them into a new survey. Make copies of the survey and distribute them to teachers, counselors, and other adults in your school. Collect the completed surveys and evaluate the results. Choose a communication style and write a brief article about its characteristics. List ways to interact with this style as a competent communicator.

Presenting As a class, choose the best article about each communication style. Publish the four articles as a series in the school newspaper or as a separate communications handbook.

CHAPTER 8 Developing Effective Interpersonal Skills

WHY IT'S IMPORTANT

Whether you are speaking to someone you would like to have as a friend or an employer, the quality of that relationship depends, in part, on the appropriateness of your speech.

To better understand interpersonal communication, view the **Communication in Action** Chapter 8 video lesson.

"The trouble with . . . is [he/she] lacks the power of conversation but not the power of speech."

—Bernard Shaw, British author

GLENCOE Online

Visit the *Glencoe Communication Applications* Web site at **communicationapplications.glencoe.com** and click on **Overview–Chapter 8** to preview information about interpersonal skills.

Section 1

Communicating Interpersonally

GUIDE TO READING

Objectives

1. Describe strategies for participating appropriately in conversations.
2. Devise clear and appropriate requests.
3. Describe strategies for giving clear and accurate directions.
4. Recognize the importance of appropriate and purposeful questions.
5. Respond appropriately to the requests, directions, and questions of others.

Terms to Learn

open-ended question
closed question
paraphrase

What if you were to meet the President of the United States? Would you greet him the same way that you greet your best friend? Of course not. You have built a more interpersonal relationship with your friend. Together you have developed a unique way of speaking and listening to each other.

As you learned in Chapter 2, interpersonal communication takes place anytime messages are exchanged between two or more people. Interpersonal communication within social and professional contexts can take place at home, at school, in the community, or at work. Every day you communicate with a number of different people. You talk to members of your family, friends, teachers, other group members, and, possibly, coworkers and employers.

Although the purpose for your communication may vary from contact to contact, one goal remains constant: You want your communication to be as successful as possible. To accomplish this, you need to learn techniques for participating effectively in conversations.

Interpersonal communication takes place between these coworkers as they have lunch. What goal remains constant for communication in any relationship?

Communication provides the means for one employee to explain a procedure to another. What is small talk?

Becoming an Effective Conversationalist

Conversations help people in an organization understand the organization's culture. In addition, conversations help people do their jobs more effectively. In social and professional organizations, conversations allow a free flow of information. They also enable people to clarify job tasks; persuade employees, coworkers, or superiors to do something; or ask for opinions on work-related issues. Finally, conversations are useful for providing guidance on procedures or policies in the workplace or organization.

Initiating Conversations

Some people find it easy to begin conversations. If you are not one of these people, it may seem awkward or difficult for you to begin talking with someone. However, by following a few simple steps, you can become a good conversationalist.

Begin with Small Talk. In many social and business situations, conversations begin with what is called "small talk." Small talk is the kind of light, social "chitchat" that initiates a conversation. Small talk simply breaks the ice and sets the tone for the communication.

Small-Talk Topics

Small talk can span a broad range of topics, but it is all similar in one respect. Small talk almost always takes on a superficial, somewhat distant tone. In other words, it does not involve strong opinions, feelings, or great detail. In general, topics for small talk tend to revolve around three categories: environment, personal characteristics, and biography.

Guidelines for Small Talk Small talk is a starting point for developing valuable social and professional relationships. To use small talk effectively for these purposes, use the guidelines in the Communication Strategies checklist on the following page.

Check Nonverbal Signals. Before you initiate any conversation, check the nonverbal signals you and your receiver are sending. If your nonverbal messages show confidence and poise, they can help to make a positive impression on the person with whom you'll be conversing. If the other person appears distant or uninterested, perhaps he or she is not interested in small talk.

Take the Lead. Often, the hardest part of small talk is the first few words. Fortunately, the more you take the initiative, the easier it gets. So, how do you start? It's simple. Just say something. Introduce yourself. Offer a sincere compliment. You might make this

COMMUNICATION
Strategies
INITIATING CONVERSATION WITH SMALL TALK
Check nonverbal signals.
Take the lead.
Ask open-ended questions.
Stick to safe topics.
Don't rush or skip the small talk.

initial contact by commenting on the weather, saying something humorous, or even asking the time.

Ask Open-Ended Questions. Once you have made initial contact, move into small talk by asking open-ended questions. An open-ended question is broad in scope, requiring more than a single-word answer such as "Yes" or "No." Open-ended questions draw answers from a person and help shy or reluctant conversationalists take an active role in the dialogue.

Open-ended questions are much more effective than closed questions in the context of a conversation. A closed question is one that requires a very specific answer, often just one word. A closed question such as "Did you see the big game last night?" requires only a "Yes" or "No."

Stick to Safe Topics. Another tip for effective small talk is to keep the conversation "safe" and light. You can talk about school, work, sports, hobbies, or other interests that you might have in common. However, you should avoid personal or controversial topics such as politics, religion, personal beliefs or values, criticisms, or topics that can be misinterpreted as reflecting bias or harassment.

Don't Rush or Skip the Small Talk. Small talk is an important buffer that allows both parties to warm up to more purposeful communication. Although it should be kept fairly brief, rushing through small talk or skipping it entirely can make your communication seem abrupt, awkward, or even rude.

Maintaining Conversations

During the small-talk phase of a conversation, the parties form opinions and impressions and decide whether they want to maintain the communication. If they decide that the communication is not worth their time, they may excuse themselves from the situation or simply stop contributing to the exchange. If they wish to maintain the conversation, the tone and topic is likely to become more meaningful, moving toward the real reason for the contact. Your goal is to maintain the conversation so it can move to a level necessary to achieve the reason for the conversation. The basic strategies for participating effectively in conversations are found in the Communication Strategies checklist on the next page.

COMMON TOPICS FOR SMALL TALK

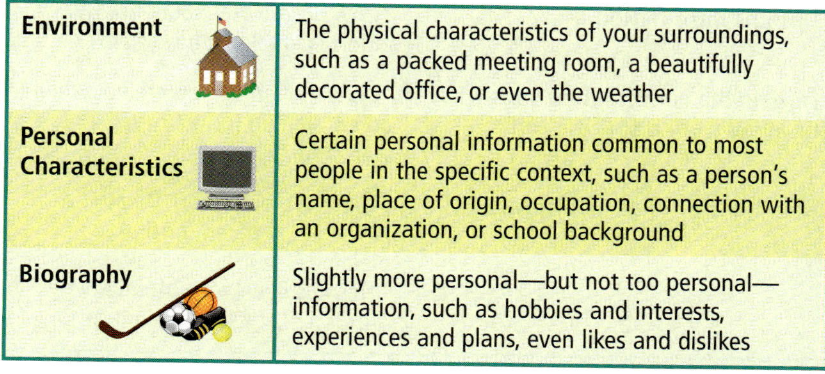

Environment	The physical characteristics of your surroundings, such as a packed meeting room, a beautifully decorated office, or even the weather
Personal Characteristics	Certain personal information common to most people in the specific context, such as a person's name, place of origin, occupation, connection with an organization, or school background
Biography	Slightly more personal—but not too personal—information, such as hobbies and interests, experiences and plans, even likes and dislikes

Choose Only Appropriate Topics. People who converse effectively often develop a set of proven topics to choose from. So, what topics are appropriate for maintaining a conversation in social and professional situations? That depends in part on the purpose and context of your communication. Is this a business meeting of new clients? Are you at a staff meeting at your workplace? Is this a club gathering or social event? While your small talk and conversation do not necessarily have to relate directly to the context, you will want to choose topics that would be of interest to someone in that specific group. Also, try to choose topics that you know something about. This allows you to contribute something of value to the conversation.

COMMUNICATION Strategies

PARTICIPATING EFFECTIVELY IN CONVERSATIONS

- Choose appropriate topics.
- Ask effective questions.
- Use tact and courtesy.
- Demonstrate confidence and assertiveness.
- Demonstrate immediacy.
- Practice ethical communication.
- Balance speaking and listening.

Ask Effective Questions. Knowing information about many different topics allows you to ask effective questions. Questions are probably the most powerful tool you can use to maintain a conversation. People enjoy talking about themselves and voicing their own opinions. They may even see questions as a type of compliment that says, "I think you're interesting. Tell me more." Questions allow you to put the other person in the spotlight. You show respect for that person's knowledge and opinions by asking him or her to share information and insights with you.

Use Tact and Courtesy. Tact is knowing what to do or say—or *not* do or say—to maintain a positive professional exchange. A tactful person uses a considerate, courteous, and respectful tone to manage difficult communication situations without offending others. He or she understands that communication is powerful. It can help solve problems or make them worse, depending on the message and how it is communicated. In addition, a tactful communicator also understands that people prefer to be treated with courtesy in day-to-day communication. The best way to call out courteous behavior from other people is to be courteous yourself.

USING QUESTIONS TO MAINTAIN CONVERSATION

Purpose of Question	Example
Draws others into the conversation	"I'm thinking about taking that class. Do you think I should?"
Obtains information	"How do you feel about our new automated telephone system?"
Directs the conversation toward or away from a specific topic	"I just thought of something. When do we sign up for the new workshop?"
Maintains or ends an interaction	"That's a great report. What else have you prepared for the meeting?" *or* "This has been very informative, hasn't it? Let's talk again next time."

Tact can be a valuable skill in professional and social contexts. When a conversation moves toward a new topic—particularly if it is unusual or controversial—pay close attention to verbal and nonverbal feedback. Look for signs of interest or boredom, agreement or disagreement. If the other person seems uncomfortable, you may wish to steer the conversation elsewhere.

Sometimes, you will be the one who feels uncomfortable or disagrees. To tactfully disagree with someone else's opinion, try to find some part of the statement with which you can agree. Then, gently and courteously lead into your perspective by saying something like, "I can see what you're saying, but what about . . . ?" You may even want to compliment the other person by saying, "That's a unique way to look at the issue. I can tell you really feel strongly about it." Either of these methods can help you maintain the positive climate of a conversation.

Global Communication

Appropriate Conversations

Although some people who live in the United States openly discuss their personal relationships and family activities, people from other cultures might consider questions about these topics intrusive. Many people from cultures outside the United States do not discuss their families, personal relationships, religious beliefs, or political opinions in the workplace. Why do you think these subjects are so sensitive? What are some other topics that might be considered offensive?

Demonstrate Confidence and Assertiveness. In conversation, it is important to offer your ideas about a topic in a clear, direct manner. Include in these comments some statements of how you hope the other person will respond to your proposal or information. For instance, if someone asks you for a report on the status of your project, you might respond with a statement such as, "I will have that to you within the hour if that is acceptable to you." Your response indicates your confidence in meeting the request, and provides a window for the listener to respond.

In addition, there are other practices that will indicate confidence and assertiveness. To show the other person that you are focusing on the conversation, use some of the suggestions given in Chapter 5, such as nodding, making appropriate gestures, and maintaining a conversational posture that is neither threatening nor distant.

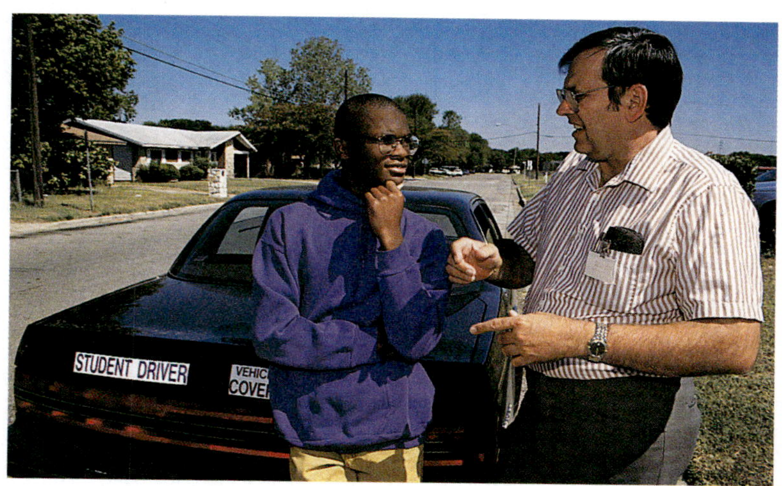

A student driver questions his instructor to learn more about driving. Besides gathering information, what do questions allow one to do?

Demonstrate Immediacy. Remember that immediacy means that you are approachable. In conversations in social and workplace contexts, you want to show the other person that you are interested in what he or she has to say. The Communication Strategies checklist can serve as a guide to demonstrating immediacy in conversations.

Practice Ethical Communication. Each person has a different set of ethical standards based on his or her priorities and values. Even so, some basic assumptions apply to communicating ethically. Generally speaking, communicators should be able to assume the following:

- What is being said in conversation is both true and complete as far as the communicators know.
- One person is not trying to deceive the other about shared information or opinions on the topic.
- Information given in confidence will be considered private and not revealed to others.
- Verbal and nonverbal messages are consistent with the meanings they communicate.

Balance Speaking and Listening. Generally, in a conversation, people enjoy revealing insight into their own experiences and opinions. However, both parties can't talk all the time, or you'd drown each other out. The art of carrying on a conversation depends on the participants' ability to maintain a balanced flow of talk.

Although this responsibility can often be shared, it is more than likely that one person will stand out as the dominant speaker. If that person is you, encourage the other participant to contribute to the conversation. If the other person is speaking more, listen carefully and try to contribute when you can. Remembering the roles and responsibilities of effective speakers and listeners will help your conversations flow easily.

COMMUNICATION Strategies

DEMONSTRATING IMMEDIACY IN CONVERSATIONS

- ✓ Establish and maintain eye contact while the other person is speaking.
- ✓ Respond nonverbally to show you are listening to and considering what the other person is saying.
- ✓ Restate the other person's comments before adding your own.
- ✓ Avoid distracting behaviors, such as looking at your watch or your papers or notes while the other person is talking.
- ✓ Keep your voice at a comfortable volume that is easy to hear but not too loud.

Listening in Conversations

Careful listening is key to maintaining conversations. Because people enjoy talking about themselves, they usually appreciate a good listener. To be an effective listener in a conversation, it is important to be able to restate the speaker's ideas in your own words. Ask questions that show you are listening and are interested in what the speaker is saying. Try to remember the person's name when you first meet, then repeat it later in the conversation. Use appropriate eye contact and other nonverbal communication to demonstrate your interest. Also, be sure to allow someone to finish speaking before you take your turn.

Listen to What Is Said. What kinds of topics interest the speaker? To find out, listen to his or her opinions, attitudes, and concerns regarding the topics that are discussed. These topics can serve as a basis for further conversation. Use your listening skills to prepare you to comment intelligently and ask good questions. In this way, you will become an active participant in the conversation.

Listen Empathically. Often, what a person says is not as important as what he or she is feeling. When you listen empathically, you pay attention to the feeling component of the message. As you read in Chapter 6, empathic listening involves listening to understand the emotions attached to a message. While you do not necessarily have to agree with or sympathize with those feelings, as an effective listener you should demonstrate an appreciation for the situation.

Listen to What Is Left Unsaid. To listen empathically, it is important to listen actively to what is left unsaid in a conversation. Nonverbal communication behaviors, such as posture and tone of voice, provide valuable clues to how a person really feels. Does the person stand tall or allow his or her shoulders to droop? Is the voice excited or dull and flat? Do the eyes look directly at you, or are they downcast?

Imagine that a friend is telling you about a job interview he just had. Your friend may say "Oh, it went really well." However, you notice that his voice is flat and his eyes are focused on your feet. You get the feeling that, despite your friend's words, the interview didn't go as well as he would have you believe. This is because his verbal and nonverbal messages don't match. When this happens, people tend to believe the nonverbal message.

Now imagine that another friend, who also interviewed, says the same words, but her response is more animated and enthusiastic. Her tone of voice is excited, she stands confidently, and she shares some of the interviewer's questions with you. Despite using the same words, your two friends' messages are very different. Paying attention to nonverbal details is a valuable part of listening. It allows you to gain insight into a conversation so you can continue it appropriately.

Listen Before You Speak. While observing nonverbal cues may help you interpret what is said, avoid making assumptions. It is important to confirm your initial perceptions because first impressions aren't necessarily accurate.

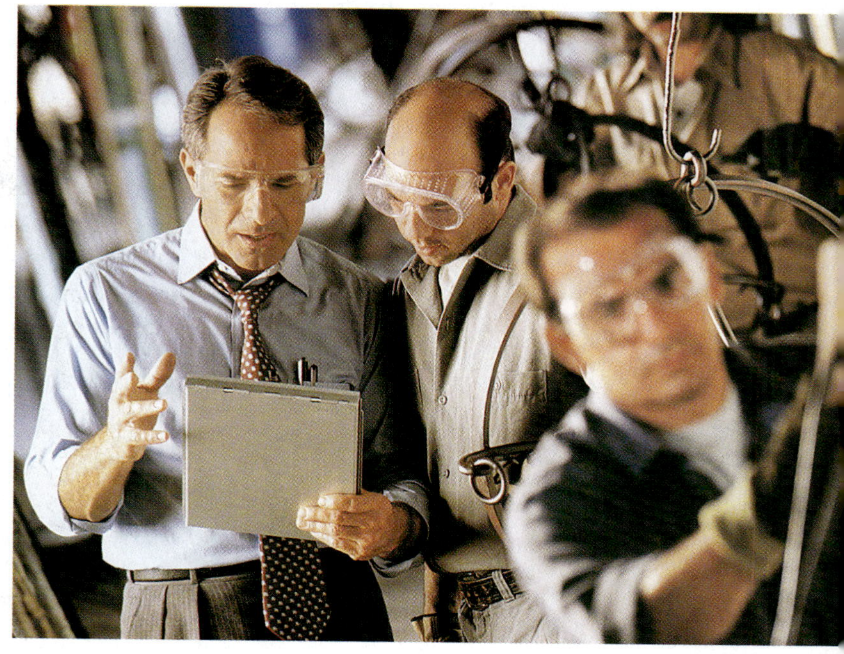

Careful listening in conversations is imperative to being a competent communicator. **Identify the ways in which you can show that you are listening effectively in a conversation.**

Consider a conversation you might have with a teacher who is the advisor for your school newspaper. As you discuss the editorial section together, the teacher may frown while listing the different articles. You "read between the lines" and wonder if the teacher disapproves of some of the topics. If you fail to investigate what the teacher is feeling, you may make a false assumption. Perhaps the advisor is frowning simply because of a headache. To confirm your suspicion, you might ask if he or she has any issues to share about the editorial page. This allows for open discussion and resolution of any questions.

TECHNOLOGY *Activity*

Using a Fax Machine With another classmate, call an advertising agency or a consulting firm in your area. Ask a representative of the company if he or she would mind if you faxed a short list of questions that focus on the communication strategies used with clients. For example, you might ask the representative how he or she uses small talk in conversation with clients. Develop a fax cover page and memo to accompany the list of questions. Ask the representative to fax the responses to the questions or telephone you to give oral answers—whichever is more convenient for the representative. Share the responses with the rest of the class.

Requests, Directions, and Questions

Often, communication extends beyond small talk to sharing information with a purpose or goal. People exchange information, make requests, give and receive directions, and ask and respond to questions. This is part of everyday interaction, whether you are at work, at school, or at home. The ability to communicate effectively in this capacity is crucial to both your personal and professional success.

Making Clear and Appropriate Requests

Whenever you ask for something, you are making a request. Sometimes, you may find it necessary to request information, such as when you ask a teacher what grade you made on a quiz. Asking incorrectly might not yield the exact information you need. Requests also may

BEFORE REQUESTING INFORMATION, CONSIDER . . .

Who has the information I need?	Not everyone in an organization has the same knowledge base or access to resources. Be sure to make your request of the person who can be the most helpful.
What is my specific question?	The more specific your question, the less margin for error. State exactly what information you need.
Why am I making this request?	Briefly explaining why you need to know something can give a person insight into exactly what you need.
When do I need the answer?	Be sure to share your deadline for a response. The best information in the world is of little use if it's a day too late.
How do I need the information?	In what form should the information be provided? Do you need a photocopy of the source, a signed report, or just a verbal answer? Describing how you need the information can save valuable time and effort.

WHEN MAKING A PERSUASIVE REQUEST . . .

Describe the problem unemotionally	Give a clear description of the situation, conveying the facts, not your personal feelings. Whining or being rude or angry will not help you persuade the listener. Instead, use your description to help the listener understand the need for change.
Suggest a solution	Act as a problem solver, offering a reasonable solution to the situation. Be specific and remain calm. Issuing threats can make the listener defensive and may reduce your chances of finding an acceptable solution.
Explain the consequences	Even if you're thinking, "Do it or else," don't say that. Instead, point out the benefits of fulfilling your request and creating a win-win solution. If the listener refuses to comply, calmly outline consequences that are realistic and appropriate.

be used to persuade someone to do something. Done improperly, this type of request can sound like a demand, and you may not get the response you seek. You can see that it is important to learn how to make effective requests.

Requests for Information Have you ever heard the saying "If you ask the wrong question, you'll get the wrong answer"? This is never more true than when you make a request for information. Reviewing who, what, why, when, and how before you make a request can help you get the information you seek.

Imagine that your friend is wearing a cap with your school logo on it. You'd like one too. If you ask, "Where'd you get that?" your friend may simply reply, "Downtown." However, if you ask, "Can you tell me where you bought that cap? I'd like to buy one myself after school," you'll be more likely to get a useful response. This question employs all the details necessary to effectively request information. Whether you are the speaker or the respondent in requests for information, make sure that your questions and responses are as clear and thorough as possible. Remember, you get what you ask for!

Requests to Persuade Persuasive requests do not ask for information. Instead, they request that some action be taken. Because you are asking another person to do something, persuasive requests can be tricky. If stated ineffectively, they may be perceived as whiny or demanding. Careful phrasing of persuasive requests can help you avoid these problems.

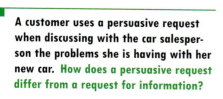

A customer uses a persuasive request when discussing with the car salesperson the problems she is having with her new car. How does a persuasive request differ from a request for information?

Imagine that you have just purchased a car that is not performing well. It is most likely that you will use a persuasive request to correct the problem. For instance, you might take the vehicle back to the dealership and say, "This car is a lemon. I want another one now, or you'll be hearing from my lawyer!" While this approach certainly would get the salesperson's attention, it also might result in your being escorted off the car lot.

A more effective request would follow the guidelines you read in the chart. You might instead say, "I just drove this car off the lot, and it stalled at every red light on my way home. I noticed that you have another car like mine on the lot. Would you like to give me that one, or would you prefer to loan me a vehicle at no charge while you repair this one?" This not only explains the problem but also suggests a logical solution.

If the salesperson refuses both of the solutions you offered, you might then ask to speak with a manager, say that you will be writing a letter to the company, or even explain that you will be withholding payment until a satisfactory solution has been reached. By remaining calm and reasonable, you have presented an effective persuasive request.

Giving Clear and Accurate Directions

From time to time, you may be asked to give someone directions. Sometimes, these directions will be geographic, involving getting from one place to another. Other times, the directions will be instructional, indicating how to do something. In either case, the foundation for good directions is communicating a logical sequence of steps to achieve a desired result.

Organize the Steps. In order to give directions, you must first understand the process clearly. Sometimes, this is more difficult than it sounds. Have you ever been asked to give directions to a particular place and

PRACTICE LAB

Making a Persuasive Request

To practice making appropriate persuasive requests, follow these steps:

Step 1 As a class, brainstorm a list of problems you have encountered as consumers. This might include receiving defective merchandise, being treated poorly by a salesperson, or other problems.

Step 2 Working with a partner, choose one of the problems from the list. Then determine who will role-play the customer and who will play the company or store representative.

Step 3 Act out a scenario in which the customer makes a persuasive request to solve the problem. The store representative should respond realistically to the request.

Step 4 Adjust the request as necessary to get the desired response from the store representative. Note the adjustments that you made.

Step 5 Carefully observe as volunteers act out their scenarios for the class. Was the customer's request effective? Was the store representative's response realistic?

Step 6 As a class, discuss the adjustments that made your requests more effective. Did you notice any common changes?

Figure 8–1 Steps in Directions

realized that you don't know the names of certain key streets? Sometimes, you may know how to perform a certain process without understanding how to describe it.

As shown in Figure 8–1, you can begin creating clear and accurate directions by listing all the necessary steps and then arranging them in order. Often, that order is time-related, as in "do this, then this, then this." For example, you explain how to bake a cake beginning with pre-heating the oven and ending with spreading the frosting. It would be very confusing to a listener to hear how to frost the cake, then how to grease the pan, then to preheat the oven, all out of order. Usually, directions for accomplishing a task need to be arranged according to the sequence in which they are to be performed.

Avoid Assumptions. One of the most important things to remember about giving effective directions is to avoid assumptions. For example, don't assume everyone speaks the specialized jargon associated with a particular field. A computer technician may speak too technically to be helpful, or a doctor may confuse patients with complex medical terms. As a result, they may miscommunicate information or frustrate the people who are trying to follow their directions.

Making assumptions can also cause you to skip steps in a process. Even though you may be very familiar with a process, don't assume the listener is. Rather, phrase your directions as though the listener is performing the process for the first time.

Use Details. For clear, accurate directions, use general language, but provide specific detail. In other words, don't just say, "Turn the knob." Say, "Turn the blue knob to the left one-quarter turn." To make sure you are providing adequate detail, pay attention to feedback. Does the listener look confused? Is he or she hesitating? One effective way to check understanding is to ask the listener to restate your directions in his or her own words. This allows you to clarify any areas of confusion and ensure that your directions are as effective as possible. Also, be careful using pronouns. Make sure you define *it, he, we,* and *they* carefully. Don't assume the listener understands.

Asking Appropriate and Purposeful Questions

Often, people hesitate to ask questions because they do not know what question to ask or how to ask it. For example, imagine that the manager at your office shows you four different forms, explains quickly when and how to fill out each, and directs you to begin using them immediately to organize some files. You understand that you need to use the forms, but you are unsure of how to actually complete the assignment. Worse still, you are afraid that if you ask questions, your manager will think that you were not paying attention or that you are not competent to complete the job. What do you do?

First, do not be afraid to ask questions. Remember the old saying "The only bad question is one that is never asked." Then, remind yourself that it is better to ask questions than to do a job wrong. The following chart provides you with some effective tips for asking appropriate and purposeful questions.

Responding Appropriately to Requests and Questions

Requests and questions are examples of communication for a specific purpose. They are intended to seek information or bring about change. If the person asking the question or making the request is unskilled in these forms of communication, they may instead sound like demands or criticisms. The most effective way to respond to a request or a question is to reply using the level of courtesy you would have liked the speaker to use.

EFFECTIVE QUESTIONING STRATEGIES

Strategy	Explanation	Example
Rephrase the message	Restate in your own words what you heard the speaker say. This allows him or her to correct any misunderstandings.	"Let me see if I understand you correctly. I add the figures in these two columns to find the total sales?"
Ask for clarification	Sometimes, a speaker will assume you are familiar with certain jargon and background information. If you are not, ask the speaker to explain.	"I'm sorry. I'm not familiar with that term. Could you clarify it for me?"
Ask for more details	Often, more information can help you better understand a concept. Ask specific questions to get specific details.	"Which products were involved in this comparison study?"
Confirm through examples	Verify that you understand with an example that summarizes or illustrates what you have heard.	If you are baby-sitting and the parents say the children can stay up for "a while," ask, "Is 9:30 OK, or is that too late?"

Responding Appropriately to Requests A request that begins with a forcefully stated solution, particularly if it is followed by some type of real or implied threat, is likely to be perceived not as a request but as a demand. However, you do not have to respond with the same level of emotion. Imagine that you work in the customer service department of a major clothing store. A customer waves a damaged item in front of you and yells, "I'm so tired of bad quality. Look at this! You need to replace it now!"

Stay Objective. As an employee and as an effective communicator, it is your responsibility to filter out the hostile emotion in a request. Focus on the message—no matter how emotionally it was communicated to you.

Assess the Situation. Determine what the problem is so you can decide what course of action is necessary. What is the item? When was it purchased? Exactly what is wrong with it? Did the customer damage it, or does it really have a fault? What is really the problem?

Use Problem-Solving Style. To respond best to requests—whether friendly or aggressive—try to use a problem-solving style of communication. After assessing the current situation, suggest that the person describe some possible solutions. Depending on your store's policy, you might say, "I can see the tear in the vest, and

This student appears to be listening defensively. **How do defensive listeners tend to hear questions?**

I apologize for your inconvenience. What can we do to make this right for you?" Join in brainstorming solutions, if possible.

State Consequences. Finally, carefully and objectively state the consequences you are trying to achieve. You might say, "I understand that you are upset, ma'am, and I very much want for you to be a satisfied customer. Could we replace the defective part or give you one of our other products instead?" Reassure the person that you are seeking a positive outcome.

Requests are part of everyday interaction whether at work, school, or home. Maintain a descriptive and objective tone and use a problem-solving style when responding to requests, no matter how harsh or unreasonable they may appear to you. This will help you build an image as a fair and competent communicator.

Responding Appropriately to Questions When responding to questions, it also is crucial to be an active—not defensive—listener. Defensive listeners sometimes hear questions as if they were criticisms.

To answer questions effectively, first determine exactly what information is being requested. Did the person just not hear clearly? You may be able to simply repeat the information. Perhaps the listener needs for you to define your terms or clarify your meanings. Maybe he or she is asking for additional information. Knowing what kind of information is needed will help you to respond appropriately to the question.

Inappropriate Questions Sometimes, you will be asked inappropriate questions. When this happens, ask yourself whether it would be unwise or unethical for you to provide the requested information. For instance, if a coworker asks you how much you earn per hour, it might be unwise to answer. The coworker might resent your wage or start feeling superior, depending on how much you make. By the same token, it would be unethical to reveal how much a friend makes per hour. Remember, you do not have to answer inappropriate questions.

When You Don't Know an Answer Occasionally, you might be asked a question for which you do not have an answer. In these cases, ask yourself who might be the best person to answer the question. Who has knowledge on the topic or access to accurate resources? Who can most efficiently communicate the answer to the question? If you suspect that no one else knows the answer either, consider how you might obtain the information for the questioner. No one knows the answer to every possible question. However, knowing when to redirect a question to a

Students follow along as their teacher provides directions for an assignment. **What can you do to make sure you respond appropriately to the directions of others?**

more knowledgeable source or to say "I don't know, but I'll find out," will make you a valuable resource.

Responding Appropriately to the Directions of Others

How many times a week does someone give you an instruction or provide you with directions? How many times each day? Following directions is a crucial part of being an effective family member, student, and employee. Whether the directions involve going somewhere or completing a task, you are expected to listen to the steps and follow them.

Listen Without Judgment

Sometimes, people are their own worst enemies when it comes to following directions. Instead of listening actively, they begin thinking of other things. They may assume they have heard it all before, or predetermine that the directions will be impossible to remember or unpleasant to follow. Think about when your teacher explains an assignment. As he or she gets to the second step, you may think, "Why are you repeating these directions?" Later, you may discover that you have done the assignment incorrectly because you did not listen with an open mind.

Listen for Steps or Main Points

Directions usually are explained in a particular order—usually in a time-related sequence or according to a certain grouping. Imagine directions for closing up a business at night. The directions may be given in a particular order in time. For example, secure the back room, lock the cash register, turn off the lights, and set the alarm. If you complete these steps out of order, you might set off the alarm or find yourself walking around in the dark. While you may be able to get by without remembering all the tiny details of directions, you need to listen carefully for the steps or main points.

Paraphrase

Even if you think you have understood a set of directions, it is important to check your own understanding. You can do this by paraphrasing.

To paraphrase is to repeat a message in your own words. As the speaker gives you directions, briefly repeat each step to yourself. If you cannot repeat the steps, it probably means that you did not understand the instructions well enough to follow them.

Ask the Speaker to Explain

Sometimes, noise can impact how a message is received. If you are unsure you have correctly understood a message, ask for confirmation. You may need to ask the speaker to repeat the message. Perhaps he or she needs to define some technical terms, or you may need to ask for more explanation. One thing is certain. Pretending to understand and remember directions is not an effective communication strategy. In some circumstances, it can even threaten your health or safety. It is always better to confirm what you know and ask for any extra information you may need. Responding to questions in this manner shows that you are a responsible and competent communicator.

Section 1 Assessment

Visit the *Glencoe Communication Applications* Web site at **communicationapplications.glencoe.com** and click on **Self-Check and Study Guide 8.1** to review your understanding of communicating interpersonally.

Review Key Terms

1. Define each term and write it in a sentence: open-ended question, closed question, paraphrase.

Check Understanding

2. What are seven strategies for participating effectively in conversations?
3. Imagine you are served an improperly cooked meal in a restaurant. Request a solution to this problem.
4. What three things should you remember when giving clear and accurate directions?
5. Why is it important to ask appropriate and purposeful questions when you are unsure of something?
6. **Apply** Imagine that a classmate asks you about a school policy that you are not familiar with. How might you respond appropriately?

Analyzing Interpersonal Communication On a sheet of paper, list at least five people you see almost every day. Choose one day of the week and monitor how effectively you converse with these people. Next to each person's name, list the communication skill you used to initiate or maintain a conversation with him or her. Use the Communication Strategies checklists on pages 240 and 242 as a guide. Study your analysis, then design a personal strategies checklist to improve your conversation skills.

Technology Skill

Using Voice Mail

Voice mail is an automated telephone answering system that companies use to conduct business more efficiently. While voice mail is useful for businesses, it also offers many conveniences for callers.

Learning the Skill

If you call a place of business that has voice mail, keep the following in mind:

- You can respond to voice mail prompts only if your telephone uses tones to communicate. If you have a rotary dial or pulse phone, you are usually instructed to wait for an operator.
- You'll need to listen carefully to a menu of choices.
- You must be prepared to leave a message. Before you call, arrange a list of points you want to discuss with the other party.

If you use voice mail to manage your calls at work or at home, follow these suggestions:

- Make your greeting short but pleasant. Explain why you are unable to take any calls. Tell your callers what information you want them to include in their messages. Always speak slowly and clearly.
- Check your messages frequently and return calls promptly.
- If your message gives several options for routing a call, make sure they are clearly stated and not confusing to callers.

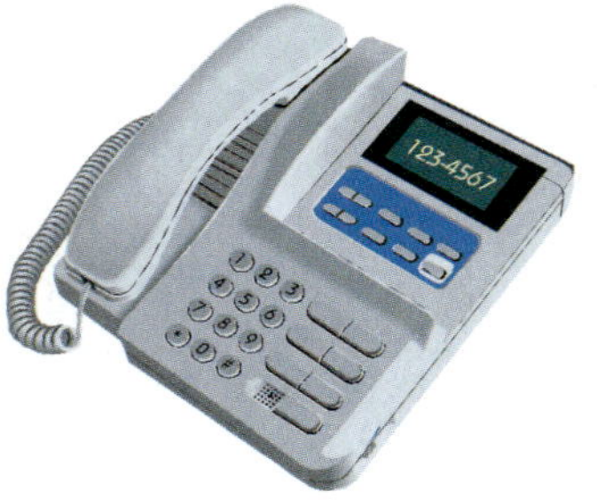

Practicing the Skill

Compare and contrast the voice mail for five companies.

Step 1 Browse through a newspaper or magazine to locate five toll-free telephone numbers.

Step 2 Decide what kind of information you want from each company.

Step 3 Call each organization. Listen carefully to the automatic announcement for directions on how to proceed.

Step 4 If you are required to leave a voice message, be cordial and speak clearly.

APPLICATION *Activity*

Assume that your school has voice mail and you will be using it to manage calls about the school play. Write an outgoing announcement that gives the following information: which play is to be performed, when the play will be staged, how to purchase tickets, how to get to the school, where drivers should park their cars, and how to speak to a person if the caller needs other information.

Section 2

Applying Professional Etiquette and Protocol

GUIDE TO READING

Objectives

1. Explain professional etiquette and protocol for making introductions.
2. Describe professional etiquette and protocol for using the telephone.
3. Compare and contrast professional etiquette for offering and receiving criticism.
4. Analyze and evaluate the effectiveness of your own and others' communication.
5. Identify and use appropriate strategies for dealing with differences, including differences in culture, gender, ethnicity, and age.

Terms to Learn

etiquette
protocol
constructive criticism
descriptive communication
evaluative communication

Imagine that you found an advertisement for the ideal summer job. You applied for the job, aced your interview, and were hired. Now you're just waiting for the job to begin. You are looking forward to this job—particularly because your interview with the boss went so well.

Imagine that the weekend before your new job begins, you are at the grocery with one of your teachers buying supplies for a band picnic. Suddenly, you see your future boss right there in the vegetable aisle. A second later, she sees you too. Now what should you do?

In the seconds that follow, a thousand questions crowd your brain: "Should I say something or shouldn't I?" "What should I say?" "Does she remember me?" "Should I introduce my teacher?" "How formal should I be?" All of these questions center on how to communicate appropriately in a professional context.

Etiquette and protocol are used when making introductions like the one shown. **What role do etiquette and protocol play in the workplace?**

How you communicate in such situations could affect how you are perceived, not only as a person, but also as a student and as an employee. Although there are no hard and fast rules, there are some generally accepted guidelines to help you make appropriate choices in a situation like this one. These guidelines are based on what is considered to be socially acceptable behavior for a specific context.

Practice for the Workplace

The Chain of Command Almost every organization is made up of people who occupy positions of power within the company. The relationships between the positions form the chain of command. This graded system is similar to the military in that certain ranks have more power than others. If a lower-ranking employee questions an action taken by the company, that person first goes to the immediate supervisor to voice his or her opinion. The employee's complaint will then be dismissed or progress through the chain of command until it is settled at the proper level.

BUSINESS PRACTICE *Activity*

What is the chain of communication in your school? To whom do you speak within your school if you want to suggest a change in a policy of your school or recognize an outstanding teacher? What if the people in your school cannot resolve your request? Identify each level of the educational hierarchy from the classroom to the district level.

Professional Etiquette and Protocol

In interpersonal communication, there are certain rules for interacting with supervisors, coworkers, teachers, classmates, and even the parents of classmates. Because these relationships tend to be more distant than our close friendships, rule violations are viewed more seriously. Mistakes can result in a lasting bad impression, a lost opportunity, a complaint from a customer, or a reputation as a poor communicator.

For these reasons, it is important to understand and follow the rules of professional etiquette and protocol. **Etiquette** is an established code of behavior or courtesy. There are different forms of etiquette for different contexts in life. Sometimes this code is written, and sometimes it isn't. **Protocol** is a code of etiquette that is written and prescribed by an organization. This particular form of etiquette typically is used for official dealings, such as business or governmental operations. The armed services, in particular, are known for prescribed behavior or protocol. For example, enlisted personnel are required to salute officers, all personnel must wear hats outdoors, and officers are not supposed to socialize with enlisted personnel.

Most other social and professional organizations do not have such rigorous, formal rules of protocol. In many cases, the expectations for your interactions may be unstated—at least until you violate them. Inappropriate behaviors can result in personal humiliation, lost customers, offended coworkers, and embarrassed employers. They also can affect your future with the organization.

How are you supposed to know what behavior is appropriate for any situation? In general, you do the thing that is the most courteous and polite for the situation at hand. There are some fairly set standards for several of the most common professional interpersonal situations. Try to keep in mind that these standards reflect the accepted norms for these behaviors. There may be situations when you need to adapt these recommended standards to be appropriate to yourself, a listener, the occasion, or the task.

Etiquette and Protocol in Making Introductions

What do you do when your boss walks out to meet a customer or client you just greeted and the two have not met before? Obviously, you have to introduce one to the other. Whose name do you say first, and how do you identify each of them? Is it the same as introducing a new coworker to your boss? How do you introduce a friend to your boss or coworker? As you can see from the chart below, according to etiquette the person who deserves the most respect in the situation is named first. You are actually presenting the other person to the one who is more respected. At work, a client usually will be introduced first, followed by your boss or other superior, coworkers, family members, and then friends. When introducing people outside the workplace, you usually introduce the person you are with to the person you encounter.

Exceptions to the Rules As with all forms of communication, the appropriateness of an introduction depends on the context. Sometimes, introductions will vary slightly from the examples in the chart. This is especially true in very informal situations and when more than one rule of etiquette applies. If you are on a first-name basis with one or both parties in an introduction, state the individuals' first names as well as their last names. When people fit into multiple categories, always defer to the person with the most power. For instance, if you are introducing a new female coworker to a male president of the company, state the president's name first, then the woman's name.

ETIQUETTE FOR MAKING INTRODUCTIONS

When Introducing . . .	Tradition	Order of Introduction	Example
Your boss to a client	Respect is shown to the client.	State the client's name first, then your boss's name.	"Ms. Sanchez, I'd like you to meet our manager, Mr. Jones."
Your boss to a new coworker	Respect is shown to your boss.	State your boss's name first, then your coworker's.	"Mr. Tong, this is our new staff member, Stacy Adams."
Your friend to your boss or a coworker	At work: Respect is shown to your boss or coworker.	At work: State your boss's or coworker's name, then your friend's.	"Ms. Majors, I would like you to meet my friend Elizabeth Maddox."
	Outside of work: Equal respect is shown to your friend and your boss or coworker.	Outside of work: State your friend's name, then your boss's or coworker's. Then, introduce your friend to your boss or coworker.	"Elizabeth, I would like you to meet my boss, Ms. Majors. Ms. Majors, this is my friend Elizabeth Maddox."
A junior businessperson and a senior businessperson	Respect is shown to the person with the most experience.	State senior businessperson's name first, then the junior businessperson's name.	"Ms. (company vice president), allow me to introduce Mr. (salesperson)."
Anyone and a guest of honor	Respect is shown to the person with the most power or authority.	State the guest of honor's name first, then the other person's name.	"Mr. (governor), please allow me to introduce our high school principal, Ms. Greene."

When performing any introduction, it is important to use your best judgment. Consider the context and the individuals involved and back up your decision with the rules of etiquette. Making wise choices will help you distinguish yourself as a competent communicator and help the person who is being introduced know with whom he or she will be meeting or speaking.

Etiquette and Protocol in Using the Telephone

Another area of communication where rules of etiquette apply is on the telephone. Although you may have been talking on the phone since you were very young, you may not have been doing so effectively. Your family and friends may have learned to ignore a lack of phone etiquette on your part. Business associates and clients, however, will expect you to be a competent communicator, following the rules of etiquette in your phone conversations.

COMMUNICATION Strategies
USING EFFECTIVE TELEPHONE SKILLS
Speak clearly and pleasantly.
Identify yourself and your employer.
Be a responsible listener.
Develop a plan for making calls.
Develop a plan for receiving calls.
Take accurate notes.

Knowing how to use appropriate telephone skills can improve your effectiveness with clients and customers and in other business interactions. Correctly answering the telephone can also make you a valuable public relations source.

interNET ACTIVITY

Cultural Etiquette Social and professional etiquette consists of written and unwritten rules that reflect cultural expectations as well as official policies and procedures. Search the Internet using the following terms: *airplane travel etiquette, dining etiquette, disability etiquette, gift-giving etiquette,* and *etiquette for making proper introductions.* Create a list of "Dos and Don'ts" based on the expectations that most people in the United States have regarding these issues. Compare your findings with those of your classmates.

If communicating on the telephone appropriately is so important to professional and organizational success, how do you do it? Just as in other types of professional interactions, there are not always defined rules. However, whether you are speaking to a person, to voice mail, or to some other type of recording system, you can follow some basic rules of etiquette and protocol when using the telephone. These skills are given in the Communication Strategies checklist.

Speak Clearly and Distinctly. Although this rule seems obvious, people sometimes forget to practice it. Have you ever called a company and been unable to understand the person who answered the phone? As Figure 8–2 on the following page shows, the person who answered may have spoken too quickly, too softly, mumbled the greeting or the name of the company, or perhaps used slang terms that were difficult for you to understand. It is very likely that this person did not make a positive impression on you. You do not want to create this same impression for yourself or your organization. Instead, make sure that you speak clearly and distinctly and use a pleasant tone. Also, if your listener is trying to write down what you say, adjust your pace accordingly.

Identify Yourself and Your Employer. As a general rule, when answering the phone, give both your first and last names and the name of your employer or organization. This assures the caller that he or she has reached the right number. Many companies also want you to identify the department or office in which you are located. It is usually appropriate to say something like, "Hello, this is Jane Smith in Receiving."

The purpose of clear identification is to make the speaker and the company recognizable and traceable. The caller should be able to refer to you by name and call you back later, if necessary. This person also should see you as a pleasant and helpful representative of the company. During a phone call, you are, indeed, the voice of your company or organization.

Be a Responsible Listener. When you answer the phone, you often are the first contact the caller has with your company or your department. No one expects you to be able to solve every problem or answer every question, but you do need to know how to handle each inquiry efficiently.

Develop a Plan When Making Phone Calls. When you need to make a telephone call for your company or organization, take the time to organize the materials you will need to make the call efficiently. It may help you to create a quick list of topics that you want to cover during the call. When you have reached the person, identify yourself and ask if he or she has time to talk with you.

Figure 8–2 Speak Clearly and Distinctly

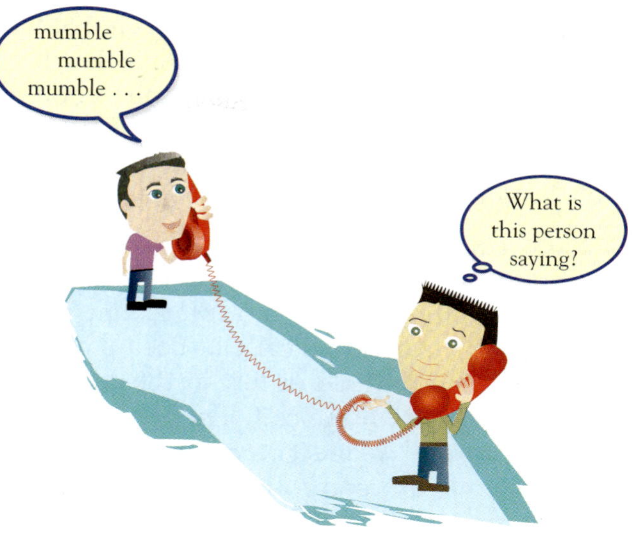

If the Person Is Available If the person is available, preview the purpose of your call, saying something like, "I have two questions" or, "There are three projects I need to discuss." Try to keep the conversation organized and on track, limiting small talk as much as possible. After you have received the information you need, briefly summarize the conversation and ask if you are clear on all the information. Then, conclude the call by thanking the person for his or her information and time.

If the Person Is Not Interruptible If the person responds that he or she does not have time to speak at that time, ask for a time when he or she might be available. It may also help if you can estimate how much time your conversation will last. "When would be a good time for me to speak with you about my current project? I will need about fifteen minutes to get your answers to two or three important questions." This helps the person plan enough time to respond. Once the person names a time for you to call back, it is important for you to remember to do so at that time.

Prepare to Receive Phone Calls. When you receive a phone call, prepare by having paper and pen or pencil ready. Find out the full name of the caller and write it down. Next, ask about the purpose of the call. If you will need to put the person on hold temporarily or call him or her back, write down the complete phone number, including the area code.

If the caller asks a question you cannot answer, route the caller to someone who can. Then, check the phone's indicator lights to make sure the transferred call has been picked up and not left on hold or lost in the wilderness of voice mail. If the call is not picked up after one minute, redirect it yourself. A well-answered call can lead to a positive evaluation of both you and your company.

COMMUNICATION *Strategies*

EFFECTIVELY HANDLING HOSTILE TELEPHONE CALLS

- Remain calm.
- Listen empathically.
- Keep your responses objective.
- Acknowledge the caller's anger or hostility.
- Let the caller know that you want to help.
- Respond with clear, logical messages that reflect empathy with the caller.

Documenting the Call When dealing with business matters, you may find it helpful to document phone calls. Documentation can help you verify any information you receive and can serve as a reminder to follow up on the purpose of the call. Many companies use a preprinted form like the one in **Figure 8-3** on which you can record information vital to a conversation. If your company does not use a preprinted form, you may want to develop one for yourself. This can help you track the caller, the caller's phone number, the date and time of the call, and any information that results from the conversation.

Figure 8–3 Telephone Message Form

MESSAGE

While you were out

_______________ called

☐ Will call back

☐ Return call

Comments:

____

____

____

Time: __________ Date: __________

Taken by: _______________

Answering the Telephone for Someone Else When answering the telephone for a supervisor or another employee, be sure to take accurate, organized notes. If the person the caller wishes to speak with is not available, simply say that he or she cannot take the call at that time. There is no need to reveal details about why the person cannot take the call.

If you have been asked to screen calls, do so with tact and courtesy. Try to avoid making promises for other people, such as "She'll call you as soon as she gets back to the office." Also, avoid making comments about policies or programs about which you lack knowledge or authority. Finally, remember to remain professional on the phone even if the person is upset and hard to deal with.

Dealing With Hostile Telephone Calls Some of the most difficult phone calls to deal with involve angry or hostile callers. Effective communication strategies in these instances are extremely important to the relationship between the person making the call and your company or organization. Use the Communication Strategies checklist on the left as a guide to handling hostile calls.

Etiquette and Protocol in Giving Criticism

In a perfect world, all people would do their jobs effectively and efficiently, generating absolutely no need for negative feedback. The real world is not quite so simple, though. Sometimes, in order to do your own job well, it becomes necessary to give criticism. When you criticize people in a manner that helps them to learn and grow, you are offering constructive criticism. **Constructive criticism** is a negative evaluation done in a way that brings about positive change. Often, people value this type of criticism because it helps them to improve. To keep criticism positive and constructive, however, it is necessary to follow certain rules.

Describe the Facts. Few people truly enjoy being criticized. However, by structuring your criticism a certain way, you reduce its unpleasantness and make the communication as productive as possible.

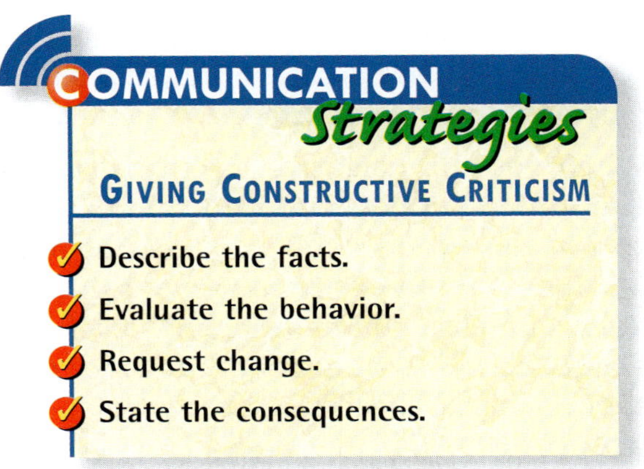

COMMUNICATION Strategies
GIVING CONSTRUCTIVE CRITICISM
Describe the facts.
Evaluate the behavior.
Request change.
State the consequences.

First, it is important to remember that constructive criticism always begins with descriptive communication—not an evaluation. **Descriptive communication** is talk that paints a picture of the facts of a situation. Starting with a simple description of the facts helps you ease into the criticism without looking as though you are attacking or judging the person unfairly.

To begin, simply describe the exact behavior or set of behaviors that are the root of the issue. At this point, try not to use any words that imply an evaluation. This can be a little tricky because so many common words fall into that category. In general, avoid words such as *good, bad, better, worse, right, wrong,* and so on.

It can be much easier to apply a label to someone than to describe the behaviors that led you to that evaluation. For example, it might be simpler to tell someone, "You are acting like a slacker," than it would be to describe his or her unmotivated behaviors. However, with a little practice, you can learn to describe the facts of a situation without passing judgment on the person.

For example, instead of calling the person a slacker, you might say, "You rarely offer to do any work other than what is strictly required." Using this kind of description not only avoids evaluation, but it also lets the person know how to improve his or her behavior. This is the only way criticism can be constructive.

Evaluate the Behavior. After you have clearly and objectively described the troublesome behavior, it is appropriate to evaluate it. **Evaluative communication** is talk that tells how you interpret a behavior and how you feel about a situation. At this point, you might say, "It seems as if you don't care much about this job anymore. Unfortunately, the quality of your work is suffering because of your attitude."

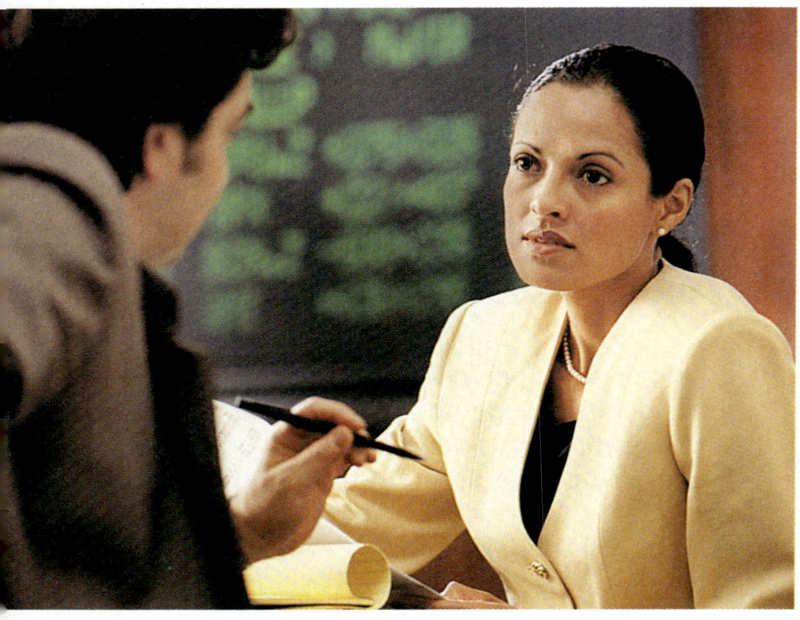

A young woman receives constructive criticism during an annual review. **What can happen if one becomes defensive when receiving constructive criticism?**

As you complete this step of the process, it is important to remember that you are evaluating the specific behavior and not the person. While a person may be unmotivated or unproductive at work, he or she still is a valuable human being. Try to keep your criticism from becoming personal.

Request Change. Immediately following a brief, direct evaluation, return to descriptive communication. This time, however, focus on the specific behavioral change you want to see. To avoid any misunderstandings, be as specific as possible in your description. For instance, if a worker has not been completing his or her duties, you might say, "Our company policy is that breaks end on time and the employee immediately returns to the sales floor. I'd appreciate it if you would be careful about this in the future." This type of detailed instruction tends to be much more effective than a general request to "shape up."

State the Consequences. Finally, you need to tell the person what will or may happen as a result of his or her behavior. Remember, you have clearly described two different behaviors: one that is the problem and another that is the solution. Now you need to mention the possible negative consequences if the problem behavior continues. For instance, "If you continue to return late from breaks, I will have to take that time out of your pay."

The focus of this step, however, should be on the positive consequences of change. You might say, "Being prompt and eager to work will help identify you as an enthusiastic employee. That's the type of person who gets promoted." Constructive criticism is based on the assumption that people want to grow and develop. By giving them some instruction for change, you can help them become more effective.

Etiquette and Protocol in Receiving Criticism

While criticism does focus on a need for change, that need can be viewed as either negative or positive. Viewing the criticism as a negative judgment can cause you to respond defensively. However, viewing it constructively can help you see the situation as an opportunity to better yourself.

When you are defensive to criticism, you put up an emotional barrier to communication. You close yourself off from change and, instead, may try to justify your own behavior or even launch a counterattack. A defensive response prevents you from growing and becoming more effective as a result of the criticism.

COMMUNICATION *Strategies*

RECEIVING CRITICISM EFFECTIVELY

- Ask for a description of the facts.
- Paraphrase the criticism.
- If possible, agree with the critic's assessment.
- Listen for the desired change.
- Focus on the positive consequences of change.

A constructive response does just the opposite. Even if the criticism itself is not expressed constructively, you can still respond in a positive way. There are several strategies you can use to get the most out of criticism.

Ask for a Description of the Facts. It can be difficult to make positive changes if you do not understand exactly what behaviors are the problem. Therefore, if a critic says that you are not doing your work, tells you that you are selfish, or accuses you of having a bad attitude, politely ask the person what caused him or her to arrive at that conclusion. If the person cannot give you any specifics, adopt a problem-solving attitude. Ask probing questions such as "When did you begin noticing this?" or "Has the problem seemed to get worse lately?" to help narrow the person's broad criticism to specific behaviors that you can change.

Paraphrase the Criticism. Stating the person's criticism in your own words can serve several purposes. First, it helps ensure that you have understood correctly. If you get off on the wrong track, the critic can clear up any misunderstandings immediately.

Second, paraphrasing can help buy time while you control your emotions. If you have received a particularly harsh criticism, you may need to compose yourself before offering a response. Rephrasing the criticism less harshly can help take the edge off of it. It also may help the critic see that his or her language is more negative than it needs to be.

If Possible, Agree With the Critic's Assessment. Some criticism is constructive; some may be unjustified. To the extent that it is possible, agree with the factual description of your problem behavior without adding any qualifiers. Qualifiers often begin with "but . . ." or "that's because. . . ."

Employees who are tardy to work may receive criticism from a supervisor. What are the benefits of paraphrasing a criticism?

If you have been taking longer breaks than you should have, avoid qualifying your behavior with statements such as "But I had a ton of homework this week that I was trying to finish up during my breaks." Instead, just say, "Yes, sir (or ma'am), I have been late returning from breaks this week."

Even if you feel that a certain behavior should not be judged negatively, you may be able to agree with the principle involved. For instance, if you were late only once because you spent your break helping your manager, you probably would not want to agree that you have made a habit of being tardy. Instead, you might say, "Yes, sir (or ma'am), I agree that people who always return late from breaks look like slackers."

Listen for the Desired Change. To view criticism as an opportunity for change, you need to know exactly what change the critic thinks is necessary. Once there is a clear understanding of what behavior is the source of the problem, there needs to be an equally clear understanding of the proposed solution. Actively listen for a description of the desired behavioral change. If you do not hear it, ask the critic for specific changes he or she would like to see.

Stay Focused on the Positive Consequences of Change. Perhaps the least pleasant part of criticism is hearing what may happen if problem behavior continues. The person making the criticism may warn or even threaten you with these negative consequences. Remember to stay calm and listen actively and politely. You can use these consequences later as a motivating force to help you change.

However, as a competent problem-solver, you will want to focus most of your energy on the benefits of change. What will happen if you change in the manner that the critic has described? Will the critic be more pleased with your performance? Will you improve your image as a valuable employee? Will you increase your chances for promotion? These questions help you put the past behind you and move ahead with positive growth and change.

COMMUNICATION PRACTICE LAB

Responding Appropriately to Criticism

To practice an appropriate response to criticism, follow these steps:

Step 1 As a class, brainstorm a list of criticisms that students might hear from parents, teachers, or employers.

Step 2 In groups of four or five, choose a few of the criticisms from the list and write them on a sheet of paper. Think of an appropriate scenario in which an annoyed employer might state these criticisms to a teenage worker.

Step 3 Working as a group, write a script of the employer's criticism and the teenage worker's response. Be sure to follow the protocol for giving and receiving criticism.

Step 4 Present your scripted scenarios to the class.

Step 5 As a class, evaluate the effectiveness of both the critic and the teenager. Did both parties seem to view the criticism as an opportunity for positive change?

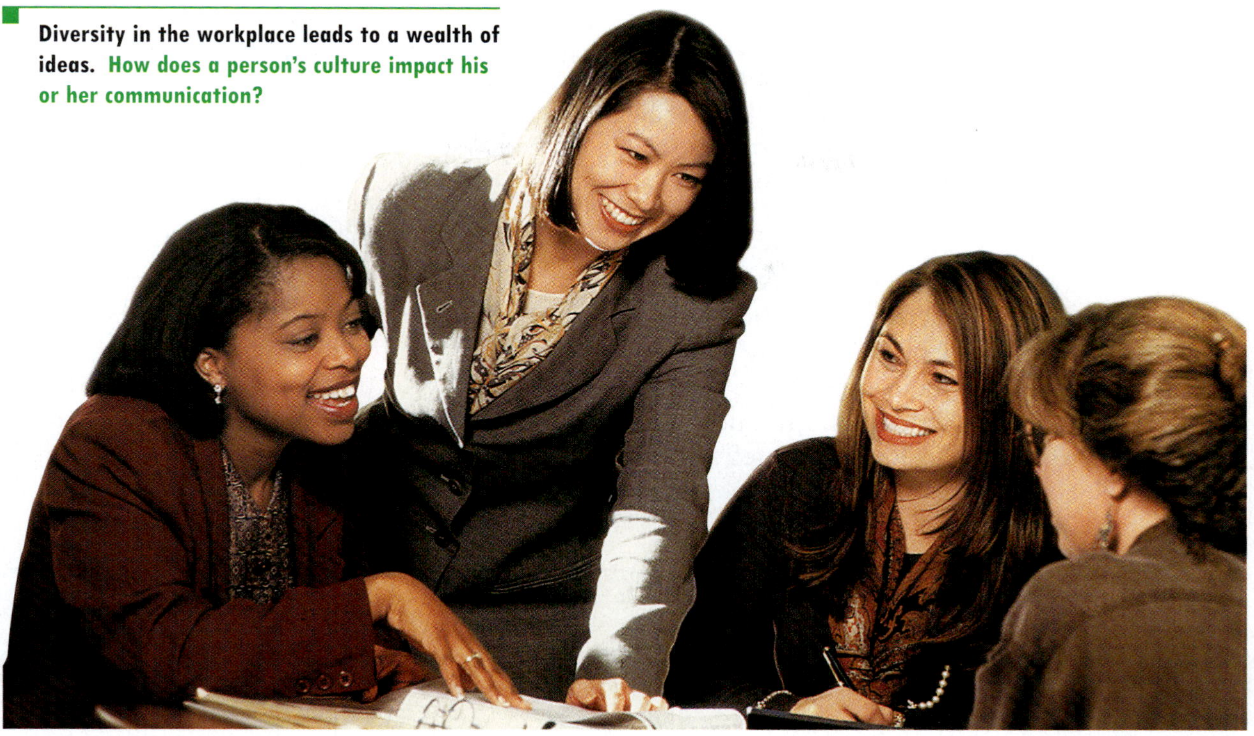

Diversity in the workplace leads to a wealth of ideas. **How does a person's culture impact his or her communication?**

Appropriate Strategies for Dealing with Differences

The United States always has been a richly diverse nation, with people from many different backgrounds and traditions living and working together. Sometimes, however, this variety can breed conflict in the workplace. People often feel threatened by ideas and people that are new or different to them. Sometimes, people prefer to shut out information that does not fit in with their personal perspective of the world.

Our taste in food often follows this same pattern. You may not like some new flavors the first time you try them. However, over time, you may grow to appreciate many different flavors. Diversity among human beings is similar. Just as a strong flavor might jump out at you at first but later add to the uniqueness of a dish, so might a person's most obvious differences seem striking and objectionable at first. However, over time, as you become more accustomed to these differences, you may come to appreciate the richness that they provide.

The trick is to be open to other peoples' perspectives. That does not mean that you need to agree with their ideas. Nor does it mean that you must do things someone else's way, rather than your own. However, skillful communicators are willing to keep an open mind when it comes to diverse ideas.

As you become a more experienced communicator, you will find that differences exist on many levels. What's more, each of these areas can have an effect on communication. Four factors that often affect people's perceptions and communication are the ones listed here:

- culture
- ethnicity
- gender
- age

Culture

In Chapter 1, you read that a culture is the life patterns of a specific group of people. It is the rules, norms, customs, values, and beliefs that allow people to define themselves—and be defined by others—as members of a particular group. Among other things, a person's cultural background may influence his or her language, food, dress, leisure activities, work ethic, traditions, and family role. It also may affect the way he or she approaches conflict, decisions, and communication. In addition, culture can affect the rules of etiquette and protocol that a person follows. In short, a person's culture strongly influences the way he or she perceives the world.

As you have grown, you have come to identify with one or more specific cultures. Your communication reflects the assumption that these cultural rules, norms, and customs are the "right" way of doing things for you. However, other cultures often can open our eyes to different and perhaps better ways of doing things.

To deal effectively with cultural differences, you need to be open to new ideas, avoid rushing to judgment, and see diversity

Elizabeth Dole is an accomplished speaker and politician. **In what ways can gender influence communication?**

as opportunity. As today's business world becomes increasingly global, those who are able to communicate effectively with people of different cultural backgrounds will surely enjoy great opportunities for advancement and success.

Ethnicity

Sometimes, when certain cultural groups share a national origin, language, religion, or other characteristic, they are referred to as an ethnic group. Very often, the people in a specific ethnic group also share certain physical traits. For this reason, people tend to judge a person's ethnicity according to the way he or she looks.

However, basing even part of a person's identity on his or her physical features can create problems. First, you may offend someone by incorrectly identifying his or her ethnicity or nationality. Second, you may tend to shape your communication to fit some unjust ethnic stereotype. This kind of mass generalization can easily lead to misunderstanding. It can also lead to communication failure.

As a rule of thumb, avoid basing your communication choices on a person's ethnicity. Instead, concentrate on communicating appropriately and effectively—just as you would in any communication context.

Gender

People typically identify themselves as belonging to a specific gender, male or female. Certain aspects of that gender influence your perceptions and communication. For instance, you may communicate a certain way with people of your same gender and a slightly different way with people of the opposite gender. To make matters even more complicated, cultural rules and norms for your gender may influence your communication.

Most cultures have developed certain rules and norms for the way males and females communicate. North American cultures typically make few distinctions between the way men and women communicate. Of course, some stereotypes still exist. For example, an outspoken woman may be viewed by some as overbearing while an outspoken man may simply be viewed by those same people as assertive. Still, the goal in communication—especially in social and professional contexts—is for men and women to behave as equals.

Sometimes, however, this attitude may come into direct conflict with the norms of other cultures. For instance, in some Asian or Muslim cultures, females are expected to defer to males. Therefore, even if a female outranks a male colleague, businessmen from one of these cultures may insist on negotiating with the male. This type of behavior may seem extremely unjust to a businesswoman from the United States. However, if she insists on doing the negotiating herself, she runs a high risk of offending the businessmen and causing the negotiations to fail.

As a competent communicator, it is important for you to recognize when a culture has different gender rules for communication. You can then adapt your communication to make it appropriate for the context. This will help you communicate as effectively as possible in any culture.

Age

Sometimes, society groups people together according to their age whether they like it or not. Just as you should not stereotype people of different ethnicities, you also should not stereotype people of different ages. People of all ages have their own unique perceptions and ways of communicating. Some teenagers tend to be extremely mature, very serious, and strikingly formal. By the same token, some elderly people are whimsical, young at heart, and up to date on the latest trends.

Rarely would every person in a particular age group perceive things the same way. Therefore, your communication choices should not be based on a person's age. Stereotyping others on the basis of age is just as dangerous as any other kind of stereotyping. It almost always has a harmful effect on communication.

Section 2 Assessment

Visit the *Glencoe Communication Applications* Web site at **communicationapplications.glencoe.com** and click on **Self-Check and Study Guide 8.2** to review your understanding of applying professional etiquette and protocol.

Review Key Terms

1. Define each term and write it in a sentence: etiquette, protocol, constructive criticism, descriptive communication, evaluative communication.

Check Understanding

2. What is the main rule of etiquette or protocol to remember when making introductions?
3. Describe rules of etiquette or protocol to remember when answering the telephone.
4. Compare and contrast the rules of etiquette for giving and receiving criticism.
5. What is one effective way to evaluate others' communication skills in an organization? How might you evaluate your own skills?
6. **Synthesize** When communicating with diverse peoples, which of the following should you pay most attention to: culture, ethnicity, gender, or age? Why?

APPLICATION Activity

Recognizing the Impact of Diversity On a sheet of paper, list the following categories related to your culture: gender, race, age, religion, native language, number of people in household, favorite holiday, favorite food, what you hope to be, and what is most important to you. Beside each category, write an answer that applies to you and another answer that is very different from yours. Now, imagine that you must carry on a fifteen-minute conversation with the second person you described. What would be most interesting and most difficult about your conversation? Discuss your ideas as a class.

Communication Self-Assessment

Evaluating Your Interpersonal Communication Skills

How Do You Rate?

On a separate sheet of paper, respond to the following statements. Put a check mark at the end of each skill you would like to improve.

KEY: **A** Always **U** Usually **S** Sometimes **R** Rarely **N** Never

1. I am able to build unique, interdependent, and irreplaceable relationships.
2. My interpersonal skills include the ability to start conversations with open-ended questions.
3. I can maintain conversations because I know how to ask tactful questions, and I can balance listening with talking.
4. I listen empathically and ask questions if I don't understand nonverbal clues.
5. When I request information, I define what I want, why I am making the request, and when I need the information.
6. When I give directions, I assume the person is performing a task for the first time.
7. When I respond to questions, I listen actively and avoid making judgments.
8. I make introductions according to the etiquette and protocol of the situation.
9. I am able to accept constructive criticism by focusing on the value of making changes.
10. In work situations, my communication follows the norms set by my superiors.

How Do You Score?

Review your responses. Give yourself 5 points for every A, 4 for every U, 3 for every S, 2 for every R, and 1 for every N. Total your points and evaluate your score.

41–50 Excellent You may be surprised to find out how much you can improve your skills.

31–40 Good In this course, you can learn ways to make your skills better.

21–30 Fair Practice applying the skills taught in this course.

1–20 Needs Improvement Carefully monitor your improvement as you work through this course.

Setting Communication Goals

If you scored Excellent or Good, complete Part A. If your score was Fair or Needs Improvement, complete Part B.

Part A

1. I plan to put the following ideas into practice:
2. I plan to share the following information about communication with the following people:

Part B

1. The behaviors I need to change most are:
2. To bring about these changes, I will take these steps:

Writing a Résumé

A résumé is a summary of your employment qualifications and work experience that is used to present your credentials to possible employers. Just as effective small talk can set the tone for a good conversation, a well-written résumé can positively influence your chances for getting the job that you want. Employers use résumés to assess your educational background, review your employment history, and evaluate your organizational skills. If your résumé shows that you can be an asset to an employer, you are likely to be offered a job interview. Your résumé should make a positive first impression for you. Use the following pointers to write an effective résumé.

Identify Yourself. Your full name, address, and telephone number are essential parts of your résumé. If you have a fax number or an e-mail address, include that as well. This information must be accurate and should be featured prominently at the top of the document. Make it as easy as possible for employers to contact you. If possible, supply the number of a phone that has an answering machine or voice mail.

State Your Objective. This part of the résumé follows your identification. Use this space to identify the position for which you would like to be considered. You may also want to briefly state your personal and professional goals or summarize your special abilities in this section.

Describe Your Educational Background. State the names of the schools you attended, your areas of study, and the degrees that you earned. Start by listing the academic degree you earned most recently or your current course of study, then work backward. Since you have not yet completed high school, include your projected graduation date. Mention any academic honors that you have received. Your education is a valuable asset—use it to your advantage.

List Your Work Experience. Your work history is an important part of your résumé because it shows potential employers that you know how to interact with other people on a professional level. List the jobs you have held by starting with the most recent one and working backward. Explain the positions you held at each place of employment and the duties for which you were responsible. Include part-time jobs and internships as well as any full-time jobs you have had.

Mention Special Interests and Volunteer Work. Volunteer work suggests to employers that you have good social skills and are willing to dedicate yourself.

For additional information about business writing, see the *Guide to Business Communication* section of the Communication Survival Kit in the Appendix.

Mention your special interests and hobbies. This information tells potential employers that you are a well-rounded person.

Give References. A reference is a person you know, such as a teacher or a work supervisor, who knows you well enough to discuss your work habits with potential employers. Ask your references for permission to use their names and advise them that they may be contacted. When listing a reference, provide the person's name, title, business address, and business phone number. If you do not include the names of references on your résumé, make sure the employer knows that you have references available. Put your reference information at the end of your résumé.

Gina M. Pandelli
230 Patterson Avenue
Ft. Collins, Colorado 80525
Phone: 970-555-8025
Fax: 970-555-3699
E-mail: gmpandelli@isp.com

Objective
To obtain a position as a teller with a national bank that will enable me to use my education and work experience to the fullest extent

Education
Mountainside High School
- Graduated May 1999
- Business-preparatory curriculum
- Honor Roll student
- Student Council treasurer

Work Experience
Gourmet Grocers, 10/97–present
Cashier
- Helped customers check out and purchase groceries
- Bagged items for customers
- Assisted with store opening and closing duties

Activities
Mountainside High School
- School newspaper staff
- Vocal music accompanist
- Varsity track and field

Volunteer at Larimer County Animal Shelter

References
Andrew Sparks, DVM
Veterinarian, Larimer County Animal Shelter
284 Springs Road, Ft. Collins, CO 80525
970-555-7387

Mr. Douglas McKee
Teacher, track coach, Mountainside High School
860 Mountaineer Lane, Ft. Collins, CO 80525
970-555-7866

WRITING Activity

Imagine that you have heard about a summer job that you really want to have. Write your résumé for this job, using the following points as guidelines:

- Put your full name, home address, and telephone number at the top of the résumé. Include your e-mail address or fax number if you have one.
- Indicate the job opening in which you are interested and why. If possible, explain how this job can accommodate your personal or career goals.
- Provide your educational background, including schools, subjects studied, graduations, extracurricular activities, academic honors, and leadership roles.
- Give the names of your past employers and the dates during which you were employed.
- Describe your responsibilities at your past jobs.
- Include your interests and activities.

CHAPTER 8 Assessment and Activities

GLENCOE Online

Visit the *Glencoe Communication Applications* Web site at **communicationapplications.glencoe.com** and click on **Chapter 8 Activity** for additional practice in interpersonal skills.

Reviewing Key Terms

Read each definition. On a separate sheet of paper, write the number of the description and the letter of the term that fits the description best.

1. Helps a shy conversationalist participate

2. Etiquette used for official business or government dealings

3. Describes communication that has no specific individual reference or connection

4. Something that is satisfying within itself

5. Requires a very specific, one-word answer

6. A negative evaluation that brings about positive change

7. Repeat a message in your own words

8. People's willingness to accept differences in status within an organization

a. impersonal

b. intrinsic reward

c. open-ended question

d. closed question

e. paraphrase

f. protocol

g. constructive criticism

h. power distance

Reviewing Key Concepts

1. List the six characteristics of interpersonal communication.

2. What makes a relationship irreplaceable?

3. How do most conversations begin?

4. What are four strategies for participating effectively in a conversation?

5. What nonverbal communication behaviors provide the most valuable clues to how a speaker feels?

6. What effective questioning strategy is being used when a speaker asks, "Will a ten-page paper on *The Scarlet Letter* be satisfactory, or should it be longer?"

7. Imagine that you are invited to an awards dinner to be honored for establishing a food pantry in your community. How would you acknowledge a public introduction by the mayor to a roomful of civic leaders?

8. Give two reasons for identifying yourself and your company when answering phone calls.

Assessment and Activities

Reading and Critical Thinking Skill

1. **Applying Information** Describe the characteristics of a unique relationship.
2. **Classifying Information** Under which topic of small talk would you classify a discussion about the temperature?
3. **Synthesis** Suppose you are the dominant speaker in a conversation about automobiles. Synthesize a question that encourages another participant to contribute to the conversation.
4. **Making Contrasts** How do requests for information and persuasive requests differ?
5. **Recognizing Cause and Effect** What are two possible effects of violating the rules of professional etiquette with a potential employer?

Skill Practice Activity

Evaluating Criticism Read the following criticism from a teacher to a student. On a separate sheet of paper, rewrite the paragraph using strategies for constructive criticism.

"Your essays are getting worse, and you obviously spend little time on them. If your lazy thinking and writing persist, your grade in this class will suffer. Improve the quality of your next paper. Otherwise, you'll fail this course."

Cooperative Learning Activity

Giving Directions As a class, organize into small groups. As a group, choose a site within the school building and write a set of directions from the classroom to that site. Address a short letter to the members of another group and leave it at the selected site. Exchange sets of directions with another group. Follow the directions you now have and retrieve the letter from the site selected by the other group. Return to the classroom and evaluate the directions you used.

Chapter Project

Planning Select a video in which culture, ethnicity, gender, or age affects the communication between two characters. Possible choices are *The Searchers, Prince of Egypt, Yentl,* and *Treasure of the Sierra Madre*. As you watch the video, write descriptions of several scenes in which characters deal ineffectively with their differences. Afterwards, rewrite the dialogue of one of the scenes to make the characters more open to new ideas and less likely to stereotype each other.

Presenting In class, show scenes from the video in which characters are dealing ineffectively with differences. Read your rewritten dialogue to the class and sum up how the movie would end differently if the characters used effective communication. Discuss whether the rewrites make the movie more or less entertaining.

CHAPTER 9

Exploring the Interview Process

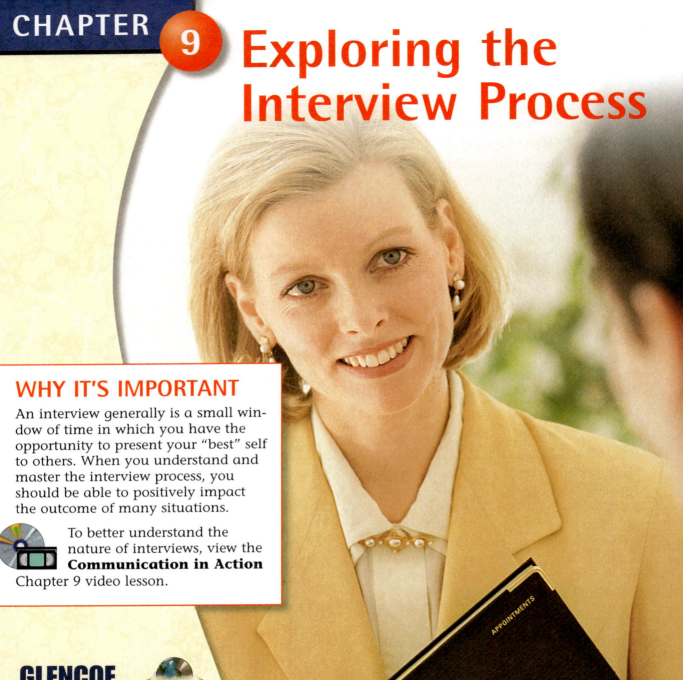

WHY IT'S IMPORTANT

An interview generally is a small window of time in which you have the opportunity to present your "best" self to others. When you understand and master the interview process, you should be able to positively impact the outcome of many situations.

To better understand the nature of interviews, view the **Communication in Action** Chapter 9 video lesson.

"The important thing is to never stop questioning."
—Albert Einstein, American physicist

Visit the *Glencoe Communication Applications* Web site at **communicationapplications.glencoe.com** and click on **Overview–Chapter 9** to preview information about the interview process.

The Nature of Interviews

GUIDE TO READING

Objectives

1. Analyze the roles in the interview process.
2. Describe the different types of interviews and identify an appropriate situation for each.
3. Explain the importance of communicating effectively in interviews.

Terms to Learn

interview
interviewer
interviewee
information-gathering interview
survey interview
investigative interview
exit interview
information-giving interview
performance appraisal
counseling interview
employment interview

You've found an ad in your hometown newspaper for part-time employment at a popular fast-food restaurant. The hours are perfect, the pay is good, and you feel that you have all the necessary skills and abilities to perform the tasks. You're qualified, but is the job yours?

People often believe that the only important consideration in getting a job is whether they can do the work. However, being qualified may not be enough. If you cannot communicate your qualifications and do not know how to conduct yourself during an interview, you may not be hired.

On the other hand, if you learn to communicate effectively and conduct yourself appropriately in an interview, you may increase your chances of getting the job you want. Not only can interviewing skills help you in the job market, but they also may help you communicate successfully in a variety of other situations.

For instance, when you question the president of your senior class for a yearbook story, conduct a telephone poll of local citizens, or try to get the perfect summer job, you are engaged in an interview situation. Although each type of interview is different, they all have set roles and a specific purpose.

A television journalist interviews Madeleine Albright. How are all types of interviews similar?

Roles in the Interview Process

An **interview** is a formal two-party communication in which at least one of the participants has a set purpose. Interviewing allows you to give and receive information through the use of questions and answers. This specific type of communication calls for using excellent listening skills, asking appropriate questions, and giving appropriate answers. It also requires an understanding of the roles people assume in an interview.

There are two main roles in the interview process: the interviewer and the interviewee. The **interviewer** is the one who determines the purpose of the interview and ensures that the discussion remains focused on the purpose. The **interviewee** is the one who provides information to the interviewer. In order to have a successful interview, both parties must participate fully. In other words, both must ask questions, listen to each other's responses, and then provide feedback to each other.

Interviewing is an effective way to find the best florist for a formal event. What does interviewing allow one to do?

Imagine that you are on the planning committee for your senior prom. Your task is to interview local florists and select one to create flower arrangements for the tables. As the interviewer, your main responsibility is to ask questions that will help you determine which florist will best meet your needs. Closely tied to this is another important responsibility: You also need to listen carefully to the florists' answers.

In this interview, both parties must participate and listen even though their goals are different. As the interviewer, you will provide information to each florist about your expectations regarding color, style, budget limitations, and date of delivery. As the interviewee, the florist needs to listen to your needs and respond by showing you examples of floral arrangements that meet those needs. In turn, you need to listen to what each florist has to say and decide which one has the most to offer. Although these roles overlap somewhat, each participant in the interview has a specific set of responsibilities.

The Interviewer

In most cases, the interviewer drives the interview. In other words, he or she has the responsibility of setting up the interview and carrying it out. The interviewer's main responsibilities are to set the goal and structure of the interview, prepare and ask questions, and control the direction of the discussion.

Set a Goal. A goal defines what you would want the outcome of the interview to be. For example, if you were to interview a veterinarian about his or her career field, your goal might be to find out what type of education and experience are required. A different goal might be to find out about new advances in animal medicine. In the workplace, an interviewer might have a goal to hire an employee to work the evening shift.

Figure 9–1 Interviewer Controls Direction

"What are your weaknesses?"
"What qualities do you have that would make you an asset to this company?"
Now, how do I want to answer . . .

Develop the Structure. The structure of an interview is the manner in which it is conducted. Most interviews involve only the interviewer and the interviewee. However, a team or group interview may be set up so that a group of people ask questions of the interviewee. This is often done in a job interview if the applicant would be working with a team or would be supervised by several bosses. Another structure might be to have the initial interview with one person and then follow-up interviews with other individuals if the first interview was successful.

Prepare and Ask Questions. A qualified interviewer does not simply arrive at an interview ready to "wing it." Instead, he or she will prepare a list of appropriate questions ahead of time. The interviewer will then ask these questions to help meet the goal of the interview.

If the goal of an interview is to determine whether the interviewee has good customer-service skills, the interviewer probably will prepare and ask questions that revolve around customer-service situations. If the goal of an interview is to determine whether a new school rule is appropriate, the interviewer's questions might focus on why the rule was created, how it will be enforced, and what the expected results are.

Control the Direction of the Discussion. As Figure 9–1 indicates, in an interview, the interviewer keeps the discussion focused and moving toward the goal. He or she makes sure that the interviewee actually answers the specific questions and does not avoid them or talk around them.

Suppose an interviewer were to ask, "Why did you leave your last job?" and the interviewee replied, "I really want to work here." The interviewee avoided the question. It is the responsibility of the interviewer to maintain focus and get the interview back on track.

The Interviewee

Many people mistakenly believe that, because the interviewer controls the direction of the interview, he or she is the only one responsible for successful communication. It is important to understand, however, that interviewees also have the responsibilities of providing clear, complete, and appropriate answers and of gathering information.

Provide Clear, Complete, and Appropriate Answers. Imagine that an interviewer asks you what duties you had in your last job. To answer, you simply say, "I had a lot of different responsibilities." Did you thoroughly answer the interviewer's question? This type of vague answer doesn't really tell the interviewer anything about your specific experience.

It is the responsibility of the interviewee to provide clearly worded, well-thought-out answers. Clear, complete answers help the interviewee convey information to the interviewer without any need for interpretation. In addition, thinking about your response before actually voicing it can help you avoid making misleading or confusing statements.

To provide appropriate answers in an interview, it is essential to listen. Often, interviewees concentrate too much on what they want to say in an interview and too little on what they need to hear. Remember, to answer a question appropriately, you need to hear and understand it first.

Practice for the Workplace

The Importance of Perspective As you prepare for a job interview, whether as the interviewer or the interviewee, it is helpful to consider the other person's point of view. Try to visualize the interview from more than one perspective. If you are preparing to hire a cook for a restaurant, for example, you may consider asking an applicant if he or she has any experience making pasta sauces. The cook, preparing for the same interview, might ask to see what pasta sauces are on the menu. Both parties have similar concerns, but they are viewed from different perspectives.

BUSINESS PRACTICE *Activity*

Suppose you are the owner of a limousine service in a major city. You need to hire a new driver. Develop a series of questions you would ask the applicants. Next, as a potential applicant for the same job, develop a list of questions you would ask the interviewer. Are the two sets of questions related in any way? Do the two sides have any mutual concerns? Compare your results.

Gather Information. Although an interviewee's main responsibility is to provide information, he or she also may need to gather certain information. This responsibility occurs most often when interviewing for a job.

Job responsibilities for employees in a grocery store range from running the cash register to bagging groceries. Why is it important for an interviewee to gather information during an interview?

The purpose of a job interview is not only to allow an interviewer to learn more about an individual. It also is designed to help the interviewee learn more about the company and the job. By asking specific, appropriate questions, an interviewee can better determine whether a company or position fits his or her needs.

For example, suppose you are interviewing for a part-time cashier position at a local grocery store. The manager explains that the job will require you to work fifteen hours per week, including some weekends. As a member of your school band, you have a standing Friday evening commitment during football season. If you tell the manager that you are unavailable Friday evenings and ask if that is a problem, you'll have a better idea if the position is a good choice for you. Your question also will help the manager decide whether you are right for the company. Realistically, if one of the two people in the interview finds that the situation is not a good match, it may be best not to offer or take a position just to have a job.

It is clear that interviewers and interviewees have specific responsibilities in interview situations. It also is clear that, in order to have a successful interview, both must be effective communicators. Listening carefully, asking questions, and answering clearly and appropriately all are important communication skills that can make or break an interview. Other factors in determining the role and responsibility of interviewer and interviewee are the type of interview being conducted and its purpose.

Types of Interviews

From what you have read so far in this section, you probably have concluded that not all interviews are alike. A job interview, for example, would be different from interviewing the principal about a new rule or interviewing florists for the prom. Interviews vary because they are conducted for different reasons. Thus, interviews are categorized by type. The three main types of interviews are as follows:

- information-gathering
- information-giving
- employment

Communication Practice Lab

Determining Roles and Responsibilities

To practice determining your specific role and responsibilities in an interview, follow these steps:

Step 1 Imagine that you are a staff member of your school newspaper and you are going to interview a fellow student about an accomplishment. You have arranged to meet tomorrow to discuss it. On a sheet of paper, write your role and the other student's role in the interview.

Step 2 List each party's main goal or purpose for the interview.

Step 3 List two specific responsibilities for each party in this interview situation.

Step 4 Share your answers as a class and discuss how your goals and responsibilities might change if the roles were reversed.

Information-Gathering

An information-gathering interview is one in which an interviewer obtains information from an interviewee. The interviewer usually does this through a survey or an investigation.

Survey Interviews Survey interviews gather information from a number of people. The information is used to draw conclusions, make interpretations, and determine future action. Survey interviews also are used to find out consumers' reactions to a product. For example, you might be asked in a grocery store to taste several different juice drinks, such as the ones shown in Figure 9–2, and give your opinion about which one you like best. This information helps the juice drink companies understand what consumers like and dislike about their product. They can then make changes, if necessary, to better meet the customers' needs.

Survey interviews also are used to gather information about people's reactions to change or new ideas. For example, imagine your school is thinking about changing its dress code to specify uniforms. The student council may conduct a survey interview to find out how the student body and parents will feel about the change. The information they gather may influence the way the school puts its new uniform rule into effect. You will receive information about preparing a survey in Chapter 14.

Figure 9–2 Product Samples

Investigative Interview An interview in which the interviewer uses questions to find out unknown information is known as an investigative interview. This information often is used to determine the cause of an event.

The types of questions generally asked in an investigative interview are *Who, What, When, Where, Why,* and *How.* For example, suppose a student in a neighboring school was awarded a four-year scholarship to a famous university. Your school guidance counselor wants to investigate how the student won the scholarship to determine if students at your school might be eligible. To make that determination, the counselor, or interviewer, might ask the following questions:

- "*Who* was the recipient of the scholarship?"
- "*What* were the criteria for the award?"
- "*When* was the deadline for applications?"
- "*Where* did the student obtain the information?"
- "*Why* was the student chosen?"
- "*How* will the scholarship monies be distributed?"

A business will often use investigative interviews among its employees to discover what is needed for the development of products and services. Journalists depend upon investigative interviews to develop the lines of information upon which they base their stories. Detectives and lawyers depend heavily upon investigative interviews while attempting to solve crimes or develop cases.

Another type of investigative interview is called an exit interview. An exit interview is used to determine why a person has decided to

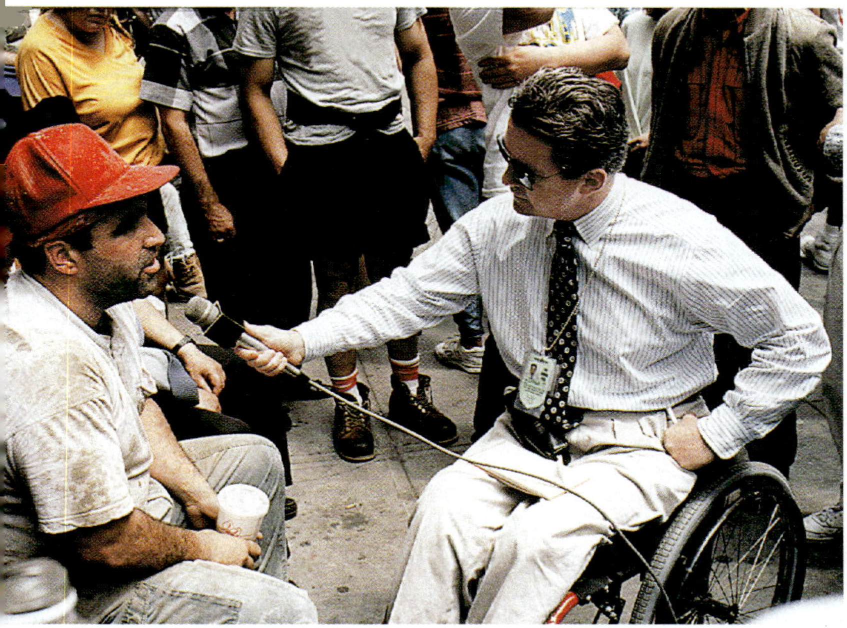

A reporter holds an investigative interview. **What types of questions are asked in an investigative interview?**

leave an organization. Companies often conduct exit interviews at the end of employment or involvement of a person in an organization to determine why employees leave for other jobs. If they discover that several employees have left because of a troublesome manager or a poor benefits package, they may decide to make changes before others leave. Schools also might arrange exit interviews to determine why students resign from school clubs and organizations. Exit interviews can give them the information they need to keep their membership strong.

Information-Giving

An information-giving interview is one in which an interviewer gives information to an interviewee. Two commonly used information-giving interviews are performance appraisals and counseling interviews.

Performance Appraisal

An evaluation of how well you have achieved your goals and objectives over a set period of time is called a performance appraisal. As Figure 9–3 shows, when you get your grade card, you have received a type of written performance appraisal. This type of interview most often occurs face-to-face, such as when an employer talks to an employee about job performance.

Counseling Interview A counseling interview generally occurs when an interviewer helps the interviewee decide on a course of action. For example, you might talk to a school counselor about scheduling your classes or choosing a college. A social worker or family counselor may use counseling interviews to help individuals solve difficult personal problems. In both cases, the counselor shares his or her expertise with the interviewee to achieve a positive result.

Figure 9–3 School Performance Appraisal

SUBJECT	GRADE
Language Arts	A+
Algebra	A+
Physical Science	A+
World History	A+

By permission of Mell Lazarus and Creators Syndicate.

Employment

A common type of interview is an employment interview. An **employment interview** is a process employers use to judge whether a job candidate is qualified and well suited for a position. During an employment interview, an employer investigates a prospective employee's experience, motivation, education, and personality, among other considerations, and decides who of the interviewees is best suited for the job.

Importance People often do not realize how important employment interviews can be. However, in a poll of personnel executives, the Bureau of National Affairs discovered that the employment interview was the single most important factor in landing a job. The executives went on to say that communication skills and a knowledge of interviewing were even more important to a successful interview than grade-point average or work experience.

Employers use interviews to size up the whole individual. Does this person know how to communicate in a professional environment? Will he or she be able to make sound decisions? Does the applicant know how to communicate appropriately and effectively? Does he or she possess the interpersonal skills to work well with others in this office? Is he or she qualified to meet the responsibilities of the job? Because so many of your qualities are being evaluated in a short period of time, it is important to make your best possible impression on the interviewer. For this reason, it is critical to master the skill of interviewing effectively.

Building Skills Now is the time to develop strong interviewing skills. The way to build these valuable skills is through study and practice. To begin, take a look at how companies advertise job openings to attract the right candidates. Notices for employment can be found in newspapers' classified advertising sections, on radio and television, through your school counselor, by word of mouth, on school or community bulletin boards, or on the Internet. Careful study of these employment ads may indicate what you need to be prepared for in an interview.

Some positions require that applicants phone first or send a brief letter with a résumé. A résumé is a brief history of your education and work experience. In many cases, an employer will review an applicant's résumé first and then only grant an interview if he or she feels the person is suitable for the job. A well-written résumé not only may get you through the door, but it may give you a strong base of information to expand upon in the interview itself.

Employment Interview Variations

Most of the time, employment interviews are conducted on-site, which means at the company where the job is being offered. However, some employment interviews may be held at a job fair, in a hotel conference room, on the telephone, at a convention center, over dinner or sodas at a restaurant, or elsewhere. Most off-site interview locations are chosen for their convenience to the interviewer or the interviewee.

In this section you have learned about the roles of the participants in an interview and about the different types of interviews. You also may have noticed that every type of interview has a specific purpose. However, how is this purpose met? Each type of interview has a special interview process, or order of events. Understanding this process will help you prepare for your own interviews in the community and the workplace.

Section 1 Assessment

Visit the *Glencoe Communication Applications* Web site at **communicationapplications.glencoe.com** and click on **Self-Check and Study Guide 9.1** to review your understanding of the nature of interviews.

Review Key Terms

1. Define each term and write it in a sentence: interview, interviewer, interviewee, information-gathering interview, survey interview, investigative interview, exit interview, information-giving interview, performance appraisal, counseling interview, employment interview.

Check Understanding

2. Compare and contrast the roles of an interviewer and an interviewee.
3. Describe the three types of interviews and give one real-life example of each.
4. Explain the following statement: Communication skills can be even more important than your qualifications when interviewing for a job.
5. **Analyze** You have been selected to write a professional profile of your communication applications teacher for the school newspaper. What type of interview would you use? Give three questions you might ask as the interviewer.

APPLICATION *Activity*

Developing Interview Goals Imagine that you would like to create a student-run computer help desk at your school. Before presenting your idea to the principal, you want to find out students' reactions to the idea. Create two columns on a sheet of paper. Label one column *Students* and one *Principal* and write the type of interview you might conduct with each. Then, in each column, list a goal you might have as the interviewer in that situation.

Applying Reading Skill

Skimming for Information

Skimming means quickly reading through a body of information in order to pick out key points or concepts.

Learning the Skill

Follow the guidelines listed below when skimming different materials.

- When skimming a book, start by looking at the table of contents or the index to get an overview of the entire body of information. Notice the titles of major chapters or sections, headings within sections, and lists. Use the index to find specific topics.
- If you are skimming an essay or other scholastic report, pay attention to the title and any major divisions.
- When skimming a memorandum, fax, or e-mail message, check the beginning of the message for a heading such as *Re:* or *Subject.*

Once you get to the main body of any source, always look for words or topics that are related to the specific information for which you are looking. Find the topic sentence in each paragraph. Always check information that is displayed in graphs, tables, charts, artwork, and photograph captions.

Practicing the Skill

Many companies supply their workers with employee handbooks. The handbooks provide information on company policies and practices. Assume that your supervisor has asked for volunteers to work on Thanksgiving Day. You are not sure what your company's policies are regarding holidays and overtime pay. In which chapters from the following employee handbook would you find information about these policies?

Employee Handbook

Table of Contents

Chapter	Page
1. About this Guide	1
2. Commitment to Diversity and Equal Opportunity	2
3. Determining Length of Service	4
4. Personnel File	7
5. Notice and Separation Pay Benefits and Exit Interviews	12
6. Business Ethics	16
7. Rewards and Recognition	21
8. Compensation Practices	28
9. Personal Time	35
10. Vacations and Holidays	45
11. Leaves of Absence	57
12. Emergency Closings	61
13. Performance Review	63
14. Tuition Refund Program	71
15. Career Opportunities Program	73
16. Financial Programs for Employees	77
17. Health Benefits	79

Obtain a copy of the handbook that describes the policies and procedures of your school. Skim the handbook's table of contents to find your school's attendance policies and procedures. Write a brief paragragh that summarizes this information.

Section 2

Understanding the Interview Process

GUIDE TO READING

Objectives

1. Identify and describe the components of the interview process.
2. Explain the steps needed to prepare for an interview.
3. Distinguish the basic components of an interview.
4. Explain the importance of the activities in the post interview.

Terms to Learn

interview process
highly closed question
primary question
secondary question
leading question
neutral question
direct question
indirect question
factual question
opinion question
hypothetical question

What would happen if you worked at a fast-food establishment where none of the employees were assigned specific tasks? Who would take people's orders? Who would order supplies? Would several people rush to get beverages while no one cooked hamburgers? How effective do you think this operation would be in the long run?

Clearly, if no one were assigned specific duties, the process of operating a fast-food restaurant would be inefficient. Customers and employees alike probably would become frustrated and go elsewhere.

Like a fast-food restaurant, almost every endeavor needs a plan or structure that the participants understand and follow. An interview is no different. It consists of more than just two people showing up to talk to each other. Instead, it is a planned process. The **interview process** is a sequence of actions that results in an effective interview. This process includes preparation, the actual interview, and the post interview.

The efficiency of a fast-food restaurant is determined by the process by which the food is prepared and served. What does the process of the interview include?

Preparing for an Interview

If your English class assignment is to write a composition about a classic novel, you probably would not begin writing before you had read the book. Just like writing an English composition, an interview requires a lot of thought and preparation.

Set a Goal

The first step in preparing for an interview is to set a goal. To do this, determine what you want the outcome of the interview to be. For instance, if one of your friends has asked your advice about an argument she is having with her brother, you will need to be prepared for a counseling interview. Your goal might be to get your friend to resolve her conflict with her brother.

Goal of the Interviewer As you learned earlier in this section, it is the responsibility of the interviewer to determine the goal of the interview. A clear goal helps him or her decide how to approach the situation.

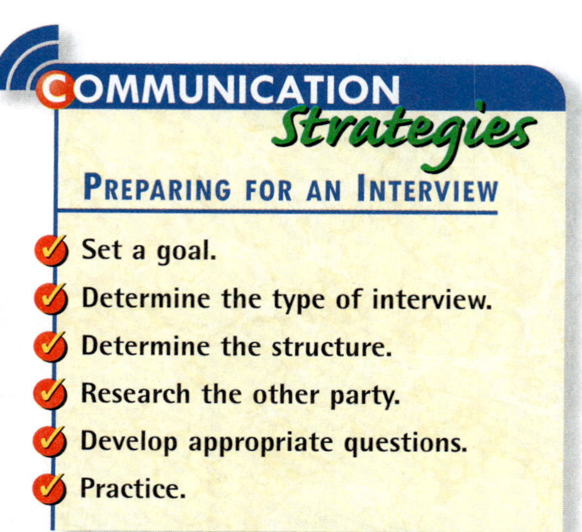

Communication Strategies

Preparing for an Interview

- Set a goal.
- Determine the type of interview.
- Determine the structure.
- Research the other party.
- Develop appropriate questions.
- Practice.

Goal of the Interviewee Like the interviewer, the interviewee also should decide what he or she wants to accomplish in the interview. Imagine you are a reporter for the local television station. Your assignment today is to interview one of the candidates running for the office of mayor. Your goal as the interviewer is to gain as much objective information about the candidate as possible. On the other hand, the interviewee has an important goal, too. That person wants to prove to local viewers that he or she is the best candidate for the office.

Determining the Type of Interview

How you prepare for an interview depends upon the type of interview situation you are involved in. This is a key step in preparing for an interview and usually is the responsibility of the interviewer.

As the interviewer, it is important for you to analyze the situation and use context clues when determining which type of interview to conduct. Choose the type of interview that will best enable you to reach your goal. For example, if your goal is to find out how many students have computers at home, it may be too time-consuming to conduct an investigative interview with every student. Instead, a survey interview might be appropriate.

However, if you are going to interview the captain of the school football team for the yearbook, you may determine that the most appropriate type of interview is an investigative interview. This type of interview will enable you to gather all the information needed to write a complete story. Once you have determined the best type of interview to conduct, you can adapt the structure and your research accordingly.

Larry King talks with Ross Perot in a prearranged interview. **What is a scheduled interview?**

Determine the Structure

Another important preparation step is to determine the structure of the interview. Again, this step typically is the responsibility of the interviewer. Because the different structures can produce very different results, it is important that interviewers base their choice on the goal of the interview. For instance, where will the interview take place? Who will be present?

A prearranged interview is one that is arranged in advance. If you are researching a topic and must interview a person who has information about your topic, make sure that you arrange the interview several days in advance. Call and ask the person for some time to discuss your topic at his or her convenience. Try to let the person know approximately how much time you will need for the interview. Give the person your phone number or a way in which he or she can contact you if the interview appointment cannot be kept. Call to confirm the appointment the day before the interview and remind the person about the topic of the interview.

Which format will produce more useful results? Would a scheduled interview, a nonscheduled interview, or one that is a little of both be the most useful?

Scheduled Interviews A scheduled interview is one in which the questions are standardized, such as in a survey or poll. A scheduled interview might include questions such as "How many juice drinks do you drink each week?" Generally, there is little flexibility for expanding upon specific questions or answers. Because of this, a scheduled interview typically takes less time than other types of interviews. It also gives the interviewer more control over the interview and its outcome.

Scheduled interviews usually strive to ask each interviewee the same questions in the same manner. Answers also tend to be limited to either a specific type—"In what year were you born?"—or even specific words—"Would you describe yourself as a heavy sleeper or a light sleeper?" Because answers are so limited, they are fairly easy to quantify. For instance, it is easier to group answers to a question such as "Do you prefer red or blue?" than it is to group answers to "What is your favorite color?"

When conducting the interview, remember to be flexible with your questions. The person you are interviewing may disclose some interesting pieces of information that you may not have heard before, or you may want to ask a question about an answer that you get. In these or other cases, you may want to get away from your plan and go with the moment. However, keep in mind that it may take you away from the original purpose of the interview.

While it may take substantial expertise to develop effective questions for a scheduled interview, the interview itself requires little interviewer skill. Information is gathered according to a strict set of guidelines, leaving little opportunity for interviewer discretion.

One example of a nonscheduled interview is a salesperson checking up on a client to evaluate the client's satisfaction with a product. What must an interviewer in a nonscheduled interview do to make the interview a success?

nonscheduled interviews. An interviewer may develop a set of questions to use as a guide, but he or she will venture away from the list as needed to pursue an interesting thought or an unusual answer. While the list of questions helps ensure that the most important information is covered, the interviewer is free to discover other information that might otherwise have been overlooked.

Regardless of which type of interview the interviewer chooses, it is important for both participants to be well prepared. An important part of that preparation involves learning as much as possible about the other party.

Nonscheduled Interviews Nonscheduled interviews, on the other hand, generally have a topic but may not involve a standardized set of questions. An example of a nonscheduled interview might be a sales representative casually calling a client to make sure he or she is satisfied with a particular product.

Finally, because of their flexible, changing nature, nonscheduled interviews require considerable skill on the part of the interviewer. He or she must know how to keep the interview on track and moving forward to meet a specific goal.

Moderately Scheduled Interviews Scheduled interviews and nonscheduled interviews tend to represent two extremes regarding structure—one is highly structured, and the other has little structure at all. Often, the most useful interview structure lies somewhere in between.

A moderately scheduled interview combines useful aspects of both scheduled and

Research the Other Party

Before you enter into an interview, it is important to find out as much as possible about the other party who will be participating. This will give you the foundation needed to engage in a successful interview. Although both parties need to prepare for each type of interview, the majority of the responsibility usually falls on one party. Whether that is the interviewer or the interviewee depends on the type of interview.

Information-Gathering Research In an information-gathering interview, it is primarily the interviewer's responsibility to prepare research. He or she is the one trying to obtain as much information as possible from the interviewee. To prepare for the interview, you will need to know some background on both the topic and the interviewee. For example, if you are preparing to interview a police officer about crime prevention, you might want to read up on crime statistics in your area and across the country. You also might want to find out about the officer's professional history, such as how long he or she has served on the force and any special honors or awards he or she has received.

*inter*NET ACTIVITY

Wanted . . . The Internet provides a wealth of employment information. For ideas on how to prepare for a job interview, do a search using the keywords *career planning, résumés, cover letters,* and *employment interviewing.* Print any interview tips, résumé and cover letter guides, job descriptions, and salary ranges that you find. Share this information with the rest of the class.

Information-Giving Research As with an information-gathering interview, in an information-giving interview, the responsibility for most of the research falls on the interviewer. In order to present accurate and complete information to the interviewee, the interviewer needs to be able to support his or her evaluation.

One common type of information-giving interview is a performance appraisal. During a performance appraisal, the manager, or interviewer, needs to be able to explain why he or she is or is not satisfied with the quality of the employee's work. To do this, the manager needs to have enough research and data to support his or her conclusion.

Although the interviewer will do most of the research for an information-giving interview, it is important for the interviewee to conduct research as well. By learning something about the topic and the speaker beforehand, the interviewee will have a better basis for understanding and critically examining any information he or she receives.

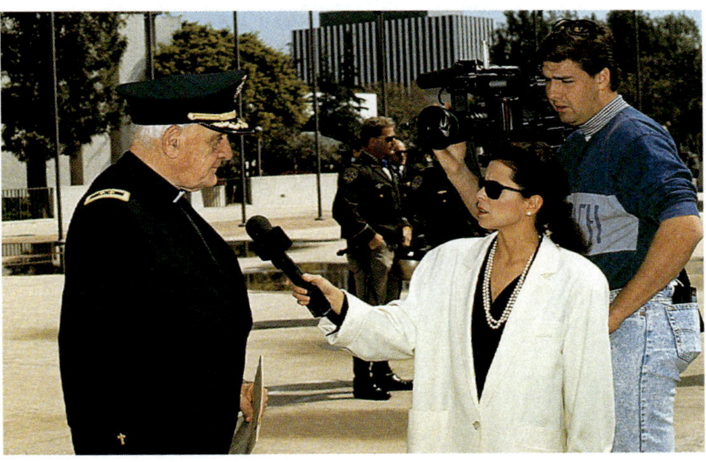

A reporter interviews a police officer to gather information on a breaking story. What is the responsibility of the interviewer in an information-gathering interview?

Employment Research An employment interview also requires preparation by both parties. However, the primary research responsibility lies with the interviewee. As an interviewee, it is important for you to research both the company and the job for which you are interviewing.

Researching the Company Usually, you can find information about individual companies at the public library, through current employees, on the Internet, or through a city's Better Business Bureau. If a company is new or very small, it is important to research at least current trends and leaders in the company's industry. Most of the time, however, you will be able to find at least some information on the businesses in your community.

As you conduct your research of the company, keep in mind the questions on the next page.

Before applying for a bank teller position, it is wise to familiarize yourself with the job responsibilities. What factors should you keep in mind when researching a position?

1. When and by whom was the company founded?
2. Who runs the company now?
3. What is the company's main line of business?
4. Have any recent changes or developments occurred at this company or in this line of business?
5. Who is the competition?
6. Approximately how many employees work for this company?
7. How does the company train its employees?
8. What employee benefits does the company offer, such as sick leave, medical insurance, vacation time, and retirement?

Researching the Job In addition to learning some basic information about the company, you need to research the job itself.

As you conduct your research, keep the following questions in mind.

1. What are the primary responsibilities of the job?
2. What role would I play in this position?
3. What skills typically are required for this type of position? Will I need any special training?
4. Where might this type of job lead in the near future? In the distant future?
5. What kind of employee performance appraisal system does the company use?

Suppose you are applying for a job as a bank teller. Prior to the interview, you will need to find out what a teller's primary

Global Communication

Gathering Information

If you are going to conduct business in a country you have never visited before, the best way to learn about it is to ask people who have lived there. Find people in your community who have lived in other countries by consulting with international companies, ethnic businesses, military bases, the chamber of commerce, or local universities. Develop a list of questions for a moderately scheduled information-gathering interview designed to learn more about other countries and their customs. Use the interview questions to ask the people in your community about another culture. Share your interview results with the rest of the class.

responsibilities are. Your main duty might be processing customer transactions, or the job could include doing daily audits, or balancing a cash drawer. You will also need to find out what your role would be when performing the tasks. For example, you may be the person to whom customers are directed when they have a problem with their deposit.

Also, you need to find out what types of skills a bank teller needs and what types of equipment you will be expected to use. In many cases, tellers use a special computer system to process transactions. How might your current skills help you quickly learn to use this system?

Benefits of Research Besides providing you with valuable background information, research has other benefits as well. First, it will help you decide whether this particular company and job are a good match for your skills and goals. Does this company seem stable and ethical? Is it a safe environment? Am I qualified for this job? Will I be challenged in this position? Answering yes to these questions may help you feel enthusiastic about interviewing for the position.

Research also can help you feel confident in your interview. Learning about the job's responsibilities can help you match them to your own skills and experience. This allows you to enter the interview confident that you can do the job and do it well.

Interviewer's Responsibilities Although the biggest burden of research in an employment interview rests upon the interviewee, the interviewer also needs to do research. As the interviewer, you need to make sure the interviewee has the qualifications and skills necessary to justify an employment interview. You also will need to carefully review the information the interviewee has provided, such as an application for employment, a résumé, or a cover letter. As Figure 9–4 shows, once you have done your research, you are ready to formulate the questions that you want to ask during the interview.

Figure 9–4 Preparing to Interview

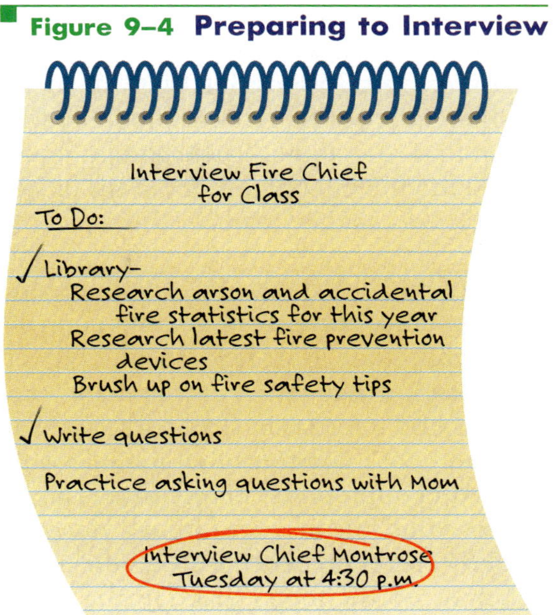

Interview Fire Chief
for Class
To Do:
✓ Library–
Research arson and accidental fire statistics for this year
Research latest fire prevention devices
Brush up on fire safety tips
✓ Write questions
Practice asking questions with Mom
Interview Chief Montrose
Tuesday at 4:30 p.m.

Develop Appropriate Questions

Based upon their research, both parties in a successful interview should develop questions as part of the preparation process. To determine which questions are appropriate, you will need to make a list of what you already know versus what you need or want to know. Then, you can better develop questions to bridge this gap.

Interviewee Questions

As the interviewee, your questions should help you achieve your goal for the interview. The goal, of course, depends upon the type of interview.

Information-Gathering Interviews In an information-gathering interview, your goal probably will be to provide accurate, interesting, and complete information to the interviewer. You may want to ask questions about how your information will be used. You also may want to ask perception-checking questions throughout the interview to make sure your meanings are clearly understood.

Information-Giving Interviews In an information-giving interview, your goal should be to learn as much as possible from the interviewer. Therefore, your questions probably will center around the topic. These might even include asking the interviewer about his or her own experiences as they relate to the topic.

Employment Interviews The questions you ask in an employment interview can be extremely important. They help the interviewer better understand who you are and where your motivations and interests lie. In an interview, it is important to ask questions that are relevant, respectful, and appropriate for the situation. In most cases, this means you would not ask about salary or certain benefits unless the interviewer brings up the topics first. On the other hand, you will show initiative by asking intelligent questions about the company, the position, and your specific responsibilities.

For instance, imagine that you are preparing to interview for a position as an assistant video technician. You know that the position requires someone who can maintain and operate video editing equipment as well as assist in other video production tasks. You also know that the company provides training on its specific video equipment, but you are interested in knowing more. Your questions for the interview might include these:

1. What specific editing equipment does this company use?
2. Will the company provide tuition reimbursement if I take courses to learn new editing techniques or programs?
3. Will I ever travel with the videographer to shoot and edit video on location?
4. In addition to my regular responsibilities, will I ever participate in planning the shoots or actually shooting a video myself?

As an interviewee, you should make sure that your questions reflect a basic understanding of the company and the position but show an eagerness to learn more. They also should imply a desire to work hard and to stay with the company for a significant length of time. In general, view your questions as another opportunity to make a good impression on the interviewer.

Interviewer Questions

As the interviewer, your questions will direct the course of the interview. Sample interviewer questions are shown in Figure 9–5. As was the case for the interviewee, the nature of your questions will depend upon your goal and the type of interview in which you are involved.

Information-Gathering Interviews In an information-gathering interview, it is the interviewer's responsibility to gather as much information as possible from the interviewee. Your questions will probably center around a central theme or topic and should be based on the research you have done.

Figure 9–5 Sample Interviewer Questions

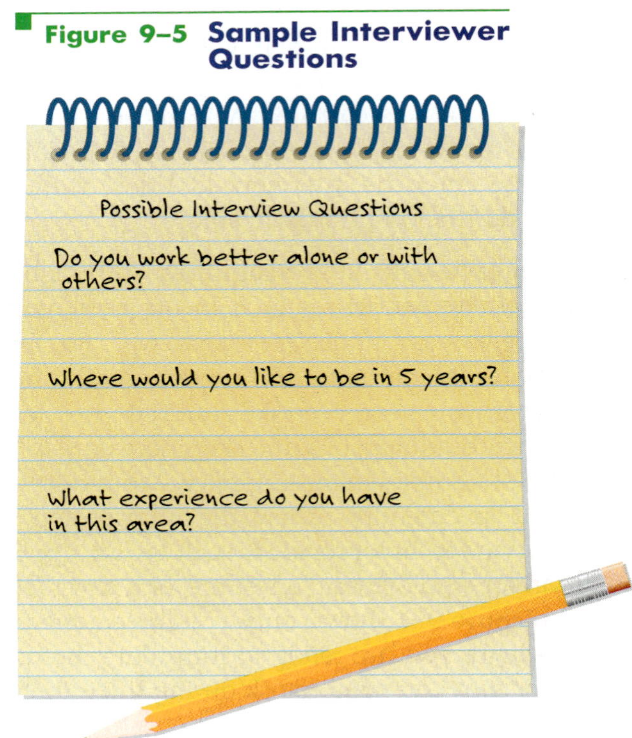

Possible Interview Questions
Do you work better alone or with others?
Where would you like to be in 5 years?
What experience do you have in this area?

TECHNOLOGY *Activity*

Seeing Is Believing One way to practice your job interviewing skills is to videotape yourself in a mock interview. Identify a career that you would like to pursue; then, choose a partner and develop ten employment interview questions for each other. Have a third student record your interview with a video camera. Watch both interviews and analyze your questions, your answers, and your nonverbal communication. Try watching the interviews with the sound turned off to more easily see and analyze nonverbal behaviors. What do you see on tape that you didn't notice before? Having seen yourself on tape, what would you try to improve upon during an actual interview?

Information-Giving Interviews In an information-giving interview, your goal is to be an information resource for the interviewee. As you explain your topic or ideas, you may want to use perception-checking questions to make sure the interviewee understands what you are saying. Depending on the tone you have set, you also may wish to ask the interviewee to contribute some of his or her own ideas to the interview.

Employment Interviews In an employment interview, the interviewer's questions should be designed to evaluate the interviewee's personality, qualifications, potential, and goals, among other things. If you are interviewing a number of individuals for the same position, you may decide to ask each a similar set of questions. However, try not to be so focused on following a routine that you fail to follow up on unusual answers or comments given by the interviewee. Many interviewers find it helpful to discuss possible questions with those who will be working directly with the newly hired person. In general, the more you can find out about each interviewee, the better equipped you will be to make a final hiring decision.

Practice

Once you have determined the goal, type, and structure of the interview, researched the other party, and developed your questions, it is time to put all these elements together. Practice allows you to experiment with the flow of the interview, correct any missteps, and adjust your behavior for maximum impact and effectiveness when it counts.

Practice Interviewing. As the interviewer, it is important for you to practice what you want to say during the beginning, middle, and end of the interview. Keep the goal of the interview in mind and practice getting the discussion back on track when it strays. In addition to practicing what you will say, take time to focus on your nonverbal behavior. Make sure it sends the right message. You also may wish to choose the clothing you plan to wear to the interview and make sure it is clean and

This person is practicing in front of a mirror before an interview. How does practicing help an interviewee?

ready to wear. Practice your note-taking skills. Practicing your role as an interviewer will help you participate in the actual interview with confidence and remain focused on your goals.

Practice Being Interviewed. As the interviewee, you will want to be prepared to respond appropriately to any situation that may arise in an interview. One way to practice this is to make up questions that you think the interviewer might ask. Have a parent or friend pretend to be the interviewer and ask you the questions so you may practice your answers. Also enlist that person's help in evaluating your nonverbal behavior. Try to use nonverbal cues that communicate honesty, openness, respect, and enthusiasm. In Section 3 of this chapter, nonverbal behaviors will be discussed.

The Actual Interview

Just as with an English composition, a business letter, or a speech, an interview has a definite beginning, middle, and end. These components are referred to as the *opening,* the *body,* and the *closing.* Analyzing how each of these components work together will help you participate more effectively in any interview.

The Opening

The opening of the interview begins with both parties establishing a rapport, or harmonious relationship, with one another. A typical beginning has both parties introducing themselves. Sometimes, this step is followed by a handshake and a few moments of "small talk" or polite conversation. The purpose of this is to develop an atmosphere of goodwill and to put both parties a little more at ease in what often is a stressful situation. Generally, this brief, initial conversation will set the tone for the rest of the interview.

Once the tone has been set, it is important for the interviewer to review the purpose of the interview. This will help both parties keep their comments on track during their

Communication Practice Lab

Practicing an Interview

To practice participating in an interview, follow these steps:

Step 1 As a class, brainstorm possible interview situations. Then, with a partner, choose one of these situations and write it on a sheet of paper.

Step 2 Determine the type of interview and write it on the sheet of paper.

Step 3 On the same sheet, write the interviewer's and interviewee's goals for the interview. Also, describe the structure and how you might research each party.

Step 4 Write three questions for the interviewer and three for the interviewee and label each with the type of question it models.

Step 5 Describe your interview situation to the class. Then, with one partner acting as the interviewer and one acting as the interviewee, practice your interview.

Step 6 As a class, discuss the strengths and weaknesses of each pair's preparation.

TYPES OF QUESTIONS IN AN INTERVIEW

Question Type	Definition	Example
Open-ended	Broad in scope, giving the respondent a great deal of freedom in his or her answer	Tell me about yourself.
Closed	Seeks a very specific answer	What hours are you available to work?
Highly closed	Not only seeks a specific answer but may even provide answers from which to choose	Would you prefer to work mornings, afternoons, or evenings?
Primary	Begins a new topic	Tell me about your hobbies.
Secondary	Helps the interviewer better understand the answer to a primary question	Why do you like that particular hobby?
Leading	Suggests the desired answer	You do want to work weekends, don't you?
Neutral	Implies no specific or "right" or "wrong" answer	Would you like to work weekends?
Direct	Straightforward; asks exactly what the interviewer wants to know and leaves no room for ambiguity	Can you work Friday evenings?
Indirect	Seeks specific information without directly asking for it	What do you usually do on Friday evenings?
Factual	Seeks information that can be proven	Where do you attend high school?
Opinion	Asks for the respondent's judgment about something	What is your opinion about employees who steal?
Hypothetical	Asks how a respondent might react in a given situation	If you knew someone were stealing from the company, what would you do?

discussion. The interviewer also may wish to explain the structure and length of the interview so the interviewee will know what to expect. The interviewee's primary responsibility during the opening of the interview is to listen, respond appropriately, and try to make a good first impression.

The Body

The body is the main part of the interview. During this time, the conversation turns to specific questioning. Unlike casual conversation with your friends, conversation during an interview is planned. The interviewer asks questions that have a specific purpose in mind. The interviewee also carefully considers each answer to make sure it is appropriate and accurate and contributes to the goal of the interview.

In a balanced interview, both parties speak and listen. The interviewer will both ask and answer questions of the interviewee. Similarly, the interviewee not only will answer questions but also may have questions to ask of the interviewer. Both parties make decisions based upon the information they receive. They do this by analyzing the answers to many types of questions.

There are several types of questions that may be asked during an interview. Some might not even seem like questions at all at first glance. The chart lists some of the different types of questions and gives an example of each.

As an interviewer, understanding the different types of questions may help you get the exact information you need. As an interviewee, knowing what types of questions you may be asked can help you answer more appropriately. In both cases, you may want to record answers given in the interview. Careful note-taking skills will help you do this. In any case, providing clear, concise answers adds to your overall effectiveness in any interview.

The Closing

The closing is a summary of what occurred during the body of the interview. In an information-gathering interview, the interviewer also may take this opportunity to summarize and verify what he or she has learned from the interviewee. For example, a college interviewer may say, "I understand that you want to earn a degree in education. You currently have a high school grade-point average of 3.3. You plan to work part time while attending school and will live on campus." This summary gives the interviewee a chance to correct any information that has been misunderstood.

This also is the time to discuss plans for future action. Usually, the interviewer will initiate these plans. He or she might say, "I will contact you by mail within two weeks." If no future plans are mentioned, the interviewee might ask if he or she may make a follow-up call to the interviewer in a few days. Whether the interview has gone well or not, both parties should express appreciation to each other for their time and consideration. It is important to leave the interview on a friendly note.

THE POST INTERVIEW

As you may have guessed from its name, the post interview is what happens following the interview. This is a key time for reconnecting with the interviewer and reminding him or her of your strong points.

Figure 9–6 Sample Thank-You Letter

386 Lakeview Street
Columbus, Ohio 12312
(614) 123-4567

November 23, 2002

Jessica Jones
Banking Center Manager
Franklin National Bank
252 Main Street
Columbus, Ohio 12312

Dear Ms. Jones:

Thank you for taking time to discuss possible employment opportunities at Franklin National Bank. I realize that Franklin National Bank has a reputation for excellence in customer service and desires energetic and effective tellers to continue this proud tradition. I believe my skills meet the needs of your company.

As we discussed, having spent two years as a cashier at East End Market has shown me the importance of quality customer service. It is for these reasons that I wish to be considered for a teller position.

I look forward to hearing from you next week. Thank you for your time and consideration.

Sincerely,

Andrea M. Smith

Andrea M. Smith

A follow-up thank-you letter or other type of business communication is a crucial part of the post interview. In this brief communication, you should summarize what you discussed in the interview and thank the interviewer for taking time to meet with you. The tone of your thank-you should be warm but professional, similar to the one modeled in the letter in Figure 9–6.

The post interview also is the best time to analyze how the interview went. After participating in an interview, ask yourself what went right, what went wrong, and how you can improve next time. The following is a list of several questions you may wish to include in your analysis.

- Was I adequately prepared for the interview?
- Did I ask clear, appropriate questions?
- Were my responses accurate and complete?
- Did I listen carefully?
- Did I seem confident during the interview?
- (Employment interviews only) Based on this interview, would I hire me?
- What behaviors, questions, or answers would I change for the next interview?

Each time you participate in an interview and evaluate your role, you learn more about the interview process. The more you learn, the better a participant you will become.

Section 2 Assessment

Visit the *Glencoe Communication Applications* Web site at **communicationapplications.glencoe.com** and click on **Self-Check and Study Guide 9.2** to review your understanding of the interview process.

Review Key Terms

1. Define each vocabulary term and write it in a sentence: interview process, highly closed question, primary question, secondary question, leading question, neutral question, direct question, indirect question, factual question, opinion question, hypothetical question.

Check Understanding

2. Identify and describe the three components of the interview process.
3. Imagine that you will be interviewing for a position as a counselor at a summer camp. Describe how you will prepare for the interview.
4. During which component of the interview would each of the following be most likely to occur? Explain your answers.
   - Questions about the interviewee's experience and qualifications
   - A summary of information
   - Small talk and introductions
5. **Predict** Imagine you have interviewed two candidates for the same job. The first sends a thank-you letter reminding you of his or her qualifications. The second sends no letter. How might this affect your decision? Explain.

APPLICATION *Activity*

Applying the Interview Process Imagine that a recruiter from your favorite college is coming to speak to your class. Each student interested in attending the college will be given fifteen minutes to speak individually with the recruiter. Working in a groups of three or four students, complete each of the following. Then, discuss your answers as a class.

- List three things you should do to prepare for your interview with the recruiter.
- Prepare five questions for the interview.
- Describe when and how you will follow up with the recruiter.

Section 3

Appropriateness in Interviews

GUIDE TO READING

Objectives

1. Explain why appropriateness is important in an interview.
2. Develop appropriate questions for an interview.
3. Recognize unlawful interview questions.
4. Determine what constitutes appropriate dress and demeanor for an interview.

Terms to Learn

demeanor
discriminate
body language

Look at the clock and count off one minute. It's not a very long period of time. It's not long enough to listen to a whole song. It's probably not even long enough to walk from one class to the next. However, when you meet someone for the first time in an interview, he or she forms an opinion about you within just one minute.

This phenomenon is called a first impression. In an interview, a good first impression can be critical. Some experts believe that up to 50 percent of an interviewer's hiring decision may be determined by his or her first impression of the interviewee. So, how can you be sure you will make a good impression? One way is to dress, behave, and speak appropriately.

It is important to make a good first impression when meeting someone for the first time. **How can you be sure to make a good first impression in an interview situation?**

Personal Appropriateness in Interviews

During an interview, appropriateness is necessary for making a positive first impression. As you learned in Chapter 1, appropriateness is what is acceptable or the norm for a given situation. Generally speaking, a person who does not act appropriately in a specific context is likely to be perceived negatively by others.

For example, it may be appropriate to yell and shout for your team at a sporting event. However, if you were to engage in this type of behavior in the school library, you probably would be in trouble—or at least be asked to leave. Loudness in the library is not appropriate.

Just as certain kinds of conduct need to be followed in the library, certain guidelines of appropriateness should be followed by both parties in an interview—especially in an employment interview. Among these are guidelines regarding appropriate appearance, demeanor, and questioning techniques.

Appropriate Dress and Appearance

As you learned in Chapter 5, clothing and overall appearance carry a strong nonverbal message. It is hard to overestimate the impact of clothing and overall appearance when you first enter an interview situation. As unjust as it may seem, people do tend to judge a book by its cover. That is, they tend to form their initial impressions based on physical appearance.

COMMUNICATION *Strategies*

FIRST-IMPRESSION CHECKLIST

- ✓ Do you have a confident posture?
- ✓ Are you smiling?
- ✓ Are you dressed appropriately?
- ✓ Are your clothes neat and clean?
- ✓ Do you appear clean and well groomed?
- ✓ Do you seem relatively calm?
- ✓ Do you seem outgoing and enthusiastic?

Figure 9–7 Appropriate Dress for an Interview

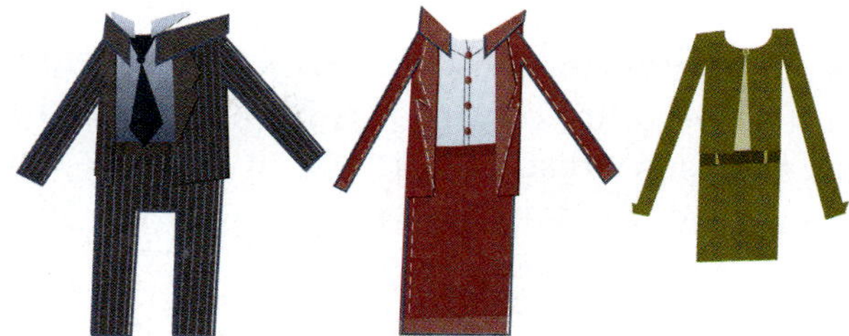

From the moment the interviewer first sees you, he or she begins forming judgments about who you are and whether you are right for the job. Before you ever even speak, you will be evaluated on several important points.

Each of these factors is important to making a good first impression. However, when surveyed, job recruiters have named clothing as the most important factor in shaping their initial impressions of applicants.

Dress How you dress for a specific interview will, of course, depend upon the context. You might dress more casually when interviewing for a lifeguard position than you would for a summer internship at a law firm. Jeans and a knit shirt might be all right for the lifeguard interview, but you surely would be underdressed at the law firm. If you think you might have to demonstrate your skills, such as in the case of applying for a welding or machinist position, make sure you have your work clothes available. Figure 9–7 shows some appropriate styles of dress for more formal interviews.

If you are unsure of how to dress for an interview, keep this rule in mind: Overdressed is usually better than underdressed. In other words, if you happen to dress too formally, you probably will be perceived as trying to make a good impression—which is a definite plus. If, however, you happen to be dressed too casually, you may be perceived as disrespectful, rebellious, or just plain lazy. In any case, the interviewer probably will see you as someone who exercises poor judgment.

Personal Appearance Although clothing usually makes the most memorable first impression, its influence can be overshadowed. Unfortunately, this probably means that some other aspect of a person's appearance was so distracting that it caused the interviewer to temporarily forget how the person was dressed.

Think about things that can be a major distraction when you meet someone for the first time. Poor hygiene, an overpowering scent of cologne, too much makeup, an unusual hair color or style, uncombed hair, or even bad breath may cause you to form a poor opinion of someone you have just met.

The rule of thumb regarding personal appearance in an interview is to always be clean and neat. Keep hair and nails neutral. Jewelry should be kept to a minimum. Wear appropriate clothing. That means dresses and skirts should be of a modest length, and pants should fit neatly. Avoid sweatshirts, tank tops, halter tops, spaghetti straps, shorts, sandals, and sneakers unless you are absolutely sure they are appropriate for an interview context.

Appropriate Demeanor

Typically, the first thing an interviewer will notice is your physical appearance. However, this will be followed closely by your **demeanor,** or outward behavior, and your verbal communication skills. For this reason, it is important to enter any interview situation poised, confident, and friendly. Use appropriate speech and body language to show that you are a professional who would be an asset to any company.

Friendliness Close your eyes and think about one person who makes you feel comfortable and welcome whenever you are around him or her. Imagine for a moment that you are meeting that person on the street or in the hallway of your school building. How does this person greet you? You probably imagine a smile and a sincere, friendly greeting. When you are trying to make a positive first impression, it is important to be friendly. Make eye contact with the other person, offer a firm handshake, and extend a sincere greeting. For example, you might say, "Hello, Mr. Brown. It's so good to meet you."

Poise and Confidence Along with friendliness, it is important to project a poised and confident attitude. A person who has an air of confidence may be perceived as mature and as having certain leadership abilities. One way to display confidence in an interview situation is to adequately prepare. You are working toward that goal now by reading this chapter. Research, practice, and the other preparation techniques you have read about are all ways to gain confidence and poise in an interview.

It is important to note, however, that although you want to be confident, you don't want to appear arrogant. An arrogant person is one who believes he or she knows everything. Arrogance, as opposed to confidence, can create a negative image.

INTERVIEWING DOS AND DON'TS

Do	Don't
Look professional.	Chew gum.
Make good eye contact.	Wear too much fragrance.
Be specific.	Wear excessive jewelry.
Be flexible.	Lie.
Listen carefully.	Mumble.
Be enthusiastic.	Brag.
Speak clearly and concisely.	Interrupt.
Smile.	Look at your watch.

Verbal Skills How you speak is another manner to consider when interviewing. Unless the job requires it, avoid using slang in an interview. Also avoid using speech fillers such as "you know," "uh," "um," and "like." Above all, do not interrupt or raise your voice to an interviewer. The key is to present yourself as a pleasant, intelligent, well-qualified professional.

When you ask or answer questions in an interview, make sure your speech is clear and straightforward. Before you answer a question, think about your answer. It is common to be nervous in an interview, which often can cause you to speak too loudly or too softly. It also can cause your speech to speed up. When this happens, put on the brakes. Take a deep breath, speak in a normal tone, and take your time. A well-thought-out answer says volumes about you as a competent communicator.

COMMON REASONS FOR REJECTING JOB APPLICANTS

Poor appearance	Overbearing, aggressive
Poor voice, diction, grammar	Lack of purpose, career goals
Little enthusiasm, passive, indifferent	Unwilling to start at the bottom
Late for interview, disrespectful	Lack of courtesy, proper etiquette
Talks too much, rambles	Poor eye contact, extreme nervousness
Unable to handle silence	Lack of poise, confidence
Negative attitude	Lack of leadership skills
Couldn't sell himself/herself to employer	Condemnation of previous employer
Talked about salary	Didn't ask for the job

Body Language In Chapter 5, you learned that body talk is a powerful communicator. **Body language** is how people nonverbally express feelings and attitudes. For example, imagine that you have arrived early for a 7:00 A.M. interview. Five minutes before your appointment, the interviewer apologizes and says it will be at least a half hour before she can meet with you. Even though you may respond politely, if you fold your arms across your chest or slump down in your seat, your body language may demonstrate that you are disappointed or angry.

During an interview, the way you use your body will send important messages. As you enter the interview situation, use positive body language. Smile. Stand tall. Your posture should be relaxed but erect. Greet the

COMMUNICATION PRACTICE LAB

Analyzing Body Language

To better understand the messages sent by nonverbal behaviors, follow these steps:

Step 1 As a class, brainstorm ten to fifteen examples of appropriate body language and list them on the chalkboard.

Step 2 Beside each behavior, write under what circumstances it might be exhibited by an interviewer or interviewee.

Step 3 Discuss why each would be appropriate in an interview situation.

Step 4 Have a pair of volunteers act out an interview using the appropriate behaviors you listed.

Step 5 As a class, draw conclusions about the possible effects of various body language in an interview situation.

interviewer appropriately. Confidently approach the chair where you will sit and settle into it as comfortably as possible.

Sit tall in the chair, making sure not to slump. Your feet should be flat on the floor so that you are balanced and comfortable. You can lean slightly forward, making appropriate eye contact. If someone is asking a question, maintain eye contact with that person. However, when you answer, your eye contact should be with everyone in the room. Your hands should lie quietly in your lap when you are not using them to make graceful, appropriate gestures while you speak. If you have a pen for taking notes, be sure that you hold it only when you are writing. Avoid playing with any object since this communicates anxiety and lack of confidence. Overall, your body should show that you are interested, attentive, and ready to participate fully in the interview.

Appropriate Questions in Interviews

An appropriate question is one that is suitable based on the situation. In order to determine if a question is suitable, you need to analyze the context and norms for that particular situation.

Interviewee Questions

In a job interview, you are the guest of the interviewer. He or she ultimately controls how much information is exchanged. However, by preparing and asking appropriate questions, you can help ensure that you will get the information you need about the job and the company.

In Section 1, you read about preparing useful questions. Following are some appropriate questions you may wish to use as a guide.

- What are the specific duties of this position?
- How might you describe a typical day in this position? At this office?
- Is this a new position, or has it recently been vacated?
- How much travel is normally involved?
- With whom will I be working most closely?
- What type of computer technology is involved in this position?
- Is any special training provided?
- Is performance reviewed on a regular basis?
- What else can I tell you about my qualifications?
- When do you expect to make a decision?

Interviewer Questions

What types of appropriate questions can you expect to hear from the interviewer? Following are some questions commonly asked in employment interviews.

- Tell me about yourself.
- What is one of your weaknesses/strengths?
- How will your specific experience and qualifications help you do this job?
- Why did you leave your last job?
- What is the most important thing you learned from your last job or from school?
- What did you like most about your last job/school? What did you like least?
- What have you done that shows initiative (taking charge) or a willingness to work?

- Why do you want to work for this company?
- Why should we hire you for this position?
- When are you available to start?
- May we contact your references?

Laws Governing Employment Questions

Many laws govern what questions are and are not legal in employment interviews. Basically, employers may not legally ask for information that can be used to discriminate on the basis of race, color, religion, sex, disabilities, marital status, national origin, or age. To **discriminate** means to treat differently based on reasons other than individual merit, or quality.

A few examples of illegal interview questions are shown in the table. Note that simply asking the question is not illegal. However, it becomes illegal if the question leads to an act of discrimination. For this reason, most interviewers consider these questions inappropriate and avoid them entirely.

Responding to an Unlawful Question Of course, just because a question is illegal doesn't mean it won't be asked. That's why it is important to know how to respond to unlawful questions in an interview. There are several ways to answer unlawful questions. They include the following.

- Simply answer the question.
- Note that you think the question is illegal but answer anyway.
- Ask the interviewer about the appropriateness of the question. "Why? Is my religion a factor in whether or not I will be hired?"
- Refuse to answer directly, but rationalize that your answer would have no bearing on your ability to do the job.
- Ask the interviewer how the question relates to the job and whether it really is lawful.
- Redirect the focus of the discussion from the question to something else, such as the job requirements.
- Refuse to provide the information.
- End the interview and leave.

ILLEGAL INTERVIEW QUESTIONS

Questions Related to . . .	Example
Birthplace, nationality, or ancestry	"Pasquale—is that a Spanish name?"
Gender or marital status	"Is that your maiden name?"
Race or color	"Are you considered to be part of a minority group?"
Religion or religious days observed	"Does your religion prevent you from working weekends or holidays?"
Physical challenges or disabilities	"Do you have any use of your legs?"
Health or medical history	"Do you have any pre-existing health conditions?"
Pregnancy or child care	"Do you plan to have children?"

Choosing a Specific Response If you are asked a question that is not legal, how do you know which of these responses to use? There are several factors to think about. First, consider why the interviewer asked the question. Many interviewers may not realize that certain questions are unlawful. The interviewer who asks about nationality or family may simply be trying to make conversation.

A second consideration is how badly you want the job.

If you feel that the interview is going well and you would like the position, you may decide to answer the question.

A third consideration is how comfortable you feel with the interviewer. If the interviewer is your age or has children your age, you may feel more comfortable discussing age issues.

Finally, consider your own personal style. You may or may not be willing to confront the interviewer or walk out on the interview. You may prefer to go ahead and answer the question but then refuse to take the job if it is offered.

Ethics in Interviewing

You can see the ethical stance interviewers need to take when asking questions. How does ethics apply to the interviewee? Imagine that you were fired from your previous job. If the interviewer asks why you left, how should you answer? The best choice is to tell the truth, briefly explaining any special circumstances or simply that you made a mistake and have learned from the experience. In all questions, honesty is best. If an employer finds that you have lied, nothing else you say will be believable.

Section 3 Assessment

Visit the *Glencoe Communication Applications* Web site at **communicationapplications.glencoe.com** and click on **Self-Check and Study Guide 9.3** to review your understanding of appropriateness in interviews.

Review Key Terms

1. Define each term and write it in a sentence: demeanor, body language, discriminate.

Check Understanding

2. Explain why appropriateness is important in an interview.
3. Write two specific questions you might ask when interviewing for a job as an editorial assistant at a small newspaper.
4. If an interviewer asked you "Would you have any problem working on Christmas Day?" how might you respond? Explain.
5. Might it be appropriate to wear jeans and a nice shirt to an interview for a construction job? Explain why or why not.
6. **Analysis** Think of an instance when you met someone for the first time. What type of impression did that person make? Describe what about their dress, appearance, and demeanor helped to create this impression.

APPLICATION *Activity*

Determining Appropriate Dress Working with a partner, discuss what type of dress would be appropriate for each of the following interview situations:

- You apply for an internship in the state capitol building.
- You audition as a singer in a local band.
- You meet a new neighbor who needs a baby-sitter.
- You apply for a summer job in your local parks and recreation department.

Communication Self-Assessment

Evaluating Your Interview Skills

How Do You Rate?

On a separate sheet of paper, respond to the following statements. Put a check mark at the end of each skill you would like to improve.

KEY: **A** Always **U** Usually **S** Sometimes **R** Rarely **N** Never

1. When I am an interviewer, I have a goal and questions.
2. In an interview, I listen carefully and answer questions directly.
3. I try to make the best impression possible in an employment interview.
4. To prepare for being an investigative interviewer, I plan questions ahead.
5. I prepare for performance evaluations by learning about my interviewer, reviewing my job description, and preparing a summary of my past work.
6. I do research about the company before an employment interview.
7. As I prepare for an interview, I think about what I want to say, focus on non-verbal behaviors, and practice the interview with someone, if possible.
8. I know how to recognize unlawful interview questions.
9. I wear appropriate clothing and choose proper demeanor when I am interviewed.
10. I am able to show poise and confidence in an interview.

How Do You Score?

Review your responses. Give yourself 5 points for every A, 4 for every U, 3 for every S, 2 for every R, and 1 for every N. Total your points and evaluate your score.

41–50 Excellent You may be surprised to find out how much you can improve your skills.

31–40 Good In this course, you can learn ways to make your skills better.

21–30 Fair Practice applying the skills taught in this course.

1–20 Needs Improvement Carefully monitor your improvement as you work through this course.

Setting Communication Goals

If you scored Excellent or Good, complete Part A. If your score was Fair or Needs Improvement, complete Part B.

Part A

1. I plan to put the following ideas into practice:
2. I plan to share the following information about communication with the following people:

Part B

1. The behaviors I need to change most are these:
2. To bring about these changes, I will take these steps:

Writing a Cover Letter

A résumé sent in with an application for work is often general and impersonal. A cover letter sent with your résumé, however, acts like a personal introduction when directed to the individual responsible for hiring new workers. Getting an interview is the ultimate goal of sending the cover letter and résumé. To write an effective cover letter, follow the procedures below.

Provide the Context. Let the employer know how you heard about the job opening. Do this near the beginning of your cover letter.

Catch the Reader's Attention Quickly. Classified advertisements in major newspapers or journals may attract hundreds of responses. Most of these responses will be discarded. Therefore, you need to give the employer a reason to call or remember you. Do this by asking a question or making a clever statement at the beginning of your letter. If you don't capture the attention of the reader right away, your full letter and résumé may not be read.

Describe Your Previous Accomplishments. Show the employer that your qualifications meet the job requirements. Since companies are interested in people who are achievers, show the reader that you take initiative. Explain to the employer how you can use your skills to fulfill the objectives outlined in the job description. By doing this, you relate your past experiences to the kind of talent the employer needs. You can refer to your résumé to support your claim.

End by Requesting an Interview. One way to ask for an interview is to say you will call on or near some future date. Suggest that you would enjoy having the opportunity to meet and talk with this person. You can also ask the potential employer to contact you. If you use this approach, provide an accurate telephone number with a message service or other reliable means of contact so the employer will be able to reach you.

Check Format and Appearance. Write your cover letter on standard $8\frac{1}{2}" \times 11"$ stationery using the format shown in the sample letter on the following page. Your cover letter should be centered on the page, and it should be only one page long. Make sure that you proofread your cover letter. Be sure to correct all errors in spelling, punctuation, and grammar before you send the letter.

For additional information about business writing, see the *Guide to Business Communication* section of the Communication Survival Kit in the Appendix.

Communication Through Writing

April 9, 2002

Hector Cruz
4510 Elm Drive
Chillicothe, Missouri 64601

Mr. Elmer Todd
Human Relations
City of St. Louis International Bank
1157 Avenue of the Arch
St. Louis, Missouri 62035

Dear Mr. Todd:

Are you interested in hiring a Spanish/English speaking person to work as a receptionist in your bank this summer? When I read your ad in the St. Louis *Post-Dispatch*, I was eager to answer because I enjoy working with people and speak Spanish and English fluently.

My résumé is enclosed. You might be interested in the fact that I am president of the Spanish Club at Chillicothe High School. I have held this position for two years. You might also note from my résumé that I spent last summer working as a travel guide in St. Louis translating English into Spanish for many Spanish-speaking groups.

I am very interested in discussing this position with you. I will telephone you early next week to talk about this possibility.

Sincerely,

Hector Cruz

Hector Cruz

WRITING *Activity*

You have learned about an entry-level position in a real estate office. Your guidance counselor informed you of this position. Use the following information to write a cover letter. Write your letter using the information you have learned in this feature and in the rest of Chapter 9.

- Applicant must have courteous phone skills and be able to direct calls to a busy staff of real estate agents.
- Applicant will need excellent word processing skills.
- Job description includes typing weekly ads about properties for sale and submitting them to a Sunday newspaper.
- You have learned many word processing programs and feel comfortable with them.
- You have had some experience answering a busy telephone in your high school business office.
- Last summer you worked for a temporary office service using your word processing skills.
- You had one two-week assignment last summer working in the advertising department of a local paper.

CHAPTER 9 Assessment and Activities

GLENCOE *Online*

Visit the *Glencoe Communication Applications* Web site at **communicationapplications.glencoe.com** and click on **Chapter 9 Activity** for additional practice in the interview process.

Reviewing Key Terms

Read each statement. On a separate sheet of paper, write whether the statement is true or false. If the statement is false, rewrite the statement so that it reads true. Underline the word or words that you substitute to make it so.

1. The interviewee determines the purpose of the interview.
2. Survey interviews gather information from a number of people.
3. Investigative is a kind of information-giving interview.
4. A counseling interview is an evaluation of how well an employee has achieved his or her goals over time.
5. A highly-closed question can provide options or a specific answer.
6. An employment interview is used to determine why a person has left an organization.
7. The interview process includes preparation, the actual interview, and the post interview.
8. An example of discriminating is turning down a job applicant for an office position because he or she belongs to a certain race.

Reviewing Key Concepts

1. In what three ways do interviewer and interviewee participate fully in an interview?
2. What are five major responsibilities of an interviewer?
3. How does thinking about a response before voicing it help an interviewee?
4. What six types of questions does an interviewer generally ask in an investigative interview?
5. Name the two kinds of information-giving interviews.
6. List six steps in preparing for an interview.
7. How does practice help the participants before an interview?
8. What are two elements of the interviewee's post interview?

Assessment and Activities

Reading and Critical Thinking Skill

1. **Applying Information** An interviewer greets you, the interviewee, with a smile, a handshake, and an offer of coffee. What responsibility is the interviewer carrying out by these actions?
2. **Synthesis** How should an interviewee respond to the ambiguous question "Can you walk long distances?"
3. **Cause-Effect** What is generally the result of sending a poorly written résumé?
4. **Classifying Information** How would you classify the following question: "At which office would you prefer to work—Dallas, Houston, or Oklahoma City?"
5. **Making Comparisons** Which type of interview generally takes more time—a scheduled or an unscheduled? Why?

Skill Practice Activity

Skimming Get an employee handbook from a business in your area, or use your school's handbook of policies. Skim the handbook for information about sick leave or procedures to follow when you are sick and unable to go to work or school. Provide a list of these policies. Discuss as a class the procedures you used to find the policies in the handbook.

Cooperative Learning Activity

Modeling Appropriate Dress Organize into groups of four. As a group, select an employment ad from the classified section of the newspaper. Then search magazines and catalogues for appropriate dress in an interview for that job. Create a poster with the title of the job at the top. Cut out the photographs of the clothing, and glue the photographs onto the poster. Beside each type of dress, explain why the outfit is appropriate for the interview.

Chapter Project

Planning Choose a company at which you would like to interview in the future. Start your preparation now by finding answers to the research questions on page 288.

Presenting Arrange the information you have researched on a flyer. Place the name of the company at the top of the flyer and include bold headings for each classification of facts. Add the facts in brief phrases. Remember to include the company's address and phone number. Make copies of your flyer and distribute them to interested classmates.

Standardized Test Practice

Read each passage and choose the word or group of words that belongs in each space. Mark the letter for your answer.

Looking for a summer job can be difficult and stressful. It is important to realize that you can always find an employer who __(1)__ a vacancy if you keep searching. Remember, thriving businesses often __(2)__ new positions as they grow and prosper. In addition, existing positions are continually becoming available, for a number of reasons. People are promoted to new positions, or sometimes __(3)__ move on to other companies. All of these factors contribute to the availability of jobs in the marketplace.

Finding a vacancy may be the __(4)__ part of the process, but it is not the last. Do not forget to prepare for your job interview. Research the organization ahead of time, so you know what they are looking for in an employee. Make a list of your accomplishments and strengths. You will be able to communicate your desires and abilities __(5)__ if you plan ahead.

1 **A** has
B have
C is having
D had

2 **F** created
G creates
H create
J is creating

3 **A** we
B they
C you
D it

4 **F** hard
G more hard
H hardest
J most hardest

5 **A** effective
B effectiver
C more effectiver
D more effectively

Standardized Test Practice

Read each passage and decide which type of error, if any, appears in each underlined section. Mark the letter for your answer.

When Cynthia recieved her first writing assignment from the *Washington High School Observer,* she was (1) excited. She decided to interview a local nutritionist for an article about keeping fit. To prepare for the interview, Cynthia asked some of her fellow students what they did to stay in shape. "On Mondays and Thursdays I go to the gym after school, said her friend Louisa." (2)

Joe, a member of the school Football Team, said, "I get plenty of exercise at (3) practice every day."

At the library, Cynthia discovered a cookbook containing healthy recipes for the following: pasta, fish, meat, and even desserts. Later, (4) she called a health club in the area and asked about their membership fees. Cynthia spent some time reading the materials that she borrowed from the library: and created a long list (5) of questions to ask the nutritionist. When it was time for the interview, Cynthia was ready!

1 **A** Spelling error
B Capitalization error
C Punctuation error
D No error

2 **F** Spelling error
G Capitalization error
H Punctuation error
J No error

3 **A** Spelling error
B Capitalization error
C Punctuation error
D No error

4 **F** Spelling error
G Capitalization error
H Punctuation error
J No error

5 **A** Spelling error
B Capitalization error
C Punctuation error
D No error

UNIT 3

Group Communication

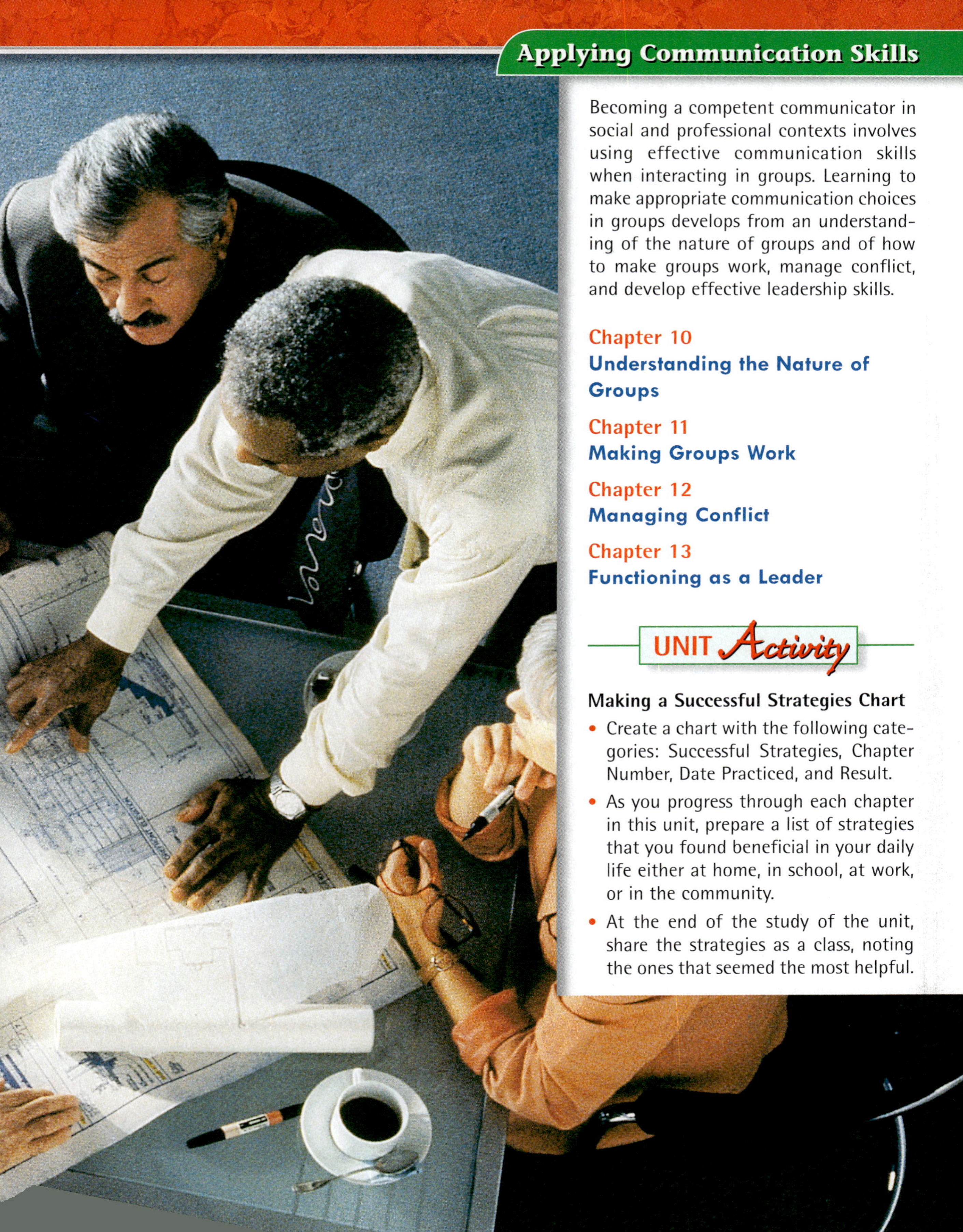

Applying Communication Skills

Becoming a competent communicator in social and professional contexts involves using effective communication skills when interacting in groups. Learning to make appropriate communication choices in groups develops from an understanding of the nature of groups and of how to make groups work, manage conflict, and develop effective leadership skills.

UNIT *Activity*

Making a Successful Strategies Chart

- Create a chart with the following categories: Successful Strategies, Chapter Number, Date Practiced, and Result.
- As you progress through each chapter in this unit, prepare a list of strategies that you found beneficial in your daily life either at home, in school, at work, or in the community.
- At the end of the study of the unit, share the strategies as a class, noting the ones that seemed the most helpful.

CHAPTER 10 Understanding the Nature of Groups

WHY IT'S IMPORTANT

Worker cooperation depends on effective communication. However, learning to communicate effectively in professional and social groups can take practice.

To better understand the nature of groups, view the **Communication in Action** Chapter 10 video lesson.

"Coming together is a beginning; keeping together is progress; working together is success."
—Henry Ford, American automotive pioneer

GLENCOE Online

Visit the *Glencoe Communication Applications* Web site at **communicationapplications.glencoe.com** and click on **Overview–Chapter 10** to preview information about the nature of groups.

Section 1

Understanding Groups

GUIDE TO READING

Objectives

1. Identify the four characteristics of a group.
2. Explain how groups are important to organizations.
3. Explain how groups are important to individuals.
4. Create an effective group goal statement.
5. Distinguish between the two main kinds of groups.
6. Compare and contrast the purposes of task groups and social groups.

Terms to Learn

group
committee
team
advocacy group
group goal
prescribed goal
emergent goal
task group
information-gathering group
policy-making group
action group
social group
informal social group
formal social group

The expression "Two heads are better than one" illustrates why so many organizations use groups to meet their goals. However, another expression, "A camel is a horse put together by a committee," indicates that working in groups is not always easy or effective!

Groups are a major part of both our professional and social lives. We often identify ourselves by the groups and organizations in which we are involved. Organizations also use groups to meet their goals. Because groups are such a large part of our lives, it is important to understand exactly what they are. It is also important to know how they are used in professional and social contexts.

DEFINITION OF A GROUP

A **group** is a small number of people who identify and interact with one another because of a common interest, bond, or goal. This definition applies to many different types of groups as well as to groups with different purposes and functions.

Members of a marching band form a group that works together to perform an entertaining show. Define group.

Groups Within Organizations

An easy way to understand how groups function within organizations is to think about a marching band. Although a marching band is a single musical organization, it is divided into different instrumental groups. Each member of each group has a common goal or task: to play—accurately and skillfully—the notes in a musical composition. As a result, the group has created a product that is greater than the sum of its parts.

Members of each section of a marching band will rehearse together to learn the notes for their specific instruments. Their notes will be different from the notes for the other groups. When the whole band plays together, the resulting sound from all these groups doing different things at the same time is a complete song, which is the goal of the band. In the same way, both individuals and organizations use groups to accomplish parts of an overall goal. These goals are often ones that would be difficult for someone to achieve individually.

Formation of Groups

Participation in a group can be either required or voluntary. An employer, governmental representative, or other authority may appoint someone to serve in a group. This would be the case if your boss appointed you to a special marketing team.

Other times, people become involved in a group because they want to be a part of what that group is doing. For example, if you are interested in improving the school's homecoming activities, you might volunteer to serve on the planning committee. If you are interested in the security of the neighborhood where you live, you might ask others who share your interests to form a neighborhood watch group. Regardless of whether participation is voluntary or required, we belong to groups in both our professional and social lives to accomplish specific goals.

Names of Groups

Just as the different sections in a marching band have different names, the groups used in social and professional organizations have a variety of names. These names are derived from the organization itself or from the nature of the particular group. Three names for different groups are committee, team, and advocacy group.

Committee A **committee** is a group with a specialized task that is part of the basic structure of an organization. A committee that is a permanent part of an organization is called a standing committee.

Team A **team** is a small group that usually is given the power to make and implement decisions. Teams may be made up of a

Figure 10–1 Characteristics of a Group

variety of people from different levels and departments in an organization. Organizations may give their teams different names too, such as management teams, work/study teams, and quality-control teams.

Advocacy Group An **advocacy group** is a group set up specifically to support, protect, defend, or lobby for a cause or group. Advocacy groups are highly specialized. They may exist either independently or within an organization.

Figure 10–2 Sample Group Goals

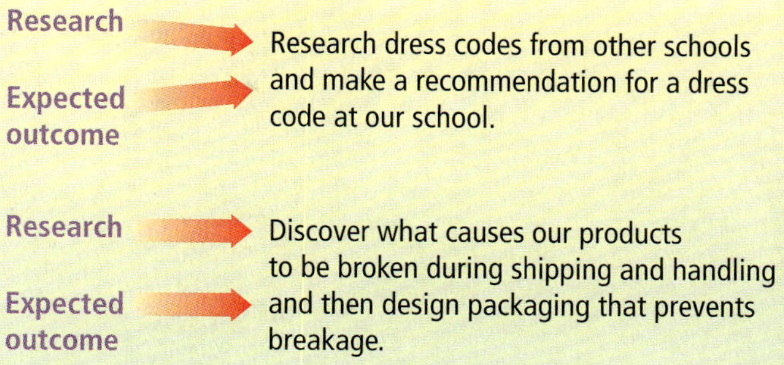

Research
Expected outcome
Research dress codes from other schools and make a recommendation for a dress code at our school.
Research
Expected outcome
Discover what causes our products to be broken during shipping and handling and then design packaging that prevents breakage.

Characteristics of a Group

A group is more than just a collection of people who happen to be in the same place at the same time. People standing on the corner waiting for a bus or people who happen to be eating at the same restaurant at the same time are not classified as a group. Rather, as Figure 10–1 shows, people in groups display a specific set of characteristics.

Limited Size

The membership of a group is limited. In fact, the best size for a group is four to six people. Imagine trying to listen to ideas and suggestions from every student in your school when planning your school prom. The process probably would be extremely frustrating. It also would be time-consuming. This is why organizations as a whole are not well suited for the kind of interaction and decision making that groups do.

With a limited size, most members of a group have the chance to voice their ideas in a typical meeting. Also, when membership is limited in a small group, members can fully explore issues and examine many different plans of action. They can then bring their work back to the larger group for approval, implementation, or evaluation.

The most productive group work is done when a limited number of people work together to discuss an issue fully, share different ideas, and explain the reasoning behind opposing ideas. This allows group members to seek new alternatives. It also allows for better combinations of ideas as members agree upon a common solution.

Shared Goal

Members of a group share a common purpose or goal. Before a group can work effectively, its members must understand and agree upon this goal. They then have to decide how best to accomplish it.

A **group goal** identifies what specific tasks are to be accomplished and what the expected group outcome is. A group goal statement might look like one of the two statements in Figure 10–2.

Both of these examples define what tasks are to be done. They also point out whether or not the group will simply make a recommendation or actually implement some action.

Types of Group Goals Sometimes, a group's goal may be prescribed. A **prescribed goal** is one that is assigned by a person in

This group is working on a common goal by creating a commercial. What takes place when group members bond?

authority. Often an organization's president, a manager, or a committee chairperson will appoint a group and issue the group goal at the same time. At other times, a group's goal may be emergent. An emergent goal is a goal set by the group itself. When a group sets its own goal, it may do so over a period of time or at its first meeting. Regardless of who sets the group goal, its main purpose is to guide a group in its work.

Importance of Group Goals

Sharing a common goal helps group members think of themselves as a group. This means they probably know one another by name. They also recognize that their group is a special unit working toward a common goal. Finally, they feel a sense of commitment and loyalty to the group, leading to a more effective group effort.

As members begin bonding as a group, they also begin to depend upon one another to accomplish their goal. In other words, they recognize that they need the input and assistance from other members to achieve the group goal. Rather than one person working alone, it is the group's charge to complete the task together.

A group in a media literacy class might have a project assignment due in two weeks. The group's goal could be to produce a persuasive thirty-second commercial to promote an upcoming school event. To accomplish its goal, the group might work together to complete a number of tasks:

- Gather all pertinent information about the event.
- Write a persuasive script.
- Determine the location of each individual video shot.
- Cast all the acting parts.
- Rehearse the script and video shots.
- Obtain the necessary video equipment and shoot the actual commercial.
- Edit the commercial and reshoot any necessary footage.

All these tasks help accomplish the group goal of making the thirty-second commercial. It's likely that no one member would be able to carry out all of these tasks within the time limitations. The members must depend upon one another to accomplish the goal together.

Face-to-Face Meetings

The third characteristic of a group is that the members generally meet face-to-face.

Benefits of Face-to-Face Meetings

Meeting face-to-face is important because it allows each member to be aware of both the verbal and nonverbal messages that other members send. Face-to-face interaction also allows members to recognize who is and who is not participating fully. This can help the group know who needs to be encouraged to contribute ideas.

Meeting face-to-face also tends to encourage spontaneous interaction that can lead to more creative ideas and solutions. Members can modify or adjust their messages based on interaction with others. When people meet face-to-face, they can give and get direct and immediate feedback, which helps them understand the verbal and nonverbal messages of others.

When Meeting Face-to-Face Is Not Possible Although the benefits are clear, it is not always possible for group members to meet face-to-face. In such cases, groups often use other methods to meet and exchange information. These may include contact via interoffice memos, postal mail, e-mail, teleconferencing, or videoconferencing. Each of these methods allows group members to maintain communication and continue progress toward the group goal even when they can't get together.

In today's busy world, teleconferences and videoconferences have become attractive methods of business communication. Both can be less expensive than face-to-face meetings that require travel arrangements for a number of group members. Also, electronic meetings often can be much more convenient for busy group members. Because no travel time is involved, meetings can be called, conducted, and adjourned relatively quickly. This often happens in a fraction of the time that it would take for members to all assemble face-to-face.

It is important to note, however, that convenience does have its costs. The direct and immediate interaction and exchange of ideas and nonverbal messages often are lost when the group cannot communicate directly. That's why the work of groups is generally more successful when conducted face-to-face.

Meetings Over Time

Rarely can the work of a group be completed in only one meeting. Therefore, groups usually meet over a period of time. Groups typically follow a specific cycle of meetings: orientation meetings, action meetings, and implementation meetings. The chart below describes this cycle.

The Importance of Groups

Groups are important to social and professional organizations as a whole. They also are important to individuals within those organizations. In general, groups have the potential to benefit everyone involved.

GROUP MEETING CYCLE

Meeting Cycle	Duration	Function	What Happens in This Cycle
Orientation	1–2 meetings	• to introduce members • to discuss group goals • to determine members' talents and expertise	This cycle helps the group develop productive working relationships.
Action	middle set of meetings	• members work on group goals • members gather information and interact on how to complete the group goal • members come to a conclusion on how to complete the goal	The group members have established their areas of expertise and are able to work from their strengths to complete the group goal.
Implementation	last few meetings	• implement solution, or • present findings to a designated management group	Group members are now at the end of their task and will either implement the solution or report their findings to another group.

Communication Practice Lab

Creating a Group Goal Statement

To write an effective group goal statement, follow these steps.

Step 1 Form a group of four to six students and create a statement that describes a group goal for each situation below. Make sure your statements identify the specific research to be done and the expected group outcome.

- Your technology department wants the school board to buy ten new computers for the lab.
- The manager at your part-time job asks employees to help find ways to get more students interested in working part time for the company.

Step 2 When your group's goal statements are complete, have one person write them on the chalkboard.

Step 3 Take turns explaining why each statement will produce the desired results.

Benefits to the Organization

Groups are a necessary part of large social and professional organizations. Organizational leaders who use groups know that they can provide very important benefits for the organization. These benefits include members or employees who are more creative, involved, motivated, and ultimately, more productive. The quality of the work also often increases when it is conducted in groups.

Benefits to the Individual

Organizations are not the only ones who benefit from groups. Participating in groups can help individuals in many aspects of their lives. This may include improving the conditions in which they work and developing better social and professional relationships.

Kinds of Groups

Most groups—those that are established and work independently and those that exist within organizations—can be divided into two basic kinds: task groups and social groups. These two main types of groups have very different purposes and operate in different ways.

Task Groups

The Macintosh computer, the stealth bomber, and even the painted ceiling of the Sistine Chapel all were created by different types of groups. However, each of these groups has a common element: Each was a type of task group.

Definition A **task group** is a group that is given a specific job, or a task, to complete. A task group may have a different name. Sometimes, it may be called a task force. At other times, it might be named a committee, team, or advocacy group. A task group might exist for only a short period of time, or it may meet for years. The amount of time depends upon the task it has been assigned. After the task has been completed, the group is dissolved.

Purpose A task group's purpose is to complete an objective or a job. Sometimes, a task group will be given the charge of finding out all the information about a problem and then suggesting possible solutions. Other times, it may be charged with creating a new policy or procedure or to perform some other type of action to solve a particular problem.

Some task groups have a very clear objective. For example, if a group is appointed to determine how satisfied parents are with the elementary school's new dress code, the task is very clear. Other times, groups do not have a clear objective to follow. A task group might be formed to anticipate what changes customers and clients might like to see in a company's product.

Some engineers at Saturn Corporation were asked to build a prototype of a three-door coupe. They were given a standard two-door car. In addition, they were given a saw and

IMPORTANCE OF GROUPS

Benefit to the Organization	Explanation
Productivity	• Individual members are motivated to perform well in front of their peers. • Individual members report that they communicate more with their group members than with employees in other departments/divisions of the organization.
Accuracy	• All group members examine each others' work, catch errors, and suggest corrections.
Creative Energy	• In groups, people tend to be more creative and enthusiastic about their work. • People tend to approach a project with more interest and excitement when it is a group endeavor.
Organizational Commitment	• Group members report higher morale than other organizational members not involved in any groups. • Group members report a higher satisfaction with their jobs and higher commitment to the organization than those not involved in groups.
Community Presence	• Community group members represent their organizations to the whole community. • These individual group members, representing their organizations, make the organization seem to be involved in and concerned about the welfare of the community at large.
Benefit to the Individual	**Explanation**
Political Influence	• Our U.S. political processes depend upon citizen participation to function democratically. • Individuals can influence governmental regulations by participating in town meetings, school board meetings, and civic and local planning groups.
Career Advancement	• Successful group participation skills help people in civic, political, and professional groups. Doing well in groups at a job increases the chances of promotion. • Doing well in groups of professional and social associations helps people network for career positions across the country.
Job Satisfaction	• Employees involved in groups report being more satisfied with their jobs and their companies. • Employees involved in groups report less work stress and more pleasant and safe work environment than those not involved in groups at work. • Employees involved in groups report they are encouraged to use their creativity and initiative, which raises their morale at work.

TECHNOLOGY Activity

Comparing Group Communication Methods
As a class, form three or four groups. Each group will identify a traditional school activity and come up with a plan for changing it. Group One should complete its task through a face-to-face meeting. Group Two should conduct all group interactions by writing memos or letters to each other. Group Three should be divided in half, with the two halves simulating a teleconference. Ask for permission to use two speakerphones at your school for your teleconference. Group Four, if feasible, should interact through e-mail.

When all groups are finished, compare your solutions and the time needed to accomplish the group goal. What were the advantages and disadvantages of each method?

the outline of a door marked with masking tape. Engineers were then told to cut on that car until they came up with a way to make the idea work. When the engineers finished, they had sawed an extra door on the driver's side that allowed drivers to easily put things in the back seat.

Types of Task Groups

Organizations use various types of task groups to accomplish different organizational goals. Each of these has a different purpose for the organization. These groups may be divided into three main types:

- information-gathering groups
- policy-making groups
- action groups

Information-Gathering Groups

All types of groups have to gather extra information or conduct research in order to accomplish their goals. An **information-gathering group** is designed specifically to gather data. After the group has gathered its information, it provides it to an administrative or managerial group or an organization for consideration. The information-gathering group has completed its task and accomplished its goal when it has turned in a summary report.

Sometimes, the duties of an information-gathering group extend beyond gathering, compiling, and reporting information. This type of group also may be asked to suggest decisions, solutions, or alternative courses of action for the organization. Financial institutions such as banks, credit unions, and savings and loans

TYPES OF TASK GROUPS

	Type of Task Group	Characteristics	Power
	Information-gathering group	Designed specifically to gather information and relay that information to the organization	Only has power to make recommendations; does not implement its decisions
OFFICIAL HANDBOOK	Policy-making group	Creates procedural rules that all members of the organization must follow; evaluates the effectiveness of those rules	Has power to implement, enforce, review, and change policies as needed
TITLE ROLL SCENE TAKE	Action group	Plans and takes action to solve a problem, create or improve something, or effect change	Has power to implement its decisions and evaluate their effectiveness

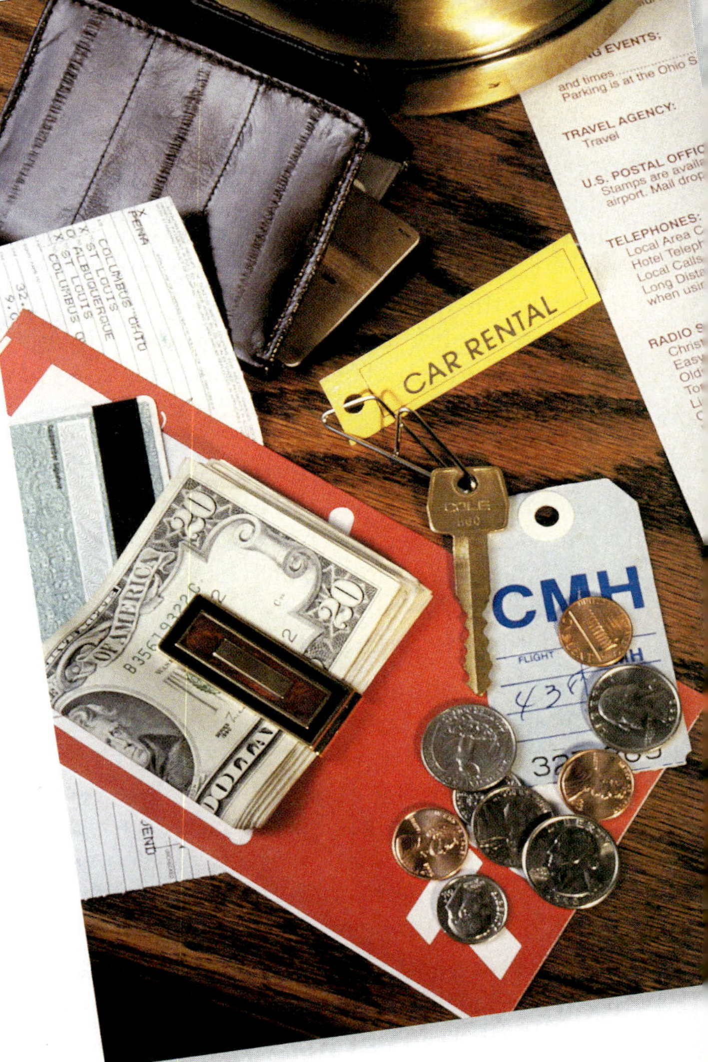

Most companies have travel policies stating that employees must provide receipts in order to be reimbursed for travel expense. What is the responsibility of a policy-making group?

often maintain loan committees. These types of information-gathering groups research the loans the institution already has made. They also compute which future loans should be made. Loan committees then provide this information to the officers of the institution so they can make the wisest lending decisions possible.

Organizations also regularly use a different kind of information-gathering group. These are called learning or study groups. These groups' task is to stay current on information that affects the organization. Group members often attend training programs, gather current information, and bring that information back to the organization. They may even plan workshops or training sessions to share the new information with other employees.

Policy-Making Groups Think about the rules you follow every day at school or on the job. Did you ever wonder where those rules came from? Chances are that a policy-making group created them. A **policy-making group** has the task of creating procedural rules that all organizational members must follow. A policy-making group might be responsible for deciding which skills and level of education or training an applicant must have to be hired. It might also decide on policies—such as hiring procedures, how to deal with customers or clients, or how often employees are expected to travel for the company.

Because policies are rules, policy-making groups need to be aware of some guidelines. Effective policies include a statement of what will happen if these guidelines are not followed. For example, many organizations require employees to travel to different cities for their work. A company may have a travel policy stating that to be reimbursed for travel expenses, employees must turn in all receipts for food, travel, and hotel costs incurred while away on company business. The policy also might state that if employees lose their receipts, the organization will not reimburse them for any of their expenses. Therefore, it is to the employees' advantage to collect and organize their receipts.

Policy-making groups also are in charge of reviewing how current policies are working. Often, policy decisions will be reviewed a year or so after they have been put into effect. This allows groups to evaluate whether their decisions are providing the intended result.

Action Groups An **action group** is appointed to plan and implement a specific course of action. Action groups often are charged with solving organizational problems. They can also develop products, improve the quality of products or services, or promote higher morale and productivity in the organization. The most common type of action group in an organization is a team.

Quality-Control Team Organizations sometimes use a type of action group called a quality-control team. This team is expected to check on the quality of work within the organization. It also does creative problem solving for the organization.

One international hotel chain had spent $6,196 on fruit baskets that were provided to corporate clients as free gifts during their stay. However, the fruit in many of these baskets was left uneaten. Since the hotel wanted to provide this service but did not want to waste money, a quality-control team in the hotel was asked to investigate and suggest a solution.

The team found that the fruit often spoiled as it sat in unoccupied rooms. Also, some guests didn't take the baskets because they did not understand that they were free. To solve these problems, the quality-control team recommended that the baskets be sealed and to be delivered to rooms only after guests checked in. This process kept the fruit from spoiling as quickly and added a personalized touch. It also made it clear that the fruit was a free gift. As a result, the hotel reduced waste and increased corporate guests' satisfaction.

Self-Managed Work Team Another type of action group is a self-managed work team. A self-managed work team is a group that works on its own to complete a particular job for an organization. These teams select their own leaders and complete their tasks with little or no supervision. They then bring back a finished product or other result. Members are assigned to this team because of the unique talents they can contribute to the group task.

Social Groups

Not all groups are task driven. Think about the groups to which you belong. In some groups, you probably don't expect anything more than friendship with the other members. You do get certain personal benefits from being part of these groups, but they do not have any particular task or job to do.

Definition A **social group** is a group that someone joins for purely personal reasons. Joining a social group is voluntary. People often join to engage in something in which they have an interest. Social groups can exist independently or be part of an organization, such as a company, school, neighborhood, or religious association. Study groups, neighborhood street hockey teams, "Monday Night Football" watchers, and your school's yearbook staff are all social groups. These groups typically have casual memberships that tend to fluctuate as members come and go.

Purpose The purpose of social groups is to allow members to follow some mutually agreeable activity with the help of a general support system. Exercise classes, poetry groups, and cycling clubs are also social groups, so long as the members participate as much for the company of the other members as for the skills they are learning. Like task groups, social groups have goals. These goals are usually related to the relationships group members desire to maintain.

Social groups are people joining together to share in something they mutually enjoy, such as rafting. **What are some of the social groups you are involved in?**

Some of the groups you belong to at school may not be related to your career goals. For example, you may hope to have a career in the computer field someday, but you also may be a member of your school band. Being in the band might not teach you much about your future career, but it can support your interest in music. It also can give you an opportunity to be around people you like. Therefore, band is one of your social groups. Several of the people who work with you at your part-time job might decide to take a self-defense class together one night each week. This, too, is a social group. The class probably has nothing to do with your work, but it allows you to spend time with coworkers you like while you all learn about self-defense tactics.

Some of your social groups will be made up of people with whom you work. Others will be made up of people from your neighborhood, church, or community. These groups can help you build valuable decision-making and problem-solving skills while participating in an enjoyable activity that is unrelated to your job.

Kinds of Social Groups

There are two kinds of social groups within organizations: informal and formal. An **informal social group** is one in which membership may be encouraged, but not required, by an organization. A **formal social group** is one in which the organization chooses members to participate in community activities.

Informal Social Groups Participation in informal social groups is not required by an organization. However, an organization may encourage its members to join a social group to build morale and help form relationships across different departments or divisions. Members of an organization might form physical-fitness groups, softball leagues, or other clubs that are made up of only organizational members. If employees at a company begin meeting at a local gym after work to play a casual game of racquetball, they have formed a social group. No one requires their attendance, but they enjoy the game and develop new friendships with coworkers.

An informal group might form at first because all the members have the same lunch schedule and happen to choose the same place to eat. These members may then begin inviting a few more friends, making it a regular practice to meet for lunch on a certain day. Eventually, the group might expand the lunch activity to include some sort of exercise, and the lunchtime meeting might become more structured for the group. At this point, the group has developed a social purpose of meeting with a particular group of people on a regular—perhaps even daily—basis.

Formal Social Groups An organization also might create formal social groups. These groups often have a regular meeting time, officers, rules for joining and participating, and agendas or schedules for their meetings.

Many company-sponsored sports teams fall into this category. If an organization is quite large, it may have several departmental sports teams, such as bowling, golf, or softball. These teams compete against other departmental teams from within their own organization or from outside organizations. If an organization is small, it might form a single company team to compete against teams from other companies in community tournaments.

Formal social groups may grow out of informal ones. For example, members of a lunch

A company team working on a community project could be either a formal or informal social group. What is the difference between formal and informal social groups?

group might decide to start devoting one lunch hour per week to a non-profit community organization such as Habitat for Humanity—a group that builds homes for low-income families. If this informal effort is successful the first year, the group may strive to make it more formal in following years. This might lead to management recognizing the effort and forming a "Habitat Team" in the organization. Thus, the informal social group has become a formal social group within the organization. A company also may encourage members to belong to various non-profit civic groups to support community projects.

Section 1 Assessment

Visit the *Glencoe Communication Applications* Web site at **communicationapplications.glencoe.com** and click on **Self-Check and Study Guide 10.1** to review your understanding of the nature of groups.

Review Key Terms

1. Define each of the following terms and write it in a sentence: group, committee, team, advocacy group, group goal, prescribed goal, emergent goal, task group, information-gathering group, policy-making group, action group, social group, informal social group, formal social group.

Check Understanding

2. List the characteristics of a group. How does each characteristic contribute to a group's effectiveness?
3. Describe how groups are important to an organization.
4. Describe how groups are important to individuals.
5. Create one group goal statement for an information-gathering group and one group goal statement for a policy-making group. How are the two statements alike? How are they different?
6. Describe the two main kinds of groups and give an example of each.
7. **Comparison** How are purposes of the two main kinds of groups alike and different?

APPLICATION *Activity*

Working as a Quality-Control Team In a group of four to six students, assume that you are a quality control team with the power to implement recommendations. As a team, solve the following quality-control issue: How do you get more parents involved in your high school events and organizations? Create a group goal statement and write an outline detailing how your quality-control team should proceed to investigate and solve this issue. As a group, use this outline to prepare and deliver a four- to six-minute group presentation on how to resolve the issue.

Critical Thinking Skill

MAKING AN INFERENCE

An **inference** is a reasoned judgment or conclusion based on a set of circumstances or facts.

Learning the Skill

No one wants to make incorrect inferences, especially when working in a group where others can witness your mistakes. The following four steps are an effective process for making intelligent, informed inferences.

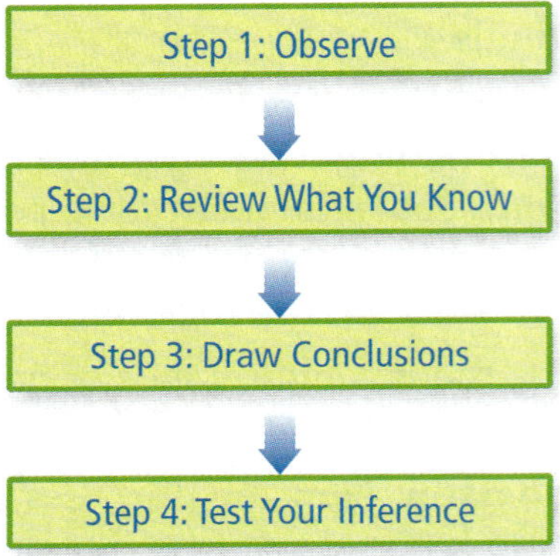

Step 1 Observe. When working in a group, pay careful attention, listen to others, read, research, and check facts to enhance your observation skills.

Step 2 Review What You Know. After making your observations, compare them to what you have observed in the past.

Step 3 Draw Conclusions. One of the best ways to make accurate inferences is to use your own common sense. Evaluate conclusions to see if they are logical.

Step 4 Test Your Inference. Whenever possible, try to gather specific information that will prove or disprove your conclusion.

Practicing the Skill

Read the quote below and answer the questions that follow.

> *A great IT [information technology] job has opened up at a local company, and you have the technical skills for the position. Unfortunately, that may not be enough. . . . At one time, companies placed a premium on technical skills and worried less about communication and interpersonal skills. . . . To assess the personality of IT job candidates, some companies are using behavioral interviewing . . . style of questioning that elicits descriptions . . . that may reveal how a candidate will perform in the future.*

1. What observations has the writer made?
2. What generalizations were made?
3. What are the reasons behind the writer's inference?
4. What inferences did you make after reading the article?

APPLICATION *Activity*

Imagine that you are the chief of police in a small community. The city council has asked you to write a report on the main cause of automobile accidents in your town and to suggest ways to reduce accidents. Your research shows that 55 percent of accidents over the past two years occurred during bad weather. Would it be accurate to conclude that bad weather causes traffic accidents? Why or why not? How might these conclusions affect your suggestions? Discuss your conclusions as a class.

Functions of Groups

GUIDE TO READING

Objectives

1. Explain why the group function of planning is important to organizations.
2. Identify the three main considerations involved in planning.
3. Describe the six steps of the problem-solving process.
4. Explain why brainstorming is useful for generating new, creative ideas.

Terms to Learn

problem
problem solving
criteria
brainstorming
decision making

Statements such as "None of us is as smart as all of us" and "Two heads are better than one" point out the advantages of working in groups. How have groups served a useful function in your life?

All task and social groups engage in planning, problem solving, or both. Why are these functions so well suited to groups? Each requires creativity. And the more knowledge and experience available, the more ideas generated.

PLANNING

One major function of a group is planning for some event, action, or change. You probably have participated in group planning for some event, action, or change. Think of the last time you worked on a group project for a class at school. You had to plan what each person would contribute and how often the group would meet. You also had to plan when each task would be completed to get the entire project done.

Groups such as the one shown are ideal for planning and problem solving. Why is it better to have a group working on solving a problem instead of an individual?

Businesses use groups to plan and organize work. **Why is planning important to a professional organization?**

Importance of Planning

Social and professional organizations depend on groups to plan the work they want to do. Without planning, social organizations can lose sight of their purpose. Businesses may not make a profit and have to close their doors.

Planning in Professional Organizations Planning is important for professional organizations because the business climate constantly changes. Companies have to plan how they are going to adapt to those changes to stay in business. They need to plan what, when, how, and who will produce, sell, and distribute their products or services. They will also plan for special events in the organization and for other company actions. Finally, they need to make both short-term and long-term plans. Some companies even have master-plan committees who do nothing but make long-term plans.

Planning in Social Organizations

Just as professional organizations have to adapt to change, so do social ones. Many communities have permanent planning commissions whose job is to predict how conditions may change over time. Commissioners might be involved in planning new schools, roads, parks, or other community services. Communities must also plan for civic events and for actions that will affect the entire city.

Considerations in Planning

A committee whose main function is planning is not usually responsible for implementing the plans it develops. Rather, its job is to envision the result of the plan and what should be done to achieve that result. Since the group plan will be implemented within either a professional or social context, the group should carefully consider the people, the occasion, and the task involved in any plan.

Consider the People. Who will be involved in the event or change proposed by your plan? A planning group should carefully consider all organizations, departments, or individuals that will be affected by a plan. The group also needs to consider the group itself and its goals.

By considering everyone who will be affected, the group can base its decisions on the most complete knowledge available. It also ensures that the group will fully consider all the consequences of its plan. For example, imagine that a group is planning to have all new employees attend a software training seminar. After speaking with several new employees, the group finds that most already know how to use that software. However, more senior employees feel they are the ones who really need the training. The planning group might then decide to make the training voluntary and offer it to all employees.

Global Communication

To Speak or Not to Speak?

When is it wise to speak up in group meetings and when is it better to remain silent? The answer to this question may differ from culture to culture. Some cultures, such as the Japanese, may respect silence while Americans typically are uncomfortable with long periods of silence. The Japanese sometimes find silence to be useful in decision making and problem solving, especially when they are uncertain about the response of other group members. How do you respond to silence in a group setting? Why?

Get the Support of the People. For a plan to achieve its goal, it must have the support and positive participation of the people affected. One way to build support for a plan is to show how it will ultimately benefit those involved. For example, when planning a community celebration, the planning group could show merchants how many tourists they expect the event to draw into the community. Support for a plan can be built by reducing people's fears. For example, a planning group might identify those employees most likely to be affected by a company's reorganization and then address their fears. By making a special effort to inform these employees in advance, the group can help remove any perceived threats.

PLANNING

To Plan Properly	Issues to Consider
Consider the People Involved	Who is needed to implement the plan? Who is affected by the plan? How will we motivate people to participate in the plan?
Consider the Occasion	What is the purpose of the action being planned? When and where will it take place?
Consider the Task	Have we considered the impact of the plan? How much time is needed to accomplish all parts of the plan? How many people must be involved in the plan? How much money will the plan cost?

Identify the Target Audience. The planning committee also will need to identify the target audience for an event and plan how to attract that audience. For a concert event, the committee might decide to provide discount admission coupons at area stores. For a business conference, the committee might mail invitations to related businesses throughout the region. By focusing its efforts, the committee can make sure that it reaches the people who will be most interested in attending.

Consider the Occasion.

Planning groups need to consider the occasion—the actual event or action being planned. Some factors to consider are the occasion's purpose, timing, location, and impact. The planning group might need to begin by asking the following questions:

- Why is this event taking place?
- What is the desired outcome?
- Does this event or activity conflict with other ongoing or traditional events?
- Will the proposed location of the event create any special difficulties?
- Have we adequately thought about the impact of the event on the community?

Consider the Purpose. Suppose a community decides to hold a summer festival to encourage tourism or to honor some historical occasion. One of the first responsibilities is to examine how the event will accomplish the stated purpose. The planning group may want to look at what other communities have done or consider some other approach. This might include establishing a new park or community center or restoring a historic building.

Consider the Timing. Event-planning committees also should look closely at community or organizational calendars to plan a successful event. The group should determine what other activities are occurring at or around the same time to avoid scheduling conflicts. If a community plans a walkathon for a local charity during the school district's spring break, it might have a small turnout for the event. Similarly, a company that plans its annual employee picnic for the same weekend on which the local high school baseball team is in the state playoffs might find that attendance at their picnic will suffer.

Consider the Location. The proposed location of an event is another factor that should be examined. Any proposed location should have adequate space and support facilities for the number of people expected to attend. Utility services such as electricity and water might be required. There also might be a need for security or police officers at the event. In addition, details such as parking, availability of food services, and rest areas also must be considered when choosing a location.

Consider the Task.

A planning group also takes into consideration the task. The task includes everything that must be done to implement the plan. The planning group must consider how the work will be done, when it will be done, and who will do it.

Event-planning committees then should decide when each part of the work is to be completed and by whom. They also should consider whether there is enough time in which to accomplish the task. These two considerations can be accomplished by developing a time line. One method for creating a time line is to

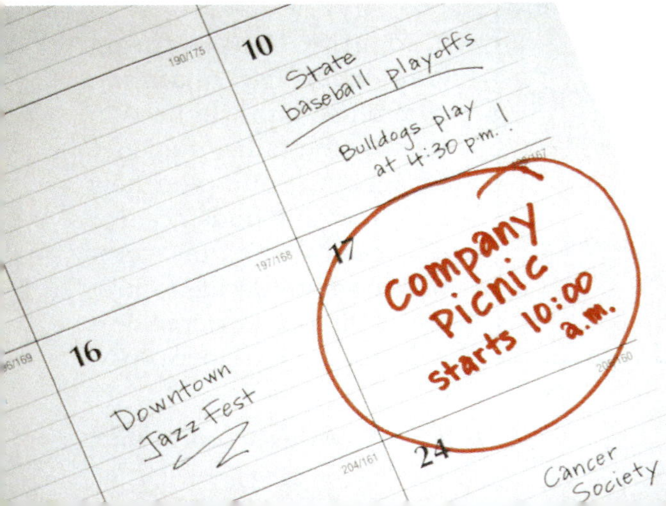

When planning an event, it is important to consider other events taking place on or around the same day. List the factors a planning group should keep in mind when planning an event.

start from the event date and then work backward in time. By incorporating how long it will take to accomplish each part, the committee can establish the start date of the task.

Sometimes, a plan may require more people than are available in an organization. Also, a plan may be too costly for the resources that are available. If the task itself is not realistic given the money, labor, or time available, then the planning will have to be adjusted.

Problem Solving

Organizations and businesses face a wide range of problems every day. A **problem** is a difficulty or uncertainty—a difference between the way something should be and the way it is. A business's problems might include determining how to cut costs, increase employee satisfaction, or keep up with the competition. An individual's problems might include how to improve grades or stick to a budget.

Definition

Problems can affect how an organization or individual meets its goals. Problems that go unsolved also can allow harmful situations to continue or worsen. Because of the need for effective solutions, problem solving is the second major function of groups. **Problem solving** is the act of understanding the nature of a dilemma, creating alternative solutions, determining which solution is best, and implementing that solution. Problem solving is a creative activity that is best accomplished through a step-by-step process.

Steps in the Process

Organizations and individuals frequently face problems in both professional and social contexts. These problems can cause emotional responses and may keep people from reaching the best solution. Therefore, it is valuable to apply a systematic process for

Medical professionals are constantly involved in problem-solving situations. What is the purpose of problem solving in groups?

moving logically and unemotionally to a solution. These steps are found in the Communication Strategies list below. Although the steps are in sequence, all six steps do not have to be done each time. Sometimes, the problem has already been defined, and the group's goal is to analyze it and solve it. In addition, all steps of the process are of equal importance.

Define the Problem. The first step is to define the problem facing the group. This can be accomplished by talking about the problem either with the group or with those involved in the problem. You cannot solve a problem that is unclear to you.

Sometimes, the problem to be solved is very clear. If management's prescribed goal is for the group to work out employees' work and vacation schedules for the next year, the problem is defined clearly. However, if the group has developed an emergent goal to improve employee morale, the problem will need to be defined before solutions can be found.

A problem's definition should fully describe what the group needs to accomplish. The problem statement often is written in the form of a question, such as "How can the company raise employee morale?" This goal of this statement is to keep the group members on track as they search for a solution.

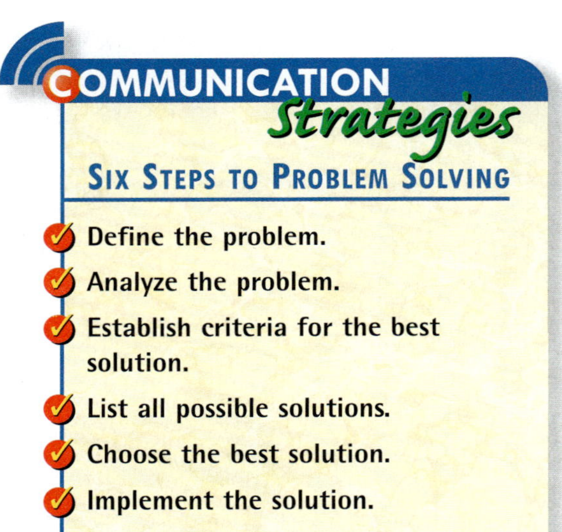

COMMUNICATION Strategies
SIX STEPS TO PROBLEM SOLVING
Define the problem.
Analyze the problem.
Establish criteria for the best solution.
List all possible solutions.
Choose the best solution.
Implement the solution.

interNET ACTIVITY

Absenteeism "How many days of school or work have you missed in the last year?" You may be asked this question in a future job interview. Employee absenteeism costs United States businesses approximately $20 billion per year. As a result, special committees are often formed to gather information or develop ways to address employee absenteeism. Using a reliable Internet search engine, enter the keywords "employee absenteeism" to learn more about this dilemma. Summarize the information you find in your own words. Share your findings with the class.

Sometimes, a problem is not exactly what it appears to be at first. A broad problem must be more narrowly defined. Consider, for example, that you have been assigned to a group of students to research the problem of an increasing number of locker thefts at your school. To move from the broad problem—"How can we stop thefts from student lockers?"—to a defined problem statement, your group might ask the following:

- Is there a specific time of day or location at which more or fewer locker thefts occur?
- Is one particular student group targeted more than others are?
- Are the lockers being broken into in any specific part of the school?

After answering these questions, your group may discover that 90 percent of all locker thefts are from the student lockers in the gym area. With that information, your group can formulate a defined problem statement focusing on a particular location of the thefts, such as, "How can we stop thefts from student lockers in the gym area?" This more accurate definition of the problem can now focus the group's work and energy and allow the group to proceed logically to the next step.

Analyze the Problem. The next step is to analyze the problem. You will try to discover its causes, how far-reaching the problem is, what conditions are contributing to the problem, and other information that may help lead to solutions.

To begin, determine what information the group needs to know. Group members can start by sharing their own knowledge and experiences that relate to the problem. Next, generate research questions about specific areas in which your group lacks information. Each member should take one or more of the research questions and find an answer to it prior to the next meeting. Members might find this information by conducting interviews or reviewing written materials available in the organization, or they might get it from the Internet or a library. At the next meeting, all members should share the answers to their question(s) and consider the answers and comments given by the other group members.

The group that has been formed to solve the problem of locker thefts in the school gym area will have several things to consider. This group might first determine if there is a specific time in which the thefts typically occur. It also might consider what is different about the gym and how that may contribute to the problem. As the group poses these questions, other issues that need investigating may present themselves. This may lead to questioning how well the locker room is supervised and how isolated the lockers are. Finally, it might consider if these lockers have a different locking system than those in other parts of the building.

The group's analysis of the problem is a vital step in the problem-solving process. This group might discover that most of the gymnasium thefts occur after school while athletic teams are practicing. It may find inadequate supervision in the gym. It might also discover that the padlocks indeed are less secure than combination locks.

Groups may be called upon to solve problems like theft in the locker room. What steps are involved in analyzing a problem?

Establish Criteria for the Best Solution. After the group understands the problem and the conditions that contribute to it, it needs to identify the characteristics of a good solution. These characteristics are known as the criteria of the solution. **Criteria** are the standards or conditions that any solution must meet in order to be acceptable. A criteria list for the locker-theft problem is shown in **Figure 10–3.**

This list of criteria should be generated before the group discusses any possible solutions. If the group tries to set criteria after it already is looking at a possible solution, it may tend to formulate criteria to fit that particular solution. Instead, the criteria should reflect what is both desirable and possible within the organization. Sometimes, the criteria are imposed, while other criteria can come from the members themselves.

After the group has listed all the criteria, it should double-check to make sure everything important is covered and there are no unnecessary criteria. Some groups might even choose to rank the criteria in order of importance. In general, the fewer criteria statements the better. This keeps the group from eliminating too many possible solutions.

Practice for the Workplace

Promoting a Sense of Community How does it feel to move to a new city, attend a new school, join a new club, or begin a new job? It is normal to be concerned about how to meet new people and how they will respond to you.

BUSINESS PRACTICE *Activity*

Planning committees in the workplace are responsible for developing activities that promote a sense of community, commitment, and inclusion among employees. In groups of five or six, work as a planning committee. Make a list of activities that would result in cooperation and a sense of teamwork among students at your school. Present your ideas to the remainder of the class. As a class, discuss which activities offered at your school might also be available in the workplace.

Figure 10–3 List of Criteria

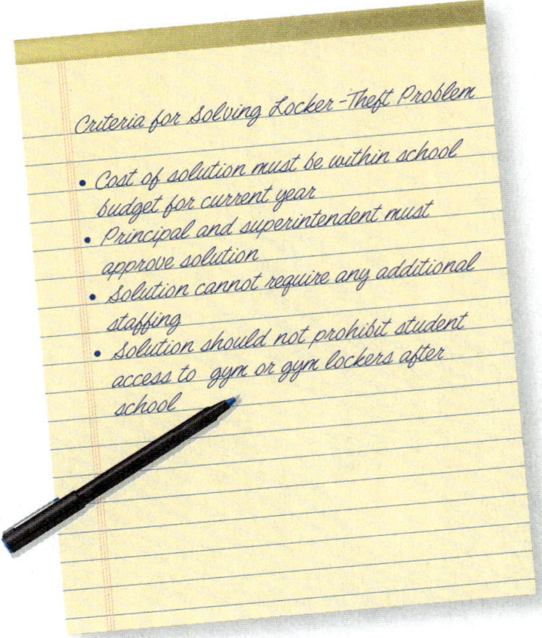

Criteria for Solving Locker-Theft Problem
• Cost of solution must be within school budget for current year
• Principal and superintendent must approve solution
• Solution cannot require any additional staffing
• Solution should not prohibit student access to gym or gym lockers after school

Occasionally, a group may identify some criteria that are essential and others that are preferable but not essential. If, for example, the group were aware of a budget limit, then a non-negotiable criterion would be cost. On the other hand, if there are ample resources for a solution, the cost criterion could be eliminated. Without this criterion, the group would not have to eliminate potentially costly solutions from its list. Therefore, the group would have more possibilities from which to choose the best solution.

List All Possible Solutions. After the group has had time to consider all the criteria carefully, it can begin looking for a solution. This step may be most effective if it is conducted in a separate meeting after all the criteria have been developed. Otherwise, a member may be so busy thinking about the criteria that he or she does not offer possible solutions.

During this step, members of the group need to be highly creative. The purpose of this step is to generate as many ideas as possible. One way to do this is through brainstorming.

Brainstorming is a process of quickly listing all ideas that come to mind regarding a specific topic. Although group members often contribute ideas in the course of everyday meetings, brainstorming refers to a particular technique. This technique begins with a warm-up session that helps familiarize members with the process. During the warm-up, members toss around ideas about a nonsense topic. Any topic will do as long as it is not related to the main group topic.

After the warm-up session, the actual brainstorming can begin. The most valuable feature of brainstorming is that you generate ideas before you judge any of them. Group members do not critique their own or others' ideas, no matter how silly or impractical those ideas might seem. The process demands that group members list ideas spontaneously—offering new ideas, building upon each other's ideas, and even combining ideas before evaluating them.

The group should continue brainstorming and listing ideas as long as it is productive—usually for no more than thirty minutes. Compare brainstorming to popping popcorn.

The students above are brainstorming. What is the most important rule for brainstorming in a group format?

When the popping slows, it's time to stop the cooking process. Similarly, when the ideas begin to slow down significantly, it's time to stop brainstorming.

After the session, the group should take a moment to clarify all the ideas that were listed, marking out any duplicates. It is not a good idea for the group to start checking these suggestions against the criteria at this meeting. Instead, the group should just post the full list of ideas and adjourn the meeting.

Choose the Best Solution. Once all suggested solutions have been listed, the group can go back and find the best solution for the problem based on the established criteria. This step is a decision-making activity. **Decision making** involves examining a set of alternatives and using reason and logic to select the best one. Decision making does not involve creating any additional alternatives. The brainstorming session has already done this.

During the decision-making session, the group first should review all the ideas to be evaluated, making sure everyone understands each idea. Next, members should carefully check all brainstormed solutions against the criteria. It usually is helpful to have a criteria checklist to make this task easier. Figure 10–4 below is a sample criteria checklist for the locker-theft problem.

In addition to considering how well each possible solution meets the criteria, the group should ask itself three questions.

1. Does the solution achieve all the desired results? If it solves only part of the problem, your group may need to change or eliminate the solution.
2. Is the implementation of this solution within the group's power? Even if it is a good solution, the group must have the ability to implement it. Otherwise, your group may need to change or eliminate the solution.
3. Are there serious disadvantages to this solution? If a solution will create additional problems, your group may need to change or eliminate the solution.

Figure 10–4 Criteria Checklist

Brainstorming Idea	Cost Is Within Budget	Likely to Get Approval	No Extra Staffing Required	Allows After-school Student Access
Have custodian lock exterior gym doors	✓	✓		✓
Equip gym lockers with combination locks	✓	✓	✓	✓
Add extra security doors to locker area and provide keys to athletes and coaches			✓	✓
Add security guard in gym locker area		✓		✓

COMMUNICATION PRACTICE LAB

Brainstorming Ideas

To practice conducting a warm-up brainstorming session, follow these steps.

Step 1 Working in groups of five or six, generate ideas for five minutes on one of the following topics or a topic of your own. Have any new topics approved by your teacher.

- New game shows you'd like to see on TV
- How to spend one million dollars
- Uses for a paper plate

Step 2 List your ideas on a sheet of paper. List at least twenty ideas.

Step 3 After your ideas have been generated, discuss as a class some of the most unusual ideas. How difficult was it to keep from criticizing others' ideas? Do you think you could have generated such a diverse list on your own in the same period of time? Why or why not?

After checking the solutions against the criteria and answering the implementation questions, the group may then cross off those ideas that do not fit. Some solutions might meet all the criteria but be unacceptable because of the implementation questions. In this stage of decision making, the group should consider combining ideas or modifying them before discarding them.

Once the group's ideas have been focused, it is time to choose the best solution. Group members should fully discuss all the remaining suggestions. They then should choose the idea or combination of ideas that best meets the criteria.

There are several ways for a group to make its final decision. The most desirable method is to reach a collective decision, or consensus, that every member is willing to support. If this does not seem possible after sufficient discussion, the group may decide to vote. Group members might also decide to ask an expert to listen to the issues and make a decision. Regardless of the decision-making method used, the final step in the process cannot be completed until a solution is chosen.

Implement the Solution. This is the last step in the problem-solving process. In this step, the group should list, in chronological order, all the tasks or jobs necessary to put the solution into effect. The group also should identify the resources necessary to make the plan work. If, for example, cost were a non-negotiable criterion, the implementation plan would need to demonstrate that the solution falls within the established budget.

Next, the group should specify individual responsibilities. Who will do each of the listed tasks? What are the deadlines for completing these tasks? What is the timeline for the plan's overall completion? Understanding these basic guidelines can play a large part in the overall success of the solution.

The implementation plan also should include a system for evaluating the effectiveness of its solution. This evaluation plan should include ways to assess the results of the solution. It should list specific standards for this evaluation as well. Finally, it is important to include a realistic time line for the evaluation.

As a final step, the group should put into place a plan for dealing with possible emergencies. Emergencies might include running over budget, having a key group member quit or move away, or taking more time than was planned. By anticipating and planning for these types of difficulties, a group can ensure that its plan will be implemented successfully.

Once the group's implementation plan has been finalized, it should be clearly explained in a report. This is a communication task for the group. The final report should be submitted to the parent organization. For example, the locker-theft group could use the information from its chart to write up a recommendation, justifying the reasoning behind each step. This report could then be turned in to the school's administration, thus completing the group's problem-solving task. In this way, the group has not only found a solution but also has carefully thought out every step toward putting it into effect.

Section 2 Assessment

Visit the *Glencoe Communication Applications* Web site at **communicationapplications.glencoe.com** and click on **Self-Check and Study Guide 10.2** to review your understanding of the functions of groups.

Review Key Terms

1. Define each of the following terms and write it in a sentence: problem, problem solving, criteria, brainstorming, and decision making.

Check Understanding

2. Why is the group function of planning important to an organization?
3. Identify the three main considerations involved in planning and give an example of each.
4. Explain the six steps of the problem-solving process.
5. **Drawing Conclusions** Why might brainstorming be an effective tool for solving problems?

APPLICATION *Activity*

Planning a Campus Radio Station Imagine that you are a member of a team charged with creating a new radio station format at your school. Working in groups of four to six people, list the different areas you should consider as you plan the new format. Base your list on a consideration of the people, occasion, and task. Once you have created your list, come to a group consensus on which are the three most important considerations. If you have trouble forming a consensus, use the problem-solving strategies you read about in this section. After all groups have completed their lists, share them as a class. Create a class list of ideas for creating a station at your school.

Communication Self-Assessment

Analyzing Your Group Communication Skills

How Do You Rate?

On a separate sheet of paper, use the key to answer the following questions. Put a check mark at the end of each skill you would like to improve.

Key: **A** Always **U** Usually **S** Sometimes **R** Rarely **N** Never

1. When I work in a group, I talk about thirty percent of the meeting time.
2. I am more comfortable when I speak face-to-face with people.
3. I express my opinions in a group whether or not I think the group will agree with me.
4. When I am on a committee or task force, I am willing to do research for the group.
5. I offer information I have about our group work at the proper point on the agenda.
6. I enjoy moving forward to meet group goals.
7. When there is tension in the group, I try to relieve it by asking people to clarify their differences.
8. If someone violates a group norm, I speak to them about this privately.
9. When new members join the group, I am eager to welcome them and bring them up to date on our work.
10. In a group, I tend to be the one who brings our group back to its goal.

How Do You Score?

Review your responses. Give yourself 5 points for every A, 4 for every U, 3 for every S, 2 for every R, and 1 for every N. Total your points and evaluate your score.

41–50 Excellent You may be surprised to find out how much you can improve your skills.

31–40 Good In this course, you can learn ways to make your skills better.

21–30 Fair Practice applying the skills taught in this course.

1–20 Needs Improvement Carefully monitor your improvement as you work through this course.

Setting Communication Goals

If you scored Excellent or Good, complete Part A. If your score was Fair or Needs Improvement, complete Part B.

Part A

1. I plan to put the following ideas into practice:
2. I plan to share the following information about communication with the following people:

Part B

1. The behaviors I need to change most are:
2. To bring about these changes, I will take these steps:

Writing a Memo

A memorandum is a communication circulated within a company. A shorter name for a memorandum is a *memo*. Memos provide employees with important information and updates. Memos can range in length from one paragraph to two or three pages.

Using the Appropriate Style Although a memo may look somewhat like a letter, its style is quite different. A memo is strictly informative and is intended to get right to the point. Typically, it does not include a greeting or closing. The wording of a memo also may be direct or indirect. Most memos use a direct style, summarizing the subject matter in the first paragraph. Then, if necessary, more detail is provided in additional paragraphs. A memo should give only the most important information on a topic.

Occasionally, a memo may have a more indirect style. This style often is effective for conveying bad news or trying to persuade someone to do something he or she may not want to do. In these cases, the first paragraph might explain a special situation or the reasons why a decision has been made. Then the memo can move on to the main information.

Tips for Effective Memos To make your memos useful and easy to read, follow these guidelines.

- Include all the necessary information in the heading. If others besides the main recipient will receive a copy of the memo, list their names beside cc: in the heading. The abbreviation *cc* means *copies.*
- Use a block style for paragraphs.
- Refer to only one topic in each paragraph.
- Do not use highly technical language.
- Use bulleted lists for important points and to convey more complex information.
- Handwrite your name, initials, or a P.S. on the memo for a personal touch.
- Proofread your work, correcting any errors in grammar or spelling.

Now, imagine that you are a sales manager whose staff must begin using a new form. To inform them of this change, you have written the following memo.

For additional information about business writing, see the *Guide to Business Communication* section of the Communication Survival Kit in the Appendix.

Communication Through Writing

Date: June 15, 2004
To: All Sales Agents
From: Marcy McDonald
Purchasing Manager
Subject: New Purchasing Procedure

As of today, June 15, 2004, purchasing order forms 123-A are outdated. We are substituting forms 123-B. Look for the new forms in your inbox today. Each of you will receive a dozen new forms.

The reason we are making this change is that we have changed our accounting procedures.

If you compare the old and new forms, you will see few differences between them. The only difference is that you will order Real Estate Contracts on line 10 of the new form (as opposed to line 1 on the old form).

Things for you to do:
- Find all copies of form 123-A in your files.
- Compare the old form with the new one.
- In addition, note the change on line 10.
- Toss out all copies of form 123-A.
- File copies of 123-B.

P.S. Sam, thanks for recommending this idea. It will make all of our jobs easier.

WRITING *Activity*

Imagine that you are an office manager for a company in a large office building. A security officer has informed you that employees at your company are illegally parking in the building's 15-minute loading and unloading zones. Using a word-processing program, follow these steps to write a memo to all employees.

- Create the heading for your memo.
- Send a copy of the memo to Mark Fields, Chief of Security.
- Using a block paragraph style, write a paragraph summarizing the reason for your memo.
- In another paragraph, remind employees that parking is allowed only along the street, in the outdoor lot, and on floors B, C, and D of the parking garage. Use a bulleted list for this information.
- In a third paragraph, explain that illegally parked cars will be towed at the owner's expense.
- Proofread your memo, correcting any errors.
- Print your memo.
- Handwrite your initials beside your name in the heading.

CHAPTER 10 Assessment and Activities

Visit the *Glencoe Communication Applications* Web site at **communicationapplications.glencoe.com** and click on **Chapter 10 Activity** for additional practice in identifying the nature and function of groups.

Reviewing Key Terms

On a separate sheet of paper, write the communication term that completes each statement.

1. A(n) ________ is a group designed specifically to gather data.
2. In order to be acceptable, a solution to a problem must meet certain ________ .
3. A(n) ________ is a group that is part of the basic structure of an organization.
4. A(n) ________ is set up to promote, protect, defend, or lobby for a cause or group.
5. The difference between the way something should be and the way it is is a(n) ________ .
6. A(n) ________ tells what specific tasks are to be done and what outcome to expect.
7. A person in authority assigns a(n) ________ .
8. Someone joins a(n) ________ for purely personal reasons.
9. The purpose of a(n) ________ is to complete an objective or a job.
10. The activity of a group choosing the best solution for the problem is a(n) ________ activity.

Reviewing Key Concepts

On a separate sheet of paper, answer the following questions in complete sentences.

1. Why do individuals and organizations use groups?
2. What are the four characteristics of a group?
3. How does limited membership help a group agree?
4. Create a statement that describes a group goal for a neighborhood cleanup committee.
5. Name one advantage meeting face-to-face has over telephone or e-mail.
6. How does working in groups benefit an organization?
7. How does working in groups benefit the individual?
8. Define the three main types of task groups.
9. Why might a company encourage its employees to join nonprofit civic groups?
10. What are the two main functions of groups?

Assessment and Activities

Reading and Critical Thinking Skill

1. **Inference** What can you infer from the following statement by an employee: "As a group member, I get to contribute so much that I wouldn't dream of looking elsewhere for work"?
2. **Cause-Effect** What effect does group work have on employee morale?
3. **Summarization** Summarize the three main considerations a group whose main function is planning must address to implement its plan.
4. **Analysis** How does a problem-solving group determine what information it needs to know?

Skill Practice Activity

Making an Inference Read the following information taken from a memo and answer the questions below.

To: Paloma Gonzalez, Lynn Tse, and Pamela Walker—customer service team

Enclosed are certificates to mark your five years as a team. Our company enjoys an excellent standing in the community because our employees are committed to their work. Recently, a rare 'unsatisfied' customer called to praise your team for your conscientious efforts to correct a delivery error.

With these certificates, the company wishes to thank you for your loyalty. We hope you are with us for many more years.

1. What observations are made?
2. Which of the following statements is an inference based on the memo?
   - **a.** The customer service team adds to the company's good standing.
   - **b.** Despite the company's excellent reputation and loyal employees, many customers call to complain.

Cooperative Learning Activity

Picturing an Organization Form teams of four to six people. As a team, consult the yellow pages in a phone book to find a business that probably has several levels of management and other employees. Brainstorm to name the kinds of groups the business might need to operate and the kinds of workers each group might need. Use the lists to create a diagram of the business's organization.

Chapter Project

Planning As a class, brainstorm a list of all the workshops, seminars, and summer camps that help students get information about or training in school activities. Form groups of four or six. Each group selects one information or training opportunity and gathers all the information it can find on the event.

Presenting Each group uses the information to create a brochure for students who might benefit from the event.

CHAPTER 11 Making Groups Work

"Make a dent in the universe."
—Steven Jobs

WHY IT'S IMPORTANT

By developing the Macintosh computer, which made personal computing easier than ever before, Steven Jobs's team made a huge impact on the universe of personal computing. And it proved once again that effective groups can accomplish great things.

To better understand how communication affects the productivity of groups, view the **Communication in Action** Chapter 11 video lesson.

GLENCOE Online

Visit the *Glencoe Communication Applications* Web site at **communicationapplications.glencoe.com** and click on **Overview–Chapter 11** to preview information about making groups work.

Section 1

Interacting in Groups

GUIDE TO READING

Objectives

1. Distinguish between prescribed and emergent norms.
2. Identify and describe the three major roles group members play.
3. Analyze and adapt group dynamics to achieve productive group participation.
4. Describe appropriate skills and strategies for participating effectively in group discussions.

Terms to Learn

group norm
prescribed norm
emergent norm
initiator
facilitator
agitator
groupthink
group dynamics
group discussion

Think about how you might be expected to behave in an English class. Now think about how you might act in athletics. Are there different expectations about your behavior in each type of school activity? What do you think accounts for these differences?

The degree to which your behavior changes from one type of activity to another depends on a number of factors. Two of these are the rules set by your teacher or coach and the roles you choose to play as a participant in the activity. Rules and roles play a large part in the way we communicate with others in almost any group setting.

Identifying Group Norms

Whether you join a group on your own or are assigned to one, you will be expected to follow some group norms while working in that group. **Group norms** are the informal, often unstated rules about what behavior is appropriate in a group. If you

Group norms determine the interaction that takes place between people when they are at work. Define group norms.

work as a stocker at a grocery store, you probably have certain duties when you begin each workday or shift. You might be expected to punch a time clock, put on a uniform, or check with a supervisor to find out what specific tasks are assigned to you that day.

As a student, you also are expected to do certain things each morning as you begin your school day. For example, you probably are expected to dress appropriately, arrive on time, gather your books and materials for your first class, and proceed to that classroom at the designated time. By behaving in this way, you are following the group norms for the student body at your school.

As you can see, the norms for one group may be very different from those for another group. However, despite their differences, most group norms can be classified into two categories. They are either prescribed norms or emergent norms.

Prescribed Norms

A prescribed norm is a rule for appropriate behavior that is routinely taught to new group members. Prescribed norms may be written or unwritten.

In School Both schools and workplaces have prescribed norms. For instance, at the beginning of the school year, some teachers give students a list of rules, or prescribed norms, for their specific classroom. This establishes the norms for students' behavior in class.

In the Workplace In the workplace, prescribed norms usually include a specific time for the workday to begin and end or when people usually have lunch. Members of the armed services have prescribed norms about which uniforms to wear on different occasions. A coach might establish norms such as how long practice will last, what uniforms will be worn for home games, and how players are expected to behave when traveling to games in other cities.

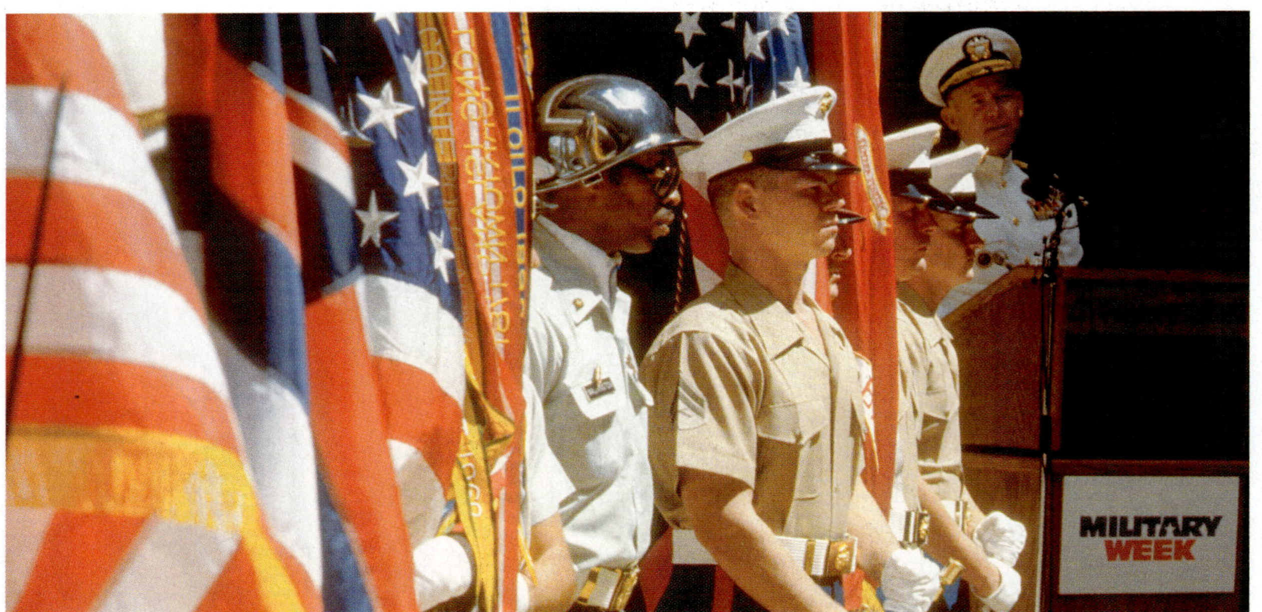

Members of the armed services adhere to a strict dress code. One individual shown above appears to be going against the dress norm. Identify the two categories of group norms.

Global Communication

Culture in Meetings

The group norms followed in meetings often vary from culture to culture. In Brazil, for example, the norm is to engage in conversation about family and friends before moving on to the business part of a meeting. A person unfamiliar with this norm might dive right into business matters first and be considered cold and unfriendly. Think about the activities and interactions that might take place in meetings. What other group norms might clash in a business meeting involving people from different cultures?

Emergent Norms

Not all norms are as basic and enduring as the prescribed norms just described. Some develop as the group grows and changes. An **emergent norm** is any group norm that develops from the group interaction and the mix of the group members' personalities. These norms usually are unwritten and arise from some need that is determined by the group members.

If a teacher assigns a group project, the group goal and project deadline would be prescribed. However, the way in which the group chooses to complete the project; details about where, when, and how often the group will meet; and decisions about who will complete each task will emerge as a result of the group working together.

Imagine that the employees of a fast-food restaurant establish the norm that they will celebrate each other's birthdays by giving cards rather than gifts. If one member of the group brings a gift, the emergent norm of the group has been violated. The behavior is not appropriate for that group's norms.

Emergent group norms make a big difference in how a group works. Positive emergent norms can make group membership more pleasant and can help the group achieve its goal. Negative emergent norms, on the other hand, can be harmful to the group. When it

Communication Practice Lab

Classifying Norms

To learn how to distinguish prescribed norms from emergent norms, follow these steps:

Step 1 As a class, brainstorm a list of group norms. Then, write the list on the chalkboard.

Step 2 Copy the list of norms onto a sheet of paper.

Step 3 For each norm, ask yourself "Would this norm be taught to all new group members?" If so, write *Prescribed* beside that norm.

Step 4 For each remaining norm, ask "Is this norm a result of group members' interactions and personalities?" If so, write *Emergent* beside that norm.

Step 5 Compare your answers as a class and discuss any differences of opinion. Then discuss whether each norm might have a positive or negative effect on a group and why.

becomes the norm to be late or to complain about the task, the group is likely to become less effective. It doesn't take long for new norms to emerge in a group.

Sometimes problems arise in a group because discussion of emergent norms happens so rarely. If a norm is not written, a person may be breaking a norm and not know it. Others in the group may assume the person knows so they don't say anything. Fortunately, however, these norms usually can be changed quickly through group discussions and action.

Productive groups set productive group norms. The members also are productive in their group roles. In other words, they interact in ways that help accomplish the goal. For instance, people in productive groups either agree with each others' ideas or disagree respectfully. They also critically examine the work of others without being rude or sarcastic. Finally, they promote the task of the group without being impatient with other members. In short, productive group members act as competent communicators.

Group Roles

Have you been a part of a group whose members really seemed to work well together? In this type of group, the work tends to be shared among all group members. Members also seem to genuinely enjoy working on the group task and working with each other, and there is a lot of positive energy.

In committees, teams, and other groups some members will have formal roles such as chairperson or manager. However, all members have communication roles that indicate the way they function in a group. The three roles that members are likely to play are initiator, facilitator, and agitator. In a single group session, it is possible that one person might switch from one role to another so that he or she actually plays all three roles during the session. In a productive group, members take turns playing these three roles to keep the group balanced and to keep it moving toward the achievement of its goal.

Communication Strategies

Displaying Positive Initiator Behaviors

- Get the discussion started.
- Offer ideas about the task.
- Try to bring energy to the interaction.
- Point out negative norms and suggest possible ways to change them.
- Ask others to contribute their skills or talents to the task.

Initiator

Within a group, a member may play the role of an initiator. An **initiator** works to get the group started toward achieving the group goal. An effective initiator contributes positive task energy to the group.

Positive Initiator Behaviors A person playing the role of initiator can contribute to the group by displaying certain positive behaviors.

An initiator in a group of students planning a school dance might suggest different tasks to group members based on their individual talents. He or she might ask someone who plays in a band to plan how and where to set up the sound equipment and band platform. The initiator also might ask a skillful writer to compose an article about the dance for the school newspaper.

Sometimes, the role of the initiator can be assumed by a member of a group who is not the group leader. Think about a time when you were in a group meeting and realized it was time to begin. However, the group leader may have been busy talking with another member, unaware that the group was ready to start the discussion. To avoid wasting time, someone else in the group needed to assume the role of initiator by saying, "Hey, it's late. Should we get started?" By helping to begin the discussion, this person provides positive energy to the group.

Negative Initiator Behaviors Initiators also can contribute negative energy to a group. If an initiator is too aggressive and tries to control what everyone in the group does, his or her actions may backfire. Often, this creates a hostile relationship among group members instead of encouraging a spirit of cooperation.

Initiators who dominate a discussion also have a negative effect on a group. When other members are not allowed to contribute, they often quit trying. This can stop the free exchange of ideas that is so important to productive groups.

Finally, initiators may display negative behavior by ignoring the feelings of others while trying to get the task done. Although it is important to keep the group moving toward its goal, it also is important to recognize the value and contributions of each individual member.

Facilitator

Another role a group member may play is that of a facilitator. A **facilitator** is a person who also adds energy to the group by helping group members follow through on tasks. The facilitator is the glue that holds a group together. This person often offers to do the tasks necessary for the group to achieve its goal.

Positive Facilitator Behaviors The facilitator can contribute greatly to the effectiveness of the committee, team, or group. To do this, he or she should display certain positive behaviors.

An effective facilitator is one who listens and cooperates. He or she also supports other members of the group. A facilitator may volunteer to do extra research, make key changes to a report, make phone calls, write letters, or assume other responsibilities needed to help the group reach its goal.

Think about a time when you tried to contribute a comment during a particularly lively group discussion. You may have had

During community meetings such as the one shown here, individuals sometimes act as initiators. Describe an effective initiator.

some difficulty making yourself heard. You may have leaned forward, possibly gestured for silence from the rest of the group, and started speaking. However, after only one or two words, someone else may have started speaking, taking the group discussion in another direction.

If someone had assumed the role of facilitator in the group, your comment might not have been lost. A facilitator would have heard that you had been cut off before you had an opportunity to be heard. He or she might have redirected the discussion by saying something like, "I think you had a comment to make when we were talking about the cost of this project. I'd like to hear your idea."

Negative Facilitator Behaviors Like an initiator, a facilitator sometimes may display negative behaviors. One common negative facilitator behavior is assuming too much responsibility and not delegating to others. A facilitator also may be so concerned about keeping the peace in a group that useful disagreements do not develop. Some conflict can benefit a group, causing group members to examine the issues more closely.

Displaying Positive Facilitator Behaviors

- Direct the discussion.
- Assume responsibility for completing tasks to attain the group goal.
- Ask for group members' ideas on the task.
- Support group members' participation by complimenting their work when appropriate in the group.
- Notice when facial expressions and other nonverbal feedback indicate a member has a problem that needs to be addressed.
- Ask for input from all group members who haven't yet spoken on the topic.
- Summarize the main points of discussion for other group members.
- Provide humor and relieve tension among members as needed.

Agitator

Some roles generally are considered to be nonproductive and negative. People who play the role of agitator inject negative energy into the group process. There are six identifiable roles typically adopted by agitators: nonparticipant, distracter, clown, complainer, critic, and absentee. These six types of agitators are described in the following chart.

Negative Agitator Behaviors As you can see, most agitator behaviors are negative. An agitator works against the group's momentum. Some may even aggressively work against the group goals. Constantly criticizing and antagonizing other group members can create conflict and disrupt the group process. If an agitator argues for the sake of argument or disagrees just to be disagreeable, barriers to group effectiveness result.

Dealing With Agitators Agitators who actively create negative energy and those who contribute only a low level of energy both become a drain on the positive energy of a group. They create dissension and frustration and hold back group progress. The general rule for dealing with the negative behaviors of

TYPES OF AGITATORS

Type	Characteristics	Effect on Group
Nonparticipant	• Unconcerned with meeting group goal • Does not contribute ideas • Invests a low level of energy to group activities and meetings • Often may be late to meetings or fail to complete tasks on time • May do work of poor quality	• Can drain positive energy from the group and lower group morale • May create frustration and dissatisfaction among other group members who have to take over nonparticipant's share of responsibilities
Distracter	• Has difficulty focusing on the business of the meeting • Equates group time with social time • May be enthusiastic and energetic, but energy is misdirected • Tends to stay off the purpose, off the topic, and off the task	• Continual interruptions can be very disruptive • Can get other members off track • Can be annoying to group members trying to focus on the task
Clown	• Diverts attention from a task he or she does not find interesting • May disrupt the group's progress with jokes, wisecracks, sarcasm, or teasing	• Can provide comic relief, but typically overdoes it • Actions interfere with group's goal and purpose
Complainer	• Has a negative attitude • Repeatedly voices doubts or opposition to whatever the group is doing • Shares his or her bad attitude with the rest of the group	• Creates an atmosphere of negative thinking that can be difficult for a group to overcome
Critic	• Constantly points out what is wrong with others' ideas • Makes a habit of putting down others' suggestions • Seldom makes suggestions of his or her own	• Creates an atmosphere of hurt feelings, defensiveness, and anger among group members • Some members may not participate for fear of being criticized
Absentee	• Is a frequent "no show" for group meetings • Often will not respond to telephone calls or other contact from group members	• Even in his or her absence, injects negative energy into the group dynamics • Other members must step up to fulfill the absentee's responsibilities

agitators is simply to move on before the agitator's negative energy has a chance to influence the group. Once the group has moved on, the problem becomes that of the agitator, not of the group as a whole.

Positive Agitator Influences There are exceptions to this rule, however. Occasionally, it may be good for an agitator to slow the momentum of the group. If, for example, the group has missed an important detail while making its decision, it may take an agitator to draw attention to the oversight. In this case, the agitator has caused the group to reexamine its work as it progresses, rather than waiting until a real mistake has been made.

Imagine that a committee has been formed to explore changes in a company's vacation policy. Most members quickly agree that employee vacations should be restricted to the summer months. An agitator in the group might say, "Shouldn't we give some consideration to individuals who want time with their families during winter holidays or who enjoy ski vacations?" With this challenge, the agitator has stopped the momentum of the group. Instead of agreeing too quickly on a solution, a more complete discussion can now occur. The agitator's comment also may have given courage to other members of the group. Those members who were silently concerned about the group's decision now have another opportunity to speak up and make their feelings known.

Groupthink Log on to the Internet and access a reliable World Wide Web search engine. Conduct a search using the keyword *groupthink* and explore the results. Note three facts about avoiding groupthink and share them with the class.

Groupthink Even though agitators cause a disruption in the group momentum, groups with no agitators may perform poorly. **Groupthink** is the name for poor decision-making in a group because group members have a stronger desire to agree with one another than to solve the problem.

A group of people who are afraid of disagreeing with one another or who want very much to be agreeable may become a victim of groupthink. If this group had a member who could play the agitator role positively, the group would have a better chance of making good decisions. It also would avoid making decisions that might cause additional problems.

Figure 11–1 Dealing with Agitators

Assuming Productive Group Roles

Although the roles of group members at first may seem very distinct, they are not set in stone. At one point in a discussion, you may be an initiator trying to move the group discussions along toward the goal. Later, you might be a facilitator encouraging a silent member to participate. At another point in the discussion, you may be an agitator, trying to get the group to consider an alternate idea. You also may have to find a way to deal with the apathetic or uncooperative agitator to safeguard the momentum of the group.

The key to assuming successful group roles is balance. Productive groups need members who can play all three roles and understand which role is appropriate at any given time. When should you change group roles? Ask yourself these two important questions: "Are we making progress?" and "What role do I need to assume to help move the group forward?"

Analyzing Group Dynamics

As you move from committees to teams to other kinds of groups, changing your behavior in each situation, you are responding to group dynamics. **Group dynamics** is the energy created as group members communicate and interact with each other in committees, teams, and other groups.

Interaction among group members may be either positive or negative. Positive group interaction moves the group toward accomplishing its goal and building cohesion among group members. Negative interaction creates barriers that can prevent the group from reaching its goal. These barriers also provide obstacles to unity within the group.

Figure 11–2 Factors Affecting Group Dynamics

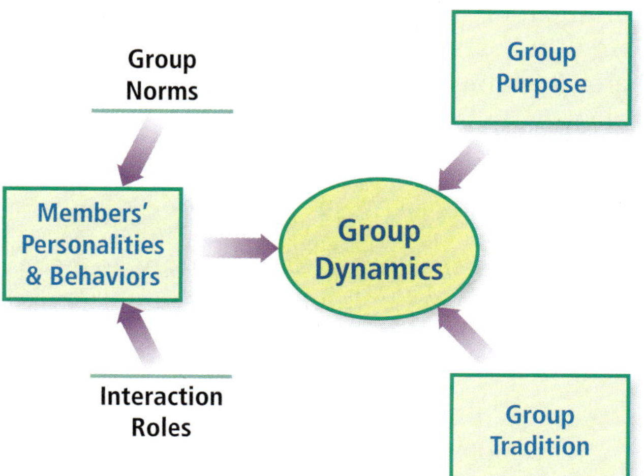

TECHNOLOGY *Activity*

Creating a Table As a class, hold a five-minute class discussion about a business topic and videotape it. Review the tape, noting each time a student speaks and what role he or she assumes. Then, working in groups of two or three, use a word-processing program to create a table from your notes. In your table, list every student in the class, the three types of roles, and how many times each student assumed each role. Share your table with the class. How do your tables look similar? How are they different?

As Figure 11–2 shows, group dynamics is the unique combination of group members' different personalities and behaviors, the group purpose, and the group tradition. Because each of these elements can change, group dynamics tend to be active, unpredictable, and constantly evolving.

Group members often influence one another's behavior, which can change the dynamics of the group. This typically occurs when they form and perform group norms or when they assume different group roles.

Impact of Norms on Dynamics

In a group, both prescribed and emergent norms should lead to achieving the group task and purpose. They also should contribute to a sense of unity within the group. A group's norms have a definite effect on the nature and quality of interaction among group members. For example, if a norm for committee members is to be courteous and direct with each other, members have a safe environment for voicing their ideas. This may make their interaction more comfortable. If the

THE FAR SIDE By GARY LARSON

The entire parliament fell dead silent. For the first time since anyone could remember, one of the members voted "aye."

norm, such as the time and place or the level of formality, creates a problem within the group, the members should discuss the issue and look for a way to change the norm.

Impact of Roles on Dynamics

All group members should try to remain aware of which roles are needed during a meeting. Once a need has been determined, the members should do their best to fill that vacant role. A productive group needs a good balance of all three roles—initiators, facilitators, and agitators—performed competently. When there are too many or too few people filling one specific role, the group dynamics suffer.

Too many initiators can lead to power struggles. Too few initiators, however, can stall a meeting or send it off track. Too many facilitators may cause the group's work to stall if nobody takes action, even though everyone is willing to help. With too few facilitators, less assertive members may not be heard. Too many agitators in a group can create disruption and focus the group's energy on its disagreements. Too few agitators, on the other hand, may keep a committee from fully examining its decisions. The group may fail to consider alternative points of view.

When every group member assumes productive roles as they are needed, group dynamics often change for the better. This type of positive adaptation can help a group to function effectively and successfully.

Group Discussion

Have you ever been to a meeting that never seemed to get down to business? Perhaps side conversations and activities made the meeting last twice as long as necessary? Using effective group discussion skills could have solved both of these problems.

In Chapter 1, you read that different contexts require different communication skills. In the context of personal interaction, communication may require conversation skills or small-talk skills. However, in the context of a group, communication requires the appropriate use of discussion skills.

Importance of Discussion

During a meeting, it is important to hear information and opinions of all group members. This can be accomplished through group discussion.

Group discussion occurs when three or more people exchange ideas on a specific topic for a specific purpose. A discussion is different from a conversation, in which people informally exchange random observations, ideas, and opinions. Rather, a discussion is focused on a particular topic. It is organized around a central idea and has a specific reason for occurring. Group discussion also engages every member of the group.

Many times in a professional or social group setting, the topics of discussion are determined ahead of time. Some groups may organize these discussion topics in a formal agenda like the one in Figure 11–3.

Many groups do not prepare agendas for their meetings but may follow a fairly predictable order of topics in their meetings. These topics may relate to the type of group it is, its task, or its purpose. Whether or not these topics are written down, they serve as a guide for group discussion.

Characteristics of Effective Discussions

You probably know from experience that not all discussions go smoothly. In fact, some are much more effective than others. Effective discussions in committees, teams, and other groups share some important qualities. They are

- interactive
- focused
- organized
- cooperative

Interactive Group discussions generally are not effective unless everyone participates. For maximum participation, group members should remember to do the following:

Prepare ahead of time. This ensures that each member will have something valuable to contribute during the group session.

Take turns speaking. If two or more members speak at once, no one can hear everything that is being contributed to the discussion. A facilitator can help make sure everyone gets a turn to speak.

Listen carefully. Remember that others have prepared for the meeting as well. They may have important information and ideas to contribute to the discussion. Listening can mean keeping an open mind until different views are completely voiced before beginning to criticize. Listening carefully helps you stay more informed and aware in the group

Figure 11–3 Formal Agenda

POOLS Inc.

Discussion of Possible Market Expansion

Monday, March 12, 2003
Conference Room A
8:30 A.M.–10:30 A.M.

Benefits of market expansion 8:30–8:45
Susan Margolis, President

Possible expansion areas 8:45–9:15
Mark Pulos, Vice President, Marketing

Cost/benefit analysis 9:15–9:30
Ian Bernsen, Vice President, Accounting

Employee suggestions 9:30–9:45

Group discussion of all options 9:45–10:20

Wrap-up, plans for next stage 10:20–10:30
Susan Margolis

discussion. Your nonverbal behavior also should show that you are interested in what others have to say.

Contribute to the discussion. You can contribute by offering information, opinions, or suggestions about the topic. You also can contribute by asking others for their information, suggestions, and opinions.

Assume different roles as needed. Group members should act as initiators and facilitators and use questioning skills to keep the group moving toward achieving its goals.

Focused Group sessions are most effective when they focus on one topic at a time. Group discussion allows all group members to fully explore the information about one topic before moving to the next one. The goal is to use each group member's critical evaluation skills to fully explore a topic before coming to a conclusion. First, the chairperson of the group or an initiator should introduce the topic to be discussed. He or she might then suggest how to start the discussion. If the initiator doesn't do this, a facilitator might make the suggestion and then keep the group on topic. For example, if a member strays from the topic, the facilitator might say something like, "Good idea, but we haven't finished with fund-raising ideas yet. Let's remember your suggestion for our next meeting." By being both direct and courteous, the facilitator can help the discussion stay productive and on track.

Organized Unlike conversation or small talk, which may jump from topic to topic, effective group discussion progresses from one

Members of a group assume different roles to keep the discussion focused.
What role does the initiator play?

logical point to the next to get the group's work accomplished. The goal of this sequence is to achieve a specific purpose. Whether a group is planning or problem solving, its interaction will be more effective if discussion is organized.

Cooperative To be effective, interaction in a committee or team should be cooperative. Group members should focus discussion time on achieving the group's stated goals. The degree to which members feel positive toward the group, its goals, and the other group members affects how cooperative the nature of any group discussion will be.

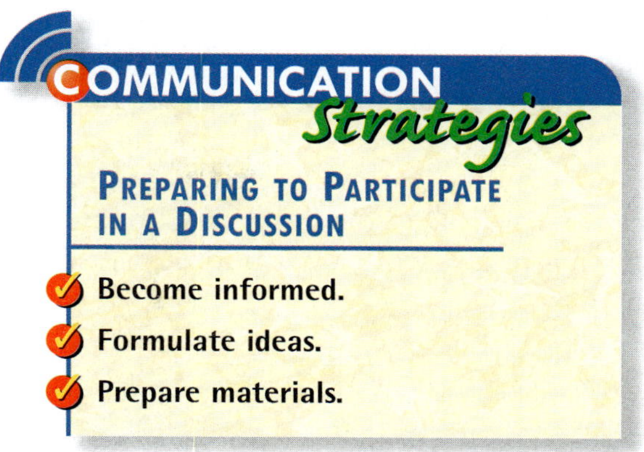
COMMUNICATION Strategies
PREPARING TO PARTICIPATE IN A DISCUSSION
Become informed.
Formulate ideas.
Prepare materials.

EFFECTIVE GROUP DISCUSSION

No one is born a discussion expert. On the contrary, participating appropriately in a group discussion is a learned skill. Quite simply, to be most effective in a committee, team, or other group discussion, you must learn how to adequately prepare for it. Preparing to participate in a group discussion involves some basic communication behaviors.

Become Informed

If you are participating in a committee, team, or other group and know the topic ahead of time, research it before the group meeting. You may want to read more about it in books, periodicals, or special publications.

You also may want to talk with someone who is familiar with the topic to get his or her ideas and perspectives. Finally, you may wish to gather information from videotapes, newscasts, the Internet, or special televised programs that deal with your topic. Throughout your research, concentrate on finding factual information about the topic that might be useful to your group.

Formulate Ideas

Prior to the group meeting, take time to think about what ideas you can contribute to the group task. Come to your committee, team, or other group meeting with questions to ask about the topic, ideas to contribute, and suggestions to make.

Use your reasoning skills to formulate ideas and questions about the topic. Depending on your group's task, you may need to think about the long-term and short-term effects of taking a particular action or adopting a particular policy. Think about how your ideas or proposals might affect different members of your group or other groups. Consider cost, time, workers, and other practical issues involved in implementing your ideas. You might even want to anticipate potential arguments to your suggestions. Once you have considered all these factors, you can properly formulate and organize your ideas to present to your group.

Prepare Materials

If, after researching and considering the topic, you have developed new ideas or suggestions, you may want to prepare certain materials to help explain them to the group. These materials might include handouts, fact sheets, charts, or graphs that clarify your position.

You also will want to consider that other group members will be bringing their own ideas and information to the group. You may want to preview all the topics on the agenda and have a list of questions and ideas that you want to voice. Do you have questions about other members' work on the group task? Be prepared to play the initiator or agitator role. Do you have extra information that might be helpful to the group regarding the topic? Be prepared to play the facilitator or initiator. By preparing adequately and participating actively in the group discussion, you will help your group achieve its task and purpose.

Section 1 Assessment

Visit the *Glencoe Communication Applications* Web site at **communicationapplications.glencoe.com** and click on **Self-Check and Study Guide 11.1** to review your understanding of the interaction in groups.

Review Key Terms

1. Define each term and write it in a sentence: group norm, prescribed norm, emergent norm, initiator, facilitator, agitator, groupthink, group dynamics, group discussion.

Check Understanding

2. Explain the difference between prescribed and emergent norms. Give an example of each.
3. Identify and describe the three major roles group members play.
4. Why is it important to maintain a balance of the roles assumed by group members?
5. How might you adapt group dynamics to help a group function more productively?
6. **Apply** How might you prepare for a discussion on possible guest speakers for this year's graduation ceremony at your school?

APPLICATION *Activity*

Determining Group Roles Work with a group of three students to play "What's My Role?" Have one student write the following words on separate strips of paper: *initiator, facilitator,* and *agitator.* Fold the strips of paper, mix them up, and have each student in your group choose one. As a group, determine a possible discussion topic for a business meeting. Then, taking turns with the other groups in your class, play your group's assigned roles in a one- to two-minute discussion of that topic. Perform your discussion for the whole class. When you have finished, the rest of the class should vote on which student was playing each role. Finally, reveal your roles to the class.

Technology Skill

VIDEOCONFERENCING

Videoconferencing uses video and audio signals to allow people in different locations to participate in a meeting. During videoconferencing, special cameras send live video images over phone lines to distant locations.

Learning the Skill

Videoconferences require preplanning. Read the planning steps below.

1. **Set the Conference Date and Time.** Contact all groups involved in the conference and arrange a meeting time.
2. **Get to Know the Participants.** Call participants before the actual meeting.
3. **Prepare an Agenda.** Create and send an agenda listing the date, time, and purpose of the meeting and detailing what needs to be accomplished.
4. **Use the Technology Effectively.** To keep communication clear, make sure all participants are visible in the camera's range. Remind everyone to speak clearly and avoid side conversations.

PLANNING

Set Date and Time

↓

Know Participants

↓

Prepare Agenda

↓

Use Technology Effectively

Practicing the Skill

Imagine that you are planning a videoconference among a marketing group in Houston, a design group in San Diego, and a production group in Tokyo, Japan. The purpose of the meeting is to share ideas about creating and marketing a new hand-held video game. Follow these steps for your videoconference.

Step 1 Imagine that, after speaking with all participants, the best time for the meeting is Thursday at 4:30 P.M. central standard time. Calculate the meeting time for each participating group. Include these times on your agenda.

Step 2 Create an agenda for your meeting. Include items that you think might be important to discuss in this type of meeting.

Step 3 Share your agenda with the class. Combine students' ideas to create a master agenda for the class.

Step 4 As a class, work in three groups—one for each group involved in the meeting. Hold a mock videoconference, taping the proceedings with a video camera.

Step 5 Watch the tape of your meeting. How could you make your next videoconference more effective?

Explain the advantages or disadvantages of videoconferencing in the following situations: interviewing for a job in another city, and people located in different cities brainstorming ideas for the development of a new product.

Section 2

Participating in Groups

GUIDE TO READING

Objectives

1. Use appropriate verbal strategies to promote group effectiveness.
2. Use effective and describe ineffective nonverbal behaviors in group meetings.
3. Use a variety of listening strategies to contribute to group effectiveness.
4. Identify and analyze the role of the group chairperson.
5. Analyze the participation and contributions of group members and evaluate group effectiveness.

Terms to Learn

task need
maintenance need

Imagine that you are part of a small group whose goal is to develop new product ideas. At the beginning of the meeting, three of the four group members sit around the table and begin to brainstorm ideas. The fourth member turns her chair away from the table and works on a report she has to turn in later that day. You and the other group members feel resentful that she is not helping the group do its work. Is the fourth person participating appropriately and making a positive contribution to the group? Is this group being effective?

If you were a member of this group, how might you improve the situation? What will it take for the group to become productive? By learning how to apply your communication skills in a group, you will learn how to answer these questions. You will learn methods for overcoming challenges to group productivity and effectiveness. You will also learn how to use effective verbal, nonverbal, and listening strategies in teams, committees, or other groups. Finally, you will have some guidelines to analyze the effectiveness of your participation and the participation of other members in committees, teams, or other groups.

Participating in groups at work offers challenges and rewards. What kind of skill must one develop in order to work with a group effectively?

COMMUNICATION Strategies
USING EFFECTIVE VERBAL STRATEGIES
Ask clear questions.
State your ideas, opinions, and position.
Use courtesy and tact.
Provide constructive criticism.

EFFECTIVE VERBAL STRATEGIES IN GROUPS

Your responsibility as a productive group member is to assume the role of initiator, facilitator, or agitator appropriately as needed. This helps your group, regardless of its purpose, take care of the task needs and the maintenance needs of the group.

A **task need** is a need that relates directly to the business and goals of the group. Task needs are met when members give and seek information that will help move the group toward accomplishing its goal.

A **maintenance need** relates to the feelings of group members and their relationships to one another. Maintenance needs are met when members are satisfied with their position in the group and the way members are interacting. The effective verbal strategies in the Communication Strategies checklist can help you meet your group's task and maintenance needs.

Ask Clear Questions

Computer programmers often repeat this important work rule: "Garbage in, garbage out." In other words, if you give a computer an unclear or faulty command, the computer won't perform the way you want it to. The same concept applies to asking questions. If you are not specific about what you want to know, you aren't likely to get the right information you need.

Ask Specific Questions. Consider the conversation below between two members of a company's planning committee.

Martina Means:
"It's time for you to share your research on the cost of each plan."
Martina Says:
"Robert, do you have any comments about these plans?"
Robert Means:
"I know what each plan costs, but I have no other comments. I wonder when she'll ask me for those cost figures?"
Robert Says:
"No. I don't have anything to add right now."

Martina and Robert are not communicating effectively. In order to communicate effectively, one should always ask clear questions. Why is it important to be specific when asking a question?

In this conversation, Martina did not directly ask for the information she wanted. Likewise, Robert did not draw conclusions about what Martina really wanted to know. To avoid this type of misunderstanding, Martina could have been more specific. At the previous meeting, she might have asked Robert, "Will you please research the cost of each plan and then distribute the figures to everyone at our next meeting?" Then, at the next meeting, Martina could have asked Robert, "Will you now share with the group your information about the cost of each plan?"

Other Uses for Questions Questions are not only used to get information. They also can be used to move the discussion forward. For example, an initiator might ask, "Shall we now consider the real nature of the problem?" or "Have we considered the disadvantages of such a program?" Regardless of whether they are seeking information or directing a discussion, well-formed questions help meet the task needs of a group.

Questions also can be used to help meet the maintenance needs of a group. For instance, a facilitator might ask, "Have we heard from everyone on this issue?" An initiator might ask, "Would you begin our discussion of this phase of the plan? I know you have some innovative ideas." In both cases, the question promotes cohesion by involving all members in the group task.

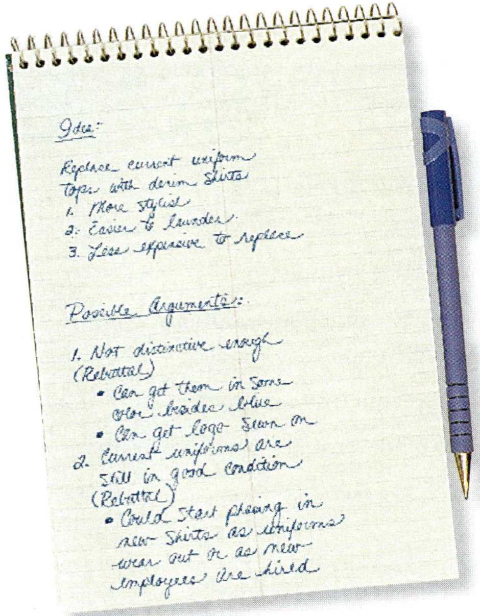

Questions can direct group members to communicate their ideas to one another. **What are other uses for questions in group situations?**

State Your Ideas, Opinions, and Position

Usually, you are a member of a committee, team, or other group because you have some experience, knowledge, or ability to offer regarding the group task. That means, what you know and think about the group task matters. Also, building group enthusiasm and support for your ideas can help bring members together, meeting the maintenance needs of the group. In either case, your information and opinions must be stated clearly and persuasively to be effective.

As you prepare for each group meeting, think about the topics to be discussed and what you might contribute. Also, consider the other group members. Will some members be opposed to your ideas? If so, try to anticipate their concerns and address them as you give your information. You might say, "I know that some members are concerned about the state of our current budget, so I think we should make this purchase after the new budget comes into effect this January because . . ." This statement then could be followed by a list of reasons why you support making the purchase.

As you state your opinions and ideas, you may be involved in an information-giving interaction. This type of interaction advances the task by providing information or opinions for the group's consideration. You might say, "I have learned that three of our competitors have tried this plan. Here is what they discovered. . . ."

On the other hand, you may be involved in information-seeking interactions. You might say, "I would be interested in hearing what you found out in your research on this issue." This statement not only advances the task, it also serves a maintenance function by acknowledging an interest in this person's ideas.

Use Courtesy and Tact

The third effective verbal strategy is the use of courtesy and tact. Courtesy and tact can make a great impact on the cohesiveness of a committee, team, or group.

Utilizing courtesy and tact can further effective communication. Compare the two photos above. Which photo suggests that a person is using courtesy and tact? Explain.

Courtesy By using courteous verbal and nonverbal language, you show respect to the other members of the group. After a short time, you'll realize that courteous language is contagious. Other members will tend to follow your lead in being courteous. Courtesy should become an emergent norm for every group.

One practical use of courtesy in a group is to praise group members for effective contributions—especially if you are filling the facilitator role. An important part of giving praise is to make it genuine and specific to the behavior or idea, not just a general statement.

Tact In group interactions, tact is a way of dealing with others so that good relations are maintained in the group. Tact is especially important when a group is discussing a controversial topic or when there are strong feelings on either side of an issue.

Tact is useful when you must disagree with someone but do not want to hurt that person's feelings or make him or her angry. For instance, if you think a group member is slowing the group down by being overly cautious about every decision, you might say, "I agree that we should be cautious, but I would like us to consider this idea."

To be tactful, try to use diplomatic language and choose your words and tone of voice carefully. Your goal is not to offend others; your goal is to accomplish a task cooperatively. Both tact and courtesy are vital to maintaining unity in a group. In this way, they fulfill important maintenance needs in a group.

COMMUNICATION Strategies

PROVIDING CONSTRUCTIVE CRITICISM

- Separate the speaker's information from any feelings you might have about him or her. Do not disagree just because you don't like the speaker.
- Try to restate the other person's point of view before adding your own comments.
- Calmly and objectively state why you disagree. Do not verbally attack the person who gave the information.
- Do not interrupt other speakers.
- If your concerns already have been answered by another group member, graciously state your agreement. Don't waste the group's time by repeating what already has been said.
- When possible, use tentative language to soften your disagreement. For instance, you might say, "Would it be just as effective if we . . . ," or "Perhaps we could look at this from another point of view as well."
- Offer an observation and then a suggestion. For example, say, "Somehow I think we have gotten off the topic. Perhaps we could finish the original discussion first and then come back to this topic."
- If there is a part of the other person's work that you can compliment or agree with, do so.

Provide Constructive Criticism

Constructive criticism is often difficult to give. If you disagree with comments made by other members, make an effort to disagree without being disagreeable. Remember that constructive criticism has two important elements: praise for appropriate choices, behaviors, and results; and positive suggestions for improvement when improvement is needed.

Offering constructive criticism requires courtesy, tact, and careful consideration of the other person. Following are some important ideas to consider when offering constructive criticism.

EFFECTIVE NONVERBAL STRATEGIES IN GROUPS

Your nonverbal behavior is as important to a group discussion as your verbal comments. In other words, what you do is just as important as what you say! Following are some nonverbal behaviors that require your special attention during group interactions. These are

- dress and grooming
- time
- space and distance
- eye contact
- volume and tone
- gestures and movement

Dress and Grooming

If you are preparing to attend a group meeting, first plan your dress and grooming so that you will fit in with the rest of the group. Is this a casual group or is it the norm to dress more formally? If you are in a group at school, there may be a time when you wear a special shirt or sweatshirt to a meeting.

If you are in doubt about what to wear, it is better to dress too formally than too casually, such as the young man in Figure 11–4. As for grooming, always appear clean and neatly groomed when participating in business or group activities.

Time

How you use time transmits a message to others around you. If you arrive late to a group meeting, your actions may indicate that the meeting is not important to you. Lateness also indicates that you are unconcerned about wasting other group members' time as they sit and wait for you.

If you miss a meeting entirely without notifying someone in advance, you convey the message that both the group and the group task are unimportant to you. Finally, if you leave the meeting early, you send the same negative message.

Space and Distance

People tend to divide space equally among the people who are occupying that space. For instance, if four people will be meeting around a square table, each person probably would sit at a different side of the table. If the table were round, the group probably would mentally divide the table into fourths, with each person taking one-fourth of the space. Crowding into another group member's space without good reason can make that member uncomfortable and, therefore, would be inappropriate behavior.

Some informal group meetings might take place in a living room, in an empty classroom, in a coworker's office, or in some other type of room that isn't equipped with a large, round table. When this happens, try to arrange the group so that everyone can see and be seen by the other members.

Figure 11–4 Appropriate and Inappropriate Dress

Eye Contact

At home, at school, or at work, eye contact commands attention. We use our eyes as nonverbal traffic signals. In a group setting, not only should members be able to see one another, but they also should work at maintaining eye contact with the other group members. Because of this, you should not examine printed materials while group members are speaking unless they are guiding you through those materials. If you are the one speaking, be sure to look at all the members of the group—one by one—on a regular basis.

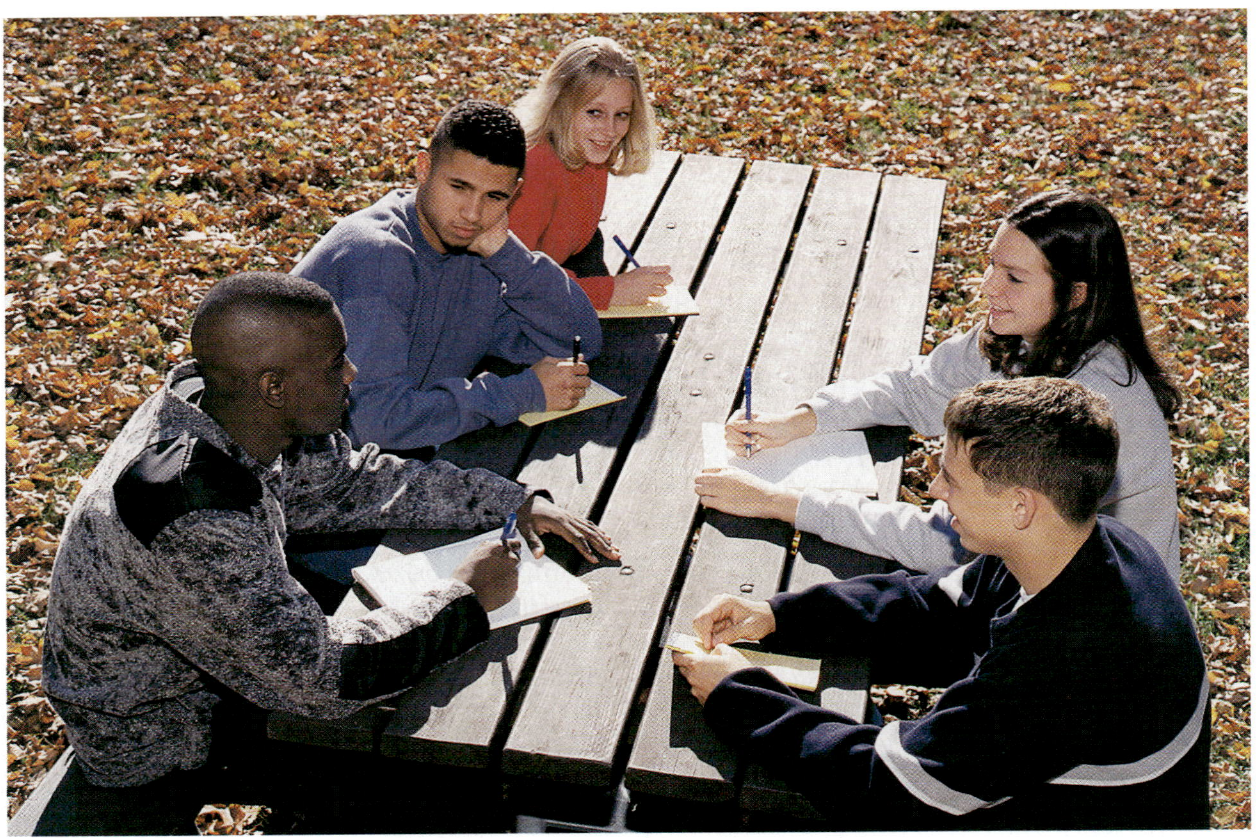

During group interactions, it is important that all members are able to hear and see each other.
What is the general rule with regard to voice volume when interacting with a group?

Volume and Tone

Most importantly, all group members need to be able to hear the discussion. Therefore, it is your responsibility to speak loudly enough for all to hear. This may require you to project your voice more loudly than you are accustomed to speaking. If this makes you a little uncomfortable, just remember: No one will complain about being able to hear you. However, they might become very frustrated if they can't. As a general rule, address a group as if you were speaking specifically to the people farthest away from you. If those people can hear you, the rest can too.

Gestures and Movement

Gestures and other body movements can add emphasis to your verbal message. Speakers also use gestures to complement their verbal message. As a listener, try to avoid any distracting movements or gestures that may take attention away from whomever is speaking.

In formal groups or groups that have a large number of members, you may have to raise your hand to be recognized. However, this usually is not the case with smaller, informal groups such as committees and teams. Generally speaking, it is not appropriate for you to move away from the group or leave the room while another member is speaking.

Effective Listening Strategies in Groups

In a group setting, effective nonverbal posture and eye contact can help you listen well. To better focus on a speaker, use all three types of listening skills—critical, deliberative, and empathic—that you learned about in Chapter 6. These effective listening strategies can help you understand and properly respond to what is being said in a group discussion.

Using Critical Listening Skills

When you use critical listening skills, you are not only listening for information but also evaluating the value and meaning of that information. Is the person's information logical? Is it accurate and useful? Do you agree with the message?

The next time a classmate speaks as a member of a group, use your critical listening skills to answer the following questions:

- What are the speaker's main ideas and how are they supported?
- Is the group member expressing facts, personal opinions, or informed or expert opinions?
- Is the information current and appropriate to the situation?
- Is there any evidence that contradicts the speaker?

As you listen, note any concerns you have about the speaker's information. Then, when he or she has finished speaking, ask questions.

Using Deliberative Listening Skills

As a deliberative listener, you should assume that a group member is offering information

Communication Practice Lab

Listening Deliberatively

To practice listening so that you know how to learn and take action, follow these steps.

Step 1 On a sheet of paper, list ideas about how you might organize a canned-food drive at your school. Spend no more than five minutes writing your ideas.

Step 2 Working with a partner, take turns explaining your plan as if you were presenting it to a group of volunteers. Presentations should last three minutes.

Step 3 As your partner explains his or her ideas, ask yourself these questions:

- What does he or she want the group to do?
- What supporting information is he or she offering to persuade me to do these things?
- What questions do I have?
- What are the advantages and disadvantages of this plan?

Step 4 Ask your partner any questions you may have.

Step 5 After you have both presented your plans, discuss as a class the benefits of deliberative listening.

he or she wants the group to act upon in some manner. With that attitude, the next time a group member speaks, try to learn what he or she is trying to tell you.

As you listen to the speaker's message, ask the following questions:

- What does this group member want me to do?
- What supporting information is he or she offering to persuade me to do this?
- Do I have questions about this information?
- What are the advantages and disadvantages to the group if I do as the member asks?

Using Empathic Listening Skills

When you listen empathically, you listen for the speaker's feelings and provide him or her with emotional support. To be an empathic listener in a group setting, assume that all group members are trying to offer helpful information and to make progress on the group task. When all group members display this attitude, a caring atmosphere is created. As a result, the group grows more cohesive.

You are listening with empathy when you listen to a friend tell you about his or her feelings and you offer emotional support. **Identify two strategies to listening emphatically.**

To listen empathically to another group member, there are two main things to remember:

- Watch the speaker's nonverbal communication. What does it indicate about his or her feelings?
- Listen to the message. How does the speaker seem to feel about information he or she is sharing?

Empathic listening can be valuable in a variety of group situations. For instance, imagine that a hard-working group member was assigned to gather information from the school principal regarding a specific security policy at the high school. However, the principal was only willing to reveal a portion of that information. As a result, the group member could not complete the assignment before the next group meeting.

This could have several different effects on the group member. He or she might feel angry, helpless, or disappointed about presenting incomplete information to the group. This, in turn, could make him or her avoid eye contact with the others, seem unenthusiastic, or send other negative nonverbal cues.

You might show empathy by saying, "You seem upset that you didn't get the information we needed. I know you did the best you could. Where do you think we might get the rest of the information we need?"

With this response, you have affirmed that he or she could not force the principal to give any more information. In addition, you have asked his or her opinion about how to finish the task. For effective empathic listening, try to put yourself in the speaker's position. It is important for you to respond to how the speaker feels about the information as well as to the information itself.

Discussions and Consensus Building in Groups

A chairperson is someone who has been appointed or elected to organize a group or preside over it. The chairperson, sometimes referred to as the chair, not only should use all the skills normally used by group members, but he or she also has some additional responsibilities that require special skills. Among these skills is the ability to plan an effective meeting.

Planning the Meeting

One of the responsibilities of a group chairperson is planning the meeting. This involves making all the necessary arrangements for the meeting, delegating responsibilities to others when necessary. First, the chair must arrange the time and place of the meeting. Then, he or she most likely will need to create a meeting agenda to organize the group discussion.

Arranging Time and Place As a group's chairperson, it is important to remember that meeting times should take into consideration all members' schedules. Of course it may be impossible to accommodate every member's schedule, but it is courteous to ask members for their scheduling suggestions, when possible. The group chair or someone chosen by the chair also is responsible for determining a meeting place and setting up the room appropriately. As you arrange the time and place of your meeting, keep in mind these considerations.

Setting Agendas Whether in an informal or a formal group, the chairperson has a plan for how the meeting should proceed from topic to topic. In informal group meetings, if you are the chair and do not wish to create a formal agenda, you should at least make a list of the goals to be accomplished in the meeting. For some informal meetings and most formal meetings, you should prepare and distribute a written agenda, if possible, a day or two before the meeting.

Meeting agendas typically include

- any announcements that should be made at the meeting
- a reading of the last meeting's minutes (This mostly applies to formal groups, such as a zoning committee, school board, or board of directors.)
- any topics which were not completely discussed or resolved at the last meeting
- the topics to be discussed at the meeting
- a request for any special announcements members may have

Practice for the Workplace

Effective Listening in Groups Surveys in the workplace reveal that listening is one of the most important communication skills in business. It also is the foremost communication skill employees wish they had been taught in school. Listening can help make a group more effective and productive on the job. Discuss as a class how you can identify an effective listener or a poor listener.

BUSINESS PRACTICE *Activity*

Imagine that you are a member of a group developing an Internet marketing plan for a CD and video store. Working with a partner, take turns brainstorming ideas for your marketing plan. Each time one partner makes a suggestion, the other partner should restate the idea in his or her own words. How accurate were your statements? How could you listen more effectively?

Communication Strategies

Arranging the Setting for Your Meeting

- Make sure every member will be able to see every other member in the meeting.
- Obtain enough chairs for all members to be seated at the table.
- Regulate the room temperature to be comfortable for most members.
- Make sure the room is ready to be used at the appointed time.
- Locate and provide any presentational equipment needed by group members. This may include a videocassette player, flip chart, overhead projector, computer with presentation software, or other audio-visual aids.

Chairing the Discussion

Once the group is gathered and ready to perform its task or engage in its social process, the chairperson will need to exercise some special verbal, nonverbal, and listening skills. Although the chair's primary responsibility is to meet the task needs of the group, he or she also should pay attention to building consensus and meeting the group's maintenance needs.

Chairperson as Initiator The chairperson has several roles to play during a group discussion. As the initiator, you should call upon members to give information or ideas. You also should encourage other members to comment on those ideas. Your goal is to allow a full discussion that results in all the members agreeing, or coming to a consensus, on some course of action for the group.

Chairperson as Facilitator To encourage full discussion, the chairperson also should play the role of facilitator. He or she should observe members' interactions and nonverbal cues. If a member wishes to comment or appears to disagree with some point of discussion, the chair should encourage that person to offer his or her ideas and opinions. The chair also should be aware of members who are not contributing to the discussion and try to get them to participate.

Also in the facilitator role, the chairperson is responsible for maintaining order in the meeting. If a member is discourteous or argumentative, the chairperson should step in and reinstate the courtesy norm for the group.

Chairperson as Agitator An effective chairperson occasionally may need to display positive agitator behavior. This may be necessary if members seem to be accepting information without fully considering it. In this instance, the leader may need to challenge the assumptions of the speaker or call upon other group members to critically examine the information.

Nonverbal Responsibilities and Skills In a group setting, it is important for the chairperson to try to maintain eye contact with any group member who is contributing information or ideas. This tells the member that the chairperson is listening and trying to understand the information. Smiling, nodding, and providing other types of acknowledgment indicate to members that their contributions are appreciated.

Listening Responsibilities and Skills All members, especially the chairperson, should listen critically, deliberatively, and empathically to the group discussion. Critical listening helps the chairperson determine the quality of information given by group members. Deliberative listening helps him or her determine whether or not to be persuaded by members' suggestions. Empathic listening also can be helpful in a variety of group situations.

For instance, if a group's task is especially challenging, it may cause group members to become frustrated. Similarly, group members may become frustrated if they have personal disagreements with one another. Group members with numerous outside responsibilities also may become discouraged when too much group work is added to their heavy workload. A chairperson who is listening empathically addresses these concerns when they come up in the group meeting.

Evaluating Group Effectiveness

Competent communicators regularly evaluate their own effectiveness and the effectiveness of their group. As a group member, are you doing all you can to help the group complete its task? Is the group operating in a way that will achieve positive results? To begin making these evaluations, examine the group results and the process the group follows to achieve those results. This not only will reveal the group's strengths and weaknesses but also will help you find new ways to build your own group participation and leadership skills.

In some group formats, a chairperson is chosen to preside over or organize the group. **Identify some of the responsibilities of a chairperson.**

Communication Strategies

Managing Conflict and Building Consensus as a Chairperson

- **Paraphrase a concern or complaint to a speaker's satisfaction. For example, when paraphrasing, you may wish to say, "I hear you saying that you disagree with the plan. Is that correct?" This demonstrates that you have understood the point the group member wished to make. If there is a disagreement between members, summarizing the different points of view helps clarify on which points the members agree and disagree.**
- **Ask questions that allow a speaker to give a full analysis of the issue. This helps prevent misunderstandings.**
- **Open the discussion to the other group members, asking if they share the same concern or complaint. If several members do, this item may need to be discussed fully in a future group meeting. If only one or very few members share this problem, you may be able to work out a solution with these members alone.**

Communication *Strategies*

Analyzing Group Results for Groups That Solve Problems

- ✓ Was the group able to identify the nature and extent of the problem?
- ✓ Did the group set up criteria for the solution that were achievable?
- ✓ Did the group measure all possible solutions against the criteria?
- ✓ Did the chosen solution solve the problem without creating other problems?
- ✓ Was the chosen solution put into effect according to the group's recommendation?
- ✓ Has the problem been solved or has it reoccurred?

Analyzing Group Results for Groups That Plan

- ✓ Was enough consideration given to the people who would be affected by the plan?
- ✓ Was enough consideration given to the occasion for which the plan was made?
- ✓ Was enough consideration given to the task or tasks involved in the carrying out of the plan?
- ✓ Was the event or change implemented according to the plans?
- ✓ Was the response of the people involved positive?
- ✓ Were the timing, location, and impact of the occasion well received?
- ✓ Were all tasks adequately performed?

Analyzing Group Results

One way to evaluate a group's effectiveness is by determining whether it achieved the desired results. Evaluating the results of a group's work requires the collection of certain information. This may include following up to see if a problem was completely solved, listening to feedback from people affected by a plan, or taking note of unforeseen consequences. The questions in the Communication Strategies checklist can help you evaluate the group's work based on the results it achieved.

Evaluating the Group Process

Your goal each time you participate in team, committee, or other group discussion is to use group skills effectively. Learning to evaluate your own participation and the participation of others is necessary if you are to improve your group communication skills.

The Effectiveness of Your Participation The most important evaluation you will make is to determine how effective you were in the group process. The evaluation of your own effectiveness will lead you to understand both your strengths and your challenges as a communicator in group discussion. You can use the following questions to guide the evaluation of your participation in a group, committee, or team.

1. Was I able to determine when emergent norms were not productive?
2. Was I able to help change harmful norms?
3. Was I able to assume the roles of initiator, facilitator, and agitator appropriately?
4. Did I make appropriate and timely contributions to the group discussion?
5. Did I use appropriate verbal and nonverbal strategies?
6. Did I use effective listening skills?

GROUP ROLES CHART

Member	Initiator	Facilitator	Agitator
Julio		✔ ✔ ✔ ✔ ✔ ✔	
Ken	✔		✔ ✔ ✔
Rae	✔ ✔ ✔ ✔ ✔ ✔	✔	✔
Kwan	✔	✔ ✔ ✔	

7. Did I perform needed research and group assignments?
8. Did I help meet both the task and the maintenance needs of the group?
9. Did I adhere to both prescribed and emergent group norms?

The Effectiveness of Others' Participation Once you have looked at your own participation, you need to look at other members of the group. Your purpose in this stage of evaluation is not to pass judgment on anyone but to identify characteristics of the participation of others that might have influenced your own.

You can answer the same questions about others' participation as you asked about yourself. Answering these questions will help you identify members who were the most effective and members who may need help in group situations. Most importantly, however, you may also identify behaviors that you want to use again and behaviors that you want to avoid as you work in committees, teams, and other groups.

Evaluating the Group Dynamics The overall effectiveness of a group process does not just depend on how effectively individual group members performed. The quality of the group dynamics also affects how effective a group will be. To evaluate the quality of the group dynamics, you will need to answer the following questions:

1. Were the emergent and prescribed norms productive and helpful to the group?
2. Did members provide a good balance in the roles they assumed?
3. Were group members' interactions positive, helping to meet both task and maintenance needs?
4. Were negative interactions dealt with in a constructive and positive manner?
5. Did all members participate and contribute to the discussion?
6. Did all members exercise good listening skills?
7. Was there enough positive energy in the group discussion?

Information for Evaluating Evaluating the effectiveness of a team, committee, or other group requires that you have information. You will need to be very aware of your own and others' participation in the group and be honest in your assessment of that participation. You will also need to be aware of the overall group dynamics.

There are several ways you can collect data you will need for this evaluation. You could audiotape or videotape several sessions of the group. You and other members could listen to and watch those tapes in order to discover the level and quality of everyone's participation.

Another useful device for collecting information about performance is to use a group roles chart like the one shown above. It allows you to count the number of times each member interacts during the group meeting. You could complete a group roles chart while watching a videotape of one or two meetings. The group could also invite an observer to chart group interaction while the discussion was taking place. A debriefing session afterwards could help you and other members of the group evaluate the effectiveness of your work. The goal of such a session is to get information that can be very useful in improving your interaction skills.

The information from a group role chart and a self-assessment checklist provides group members with feedback on how they interact in the group. Often, group members are surprised to find that their actual group behavior is quite different from how they thought they acted.

As a competent communicator, you will want to use all the information gathered during your evaluation of group process. This information helps you build better group interaction skills and eliminate negative interactions.

Section 2 Assessment

Visit the *Glencoe Communication Applications* Web site at **communicationapplications.glencoe.com** and click on **Self-Check and Study Guide 11.2** to review your understanding of participating in groups.

Review Key Terms

1. Define each term and write it in a sentence: task need, maintenance need.

Check Understanding

2. Use an effective verbal strategy in an example scenario. Explain your answer.
3. Give six examples of effective nonverbal strategies for group members.
4. Give an example of one type of listening skill and how it has helped you function effectively in a group.
5. Why is the role of group chairperson important?
6. **Synthesis** Why is it important to evaluate your own effectiveness and the effectiveness of your group?

APPLICATION *Activity*

Acting as Group Chairperson Imagine that you are the chairperson of a six-member group at your school. Choose one of the following group tasks and prepare your group for the first group meeting.

- Plan how to raise money for someone in the community who needs kidney dialysis or some other costly medical treatment.
- Solve the problem of low student attendance at high school athletic events.

Assume that your group must meet after school hours somewhere on school property. How will you prepare yourself, other group members, and the meeting location for this meeting? Write a paragraph explaining your answer.

Communication Self-Assessment

Analyzing Your Participation in Groups

How Do You Rate?

On a separate sheet of paper, use the key to answer the following questions. Put a check mark by each skill you would like to improve.

KEY: **A** Always **U** Usually **S** Sometimes **R** Rarely **N** Never

1. When I am in a group meeting, I try to keep eye contact with the person speaking.
2. I give and seek information that contributes to the unity of the group.
3. I track nonverbal communication and try to find out what it indicates.
4. I prepare for group meetings and present my suggestions by anticipating group objections.
5. When I act as an initiator, I try to let the group reach a decision on its own before I interject my own thinking.
6. When a person in the group is an agitator, I cause the meeting to go forward.
7. When I am a facilitator, I try to cause full discussion in a group.
8. When I express disagreement, I do so calmly and objectively.
9. As a group member, I listen critically to learn what I think about suggestions given.
10. I believe it is important to evaluate how my group works together and how well we reach our goals.

How Do You Score?

Review your responses. Give yourself 5 points for every A, 4 for every U, 3 for every S, 2 for every R, and 1 for every N. Total your points and evaluate your score.

41–50 Excellent You may be surprised to find out how much you can improve your skills.

31–40 Good In this course, you can learn ways to make your skills better.

21–30 Fair Practice applying the skills taught in this course.

1–20 Needs Improvement Carefully monitor your improvement as you work through this course.

Setting Communication Goals

If you scored Excellent or Good, complete Part A. If your score was Fair or Needs Improvement, complete Part B.

Part A

1. I plan to put the following ideas into practice:
2. I plan to share the following information about communication with the following people:

Part B

1. The behaviors I need to change most are:
2. To bring about these changes, I will take these steps:

Writing a Meeting Agenda

In meetings, people communicate with one another to share ideas and relay progress on specific activities. To keep this communication on track, it is a good idea to have a meeting agenda. A meeting agenda is an order of discussion that allows all group members to know the sequence and direction of a meeting. It also provides a springboard for discussion so the group may make decisions, vote, reach consensus, and take action.

Determine the Type of Meeting. What type of meeting is needed to accomplish your group goal? Is the purpose of the meeting to make decisions, solve problems, resolve conflicts, or accomplish some other goal? Will your meeting be formal—that is, conducted according to parliamentary procedure—or informal? Once you have determined the purpose, you can begin structuring your agenda.

Specify the Meeting Basics and Order Agenda Items. First, the agenda's title should reflect the basic purpose of the meeting. Additionally, the time and place of the meeting should be specified. Next, you may begin listing the items to be discussed.

In a formal meeting, the items on an agenda might not be listed in the order in which they are discussed. The chairperson may accept requests to give certain items priority in the meeting. In an informal meeting, however, the most important items are usually listed first on the agenda. This way, if time is limited, at least the most possible time can be dedicated to the main points of the meeting.

Set Time Limits. For both formal and informal meetings, the agenda should include a time limit for each topic. It also should include the estimated length of the overall meeting so attendees can schedule their time accordingly.

Encourage Member Participation. When group members actively participate in meetings, they often feel more committed to the work being done. If group leaders wish to have everyone participate in specific activities and discussions, these items should be listed on the agenda. The agenda also should note whether participants are to prepare any information before the meeting begins. For this reason, it is a good idea to send a copy of the agenda to all expected attendees beforehand. Well-prepared group members result in more productive meetings.

For additional information about business writing, see the *Guide to Business Communication* section of the Communication Survival Kit in the Appendix.

Communication Through Writing

Following is an example agenda for a sales manager's meeting at a clothing manufacturing company. See if you can identify all the basic elements of an effective meeting agenda.

Introducing the *Casual on Friday* Collection

February 25, 2003
8:00 A.M.–5:00 P.M.
The Conference Lodge
Louisville, Kentucky

Fashion Show . . . . 8:00 A.M.
(Develop notes/questions) Main Ballroom

Morning Break . . . . 10:00 A.M.

Guest Speaker: Marta Bianco . . . . 10:30 A.M.
(Followed by question/answer session) Main Ballroom

Lunch . . . . 12:00 P.M.
Poolside Cafe

Marketing Presentation . . . . 1:30 P.M.
(Followed by question/answer session) Suite 450

Afternoon Break . . . . 3:00 P.M.

Discussion: Sharing Ideas About Selling . . . . 3:30 P.M.
Suite 1000

Free Time . . . . 5:00 P.M.
(Fill out meeting evaluation)

Dinner and Live Music . . . . 6:30–9:00 P.M.
Main Dining Room

WRITING *Activity*

Imagine that you are a manager at an employee recruitment firm called Super Staffers. Create an agenda for an informal planning meeting. The purpose of the meeting is to plan an upcoming job fair. A job fair is usually a day-long event in which area businesses set up information booths and interview prospective employees. People attend the fair to explore job opportunities with these companies.

- Use the agenda on this page as a guide to create an agenda template of your own.
- Create a descriptive title for your meeting.
- Specify that the meeting will last from 9:00 A.M. to 5:00 P.M. on this coming Tuesday. The meeting will be held in Conference Room B at the Super Staffers office in your hometown.
- Point out that members of your staff will be asked to share information about local employers who might participate in the job fair.
- Tell attendees how much time they will have to share their information.

Besides these items, your agenda should list the other details of the meeting. This may include group discussions, lectures, breaks, and other activities. By the end of the meeting, the group should have planned, voted, and assigned duties to accomplish the upcoming job fair. When you have completed your agenda, share it with the class.

CHAPTER 11 Assessment and Activities

Visit the *Glencoe Communication Applications* Web site at **communicationapplications.glencoe.com** and click on **Chapter 11 Activity** for additional practice in making groups work.

Reviewing Key Terms

On a separate sheet of paper, write the vocabulary term that fits each description. The number of spaces indicates the number of letters in each answer.

1. Group member who gets the discussion started - - - - - - - - -

2. Different from a conversation because it is an exchange of ideas on a specific topic for a specific reason - - - - - - - - - - - - - - -

3. A need that promotes unity in the group - - - - - - - - - - - - - - - -

4. Group members' strong desire to agree with one another, even if it means making a poor decision - - - - - - - - - - -

5. Group member who questions others' decisions, facts, or research - - - - - - - - -

6. The energy created as group members communicate and interact with one another - - - - - - - - - - - - -

7. Group member who may negatively affect the group by dominating the discussion - - - - - - - - - -

8. Rule of behavior that develops from group interaction - - - - - - - - - - - -

Reviewing Key Concepts

On a separate sheet of paper, answer the following questions in complete sentences.

1. What are group norms? Give an example of a positive norm and a negative norm.

2. What is one way an initiator's actions might influence group dynamics?

3. What is meant by the statement "An agitator goes against the momentum of a group"?

4. What steps should a group member take to prepare for discussion?

5. How might you use tact to inform a group member that his or her habit of interrupting others is inappropriate behavior in group discussions?

6. Why do you think feedback is an important tool for evaluating group results?

7. Describe one way to collect information for evaluating group process.

Assessment and Activities

Reading and Critical Thinking Skill

1. **Predicting** Imagine that several members of a group have begun skipping meetings. How might the group change this harmful norm?
2. **Inferring** Why is it important for a facilitator to understand people's nonverbal behaviors?
3. **Applying** As the president of a fan club, what question might you ask the treasurer to find out about the state of the club's finances?
4. **Making Comparisons** Explain the difference between criticizing and offering constructive criticism.

Skill Practice Activity

Writing a Meeting Agenda Imagine that you are the chairperson of a citizen group charged with cleaning up litter and debris around a local lake. During your first meeting, the group will need to determine individual tasks such as which areas to clean up, where to begin the cleanup, how to dispose of different types of debris, and what tools will be needed. Write an agenda for this meeting.

Cooperative Learning Activity

Evaluating Group Results Working with four or five other students, imagine that your group is charged with cleaning up around a local lake. Participate in a five-minute discussion about the cleanup. If you completed the *Skill Practice Activity* above, base your discussion on one or two points from your agenda. As you discuss, notice how the roles of initiator, facilitator, and agitator are being filled. Also, notice the effectiveness of group members' verbal, nonverbal, and listening skills. Finally, work together to write a one-page evaluation of the group process. Share your group evaluations as a class.

Chapter Project

Planning Divide your class into three groups. Decide which group will give a five- to ten-minute presentation on verbal skills, which will present nonverbal skills, and which will present listening skills. Once you have chosen a topic, work with your group to brainstorm a list of effective and ineffective skills in that area. Divide the list, assigning each listed skill to two or three students. Work with group members to research your assigned skill. Use visual aids and brief skits or dramatizations to effectively demonstrate and explain your assigned skill.

Presenting As a group, present your dramatizations and visual aids to the rest of the class. Explain why each skill is effective or ineffective and what impact it can have on a group. Ask your classmates if they have any questions.

CHAPTER 12

Managing Conflict

WHY IT'S IMPORTANT

Conflict plays a part in all of our lives. Learning how to manage conflict can help you be sure that it doesn't play the starring role.

To better understand how to manage conflict, view the **Communication in Action** Chapter 12 video lesson.

Visit the *Glencoe Communication Applications* Web site at **communicationapplications.glencoe.com** and click on **Overview–Chapter 12** to preview information about managing conflict.

"How many a dispute could have been deflated into a single paragraph if the disputants had dared to define their terms."

—Aristotle, Greek philosopher

Section 1

Diagnosing Conflict

GUIDE TO READING

Objectives

1. Describe possible advantages and disadvantages of conflict.
2. Determine the level on which a conflict exists.
3. Analyze how relationships and interdependence impact conflicts.
4. Determine types of conflicts.

Terms to Learn

conflict over facts
conflict over values
conflict over policies

You may know someone who always seems to be "looking for a fight." You probably know someone else who will go to great lengths to avoid the smallest disagreement. Which is the better approach to conflict? Neither one is very productive in the long run.

It takes courage, along with well-developed communication skills, to confront conflict. People who are afraid of disagreement can be as destructive to relationships as people who are consistently confrontational. Letting your problems simmer inside of you can eventually make you angry, resentful, or perhaps argumentative. However, these actions aren't always directed at the person your original conflict involves. Often, unresolved conflict interferes in other relationships, both at home and at work. The key lies not with having conflict, but managing it.

Understanding Conflict

As you learned in Chapter 1, conflict is a struggle between two or more parties who sense interference in achieving their goals. At various times, you may find yourself in conflict with other people or with an organization if its needs or values directly contradict your own. Your conflict may be an obvious one, with loud arguments and slammed doors. It may be less emotional, marked by calm discussion. It may even continue unnoticed by others, simmering below the surface.

In order to build effective relationships, one must develop conflict management skills. What is conflict?

Just as conflicts may take on many appearances, they also may involve a variety of relationships. You may deal with internal conflict. That is, you may have conflicting emotions, loyalties, or goals within yourself. Conflicts also can occur between two individuals, such as coworkers, family members, or friends. In addition, conflicts may occur between an individual and a group, or between and among different groups and organizations.

Whether your conflicts are emotional or rational, angry or calm, external or internal, they can be managed in much the same way. Once you understand what conflicts have in common, you'll be well on your way to examining, diagnosing, and resolving the conflicts that arise in your social and professional lives.

Conflict Is Inevitable

While most people would prefer not to have conflicts, they are a part of life. Over the years, you'll find it impossible to escape conflict in your personal relationships or working environment. Therefore, in order to be successful, you must learn to diagnose the conflicts in your life and work to manage them.

Conflict may occur in any relationship. **How can conflict be beneficial?**

Conflict May Be Beneficial

Although conflict typically is thought of as negative, it can sometimes be beneficial. The seemingly contradictory nature of conflict is clearly illustrated in the Chinese language. In Chinese, the symbol for the word *crisis* consists of two characters. One character represents danger, and the other represents opportunity. Just as in a crisis situation, the outcome of conflict can be either negative or positive.

The frustration of a conflict situation often motivates people to confront and solve problems that face their relationships or working environment. By working through a conflict, you are likely to learn something about yourself and the others around you. The process of finding a constructive resolution for a conflict may help you feel revitalized or empowered as a problem-solver. The organizations you belong to also may benefit from improved organizational policies and procedures. This, in turn, can lead to streamlined processes, higher profits, and better working conditions.

Conflict May Be Destructive

If a conflict is not effectively managed, it can damage or destroy relationships and, potentially, entire organizations. Friendships can end. At work, morale can suffer, which can cause a decrease in productivity and quality. Employees with pent-up frustrations may be abrupt or even rude to customers. They may put less effort and energy into their work, either consciously or subconsciously.

In addition, the benefits of working to resolve conflict are not absolute. They often come at a price. For example, you may feel like a problem-solver each time you resolve a conflict with a coworker. However, if this is the fourth conflict you have been involved in this month, you may gain a reputation as a troublemaker. At this point, you might want to do some self-analysis. When conflicts occur too often between the same two parties—even if each conflict is successfully resolved—the relationship is likely to suffer. The emotional toll of constant tension or repeated problems with another can easily overshadow the benefits of any single conflict.

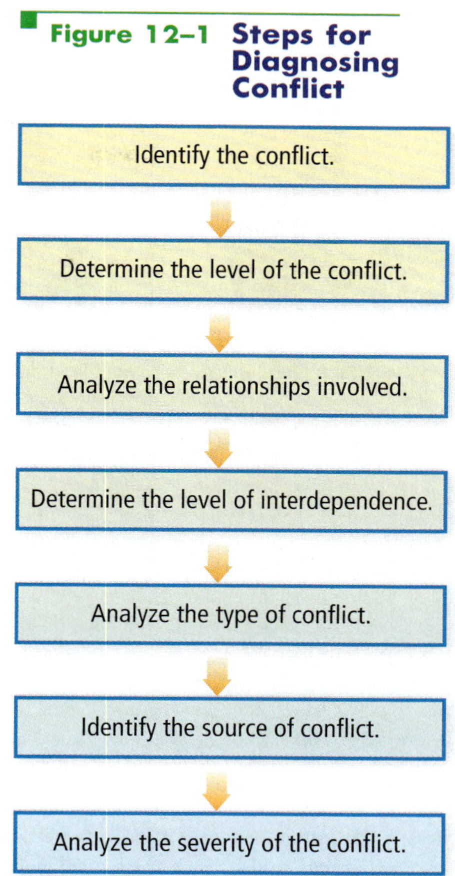

Identify the conflict.
Determine the level of the conflict.
Analyze the relationships involved.
Determine the level of interdependence.
Analyze the type of conflict.
Identify the source of conflict.
Analyze the severity of the conflict.

Figure 12–1 Steps for Diagnosing Conflict

Steps for Diagnosing Conflict

To develop skills for managing the conflicts in your life, you need a systematic procedure to diagnose them. By breaking down a conflict into its separate elements, you can make it seem less overwhelming. The steps in Figure 12–1 can help you systematically diagnose each conflict you face.

Identify the Conflict

Have you ever found yourself well into an argument and then realized you were unable to remember what you were arguing about? Have you ever snapped at a family member over something insignificant, when your real source of irritation was a problem at school? Conflict often has a way of hiding or disguising itself. After all, it's much easier to wage a minor battle with your little sister than to tackle an issue with your teacher or boss. The first step toward resolving a conflict is identifying the actual conflict at hand.

Start diagnosing your conflict by stating and describing the problem. Along with the problem-solving skills you read about in Chapter 11, the questions in the following activity can help you clarify the conflict from your point of view.

A clear definition of the conflict at hand is essential. Knowing what is really bothering you can help you eliminate emotional distractions. Then, once you've identified the issue at the heart of your conflict, you're ready to move on to managing it!

Businesses that promote competition between employees can inadvertently cause conflict by pitting employee against employee. **What is a good rule to use when handling conflict?**

Determine the Level of the Conflict

Conflict can occur on any of the five levels of communication:

- intrapersonal
- group
- environmental
- interpersonal
- organizational

Each time additional people or groups are brought into a conflict, the level of that conflict progresses. An effective rule of thumb is to manage conflict on the smallest level possible. That means that it is most desirable to handle a conflict by yourself or with the fewest people necessary to come to a true resolution.

Intrapersonal Conflict All conflicts begin on the intrapersonal level with your perception of a situation. Some situations may be purely intrapersonal; that is, no other individuals, groups, or policies are involved. For example, you may be in conflict over whether to keep a higher-paying job or accept another with better potential for promotion. This conflict is an internal one. In other words, you must decide for yourself. Even with outside advice, this type of conflict remains intrapersonal.

Here's another example. Imagine that, at your office, you and your coworkers share telephone-answering duties. You may feel that you answer the phone for one or more of your coworkers much more often than they do for you. If you have not yet spoken to your coworkers about what you perceive to be a problem, this conflict is still on the intrapersonal level. Is this an important conflict to you? Are you willing to "get over it" and just let things continue as they are now? Is the conflict important enough for you to consider quitting your job?

You must analyze your own needs in this situation and determine whether or not you will resolve the conflict yourself or share your feelings with your coworkers. If you choose to discuss the conflict, you take it to the next level of communication.

Interpersonal Conflict Interpersonal conflict occurs when two or more people openly express their perceptions of a problem. Once a conflict becomes interpersonal, it is more complex than before. There are at least two sets of goals, needs, values, and feelings to be considered and dealt with.

In the earlier telephone example, your coworkers may surprise you with their perception of the situation. They may each believe that they, too, do more than their share of answering the telephone! On the other hand, your coworkers may think your answering the phone more often is a sign that you prefer to answer it. They may even be irritated at you for answering more than your share of the calls. You should be prepared to listen to very different perceptions of the situation from the others' points of view.

Group Conflict Group conflict may occur in different ways. It may involve one group member who perceives a conflict between himself or herself and the rest of the group. Conflict also may occur between or among subgroups within the same group. Additionally, conflict can occur between or among different groups within an organization. If properly managed and resolved, conflict actually can strengthen a group. If improperly managed, that same conflict can have the power to destroy the group.

Imagine that you have a new player on your high school hockey team. If the rest of the team has played hockey together since you were in elementary school, group conflict may occur as the new player tries to fit in. Since the rookie doesn't know the formations and lines most often used by this team, his or her awkwardness at practices may cause the group to feel resentment or anger. This kind of group conflict is much more complex than interpersonal conflict; the individual may feel as if everyone else is working together against him or her. The person also may feel excluded and victimized. Adding to the complexity of the situation is the fact that not just one or two sets of emotions and needs are at stake. In this case, there are many.

Equally complex are clashes between subgroups within a larger group or between groups in the same or a different organization. The afternoon shift at the restaurant where you work may clash with the morning shift over the cleanliness of the break room; the Spanish Club may feel threatened by the French Club's continual use of the school's language lab. When many people share their opinions and feelings regarding an uncomfortable situation, emotions can escalate, making resolution more difficult.

COMMUNICATION PRACTICE LAB

Identifying Conflict

To identify the true source of a conflict, follow these steps:

Step 1 List any conflicts you have been involved in over the last month.

Step 2 Choose one of the conflicts listed. Write what you remember or know about the conflict.

Step 3 Answer the following questions about the conflict you have described: What did you want? What prevented you from getting it? Which of your goals, needs, values, or emotions were involved? What people and/or policies were involved?

Step 4 How did your answers in Step 3 compare with your description in Step 2? Were you honest with yourself and others about the true issue or issues in conflict? If the conflict has not been resolved yet, you may wish to use this information and the skills you'll learn in this chapter to bring it to a close.

Sometimes, organizations hold competitions that can unintentionally turn into conflict situations. Companies that hold competitions to determine star sales representatives may unintentionally pit employee against employee, department against department, or work shift against work shift. The competitive conflict may have its benefits: increased productivity, sales, and bottom line. However, it also can result in employee resentment, backbiting, anger, and job dissatisfaction.

Organizational Conflict Organizational conflict occurs between an organization itself and individuals or groups of individuals within that organization. For instance, individuals or groups may determine that the organization uses unfair policies. When employee advocacy groups come into conflict with an organization's management, it usually is over policy matters such as hiring practices, benefits, or salary rates.

Other sources of organizational conflict may be unsafe, outdated, crowded, or otherwise inefficient conditions at a worksite. A construction site may be without first-aid equipment, or several lab technicians may have to share one computer. Employees may demand that the organization make changes to improve conditions, opening a conflict between labor and management divisions.

Sometimes, organizational change fosters conflict. Any time a company changes how work is done, employees may need to be retrained. They also may need to be motivated to embrace these new work conditions. When these important steps are ignored, employee frustration, confusion, resentment, and, ultimately, conflict can occur. Left unresolved, all these conflicts can be very costly.

Environmental Conflict If a conflict is environmental, it is important to identify it quickly. Many times, we blame other people when our conflict is truly environmental. For example, you and the two students in your class who share an area of a biology lab may be in constant conflict. While you believe it is their rudeness or lack of organization that is the cause of the conflict, it may actually be the result of too little personal working space. The cramped quarters may be amplifying any differences in work style and adding tension to your working relationship. Understanding that the conflict has nothing to do with your classmates but rather with your surroundings helps take some of the emotion out of the situation.

At any of these different communication levels, you may make the decision not to engage the conflict but just to cope with the situation as it stands. However, if you do choose to resolve the conflict, the next step is to analyze what relationships are involved.

THE BORN LOSER reprinted by permission of Newspaper Enterprise Association, Inc.

Analyze the Relationships Involved

Is there a difference between a conflict with a family member and one with a good friend? What is the difference between a conflict with another player on your team and one with your coach?

The relationships of the parties involved in a conflict matter a great deal. Regardless of the outcome of your family dispute, you probably will still be considered a family member. However, can you be certain that your friendship will withstand any conflict? Likewise, a conflict between teammates may be uncomfortable and result in poor teamwork at times, while a serious conflict with the coach can put you on the bench or off the team entirely.

People Involved

Determining who is involved in the conflict and what relationships they have with one another is important. In the workplace, conflict tends to be more serious if those involved work in the same department rather than in different ones. It can become even more difficult if they hold different levels of authority, such as a supervisor and an employee.

Relationships of Those Involved

The relationships of those involved in a conflict often have a major impact on whether or not it can be resolved. In some cases, conflict with a supervisor may be better left alone. You might decide that coping with it intrapersonally is preferable to addressing it openly and risking your future at your job. Likewise, ruining a lifelong friendship may be too great a price to pay to resolve a minor difference. It is important to take an honest look at how you feel about that person, how much you want to maintain the relationship, and what each person's role is in the relationship. You then want to weigh the risks of pursuing a resolution or coping with the conflict.

TECHNOLOGY *Activity*

Analyzing the Message Channel Technology can have a significant impact on communication. A receiver often will interpret a message based partly on the channel of communication chosen to communicate it. When discussing a conflict, how is a face-to-face meeting different from a discussion through e-mail, voice mail, or memos? Discuss your answers in groups of four or five.

Determine the Level of Interdependence

How interdependent are the parties involved in a specific conflict? That is, how much do they need one another in order to get their work done? It is more important for two basketball teammates to resolve their differences than it is for a basketball player and a tennis player to resolve theirs.

So, how do you determine the interdependence of parties in conflict? First, analyze how much space and equipment they must share and how much time they must spend together. Also, determine whether or not one of the participants has some control or supervisory power over the other. It is particularly important to resolve differences if the cooperative decision making is a major function of the parties involved, such as with the administrators at your school.

Imagine a situation in which two coworkers are in conflict because they must share a telephone, a computer, and other office equipment. The costs of not resolving their conflict may be that one of them refuses to share what the other needs. In this case, each person's ability to do his or her job is likely to be affected by the conflict. Therefore, it may be to everyone's advantage to address the conflict.

Analyze the Type of Conflict

The next step in the analysis of a conflict is to look at the type of conflict it is. Most conflicts occur over differences in factual information, personal values, or policies. Analyzing your conflict can help you classify it in one of these categories and better understand what issues are at stake.

Facts A **conflict over facts** is a disagreement over something that can be proven to be true or false. These conflicts are the easiest to resolve because they are the result of inadequate information or misinterpretation. Once you uncover the facts, the conflict is settled. If the conflict is over whether or not you can purchase a new copy machine for your department or club, looking at the funds provided in the budget probably will provide the answer. Once those in conflict understand the factual information, the conflict can be resolved.

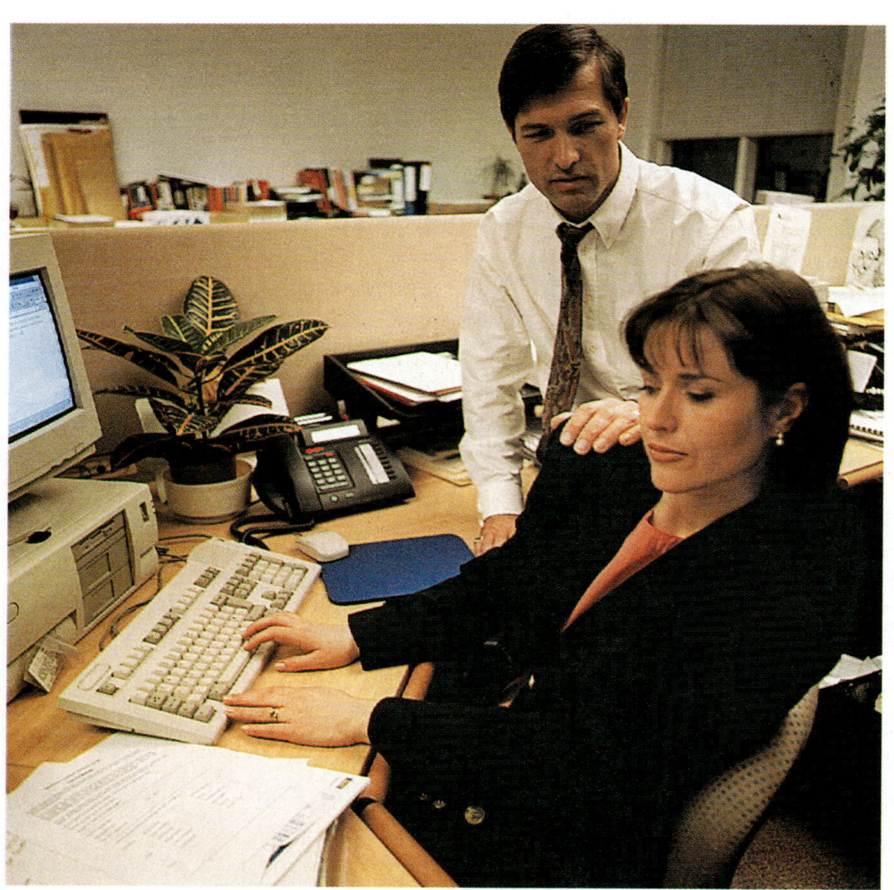

Interdependence between coworkers can lead to conflict. What causes most conflicts to occur?

Conflicts over facts also are the easiest to avoid altogether. Making sure you have gathered as much information as possible can help you avoid unnecessary conflict. It also can save you from the potential embarrassment of appearing uninformed.

Values As you learned in Chapter 1, a value is something you find important. A **conflict over values** is a disagreement over priorities. Unlike facts, values and opinions are not verifiable. Rather, they are deeply personal and rooted in what someone believes.

Imagine that you and a classmate are in conflict over when to work on an assigned team project. You place a priority on time with your family; you'd rather not meet on Saturday or Sunday. Your

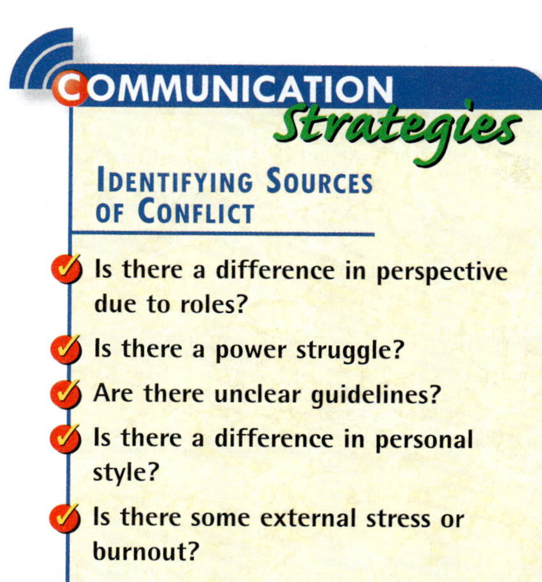

partner, on the other hand, values school athletics and would rather not meet during game time.

COMMUNICATION
Strategies
IDENTIFYING SOURCES OF CONFLICT
Is there a difference in perspective due to roles?
Is there a power struggle?
Are there unclear guidelines?
Is there a difference in personal style?
Is there some external stress or burnout?

Each person in a conflict over values will be emotionally involved in and committed to his or her personal stance. Therefore, each person in the conflict needs to listen empathically and try not to be judgmental or accusatory about other points of view. If you decide to resolve the conflict using the strategies found later in this chapter, it will help if you take into account the feelings and emotions of each person involved.

Policies A **conflict over policies** is a disagreement that deals with differences over how to best complete a task. Such a conflict does not concern the end goal of the task, but rather how to get to that goal. For example, a goal at your workplace might be to hire the best-qualified managers for the company. The hiring policy might require that all job openings be advertised nationally to attract a large group of qualified applicants from across the country. On the other hand, your employees might feel that experienced workers who have done well in your company should be given more consideration than "outsiders" whose true work record and abilities are unknown. Everyone agrees that the company needs good managers; they disagree on how to go about hiring those managers.

Resolving a conflict over policies generally requires the willing cooperation of the administration or management of an organization. Therefore, when you diagnose this type of conflict, be sure to include an analysis of the people who will need to be consulted and involved if you try to resolve this conflict.

Identify the Source of the Conflict

One of the most important steps in diagnosing a conflict is identifying what produced the conflict in the first place. Remember that all people perceive things differently. Therefore, no two people will perceive a conflict the same way. As part of your perception check, ask the questions in the Communication Strategies checklist to get to the source of the conflict.

Roles Some conflicts may be caused by roles. The role you play in a particular situation tends to give you a perspective that is different from that of someone in another role. Employers and employees may view what happens at work differently. Coaches, athletes, and parents may all view the purpose of school sports differently. Conflict may result from these different points of view.

Power Struggle The conflict might be over a struggle for power. You and a coworker may be competing for recognition, rewards, bonuses, or promotions. Competitive activities often lead to conflict because both of you may not be able to achieve the same prize.

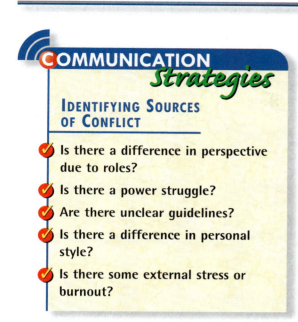

Garfield ® **by Jim Davis**

Unclear Guidelines If you have not been given clear guidelines on how to proceed with a task, you may make some mistakes in trying to do your job. When this happens, your expectations for a task may differ from that of a supervisor, causing conflict. You may get angry with your supervisor because you feel he or she should have given a better explanation of your responsibilities. Your supervisor may be upset with you for taking too much time or using the wrong materials. He or she may have thought you would ask questions if you were unclear about how to do this part of your job.

Personal Style Sometimes, the source of a conflict simply may be different personal styles. Different cultural backgrounds, personal biases, or prejudices all can lead to conflict situations. You like to talk through problems; your coworker likes to work through problems alone. You may enjoy listening to music while you work, but the coworker in the next cubicle prefers silence. Since we don't often identify or talk about all the pieces that make up our personal style, we may expect others to behave as we do. These unmet expectations can lead to conflict situations.

External Stress Often, external stress can creep into unrelated situations and cause conflict. Feeling "burned out" at your job or school may cause you to become irritable and create conflict at home. In the same way, family issues may follow you to the office or school, creating problems there.

Analyze the Severity of the Conflict

Now that you've identified and described the conflict and analyzed the people and issues involved in it, your final step is to determine how serious the conflict is to you. To do this, imagine the degrees of severity, as shown in Figure 12–2.

After completely diagnosing and understanding a conflict, you may find that you are no longer bothered by it. You may recognize, for example, that the conflict stems from the different roles you and the other person play. You may be willing to allow that person to continue his or her behavior because it is reasonable in the context of his or her role. On the other hand, you may have discovered the facts underlying the dispute and can now put the conflict to rest. If so, you may determine that there is no longer a conflict and, therefore, decide to take no action on the issue. You have resolved the conflict on the intrapersonal level.

At the interpersonal level, you may determine that there is a problem, but you don't find it to be serious enough to bother others with it. Perhaps you view this as something that happened only once under special circumstances and is not likely to happen again. If the conflict is due to differences in interpersonal style, you now may feel you know how this person acts. Therefore, you think you can avoid clashes in the future without bringing the issue to the other person's attention.

On the other hand, as the result of your diagnosis, you may view your problem as being fairly serious. You still have the option of coping with the conflict yourself, or you may choose to address it with the other parties involved. If you decide that the price of confronting the other party is greater than the benefit of having the conflict resolved, you may decide to just cope.

If you view the conflict as potentially devastating to you, consider whether or not you are engaged in a crisis situation. If so, you may want to have others trained in this type of crisis to help you diagnose and resolve the conflict. At times, people are trapped in serious situations which are outside their direct control. Abuse, harassment, and discrimination are crisis situations. In these cases, you may want to consult a social service organization or a trained counselor or minister. Another alternative would be to report this problem to a special office within your organization. Personnel or human resources departments typically help employees deal with such issues. Some employees belong to unions that help them resolve such conflicts.

To Resolve or Not to Resolve

Each step in the analysis of conflict is important because it shows a very different aspect of the issue that is troubling you. You do not need to complete each one in order to resolve your conflict, however. At any step along the way you may decide that the risks involved in confronting the others involved or in pursuing a resolution are simply too great. If your job is on the line or a family relationship is in jeopardy of being strained, you may decide to let the issue go and learn to cope with the situation as it stands.

On the other hand, you may decide at any step in the diagnosis process that a conflict definitely needs resolution. For example, in analyzing the interdependence of coworkers involved in a conflict you may realize that without resolution, very little work will get done. At that time, there would be no further need for

Figure 12–2 How Serious Is This Conflict?

analysis. Instead, you should act to resolve the conflict between the coworkers. Napoleon Bonaparte, emperor of France, is quoted as having said, "Take time to deliberate, but when the time for action has arrived, stop thinking and go in." Any stage in your analysis may be the one that moves you to stop thinking about your conflict and to start resolving it.

Section 1 Assessment

Visit the *Glencoe Communication Applications* Web site at **communicationapplications.glencoe.com** and click on **Self-Check and Study Guide 12.1** to review your understanding of diagnosing conflict.

Review Key Terms

1. Define each term and write it in a sentence: conflict over facts, conflict over values, conflict over policies.

Check Understanding

2. Describe two advantages and two disadvantages of conflict.
3. Imagine a group of your coworkers is concerned about your company's policy regarding overtime hours. At what level is this conflict occurring?
4. How might the relationship and the interdependence between a supervisor and his or her employee affect their conflicts?
5. **Classify** Imagine that you and a partner must complete a history report together. Your partner suggests copying a report her sister wrote several years ago. You say that is cheating and that you should work together each night to finish the report. What type of conflict is this? Why?

APPLICATION *Activity*

Charting a Diagnosis Think of a conflict you have experienced. You may wish to refer back to the list you created in the Communication Practice Lab. Create a chart that shows how each of the nine diagnosis steps applies to your conflict. Use your chart to determine at which stage you could have ended the conflict analysis. At that stage, would you have chosen to resolve the conflict, cope with it, or acknowledge that the conflict no longer existed? Explain the reason for your choice.

Applying Reading Skill

Finding the Main Idea and Supporting Details

To fully understand the things that you read, it is important to know how to recognize the main idea or ideas. The main idea is a sentence that tells what the whole paragraph, story, article, or other written work is about.

Closely related to the main idea are the supporting details. Supporting details confirm the main idea and provide additional information, clarity, interest, or proof.

Learning the Skill

To find the main idea and supporting details, it is important to first ask yourself, "What is the purpose of this information?" Before beginning to read the text, glance at any titles or visual aids that might be included. Photos, illustrations, charts, graphs, tables, and other visuals are added to a text to enhance the main idea or ideas. Study these graphics before beginning a new section of text to help you anticipate what you will learn. Look for a common theme among sentences or paragraphs.

Finally, look for sentences that tell something about the main idea. Each time you learn something more about the main idea, you have found a supporting detail. To understand this relationship better, write the main idea at the top of a sheet of paper. Then, list each supporting detail below the main idea.

Practicing the Skill

Read the following advertisement for a veterinary hospital and answer the questions that follow.

1. What is the main idea of this ad?
2. What other information in the ad supports that idea?
3. What information is not necessary to the ad?

Purr-fect Care Veterinary Hospital

Your pet will receive the very best care at Purr-fect Care Veterinary Hospital. Specializing in small-animal care, our veterinarians treat your pet as if it were their own. Plus, each member of the Purr-fect Care support staff is trained to provide you with all the information you need. We also work hard to keep our kennels comfy and clean. Puff, the Purr-fect Care mascot, says,

"Come on in. We'll take the 'ow' out of 'meow.'"

APPLICATION *Activity*

Study an advertisement from a newspaper or magazine. Write the main idea of the ad at the top of a sheet of paper. Then, in one column below the main idea, list all the supporting details. In a second column, list any nonsupporting details found in the ad. Share your lists as a class.

Section 2

Confronting Conflict

GUIDE TO READING

Objectives

1. Describe possible losses and gains in conflict resolution.
2. Classify forces behind conflict resolution as helpful or hindering.
3. Justify a decision to resolve conflict.
4. Compare and contrast conflict-resolution strategies.
5. Organize a conflict-resolution meeting.
6. Develop strategies for coping with unresolved conflict.

Terms to Learn

avoidance
accommodation
coercion
compromise
negotiation
collaboration

Imagine your history class group project is due next Monday. You think your group should work together every night until you complete the project. Another member argues that the group should just wait and work together all day Saturday. You've analyzed the people and the issues involved in the conflict. But now what do you do?

Now that you've analyzed the different elements of the conflict, it's time to decide on a course of action. Do the benefits of resolving the conflict outweigh the costs of confronting your friends? The answer may help you determine whether to try to resolve it or to cope with it. If you decide to resolve the conflict, you will need to know how to analyze the forces behind resolution and determine which resolution strategy to use. In any case, you'll need to develop a plan and polish your communication skills.

Part of working on a group project involves taking responsibility for your part of the work. **If there is conflict in a group, what questions would you ask to decide on a course of action for dealing with the conflict?**

Outcomes of Conflict Resolution

Before you begin to resolve a conflict, you'll want to consider what you and the other people involved have to gain or lose. If the others have nothing to gain and something to lose by resolving the conflict, your work toward finding a resolution is likely to be opposed. However, if you can imagine a resolution that allows everyone to gain something, you may have a better chance at bringing the conflict to an end.

Identifying Gains

Imagine that you and a coworker are in conflict over the use of an office computer. Computer time currently is decided on a first-come, first-served basis, which means one of you is left waiting a great deal of the time.

Since you currently use the computer more than half of the time, you may want to keep the situation as it is. Resolving it means you risk losing some computer time. On the other hand, if giving up some computer time will greatly improve your relationship with your coworker, you might be willing to work it out. You'll want to look at the conflict from all sides to see what everyone has to gain from the present situation as well as what each party might gain from a resolution.

Social gains, such as enjoying a pleasant working environment or making a positive impression on someone, may be worth some sacrifices. At home, you might do some chore that you dislike, such as folding the laundry, because it makes your family members, whom you care about, happy. Work gains also are important incentives for conflict resolution. Two coworkers in conflict may be less helpful to one another on a major project than they would be if the conflict were resolved.

Identifying Losses

What will a resolution cost you and the others involved in a conflict? Is there some way that this conflict works in your favor? If so, you may lose that benefit if you

Being late for a meeting can cause conflict with group members. **What costs must you consider when deciding whether or not to resolve a conflict?**

successfully resolve the conflict. Is there some danger involved in confronting the other party or parties in the conflict? If the person you're in conflict with is your supervisor at work, you may put a possible promotion or even your job in jeopardy. Is it possible that the other person will be angered by your confrontation and create different problems for you? For instance, if you confront a coworker today, will he or she undermine you in a future project?

Imagine that you and a close friend work together on the yearbook staff. Your friend always arrives late for group meetings and rarely completes his assigned tasks. Should you confront him over his conflict with the group? Would your friendship, both with him and with mutual friends, possibly suffer? If he doesn't distinguish between your roles as members of the yearbook staff and as friends, he may have trouble with the confrontation. However, he might appreciate your talking to him privately so that he's not embarrassed by a group confrontation. Try to consider both the possible benefits and costs to your goals before deciding whether to cope with or to resolve the conflict.

Forces Behind Resolution

Imagine that you are involved in a conflict over limited supplies at your job. Your coworkers are generally cooperative, and you anticipate they would be willing to find a solution to this problem. However, your boss is not generally open to new ideas and has reacted defensively to suggestions from the staff in the past. Many forces are at work behind the situation. They can either help you achieve a resolution or make the process much more difficult.

> **Communication Strategies**
>
> **Deciding Whether to Resolve a Conflict**
>
> - ✓ Look at the severity of the conflict. Is it serious?
> - ✓ Determine whether resolving the conflict will result in gains or losses.
> - ✓ Analyze the risks involved. Is a resolution worth the risk?
> - ✓ Analyze what forces might support or hinder a resolution.
> - ✓ Determine what information and communication skills are necessary to proceed toward a resolution.

Forces That Help Resolution

After examining the office-supplies conflict, you may find that conditions are favorable for a resolution. For example, one argument may be that budgets are being cut throughout your company. Therefore, there is only a limited amount of money available for supplies. However, after investigating the issues, you have discovered that your company already has purchased plenty of supplies. Furthermore, you think you have developed a plan for sharing them that should not inconvenience other departments. If you were to analyze what is in favor of finding a resolution, you might note that

- most of the time everyone in the office tries to cooperate and work together
- there seem to be enough resources for everyone
- you have a plan you think will work

Each of these points is a positive force that would help you resolve your office-supplies conflict. However, before you begin working toward a resolution, you need to consider one more thing: What might work against the resolution of this conflict?

Forces That Hinder Resolution

Sometimes, a specific set of circumstances can present a barrier to conflict resolution. Some potential barriers to resolving the office-supplies conflict might include that

- your boss is not generally open to new ideas for the company
- your boss is anticipating more budget cuts in the near future
- your boss sometimes reacts defensively to suggestions from staff members

Each of these barriers may present quite a challenge. At this point, you'll need to ask yourself if pursuing the solution in the face of these difficulties is worthwhile.

Once you have a clear idea of the forces at work behind your conflict, the time has arrived for a decision. Should you try to resolve it or learn to cope with it?

RESOLUTION STRATEGIES

Consider	When One of These Is True
Avoidance	• The issue is trivial. • You cannot win. • The negatives of confrontation outweigh the benefits of resolution. • It is possible to unobtrusively avoid the others involved.
Accommodation	• You find out you were wrong and others were right. • The issue is less important to you than to the others involved. • Harmony is more important to you than the issue.
Coercion	• It is imperative that you have your way on the issue. • You are willing to live with the consequences of coercion. • You have sufficient perceived power to force your will upon the others.
Compromise	• Your goals are more important, but you can give in on some issues. • You can achieve a temporary settlement for a complex issue. • It becomes clear that no party will give up its entire position.
Negotiation	• You have something to trade for what you want to accomplish. • The others involved are willing to bargain.
Collaboration	• All involved have concerns that are too important to be compromised or negotiated away. • A long-term relationship between/among the parties is important. • A goal is to build consensus among all parties. • The others involved are willing to collaborate.

Choosing a Resolution Strategy

Imagine that you have weighed the possible outcomes of a conflict resolution. Because the positives outweigh the negatives, you have decided to try to resolve the conflict. However, you still have another decision to make. What strategy will you use to reach a resolution?

There are many different ways to approach a conflict. Consider the advantages and disadvantages of each before choosing the one that's right for your situation. The six most commonly used resolution strategies are

- avoidance
- accommodation
- coercion
- compromise
- negotiation
- collaboration

Avoidance

One way to deal with a conflict is to avoid it altogether. **Avoidance** is keeping away from or withdrawing from something. Avoidance can be physical or psychological. At times, there are advantages to using avoidance. Sometimes, however, avoidance can be a negative resolution strategy.

Physical Avoidance You might choose physical avoidance of your conflict. That is, you may try to stay away from the others involved in the conflict. This is different from coping because you are not deciding to "live with" the current situation. Rather, you are taking action to end the conflict.

For example, you may be in conflict with a friend who is raising money for a charity event. Every day, the friend asks you for a contribution, even though you have explained it is not in your budget. You are becoming increasingly irritated by the friend's requests. However, by choosing to avoid the friend and not return his or her phone calls, you are resolving the conflict. The friend is no longer able to bother you. Once the event is over, you can stop avoiding your friend and resume your relationship.

Psychological Avoidance Avoidance also can be psychological. You can choose to ignore whatever the others say or do that brings up a conflict by refusing to respond to their words or actions. You might even deny that there is a conflict at all.

Problems with Avoidance Because avoidance is a one-sided approach to conflict resolution, it can have some negative effects. Instead of resolving a conflict, avoidance actually may intensify it. If the parties involved in the conflict are highly interdependent, avoidance can create even more problems. For instance, even though you may avoid discussing the issue in conflict, you cannot force others to stop discussing it. This can make you appear detached or uninformed and can provide fuel for harmful gossip and rumors. Avoidance may not be the best choice if you must be in continual contact with the others involved.

Avoidance may require a strong self-image. It can take a great deal of positive self-talk to manage the resentment and frustration you may feel from others involved in a conflict. Without managing your feelings, you may reach a point at which the avoidance of one conflict creates new conflicts intrapersonally and in many other contexts in your life.

Businesses utilize accommodation to resolve conflicts with customers. Define conflict accommodation.

Advantages of Avoidance Even though avoidance as a strategy has its drawbacks, there are some circumstances in which it might be a wise response. Avoidance tends to work more easily in social contexts than at work. However, if your boss tends to put you down each time you make a suggestion, you might choose to remain silent for a while. This can help you avoid conflict until you can determine what to do about the situation.

Accommodation

Conflict **accommodation** is maintaining harmony with others by giving in to their wishes. This is a variation of the avoidance strategy. In effect, you are avoiding conflict by choosing to do what the others want done in the situation, regardless of your ideas or feelings. To accommodators, relationships are more important than issues.

There are some good reasons to choose accommodation as a conflict-resolution strategy. You might choose this strategy if you discover you have made a mistake. Admitting your error and accommodating the others would be a sign of strength and intelligence. You might also choose accommodation if the issue you disagree upon is of relatively little importance to you and seems to be of great importance to someone else. You might also choose accommodation if the rewards for putting up with the others' demands are greater than the cost of asserting your rights. For example, you might put up with a rude, but reliable, customer in order to keep his or her repeat business.

A disadvantage to choosing accommodation is the possibility that you will resent having to accommodate the other person, particularly if you feel he or she does not often accommodate your wishes. If so, resentment may build and harm your relationship in the long run. Also, if you choose accommodation to resolve a conflict over values, you are likely to both resent the other person and be angry with yourself for not living up to your personal standards. Accommodation, in these instances, may be very costly to you.

Coercion

Coercion is another way to resolve conflict. **Coercion** is trying to force others to go along with your wishes. If you are a manager or supervisor, you may use your position of authority to make others agree with your decisions. Coercion is only possible if one person involved in a conflict is perceived as more powerful than the others.

The obvious advantage to coercion is the possibility of getting your way. The disadvantages are equally obvious. People forced into an agreement won't like it and may even try to retaliate against you some other time. This may take many different forms, including not cooperating with you in the future because you coerced them on this issue.

Even those who agree with you on the issue may be offended by your tactic of forcing their cooperation. If so, they may speak out against your methods and join those who oppose you. At best, coercion may let you "win" this issue, but you are very likely to pay a price for it later.

Compromise

Compromise is a resolution choice that may not be as costly as coercion, accommodation, or avoidance. **Compromise** is settling differences by having each party give up something. When you compromise, you say that you are willing to "give in" on certain issues if the others involved will make similar sacrifices.

COMMUNICATION PRACTICE LAB

Choosing Accommodation

To practice using accommodation as a conflict resolution strategy, follow these steps:

Step 1 Working with a partner, create a list of adjectives you might use to describe an accommodator.

Step 2 Discuss which of these adjectives might be considered positive attributes, such as *generous*, and which might be negative, such as *wimpy*.

Step 3 With your partner, brainstorm a situation when accommodation would be a good choice for conflict resolution.

Step 4 Act out your chosen situation for another set of student partners. First, portray the accommodator in a way that highlights the positive aspects of accommodation. Then, switch roles and portray the negative aspects of accommodation.

Global Communication

Competition vs. Cooperation

American, Swedish, and Norwegian cultures are sometimes described as individualistic, direct, independent, and competitive and sometimes may challenge authority. Japanese, Arabic, and Latin American cultures typically avoid openly challenging authority and practice indirect communication approaches and cooperative problem solving. Imagine two people from these diverse cultural categories having a difference of opinion on an issue. What conflict resolution strategies would you use to encourage a solution?

Generally, the compromisers cooperate on all issues except for those that are most important to them. Compromise is a very common strategy among political factions and groups that make budget decisions.

Compromise is a worthwhile choice when you have no hope of attaining everything you really want and are willing to settle for a little less. Before deciding on entering a compromise, you should be sure about what you are willing to give up and what you refuse to sacrifice.

The advantage of compromise is that usually each person involved is at least partially pleased with the resolution. The disadvantage is that it may result in a "watered down" version of what might have been accomplished without compromise.

You might choose to use a compromise strategy if you reach a stalemate and cannot move on until an issue is resolved. If you feel you cannot give up any part of your position simply to reach agreement, compromise may not be the best choice.

Negotiation

Conflict **negotiation** is bargaining with others to gain what you want. As with the compromise strategy, negotiation requires you to determine what you are and are not willing to give up in the final solution. Unlike the compromise strategy, however, all trade-offs may not be directly related to the conflict issue. For example, labor negotiators bargaining for a pay increase may accept better benefits or vacation time instead. Similarly, when negotiating with your brother or sister over mowing the lawn, you may agree to do that chore if he or she will loan you his car for one day. Negotiation often involves giving up your entire position on an issue in order to get something else.

The Congress of the United States practices compromise when passing a bill. When is compromise a good choice?

In negotiation, you assertively bargain for the best deal you can get. The others involved do the same. The goal is to grant something that each person involved wants. Negotiation only works if each party is willing to trade with the others in the dispute.

Negotiation is a more assertive approach to conflict resolution than compromise because it is competitive. Each party gives up items equally in a compromise. However, negotiation involves trying to make the most favorable deal for yourself that you can.

Collaboration

Put simply, **collaboration** is working together to achieve some result. People who choose to collaborate believe that working with others will create the best possible solution to the conflict. Collaboration does not involve competition. Rather, collaborators know that they will have to work together over a long period of time. Therefore, they try to maintain positive relationships with the others involved in a conflict. The parties involved genuinely try to understand what each other wants out of the interaction. They also try to explain clearly what they want. They then work together to accomplish all goals.

In collaboration, everyone agrees that there is a problem. They also all agree that the problem is causing an undesirable conflict. No one likes having the conflict, so they agree to work together to find a way to resolve it.

interNET ACTIVITY

Negotiating As a class, brainstorm a list of school issues and then choose one that seems to be of most concern to students. Use information found in your text and through a reliable Internet search engine to prepare to negotiate a win/win solution to the conflict. Set up a meeting between the parties involved. Develop a plan to bring the concerned parties together. Then, prepare a list of ten meeting guidelines for distribution to meeting participants.

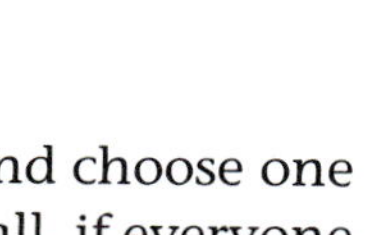

Implementing Strategies

Once you have chosen the strategy that will best resolve your conflict, you may think the difficult part is over. What happens if one of the others involved has chosen a different strategy? It's important to learn how to bring everyone together in a conflict-resolution meeting where you can share strategies and choose one that meets the most needs. After all, if everyone agrees with the plan, they will be more likely to work toward making it happen.

Preparing for a Conflict-Resolution Meeting

At times, the best plans for conflict resolution may be ruined by poor attitudes, unrealistic expectations, or poor communication skills. By taking action early, you can help ward off these barriers to resolution.

Assume a Positive Attitude. Before undertaking a conflict-resolution meeting, arm yourself with a win/win attitude. That is, come to the meeting with the attitude that everyone can gain something by working together. Rid yourself of biases and try to see others' points of view in a positive light.

To do this, try to think of others in positive terms—and always speak of them that way. Avoid being defensive. Instead, try to be objective and open-minded. Also, make up your mind to cooperate with others in the meeting.

Behave Realistically. Make sure you understand what you are trying to resolve so that you can offer realistic solutions. Also, as you found out in Chapter 3, realize that your point of view, or your perception, may not be shared by others in the conflict. The more reasonable your proposal and behavior, the more acceptable your ideas will seem.

Plan for the resolution to take time. It requires patience to listen carefully to the issues and to propose realistic solutions. Understand that the conflict may not be resolved in one meeting. Be realistic about what you can accomplish each time you meet.

Communicate Clearly. In a conflict, you and the other parties involved already disagree. You do not want to complicate matters

Communication Strategies

Communicating to Achieve a Resolution

- Listen actively.
- Seek clarification when you don't understand.
- Use frequent perception checks.
- Express your ideas as clearly as possible.
- Pay attention to feedback and clear up misunderstandings early.
- Be courteous.
- Use nonverbal behavior that is appropriate for achieving a resolution.

Conflict resolution is affected by the communication skills of group members. What communication skills will help you in a conflict resolution meeting?

with poor communication and frequent misunderstandings. To avoid these problems, remember the important suggestions in the Communication Strategies checklist on the previous page.

Conducting the Meeting

Sometimes, conflict resolution takes place in a formal meeting called just for that purpose. Other times, however, this meeting may be much less formal. For example, imagine that you typically see the person you're in conflict with at the same time each day at work. You may try to initiate the conflict resolution on one of these occasions, rather than scheduling a more formal meeting.

Take the Initiative. Before a formal or informal meeting can begin, someone must take the first step. By initiating the discussion, you show your willingness to work toward a resolution of the conflict.

After your initial statement or question, you may choose to patiently listen to what the others have to say about the conflict. This can serve as a valuable perception check, helping to clarify the issues at stake.

Remember to remain as objective as possible during the discussion. At times, the ideas and responses of others may surprise you. Use critical listening skills to discern the basis for their points of view. Also, use deliberative listening to consider what the others want you to do about the conflict. Finally, use empathic listening skills to try to understand how the others feel about the conflict.

Often, it is valuable to use a feed-forward technique to prepare the others to hear your point of view. For example, you might say, "If I understand correctly, you said . . ." Then, state your feelings clearly, avoiding defensive or accusatory language. Use this opportunity to resolve any misunderstandings the others may have about your point of view. Convey a general attitude that you are open to other ideas and genuinely want to achieve a solution.

Practice for the Workplace

Choices and Consequences In the workplace, as in school, you will have to make choices in determining the best way to resolve conflict. Unresolved conflict can be stressful and it is important that you assertively, but not timidly or aggressively, express yourself in order to get your needs met in the workplace.

BUSINESS PRACTICE *Activity*

In groups of three or four, develop three types of responses—timid, assertive, and aggressive—to the scenarios given below.

- Other students repeatedly ask to copy my homework. This bothers me, but I also don't want to make them mad at me.
- My friend and I carpool to work. He is late at least twice each week, which makes me late and often gets me in trouble.
- My coworker repeatedly asks me to put his name on the weekly reports that I develop.

Employ a Resolution Strategy. Your next step in the meeting is to decide upon or implement an appropriate resolution strategy either by suggesting one yourself or by developing it as a group. Remember that even though you may decide on one particular strategy, this decision may change over the course of resolving the conflict. For example, everyone may begin with a desire to collaborate. However, at some point, you may hit a stalemate, try to negotiate, and finally determine that the best chance of resolving the conflict is through compromise. For this reason, try to remain flexible and positive about the conflict-resolution process as it unfolds.

Meetings can be used to generate ideas for conflict resolution. **What are some strategies for assuming a positive attitude during a meeting?**

As you work toward a resolution, remember that all sides need to cooperate in the effort. You'll be more successful if everyone stays flexible, considers a variety of options, and works toward a logical and reasonable resolution to the conflict.

Know When to End. There is little to be gained in very lengthy "marathon" meetings. Particularly in the case of collaboration, but also in compromise and negotiation, you may create too many alternatives to sort out at one meeting. In these cases, summarize all the alternatives generated and suggest postponing a decision on any of them until another meeting time. This allows both sides to fully consider all the possibilities.

Another reason to avoid lengthy meetings is that people generally do not work well under stress for long periods of time. The emotions, concentration level, and intense discussion involved in resolving a conflict can create a great deal of stress. After a while, tempers can flare and communication can become careless. For this reason, it is best to limit conflict-resolution meetings to no more than one hour. Then, if you must postpone the final decision, do so on a positive note. Be sure to congratulate everyone for working hard to resolve the conflict.

If Conflict Flares During the Meeting If one or more parties become too emotionally involved in the conflict discussion, communication can become hostile or otherwise unproductive. In some instances, the discussion can actually renew the conflict or introduce new areas of disagreement. If any of these situations occurs, end the interaction quickly. If possible, you should delay setting another meeting time until after everyone has had a chance to cool down.

If a Stalemate Is Reached It is possible that your conflict-resolution meeting will result in a stalemate. Particularly during compromise or negotiation, the members may reach a point where they "dig in" and refuse to budge on an issue. At this point, you can remark that this particular issue seems to be the main point under contention and may need a little more thought. Again, end on a friendly note. Restate that you are confident that the conflict can be resolved in some mutually-agreeable way and set another meeting time.

If Agreement Is Reached Congratulations! If you were able to find a solution, get everyone involved in implementing it. Often, even when compromise and negotiation are used, the solution will not be enthusiastically approved by everyone. However, by helping everyone focus on their obvious gains—as well as the benefit of no longer having to deal with the conflict—you will gain their cooperation in quickly and easily implementing the resolution.

Coping with Unresolved Conflict

Unfortunately, not all conflicts are resolved. Sometimes, even your best attempt at conflict resolution can fail. No resolution strategy comes with a guarantee of success. Also, after your initial analysis of a conflict, you may decide to skip the resolution process altogether. When a conflict goes unresolved, you may have to cope with the difficult people and difficult situations involved in it.

The Communication Strategies checklist points out just a few strategies for coping with unresolved conflict. You likely have developed a few of your own that meet your specific needs. Whatever strategy you use, it is important to move on. Situations usually don't improve if you dwell on the negative.

To let a conflict go and get on with your work or relationship, it helps to focus on intrapersonal management. Be sure that you

Communication Strategies

Coping With Unresolved Conflict

- Develop an attitude of self-confidence, respect for the others involved, and understanding of both your position and theirs.
- Maintain a realistic perspective about the situation. Try to keep the big picture in mind.
- Maintain a respectful attitude toward others who disagree with you, viewing them as your equals. This will help you avoid bitterness and disillusionment.
- Try to be supportive of others and continue to care for them. This may help you salvage worthwhile relationships.
- Be positive. Look for something good even in a bad situation. This can help you put the conflict behind you.
- Realize that you are bigger than this one conflict. While it may impact your life in some way, it does not determine your destiny.
- Learn from this adversity, growing in self-understanding and wisdom. This will help you move on to greater things.

have a positive mind-set. Don't waste time thinking about a past conflict, but rather look to the future. Allowing an unresolved conflict to rule your emotions not only may destroy valuable relationships or enthusiasm but also can harmfully affect other aspects of your life. Learning to cope when situations aren't ideal is a very valuable life lesson—one that you may be called upon to use more often than you'd like. As you develop the skills of a competent communicator, you will have a knowledge base to draw from when faced with conflict situations in professional and social contexts.

Section 2 Assessment

Visit the *Glencoe Communication Applications* Web site at **communicationapplications.glencoe.com** and click on **Self-Check and Study Guide 12.2** to review your understanding of confronting conflict.

Review Key Terms

1. Define each term and write it in a sentence: avoidance, accommodation, coercion, compromise, negotiation, collaboration.

Check Understanding

2. What might be gained by confronting your neighbor about his or her barking dog? What might be lost?
3. Think of a recent conflict. List at least two forces at work behind that conflict. Classify each as helpful or hindering to the resolution of your conflict.
4. Imagine that one of your coworkers does not always wash his or her hands when preparing customers' sandwiches. Should you try to confront your coworker and resolve the conflict? Why or why not?
5. How are accommodation and compromise alike? How are they different?
6. Imagine that you are in conflict with the other members of your soccer team over where to purchase your new jerseys. What steps should you take to prepare a conflict-resolution meeting with your teammates?
7. **Apply** Imagine that you have a basic personality conflict with your boss. Because of the risks involved, you decide to cope with the conflict rather than to resolve it. Describe five things you can do to effectively cope with this unresolved conflict.

APPLICATION *Activity*

Coping With Conflict Talk with a parent or friend about a time when it was necessary for him or her to cope with a conflict. Inquire about specific intrapersonal management skills that helped make the situation tolerable. Share your findings as a class. Notice which skills were most used and brainstorm as a class how to develop or improve those skills for yourselves.

Communication Self-Assessment

Evaluating Your Conflict Management Skills

How Do You Rate?

On a separate sheet of paper, respond to the following statements. Put a check mark beside each skill you would like to improve.

KEY: **A** Always **R** Rarely
U Usually **N** Never
S Sometimes

1. I approach conflict from the point of view that it is a manageable part of life.
2. Before I act, I break conflicts down into sub-elements.
3. I think it's okay not to work at resolving some conflicts.
4. I carefully analyze my relationship to another person before I react to a conflict situation.
5. I analyze the source of the conflict before I decide how I will approach it.
6. I decide to confront a conflict only when I think the benefits of taking action outweigh the costs.
7. To me, negotiation and collaboration are better ways to resolve conflict than avoidance and accommodation.
8. If I were to chair a conflict resolution meeting, I would stop the meeting immediately if tempers started to flare.

How Do You Score?

Review your responses. Give yourself 5 points for every A, 4 for every U, 3 for every S, 2 for every R, and 1 for every N. Total your points and evaluate your score.

31–40 Excellent You may be surprised to find out how much you can improve your skills.

21–30 Good In this course, you can learn ways to make your skills better.

11–20 Fair Practice applying the skills taught in this course.

1–10 Needs Improvement Carefully monitor your improvement as you work through this course.

Setting Communication Goals

If you scored Excellent or Good, complete Part A. If your score was Fair or Needs Improvement, complete Part B.

Part A
1. I plan to put the following ideas into practice:
2. I plan to share the following information about communication with the following people:

Part B
1. The behaviors I need to change most are:
2. To bring about these changes, I will take these steps:

Responding to Letters of Complaint

Have you ever written a letter of complaint? If so, what type of response did you receive? The way an organization responds to complaints can affect its professional reputation and, ultimately, its ability to attract customers.

Often, dissatisfied consumers send complaint letters to businesses. Sometimes, these letters are to voice a concern about some aspect of the company. Other times, the customer is seeking compensation for inferior merchandise or service. By responding appropriately to letters of complaint, a company can build good public relations and, hopefully, avoid losing a customer. When you respond to a letter of complaint, be sure to follow these steps.

Restate the Problem. What is the specific reason why the customer is unhappy? Was he or she treated poorly? Did the merchandise not live up to its promise? Focusing on the problem and restating it at the beginning of the response letter shows the customer that you are taking the complaint seriously.

Express Your Regrets. Let your customer know you are sorry the problem occurred. This affirms that you want him or her to be satisfied. This statement can be brief and may appear early in the letter or in the closing.

Explain What Actions You Will Take. Tell the customer how you will correct the problem, whether it is by making changes at the business or by compensating the customer. Before stating what will be done, be sure you know the company policy regarding this type of complaint. The customer may be entitled to a refund or credit, or he or she may have to trade the unsatisfactory merchandise for something else of equal value. For complaints about poor service, the company might offer to do the job over or provide a gift certificate for a free service in the future.

Thank the Person for Writing. Your customer has done you a service by writing a letter of complaint. He or she could have simply walked away, refused to do future business with your company, and complained about your company to other potential customers. Sometimes, the only way a business can know about a problem is through customer complaints. This can help a company know whether to recall an unsafe product, remove a product from the shelves, lower prices, or improve services.

For additional information about business writing, see the *Guide to Business Communication* section of the Communication Survival Kit in the Appendix.

Communication Through Writing

The following letter is an example of an appropriate response to a letter of complaint.

United Motors, Inc.
8415 Sandhill Road
Lafayette, IN 47901

March 14, 2003

Mr. Drew Brooks
575 Olympic Street
Seattle, WA 98060

Dear Mr. Brooks:

I recently received your letter stating your dissatisfaction with your new United Motors automobile. We at United Motors understand the high cost of repairing your car's steering column and apologize for the inconvenience this has caused. It is our goal to resolve this problem to your satisfaction.

For your safety, we request that you take your car to the nearest United Motors dealership as soon as possible. This will allow our repair technicians to ensure that your car will be fully repaired to the highest standards. Any necessary repair work will, of course, be free of charge. Also, please send me a copy of the original bill for repairing the steering column assembly. We will reimburse you for this cost.

Thank you for pointing out this problem. Letters such as yours give United Motors the opportunity to provide better service to our valued customers.

Sincerely,

Janet Green

Janet Green
Director, Customer Relations
United Motors, Inc.

WRITING *Activity*

Use the steps outlined earlier and the following facts to write a letter of response to a dissatisfied customer.

- The customer bought a new set of your company's dishes at a local department store last December. Some of the plates now show dark scratches from use with stainless steel utensils.
- Marks-Be-Gone is a stoneware cleaner that sells for under $10 and is very effective at removing discoloration. The product is available in the kitchenware department of most department stores.
- Your company's policy is to give customers a free sample of Marks-Be-Gone and a $2-off coupon for a full-size bottle of the cleaner.
- If the customer is still dissatisfied after using Marks-Be-Gone, the company will replace the dishes.

Write your response letter and then share it with the class. As a class, discuss how you might respond to various students' letters if you were the customer who issues the complaint.

CHAPTER 12 Assessment and Activities

Visit the *Glencoe Communication Applications* Web site at **communicationapplications.glencoe.com** and click on **Chapter 12 Activity** for additional practice in managing conflict.

Reviewing Key Terms

Read each statement. On a separate sheet of paper, write whether the statement is true or false. If the statement is false, change the word that will make it true and underline the word that you substitute.

1. A conflict over policies is a disagreement over priorities.
2. A conflict over facts is a disagreement over something that can be proven true or false.
3. Each person in a conflict over facts will be emotionally involved in his or her stance.
4. Avoidance is dealing with a conflict by withdrawing from it.
5. Maintaining harmony with others while giving in to their wishes is called coercion.
6. If you discover that you have made a mistake, choosing accommodation to settle conflict is a sign of strength.
7. Coercion is only possible if one person is perceived as more powerful than the others involved in a conflict.
8. Negotiation is settling conflicts by having each party give up something.
9. In compromise, trade-offs may be unrelated to the conflict issue.
10. Competition means working together to find a way to resolve conflict.

Reviewing Key Concepts

1. What may happen if conflict is ineffectively managed?
2. Why is a conflict between a group and an individual more complex than an interpersonal conflict?
3. What often has the biggest impact on whether a conflict can be resolved?
4. Which type of conflict is easiest to resolve? Why?
5. What term describes the source of conflict between two friends who are competing for a place on the school basketball team?
6. Identify a conflict you have with a parent or teacher. Name one force that will help and another that may hinder the conflict's resolution.
7. How might a person use psychological avoidance to resolve a conflict?

Assessment and Activities

Reading and Critical Thinking Skill

1. **Summarizing** Summarize steps used to diagnose conflict.
2. **Classifying Information** Dirk and his brother are angry because each borrows the other's CDs without asking. At what level of communication is their conflict?
3. **Making Comparisons** Of the following strategies—coercion, accommodation, and compromise—which is least costly? Why?
4. **Inferring** What can you infer about the personalities of people who prefer to negotiate rather than compromise?

Skill Practice Activity

Finding the Main Idea and Supporting Details Identify the main idea and the supporting details in the following paragraph. On a separate sheet of paper, restate them in your own words.

While most people would prefer not to have conflicts, they are a part of life. Over the years, you'll find it impossible to escape conflicts in your personal relationships or working environment. Therefore, in order to be successful, you must learn to diagnose the conflicts in your life. Once you have the diagnosis, you can begin to work to manage them.

Cooperative Learning Activity

Analyzing the Relationships Involved in a Conflict As a class, organize into groups. Each group should have a copy of an advice column from the newspaper. The members of each group should choose and discuss a letter from the column that describes a conflict. The discussion should determine who is involved in the conflict and what relationships these individuals have with one another. As a group, decide which resolution strategy should be suggested to resolve the conflict. Provide reasons for the choice of strategy.

Chapter Project

Planning Design a conflict management workshop. For each major section in Chapter 12, write note cards that cover the main ideas and supporting details in the material. Make posters or overhead transparencies that list the steps for diagnosing conflict and the different resolution strategies. Plan audience participation.

Presenting Give the workshop for your family or close friends. Speak to them from your note cards and use your visual aids to emphasize important points. After you have spoken to your family or close friends about conflict, record your family's or friends' responses to the workshop and report them to the class.

CHAPTER 13 Functioning as a Leader

WHY IT'S IMPORTANT

It's not easy to be a leader. Becoming a positive and effective leader requires you to examine and emphasize your strengths and work hard to improve your weaknesses, all while working to organize and inspire your followers.

To better understand effective leadership, view the **Communication in Action** Chapter 13 video lesson.

GLENCOE Online

Visit the *Glencoe Communication Applications* Web site at **communicationapplications.glencoe.com** and click on **Overview–Chapter 13** to preview information about effective leadership.

"A leader takes people where they want to go. A great leader takes people where they don't necessarily want to go but ought to be."

—Rosalynn Smith Carter, former U.S. First Lady

Section 1

Identifying Leaders

GUIDE TO READING

Objectives

1. Distinguish between appointed and emergent leaders.
2. Describe the three approaches for identifying potential leaders.
3. Determine which leadership style is the most effective in specific situations.

Terms to Learn

leader
appointed leader
emergent leader
trait approach
style approach
authoritarian leader
democratic leader
laissez-faire leader
balanced leader
functional approach

Imagine that your debate team advisor has come down with the flu the week of your state tournament. Instead of your teammates all working together to get ready for the big event, practice turns into a chaotic argument.

How can this group function without its leader? Do you consider yourself a leader? Are only teachers, bosses, or presidents leaders? Leadership is not only earned through a promotion or an election. Very often, the quick actions of a confident group member propel him or her into a position of leadership.

TYPES OF LEADERS

A **leader** is someone who influences or inspires others to act in specific ways to accomplish a common goal. Many leaders are easy to identify. The chair of the homecoming committee, the principal at your school, and the manager at your local movie theater are all obvious leaders. All of these leaders were appointed to their positions. An **appointed leader** is given his or her leadership position by a person in authority.

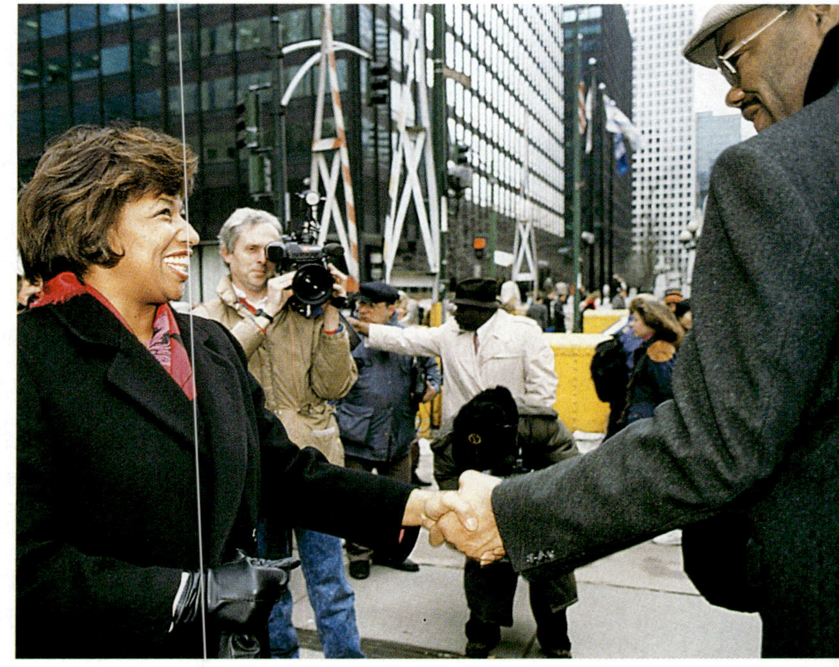

Political candidates campaign to convince voters to choose them as their leader. What is a leader?

However, not all leaders are appointed by a supervisor or boss. An emergent leader is chosen by peers or members of his or her group because of his or her personality, power in the group, or the special circumstances of the group task. Emergent leaders may be chosen officially, such as in an election of class officers or the chair of a PTA committee. They also may be chosen informally. For example, a classmate who steps forward to organize a class trip may attract many followers. Simply by choosing to go along with your classmate's plans, you informally have chosen him or her as your leader.

Some leaders, like the first woman vice president of Ecuador, Rosalia Arteaga, are chosen through election. **Explain the trait approach.**

Successful Leaders

In many organizations, leaders are appointed, promoted, or elected to their positions. What makes these specific individuals get selected? The answer is that they exhibit the characteristics of a leader. There are three ways to determine what type of person typically makes a successful leader:

- leadership traits
- leadership styles
- leadership functions

Communication Strategies

Emerging as a Group Leader

- Participate early, often, and with quality and purpose in group meetings.
- Demonstrate your ability to do a job well.
- Don't push too hard to get your way.
- Provide a solution for group dilemmas.

Leadership Traits

Can you tell who will make a good leader just by observing his or her personality? The trait approach assumes that leaders share certain personality traits that help them lead successfully. Many times, the necessary traits for leadership are determined by the type of job that needs to be done. These traits may vary from job to job and from organization to organization. A few traits, though, seem to be common in most leaders in a variety of types of organizations. These traits are as follows:

- effective communication skills
- the desire to be a leader
- originality or creativity
- intelligence

While these qualities are present in most leaders, they are not a guarantee of leadership. Why? Even though some individuals may exhibit these traits, they may be weak in other important areas, such as sensitivity to others, ability to organize self and others, knowledge of the organization, and leadership style. Strengths in all these areas can help you utilize your leadership traits to the fullest.

Developing Leadership Traits What if you have a great desire to be a leader, and you're intelligent and creative, but your interpersonal communication skills need work? On the other hand, what if you are often seen as a leader, but your strengths lie in other areas? There are two important points to consider.

First, as the old saying goes, good leaders are made, not born. By constantly working to improve your skills, you may build the strengths you need to serve as a leader.

Second, a leader is simply someone who leads. Therefore, if your skills allow you to lead others effectively, you must be doing something right. The leadership traits listed here may give you some direction for continued improvement since they are ones that researchers have identified as common to most leaders.

Leadership Style

The **style approach** to leadership assumes that the leader's communication method and use of power with followers determines his or her success. Most successful leaders choose styles that parallel the traditions and policies of their organization. There are at least four major styles that leaders might choose. They are as follows:

- authoritarian
- democratic
- laissez-faire
- balanced

Authoritarian A leader who uses power to force followers to do what he or she wants them to do is an **authoritarian leader.** Authoritarian leadership is used very effectively by military organizations, prison systems, and any type of organization that needs the power to make quick decisions or to have strong control over the group.

COMMUNICATION PRACTICE LAB

Analyzing Leadership Traits

To analyze and strengthen your leadership traits, follow these steps:

Step 1 Make a four-column chart and label each column with one of the leadership traits listed on page 414.

Then, in each column, list examples of each trait as it applies to you. For example, under *Originality and Creativity,* you might write "Thought of theme for Prom."

Step 2 Using your chart, rate yourself from one to ten (with ten being the highest) on how well you display each leadership trait.

Step 3 Identify which trait is your strongest and which is your weakest.

Step 4 As a class, brainstorm specific ways to develop or strengthen each of the personality traits most often found in leaders. For example, to build up your intelligence, you might take a study skills or a speed-reading class.

Step 5 On your own, apply your classmates' suggestions to any weaknesses you determined in Step 3. Develop a plan for improving your skills so that you can be an effective leader.

Democratic A democratic leadership style is very different from an authoritarian style. A **democratic leader** invites followers to participate in decision making, trying to get a majority to agree with and commit to decisions. Most organizations only experience crisis or extreme stress from time to time. Therefore, they often have time to deliberate about how to proceed with the organization's tasks. For example, newspapers often are led democratically. Rather than the publisher or one editor making all the decisions about content, the publisher, editors, and reporters typically work together to decide what news stories to cover.

interNET ACTIVITY

Famous Leadership Quotations
Use a reliable search engine to scan the Internet for quotations about leadership using words such as *leadership, motivation,* and *quotations.* In groups of four, analyze the meanings of eight quotations you have read. As a group, write a quotation that reflects your group's understanding of effective leadership. Present the quotations you found on the Internet and your interpretations of them to the class. Print the quotation that your group developed and post it for others to read.

Laissez-faire Laissez-faire is a French term meaning "to let people do as they choose." A **laissez-faire leader** gives up his or her power to the members of the group. He or she leads with a distinctly "hands-off" style. A laissez-faire leader provides the members of his or her group with the task or purpose of the group and then steps back to let the group accomplish the task or purpose on their own. The group will generally meet together only two or three times, but individual members will keep the leader informed of their individual progress toward the completion of the project. This type of leadership style is effective only when a group is comprised of self-directed members who are capable of working on a project alone or in a subcommittee. For example, the chairperson of the prom committee can be a laissez-faire leader if he or she has strong group members who head up subcommittees such as time and place, entertainment, and refreshments.

Figure 13–1 Balanced Leadership Grid

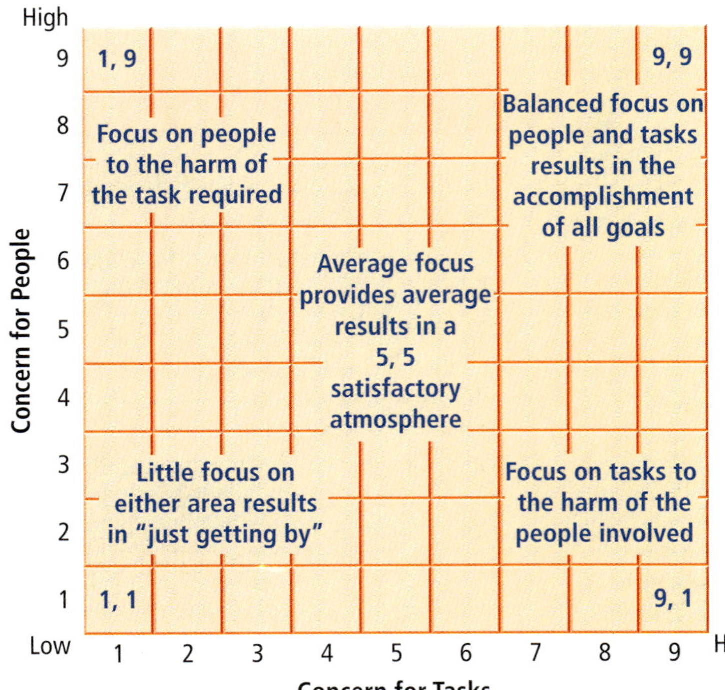

Balanced A fourth style of leadership is one that is balanced according to the grid in **Figure 13–1.** A **balanced leader** strives for an equal focus on both tasks and relationships in order to be most effective.

Leaders who are overly concerned with getting a task done may have a tendency to "run over" the people who are connected with the work. At the other extreme are leaders who are overly concerned with what everyone involved might think or feel about the work. These leaders may be more preoccupied with the relationship issues of the group and may not get very much work done. Leaders who typically get the most done are those who can get tasks accomplished while being sensitive to the relationships and feelings of those connected to the tasks.

A balanced leader can, in times of crises, initiate ways to complete the task. When time is not so critical, the leader needs to be able to facilitate discussion, spending more time listening to how group members feel and thinking about how to best complete a task.

Functional Leadership

The **functional approach** to leadership suggests that successful leaders both recognize and actively perform needed tasks. In other words, leaders see a job that needs to be done and either do it or get it done by others. Very often, emergent leaders are born out of this kind of assertiveness or take-charge attitude. A person who has leadership potential needs to work hard to develop the behaviors and communication skills necessary for success as a leader.

Section 1 Assessment

Visit the *Glencoe Communication Applications* Web site at **communicationapplications.glencoe.com** and click on **Self-Check and Study Guides 13.1** to review your understanding of identifying leaders.

Review Key Terms

1. Define each term and write it in a sentence: leader, appointed leader, emergent leader, trait approach, style approach, authoritarian leader, democratic leader, laissez-faire leader, balanced leader, functional approach.

Check Understanding

2. How are appointed and emergent leaders different?
3. Describe the three approaches for identifying potential leaders.
4. **Predict** Imagine that your school yearbook staff must finish the layout for the advertisement section by tomorrow. The yearbook editor has chosen the democratic style of leadership during this stressful time. How do you think staff members might respond to his or her requests? How effective will his or her chosen style be in this situation?

APPLICATION Activity

Preparing a Campaign Poster Imagine that you are running for a class office. Apply the three approaches for determining effective leadership to yourself. Then, prepare a poster for your campaign, highlighting your strengths.

Critical Thinking Skill

Predicting Outcomes

A leader often has the responsibility to provide guidance when the outcome of a decision may not be completely apparent. When you predict an outcome you are trying to determine how an event will turn out before it takes place. Although no one can be completely sure of any future event, there are ways to help you make more accurate guesses and, therefore, become a more skillful leader.

Learning the Skill

Use the following steps to predict outcomes:

Step 1 Start with what you know. Carefully review the information with which you are already familiar. Then decide what other information you will need to make a good prediction.

Step 2 Research what you want to know. Try to determine how people will feel about an event and why. Find out everything you can about similar situations and look for patterns. You can use surveys or opinion polls to determine a variety of people's thoughts about an idea.

Step 3 Study the past. It is often useful to use information from the past, especially if you are doing something that has been attempted before. Study the history leading up to the event, and guess what should happen based on that information.

Step 4 Consider the cost of being wrong. When you are predicting an outcome, remember to consider the effects of a poor prediction.

Practicing the Skill

Suppose you own a small pizza shop. Increased competition has recently hurt your business. You have decided you'll have to either raise your prices or start charging for delivery service in order to increase your profits. Answer the following questions to predict an outcome for your business.

1. As the owner, what are some things you already know about your business?
2. What else do you need to know before making your decision? How can you research this information?
3. If you make the wrong decision, how will it affect your business?

APPLICATION *Activity*

You are a student council member at your high school and you need to set a date on which to start a month-long fund-raising campaign that will support the building of a new gymnasium. You have the choice of starting your fund-raising campaign on the same night as a basketball game or the following week.

1. When should you host the event? Why did you make that choice?
2. What is the cost of making a wrong decision?
3. What information did you consider in making your decision? Why did you consider this information?

Leading Others

GUIDE TO READING

Objectives

1. Explain the importance of preparation and communication skills for effective leadership.
2. Analyze the six types of power.
3. Recognize seven communication methods shared by effective leaders.

Terms to Learn

power
resistance
legitimate power
reward power
coercive power
expert power
informational power
referent power

Think about General Norman Schwarzkopf, professional quarterback John Elway, the Reverend Jesse Jackson, and former prime minister Margaret Thatcher. What do all of these leaders have in common? What sets each of them apart from their followers?

Schwarzkopf, Elway, Jackson, Thatcher—each of these names brings to mind exceptional leadership qualities. These leaders all possess certain traits and styles that have made them successful, whether leading an army or a sports team. Each of these leaders exhibited intelligence and knowledge about his or her organization and program, creativity in solving problems, and communication and sociability skills that matched the needs of the situation. Jesse Jackson, for example, is known for his gift of public speaking, while John Elway used incredible drive to inspire his football teammates to greatness both on and off the field. What is it, then, that ties these leaders together?

Jesse Jackson, who exhibits a gift for public speaking, possesses many leadership qualities. Identify other leaders in society.

Skills for Effective Leadership

Once you have been appointed to lead or have emerged as a leader, what do you do next? A good first step might be to examine your knowledge and specific skills as they relate to the position you are in. If you are like most people, you will realize that successful leadership requires strong skills in preparation and communication.

Preparation

An important aspect of leadership is motivating followers to do whatever is necessary to accomplish specific goals. Effective leaders first make sure they understand what needs to be done before asking their followers to take action. This requires planning ahead for the tasks or events facing the group.

To adequately prepare, leaders should do the following:

- plan tasks
- evaluate followers
- evaluate resources
- plan communication

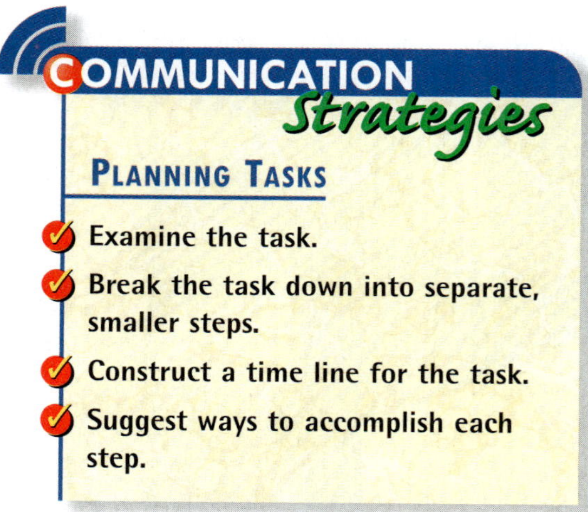

COMMUNICATION Strategies
PLANNING TASKS
Examine the task.
Break the task down into separate, smaller steps.
Construct a time line for the task.
Suggest ways to accomplish each step.

Figure 13–2 Publicizing an Event

CAR WASH
WHEN: SATURDAY
WHERE: SCHOOL PARKING LOT
• DONATIONS WELCOME
• PROCEEDS WILL HELP PAY FOR MARCHING BAND UNIFORMS

Plan Tasks. A leader's first step in preparation is to plan what needs to be done. You read about planning procedures in Chapter 10. The Communication Strategies checklist on this page summarizes the most important elements of planning.

Evaluate Followers. What are the talents of the people involved in the task? If certain individuals already have demonstrated talent in certain areas, use those talents! This not only makes for smooth work, but it also builds the self-confidence of those group members. Being called upon as an expert can help motivate them to do their jobs as effectively as possible. For example, suppose you were the leader of a project planning a special event at school. To publicize the event, you might call on one of the group members who has artistic talent to create flyers or posters, such as the one in Figure 13–2. Leaders in social and professional organizations who use the talents of group members effectively often have greater success achieving group goals.

Just as it is important to be aware of individual group members' strengths, it also is important to analyze their weaknesses. Suppose you have a job that must be completed quickly and know someone who could do very good work on this task. However, that person is not very good at meeting deadlines. You should probably find someone else to do

A factory supervisor gives instructions to employees. **What should a leader do in order to adequately prepare to communicate?**

the work. What help do you think a specific group member will need to accomplish his or her part of the task? Knowing this can help you plan for any special training or support workers might require along the way.

Evaluate Resources. A leader must be prepared to seek out anything needed to accomplish the goals of the group. For example, it is the responsibility of a highway construction project leader to request new equipment if older equipment breaks or wears out. Successful leaders in any group not only anticipate what supplies, equipment, and physical space are required for a job but also seek to provide workers with needed tools to complete the job.

Plan Communication. Finally, to adequately prepare, a leader needs to determine how and what to communicate. For example, a factory supervisor not only needs to share new instructions with the workers, but he or she also will report the group's progress to upper management. The leader is a communication link between his or her group and other leaders in the organization. This link also may extend beyond the group or organization to the community as a whole. A leader may communicate on behalf of his or her followers on many different levels, through a variety of channels, and in a number of different contexts.

GLOBAL COMMUNICATION

Giving Gifts

In the United States, policies concerning the acceptance of gifts by employees are often stated in a company's handbook. Americans representing their organizations in other countries, however, must be aware of cultural traditions regarding gifts. For example, while clocks or watches are a common workplace gift in the U.S., this gift might not be appropriate in China because a clock is a symbol of bad luck to some people there. Survey teachers, friends, and relatives who have worked with people from other cultures. Find five examples of occasions when it is appropriate to offer gifts in other cultures. Are there people to whom you should not give gifts? Are there things that should not be presented as gifts, like the clocks mentioned in the example?

Communication

Leadership is more than just envisioning a goal and then making sure the work gets done to reach that goal. It also involves communication. An effective leader takes steps to

Figure 13–3 Effective Leaders Consider the Appropriate Channel

ensure clear communication on all levels of the group. Depending upon the type of group and the nature of the task, a leader may need to do some or all of the following:

- gather and analyze feedback from followers
- conduct problem-solving or other group meetings
- provide performance reviews
- preside over meetings
- explain (and perhaps demonstrate) new tasks
- represent the group to others
- speak out in favor of needed organizational changes

Each of these tasks requires effective communication skills on the part of the leader. They may require the leader to create and express messages to followers, peers, supervisors, or even the community. They also may require him or her to listen critically, deliberatively, and empathically to others. Most of all, these communication tasks require a leader to demonstrate ethical judgment about what to say and when to say it.

Good judgment is especially necessary when performing the first three communication tasks listed above. Listening to feedback, solving problems, and evaluating others' performance can involve sending and receiving negative messages as well as positive ones. Dealing with negative messages can pose a special challenge to leaders who feel threatened when followers disagree with them. If you find yourself in this situation, use the perception checks you read about in Chapter 3 and the conflict management skills you learned in Chapter 12 to work through any difficulties.

The last four tasks listed above can require, in addition to other communication abilities, special skills in diplomacy, or the art of reaching an agreement that suits all parties. As a leader, you may find that your position will be very threatening to some people. An effective leader will be sensitive to the feelings of others and will try to anticipate ways to help them feel more comfortable with his or her leadership. To keep these people working effectively toward the group goal, you may need to experiment with different styles and methods of communication.

As **Figure 13–3** shows, a successful leader will consider the special needs of group members when determining the best ways to organize and communicate his or her wishes to them. For example, it may be helpful to use more than one communication channel to introduce new procedures or policies at work. Some employees may be satisfied to read about the change in a memo, while others might prefer to hear about it in a small group meeting, receive detailed written instructions about the change, attend a training session on the new process, or even have the opportunity to be trained individually. The leader should determine, given the context, which method or methods of communication will be most effective for the group and then carry out that plan.

TECHNOLOGY *Activity*

Creating a Spreadsheet Leaders, such as company managers, must keep detailed records of many workplace activities. In many businesses, all incoming calls are logged by a receptionist. Other businesses require all visitors who enter their building to sign in at a security desk. Information like this is sometimes entered into a database. The data can be recorded and analyzed using spreadsheet software. Think of three types of information that you could record and analyze over a period of time. Choose one of them and create a log or database by recording this information for one month. After one month, review your data and provide a one-page analysis of the information you gathered.

USING POWER

Power is available at some level to all leaders. **Power** is the ability of one person to get others to behave in a particular way or to carry out certain actions. How willingly followers work with a leader may be determined by the type of power that leader uses.

The six main types of leadership power are as follows:

- legitimate power
- reward power
- coercive power
- expert power
- informational power
- referent power

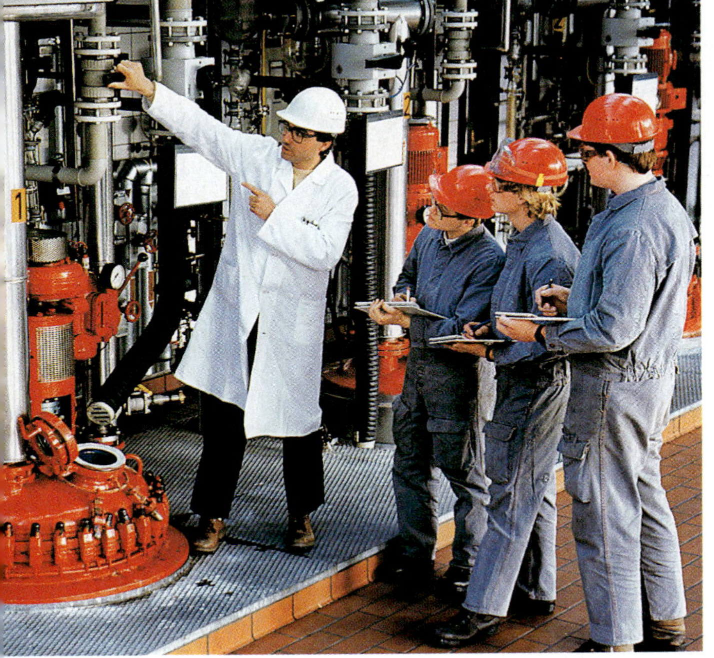

As a leader, the type of power you choose will affect the amount of resistance you are likely to encounter from others in the organization. **Resistance** is the force generated within a person that keeps him or her from accepting another's use of power. Power is something that one person allows another to have. Leaders depend upon their followers to acknowledge their power. Followers may choose to ignore or deny a leader's power. However, if power is used well, most followers will offer very little resistance to a leader's requests.

Legitimate Power

Within any organization, some individuals will be given specific titles or offices. With these assignments come certain responsibilities and

It is necessary for a supervisor to practice effective communication skills in order to lead or train others. How does an effective leader handle others who may feel threatened by his or her position?

decision-making powers. **Legitimate power** is the power assigned to anyone who holds a particular position, office, or title. For example, principals have legitimate power to oversee teachers and students. Supervisors often have the power to hire and fire workers in their department. Legitimate power allows supervisors to demand that employees come to work on time, follow company policies, and complete their work according to some standard of quality. If employees fail to meet these requirements, the supervisor may legitimately use his or her own judgment to correct the problem.

Using Legitimate Power Appropriately It is possible for a leader to abuse legitimate power by the way he or she uses it. For instance, a leader may have the legitimate power to call meetings whenever he or she wishes. However, yelling for an employee to "Get in here now!" would be inappropriate in most cases. The leader may be overstepping his or her power by being rude or overbearing while making what would otherwise be a reasonable demand.

Another misuse of legitimate power occurs when a leader tries to extend his or her influence beyond where it is appropriate. For instance, a supervisor at work cannot legitimately require you to join a particular political party, social organization, or recreational association. It may be within his or her power, however, to ask you to belong to professional associations that would help you stay current on developments in your career field.

Employees both understand and expect supervisors to use their legitimate power to get work accomplished. To use that legitimate power in a way that provokes the least resistance, leaders should be courteous in explaining their expectations to employees. A good rule of thumb is to try to give instructions in the same way you would like to have them given to you.

Reward Power

Reward power is the ability to repay others in exchange for complying with a given direction. Rewards at work might include pay raises, promotions, improved workspace, or special recognition, such as the Employee of the Month award shown in Figure 13–4. Unlike legitimate power, everyone in an organization—not just the leader—has some amount of reward power. For example, almost any employee has the power to reward coworkers by helping out with a different project, sharing office equipment, or simply making the work environment especially friendly and pleasant.

Using Reward Power Appropriately One danger with reward power is that it can appear to be bribery. Few people like to feel they can be bought. To use rewards appropriately, the reward should directly reflect the task completed. For example, if an employee finds an innovative way to use computers to ease everyone's workload, an appropriate reward might be to update the office computers and give that employee the best system.

Coercive Power

Coercive power can be thought of as the opposite of reward power. **Coercive power** is the ability to force others to do something by

Figure 13–4 Use of Reward Power

Employee
of the Month
Robin Juarez
June 2002

A supervisor gains respect from employees by being courteous when explaining expectations. What is reward power?

punishing them if they do not comply. If the person making the demand can withhold pay raises, deny promotions, change your job to include some unpleasant duty, or even fire you, that person has coercive power over you.

Like reward power, almost everyone has some level of coercive power. Your coworkers have the ability to make your work environment either pleasant or unpleasant depending on how they treat you at work. Team members can make meetings tedious by arguing over every item on the agenda, if they choose to do so. However, while your peers can make some aspects of your tasks inconvenient or unpleasant, they probably can't punish you with any severe consequence.

Using Coercive Power Appropriately The use of coercive power usually is not the most effective way to lead a group. Followers may become resentful or angry toward a coercive leader. This negativity usually results in a leader who gets little respect and a lot of resistance from followers.

While it generally is undesirable to use coercion, a leader may find that it is the most effective last resort for getting a particular job done. The best use of coercion is to allow the consequences of doing a bad job fall upon those who did the poor work. For example, imagine that the special events committee at your school failed to arrange for the custodial department to clean up after the fall dance. The committee's sponsor might require members to remain after the dance and take down decorations and clean up the area. If the committee members learn from this the importance of careful planning and responsibility for tasks, the coercion might work.

Expert Power

A group's designated leader may not be the person with the most knowledge about a particular project, task, or situation. **Expert power** is held by the person who knows the most about the work that must be done.

Imagine that you are a part of a small group whose task is to design and produce publicity for an upcoming fund-raiser at your school. One group member can draw well, another is an announcer on a local radio station, and a third works for the student newspaper. You, in turn, have experience in producing computer-generated, full-color flyers. Each group member holds some expert power over the others.

Using Expert Power Appropriately One drawback of expert power is having a leader who doesn't recognize the expertise of his or her workers or who refuses to allow the experts to act. Equally dangerous is a leader who assigns expert status to someone who is not truly an expert. A wise leader will determine the true expertise of his or her group members and give them the freedom to do what each does best.

Informational Power

Just as expert power consists of knowing how to do something very well, informational power consists of knowing where to learn about it. In other words, **informational power** is held by individuals who have access to needed information. These individuals are not necessarily experts in the subject, but they have either a position or some special skill that allows them to get the information that is needed. In a mock trial, a participant who knows how to conduct research using government documents will be useful in providing statistical information. Likewise, a new employee just hired from a competing firm may possess valuable information about what that competitor is developing.

Using Informational Power Appropriately The more an individual knows how to access scarce or difficult-to-locate information, the more valuable he or she can be. However, that person must be careful not to violate ethical standards in revealing specific information or sources of information. An effective leader will not ask that person to provide information that might harm any relationships he or she wishes to maintain. This usually includes information that was given to the individual in confidence.

Practice for the Workplace

Power and Leadership Everyone takes on leadership responsibilities and is empowered in different situations. Think about the following list of people in your school and identify the types of power each one possesses.

Counselors	Students
Teachers	Cafeteria manager
Principal	Coaches
Librarian	Club advisors
Team captains	Music section leaders
Class valedictorian	Student council president
Newspaper/Yearbook editors	

BUSINESS PRACTICE *Activity*

Sometimes people who seemingly have little power within a company can be your greatest sources of information. Consider the following employees. What types of power do they possess?

Custodian	Company accountant
Receptionist	Senior employee
Security officer	Computer network administrator

Revealing confidential information might very well cost the person a friendship, a business contact, or some other valuable relationship. Not only might this cause significant personal conflict for that person, but it also erodes his or her power. A person retains informational power only as long as he or she can keep the confidence of potential sources and continue to provide information.

Mother Teresa was a referent leader. **Describe how a person gains referent power.**

Referent Power

Most leaders hope to gain the respect of their followers. **Referent power** is the influence held by someone who is respected, liked, or otherwise admired by his or her followers. The name "referent" comes from the fact that the followers refer power onto the individual. They make the leader powerful through their willingness to follow him or her. A leader has referent power only if followers hope to become like him or her.

Of all the types of power, referent power is the most desirable for a leader to hold. Leaders with this power don't have to point out who is in charge, resort to rewards or threats, or claim some special expertise or information connections to get others to follow. Workers accept this leader's direction because they want to help the leader accomplish the work and are pleased to work for and with that person.

Most friends hold a certain amount of referent power over each other. You probably do what your friends ask because of your respect and affection for them, not because you fear them or hope to be rewarded. The same is true when it comes to your heroes as well. Anyone you admire as a hero has referent power over you. When you look up to someone for their athletic ability, musical talent, or knowledge about something, you have given him or her referent power.

Using Referent Power Appropriately Unlike legitimate, reward, and coercive power, which partially stem from a position you hold, referent power is given exclusively by the followers. As a result, they can choose to withdraw it at any time. If you have referent power over others and then disappoint them by doing something unethical or by letting them down when they are counting on you, you probably will lose some or all of that power. To maintain this type of power, you should always try to work in the best interests of those who admire, trust, and respect you.

COMMUNICATION PRACTICE LAB

Understanding Power

To analyze and understand power, follow the steps outlined here:

Step 1 As a class, brainstorm a list of leaders, including local, national, and world leaders, school officials, and other students. Write your list on the chalkboard.

Step 2 Working in groups of three or four, choose one person whom you believe to be the most effective leader on the list. Make sure you do not choose the same leader as another group in your class.

Step 3 Analyze how your chosen leader uses each of the six types of power you just read about.

Step 4 List the six types of power on a sheet of paper in the order you think your leader uses them. Then, assign a percentage value to each type. For instance, 30 percent of your chosen leader's influence may be legitimate power. Create a circular graph using the percentages you assigned.

Step 5 Share your graphs as a class. Which type of power is used most by the leaders your class chose? Which type is used the least? Do most effective leaders use every type of power at some point? Why or why not?

Any leader may lose his or her power in the eyes of followers. Making numerous mistakes or poor decisions, treating others unfairly or rudely, or requiring that followers adhere to a set of standards that the leader does not personally follow all may diminish a leader's power. It is important for a leader to be aware of and to adjust to feedback from followers so that he or she may lead as effectively as possible.

Effective Communication Methods for Leaders

So far in this section, you have analyzed and addressed your communication and preparation skills and looked at the wide variety of power that a leader can have over his or her followers. You now have the knowledge base you need to perfect your leadership skills.

Effective leaders focus the energy of their followers on the mission, or the vision, of the organization and inspire their followers to do their best work. Remember that the purpose of an organization of people is to combine their talents to accomplish much more than any of them could possibly accomplish by acting alone. Leaders should facilitate the strategic plan—that is, they should try to create the best working situation and conditions so that all the members of the organization can do their best work.

What distinguishes a good leader from a great one? How can you be like those leaders who have made such a difference in your own life? If you examine these leaders' communication methods closely, you will find some common ideas. The Communication Strategies checklist on this page lists a few of their secrets for leading effectively.

Communication Strategies

Leading Effectively

- Make others feel important.
- Promote a vision.
- Focus workers on the task.
- Treat others with respect.
- Admit mistakes.
- Criticize others only in private.
- Stay visible to your followers.
- Celebrate achievement.

Make Others Feel Important

The purpose of any organization is to combine the talents of all the members to accomplish more than any one of them could possibly accomplish on his or her own. Effective leaders try to find each member's particular strength and use it. By emphasizing the strengths of the members rather than your own skill as a leader, you will encourage each follower to give the best he or she has to offer.

Promote a Vision

Effective leaders focus the energy of their followers on the mission of the organization and inspire their followers to do their best work. Not only does an effective leader provide a blueprint of the goals at hand; he or she also shows the value of those goals to his or her followers.

For example, one major corporation has a motto that places a value on the safety and health of customers. The motto is framed and placed in all offices and break rooms, typed on notices to employees, and often quoted in meetings.

An effective leader provides structure to guide the work. **What else does an effective leader do?**

Focus Workers on the Task

An effective leader creates a structure to guide the work to its completion. In addition, an effective leader continually gives information to and seeks information from employees while the work is progressing.

Initiate a Structure. Workers usually want to be certain of which of their duties are of the most importance, how quickly they should proceed with the work, what standards of quality are expected, and the process by which they should do the work. Any time you do an assignment for a teacher, you probably want to know what the end goal is, whether it is a speech, a research paper, or some type of project. You will want to know how you are to proceed on the project, when it is due, and how it will be graded. The assignments leaders give their workers should be as clear as the assignments your teachers give you.

Request and Give Feedback on the Work's Progress. Effective leaders ask workers for their opinions about how the work is proceeding, whether they need additional equipment to do the job, what is going well, and what is causing them difficulty on the job. A leader can also do perception checks to be sure that what he or she hoped to communicate to the workers is what they also understand to be important about the job. If there are problems to be solved during the work progress, the leader collaborates with the workers and they implement whatever solution is decided upon.

Treat Others With Respect

It is always important to treat others the way you wish to be treated. Treating followers with kindness and respect will lessen any resistance you might encounter. On the contrary, it will probably increase the respect others have for you.

Admit Mistakes

You will seem more approachable and likable if you are willing to admit your errors. Your honesty will also encourage followers to take chances without fear of failure. Finally, if your followers suspect that you are covering up your own errors, they are likely to try to cover up their own as well.

Criticize Others Only in Private

Some have said, "Public praise, private criticism." Public criticism has the tendency to embarrass everyone involved, not just the person being criticized. It also reflects poorly on you as a leader. On the other hand, public praise encourages everyone to do his or her best for continued success.

Stay Visible to Your Followers

Staying in touch allows for a free flow of information as well as a constant source of feedback and ideas. Talking to followers, visiting work sites, asking questions, and observing interactions all provide a leader with valuable insight into current conditions and how to improve them.

Celebrate Achievement

When you reward the accomplishment of a goal, you encourage followers to work that much harder on future goals. While failures can be examined carefully and learned from, successes should be celebrated openly and enthusiastically.

One thing is certain: You will have many opportunities in life to lead others. You may be called upon to lead as the result of an official election or a job promotion. Alternatively, your call to leadership may be less formal. You may lead your family through a difficult decision or your study group through a tough problem. In any case, you'll find it important to keep in mind these valuable skills for being an effective leader.

Section 2 Assessment

Visit the *Glencoe Communication Applications* Web site at **communicationapplications.glencoe.com** and click on **Self-Check and Study Guide 13.2** to review your understanding of leading others.

Review Key Terms

1. Define each term and write it in a sentence: power, resistance, legitimate power, reward power, coercive power, expert power, informational power, referent power.

Check Understanding

2. What two skill areas are most important for effective leadership?
3. Identify the source of each type of leadership power.
4. **Classify** Think of the different ways your teacher communicates in a typical class period. Classify each task by the communication method it best illustrates.

APPLICATION *Activity*

Communicating Effectively as a Leader Talk with a parent or older friend about leadership positions he or she has held. Ask the person to describe different types of power and specific communication methods he or she found most effective in that leadership role. Write a brief summary of how that person's experience illustrates the concepts of this section. Discuss your conclusions as a class.

Communication Self-Assessment

Evaluating Your Leadership Skills

How Do You Rate?

On a separate sheet of paper, use the key to respond to the following statements. Put a check mark at the end of each skill you would like to improve.

Key: **A** Always **U** Usually **S** Sometimes **R** Rarely **N** Never

1. I am seen as a leader when I participate in groups.
2. When I work in a group, I try not to be so concerned about pleasing people that nothing gets done.
3. I know how to motivate people to accomplish specific goals.
4. When I have legitimate power, I use it wisely. I am not rude or overbearing.
5. My leadership style is balanced. In times of crisis I can make a decision, but at other times I am a facilitator.
6. I choose experts to lead my group only when I know they have true competence.
7. I try to establish referent power so that workers enjoy working with me.
8. When I am in a leadership role, I give the members of my group the opportunity to do what each does best.
9. I deliver criticism to group members only in private.
10. I work hard to develop the communication skills needed for leadership success.

How Do You Score?

Review your responses. Give yourself 5 points for every A, 4 for every U, 3 for every S, 2 for every R, and 1 for every N. Total your points and evaluate your score.

41–50 Excellent You may be surprised to find out how much you can improve your skills.

31–40 Good In this course, you can learn ways to make your skills better.

21–30 Fair Practice applying the skills taught in this course.

1–20 Needs Improvement Carefully monitor your improvement as you work through this course.

Setting Communication Goals

If you scored Excellent or Good, complete Part A. If your score was Fair or Needs Improvement, complete Part B.

Part A

1. I plan to put the following ideas into practice:
2. I plan to share the following information about communication with the following people:

Part B

1. The behaviors I need to change most are:
2. To bring about these changes, I will take these steps:

Writing a Meeting Summary

Meetings are held every day throughout the world. Any meeting that addresses important issues should document its activities. A **meeting summary** is a record of a meeting.

Formality Some meeting summaries are written in a more formal style than others. The degree of formality depends on the participants, the issues, and the environment in which the meeting is held. Many companies have formal summaries, called minutes, prepared after meetings of boards of directors or major committees. Less formal summaries are prepared for other types of meetings, such as weekly team meetings or project planning meetings.

Meeting Details When writing a meeting summary, you must carefully attend to the communication taking place during the meeting. Focus on the people, the issues, and the verbal and nonverbal messages being relayed. Maintain eye contact with each speaker and ignore any distractions. Be an active listener.

Meeting Notes If you are responsible for preparing a meeting summary, you will need to take accurate notes of the meeting's activities. Include the following details in your notes:

- The name of the group holding the meeting and the reason for the meeting. Note any specific goals.
- Date, time, and place of the meeting. This information is an important part of the summary. If someone misses a meeting, he or she can use this information later as a reference point to trace progress. Identify yourself as the writer of the summary.
- Who was present and absent. These lists may be important if a question of who attended arises later.
- Reports presented and major points of discussion. State the facts objectively. Listen to the discussion and ask questions when something is unclear. Any decisions that are made should be stated accurately in your summary.
- Follow-up. Include any decisions, assignments, and deadlines made during the meeting. This will remind people of the responsibilities they have taken on as a result of the meeting.

Once you have your notes, you can develop them into a meeting summary like the one that follows. You can then use the summary as a record of the proceedings of the meeting.

For additional information about business writing, see the *Guide to Business Communication* section of the Communication Survival Kit in the Appendix.

Communication Through Writing

VIP Company
Company Supplies Task Force
MONTHLY MEETING SUMMARY
June 14, 2002

TIME AND PLACE: 1:30–2:00 p.m.
Conference Room C
PRESENT: Josephina Myers, Thomas Blevins, Christina Jones, Dillon Smith, Tanisha Evans
SUMMARY BY: Dillon Smith
REPORTS: Christina presented the Company Supply Budget Report to the team.

After the report was presented, Thomas led a discussion about the amount of money that is available for supplies. He noted that the budget has been reduced, yet suppliers have increased their prices on many of the major items the company purchases, such as paper and pens.

Christina said that her department is using more supplies than in the past. Tanisha stated that one of the suppliers has a new catalog.

It was decided after the discussion that Tanisha and Thomas would research other suppliers to find out if the company can buy supplies at a lower cost. A report of their findings will be presented at next month's meeting.

Discussion was then held about the quality of the new disks that were ordered last month. Everyone agreed that the disks were of higher quality than those used in the past. This factor will be considered as we search for new suppliers.

WRITING *Activity*

Use the following steps to create minutes of a class session, a club that you belong to, or a workplace meeting that you have attended.

- State the name of the group.
- State the reason for meeting.
- State the date, time, and place of the meeting. Identify yourself as the writer of the summary.
- List the people who attended and those who were absent from the meeting.
- Briefly describe any reports presented and tell who presented them.
- Briefly describe the major points of discussion, noting each speaker's remarks. Avoid making any judgmental comments on the discussion.
- Report any votes taken during the meeting, and detail the result of the voting.
- Describe any follow-up that will be accomplished after the meeting, and include everyone's responsibilities.

CHAPTER 13 Assessment and Activities

Visit the *Glencoe Communication Applications* Web site at **communicationapplications.glencoe.com** and click on **Chapter 13 Activity** for additional practice in functioning as a leader.

Reviewing Key Terms

Read each definition. On a separate sheet of paper, write the number of the definition and the letter of the term that fits the definition best.

a. balanced leader
b. laissez-faire leader
c. authoritarian leader
d. resistance
e. style approach
f. power
g. democratic leader
h. emergent leader

1. Is chosen by peers of his or her group
2. Identifies leaders by how they choose to communicate with followers
3. Forces followers to do what he or she wants
4. Invites followers to join in decision making
5. Ability of one person to get others to behave in a particular way
6. Force that keeps a person from accepting another's use of power
7. Gives up his or her power to the followers
8. Strives to be more effective by focusing equally on tasks and relationships

Reviewing Key Concepts

1. Give examples of appointed leaders.
2. In what four ways might a person emerge as a group leader?
3. What four traits are common among leaders?
4. In what kind of organization does the authoritarian leader work best?
5. Why does a balanced leader typically get more done than other kinds of leaders?
6. When does a balanced leader need to act as an initiator rather than a facilitator?
7. Why should a leader analyze the weaknesses of group members?
8. Why is a leader's good judgment especially necessary when listening to followers' feedback?

Assessment and Activities

Reading and Critical Thinking Skill

1. **Classifying Information** Mr. Byrnes is the principal of Hamilton High School. When a teacher or student asks for direction, he says, "Do what you think best." What is Mr. Byrnes's leadership style?
2. **Summarization** Sum up the steps an effective leader uses to plan ahead for the tasks facing his or her group.
3. **Synthesis** Imagine you are the leader of a group that must solicit members for a school club on a day especially set aside for school club recruitment. Synthesize a list of the resources you will need to have a successful membership campaign.

Skill Practice Activity

Predicting Outcomes Seniors at Montcalm High School have traditionally skipped school on the Friday before homecoming weekend. This year the school has a new principal who is unaware of the tradition. Nevertheless, the seniors stay away from school on Friday. Compare the methods an authoritarian principal and a democratic principal might use to exert leadership when the seniors return to school on Monday. Which methods do you think would be more successful? Why?

Cooperative Learning Activity

Planning Tasks As a class, organize into groups of three. Each group should decide on a simple craft, such as making paper flowers, that uses materials already in the classroom. Each member should assume that he or she is the group leader and write out a plan for accomplishing the task. In constructing your plan, follow the four steps given in the chapter. Take turns as a group following one another's plan. Then rate the plans from one to three, one being the most efficient.

Chapter Project

Planning Choose a school or social organization to which you belong and follow the strategies for emerging as a leader:

Participate early and often in group meetings.
Demonstrate your ability to do a job well.
Don't push too hard to get your way.
Provide solutions for group dilemmas.
Keep a journal of your efforts and the feedback you get from other group members.

Presenting Share your journal entries with other members of the class who are participating in the project. Compare your approaches and decide whether to adopt methods that worked for them.

Standardized Test Practice

THE PRINCETON REVIEW

1 $\sqrt{150.6}$ is between which pair of consecutive integers?

A 28 and 29

B 27 and 28

C 12 and 13

D 9 and 10

2 Sarah is preparing to present a three-month series of lectures on value and belief systems. In the past, it has taken her 2 hours to cover 7 main points. If she has 168 main points to cover, how many hours will it take her?

F 108

G 48

H 24

J 12

3 Lines p and q are parallel. If the measure of $\angle 2$ is 81°, what is the measure of $\angle 4$?

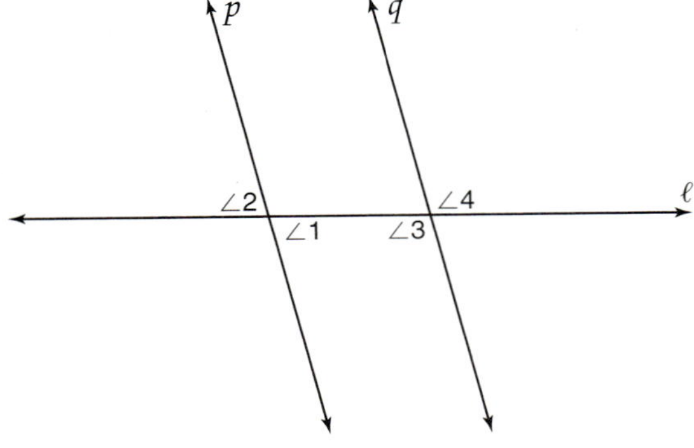

A 9°

B 81°

C 99°

D 109°

4 Tom has put together a conflict mediation pamphlet for his classmates. He will pack the pamphlets vertically in a box that is 6 inches high, 6 inches wide, and 1 foot long. If each pamphlet is 6 inches high, 3 inches wide, and 1 inch thick, how many pamphlets will Tom be able to fit into the box?

F 18

G 24

H 36

J 378

5 Margot has taken a poll of how many hours in one day that her friends spend outside of school with people from the same high school. Her friends agreed to keep track of the time that they spent. The times were 3.7hrs, 3.9hrs, 4.5hrs, 3.1hrs, 4.7hrs, 4.6hrs, and 3.3hrs. What was the median amount of time that these seven friends spent?

A 3.3hrs

B 3.9hrs

C 4.0hrs

D 4.6hrs

6 The Cross-Cultural Club had a bake sale. They sold 40 empanadas for \$8.75 total, two multinational cook books for \$10.90 each, and a dozen packs of greeting cards in several languages for \$24.00 total. How much money did the Cross-Cultural Club make at the bake sale?

F \$24.70

G \$43.65

H \$54.55

J \$395.80

K Not Here

7 Martin and Francis are playing a game called "Guess What Strategy I'm Using." Francis is the first to explain 4 different conflict resolution strategies. Today, Martin correctly identified the 4 strategies in 28.3 seconds. Yesterday, he correctly identified the 4 strategies in 48.1 seconds. How much faster did Martin identify the strategies today?

A 19.2 sec

B 19.8 sec

C 20.2 sec

D 20.8 sec

E Not Here

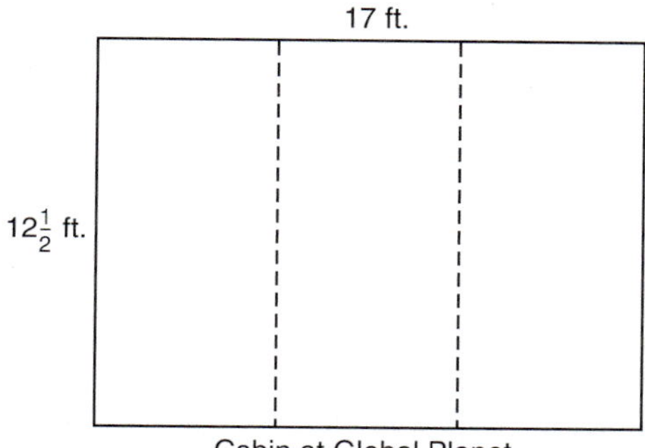

Cabin at Global Planet

8 The cabins at Global Planet, a camp for teens, are each $12\frac{1}{2}$ feet by 17 feet. They will each be divided into thirds, as shown, for the three campers.

If the three campers per cabin can share the space equally, what are the dimensions of one camper's area?

A $4\frac{1}{3}$ ft. by $5\frac{2}{3}$ ft.

B $6\frac{1}{2}$ ft. by $8\frac{1}{2}$ ft.

C $5\frac{2}{3}$ ft. by $12\frac{1}{2}$ ft.

D $5\frac{2}{3}$ ft. by 13 ft.

9 A youth anti-violence seminar paid $412 for 192 non-violence posters. Which is the best estimate of how much the seminar paid per poster?

F $2.00

G $.25

H $2.50

J $3.00

K $3.50

10 Toby makes 11 phone calls to get 5 job interviews. What proportion could be used to determine the number of phone calls, *n*, needed for 13 interviews?

A $\frac{13}{11} = \frac{n}{5}$

B $\frac{5}{13} = \frac{n}{11}$

C $\frac{11}{13} = \frac{n}{5}$

D $\frac{5}{11} = \frac{n}{13}$

E $\frac{11}{5} = \frac{n}{13}$

11 At the beginning of the school year, Meredith drew a diagram that included the names of her immediate friends. After interacting with the rest of her classmates for the rest of the year, Meredith made another diagram to include her new friends. If Meredith doubled the number of friends that she originally started with and ended up with 58 friends at the end of the year, which equation can be used to find *y*, the number of friends that Meredith had at the beginning of the year?

F $3y = 58$

G $58(y + 2) = 0$

H $y = 58 \times 2$

J $106 - y = 58$

K $2y = 58$

UNIT 4 Presentation Communication

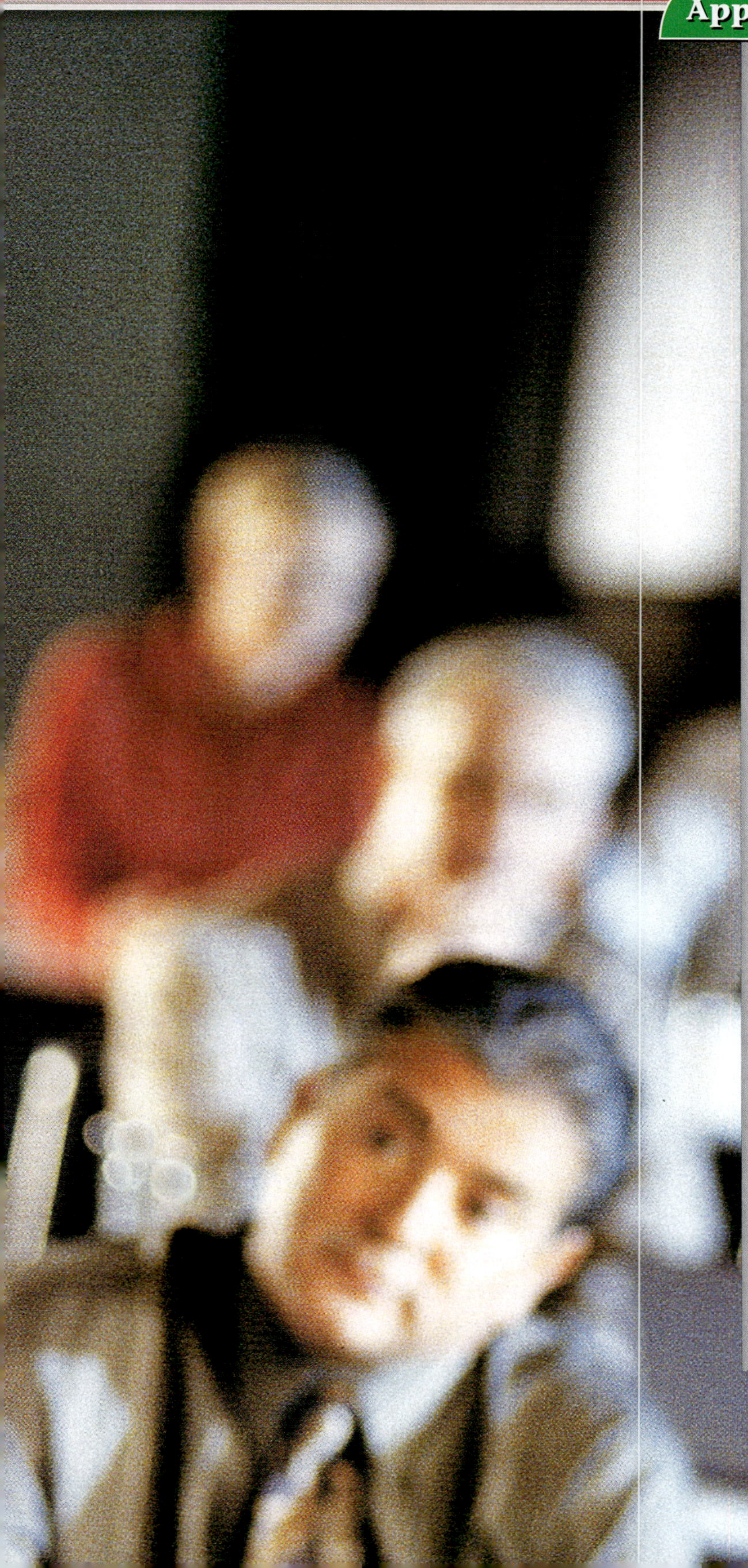

Applying Communication Skills

Making presentations in today's world is more than an art—it is a life skill applied to almost every social and professional context imaginable. To make effective presentations, it is important to study and practice the crucial steps of the presentation process, which include preparing, researching, practicing, delivering, and evaluating the presentation.

Making a Successful Strategies Chart

- Create a chart with the following categories: Successful Strategies, Chapter Number, Date Practiced, and Result.
- As you progress through each chapter in this unit, prepare a list of strategies that you found beneficial in your daily life either at home, in school, at work, or in the community.
- At the end of the study of the unit, share the strategies as a class, noting the ones that seemed the most helpful.

CHAPTER 14 Preparing for Professional Presentations

WHY IT'S IMPORTANT

Sometimes, the best way to communicate ideas is through a formal or informal oral presentation. By mastering the presentation process one step at a time, you can communicate even the most complex idea clearly and effectively.

To better understand the how to prepare for presentations, view the **Communication in Action** Chapter 14 video lesson.

GLENCOE Online

Visit the *Glencoe Communication Applications* Web site at **communicationapplications.glencoe.com** and click on **Overview–Chapter 14** to preview information about preparing for presentations.

"You can have brilliant ideas, but if you can't get them across, your brains won't get you anywhere."

—Lee Iacocca, automobile executive

Section 1

Introducing Professional Presentations

GUIDE TO READING

Objectives

1. Compare and contrast formal and informal presentations.
2. Describe a presenter's responsibilities.
3. Analyze the context for a professional presentation.

Terms to Learn

professional presentation
formal presentation
informal presentation
ethos
demographics

Help Wanted: Individual with strong communication skills to make frequent presentations before small and large groups. Must be able to inform, persuade, and motivate. Salary negotiable. Position open immediately.

Would you consider responding to an advertisement like this one? If the answer is no, why not? If you are like thousands of others, you may fear making a presentation almost more than anything else. What makes you uncomfortable speaking in public?

If you have ever given a presentation, you may have felt awkward being the center of attention. You might also be unsure about the information you were presenting. Whatever your discomfort, there are ways to overcome it through practice and preparation. The ability to produce and give quality oral presentations is a basic social and professional skill.

Public speaking is a necessity in some careers. **Name two ways to overcome anxiety with regard to public presentations.**

Professional Presentations

A professional presentation is an informed, organized oral statement made to a group of professional or social peers, supervisors, clients, or members of the general public. Most presentations in professional and social contexts fall into one of two categories: formal or informal.

Formal Presentations

A formal presentation is scheduled in advance and usually involves individual or team research and audiovisual, or AV, support. Formal presentations usually require a carefully structured format and outline. They also require formal language strategies and delivery techniques. These presentations might be made by a salutatorian at a high school graduation, by a corporate executive to stockholders at an annual meeting, or by project managers requesting funding for a specific project. Sales presentations, product demonstrations, reports to executive boards, committee project reports, and assigned classroom presentations all are examples of formal presentations.

Informal Presentations

An informal presentation may occur on a daily or ongoing basis. It usually is shorter and more spontaneous than a formal presentation and may involve a smaller audience.

You might give an informal presentation to your teacher or boss when you are casually asked for an update on your current project. At work, informal presentations might occur when showing a new employee around the office, when explaining a bill to a client, or when telling the principal your opinions on a proposed change in school policy. Each of these situations requires you to make an informal presentation on relatively short notice.

Global Communication

Oral Cultures

In ancient oral cultures that did not have a systematic form of writing, minstrels, poets, and storytellers created and narrated stories that described traditional practices and recounted historical events. What aspects of ethos do you think these presenters conveyed? How do we capture and preserve cultural traditions today?

Presenter's Responsibilities

As in other forms of oral communication, the competent speaker has a specific set of responsibilities that relate to the context of his or her presentation. These responsibilities include developing basic speaking skills and creating an image as a competent presenter.

Basic Skills

The basic skills most needed by professional presenters fall into five categories. These are:

- selection
- organization
- style
- memory
- delivery

Selection A presenter's first responsibility is to select topics, ideas, and supporting information carefully. Topics and ideas should be well supported through sufficient research. It also is critical that topics and ideas be carefully tailored to meet the demands of a particular audience, occasion, and task. If the topic has been selected for you, you still need to select additional ideas and support information that are appropriate to the topic.

Organization Presenters are responsible for making sure their presentations are put together well. Effective presenters take time to learn how to properly organize their presentations for maximum effectiveness.

Style It is important for speakers to use appropriate language in their presentations. Selecting the words and language style for a presentation is like selecting the clothing you will wear to a certain event. Just as some types of clothing are appropriate to specific situations, so are some types of language. Effective presenters evaluate what is needed and then use language that is appropriate for their topic, audience, task, and occasion.

Memory Presenters need to possess a variety of speaking and language skills that they can adapt to different speaking situations. This allows them to "think on their feet" as specific needs arise during a presentation. You can accomplish this by mentally filing away information and ideas on a topic as you do your research. Committing information to memory provides you with a bank of knowledge that you can draw from during a presentation whenever you need it.

Delivery Presenters also are responsible for using appropriate verbal and nonverbal skills. For example, even the best-prepared presentation can fail if the presenter does not speak loudly enough. Additionally, if a speaker does not establish eye contact, an audience may feel ignored or unimportant or become skeptical. In many cases, the success or failure of a presentation is determined by the presenter's delivery skills.

An Appropriate Image

In addition to developing and polishing essential speaking skills, a responsible presenter gives careful consideration to the image he or she conveys to an audience. Aristotle, a Greek philosopher, taught that a speaker's image is directly related to whether or not an audience will accept and believe a message. If an audience has a poor image of a speaker, it may not believe his or her message. A speaker with a credible image is more likely to be believed.

Aristotle stressed that a speaker has a responsibility to develop and convey a positive ethos. **Ethos** is the image a presenter displays to an audience. There are four main aspects of ethos that presenters should try to

Aristotle taught that a speaker was more believable if he or she established a positive ethos, as General Schwarzkopf has done. Identify the four aspects of ethos that a presenter should consider.

consider: knowledge, character, good intent, and genuineness. In his teachings, Aristotle discussed the first three aspects. Modern researchers have added the fourth.

Knowledge An audience has the right to expect complete and accurate information in a presentation. Therefore, a presenter should be well informed about his or her subject. It is the presenter's responsibility to study all aspects of a topic so that he or she can speak ethically. In addition to being informed, a presenter must let the audience know that he or she is knowledgeable about the subject matter. For example, before proceeding with a presentation on grandparenting, General Norman Schwarzkopf might explain his relationship with his own grandchildren.

Character For an audience to believe a message, it must feel that the presenter is of sound character. That is, the listeners must believe a presenter would not intentionally mislead them by telling untruths or omitting important information. They must trust the presenter to believe his or her message.

Good Intent A presenter should demonstrate good intentions when relating a message to an audience. Listeners will be more receptive if they feel that a speaker has their best interests at heart. They also want to feel that information is being presented fairly and that the speaker sincerely cares about the outcome of the presentation.

Genuineness Today's audiences also want speakers who are genuine, sincere, and truly interested in the audience and the topic. They want to believe that the emotions, attitudes, and ideas presented are those of the presenter; this helps them trust both the speaker and the message. However, audiences tend to reject the ideas of presenters they think are arrogant or insincere.

Context of the Message

As you prepare a presentation, you will make choices that reflect your ideas and knowledge about a topic. These choices are based on the specific context of your presentation. This includes what you know about yourself as a speaker, your audience, the occasion for your presentation, and the task, or purpose, you want to accomplish.

Consider the Speaker

When you begin to prepare a presentation, think about why you were selected to make it. Are you an authority who will have immediate credibility with the audience, or will you need to build your audience's trust? Are you a recognized member of the group to which the presentation will be made or will you have to select information that establishes who you are? Have you been selected to make the presentation because of your role on a project at work? What will you or your organization gain from this presentation?

After answering these questions, consider your own personal interest in the topic. How long have you been involved with this particular topic? How extensive is your knowledge of the subject? What do you have to gain from the presentation? The answers to these questions will help you make choices that will build your personal ethos with your audience and set the stage for your presentation.

Consider the Audience

Many of the responsibilities of the presenter are based on a thorough analysis of the audience. Therefore, the more you know about your audience, the better choices you can make to meet your responsibilities.

Audience Demographics One important consideration for a speaker is the demographics of the audience. As shown in Figure 14–1, **demographics** is information about a group's age, gender, education, group affiliations, ethnicity, and sociocultural background.

You can use audience demographics to make generalizations about listeners' interests and needs. For example, if your goal is to get approval for a skating park in your community, you might first study the demographics of area residents to get an idea of who you need to convince. To get help convincing community leaders, you could meet with local students and make a presentation that focuses on the fun, recreational aspects of skateboarding and inline skating. You also might make a presentation to local business people pointing out how the park might keep young people from skating on public sidewalks and streets.

In both cases, your goal as a presenter is the same: build support for a public skating park. However, by knowing your audience's unique perspectives and concerns, you can customize your message for maximum effectiveness. In other words, you can focus on what is most important to each group.

Demographics Speakers must consider the demographics of their audiences. Use a reliable search engine or log on to www.census.gov to find information about the demographics of your community or state. How would demographics affect your giving a speech to community leaders in your community or state?

Figure 14–1 Elements of Demographics

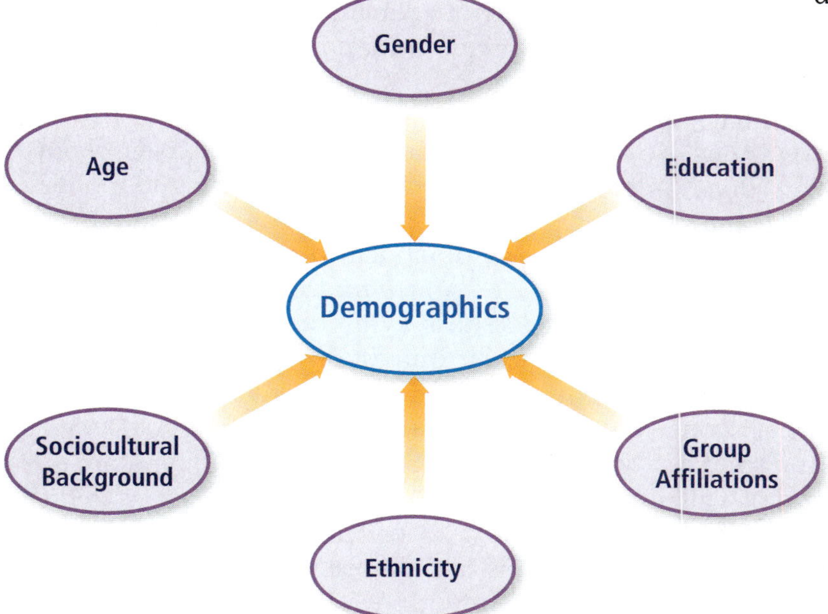

Age People of different ages typically have different interests. Because of this, they may be interested in different aspects of a topic. For instance, when the audience is a group of young employees, a presentation about a company's benefits package might focus more on family benefits and disability protection. A benefits presentation to a group of older employees may focus more heavily on retirement options and long-term medical care.

Gender Although gender once was a major consideration in audience demographics, attitudes about gender roles have drastically changed. Today, it is important not to make judgments about your audience based on gender. One possible exception is if the topic is based on statistics that categorize men

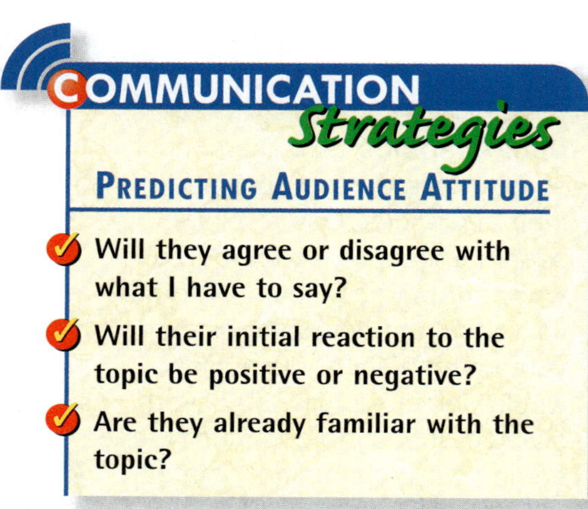

and women differently. For example, auto insurance companies use data about age and gender to determine car insurance rates. Based on statistics, young male drivers under the age of twenty-five usually pay more for auto insurance coverage. That is because this group, statistically, is more likely to be involved in an auto accident than a member of another age group or gender. In general, however, making generalizations about gender not only may offend your audience, but they also may be inaccurate.

Education Sometimes, audiences with a higher level of education may have a broader knowledge base on a specific topic. However, listeners who have a great amount of interest or experience in a topic may be just as knowledgeable, regardless of their level of education. It is important to find out how much an audience actually knows about a topic so you can either provide more information or avoid talking down to them.

Group Affiliations Knowing which groups audience members identify with can help you understand their common interests. It also can help you select examples and ideas that will relate to those interests. This information also can help you quote appropriate authorities to establish your credibility on a topic.

Sociocultural and Ethnic Backgrounds The sociocultural background of an audience helps you better understand the listeners' experience with your topic. Audiences from different backgrounds may have different ways of looking at a topic. For example, an audience from a neighborhood in a very large city may think of mass transit as a necessity while an audience from a rural area may feel that mass transit is an unnecessary expense for its community. Audiences with differing social, economic, ethnic, or cultural backgrounds may have different ways of identifying with a topic based on how they are affected by it.

Audience Attitude

In addition to knowing the demographics of your audience, it is important to determine in advance how listeners feel about the topic. Ask yourself the questions in the Communication Strategies checklist to help predict their attitude.

The answers to these questions will help you predict how your audience will accept what you have to say. If you think they might initially disagree with your main topic, you might focus on certain aspects of the topic with which everyone can agree. If your audience already knows something about a topic, your goal may be to share new information.

Gathering Audience Information

The more information you can discover about your listeners, the more you can adapt the topic, select information, and determine the appropriate approach to suit their needs and expectations. You want to put yourself in your audience's shoes. What do they need to know? What is their interest level? One way to find out this information is to contact several members of the audience before presenting. Discuss your plans with them to find out if you are on the right track. Another, but sometimes more difficult, way to get information about your audience is to administer an audience survey prior to preparing your presentation. The information you get from the survey can provide you with important insight into your audience's attitudes and knowledge about your subject.

Considering the Occasion

What is the occasion for your presentation? Is it a special ceremony to honor some person or the accomplishment of a goal? The beginning of a special campaign or sales drive? An informational presentation? Given in the morning or evening? Given around a small conference table or at a particular work site? The more you know about the occasion, the better you will be able to adapt your message and choose appropriate ideas and information.

Attendance Why are people gathering to hear your presentation? Is it a regularly scheduled social meeting, or is it a business meeting that employees are required to attend? Knowing the occasion helps you determine whether the audience is there because it wants to be or because attendance is required.

Usually, audience members who attend because they want to be there will be more interested in your topic than those who are required to attend. It is your responsibility as a presenter to include both groups and motivate them to listen to what you have to say in your presentation.

Time Time, especially in a business setting, is an important context consideration. As you can see in **Figure 14–2** on page 448, you need to think about how much time is allotted for your presentation and at what time of day you will make it. A five-minute presentation requires a much more specific topic than a twenty-minute presentation. It would be difficult to fully explain an entire budgeting process in only five minutes. However, if you've been allotted twenty or thirty minutes, you can easily cover more information. Because of these considerations, a shorter presentation may take more time to prepare than a longer one. It can take considerable effort to limit a topic to the bare essentials.

COMMUNICATION PRACTICE LAB

Considering the Context

To practice taking context into consideration when preparing to present, follow these steps:

Step 1 Imagine that you have been asked to speak about a school organization to which you belong. The organization can be athletic, academic, work-related, social, or community-based. Create a brief description of the information you will present and how you will present it.

Step 2 Determine how the following circumstances might affect your presentation.

- You are giving a fifteen-minute presentation in the high school auditorium to a group of students who will be freshmen next year.
- You are giving a five-minute presentation in a high school classroom to a group of parents.

Step 3 Make lists of ways you might adjust your presentation based on each context in which it will be given.

Step 4 Discuss your lists as a class. Did most students make similar presentation choices?

Figure 14–2 Time Considerations

As noted, another consideration is the time of day during which you will make your presentation. What will the audience be doing before and after your presentation? An audience will tend to compare your presentation to another it has just heard. If listeners are eagerly anticipating whatever comes afterward, you may have a hard time holding their attention.

Will your presentation occur first thing in the morning? Audience members may arrive late or need time to adjust to the workday. Will you present just before or after lunch? If your presentation is just before lunch, listeners may be too hungry to concentrate. If it is right after lunch, they may be sleepy or easily bored. What if your presentation occurs at the end of the day? In this instance, listeners' attention may drift to what they will be doing after work.

As you can see, all these time periods can impact a presentation. There is no ideal time for a presentation. As a presenter, you will always face the challenge of maintaining your audience's attention. Regardless of when you give your presentation, try to be as interesting and enthusiastic as possible and pay attention to your audience's responses to you. Provide breaks during long presentations, pause periodically to allow opportunities for questions, and use visuals to keep your audience focused on the topic.

Location Consider where you will be giving your presentation. The location affects your delivery and possibly any visual aids you plan to use. Will you be presenting to a small group around a conference table? To a large group in a small room? To a small group in a large room? There are many variations on room and group size, and each presents a special set of needs. For example, the larger the audience, the more formal the presentation because there may be less opportunity for audience interaction. However, your presentation may not be held in a room at all. A five-minute informal presentation at a company picnic will require you to make different presentation choices than will a five-minute formal presentation in an executive conference room.

There are other location concerns as well. What noise can you expect in the area designated for your presentation? Are phones likely to ring? Can you overhear others in

The location can greatly affect the delivery of a presentation. **What possible problems should speakers consider if their presentation is to be held outdoors?**

the next room? If you must give a presentation in a setting that is uncomfortable or distracting to your audience, try to focus on the positive elements surrounding the presentation.

Effective presenters try to be considerate of their audience as they communicate their message. Keep your message lively, allow for frequent breaks, and encourage participants to stretch regularly during longer sessions. When you do this, your listeners will appreciate your thoughtfulness and will reward you with their attention.

Considering the Task

A fourth context consideration is the task itself, or the nature or reason for the presentation. What are you being asked to do, and what will it take for you to accomplish it? Will your presentation need to be formal or informal? A five-minute presentation highlighting why a client should buy your product is different from a short presentation to someone who has never heard of your product. Although the goal in both of these situations is to get the client to buy the product, the form of each presentation will be dramatically different.

Section 1 Assessment

Visit the *Glencoe Communication Applications* Web site at **communicationapplications.glencoe.com** and click on **Self-Check and Study Guide 14.1** to review your understanding of preparing for presentations.

Review Key Terms

1. Define the following terms and write each in a sentence: professional presentation, formal presentation, informal presentation, ethos, demographics.

Check Understanding

2. How are formal and informal presentations similar? How are they different?
3. What are the responsibilities of a presenter? Explain.
4. **Synthesis** What should a presenter consider before preparing a presentation and why?

APPLICATION *Activity*

Developing Evaluation Criteria You hear all kinds of presentations—so many that you likely are unaware that each is, in fact, a presentation. School announcements, oral reports, and even your teachers' lectures are all types of presentations. Think about a recent presentation you experienced. Now, consider the responsibilities of the presenter. What criteria might you develop to evaluate whether that person has met his or her responsibilities as a presenter? Apply these criteria. Which responsibilities were met and which were not? Discuss your criteria as a class. Together, make a class list of criteria for determining whether or not a presenter has met his or her responsibilities. Copy your list in your notebook for future reference.

Beginning the Presentation Process

GUIDE TO READING

Objectives

1. Explain the relationship between context and the selection and limitation of a topic.
2. Describe how to limit a topic by classification.
3. Determine the purpose for a professional presentation.
4. Compare and contrast the characteristics of the three purposes of presentations: informative, persuasive, and motivational.

Terms to Learn

informative presentation
persuasive presentation
motivational presentation

An ancient Chinese proverb states that "a journey of a thousand miles begins with but a single step." When confronted with the idea of making a presentation, you may have no idea where to begin. Like a journey of a thousand miles, a presentation also begins with a single step.

You already have learned that many of your daily communication activities are accomplished through a series of steps or processes. Just as there is a process for giving and receiving information and a process for listening, there is also a process for preparing an oral presentation.

Whether you are Jimmy Carter, former president of the United States, or a student giving a speech for the first time, one thing remains constant: Process is important to preparing for a presentation. What is the first step in the presentation process?

UNDERSTAND THE PROCESS

When considering the steps involved in organizing an effective presentation, it may be helpful to think of the process in reverse. In other words, before you can give a presentation, you need to plan and organize it. Before you can plan and organize it, you need to research it. Finally, before you can research a presentation, you determine and organize a topic and a purpose.

By approaching presentations in a step-by-step way, you focus on one part of the presentation at a time. You have time to pay attention to the details that inexperienced or untrained presenters may overlook. If you become confused, you can go back a step to clarify the choices you have made so far. The result can be a presentation that is clear and to the point and accomplishes its task. An added benefit is that you can approach a presentation knowing that you are fully prepared. If you are well prepared, you may experience less communication apprehension.

Preparing for a presentation involves nine basic steps, as shown in Figure 14–3. The first four of these steps are covered in this chapter. The remaining steps will be explained in Chapters 15 through 18.

Figure 14–3 Steps of the Presentation Preparation Process

1. Determine a topic.
2. Limit the topic.
3. Determine the purpose.
4. Research the topic.

5. Organize and outline the presentation.
6. Select supporting information.
7. Prepare notes and manuscript for delivery.
8. Rehearse the presentation.

Determine a Topic

The first step in the preparation process is to determine a general topic for your presentation. As you read in Section 1, your topic should be one in which you are interested and qualified to speak. It also should be a topic that is relevant to the audience. In addition, it should be suitable for the occasion and meet the requirements for your task.

Many speakers in professional and social contexts have their topic chosen for them. Former President Jimmy Carter is often asked to speak about his experiences during the Mid-East Peace Accords. An employee may be

Communication Practice Lab

Determining a Presentation Topic

To practice determining a presentation topic, follow these steps:

Step 1 Brainstorm a list of topics about which you are qualified to speak or interested in presenting. Your list might include classes, sports, jobs, relationships, or personal experiences.

Step 2 Beside each item on your list, jot down why you are interested in the topic. What qualifies you to speak on that topic? Is it experience, interest, or something else?

Step 3 Exchange lists with a partner. One-on-one, explain your qualifications and knowledge of each topic.

Step 4 Have your partner draw a check mark next to each topic you appear qualified to present.

Step 5 Switch roles and repeat steps 3 and 4.

asked to update a supervisor on the project he or she is working on. The captain of the football team may be asked to speak about the team. In short, individuals usually are asked to speak on a topic because of who they are, what they do in the workplace or community, or what they know about the topic.

Other times, however, you are responsible for choosing your own topic. In these instances, speak about what you know. You will make the best presentations about topics with which you are personally involved in some way. You have a commitment to the topic. Therefore, the first consideration for selecting a topic is for the topic to suit the speaker: YOU!

Limit the Topic

Once you know the general topic for your presentation, consider how you can focus it for your specific audience, occasion, and task. When you limit a topic, you narrow it to a specific aspect of the general topic. Limiting the topic will help the audience follow, understand, and remember what you have to say.

Apply Your Analyses to Narrow the Topic

Before you began preparing your presentation, you analyzed the specific audience, occasion, and task. As shown in Figure 14–4, these analyses will help you focus your topic.

Analyzing the Audience The more you know about an audience, the more directly your presentation can relate to it. For example, when presenting a company's policy on summer hours, a presenter might narrow the topic by referring to benefits that employees might not have considered. Explaining how different options might benefit different workers, such as part-time staff and working parents, can also help the presenter relate directly to the audience.

Analyzing the Occasion Similarly, the more you understand about the occasion for your presentation, the better you can prepare for what your audience expects. Analyzing the occasion can help you avoid situations like the one encountered by a recent group of premed students. The group was scheduled to speak at a local luncheon meeting just before lunch was served. Unfortunately, the group's presentation about the importance of donating organs included

When preparing a presentation, it is always a good idea to consider the occasion in relation to your topic. **What else should the speaker analyze before preparing for a presentation?**

Figure 14–4 Narrowing a Topic

Limited Topic	Category
Campus and plans for expansion	Places
History of college and academic traditions	Events
Faculty members and their academic reputations	People
Improved admissions procedures	Processes
University's position on academic integrity and ethics	Policies

a very graphic explanation of how donated organs are harvested. Needless to say, few audience members felt much like eating at the conclusion of the presentation. These students did not do a good job of limiting their topic for the occasion of the presentation.

Analyzing the Task

Another important factor is your analysis of the task that you want to accomplish. Imagine that you have been asked to be the keynote speaker at a picnic to kick off a community fund-raising drive. The audience includes many people who have taken time off from work to attend. The picnic is held on a warm day in May in a park with little shade. After speaking for almost an hour about your personal political views, you begin to wonder why people are walking away from your presentation.

This problem could have been avoided with a better analysis of the context of the presentation. Given the warmth of the afternoon sun, the audience's time considerations, and the reason for the presentation, you might have made wiser choices. Your keynote address should have been brief, focused on community spirit, and intent on building support for the cause.

Classify the Topic

If, after considering the audience, occasion, and task for your presentation, you still are not sure about how to limit a topic, try classifying it. Almost any topic fits into one of the following categories:

- people
- places
- things
- events
- problems
- processes
- policies
- concepts

Think about a college president who has been asked to give a ten-minute presentation on the state of the school. The presentation might focus on the campus and plans for expansion, the history of the college and its academic traditions, the faculty members and their academic reputations, improved admissions procedures, or the university's position on academic integrity and ethics. To help determine these potential topics' classifications, you might create a classification chart like the one shown here.

Once you have classified the various aspects of a topic, consider which best fit you, your audience, the occasion, and the task. Develop your presentation about one of these limited aspects of the overall topic.

Survey the Availability of Information

Another consideration when focusing your topic is how much information is available. A presenter's responsibilities include being well informed about a topic. No matter how good a topic may seem, if little information is available to the presenter, the presentation is likely to suffer.

How do you determine whether enough information is available to make an effective presentation? Do a quick survey in the local library to see what information you can find in its books and magazines. Also, enter keywords about your topic in a search engine on the Internet. This quick survey can help you assess the amount of information that is readily available. It also may help you discover different aspects of your topic that you might not have considered previously.

Once you have limited your topic to the one aspect that is most appropriate and acceptable to your audience on this specific occasion, you are ready to move on to the next step in the process. Now you can begin to consider the purpose of your presentation.

Determine the Purpose

You have looked at the various elements of your task, considering length, nature, formality, and overall purpose. Now you need to determine the specific purpose you will try to accomplish in the presentation. Most professional presentations have one of the following purposes: to inform, to persuade, or to motivate.

Purpose: Informative Presentation

An **informative presentation** conveys ideas and information in a clear, accurate, and objective manner to gain the audience's interest. When you give an informative presentation, you assume the role of a teacher or newscaster. Your goal is to increase your audience's knowledge by providing them with new information. Informative presentations convey information that is

- easy to understand
- accurate
- interesting
- relevant
- objective and without bias

Many different situations call for informative presentations. When an employee gives a status report on a current project, his or her purpose is to inform. Similarly, when someone explains how to use a specific piece of equipment, or when your teacher introduces new material in class, he or she is making an informative presentation.

Purpose: Persuasive Presentation

A **persuasive presentation** attempts to get an audience to voluntarily change its thoughts, beliefs, or actions on a topic. Just as

Television newscasters give informative presentations every time they relay the news to their viewers. ***What is the main goal of an informative presentation?***

in an informative presentation, the presenter should provide thorough information to support his or her message. However, in a persuasive presentation, the speaker then attempts to convince the audience to take some action based on the information provided during the presentation.

The difference between informing and persuading an audience is the difference between explaining an idea and encouraging others to support it. Persuasive presentations urge one or more of the following:

- acceptance of facts, values, or ideas
- action
- changes in attitude or behavior

A persuasive presentation may urge an audience to vote for a specific issue or contribute to a specific cause. A speaker may try to persuade an audience to accept his or her viewpoint or values about something. Candidates for political office, for example, give persuasive presentations so voters will be inclined to vote for them. A presenter's goal also may be to change audience members' attitudes on a topic. For example, someone might give a presentation to convince people that soccer has replaced baseball as America's favorite sport.

Many of the everyday presentations that you hear from salespeople, politicians, friends, and family members are persuasive presentations. When someone tries to influence your

TECHNOLOGY *Activity*

Persuasion and Context Technology is responsible for many of the messages we receive each day. Consider the following channels of communication and determine the effectiveness of each in persuading you to join a health club: a funny television ad, an enthusiastic telephone solicitor, a direct mail ad, a door-to-door sales rep, an Internet ad, voice mail from a friend, a magazine ad, a colorful billboard, and a sales representative who speaks to your class. Think about what motivates you to pay attention to various forms of persuasive messages. How can you incorporate those strategies into your oral presentations?

COMMUNICATION PRACTICE LAB

Recognizing Persuasive Presentations

To practice recognizing the characteristics of persuasive presentations, follow these steps:

Step 1 As a class, separate into three groups.

Step 2 Divide the following categories among the groups so that each group has a different category:

- acceptance of facts, values, or ideas
- action
- changes in attitude or behavior

Step 3 Brainstorm a list of at least ten persuasive topics based on your group's chosen category. Choose a volunteer or volunteers to write down the topics as they are suggested.

Step 4 Share your lists as a class. Discuss the types of information that would be needed to give a persuasive presentation on these topics. Which category might present the largest challenge for persuading an audience?

buying habits, asks you to donate to a specific cause, or convinces you that something is right or wrong, that person is giving a persuasive presentation.

Purpose: Motivational Presentation

A **motivational presentation** inspires or encourages an audience. Motivational presentations usually are more persuasive than informative. Although motivational and persuasive presentations may seem similar, motivational presenters tend to rely more on emotion than on information to make their point. These presentations are designed to directly affect the audience in some way. Motivational presentations encourage one or more of the following feelings:

- happiness
- confidence
- self-worth

Some examples of motivational presentations are speeches that encourage students to stay in school until they graduate or to volunteer in a community program. Others might include encouraging sales personnel to meet a monthly or yearly goal, giving players an emotional pep talk at half-time of

Motivational speakers use their presentations to inspire or encourage the audience. What is the difference between a motivational presentation and a persuasive presentation?

a football game, or providing a positive evaluation for a hard-working employee. Many motivational presentations focus on improving job performance or goal achievement.

Competent speakers determine the purpose for their presentation—to inform, persuade, or motivate an audience. These presenters then use their knowledge of the context—information about the content, audience, occasion, and task—to guide how they prepare for their presentations. Once they have determined the basics, they are ready to move on to the next step of the presentation process: research.

Section 2 Assessment

Visit the *Glencoe Communication Applications* Web site at **communicationapplications.glencoe.com** and click on **Self-Check and Study Guide 14.2** to review your understanding of the beginning of the presentation process.

Review Key Terms

1. Define each of the following terms and write it in a sentence: informative presentation, persuasive presentation, motivational presentation.

Check Understanding

2. What considerations should influence the selection and limitation of a topic?
3. Create five different limited topics from the general presentation topic "the environment." How would each limited topic be classified?
4. What is the main difference between informative presentations and persuasive presentations? Between informative presentations and motivational presentations?
5. **Apply** Imagine that at this year's graduation ceremony, the high school principal gives a speech encouraging young people to give back to their school. He or she suggests that students volunteer their time and money to organize and set up a scholarship fund for deserving students. What is the purpose of this presentation?

APPLICATION *Activity*

Choosing and Limiting a Topic List at least three topics on which you are qualified to speak. If you completed the Communication Practice Lab on page 451, refer to the list you created earlier. Next, choose one of the topics to use for a three-minute presentation to your class. Consider the context of your presentation and limit your topic appropriately. Then determine the purpose of the presentation. Finally, list some of the available resources for researching your topic. As a class, share your topics, your reasons for choosing them, and how you plan to gather information.

Section 3

Researching the Presentation Topic

GUIDE TO READING

Objectives

1. Recognize the importance of gathering and using accurate and complete information as a basis for making communication decisions.
2. Explain how to use surveys and questionnaires to secure information about a topic.
3. Determine appropriate sources of information for a presentation.
4. Analyze sources for qualifications, credibility, competence, and accuracy to support a presentation.

Terms to Learn

secondary source
primary source
sample

Think about the last time a speaker made a presentation and you really learned something valuable. How did you feel about the presenter and the information that was shared with you?

Effective communicators know that much of their communication success depends on the information they use. Reliable, current, unbiased, interesting information lays the foundation for an effective presentation.

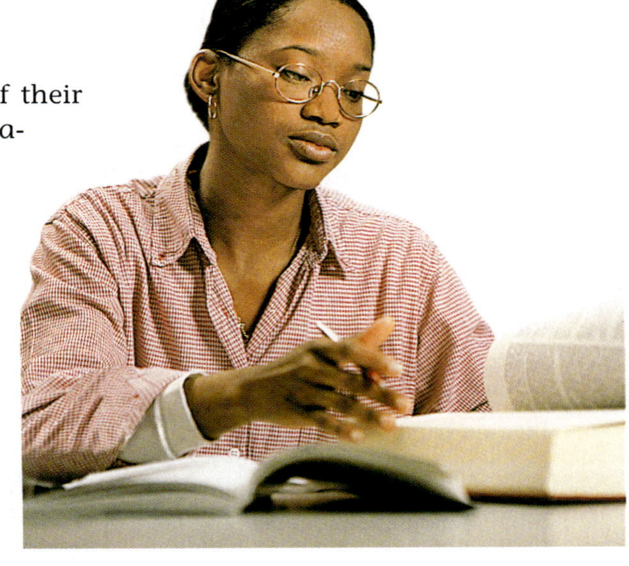

A well-informed presenter is one who has done research, like this student in the library. What provides the foundation for an effective presentation?

RESEARCH THE TOPIC

What information will you need for your presentation? One way to determine this is by reviewing the decisions and considerations you already have made. What do you know about your audience, occasion, and task to indicate the kinds of information you will need? What information will your audience expect you to know in order to make your point and to accomplish your purpose?

Communication Strategies

Questions to Guide Research

- What is the value of my topic to my audience and me? What do they want to know? What do I want to tell them?
- What is the most current information about my topic?
- What is unique or unusual about my topic?
- What is the background of my topic?
- Who are the people associated with my topic? What are their contributions and how much influence have they had? How has this topic affected them?
- To what other topics does my topic relate?
- What forces have contributed to or distracted from the development of my topic?
- What are the strengths and weaknesses of my topic?

After considering these questions, you may find that you know or have much of the information you need. Your responses to the questions in the Communication Strategies checklist should give you an idea of additional information you will need to gather.

Research is a process of discovery that is best approached with an open mind. Looking only for information that supports your ideas can cause you to overlook something important. It also can make you appear biased and, if you only choose to reveal certain facts, deceptive or unethical when questioned. An effective researcher looks for all kinds of information about his or her topic. You might discover a new or different aspect of your topic that you had not previously considered, or you might even discover that your initial ideas were flawed or incorrect. An effective presenter uses research as a tool to discover new ideas as well as to confirm old ones.

Locating Information

What is the first thing you usually do when you need to find information or conduct research for a specific project or class? Imagine that you want to buy a car. You might head to the library or log on to the Internet and look for information about the make, model, and year of the car. You might look for books, articles, and reports that other people have written about your topic. The information you get is from secondary sources.

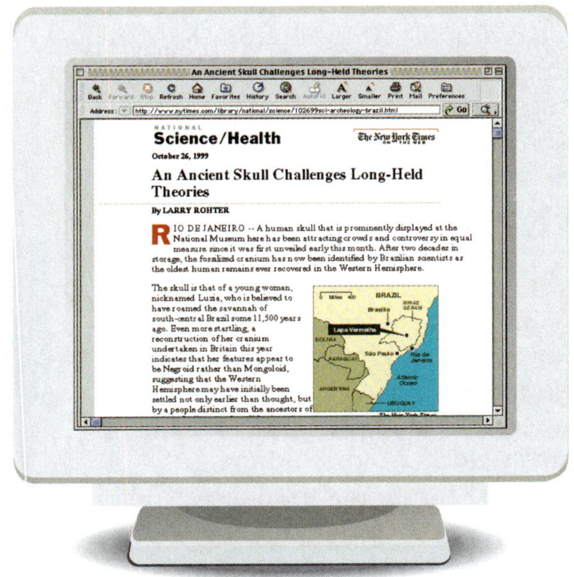

NATIONAL
Science/Health

The New York Times on the Web

October 26, 1999

An Ancient Skull Challenges Long-Held Theories

By LARRY ROHTER

RIO DE JANEIRO -- A human skull that is prominently displayed at the National Museum here has been attracting crowds and controversy in equal measure since it was first unveiled early this month. After two decades in storage, the fossilized cranium has now been identified by Brazilian scientists as the oldest human remains ever recovered in the Western Hemisphere.

The skull is that of a young woman, nicknamed Luzia, who is believed to have roamed the savannah of south-central Brazil some 11,500 years ago. Even more startling, a reconstruction of her cranium undertaken in Britain this year indicates that her features appear to be Negroid rather than Mongoloid, suggesting that the Western Hemisphere may have initially been settled not only earlier than thought, but by a people distinct from the ancestors of

Today's technology, such as the Internet, has made research more convenient. **Describe an effective researcher.**

Secondary Sources

A secondary source is an information source such as a book, periodical, radio or television program, or an Internet article that has been written by someone else about a particular topic. In essence, you are obtaining information on your topic secondhand. You are not speaking directly to the source or hearing his or her own words. You are not reading the source's autobiography. Instead, your information comes from someone else who is reporting on a subject he or she has researched.

Common Secondary Sources Books probably are the most commonly used secondary source. Books relating to your topic may not provide the most recent information, but they can provide you with extensive detail and often a historical perspective.

Most periodicals provide current information on a variety of subjects. Periodicals are publications such as magazines, newspapers, journals, or newsletters that are published at regular intervals. When researching issues related to the local community, local newspapers usually are available in the library and can provide valuable information. Many current and back issues of major newspapers published in large cities also are available in the library and on the Internet.

Secondary Sources at Work At work, you may be asked to research information for a report or presentation to be shared with a work group. Perhaps you need to use a summary of last year's sales figures found in your company's annual report. At work, informational reports and business documents, such as company handbooks or benefits information, are two other common types of secondary sources.

Secondary Sources Online The Internet can be thought of as the world's largest library. Figure 14–5 shows the number of online households in the United States. Using the Internet, you can read electronic versions of newspapers and magazines, visit world-famous art museums, get up-to-the-minute broadcast news updates, check activity on the stock market, and find out what tomorrow's weather will be like at home or halfway around the world.

Unlike your local library, however, there is no research librarian to help you locate specific information or evaluate it for accuracy and validity. Unfortunately, some of the information on the Internet comes from unreliable sources. In fact, one of the issues facing the Internet is the unregulated availability of information that may be inaccurate or harmful. As a competent communicator, it is your responsibility to verify any information you find online.

Figure 14–5 Going Online in the United States

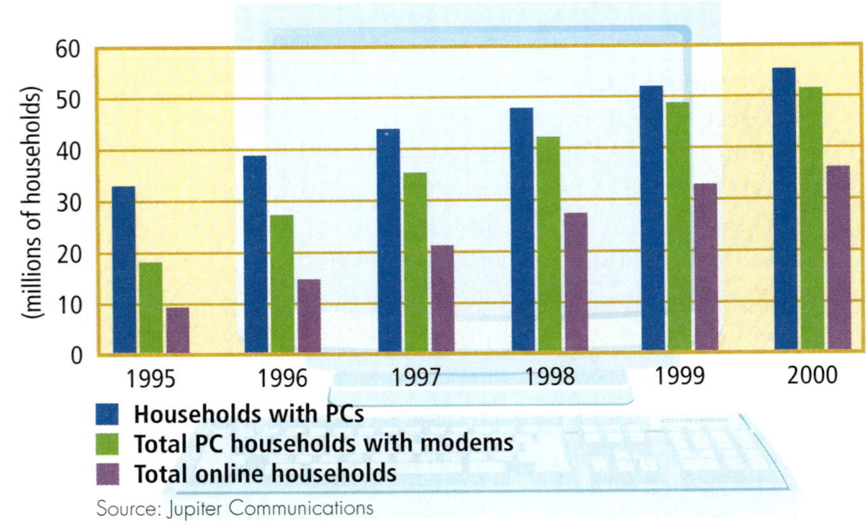

The World Wide Web The World Wide Web makes it much easier to locate information on the Internet. The World Wide Web, also known as WWW or the Web, is an easy-to-use interface to the Internet. Using the Web requires a personal computer with a modem and a software program called a "Web browser." Web browsers provide you with access to computerized indices called search engines. Search engines allow people to use keywords to locate information available from individual Internet sources called Web sites.

Some Web sites allow you to communicate with the originator of the Web site, the Webmaster, through e-mail. A Web site with linked e-mail can allow you to send and receive information on a topic, ask questions of experts on the subject, survey or poll selected populations for their opinions, and contact others to brainstorm new ideas.

RECORDING INFORMATION ACCURATELY

Procedure	Description
Copy the information exactly as it is written.	To do this, photocopy, print, or carefully recopy the information. It is important to reread each item as you write it down. This will help you avoid errors. Accidentally misquoting information is sloppy research and can mislead you and your audience. Intentionally misquoting a source is unethical. As you conduct your research, make sure you get all the facts and write them down precisely. It is your responsibility to accurately quote every source you use.
Include a complete source citation with each piece of information.	It is unethical to claim someone else's work or ideas as your own, so it is important to credit your sources. Include the name of the sources. Include the name of the author or other originator, the title of the quoted material, the title of the publication, the publisher, the city and date of publication, and the page number.
	For Internet sources, include the full Internet address, such as *www.communicationapplications.glencoe.com.* Write down the date you found the information, what search engine you used, the author and title of the information, and what keywords you used to locate these sources. This will help you and others verify your information. You also should note the date the Web site was last updated and who maintains the site. You might also want to print the information to save as a reference.
Note the author's qualifications.	This can help establish the source's credibility. You also can help establish the context of quoted material by citing the specific audience and occasion, such as: Quoted from a speech given by President Harry S. Truman to a joint session of the U.S. Congress, Washington, D.C., March 12, 1947.

Other Secondary Sources In addition to providing access to books, periodicals, and the Internet, libraries and media centers offer other secondary information sources. Many libraries also maintain vertical files of information about topics. Vertical files usually contain pamphlets and brochures about a topic, magazine or newspaper articles from little-known or non-indexed publications, and any other information that may relate to a topic. The information in these files generally is not listed in an index.

Documentary films and videos also can provide valuable information for projects and presentations. A librarian can be a valuable source for trying to locate much of the information in a library or media center. Often, a librarian can lead you to sources on your topic that you may not have realized were available. Your school library or media center may maintain various media resources for research purposes.

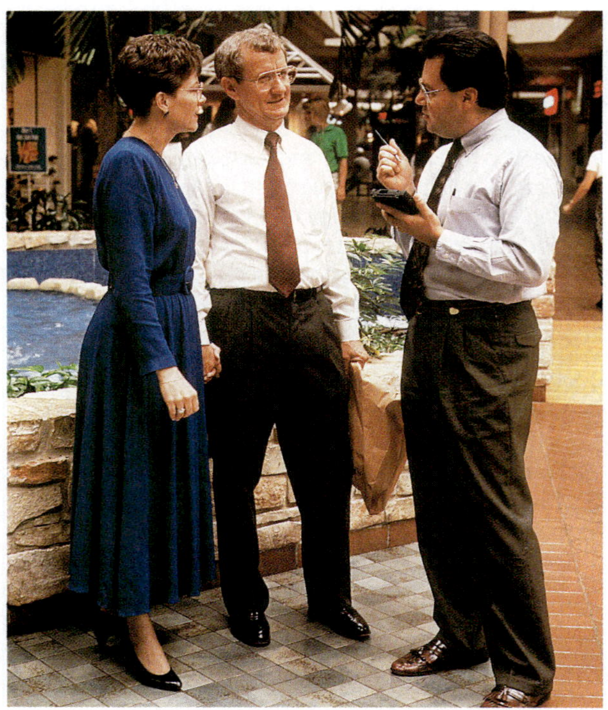

Interviews, such as this one in a mall, can be a form of primary research. **Besides interviews, what other primary sources allow the researcher to gather information personally?**

Organizing Secondary Information

As a researcher, it is important to develop a systematic method of organizing the information you find. Some researchers record their information on computer. Others use index cards or notebooks with different sections for the different types of information they find. Still others use file folders for each category of information. Regardless of which system you use, it is a good idea to follow these guidelines for accurately recording your information.

Following these guidelines will help you record your researched information so that it can be used in an ethical and responsible manner. It also will allow you to find the information again at a later date, if necessary.

Primary Sources

After searching secondary sources on your topic, you may discover that you can't locate some of the information you need or want for your presentation. You may need to talk to experts on your topic or ask people firsthand how they feel about a specific issue. This type of information comes from a primary source. A **primary source** is someone, including yourself, who has firsthand knowledge or experience regarding a topic. A quote from one of your favorite musical performers is a primary source. So is information a person tells you directly. However, once you read the musician's words in a magazine or hear a news story about the performer's musical style, this becomes secondary-source information.

Obtaining information from primary sources is referred to as primary research. Primary research also includes any personal experiences and insights that you may have with a topic. Primary research can provide important information for many different types of presentations. If you have knowledge of a topic, your audience's perception of your credibility is likely to increase. Information in books and magazines can easily become outdated. However, primary research provides the most up-to-date information available.

Some primary sources can be found in libraries or on the Internet. Diaries, journals, autobiographies, and film and video footage of actual events as they occurred provide a firsthand perspective of an event. Other primary sources, such as interviews, allow the researcher to personally gather information.

Interviews Interviews are an excellent way to gather information on a topic. In addition, interviewing a primary source—such as an expert—can help you better understand the information and the people involved.

Figure 14–6 Sample Questionnaire

CAFETERIA QUESTIONNAIRE

In an effort to better meet your menu preferences, the cafeteria staff would like your responses to the following questions. Your input will be considered when next semester's menus are being planned. Please place your completed questionnaire in the box at the end of your serving line. Thank you!

1. How many times each week do you eat in the cafeteria?
   ___ 0 ___ 1 ___ 2 ___ 3 ___ 4 ___ 5
2. What type of meal do you usually purchase?
   ___Full meal ___Sandwich ___À la carte
3. What is your favorite food served in the cafeteria?
   ____
4. What is your least favorite food served in the cafeteria?
   ____
5. What food would you like to have served that currently is not offered?
   ____
6. Would you prefer more fast food to be served in the cafeteria?
   ___ Yes ___ No ___ No opinion
7. Would you be willing to pay more for fast food than for a standard cafeteria meal?
   ___ Yes ___ No ___ No opinion
8. How would you rate the quality of the food served in the cafeteria?
   ___ Excellent ___ Good ___ Average ___ Poor
9. What is your grade level?
   ___ Freshman ___ Sophomore ___ Junior ___ Senior

So, when is an interview an appropriate source for your research? Consider your topic. Would direct statements or opinions from a primary source add clarity, interest, or credibility? If so, what information do you need, and who can provide it?

Once you have determined who is the best available resource, you can begin planning the actual interview. For information on conducting interviews for primary research, refer to Chapter 9, Communicating in Interviews.

Survey Research Groups and organizations often conduct surveys to determine the public's understanding, opinion, or knowledge of an issue. They may survey individuals by asking them questions one-on-one, or they may administer a written survey, known as a questionnaire.

Oral surveys and written questionnaires are good tools for obtaining local and regional information that may not be available anywhere else. Careful planning can help you design a survey or questionnaire to obtain the exact information you need. Just as with interviews, first determine the purpose of the survey or questionnaire and the type of information you are seeking before you get to work. Do you want to know what presidential candidate people support? How your coworkers feel about your company's new vacation policy? What team most of your classmates want to win the Super Bowl? Each of these questions can be answered through a survey or questionnaire.

Survey Questions Once you have determined the purpose of your survey or questionnaire, ask yourself what types of questions will result in the information you need. Most questions used on surveys and questionnaires are formulated to generate a specific type of response. Look at the variety of questions in Figure 14–6. Some of the questions ask the respondents for a specific response, while others ask them to respond freely. Notice that respondents have been given the choice of answering "No opinion" when asked to indicate their feelings. It is important to offer a neutral response choice to keep results accurate.

As a rule, people do not want to spend a lot of time responding to surveys or questionnaires. For this reason, limit questions to those absolutely necessary to get the desired information. Questions also should be phrased as objectively as possible to avoid leading respondents to answer a certain way.

Format of Questions Once you have determined the questions to ask, you must determine the format you wish to use. Will you use a person-on-the-street approach in which you ask the questions directly? If so, a survey may be the best format to use.

Prior to administering your survey, create a master list of questions, leaving space to record the responses you will receive. When administering the survey, be sure to ask the questions in the same sequence to each respondent. This will help you obtain consistent results. This is particularly important if more than one person will be administering the surveys.

Do you need more responses than are possible through a limited one-to-one survey? Perhaps a questionnaire is your best choice. Questionnaires can be distributed to many respondents at once, collected in an orderly manner, then tabulated at your convenience.

To begin, write down your questions in a logical sequence, make photocopies, and distribute the questionnaire to the number of people you want to poll. As an alternative, you may wish to create the questionnaire electronically and then e-mail it to respondents or allow them to answer it online. Be sure to tell respondents how much time they will have to answer. Then, at the end of that time, collect the completed questionnaires. As with a face-to-face survey, you will need a master list of questions or a master response form on which to tabulate the results.

Determining Whom to Poll How do you determine who will be the sample for your poll? Because it would be extremely expensive and time-consuming to survey everyone who has an opinion about a particular topic, researchers only poll specific samples. A **sample** is the set of people you select to respond to a survey or questionnaire. They represent a smaller segment of the larger population the researchers are unable to poll.

Demographics After they determine which segment of the population will provide the most useful information, researchers study demographics that identify where that group exists. Researchers then select a representative percentage of that population as the sample for their survey or questionnaire. Usually the larger the sample, the more accurate the results of a survey.

Practice for the Workplace

Market Research Manufacturers and advertisers often conduct market research to determine market needs and learn customer reactions to new products.

BUSINESS PRACTICE *Activity*

Assume that you want to introduce a new product to students in your school. In groups of four or five, brainstorm a fictitious product, then develop a market survey to determine whether this product would sell to students in your school. For the market survey, list the number of people you would sample and provide ten questions to poll your sample population. Share your group's survey with the remainder of the class. As a class, evaluate the relevance of each group's survey.

Figure 14–7 Demographic Representations

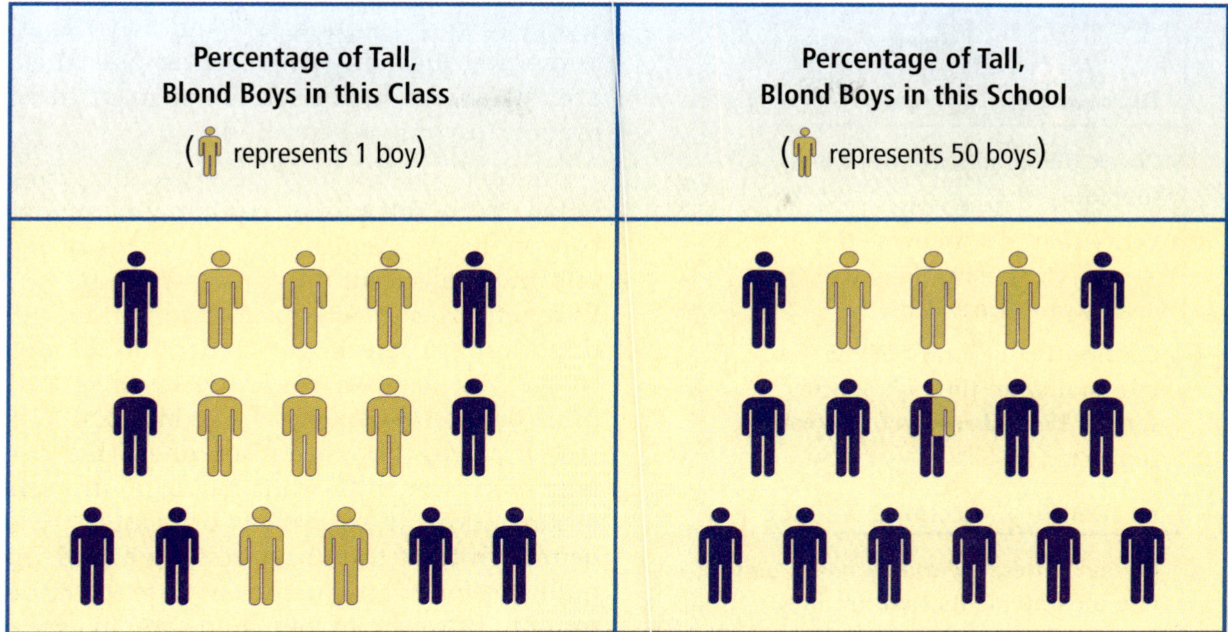

Percentages The relationship between the size of a sample and the size of a total chosen population indicates how accurate your conclusions may be. Look at the two representations in Figure 14–7. If eight of the sixteen boys in your class are tall with blond hair, would it be safe to assume that one-half of all boys in your high school are tall and blond? Probably not, because your sample is too small to reflect reality. However, if you sampled 20 percent of the student body of your school, you could probably make a credible prediction.

Analyzing Results Once you have administered your surveys or questionnaires, you will need to tally the results. Was the information what you expected? Was one response given more than the others? Could anything about the survey or questionnaire or the way it was administered have affected the results?

Evaluating Source Material

When you research a project or presentation, you owe it to your audience to use the most ethical information available. Even the best-prepared presentation or project can be a disaster if the information is outdated, misleading, or incorrect. How do you sort through primary and secondary sources to find out what information is accurate and what is not? How do you determine whether the books, periodicals, tapes, films, and memos you've found are credible? Can you confirm that the conclusions of the writer are his or her own and aren't plagiarized from other sources?

Source Qualifications

Just because a person writes and publishes a book or article on a topic does not mean he or she is a qualified source. Following a sensational

COMMUNICATION *Strategies*

Determining Reliable Sources

- Check the qualifications of your sources.
- Verify that your sources—the writers, the publications, and the details—are trustworthy.
- Confirm the accuracy of the information in through another source. Discard research you can't support.

Becoming a Reliable Source

- In your notes, accurately quote and cite all statements that are not your own.
- Reread your research and restate the information in your own words. Make sure you don't misquote, plagiarize, or twist facts to draw false conclusions.
- Check to make sure that you clearly state your point, document your information with reliable research, and summarize your conclusions. Revise your presentation as necessary.

trial, a natural disaster, or some other dramatic news event, publishers, broadcasters, and the Internet often are flooded with information from would-be experts. Many of these individuals have no firsthand knowledge of the event, but instead rely on newscasts, unreliable sources, or their own opinions for information.

On the other hand, some sources actually conduct interviews, investigate the event, and communicate with law enforcement and other agencies to acquire as much knowledge as possible. Of these two types of sources, who is qualified and who isn't? These are questions you need to ask whenever you want to include an item of information in your presentation.

Internet sources may be especially unreliable. With the proper equipment, anyone can publish a Web site and have his or her information—accurate or not—read by any Internet surfer. As with printed materials, it is important to check the credentials of any source you use. An easy way to check any print or Internet source is to conduct a Web search using the person's name. This can help you see with what publications and organizations the person is associated. As a general rule of thumb, if you can't find the qualifications of a source, don't use the information. However, to help guide you in evaluating the qualifications of a source, ask the following questions about the source:

- What is the author's education or training related to this topic?
- What is the author's experience with this subject?

Source Credibility

The credibility of a source is a reflection of how others perceive his or her honesty and reliability. Some sources may be very well qualified to speak or write on a subject but may not be credible because of their public perception. No matter how accurate they may be, an audience will not believe what they are saying. For example, a legislator who has consistently voted against conservation legislation may know a great deal about the environment. However, he or she probably will have little credibility with an environmental action group.

Credible sources take care not to mislead their audience. They acknowledge their bias and try to document their ideas as objectively as possible. They also may have firsthand experiences that elevate their credibility. They may be known for their attention to detail and for conducting in-depth research. Tabloid publications often are criticized for doing weak research and printing unconfirmed rumors as fact. Many other publications, however, enjoy good reputations for checking facts and confirming their sources.

As you evaluate your sources, keep in mind that some people who communicate on specific issues do so to promote a particular viewpoint. This does not make what that person says right or wrong; it simply means that you, as an ethical communicator, must recognize that the information reflects someone else's bias. Everyone is entitled to an opinion on a topic. In fact, including a variety of viewpoints can lead to interesting interaction and discussion.

However, some sources are so biased that they discount or completely disregard facts or opinions that disagree with their point of view. These sources lose credibility. Remember, opinions are not facts, no matter how well they are presented. To evaluate the credibility of a source, consider the answers to these questions.

- What is the professional reputation of this source?
- What is the personal reputation of this source?
- What is the known bias of this source? Does that bias affect the source's information?

Source Competence

When you assess the competence of a source, you are assessing the ability of the source to make a qualified observation or judgment about the topic. A lawyer may attack the competence of witnesses in a court case by asking a series of questions: Were the witnesses in a position to actually see the crime? Did they really see what they think they saw? Did the witnesses have any conditions that impaired their ability to make accurate observations? When you are reading research materials, ask the same kinds of questions to evaluate the competence of each source.

Relevance of Information

When developing presentations, communicators need to structure their ideas carefully so that it is clear how each idea relates to the others. It also is important for supporting information to relate to the claims or conclusions you make in your presentation.

Someone who is biased and unwilling to listen to another's point of view is not a credible source.
Describe a credible source.

Irrelevant ideas distract from the purpose of a presentation and can keep you from achieving your presentation goals. Sometimes, audience members may introduce irrelevant issues on purpose to throw a presentation off course. However, if a presenter is well prepared and focused, he or she usually can stop such interruptions and bring the presentation back to the topic at hand.

The best question to ask yourself to determine the relevancy of the information is "How does this idea really relate or apply to my topic?" If you have trouble determining a link, then the information probably is irrelevant to the topic and you don't need to include it in your presentation.

Timeliness of Information

Because the accuracy and completeness of information can change over time, you should use the most recent information available to research your topic. In addition to sources in libraries, many presenters find the Internet to be a good source for recent information because it can be continually updated.

When determining the timeliness of your information, ask yourself, "Have I located the most recent information available on this topic?" If you have, then your information is as timely as possible and can be used to support your presentation.

Evaluating Your Research

Once you have located and evaluated the information for your presentation, it is time to revisit some of the decisions you have already made. Using what you have discovered in your research, step back and look at everything you have gathered. Have you located sufficient information to support your initial thoughts or choices for your presentation? Have you verified your initial

COMMUNICATION PRACTICE LAB

Evaluating Sources

To practice gathering and analyzing sources, follow these steps:

Step 1 With a partner, choose a recent historical event to research.

Step 2 Have one person gather information on your topic using resources in your library. Have the other partner search the Internet for information on the same topic.

Step 3 Collect at least five sources per person, using the guidelines for recording accurate and complete information in the chart on page 461.

Step 4 Evaluate each source for accuracy and completeness. Identify the author, his or her related training or experience, and the quality of the information. Is the source outdated, misleading, or inaccurate?

Step 5 Exchange sources. Confirm each other's evaluations.

Step 6 On a separate sheet of paper, list the facts that appear in two or more of the sources.

Step 7 Present your findings to the remainder of the class. Why is it important to use accurate and complete information when making communication decisions?

choices or discovered new information that requires you to rethink things? If so, now is the time to change the focus of your topic or the purpose of your presentation. You will want to do this before you have a great deal of time invested in the preparation of the presentation itself. However, remember that the changes you make still must fit the needs of your audience, occasion, and task as well as your own needs.

Researching a presentation is a task that lasts throughout the preparation process. As you complete each step, you need to reevaluate the communication choices you have already made. When you make additional choices about other steps in the process, you will need to conduct research to support those choices. Your time will be well spent, however, leading to a well-thought-out presentation supported by accurate and complete research.

Section 3 Assessment

Visit the *Glencoe Communication Applications* Web site at **communicationapplications.glencoe.com** and click on **Self-Check and Study Guide 14.3** to review your understanding of research.

Review Key Terms

1. Define the following terms and write each in a sentence: secondary source, primary source, sample.

Check Understanding

2. Why is it important to gather and use complete information when researching a presentation?
3. Compare the advantages of spoken surveys to written surveys, or questionnaires.
4. What should you consider when determining what information sources are appropriate for a presentation?
5. **Compare and Contrast** What is the difference between a source's qualifications and its credibility? Why are both important?

APPLICATION *Activity*

Comparing Primary and Secondary Sources Using secondary sources in your school or local libraries, find at least two references to teenagers' use of the Internet. Read the sources. On a sheet of paper make a list of the criteria evaluating the information you read. Assess your sources against the criteria.

Next, work with your classmates to create a questionnaire about the Internet to distribute in your school. Find out who uses the Internet, how often, and why. Collect and tabulate your data.

As a class, compare the information you gathered from your secondary sources to what you learned through primary research. What conclusions can you draw?

Technology Skill

Researching on the World Wide Web

The amazing growth of the World Wide Web has led to an explosion of information. To research the Web most effectively, it is important to learn how to use a search engine.

Learning the Skill

To begin researching on the Web, first select a search engine. On the search engine's home page, you will find a query box into which you can type words. In this box, type one or more words or a question that describes the type of information you are seeking. These are known as the keywords for your search.

When typing keywords, make them as specific to your research topic as possible. For example, to find information on becoming a biologist, you might use keywords such as *biologist, biology careers,* or *How do I become a biologist?* To further narrow your search, you can sometimes add more specific words or put quotation marks around your entry.

Once you have entered your keywords, click on the search button beside the query box. The results of your search appear, listed in order from the most accurate to the least accurate match. To investigate a search result, simply click on its title or Web address. This takes you directly to that Web site and instantly connects you to the world of information available on the Web.

Practicing the Skill

Imagine that you need to give a presentation on how to start a small business. Follow these steps to research your topic.

Step 1 Log on to the Internet.

Step 2 Choose a search engine by typing its address in the **Address**, **Location**, or **Go To** box. Press **Enter.**

Step 3 Search by typing the keywords *small business.* Press **Enter.**

Step 4 Look at the number of results. Were there hundreds? Thousands? Scroll down the list to view some of the results.

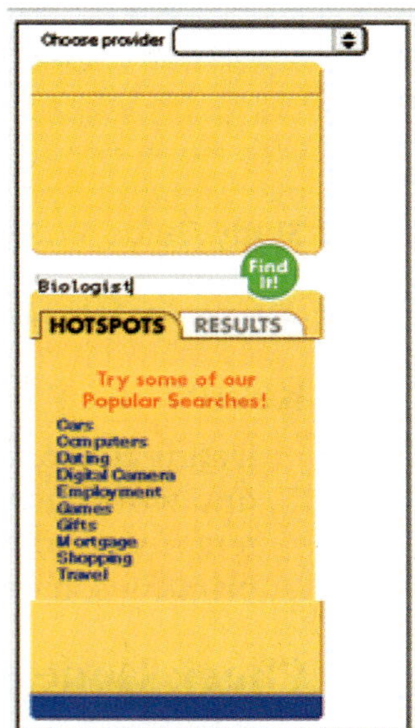

Step 5 Narrow your search by changing your keywords to *"starting a small business"* or by typing the query *"How do I start a small business?"*

Step 6 Look at the number of results now. Did you narrow your results? Click on a selection to begin your research!

APPLICATION *Activity*

Use a search engine to learn about finding a job in a field that interests you. Write a one-page essay describing the information you found in your research. Deliver your essay orally to the class.

Communication Self-Assessment

Analyzing Your Presentation Preparation Skills

How Do You Rate?

On a separate sheet of paper, respond to the following statements. Put a check mark beside each skill you would like to improve.

KEY: **A** Always, **U** Usually, **S** Sometimes, **R** Rarely, **N** Never

1. I consider the amount of information available before I choose a professional presentation topic.
2. I try to speak only about topics that I know best.
3. Even if I know a topic well, I still research it thoroughly to find the latest information and to validate what I already know.
4. I analyze the information I gather and discard any that is not factual, credible, and verifiable.
5. I try to ask objective questions when conducting a survey.
6. Whenever possible, I conduct primary research to gather information.
7. I choose samples that accurately represent an overall population.
8. I work at all four aspects of being a good presenter: knowledge, character, good intentions, and genuineness.
9. I try to develop basic speaking skills so that I will be considered a competent presenter.
10. I choose effective language appropriate for the presentation topic, occasion, and audience.

How Do You Score?

Review your responses. Give yourself 5 points for every A, 4 for every U, 3 for every S, 2 for every R, and 1 for every N. Total your points and evaluate your score.

41–50 Excellent You may be surprised to find out how much you can improve your skills.

31–40 Good In this course, you can learn ways to make your skills better.

21–30 Fair Practice applying the skills taught in this course.

1–20 Needs Improvement Carefully monitor your improvement as you work through this course.

Setting Communication Goals

If you scored Excellent or Good, complete Part A. If your score was Fair or Needs Improvement, complete Part B.

Part A

1. I plan to put the following ideas into practice:
2. I plan to share the following information about communication with the following people:

Part B

1. The behaviors I need to change most are:
2. To bring about these changes, I will take these steps:

Writing an Inquiry

Have you ever written an inquiry? An inquiry simply is a request for information. If you have sent a letter, e-mail, fax, or memo requesting information from someone, you have written an inquiry.

Because inquiries help you learn more about a subject, they are an important part of day-to-day research. You might use an inquiry to gather information for a project or presentation, to find out about a product or service, or to test the marketability of a product.

Determine Your Objectives and Purpose. Before writing an inquiry, it is important to understand exactly what you need to know and why. One way to clarify this is to write a purpose statement and objectives. A purpose statement concisely states what information you need. Objectives are the goals you hope to achieve with that information. A purpose statement and objectives provide direction for your inquiry.

Write Your Letter of Inquiry. Sometimes, it is difficult to find a source for the information you need. Other times, however, the amount of available information can be overwhelming. In these instances, it is important to narrow your research to only those sources that will be most helpful.

Begin your communication with a brief paragraph stating the purpose of the inquiry. Base this paragraph on your purpose statement.

In the second paragraph, address your objectives. It is important to make your request as clear as possible. Never assume that the reader will infer what you need to know.

Use a proper business-letter format for your inquiry. Be courteous, brief, and reasonable in your request. Remember, you are asking the reader for a favor: to provide you with information. If you are asking to meet with the person for a personal interview, suggest some possible dates, but remain flexible.

Finally, be sure to include your phone number and e-mail address, if applicable. Also, if you need the information by a certain date, politely mention this in your closing paragraph.

By following these few basic rules, you will be more likely to receive a positive response to your inquiry. Then you will have mastered another important skill for communicating in social and business contexts.

For additional information about business writing, see the *Guide to Business Communication* section of the Communication Survival Kit in the Appendix.

Communication Through Writing

The following letter is an example of an effective inquiry.

1351 High Street
Hometown, USA 76543

March 26, 2003

Ms. Jonna Butler
Butler Research Associates
1395 Central Road
Corpus Christi, Texas 78350

Dear Ms. Butler:

I am writing to inquire whether your research company does marketing research studies for small insurance firms. Star Financial Group is a market leader in insurance sales, ready to expand its business even further.

The research we are seeking would help us increase our sales of life insurance to more customers in the 35–50 age group. Although sales are strong in that area, we want to pinpoint new geographic areas in which to expand our efforts. We also would like to explore the demand for college savings plans. Would your firm be able to supply us with research in these areas?

I am anxious to hear how Butler Research Associates might be able to meet our needs. Please contact me at your earliest convenience. My phone number is 817-555-3232. Thank you for your time and attention.

Sincerely,

Reuben Garza

Reuben Garza
Marketing Director
Star Financial Group

WRITING *Activity*

Use the following steps to write an effective letter of inquiry.

- Think of a U.S. city that you might like to visit. Use the Internet or another source to research the address of that city's travel and tourism bureau or chamber of commerce.
- You will write an inquiry to this organization requesting information about hotel accommodations for an upcoming vacation. Determine a date for your trip and decide on a preferred price range for your accommodations: budget, mid-range, or luxury.
- Use this information to write a purpose statement and objectives for your letter.
- Write your letter. Begin by explaining the purpose of your inquiry.
- Request the exact information you need to meet your objectives. Provide any details the reader will need to know.
- Provide your own phone number, and e-mail address, if applicable.
- Suggest a possible response time.
- Thank the reader for his or her help.
- Write a business-style closing. Print and sign your letter.

Discuss all letters as a class. Did you discover ways to make your request clearer? Edit your letter to make it as reader-friendly as possible.

CHAPTER 14 Assessment and Activities

Visit the *Glencoe Communication Applications* Web site at **communicationapplications.glencoe.com** and click on **Chapter 14 Activity** for additional practice in preparing to make presentations.

Reviewing Key Terms

Number a sheet of paper from 1 to 10. Beside each number, write the letter of the vocabulary term that best fits that example.

1. a demonstration of how to use a printer
2. a group of shoppers responding to a mall survey
3. a review of a new best-seller
4. a pep talk to a company's sales force
5. a brief explanation of budget concerns to a small group of coworkers
6. an interview with a war veteran
7. the image projected by a respected newscaster
8. female college graduates, age 25–45, who are registered democrats
9. a campaign speech
10. a multimedia presentation to a group of computer professionals

a. ethos
b. primary source
c. formal presentation
d. persuasive presentation
e. demographics
f. informative presentation
g. professional presentation
h. motivational presentation
i. informal presentation
j. sample

Reviewing Key Concepts

On a separate sheet of paper, answer the following questions in complete sentences.

1. Describe the characteristics of a presenter who has a positive ethos.
2. How does a presenter decide on the style of language to use in a presentation?
3. What type of information is conveyed in a successful informative presentation?
4. Why might a presenter skip the steps of selecting and limiting a topic?
5. Name three types of secondary resources. Name three types of primary resources.

Assessment and Activities

Reading and Critical Thinking Skill

1. **Inferring** Imagine you are presenting information on current fashion trends to a group of teens. How might you vary your presentation for the teens' parents?
2. **Evaluating** What are three questions you might use to evaluate whether someone has met his or her responsibilities as a presenter?
3. **Predicting** If a presenter appears to be very knowledgeable about his or her topic, how might it affect the audience at an informational presentation? A persuasive presentation? A motivational presentation?

Skill Practice Activity

Writing an Inquiry Imagine that you are in charge of reserving a meeting place for your company's annual awards banquet. This formal dinner meeting will take place on December 12 from 7 to 10 P.M., and sixty people will attend. Write a letter to a local hotel or convention center seeking information about appropriate meeting accommodations. Address your letter to the group sales manager or event planner. Create a purpose statement and objectives based on the questions you will need to ask. Then, use your purpose and objectives as a guideline for your letter.

Cooperative Learning Activity

Choosing a Sample Working in a group of three or four students, determine a survey topic related to teens and automobiles. What group of teens is represented by your topic? All teens everywhere? Only U.S. teens? Only males or females of a specific age? With this in mind, work with your group to choose a representative sample for your survey. Give a three-minute presentation explaining the accuracy of your survey sample and a realistic plan for surveying these individuals.

Chapter Project

Planning Using library resources and the Internet, locate secondary information on the topic of school uniforms. Evaluate the information in at least five of the sources you find. Take careful notes on the information that you decide is credible.

Create a class list of questions to ask your principal about a school-uniform policy. Create another list of questions to survey students, teachers, and parents about your topic. In groups of five or six, administer the surveys.

Presenting After compiling the survey results, each group should present its information to the class and answer these questions: What did your group learn from its survey? What did your group enjoy most about the research process? What would your group do differently next time?

CHAPTER 15

Organizing Presentations

WHY IT'S IMPORTANT

The key to delivering a well-organized presentation lies in taking the time to understand the parts of your presentation and putting them together in the most effective way.

To better understand how to organize an effective presentation, view the **Communication in Action** Chapter 15 video lesson.

GLENCOE Online

Visit the *Glencoe Communication Applications* Web site at **communicationapplications.glencoe.com** and click on **Overview–Chapter 15** to preview information about organizing presentations.

"Begin at the beginning and go on till you come to the end; then stop."

—The King, Lewis Carroll's *Alice in Wonderland*

Section 1

Parts of a Presentation

GUIDE TO READING

Objectives

1. Identify the five purposes of an introduction.
2. Apply effective methods for getting an audience's attention.
3. Develop clear thesis statements.
4. Explain three reasons for audience orientation.
5. Identify and explain the three purposes of a conclusion.

Terms to Learn

attention device
thesis statement
audience orientation

Have you ever sat through a presentation wondering when the speaker would get to the point? Have you left a presentation confused—not knowing what the speaker was trying to say? You may have even questioned whether or not the speaker really knew what he or she was talking about.

In all of these cases, it probably was the lack of organization that left you confused and questioning the credibility of the speaker. Disorganized presentations are usually ineffective. Once a presenter has determined the specific topic and purpose for a presentation and has gathered sufficient information, he or she should consider how to organize and outline it, or put it together effectively—the fifth step in the presentation preparation process, as shown in **Figure 15–1** on the next page.

Competent communicators want to give presentations that their audiences can follow, understand, and remember. A well-organized presentation, therefore, is clear and simple to understand; has a limited number of main ideas; and flows logically from point to point.

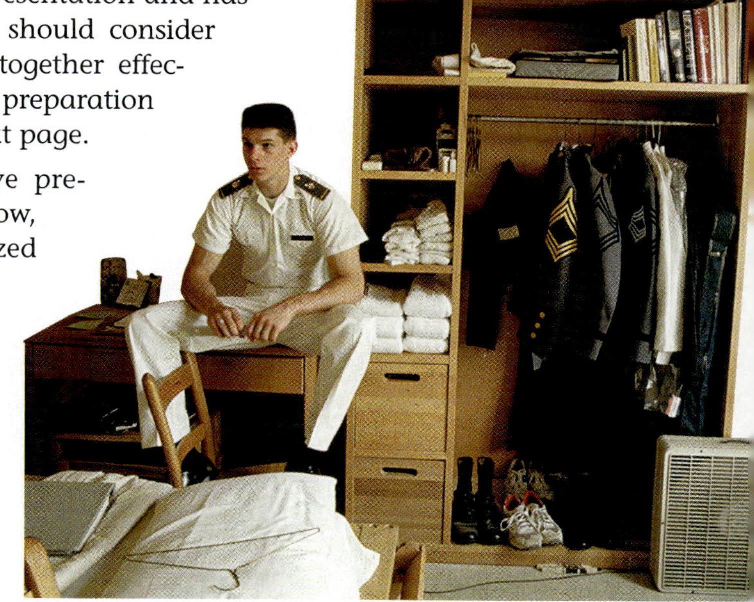

An effective presenter must exhibit organization in a presentation much like military personnel must organize their belongings in a small space. Describe a well-organized presentation.

Figure 15–1 Steps of the Presentation Preparation Process

1. Determine a topic.
2. Limit the topic.
3. Determine the purpose.
4. Research the topic.
5. Organize and outline the presentation.
6. Select supporting information.
7. Prepare notes and manuscript for delivery.
8. Rehearse the presentation.

Most presentations consist of three main elements:

- introduction
- body
- conclusion

By carefully structuring these elements, the speaker makes it easier for the audience to understand the ideas.

Simply knowing the parts of a presentation, however, doesn't necessarily result in an effective presentation. A presenter also needs to understand the purpose of each part of a presentation, the strategies to use in preparing each part, and how to relate it to the other parts of the presentation.

The Introduction

It is often said that first impressions are the most important. This is especially true for presentations. Therefore, you should devote the first 5 to 10 percent of your presentation time to the introduction.

During this brief period, you can play an important role in determining how your audience will receive your presentation. An audience who is turned off will be hard to win back. In the same way, an audience that has been grabbed by an interesting beginning, knows what to expect, is in the right frame of mind, and believes in your credibility will be attentive throughout your presentation.

The introduction of a presentation has five purposes. It serves to

- get the audience's attention
- state the thesis
- establish your ethos as a speaker
- orient the audience
- preview the main points

Get the Audience's Attention

By introducing your presentation, you have an opportunity to grab your audience's attention before getting to the important information of your topic. Audience members tend

This audience member has just lost interest in the presentation and is now considering what is on the menu. How can you prevent loss of attention during your own presentation?

"I wonder what they are serving during the break. . . ."

AUDIENCE ATTENTION DEVICES

Attention Device	Sample Main Topic
Humor	Commitment to this month's sales goal Many people enjoy steak and eggs for breakfast, but have you ever thought about the roles of the steer and the chicken in that breakfast? Yes, the chicken was involved, but the steer was definitely committed to feeding us!
Quotations	United States space program Space—the final frontier. These are the voyages of the *Starship Enterprise.* Its five-year mission: To explore new worlds. To seek out life and new civilizations. To boldly go where no man has gone before.
Personal Experiences	Importance of extracurricular activities As a member of my high school drum corp, I developed some of my closest relationships. In fact, two of the guys who were in corp with me later became groomsmen in my wedding.
References to the Occasion, Audience, or Topic	Need for additional funds for science equipment at your school I would like to thank the members of the school board for allowing me to be with you this evening.
Rhetorical Questions	Internet addiction Do you surf the Web for hours on end? Do you spend more time scanning bulletin boards in cyberspace than reading books for your classes? Are you more connected emotionally with people in your chat groups than with friends or family members?—If so, you may be part of that growing portion of the population whom psychologists identify as Internet addicts.
Startling Statements	Importance of arts programs in public schools Ricardo seems like an average six-year-old boy. He loves to play soccer and ride his bike with his brother. He is also a gifted pianist and was recently invited to play at Carnegie Hall.
Stories	Need for handicap-accessible playground equipment at a neighborhood park Picture a warm spring day. Young children are enjoying the playground at Prestonwood Park. The laughter is contagious; the smiles on their faces beam. Elizabeth is a four-year-old who comes to the park nearly every day. She loves to swing. She sees other children who are running and playing. Elizabeth can't run. She is physically challenged and is in a wheelchair. There is no equipment in the park for Elizabeth.

to have little mental patience. If you fail to gain their attention within the first few moments of your speech, their minds will quickly wander.

Attention Device How do you compete with whatever is already on their minds—sports practice, family issues, lunch? You can easily and appropriately demand their attention by using attention devices. An **attention device** is a tool used by speakers to grab the interest of an audience. Seven popular attention devices are

- humor
- quotations
- stories
- references to the occasion, audience, or topic
- rhetorical questions
- startling statements
- personal experiences

Choosing an Attention Device The attention device you choose will depend largely on your topic, your audience, and on the mood you want to set for your presentation. You probably would not want to begin a speech about an American war with a joke. Choosing an appropriate attention device will engage your audience and get it ready for the presentation you have prepared.

You may choose to follow the example of the following speaker. By asking audience members to picture a specific scene, this speaker places them directly in the action.

> *I want you to imagine this scene: It's a damp morning during the Christmas season in London. The city awakes to see streets swirling in a thick gray mist. But this is no ordinary London fog. As the clouds roll through the streets and seep into the houses, men, women, and children are gasping for breath. Within hours, hospital emergency rooms are crammed with people complaining of stinging lungs. When the fog finally lifts five days later, thousands are dead.*

By using a story, you can immediately get the audience involved in a topic that otherwise might have seemed abstract to them. If you use a true story, you can achieve further startling impact by pointing out that the scene actually occurred. This specific story also establishes a serious tone for the presentation.

Getting the audience's attention is just the first step in the introduction of a presentation. However, if you fail to grab the audience's interest, the rest of your introduction might just as well be your conclusion.

An audience member may have pictured this scene of London on a foggy morning as a result of the presenter's attention device. What factors must one consider when choosing an attention device?

State Your Thesis

A thesis statement is a clearly written, simple sentence or question that states the point you expect to make in your presentation. The thesis statement lets an audience know from the beginning the one thing you expect them to get from your presentation. So, how do you determine your thesis? If you only had the time to say one sentence to your audience, what would it be? The answer is your thesis statement. Examples of clear thesis statements include the following:

- Employees will be able to select new health plan options next month.
- How can the band raise money to participate in the upcoming music festival?
- A new photocopy machine would be a wise investment.

This single statement or question will guide your entire presentation.

Establish Your Ethos as a Speaker

An introduction also provides the opportunity for the presenter to introduce him- or herself to the audience. During the introduction, the presenter begins to establish credibility and genuineness as well as a common bond with the audience.

In establishing your ethos, you may wish to provide information about yourself, your specific expertise, or the research you have done on the topic. For example, if you are reporting the results of a recent walkathon to your local school board, it would be important to state that you were the chairperson of the fund-raiser. If you were a doctor speaking on the future of medical research, you could establish a positive ethos by mentioning your years of work in that field. Whatever your experience or expertise, be sure to share it with your audience. Be careful, however, not to brag. Simply state what you have done to gain the knowledge to be able to speak on your chosen topic.

Not all speakers need to share their expertise or background. Well-known speakers, for example, often are introduced to the audience by another person. However, these speakers may still have to build an ethos or convince the audience of their sincerity. Showing the audience that you are not only qualified to speak on a subject but also excited to do so will help you create a positive image as a speaker.

Orient the Audience

After hearing your thesis statement and establishing your ethos, you may need to include an audience orientation. An **audience orientation** provides audience members with information they likely do not already have but will need in order to understand a presentation. Not all presentations require this sort of audience preparation. A quick analysis of your audience will help you determine whether or not to provide an orientation. For more on audience analysis, you may wish to refer to Chapter 14.

In determining if an orientation is necessary, there are several different audience needs to consider. The three main types of audience orientations are

- definition
- background information
- motivation

Definition As an audience member, there are very few things as frustrating as listening to a presentation during which the presenter uses terms you don't understand. You may accept a single unfamiliar term that a presenter uses only once or twice; however, if several unfamiliar terms are used throughout a presentation, you may become confused or completely lose interest. This is particularly true if the unfamiliar term is used in the thesis statement. In addition, you may see the presenter as showing off an impressive vocabulary at the expense of the audience.

To avoid this confusion in your own presentations, consider the answers to the questions on the following page as you prepare.

Betty Ford has a well-known reputation as a speaker.
How can an effective presenter establish ethos?

- Are there any terms I have used in my thesis statement that may be unfamiliar to my audience?
- Do I want my audience to consider a term from my thesis statement in light of my personal definition rather than the dictionary definition?

If the answer to either of these questions is "yes," you will need to make some adjustments to your speech. Include adequate definitions during an audience orientation or provide a handout that lists and explains each term.

Background Information What information does the audience need in order to understand your presentation? Background information can include the history of the topic, the current status of the topic, or the criteria by which you want the audience to evaluate your presentation. Frequently, the background information is a main point that does not fit in the organizational plan for a presentation. Remember that to the majority of the audience you are the expert on the topic. Provide listeners with enough information to understand your topic as well as you do.

Motivation If, after analyzing your audience, you feel audience members may be negative or apathetic to your topic, it is important to take action. You will need to include some additional or more in-depth information to motivate them to listen to and embrace your presentation.

Refer again to your analysis. What concerns or interests do your audience members have in common? How can your topic be related to those concerns or interests? What do these individuals have to gain by listening to your presentation? Stating the audience's motivation for attending your presentation often can help you "win over" those reluctant listeners. You might say, "Today, I am going to ask you to set aside the opinions and impressions you have about the problem of the homeless. I am going to ask you to look at the issue from a new perspective."

interNET ACTIVITY

Jargon Sometimes, speakers who are very knowledgeable about a topic forget that audience members may not be familiar with the jargon being used. Log on to a reliable Internet search engine to access a site that provides information on jargon. Go to one of the sites and make a list of words associated with a particular field, such as medicine, law, finance, sports, or computer technology. Share your lists as a class.

Many of the attention devices explained earlier can be used to motivate an audience and build its interest in a topic. In fact, an interesting story, joke, or quote that also is tied closely to your topic can serve two purposes. It can both grab your audience's attention and motivate people to focus on your topic. You also might wish to point out how you are like your audience and why you are concerned about the topic. This can motivate listeners to feel it is important for them as well.

Evaluating Orientation Needs It is up to you to determine which of these audience orientation steps will be necessary for your individual presentation. If you are speaking to a group of professional peers, it may not be necessary to define any of the terms in your thesis statement. If you are speaking to people who already are aware of the background of your topic, you may find that they already are motivated to listen. In other words, there may be times when you need to use these steps and other times when you don't; the analysis you have made of your audience should be your guide.

Preview Your Main Points

Along with the thesis statement, the introduction should include a preview of your main points. This is a courtesy that you provide for your audience to let them know what to listen for in your presentation. This preview can be a single sentence, such as "Employees will be asked to select from three benefit plans next week." Or, it can actually list the main points separately: "Next week employees will be asked to select either the employee-only benefit package, the full-family benefit package, or the partial-family benefit package." Either way, the audience is alerted to listen for three main points to be covered in your presentation.

Put It All Together

At the end of your introduction, the audience should have no doubt about what it will gain by listening to your presentation. Audience members also should have a good idea of your relationship to the topic. With a well-planned and complete introduction you should gain the momentum you need to get through the longest part of your presentation: the main body.

The Body

In a presentation, you will rarely be able to share everything you know about a topic. To determine what information to include, focus on exactly what the audience needs to know to meet both your objective and theirs. The body of a presentation is made up of only two to five main points, each with supporting details and each connected with smooth transitions.

The general rule for deciding how many main points to develop in a presentation is that less is better. The time you are allowed for your presentation will be an important factor in determining how many main points to include. The body of a presentation usually makes up 75 to 85 percent of the presentation time. Obviously, this is the part of the presentation which will require the most preparation time and effort. Some suggestions to determine main points and make smooth transitions follow. Section 2 of this chapter will explain in more detail how to organize the main body of a presentation.

Determine the Main Points

The first step in determining the main points of a presentation is to consider the purpose of the presentation. What ideas do you need to communicate to the audience to accomplish this purpose? If you are asked to

Global Communication

Cultural Diversity

As a speaker, you can address, minimize, and demonstrate appreciation for cultural differences in your audience. First, research cultural practices so you can avoid offending audience members with inappropriate nonverbal gestures, attire, or language. Assume that you have been asked to give a brief presentation at a seminar in another country. The purpose of your presentation will be to describe your school traditions to your audience. Choose a country that you would like to visit. Research that country's greetings, customs, and any other cultural traditions that you would need to be aware of to make a presentation there.

train someone to change the bottle on the water cooler in the employee break room, your main points will be the steps necessary to change the bottle.

The second step in determining the main points of a presentation is to refer to your thesis statement. Each main point in a presentation must support the thesis statement and relate to the other main points. If you are making a presentation to the soccer team with the thesis statement "How can we raise money to participate in the state tournament?" each main point will be a way for the team to raise money. A main point about whether to drive individual cars or charter a bus to the tournament would not be appropriate.

The third factor in determining the main points for a presentation is the availability of information. No matter how important an idea may seem, if you do not have the information to support it, it should not be a main idea. Main ideas should be those that you can effectively back up with evidence.

TECHNOLOGY *Activity*

Analogy One way we learn new concepts is to relate them to knowledge we already possess. You can effectively use analogies in a presentation to compare or associate two unlike objects or concepts. During one week, view commercials on TV or radio and advertisements in magazines or newspapers. Find three analogies used to advertise your favorite products. What words or pictures do you associate with your favorite products? As a class, discuss how analogies are used to market products.

Make Smooth Transitions

Transitions not only join the main points together but also link the introduction and the conclusion to the main body. Weak transitions can leave your audience feeling lost or wondering where you are heading for your next point. On the other hand, smooth transitions allow you to move effortlessly from one point to another. This smooth flow of ideas is important because it allows the audience to remain focused on the issues of your presentation, not the organization of it.

Transitions may be a word, a phrase, or even one or more sentences. Expressions like "first of all," "next," and "on the other hand" all are commonly used transitions. A smooth

COMMUNICATION PRACTICE LAB

Creating Smooth Transitions

To practice creating smooth transitions in a presentation, follow these steps:

Step 1 In small groups, look at the list of the purposes transitions can serve in a presentation.

Step 2 Brainstorm words and phrases that apply to each of these purposes. For example, a phrase that relates points through time might be "later that week."

Step 3 Use each word or phrase to create a complete transition sentence for a presentation on computer technology.

Step 4 Discuss your transitions as a class. Was it more difficult to form transitions for some purposes than others?

transition is one that clearly shows the relationship between the two points being linked. Using transitions can help you

- put ideas together
- illustrate a point
- compare or contrast points
- emphasize a point
- arrange points in order
- repeat or provide a summary of the important points
- relate points through location or time

By including a variety of transitions in your presentations, you can keep an audience on the right track.

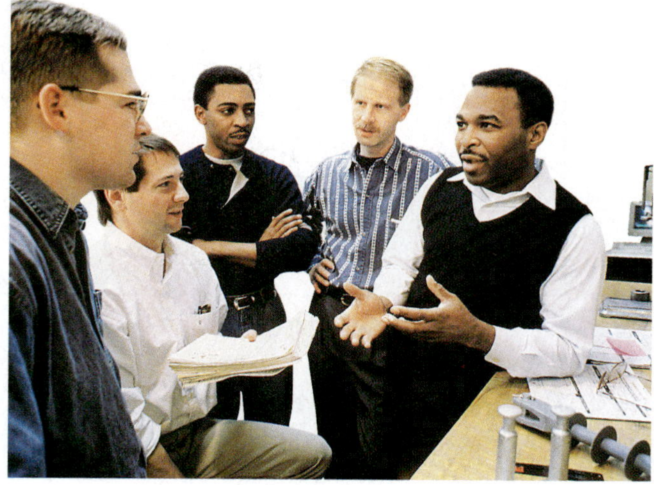

It is not always necessary to define technical terms in the thesis when presenting to professional peers. What is the purpose of the conclusion in a presentation?

The Conclusion

The conclusion of a presentation is the ending that pulls the presentation together and makes it memorable for the audience. While it is often overlooked by presenters, the conclusion is no less important to an effective presentation than any one of the main points. The conclusion leaves the audience with something to think about and remember. It also should be brief—no more than approximately 10 percent of your total presentation time.

A conclusion serves three purposes. It should

- summarize the main points of the presentation
- restate the thesis
- provide a clear ending to the presentation

Summarize the Presentation's Main Points

The summary of the presentation wraps up the main ideas of your presentation. It can be a simple restatement of your main points, such as "As you can see, we can raise money for the upcoming music festival by selling candy bars at football games, having a community citrus fruit sale, and sponsoring an Autumn Festival." The summary also can be a strong appeal that reinforces the central theme or value of your presentation. You might say, "No matter what methods of fund-raising we decide on, all band members must contribute their time and effort or no one will be able to attend the festival." Whatever form it takes, the summary leaves no doubt in the minds of the listeners about what they just heard.

Restate the Thesis

During the conclusion, you should restate the thesis of your presentation. This final statement of your topic or purpose serves as a vehicle to pull the entire presentation together.

This second thesis statement does not have to be identical to the first, but it must be clearly related. For instance, if your initial

Peanuts reprinted by permission of United Features Syndicate, Inc.

thesis statement was phrased as a question, the second thesis statement might provide the answer. Imagine that your first thesis statement was "What is the biggest problem facing today's college students?" In this case, your second statement might be "The biggest problem facing today's college students is academic apathy." The second thesis also may serve to focus, provide a twist to, offer a solution for, or add specifics to the first thesis.

If you already have reviewed the main points of your presentation, you may be wondering why you need to restate the thesis. Shouldn't it be obvious? The truth is that, even after reviewing all the main points, your summary may fail to impress your purpose into the minds of audience members. Restating the thesis helps ensure that your audience will be fully informed before leaving your presentation. Don't leave your message to chance! Make it clear to your audience what you were trying to accomplish.

Provide a Clear Ending to the Presentation

Before ending the presentation, it is important to involve the audience in your topic one last time. This is your final chance to make a lasting impression. Many of the attention devices explained earlier can be used to end your presentation. As a presenter, it is up to you to decide how you will organize the conclusion and what special strategies you will employ.

Order of Elements Some presenters state their second thesis before their summary of main ideas. Other presenters prefer to switch this order. Deciding on which elements to put first and last should be based on what you feel will best suit your presentation and have the most impact on your audience.

Special Strategies There are as many special ways to conclude presentations as there are ways to begin them. Many effective speakers refer back to their introductions as a way of providing closure to their message. If they use a story as a narrative introduction, they may give it a different ending in the conclusion. If a presenter began with a quotation, he or she may refer to the same quotation or use another related quote in the conclusion.

A speaker might also use humor. For example, if you are presenting around lunchtime, you might follow the suggestion of one seasoned presenter. She recommends acknowledging in the introduction that the presentation is right before the lunch break. Then, you might end your conclusion by asking "What's for lunch?" In addition to interjecting a bit of humor into your presentation, this strategy builds your rapport with audience members because they know that you too are ready for a break.

Finally, some presentations end by issuing a challenge to the audience. This focuses the content of the presentation back on the individual audience members by asking them to do something with what they have just heard. Asking them to take some action regarding the topic of your presentation is a great way to keep them thinking about your speech long after it has ended.

Competent communicators organize their presentations carefully so that their audiences will understand and follow the main message. Effective presenters know that the better an audience understands their message, the more likely they are to be influenced by that message.

Section 1 Assessment

Visit the *Glencoe Communication Applications* Web site at **communicationapplications.glencoe.com** and click on **Self-Check and Study Guide 15.1** to review your understanding of the parts of a presentation.

Review Key Terms

1. Define each term and write it in a sentence: attention device, thesis statement, audience orientation.

Check Understanding

2. Name the five purposes of an introduction.
3. Imagine that you are giving a presentation about year-round school. Use one of the seven devices you read about to get the attention of your audience. Explain your decision.
4. Write a thesis statement for each of the following presentations:
   - an informative presentation to a group of new students explaining the extracurricular activities at your school.
   - a persuasive presentation to a group of parents convincing them to volunteer to chaperone school activities.
5. Why might a presenter need to orient his or her audience?
6. **Analyze** What purpose does the following conclusion sentence serve? Explain your answer.

   To reduce the budget for this project, I suggest we use cheaper paper, switch overnight delivery companies, and train our staff to research effectively online.

APPLICATION *Activity*

Analyzing a Presentation Select one of the presentations found in the Appendix on pages 649–658. Work together in small groups according to the presentation chosen. Analyze the introduction and conclusion of your chosen presentation according to what you have read in this section. As a class, discuss your analyses.

Critical Thinking Skill

SYNTHESIZING INFORMATION

After you have researched your presentation, you may have a great deal of information about your topic. To organize the information, you will first want to synthesize it, or combine it, into logical groups.

Learning the Skill

Use the steps listed below to synthesize information:

Step 1 Make a Random List Write your facts on a list as you gather them.

Step 2 Combine Information into Groups or Headings Mark the items on your list in some way, for example with a star or a dot. On separate paper, write headings and then transfer your items to the new list. Cross these items off your first list. Continue until you have transferred all items.

Step 3 Order the Headings Choose one of the patterns of organization discussed in Section 2. Make sure that you settle on a pattern of organization that makes sense and works to prove or disprove your thesis.

Practicing the Skill

Synthesize the information about productivity in the online order division of a clothing company by following the steps below the list.

- Average productivity for January and February was 40 orders.
- Average productivity for March, April, May, and June was 100 orders.
- The company bought new order entry software in March.
- All workers have been trained on the new software system.
- Average productivity per worker after software training is 10 orders.

1. Combine the facts from the random list into related groups. Give each group a heading.
2. Order the headings according to one of the patterns of organization.
3. Put the information into a different pattern of organization. Reword your headings so they make sense within the new organization model.

APPLICATION *Activity*

Imagine you have a summer job working as an intern for a clothing company. Your supervisor asks you to gather information on the number of Internet orders filled in the six-month period from January through June. Using the information you just synthesized, write a one-paragraph summary of recommendations that you could present to your supervisor.

Section 2

Patterns of Organization

GUIDE TO READING

Objectives

1. Select appropriate strategies to organize a presentation.
2. Explain Monroe's Motivated Sequence.
3. Use effective strategies to outline a presentation.

Terms to Learn

chronological order
sequential order
spatial order
topical order
Monroe's Motivated Sequence

Imagine that you are listening to a presentation on how to set up your new computer. The presenter grabs your attention with a great joke. She then begins explaining how to load software, moves to connecting the power cables, and ends with attaching the mouse to the keyboard. Because the instructions are not in order, you are completely confused by the end of the presentation.

In the previous section, you learned that determining the main points included in the body is primarily based on providing adequate support for your thesis statement. Equally important to the successful presentation is a clear and logical organization of those main points.

As you determine the main points for your presentation, you probably will notice that they are connected to each other in various ways. By considering how your ideas relate to each other, you can decide how to arrange them in your presentation. The purpose of your presentation and the thesis statement will determine which pattern of organization will be most appropriate and effective. As **Figure 15–2** shows, there are several patterns from which to choose.

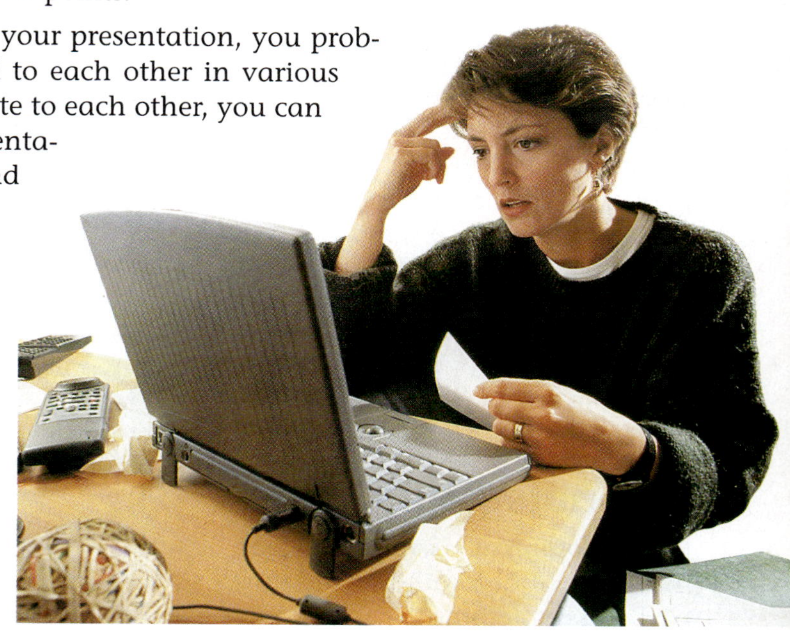

As in the example of installing a new computer, disorganized presentation of information can leave audience members confused. What determines which pattern of organization will be most effective?

Figure 15–2 Patterns of Organization for Presentations

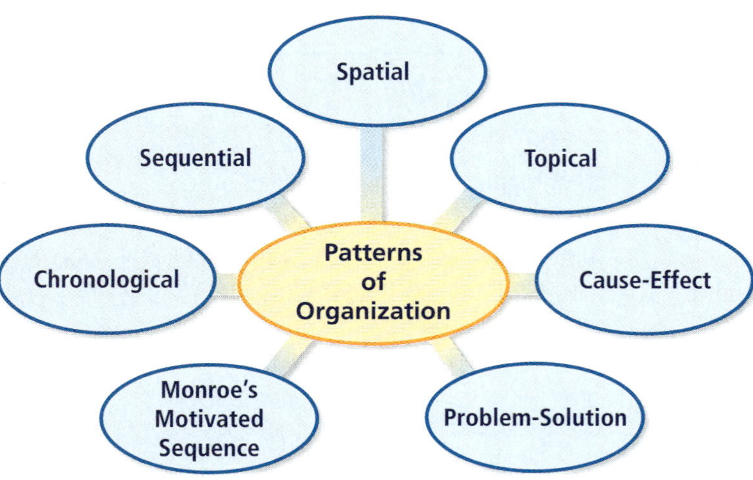

Patterns of Organization for Informative Presentations

An informative presentation is designed to provide an audience with new ideas and new information about a topic. It is important to present that information in such a way that the audience can easily understand and relate to what you have to say. As Figures 15–3 through 15–6 show, there are four major patterns of organization used mainly in informative presentations. These patterns are:

- Chronological
- Sequential
- Spatial
- Topical

Chronological Order

Chronological order is an arrangement according to the time in which something occurs. When used in presentations, this pattern categorizes the main points as past, present, or future.

Chronological Order in Formal Presentations In presentations, chronological order is particularly useful if the purpose is informative, such as to explain the history of something. In a presentation on the history of a company, for example, you might begin by explaining how and when the company was formed, move on to the company's expansion over the years, describe its current status, and finish with what it plans for future development.

Chronological Order in Informal Presentations Chronological order also is appropriate for some informal presentations. Imagine that your supervisor has asked you for an update on a project to which you've been assigned. You will want to provide him or her with a summary of what you have accomplished up to that point in time. It will

Figure 15–3 Chronological Order

December 1963

Thesis Statement:	Our corporation has come a long way in the last forty years.
Main Point #1:	The company was organized in 1963.
Main Point #2:	The company expanded into two divisions in 1975.
Main Point #3:	The company merged with a smaller competitor in 1997.
Main Point #4:	The company has grown to meet the challenges of the new millennium.

COMMUNICATION PRACTICE LAB

Using Sequential Order

To practice using sequential order to organize a presentation, follow these steps:

Step 1 Choose an object that you use on a regular basis, such as a pencil sharpener or a hair dryer.

Step 2 Without actually using the object, explain to the class how to operate it. Be sure to include every necessary step and arrange the steps correctly.

Step 3 Ask for a volunteer to use the object exactly as you explained.

Step 4 Discuss your explanation with your classmates. Were your instructions clear and complete? Were they in the correct order? Could you have added any steps to make your classmate's task easier?

be much easier for your supervisor to understand your presentation if you can explain the project's progress chronologically.

Sequential Order

Sequential order is an arrangement according to the steps of a process. Sequential order is closely related to chronological order. However, instead of arranging information by time, information is arranged according to a particular succession. Any presentation that instructs someone how to do something from beginning to end might be structured sequentially. The number of main points will depend on the number of steps necessary to accomplish the object of the presentation. Other informative presentations may also be placed in sequential order.

Imagine that you have asked a friend for directions to his or her house. What if your friend were to list all the right turns you should take and then the left turns and then how many traffic lights you will pass on the total journey to his or her house? You might not be able to get there. Instead, you need the different turns and stoplights listed in the order that you will reach them. This allows you to know what step to take next.

It is also important to use sequential order when giving instructions for a task. If you omit a step or explain things out of order when explaining a task at work, the person you instruct may not be able to do his or her job.

Figure 15–4 Sequential Order

Thesis Statement:	It is easy to change the bottle on the water cooler.
Main Point #1:	Remove the empty bottle.
Main Point #2:	Open the full bottle of water.
Main Point #3:	Carefully lift the full bottle above the reservoir.
Main Point #4:	Quickly place the bottle opening into the reservoir opening.
Main Point #5:	Clean up any water spilled during step #4.

Instead, he or she may have to find someone else who can explain the task better. This wastes valuable work time and can ultimately reflect poorly on you as a communicator.

Spatial Order

Spatial order is an arrangement according to how a topic is put together or by the physical location of its elements. Types of spatial arrangement include describing something from top to bottom, side to side, north to south, or east to west. A presentation that analyzes a company's quarterly sales might provide information sales district by sales district. Also, most television weather forecasters present the weather in a spatial pattern.

Television weather forecasters, like the one above, present the weather in spatial order. List different types of spatial arrangements.

Topical Order

Sometimes, the main points for a presentation are related only by the fact that each is a part of the general topic. **Topical order** groups ideas by some logical theme or division. For example, imagine that you were asked to speak about deteriorating facilities at your high school. You might decide to limit your presentation to a discussion of the gymnasium, the cafeteria, and the science classrooms. Each is a valid point that fits your topic and thesis, but the only thing that connects them is the topic of deterioration. This presentation would definitely be suited to topical arrangement.

Figure 15–5 Spatial Order

Thesis Statement:	Tri-Core's processor sales are up in every region of the country.
Main Point #1:	Sales are strongest in the Western Region.
Main Point #2:	Sales are growing at a rate of 20 percent in the Mountain Region.
Main Point #3:	Sales are up 9 percent in the Central Region.
Main Point #4	Sales increases in the Eastern Region are behind those in the other regions.

Arranging a Topical Presentation When using topical order, how do you know what point to present first, second, and last? Points in a topically arranged presentation usually are presented in order of their importance. Some will begin with the least important point and build to the most important. Others may place the most important information at the beginning and end of the presentation. This type of arrangement is based on the idea that an audience remembers the first and last things it hears better than the information in between.

The topical method of organizing an informative presentation provides a presenter with a lot of flexibility. In fact, the topical pattern of organization is sometimes used to persuade audiences to accept facts, values, or ideas. As such, you might choose it for a persuasive presentation, or you might want to choose one of the other patterns normally used for persuasive presentations.

Figure 15–6 Topical Order

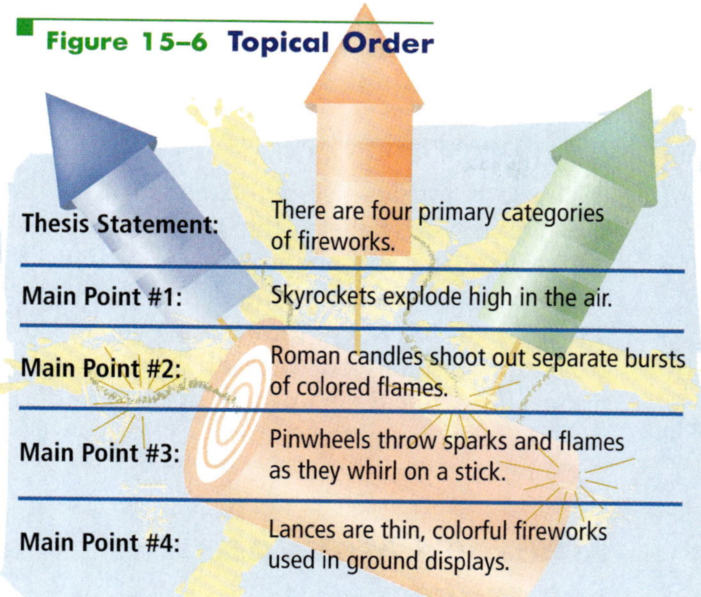

Thesis Statement:
There are four primary categories of fireworks.
Main Point #1:
Skyrockets explode high in the air.
Main Point #2:
Roman candles shoot out separate bursts of colored flames.
Main Point #3:
Pinwheels throw sparks and flames as they whirl on a stick.
Main Point #4:
Lances are thin, colorful fireworks used in ground displays.

Patterns of Organization for Persuasive and Motivational Presentations

As you've read, topical organization helps you put your thoughts in a logical order. However, a topical organization may not always be the most effective choice. Some persuasive presentations may need to be organized differently. Other patterns of persuasive presentations, as shown in **Figures 15–7 through 15–9**, are:

- Cause-effect
- Problem-solution
- Monroe's Motivated Sequence

Cause-Effect Organization

Cause-effect organization in a presentation consists of two parts. The first part—the cause—brings about some action, event, or situation. The second part—the effect—is the consequence of that action, event, or situation. This organizational pattern may be used for informative or persuasive presentations. It is also very effective for creating concern for a problem.

For example, in a presentation about a lack of employee parking at a work site, the first main point might be that local construction around the area has caused the situation. The second main point would then focus on the effects of the lack of parking, such as employee tardiness and morale problems. At this point, you have creative concern for the problem. Another persuasive use of cause-effect organization is found in **Figure 15–7.**

Problem-Solution Organization

Like the cause-effect pattern, the problem-solution pattern of organization is a two-step logical plan describing first a problem and then

Figure 15–7 Cause-Effect

Thesis Statement:	Students should have three weeks off for winter break.
Main Point #1:	Many families today are spread out throughout the country.
Main Point #2:	Travel to family gatherings is more time-consuming, giving students and their families less time to spend with loved ones.

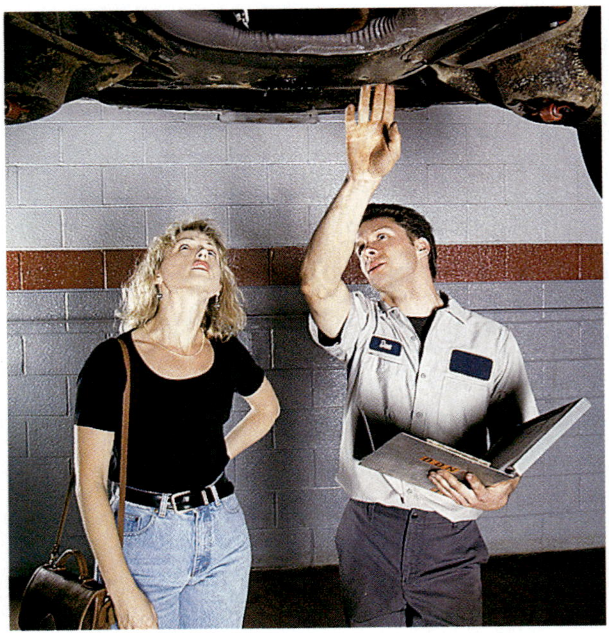

An auto mechanic explaining a problem to a customer, then offering a solution is similar to problem-solving organization. What type of presentation tends to require problem-solving organization?

a solution to this problem. It is usually used for presentations that persuade an audience to solve a problem or improve a situation. In a presentation in which you want the audience to sign a petition for more employee parking, for example, the first point would be the explanation of the problem. The second point would be the explanation of how increasing the number of parking spaces would solve the problem and benefit the audience.

When a presenter tries to show why one solution to a problem is better than another one, he or she will often describe the advantages and disadvantages. To convince the audience that the advantages outweigh the disadvantages, he or she probably would explain the disadvantages briefly and then spend the rest of the presentation describing the advantages. The presenter also may want to consider a visual depiction of how the advantages outnumber or outweigh the disadvantages.

The advantage-disadvantage strategy is effective if you believe the audience to be unlikely to accept your proposal. You will be better able to overcome audience members' resistance if you show that you have considered their point of view. Share that your proposition will affect them in a positive way and will be more beneficial than the action they had previously considered.

Monroe's Motivated Sequence

Monroe's Motivated Sequence, named after communication expert A. H. Monroe, is a five-part organizational strategy designed for speeches that seek to persuade or motivate an audience to take immediate action. It is based on two assumptions: all people have needs, and people can be persuaded by claims that satisfy those needs. The steps of Monroe's Motivated Sequence are

- attention
- need
- satisfaction
- visualization
- action

Figure 15–8 Problem-Solution

Thesis Statement:	We should purchase new computers for all of our customer service representatives.
Main Point #1:	Customers have to wait an average of 15 minutes before an employee can pull up the information and begin discussing a specific account.
Main Point #2:	Updated computers with faster processors would cut down on customer delays.

Attention The attention step is very much like the introduction section of a standard presentation. According to Monroe, you cannot possibly hope to convince anyone of anything if you do not have his or her attention. The first step of the sequence is to create audience interest in learning or knowing more.

Need Once you have the interest of your audience, move into the "need" stage of the presentation. At this point, you make the audience aware that a problem or need exists. The problem is then related directly to audience members so they personally identify with it or perceive personal need. By the conclusion of this step, your audience should be ready to hear what is necessary to satisfy this need.

Satisfaction This is where you present the solution for the problem you just explained. As you show how this solution will work, you should include enough details for the audience to completely understand what you are talking about.

Visualization In this step, you help your audience visualize the benefits of your solution. This will help listeners "buy into" your plan. The key to developing an effective visualization step is the use of vivid imagery that makes your audience a part of the solution. Audience members should know how they will profit from your solution and how much better things will be once the solution is enacted.

Action Once the audience members are convinced your solution is beneficial, you are ready to ask them to do whatever is necessary. Tell people *exactly* what you want them to do and how to do it. For example, give them the address to write, the schedule for volunteers, or a pen they'll need to write a check. Make it as easy as possible for audience members to do what you want them to do. Complete the action step by reinforcing people's decision to do what you want. Remind them of how they will benefit by contributing their time, energy, or money. Make them feel good about their decision. Monroe's pattern for organizing persuasive messages is effective because it follows the natural process of human thinking and leads the audience step-by-step to the desired action. It is widely used in marketing. Think about the following commercial.

- Scene One—Attention: A young woman is running through the park. She is wearing jogging gear and is perspiring.
- Scene Two—Need: The jogger pauses, feeling as if she cannot continue another step. She is extremely thirsty.
- Scene Three—Satisfaction: She sees a vendor selling ice-cold bottled water.
- Scene Four—Visualization: She imagines how refreshing a bottle of water would be.
- Scene Five—Action: The commercial ends with the jogger heading toward the water stand. The logo for the brand of bottled water appears over the final scene, urging viewers to take the same action the young jogger did.

Figure 15–9 Monroe's Motivated Sequence

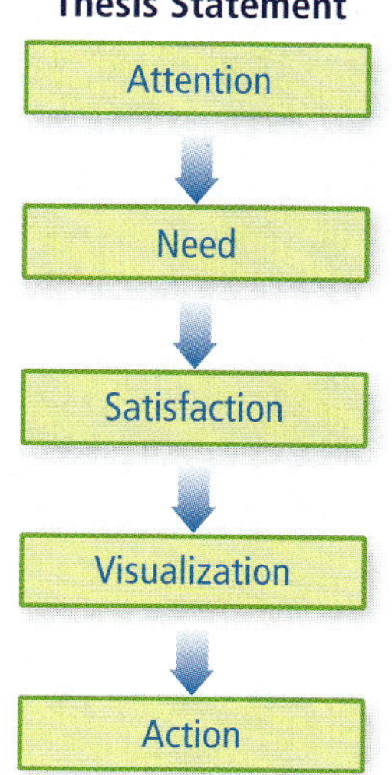

Organization in Informal Presentations

Most of the presentations that have been discussed in this chapter are formal presentations, consciously prepared over a period of time. However, organization is just as important for informal presentations. When you are asked to show a new student around your school, you need to think about the most logical tour so that it will be easy for him or her to remember. A mechanic needs to explain what is wrong with the engine of a car in clear, logical sequence so that the owner will understand what repairs are needed and why. A medical office assistant needs to be able to explain to a patient how to take a prescribed medication so that the patient will get well. The success or failure of all these tasks will likely depend on how well organized and thought-out they are. Remember that the purpose of organizing your ideas is to present a message that is easy for your audience to follow, understand, and remember.

Workers attend a trade union presentation on improving facilities and salaries. What is the main purpose of preparing a presentation outline?

Practice for the Workplace

Organizational Patterns In the workplace, you may be asked to give presentations on a variety of topics. For each presentation, you will want to select the best organizational pattern for your topic.

BUSINESS PRACTICE *Activity*

Identify the type of organizational pattern you would use to develop a presentation on each of the following topics:

- seven steps to developing successful advertising on the Internet
- national sales quotas in retail sales reflect weather patterns across the United States
- Employee Assistance Programs: a positive response to employee stress and psychological wellness

Preparing Your Presentation Outline

Now that you have decided on the organizational pattern you will use, you are ready to outline your presentation. An outline serves as the road map of your presentation. Once you have prepared your outline, you may need to revisit one or more of the first four steps of the preparation process. Your outline may even show you the limitations, flaws, or difficulties in your topic, taking you back to step number one. A good outline, however, provides your presentation with a direction, supporting information, and logical sections.

An outline for a presentation follows the structure of your presentation. Notice how the organization of the presentation is incorporated into the following outline.

I. Introduction
  A. Introductory Device
  B. Thesis Statement
  C. Establish Speaker Ethos
  D. Audience Orientation
    1. Definitions
    2. Background
    3. Motivation
  E. Preview Main Points
II. Body
  A. Main Point 1
  B. Main Point 2
  C. Main Point 3
III. Conclusion
  A. Summary
  B. Second Thesis Statement
  C. Concluding Device

When sharing with your audience, you fill in this basic structure with added support, humor, audio-visual aids, and more.

Preparing an Outline

There are many ways to begin preparing an outline for your presentation. One way is to begin by writing the names for the three main divisions of your speech—introduction, body, and conclusion—at the top of separate sheets of paper or note cards. Then, you can list the main points and any information from your research on the corresponding sheet of paper. If a piece of information supports more than one main idea, you can include it with each idea to which it applies.

Traditional outlines follow a specific format. Begin your outline with either the title or the thesis statement of your speech. Then, list each of the sections, indicated by Roman numerals. For example, for a presentation to inform your audience about the three top job opportunities for teenagers in your town, your main ideas in the body of the presentation might read:

II. Body
  A. Burger Town
  B. Kit 'n' Kapoodle
  C. Ed's Locker Room

Supporting Information Under each main idea, list your supporting information. This is where you should begin to include the results of your research. Each piece of supporting information will be indicated by a capital letter. The supporting material about Burger Town might look like this.

A. Burger Town
  1. Flexible hours
  2. Good benefits
  3. Fun atmosphere

An outline may be made up of phrases, like the ones above, or of complete sentences. A sentence outline of the section on Burger Town might look like this.

A. Burger Town is a restaurant that is a great place for teenagers to work.
  1. Employees are able to work flexible hours.
  2. Burger Town provides employees with good benefits.
  3. The working atmosphere at Burger Town is fun.

Details Details provide each of your supporting points with the content and interest you will need to keep an audience's attention. The detail part of your outline should include names, numbers, dates, events, and other specifics necessary to make your point to audience members.

You may include many levels of details in your presentation, depending upon how intricate or extensive your research is. The first level of details is indicated in an outline by numerals; the second level is marked by lower case letters. Following is a partial outline with details included.

- **A.** Burger Town
  - **1.** Flexible hours
    - **a.** Open weeknight evenings until 10 P.M.
    - **b.** Open Saturdays and Sundays from 9 A.M. until 11 P.M.
  - **2.** Good benefits
    - **a.** Up to two free meals per day per employee
    - **b.** Health insurance available for around $50 per month
    - **c.** Discounts at other Burger Town-owned companies
      - **(1)** 25 percent off at Pizza Village
      - **(2)** 15 percent off at Steak City

Proper Outline Form Besides the use of Roman numerals, letters, and numbers, you may have noticed other details about the outlines you have seen. Each level of detail, for example, is indented further. These indentions give you visual clues as to the general nature of each piece of information in your outline. The more broad or general the idea, the less indented it is.

It also is important to note that each section of your outline must have at least two parts. That is, you must begin with at least two main ideas. If a main idea has one supporting idea, it must have another. For every *A*, you need a *B*, for every *1* you need a *2*, and so on.

Section 2 Assessment

Visit the *Glencoe Communication Applications* Web site at **communicationapplications.glencoe.com** and click on **Self-Check and Study Guide 15.2** to review your understanding of patterns of organization.

Review Key Terms

1. Define each term and write it in a sentence: chronological order, sequential order, spatial order, topical order, Monroe's Motivated Sequence.

Check Understanding

2. Using one of the following organization methods—chronological, sequential, spatial, topical, cause-effect, problem-solution, advantage-disadvantage—organize a short presentation on developing good study skills.
3. Explain how Monroe's Motivated Sequence could be used for a speech asking your classmates to help solve the problem of litter on campus.
4. **Apply** Using what you have read, prepare an outline for a presentation on the importance of developing good study skills.

APPLICATION Activity

Analyzing Advertisements Select an advertisement from a newspaper or magazine and diagram it step by step using Monroe's Motivated Sequence. Next, develop a one- to three-minute presentation for that product using the diagram as a guide. Be sure to include all the steps of the sequence in your presentation. Share your presentations as a class or in small groups.

Communication Self-Assessment

Evaluating How You Organize Presentations

How Do You Rate?

On a separate sheet of paper, use the key to respond to the following statements. Put a check mark at the end of each skill you would like to improve.

Key: **A** Always **U** Usually **S** Sometimes **R** Rarely **N** Never

1. I organize my presentations well.
2. When I work on the introduction to presentations, my first concern is involving the audience.
3. I preview the main points of my presentation to encourage the audience to listen for these points.
4. When I give a speech or a demonstration, I know how to give a concise statement of my thesis.
5. I am able to build interest in a topic by using definitions, background information, and motivation.
6. As I prepare a presentation, I choose the main points according to my thesis and what the audience needs to know.
7. When I give a presentation, I know how to use attention cycles and memory aids.
8. I use audience reaction to modify my presentation.
9. As I conclude a speech, I summarize the main points.
10. As I end a speech, I use an appropriate attention catcher.

How Do You Score?

Review your responses. Give yourself 5 points for every A, 4 for every U, 3 for every S, 2 for every R, and 1 for every N. Total your points and evaluate your score.

41–50 Excellent You may be surprised to find out how much you can improve your skills.

31–40 Good In this course, you can learn ways to make your skills better.

21–30 Fair Practice applying the skills taught in this course.

1–20 Needs Improvement Carefully monitor your improvement as you work through this course.

Setting Communication Goals

If you scored Excellent or Good, complete Part A. If your score was Fair or Needs Improvement, complete Part B.

Part A

1. I plan to put the following ideas into practice:
2. I plan to share the following information about communication with the following people:

Part B

1. The behaviors I need to change most are:
2. To bring about these changes I will take these steps:

Designing a Checklist

To plan, prepare, and deliver an effective presentation, you'll need to keep track of many details. One of the best ways to make sure you don't forget something is to make a checklist. A checklist acts like a schedule to organize your preparation. By looking at a checklist, you can quickly see what you have done and what still needs to be completed. Criteria for a useful checklist is found in the list below.

Checklist Format Options

- Check that the information is not outdated.
- Is the information outdated or current?
- Info current

Useful Checklists

- are easy to read
- include all important elements
- have all steps listed in order
- have room to add new items or notes

Making a Checklist The first step in making a checklist is to write down each step in your preparation. Mark off the steps as you complete them. If possible, keep your checklist under one page. If you have several different categories of information, classify the steps under subheads so that there are only a few steps in each group. You may choose to write each item as just a word or two, or you may want to make each item a statement or even a question. Which of the styles above might you use to remind yourself to check whether your information is current?

Using Your Checklist One of the most useful functions of your checklist is its ability to help you manage your time. Listing each individual task that you need to complete keeps you from being overwhelmed by the work that needs to be done. Listing the steps in the order they should be completed allows you to proceed down your checklist as you work. This prevents you from having to skip steps and come back to them later. It also means you can tell by glancing at your checklist approximately how well you are progressing. If you have four weeks to prepare a presentation, but you are only a tenth of the way through your checklist after three weeks, you will see that you need to work harder over the next week.

For additional information about business writing, see the *Guide to Business Communication* section of the Communication Survival Kit in the Appendix.

Building Your Own Checklist Many of the steps listed in this text can serve as checklist items for you. For example, the list of the Steps of the Presentation Preparation Process, which appears on page 478 in this chapter, is a good start for a checklist. You can expand each step as necessary for your particular presentation. The sample checklist that follows expands on the step of recording your research.

If you are just learning to cite sources, you may want to expand that checklist item to include each element of the source citation. Personalize your checklist so it fits your own needs.

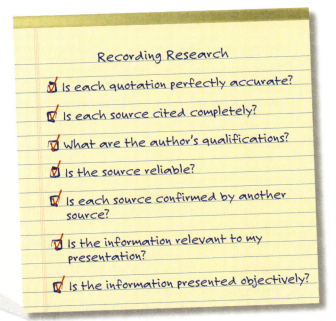

Recording Research

- ☑ Is each quotation perfectly accurate?
- ☑ Is each source cited completely?
- ☑ What are the author's qualifications?
- ☑ Is the source reliable?
- ☑ Is each source confirmed by another source?
- ☑ Is the information relevant to my presentation?
- ☑ Is the information presented objectively?

WRITING Activity

Use the following steps to make a checklist for something you know how to do that involves several steps.

- Brainstorm things you know how to do. For instance, you probably know how to pack a suitcase or set up a tent.
- Choose one of the things on your list and draw up a checklist for it. Assume that someone who has never performed the task before will be using your checklist to perform the task for the first time.
- What are the essential steps?
- In what order should the steps be performed?
- How might the steps be classified into subheads?
- Look over your work. Revise your writing so that each step is clear, in the right order, and complete.

Visit the *Glencoe Communication Applications* Web site at **communicationapplications.glencoe.com** and click on **Chapter 15 Activity** for additional practice in organizing presentations.

Reviewing Key Terms

On a separate sheet of paper, write the communication term that completes each statement.

1. Presentations arranged as a series of actions that lead to a specific result are in ______ .
2. ______ is a five-part strategy designed for speeches that seek immediate action.
3. ______ groups ideas by some logical theme or division.
4. A simple sentence that states the point of your presentation is called a(n) ______ .
5. Listeners get the information they need to understand a presentation from the ______ .
6. Presentations arranged by the physical location of the topic are organized in ______ .
7. A rhetorical question is an example of a(n) ______ with which to begin a presentation.
8. Presentations arranged by the time in which the points occur are organized in ______ .

Reviewing Key Concepts

1. Why should a presenter carefully organize a presentation?
2. What must a presenter do in the first few minutes of his or her speech?
3. Which are the three main elements of a presentation?
4. How do presenters establish their ethos with an audience?
5. How long should a presenter make his or her conclusion?
6. What three factors determine the main points of a presentation?
7. In a topically arranged presentation, how are points usually ordered?
8. Imagine your job is selling memberships to a health club. How might you use cause-effect organization in your sales presentation?
9. Give examples of informal presentations that need to be organized.

Assessment and Activities

Reading and Critical Thinking Skill

1. **Synthesis** Imagine you are speaking to a group of people about preserving wildlife in their region of the country. Create an attention device to use in the introduction.
2. **Cause-Effect** How do many effective speakers provide closure to their message?
3. **Classifying Information** Which pattern of organization should you use to report the progress of a cross-country bike race?
4. **Applying Information** When is the advantage-disadvantage strategy an effective way to order a persuasive presentation?

Skill Practice Activity

Synthesizing Information In groups of four or five, brainstorm why it is or is not important to buy American-made goods. Supplement the discussion with information found in recent magazine or newspaper articles about the United States' role in world trade. Synthesize the information into logical segments. Prepare a thesis statement and an outline as if you were going to give a two-minute persuasive presentation on the topic.

Cooperative Learning Activity

Creating Concern for a Problem With a partner, brainstorm an environmental problem, such as the disappearance of the rain forests, that you believe poses a threat to humans. Use the following as a model to develop three main points for your chosen topic:

- Fewer forests means less habitat for endangered animal species
- Reduced forestland means fewer oxygen-producing plants
- Fewer rainforest plants can reduce medical research possibilities

Chapter Project

Planning Use the thesis statement your group developed in the Skill Practice Activity to prepare a two-minute persuasive presentation on the topic. Decide which organizational strategy best fits the topic, your thesis statement, and your audience of high school students. Have each member of the group try to develop an attention-grabbing introduction and a memorable conclusion. Vote for the most effective ones.

Presenting As a class, compare the thesis statements and organizational strategies of the different groups. How are they alike and how are they different? After the class has completed the comparison, listen to the groups' introductions and conclusions and evaluate how effective they are in getting audience attention and making the audience remember the group's message.

CHAPTER 16

Supporting Presentations

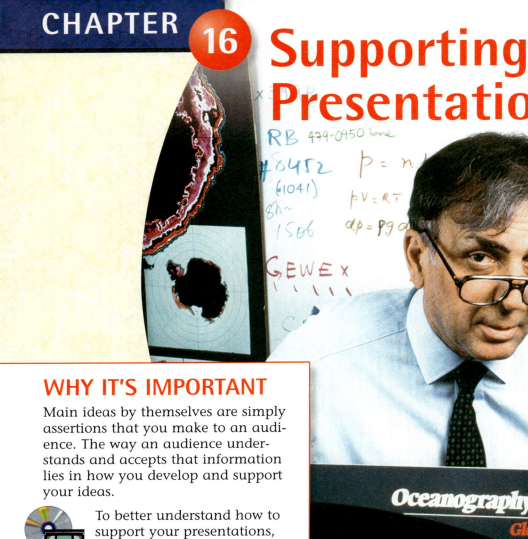

WHY IT'S IMPORTANT

Main ideas by themselves are simply assertions that you make to an audience. The way an audience understands and accepts that information lies in how you develop and support your ideas.

To better understand how to support your presentations, view the **Communication in Action** Chapter 16 video lesson.

"The proof of the pudding is [in] the eating."
—Miguel de Cervantes, Spanish author

GLENCOE Online

Visit the *Glencoe Communication Applications* Web site at **communicationapplications.glencoe.com** and click on **Overview–Chapter 16** to preview information about supporting presentations.

Section 1

Using Support Materials

GUIDE TO READING

Objectives

1. List and provide examples for the three types of proof.
2. Select information to support and clarify main points.
3. Develop effective audiovisual aids to enhance presentations.

Terms to Learn

logical proof
statistic
specific instance
testimony
ethical proof
pathetic proof
amplification device

What structures give the Golden Gate Bridge the support it needs to keep from collapsing? How do the foundation and construction of a skyscraper support its many floors? How does a cast provide support for a broken bone? How do family members, friends, and teachers help support you?

Just as bridges need support to function, so do ideas. An idea has little meaning if there is no supporting information to help prove it. When sharing your thoughts and ideas with an audience, the amount and quality of support that you provide will largely determine your success.

At this point in your presentation preparation, you have determined your main points, know what pattern of organization you will use, and probably have a very basic outline. You now need to think about how you will develop each of those main points.

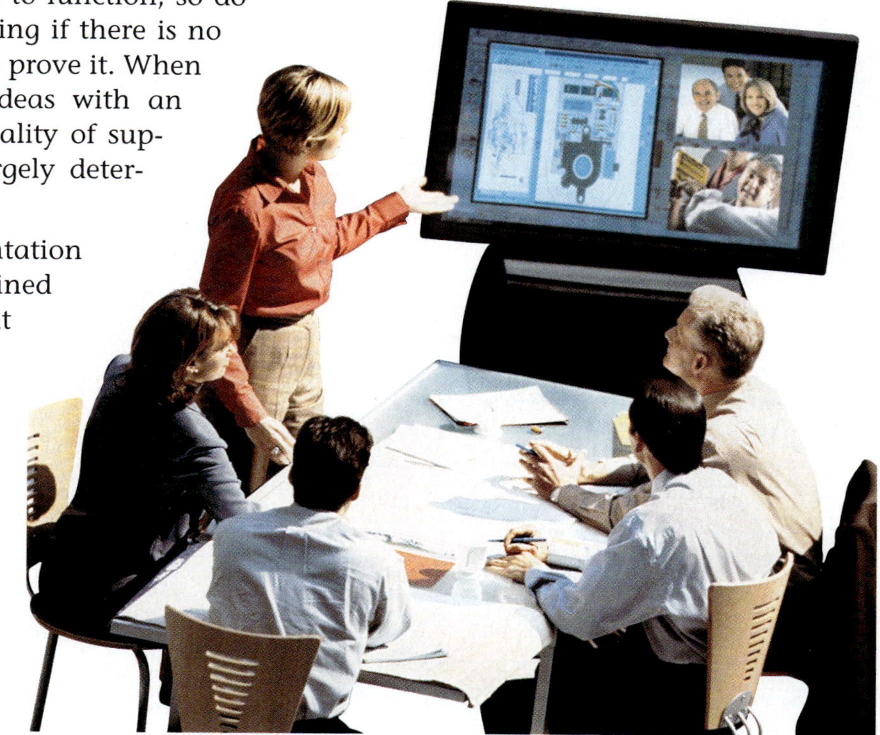

This presenter uses the support of a visual aid during her presentation. How do support materials affect a presentation?

Steps for Developing Main Points

There are three basic steps to developing a point in a presentation. First you state the point, then you support and amplify the point, and finally you restate and relate the point.

When you introduce a point to your audience, you can state it as either a simple declarative statement or a question. Then, you support your point with whatever information your audience needs to accept that your point is accurate. If you have stated your point as a question, your supporting information should answer it. Finally, after going through the first two steps, you will restate your original point with a brief summary and relate it to your thesis statement and the other points in your presentation.

These procedures have little meaning unless each of your points is supported. Meaningless statements waste an audience's time and energy. An extension of this idea is that a point is no more valid than the information that supports it—and a support element is no better than its source. With the skeleton, or outline, of your presentation prepared, you are ready to examine your research and ensure that each of your points is fully and accurately supported. Thus, as shown in Figure 16–1, you are ready for the sixth step of the presentation preparation process: selecting supporting information.

Figure 16–1 Steps of the Presentation Preparation Process

1. Determine a topic.
2. Limit the topic.
3. Determine the purpose.
4. Research the topic.
5. Organize the presentation.
6. Select supporting information.
7. Prepare notes and manuscript for delivery.
8. Rehearse the presentation.

Selecting Supporting Information

The way you develop and support your main points can make or break your credibility with an audience. In any presentation, you are educating your audience. Well-developed main points that are adequately supported will help you to achieve this goal. The support materials you select can help you overcome barriers between you and your audience for a successful presentation.

Supporting a Point

The support materials that you select should reinforce your main points, making them more meaningful and persuasive. In other words, your support information should prove your points. Three types of proof that support information can provide are as follows:

- logical proofs
- ethical proofs
- pathetic proofs

Logical Proofs A **logical proof** is a specific piece of verifiable information that supports a statement. This type of information adds the strongest support to a point. There are three types of logical proofs. These are:

- statistics
- specific instances
- testimonies

Statistics A statistic is an item of information that represents numerical data. Statistics can be used effectively to reduce large amounts of information into general categories, as with average test scores or education levels. Statistics also can emphasize the size or amount of something. In addition, statistics are useful for indicating trends. For example, "From 1995 to today, spending has increased by $2 million."

Sometimes, statistics are the result of a thorough, scientific study or poll. Other times, statistics can be flawed or incomplete. Even if a statistic comes from a respected source, it may be open to question. For instance, two different sources may make conflicting claims. Imagine that one source claims the cheetah is the fastest animal in the world, while another source gives that distinction to the pronghorn antelope. The truth is that the cheetah runs faster, but it does so for only very short distances. In other words, the cheetah would win the 100-yard dash, but the antelope would win the marathon.

Variations in statistics also may be due to the demographics of the group polled, the specific wording of the questions, or the influence of the pollster on the respondent. Each of these factors can have an impact on a poll's results. Remember, the statistics you use to add interest or support to a presentation need to be thoroughly verified, but still may not provide absolute proof.

Specific Instances A specific instance is an account of an actual event or occurrence. Specific instances tend to relate information more directly and more personally to an audience than do statistics.

If you were making a presentation to a group of fellow students to convince them of the importance of learning the Heimlich maneuver, you might include the specific instance of the second-grade student who saved his principal from choking in the school cafeteria. The example provides dramatic proof to support your point.

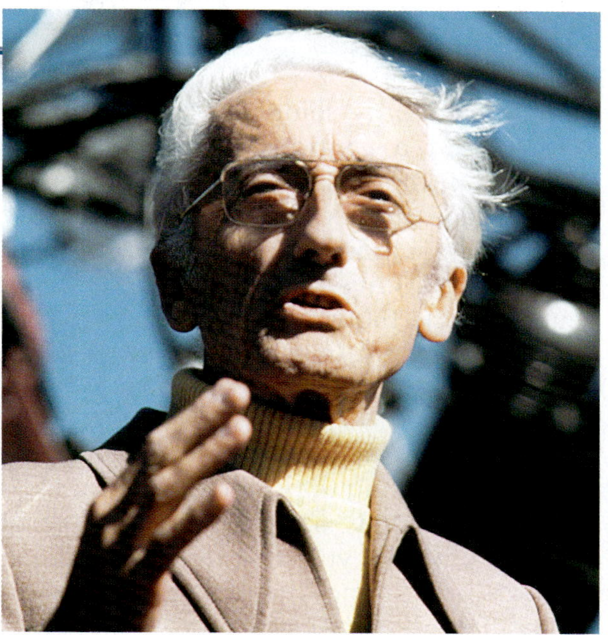

A testimony from Jacques Cousteau would be useful in a presentation on undersea exploration. How is an expert testimony effective in creating credibility?

Testimonies A testimony is a direct quotation or a summary of a quotation. When you think of testimony, you may think of quotations from people who are experts or authorities in their fields. This expert testimony is particularly effective for establishing credibility on topics you don't know much about. Quoting authorities whom your audience recognizes and respects also can be helpful when your topic is controversial or when the audience is skeptical of your personal motives or involvement.

The challenge to using testimony effectively in a presentation lies in determining exactly whom you should quote. Refer to the analysis of your audience when selecting quotations. When possible, select quotations from well-known authorities on your topic or from sources whom you know your audience admires and believes. Testimonies from well-recognized and respected sources will help you to be accepted by the audience.

Remember this, however: Just about any time you support your ideas with a quotation from one authority, someone probably will be able to find a contradictory quotation by another authority. You may decide to acknowledge the existence of contradictory information in order to illustrate to your audience that you have considered all aspects of your topic and that you are not trying to mislead your listeners. In general, however, select information that supports your ideas.

Ethical Proofs An **ethical proof** is a piece of supporting information that builds a speaker's credibility on a topic. Ethical proof demonstrates that you are uniquely qualified to speak on the topic. The most common ethical proof is personal experience. If a speaker making a presentation on overcoming learning disabilities reveals that he or she has dyslexia, that person may have more credibility than a speaker who has no learning disability.

A speaker does not have to personally experience some aspect of a topic to be credible, however. There are other ways to build ethos in a presentation. The speaker can explain his or her own personal concerns or interests in the topic, how he or she became interested in the topic, or what motivates his or her presentation.

Pathetic Proofs A **pathetic proof** is support material that gives emotional appeal to a presentation. A pathetic proof may appeal to an audience's sense of compassion, dignity, justice, pride, love, or generosity, as well as to other emotions. It asks audience members to react with their hearts as well as with their minds.

The number and type of pathetic proofs you use should be determined by how you want your audience to feel about your topic after your presentation. Be careful not to overuse emotional appeals, however. Listeners tend to be skeptical of speakers who rely heavily on pathetic proofs instead of logical ones. In addition, appeals to negative emotions, such as fear, hate, or prejudice, can create negative reactions in your audience. Audiences usually have a more immediate response to emotion, but eventually their logic prevails.

COMMUNICATION PRACTICE LAB

Supporting a Presentation

To practice supporting a presentation, follow these steps:

Step 1 In groups of four or five, discuss extracurricular activities at your school.

Step 2 Use the information from your discussion to choose three activities.

Step 3 Imagine that you will make a presentation to classmates persuading them to participate in the activities you have chosen. What skills can they learn from these activities? What types of people will they meet? Include these types of details in your presentation. Be sure to provide enough information to convince your classmates.

Step 4 Use proper form to create an outline with at least three main points for your presentation. Are there any points that need more information?

Step 5 Determine the type of proofs you will use to support each main point. Place these into your outline.

Step 6 Share your outlines as a class. Discuss whether each provides enough detail to create a convincing presentation.

Amplification Devices In addition to using logical, ethical, and pathetic proofs to support the main ideas in your presentation, you can add interest and depth to your ideas by amplifying them. To do this, you can use amplification devices. An **amplification device** is information that extends or clarifies an idea for an audience or does both. There are numerous amplification devices from which you can choose. Four of them are as follows:

- descriptions
- comparisons
- contrasts
- examples

Descriptions A description can help a listener better relate to the ideas you are presenting. It can also clarify an idea for your audience by providing details that other proofs may not have supplied.

For example, if you want to convince an audience that skiing is an exciting sport, you might help the listener feel the excitement through a vivid description. What details make the sport enjoyable for you? Create a description that helps your audience imagine the experience. Help the audience feel the chill of the wind, see the sparkling snow, experience the anticipation while riding the lift over the trees to the top of the slope, and feel the thrill of speeding down a winding, steep trail.

Practice for the Workplace

Picture This Although visual aids are key elements of effective presentations, sometimes the most influential picture you can provide in a presentation is the one you create with your own words. By using the amplification devices described in this chapter, you can create a powerful mental image for your audience.

BUSINESS PRACTICE *Activity*

Assume that your school administrators have suggested that a local restaurant chain should replace your school cafeteria's lunch service. Your class has been assigned the task of debating the positive and negative effects of this proposal. Decide whether you would be for or against this proposal, then compose a statement that defends your position. Develop vivid descriptions of the current cafeteria's food and that of the proposed food service. Draw comparisons between the cafeteria's food and the restaurant's food. Show contrasts between the two services. Give examples of why your current cafeteria's service should or should not be replaced.

Comparisons A comparison can clarify information and ideas for your audience. If you want your audience to understand an aspect of your topic that may be unfamiliar to them, compare it to something you know your audience is familiar with. Explaining how one thing is like another can give the audience insight into what you mean.

Contrasts Just as comparisons can help an audience understand an idea by showing how two things are alike, contrasts can sharpen a listener's understanding by pointing out differences. Sometimes, it is just as important to tell the audience what something is not as it is to tell them what it is. Be careful, however, not to base all your descriptions on contrasts. Overusing contrasts can give your presentation a negative tone and can leave the audience confused.

Examples Not all examples are as factual as the statistics, specific instances, or testimonies in a logical proof. You also may choose to use hypothetical or fictional examples to clarify an idea in a presentation.

As you are preparing your presentation, you may realize that a scene from a movie could explain your ideas perfectly. Maybe a character in a book you have read faced a situation similar to the one you are describing. Hypothetical and fictional examples can be interesting ways to relate and expand your ideas for your audience. Examples can come from movies, plays, sports, music, history, or any other area that will help you relate to your audience and reflect their interests.

When choosing proofs to support the details of your presentation, take care to test their reliability. The Communication Strategies checklist provides some important questions to help you test your support materials.

DEVELOPING AUDIOVISUAL AIDS

It is often said that a picture is worth a thousand words. Most audiences will find a presenter's message more interesting, understand it more easily, and remember it longer if that message is presented visually as well as verbally.

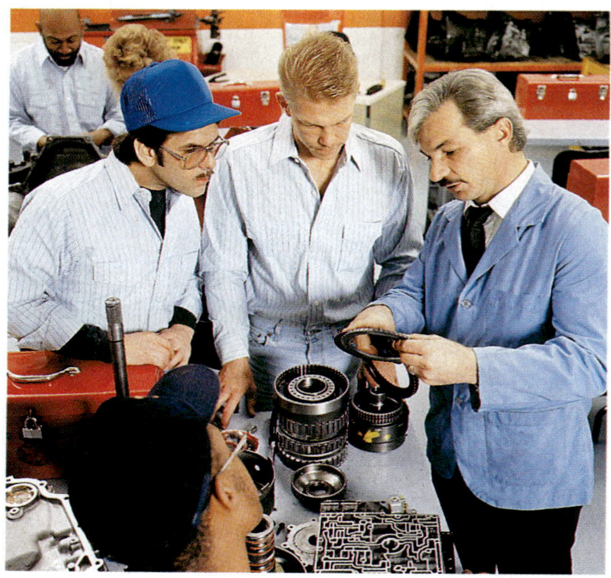

This presenter is using a visual aid to explain a process. What effect does using audiovisual aids have on the audience?

COMMUNICATION Strategies

TESTING SUPPORT MATERIALS

- ✓ Were enough people sampled for the statistic to be worth citing?
- ✓ Were the results completely reported and recorded?
- ✓ Is the source biased? Does the bias affect the accuracy of the information?
- ✓ Is this information consistent with information from other sources? If not, what could account for the differences?
- ✓ Is the information the most recent you can find on the subject?
- ✓ Is the source reliable?
- ✓ How is the source qualified to make this observation or conclusion?
- ✓ Are the cases and examples typical? Were negative examples allowed or explained?

Reasons for Using Audiovisual Aids

Of course, presentations come in all shapes and sizes. Some may last only for a minute or two, while others can be quite lengthy. However, no matter what length a presentation is, it might benefit from the use of audiovisual aids. Following are a few reasons for using these effective tools:

- clarity
- interest
- retention
- professionalism
- presenter support

Clarity Audiovisual aids are used in presentations for a variety of reasons. The primary reason is for clarity. If you are discussing an object, you can make your message clearer by showing the object itself or a representation of the object. If you are citing statistics, showing how something works, or demonstrating a technique, a visual aid can make your information more concrete for your audience. Television and movies have conditioned us to expect a visual image. A visual aid can often clarify an idea for an audience when words are not completely effective.

Interest Audiovisual aids also add interest to your presentation. Which book would you rather read: one with page after page filled with nothing but writing or one that includes pictures throughout? Over five hundred pages of text or a condensed version read by a celebrity on audiocassette? If you are like most people, you often prefer the versions that include interesting sights and sounds. Audiovisual aids have the same effect in a presentation.

Retention A third reason for including audiovisual aids in a presentation is retention. A visual image tends to remain with an audience longer than a verbal image. This is why advertisers often use vivid color and unusual images in advertisements. Consumers may not remember everything that a product claims to do, but they are very likely to remember the images conveyed by its advertisements.

Professionalism A fourth benefit to using audiovisual aids is that they can give your presentation a professional image. High-quality visuals give an audience the impression that you have approached this presentation with a professional attitude. Sometimes, that alone can increase your ethos. Of course, poorly produced, messy, or illegible visual aids can have the opposite effect.

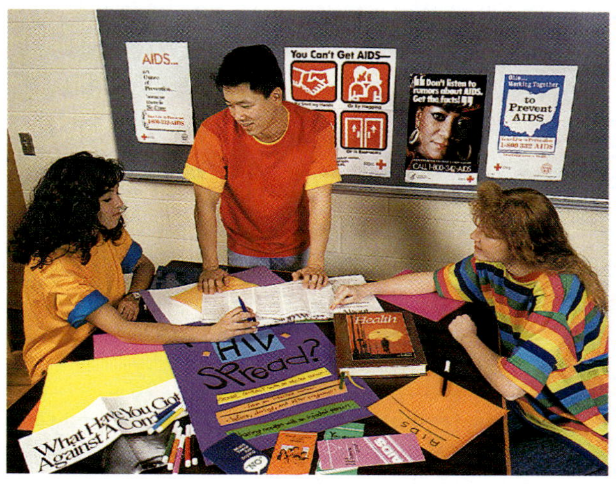

These three individuals are developing visual support to use in a presentation on AIDS. **How does the use of an audiovisual aid add clarity to a presentation?**

Presenter Support A fifth benefit to using audiovisual aids is that they are an excellent way to combat apprehension or stage fright. Visual aids heighten an audience's interest in your topic and shift the attention away from you as the presenter. Visuals also can serve as a prompt to jog your memory or as a visual representation of your notes. You might even create an organizational visual (a list of your main points, for example) that can add to the information in your notes.

Finally, preparing your visual aids gives you more opportunity to become familiar with the ideas of your presentation. The more familiar you are with what you plan to say, the less anxiety you are likely to feel about presenting it.

Types of Visual Aids

Most visual aids fall into one of three categories. These are as follows:

- objects and models
- pictorial reproductions
- pictorial symbols

This presenter is projecting information on an overhead screen. **Why is it a good idea to use an overhead projection for a pictorial reproduction instead of passing it around the room?**

Your decision to use a particular type of visual aid depends on a number of factors. Most importantly, each aid should be based on the content of your presentation, the audience, and the occasion.

Objects and Models Objects and models add substance and precision to your presentation. Objects can be either live, like a tarantula, or inanimate, like a rock. Showing the actual subject of your presentation to audience members can clarify any descriptions you make of the object and help listeners to understand your explanations more fully. Allowing an audience to see, feel, and smell the object can reveal information that will often save a presenter time. It also actively engages an audience in the presentation.

Sometimes it is impractical to bring the actual subject of your presentation to the presentation itself. It may be too large or small, too dangerous, too rare, or too delicate to be handled. In these instances, you might want to consider using a model or representation of the object.

A model usually refers to a three-dimensional, scale-sized representation of an object. A model can give your audience a sense of depth and proportion that pictures might not provide. Architects frequently use models of buildings to illustrate to an audience how a building will look before construction begins. Auto mechanics may use a model of an engine or transmission to explain to a client what needs to be repaired.

Models often enhance and clarify information for your audience. Sometimes, however, they can be a distraction, taking the audience's attention away from your message. This is particularly true for live objects. Even the slightest movement from a snake in a cage can distract a front-row audience member. He or she instantly focuses on the thought of the snake getting out of the cage and stops hearing what you are saying.

Audiences can also become so absorbed in a model of an object that they lose track of what you're saying. After a presentation, they may be able to describe the model in detail but not remember a word of your message. It usually is wise to keep the object or model out of sight any time you are not actively using it in your presentation. This keeps it from becoming an unnecessary distraction.

Pictorial Reproductions Photographs, slides, sketches, videotapes, cartoons, and drawings are all pictorial reproductions. In the absence of an object or a model, a picture can help the audience visualize some aspect of your topic.

The drawing in Figure 16–2 was used by a student to illustrate the types of problems

Figure 16–2 An Illustration of Dyslexia

This si wrdat a
qerzon with dyzlexia
mihgt ze wrdem
reding this zentnce.

TECHNOLOGY *Activity*

Making a Graph Graphs can be used to show trends, illustrate relationships, or compare data. Many computer programs can convert numerical data into a visual aid, such as a circle graph, bar graph, or line graph. You, however, have to choose the type of graph that best illustrates your data. Find out the number of freshmen, sophomores, juniors, and seniors at your school. Create a line graph, a circle graph, or a bar graph to illustrate the data. Which type of graph did you choose? Why? Which graph would work best if you displayed the data in percentage form? Why? Which type of graph would work best if you were to compare enrollment information over the last ten years?

faced by people with dyslexia. This was particularly effective because it allowed the presenter to translate complex ideas into visual terms that the audience could easily grasp.

Unless you are presenting to only one or two people, pictorial reproductions will probably need to be enlarged for easier viewing. Many photographs and drawings are not large enough to be seen unless they are enlarged or passed around a room. Passing the picture around diverts the attention of the audience away from what you are saying during your presentation. Many copy centers have equipment for making enlargements. As an alternative, you might make a transparency of your visual and use an overhead projector to enlarge it during your presentation.

Pictorial Symbols Abstract concepts and statistics are frequently presented through pictorial symbols. Pictorial symbols most commonly are used in graphs, charts, and diagrams.

Graphs Graphs are a good tool for simplifying and clarifying statistics. Audiences frequently have trouble understanding complex series of numbers. You can increase their understanding by using graphs to represent numerical data in visual form. Graphs are useful tools in a presentation because they can illustrate relationships among individual units and show statistical trends and patterns.

A line graph, such as the one shown in Figure 16–3, uses one or more lines to show change over a period of time or space. A single line graph can indicate an upward or downward trend in sales, production, profits, or employee productivity. A multiple line graph can show a relationship between two or more trends.

A bar graph is a good way to show comparisons between two or more items. It is also very easy to understand—even if your audience has no experience in reading graphs. A circle graph is a depiction of the various individual components of a whole. A circle graph looks like a pie. It is then divided into proportional segments—like pieces of pie—representing different parts of your information. A pie graph is a good way to show how all the parts of your topic fit together or what portion of a group or population is affected by your topic.

Figure 16–3 Line Graph

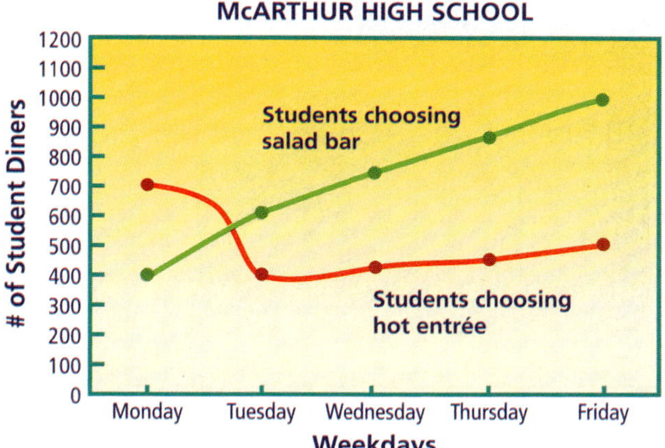

Charts While graphs are visual depictions of statistics, charts illustrate complex information that is not numerical. A flowchart, for example, may be very effective for a presenter who is explaining how something is done. A flowchart is a step-by-step diagram of the process that shows how each step leads to the next. This type of visual aid can help simplify even the most complex task.

The most common chart you will use is a table of information. A table groups information into columns and rows. Although tables may not always be particularly pretty to look at, they can help an audience grasp what you are talking about fairly quickly. They are also good for information that you may want your audience to write down, such as telephone numbers or addresses.

Computer-Generated Visual Aids

If you have access to a computer and printer, you may be able to create professional-looking visuals for your presentations. Depending on the software you have, you may be able to create anything from simple diagrams and tables to extremely sophisticated, full-color charts and graphs. Most of the graphics software that is available includes ready-made drawings, symbols, and other art elements to add color and emphasis to your main points. Some presentation-software packages will even allow you to add sound effects to your ideas. Using these tools effectively can help you make the most of your presentations.

COMMUNICATION *Strategies*

CREATING EFFECTIVE AUDIOVISUAL AIDS

- ✓ Prepare audiovisual aids in advance of your presentation.
- ✓ Create audiovisual aids that can easily be seen or heard by your entire audience.
- ✓ Make visual aids easy to read. Use a limited number of fonts and designs. Choose a font that is easy to read. Use color to make your visuals clearer.
- ✓ Create visuals that are easy to use and understand.
- ✓ Practice using your visual aids before the presentation.

One of the ways to present a visual aid is through the use of a VCR. **Identify other ways to present a visual aid.**

Presenting Visual Aids

There are many ways to present visual aids. You can be as creative as you want, as long as your support materials enhance your presentation rather than replace it. As **Figure 16–4** shows, you may wish to present your visual aids using any of the following:

- flip charts/poster boards
- transparencies
- slides
- handouts
- video/audio cassettes
- computerized displays

Figure 16–4 Visual Aids

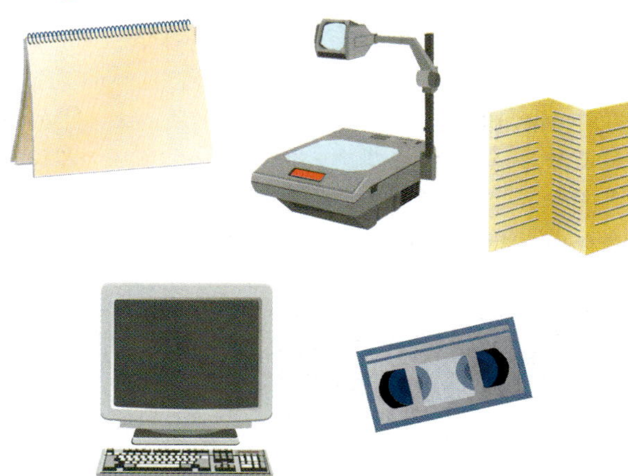

Choosing how to share your visuals with your audience will depend on a number of things. The style and tone of your presentation, as well as the occasion, audience, and purpose, all play a part in your decisions. In addition, you should try to take full advantage of your own artistic talents and the equipment you have available to you.

Using Computerized Displays

When using computerized displays, keep in mind some important cautions. First, it is very easy to get carried away with these technological wonders. The result can be a presentation that audience members remember for its special effects rather than for what you said.

You also need to think about what facilities you will need to allow your audience to properly view your display. Most computer monitors are too small for an audience larger than one or two people. Therefore, make sure a projection system is readily available before developing computerized graphics for a larger audience. If you do not have access to this type of equipment, you may

Presenting Audiovisual Aids

- Make sure any equipment you need (projector, easel, and so on) is available and operating correctly.
- Show visual aids at the time they are being discussed.
- Place audiovisual aids where your entire audience can clearly see or hear them.
- Avoid turning your back to your audience. Speak to your audience, not to your audiovisual aid.
- Do not hide behind your visual aids.
- Do not fidget with your audio-visual aids.
- Thoroughly explain all of your audiovisual aids.
- Do not pass visual aids around to the audience.

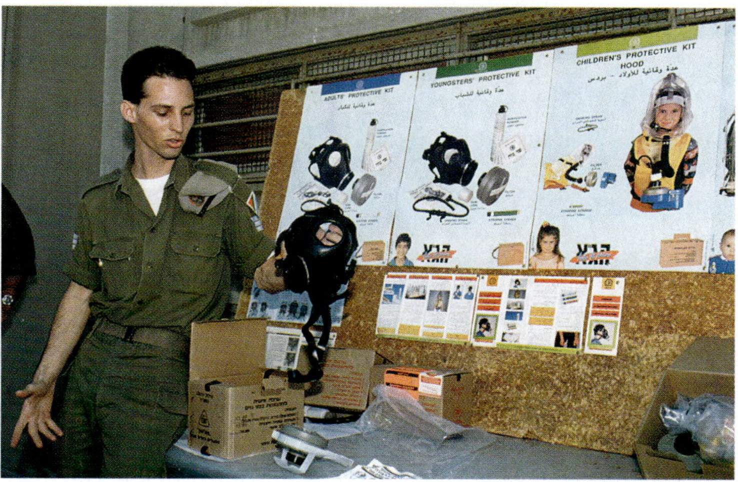

Different presentations call for different types of visual aids. **Identify the two types of visual aids utilized in this presentation.**

wish to print the graphics you design onto transparencies and use an overhead projector to display them during your presentation.

Regardless of what types of audiovisual aids you use, be sure to present them in a professional manner. Make sure text and images are easy to see and sound is easy to hear. Also, pay attention to feedback from your audience. Feedback from your audience is one of the best ways to judge the effectiveness of your audiovisual aids. Make mental notes about which types of aids are most effective. Then, use this knowledge in the future to become an even more effective presenter.

Placing Support Materials into Your Presentation

Now that you know the types of materials available to support the main points of your presentation, you will need to place the materials into the presentation. You might want to go back to your original outline and use it or pull the main points out of the outline and list them on a separate sheet of paper. In either case, review the information you have up to this time and list the support materials under the appropriate point. Be sure to include any ideas that you have for audiovisual aids as well.

Section 1 Assessment

Visit the *Glencoe Communication Applications* Web site at communicationapplications.glencoe.com and click on **Self-Check and Study Guide 16.1** to review your understanding of using support materials.

Review Key Terms

1. Define the following terms and write each in a sentence: logical proof, statistic, specific instance, testimony, ethical proof, pathetic proof, amplification device.

Check Understanding

2. How might you use each of the three types of proof to persuade your local school board to make improvements to your school's cafeteria? Give one example of each.
3. Use an amplification device to support, clarify, and extend the main point "Swimming is a great way to get in shape."
4. **Apply** Imagine that you have been asked to share with one hundred teenagers your experience volunteering at a children's camp. What audiovisual aids might you use to enhance your presentation? List at least three and describe the reasons for your choices.

APPLICATION *Activity*

Using Audiovisual Aids Using markers and posterboard, craft materials, or the computer, create one of the audiovisual aids from your answer to Question 4 above. Practice your audiovisual aid with a classmate. Was it easy to use? Did your partner easily understand it? As a class, discuss any difficulties you encountered and brainstorm possible solutions. Make any improvements that might be needed.

Technology Skill

Creating Computer Graphics

This chapter describes some of the numerous techniques that you can use to support a presentation. Many speakers generate computer graphics as visual aids for presentations.

Learning the Skill

Before you create any computer graphics, you will have to make some decisions about how they will work with your presentation. Review an outline of your presentation, then decide where visual aids will support an important or difficult point. Next, decide what kind of graphic is best suited to illustrate this point. Make a rough sketch of it so you have an idea of how it should look. Add a title and necessary labels now.

When your sketch is complete, go to the *Insert* menu on your graphics program and select the option that allows you to add pictures or art to your document. Many programs will allow you to either choose from a selection of images or create your own. Select or design the image you want to use, then follow the directions on the screen to insert it into the document.

After inserting the graphic, you can change its size by clicking on and dragging one of the corners of the image. To move the graphic, click on it and drag it to the desired location.

Once you have completed your graphic, ask yourself the following questions: Is the information accurate? Does it add to the clarity of a concept? Are the labels in the right places? Is the graphic in the right place within your presentation?

Practicing the Skill

Assume you are conducting a training seminar for new employees of a chain of pizza shops. Decide what kind of graphic will work best to describe how to make a pepperoni pizza, then make a sketch of it. Perform the following steps to make your sketch into a computer graphic.

Step 1 Go to the *Insert* menu.

Step 2 Choose *Add Pictures* or *Add Art.*

Step 3 Select or create the image that you want to use.

Step 4 Insert the graphic into your presentation document by following the directions on the screen.

Step 5 If necessary, change the size or position of the graphic.

Step 1
Go to
Insert menu

Step 2
Select
Add Art or *Add Picture*

Step 3
Choose
an image

Step 4
Insert
image

Step 5
Adjust
size or position

Choose *Add Table* from your *Insert* menu. Some programs have a separate *Table* menu. Create a table that shows your school classes and after-school activities for next week. Provide the days of the week, the name of each course or activity, and the time that you will be spending on each. Use your name in the title.

Developing Your Oral Presentation Style

GUIDE TO READING

Objectives

1. Identify the three elements of oral style.
2. Use language devices to enhance presentations.
3. Explain the relationship between oral style and presentation effectiveness.

Terms to Learn

oral style
parallelism
antithesis

Do you know someone who is described as "having style"? What does that mean? It probably refers to the way he or she dresses, walks, styles his or her hair, or even the way that person acts. What do you consider to be the elements of style? How can you determine and develop your own style?

Believe it or not, everyone has style. Style is simply a way of doing things. However, whether someone's style is good or bad, updated or old-fashioned, exciting or boring is up to interpretation. Everyone who comes into contact with you—as you work, play, or even give a presentation—personally evaluates your style.

Elements of Oral Style

The idea of what is stylish is determined by individual preferences. For instance, you may find a speaker terribly dull while your best friend finds the same person interesting. There are some style basics, however, that can help ensure a positive reaction. This is especially true for oral style.

Maya Angelou is well known for her oral style. What is oral style?

Oral style is the way a presenter uses language to express ideas. All of the effort you have put into planning your presentation can be lost if the language you use is too vague or is inappropriate for your audience and task. To begin developing oral style, consider the following three elements of style:

- clarity
- force
- beauty

> **COMMUNICATION *Strategies***
>
> **MAKING CLEAR PRESENTATIONS**
>
> - ✓ Choose words that are not too technical or difficult for your audience to understand.
> - ✓ Consider the connotations of the words you use.
> - ✓ Use standard subject-verb-object sentence order as much as possible, and be sure all modifying words and phrases are as close as possible to the words they modify.
> - ✓ Use perception checks to confirm audience understanding.

Clarity

Clarity is essential to effective communication. If an audience gets confused and does not understand what you are trying to say to them, your presentation is likely to be a failure. Clear word choice and clear organization are essential for presenters and audiences alike.

Word Choice The necessity of clear, easy-to-understand language can be illustrated in a true story. A plumber wrote to a government agency to ask whether there was anything wrong with using hydrochloric acid to clean out drainpipes. The agency responded, "The efficacy of hydrochloric acid is indisputable, but the corrosive effect is incompatible with metallic permanence."

The plumber thanked the agency for approving his idea. Alarmed that the plumber had misunderstood their response, the agency replied, "We cannot assume responsibility for the production of toxic and noxious residue with hydrochloric acid and suggest you use an alternate procedure."

Again, the plumber thanked the agency for its approval. Appalled by the prospect of a plumber ruining hundreds of drainpipes, the agency sent a third reply: "Don't use hydrochloric acid. It eats holes in metal pipes!"

In a presentation, you do not have the luxury of repeating a message until you are sure the audience understands. You have one chance to communicate your idea. Therefore, the language you use must be as clear and easy to understand as possible.

Word Meanings You also need to consider the meanings of the words and phrases you plan to use. Many words carry connotations that go beyond their definitions. In general, presenters tend to use dictionary definitions when their task is to inform an audience and connotations when they want to get the audience emotionally involved in a topic.

Word Order Ideas should be phrased as simply as possible. This typically means using standard subject-verb-object order so that listeners can easily understand and follow your message. Misplaced modifiers often make a message confusing for your audience. Consider this example from a newspaper headline: "Lost Sisters Reunited After Eighteen Years at Grocery Checkout Counter." In this case, word order implied that the people who discovered that they were related had spent years standing in line together.

Of course, incorrect word order sometimes can have a humorous effect in a presentation. More often, however, the result of unclear phrasing is confusion and embarrassment for both you and your audience.

Force

When considering the clarity of your presentation, there really is only one goal: the clearer, the better. However, in the area of force, you have a number of choices.

Force refers to the intensity or energy of your message. A presentation may be intense or relaxed, depending upon your purpose. If you plan to make an impassioned appeal for a worthy cause, your language needs to reflect intense emotion. You might choose words like *urgent* or *struggle* to engage your listeners. On the other hand, a presentation about using yoga to relieve stress might employ words like *tranquil* and *calming* to help set the tone.

Sentence structure also can have an effect on the force of a presentation. Short, choppy sentences tend to give an audience a sense of intensity or urgency. Long, fluid sentences tend to have the opposite effect, adding a relaxed tone to a presentation.

Beauty

It is important to consider the language of your presentation as carefully as an artist considers the colors for a painting. Like an artist's colors, the language you choose can add beauty and life to your message. In the context of a presentation, beauty usually refers to the following:

- visual image
- emotion element
- sound

COMMUNICATION PRACTICE LAB

Creating Visual Images

To practice creating visual images with words, follow these steps:

Step 1 Think of your favorite season. Imagine how a perfect day at that time of year might look.

Step 2 Brainstorm a list of words or phrases to describe that day.

Step 3 Using the words from your list, write one or two paragraphs to create a visual image of that day. Imagine that your audience has never experienced this type of day before.

Step 4 Trade descriptions with a classmate. Using your partner's description, sketch a picture of what he or she described.

Step 5 Look at your classmate's drawing of your perfect day. How complete was your description? Was your language precise enough to convey the right visual image?

Step 6 As a class, discuss what kinds of words tend to create the most vivid images. Create a class list of descriptive words to use as a reference when giving presentations.

Global Communication

Translations

If you go to work for a multinational corporation, you may be involved in manufacturing or selling products in other countries. This means that you will have to pay close attention to word meanings when you are developing product instructions, logos, or advertisements. For example, if you ask for directions to a library in France or Spain, you will probably be shown to a bookstore. Ask the foreign language teachers at your school about other translation errors that occur in international communications.

Visual Image Competent communicators work to paint pictures with their words. The visual image a presenter creates in the minds of audience members can have a tremendous impact on a presentation's effectiveness.

Think, for example, about a presentation on preserving old-growth forests. Which paints a more effective image in your mind—a description of "mighty giants, towering over the forest floor" or "really big trees"? Using vivid and descriptive imagery in your language makes a presentation not only more interesting but also more persuasive and memorable.

Emotional Element Language also has an emotional impact on an audience. For example, the word *house* tends to elicit a fairly neutral response from an audience, but the word *home* can evoke much more positive emotions. Short, rapidly spoken sentences may convey a feeling of impatience or urgency, while longer, more leisurely spoken sentences can have a relaxing effect on an audience. As a presenter, try to choose and arrange your words to elicit an appropriate emotional response from members of your audience.

Sound Poets, in particular, know how to master the specific sound of language. Since language is based on sound, it makes sense that the acoustic appeal of language is an important element in writing and speaking. Harsh, guttural words, such as *dark* and *growling*, tend to evoke negative responses from an audience. Soft, tender words, such as *lush* and *purring*, tend to bring more positive responses. Again, choose language sounds that will add to the overall impact of your message.

Improving Your Oral Style

One way to improve your oral style for a presentation is to write parts of the presentation in manuscript form. Because writing takes longer than speaking, you will have more time to make conscious decisions about the words and phrasing you will use in your presentation. This is particularly helpful if you have some communication apprehension about what you plan to say in the introduction or the conclusion of your presentation.

Using Language Devices

Now that you have read about the basic elements of oral style, what can you do to develop a style of your own? You can begin to develop your own style by incorporating figurative language and stylistic devices into your presentations.

Figurative Language

Figurative language can make your speech more artistic, visual, and memorable. Similes, metaphors, and personification are three effective ways to add interest to presentations.

Similes A simile is a device used to compare two things that are essentially different but that have something in common. A simile usually includes the word *like* or *as*, for example, "ran like the wind" or "white as snow." This type of comparison is very effective for helping an audience relate something it knows little about to something with which it is more familiar.

Be careful, however, when you use similes in your presentation. Some similes have been overused and sometimes can make a presentation seem somewhat stale. These include similes such as "fresh as a daisy," "fit as a fiddle," "busy as a bee," and "happy as a lark."

Metaphors A metaphor is a different kind of device for showing what two things have in common. Unlike a simile, however, a metaphor does not use the word *like* or *as*. Rather, a metaphor literally substitutes one kind of object or idea for another to suggest similarity. For example, "Her hands were ice cubes" and "a pillow of air" are metaphors. Metaphors tend to be subtler than similes, and, therefore, may not always be universally understood. However, a well-phrased metaphor can create a vivid image in the mind of your audience.

Sometimes, a single metaphor can be expanded and developed throughout an entire section of a presentation. These extended metaphors are called analogies. Analogies are effective tools to use when you are explaining a concept or process that is completely new to your audience. By comparing the entire idea or process to something that the audience already knows, you will increase their understanding of your message.

Personification Another way to add style to your language is to use personification. You personify an inanimate, or nonliving, object by giving it human characteristics. Shown in **Figure 16–5,** "The wind whispered through the trees" assigns the human characteristic of whispering to an inanimate object, the wind. Ronald Reagan personified the government when he said, "Government growing beyond our consent had become a lumbering giant, slamming shut the gates of opportunity, threatening to crush the very roots of our freedom."

Personification is useful for adding interest and intensity to your language. It also can help you relate even the most abstract concept to audience members by giving that concept familiar human traits.

Learning about language devices helps a speaker develop oral style.
When is an analogy effective in a presentation?

Figure 16–5 **Personification of Wind**

Stylistic Devices

Your presentations can be made even more interesting through the use of stylistic language devices. Stylistic devices add appeal to your ideas through the use of sound. Two of the most effective stylistic devices are rhythm and alliteration.

Rhythm Rhythm doesn't necessarily add to the meaning of a message. However, it can add appeal to your presentation. Rhythm helps words fit together with an almost musical style. Jesse Jackson, an American activist, minister, and gifted speaker, is well known for his use of rhythm, as well as other stylistic devices, in his speech. One of Jackson's most popular quotes is, "If [today's students] can conceive it and believe it, they can achieve it. They must know it is not their aptitude but their attitude that will determine their altitude." By carefully sequencing words to develop an interesting string of sounds, Jackson enhances the impact and memorability of his words and ideas. You can do the same through the use of rhythm in your presentations.

Of course, a presentation is not a poem and, therefore, should not emphasize sound and rhythm at the expense of meaning. The meaning of your message should always take priority over style, but rhythm can add great acoustic appeal when used sparingly.

Alliteration A good way to make your ideas easy for your audience to remember is to use alliteration. Alliteration is the repetition of beginning consonant sounds in a series of close or adjoining words.

"The serpent slithered silently" is a particularly effective use of alliteration. Not only does the repeated *s* sound make an impact, but it also mimics the hissing sound classically associated with snakes. You probably remember many of the tongue twisters you learned as a child because of the alliteration they use.

Used sparingly, alliteration can add interest to your presentation and make it more appealing to your audience. Too much alliteration, on the other hand, can have an unintentionally humorous effect. It may draw so much attention to itself that the meaning of your message gets lost.

Rhetorical Devices

Rhetoric is a skilled, effective use of speech. A rhetorical device, then, is a tool for making speech more effective. These special tools,

Figure 16–6 Rhetorical Devices

Rhetorical Questions:	Questions asked for effect to encourage listener participation.
Parallelism:	Arranging sentences so words or phrases are similar in structure and length to add rhythm to presentation.
Antithesis:	Pairing opposing words and ideas to produce clever or memorable phrases.

shown in Figure 16–6, not only can help you make your ideas clearer, but they also can help make your speech more memorable to your audience.

Rhetorical Questions As you read in Chapter 15, a rhetorical question is a question asked simply to achieve an effect. It is not intended to be answered aloud. Speakers often use rhetorical questions to state their main ideas in an effort to draw the audience into a presentation. Even though audience members don't answer a rhetorical question aloud, they are likely to form a mental response. In this way, a rhetorical question encourages listeners' participation in a topic.

Parallelism Presenters use parallelism to add structure and rhythm to a presentation. **Parallelism** is arranging sentences so that words and phrases are similar in length and structure. For example, two or more sentences may begin with the same noun, each may begin with a gerund, or each may contain the same prepositional phrase.

In some cases, parallelism is as simple as repeating a key word or statement throughout a topic point or an entire presentation. In his "I Have a Dream" speech, Martin Luther King Jr. used the phrases "I have a dream" and "Let freedom ring" as parallel elements. So effective were these devices that they have become icons for the civil rights movement in the United States.

Parallel structure is effective because it adds rhythm to your presentation. As you read earlier, rhythm helps make your ideas more memorable. It also can make your presentation clearer and more enjoyable for an audience.

Antithesis A third type of rhetorical device is antithesis. **Antithesis** involves pairing opposing words or ideas together. It has long been a favorite of accomplished presenters because it tends to produce clever, memorable phrases. "Sink or swim" is a famous example of antithesis.

You may be thinking that oral style is great for famous speakers who make many presentations. However, even an everyday presentation can be livened up with a little creative style. Whatever you can do to help your audience enjoy and remember your words will bring you closer to achieving the overall goal of your presentation.

Developing Continuity

Once you have developed your main ideas and have experimented with the language you want to use in your presentation, you need to decide how to link your ideas together for your audience. You can do this by using the following tools:

- transitions
- signposts
- previews and summaries

Transitions As you learned earlier in Chapter 15, smooth transitions help you and your audience move effortlessly through your presentation. A clear transition (1) clarifies the relationship between the two thoughts it bridges, (2) brings closure to the previous point before beginning the next, and (3) alerts the listener that you are changing points.

The language of transitions includes transitional adverbs and conjunctions. "Having just seen . . . let's proceed," "On the other hand," "In addition," and "Finally," are all transitional phrases that are used to begin statements that bridge ideas together. Rhetorical questions can also be used to link one idea to another. "If this is really true, then what about . . . ?"

A transition may relate to what has just been said and may serve as a summary before going on to the next idea. For example, Raymond Smith, in his presentation on Cyberhate, uses this summary type of transition when he says, "Internet access alone, however, won't build bridges of understanding between people—or level the playing field between cyberhaters and the targets of their hate." He summarizes one idea, Internet access, but lets the audience know that more about creating understanding between people is to follow.

You can think of more transition strategies as you write your presentation and encounter the shifts and ideas that need linking. If you develop your statements and restatements carefully, clear transitions usually emerge naturally.

Signposts Signposts label main ideas as main ideas. In some cases this is as simple as saying, "My first point is . . . ," "My second point is . . . ," and so forth. Katherine Clark in her presentation *The Great Equalizers* simply numbers her main points 1, 2, 3, and so on and uses the numbers in her presentation as signposts.

Some transitional adverbs also stand alone as signposts. "Next," "Second," and "Finally," each can stand alone to signal a new idea. If all your main ideas (and nothing else) are stated as rhetorical questions, your audience should catch on fairly quickly that every time you ask a rhetorical question, you are beginning a new idea.

Previews and Summaries Previews and summaries can also be used to provide listening cues or memory hooks for your audience. If you follow the tradition of "tell them what you're going to tell them, tell them, and then tell them what you've told them," then you already know the importance of previews (tell them what you're going to tell them) and summaries (tell them what you've told them). Previews and summaries help an audience to follow your presentation and prevent them from getting lost in the information.

Internal previews can provide listening cues for your audience. If, for example, you have divided a main point explaining a problem into two sub-points, you may want to preview the sub-points to let the audience know what to listen for. "As I discuss this problem, I will focus on the conditions that underlie the problem and their causes." As a different preview, you could say, "I want you

interNET ACTIVITY

I Have a Dream Dr. Martin Luther King Jr.'s equal rights speech presented in Washington, D.C., in 1963 is one of the most compelling and eloquent speeches of the twentieth century. You can access the text of this speech on the Internet by entering the phrase *I Have a Dream* into a search engine. Read the speech and identify examples of figurative language, stylistic devices, and rhetorical devices.

to consider three causes for this problem." In either instance, you are giving the audience a clue as to what you want them to get from the point.

Internal summaries keep the audience from getting lost during your presentation. It gives the audience a chance to catch up with you and refreshes their memory about what you just said that was important. Internal summaries are often used just before the last point of a presentation to summarize the content to that point. It keeps the audience focused on what you want them to take as important from your presentation.

Effective transitions, signposts, and internal previews and summaries are evidence of clarity in speaking. These are strategies that can prove to be useful in your writing, but they are essential to you and your listeners as they attempt to follow and understand your presentation. The skillful use of these strategies indicates that you fully appreciate the value of a clear, polished presentation style and that you recognize your audience's hard work.

Section 2 Assessment

Visit the *Glencoe Communication Applications* Web site at **communicationapplications.glencoe.com** and click on **Self-Check and Study Guide 16.2** to review your understanding of oral presentation style.

Review Key Terms

1. Define the following terms and write each in a sentence: oral style, parallelism, antithesis.

Check Understanding

2. Identify and describe the three elements of oral style.
3. Choose a language device and use it to enhance a presentation on roller coasters.
4. **Predict** How might oral style make a difference in the effectiveness of a presentation?

APPLICATION Activity

Developing Oral Style As a class, brainstorm a list of presentation topics. Choose one of the topics and create an example of each type of language device for that topic. Share your examples as a class. Discuss which language devices were the most difficult to use and which were the easiest. Work together to develop helpful tips for creating language devices.

Communication Self-Assessment

Supporting Presentations

How Do You Rate?

On a separate sheet of paper, use the key to respond to the following statements. Put a check mark at the end of each skill you would like to improve.

KEY: **A** Always **U** Usually **S** Sometimes **R** Rarely **N** Never

1. When I develop ideas, I introduce, amplify and support, and then restate them.
2. I try to balance evidence that supports my ideas by using logic, personal experiences, and emotional appeals.
3. When I amplify an idea, I use vivid descriptions and examples.
4. I use visual aids to give my presentation clarity, interest, and appeal.
5. I know when a model, videotape, graph, or pictorial image is the best means of supporting an idea.
6. My presentation skills include knowing where to put audiovisual materials and using audience feedback to assess their effectiveness.
7. My presentation style is clear because I use words my audience can understand and sentences that are concise and clearly constructed.
8. To involve the audience, I pair opposing words or ideas, ask rhetorical questions, and use sentences of similar length and structure.

How Do You Score?

Review your responses. Give yourself 5 points for every A, 4 for every U, 3 for every S, 2 for every R, and 1 for every N. Total your points and evaluate your score.

31–40 Excellent You may be surprised to find out how much you can improve your skills.

21–30 Good In this course, you can learn ways to make your skills better.

11–20 Fair Practice applying the skills taught in this course.

1–10 Needs Improvement Carefully monitor your improvement as you work through this course.

Setting Communication Goals

If you scored Excellent or Good, complete Part A. If your score was Fair or Needs Improvement, complete Part B.

Part A

1. I plan to put the following ideas into practice:
2. I plan to share the following information about communication with the following people:

Part B

1. The behaviors I need to change most are:
2. To bring about these changes, I will take these steps:

Writing a Thank-You Letter

A thank-you letter is a way of expressing gratitude for a gift or an opportunity. It serves as a way to strengthen a professional relationship. For example, a recent high school or college graduate might write a thank-you letter to a possible employer after an interview. A supervisor might write a thank-you letter to an employee to show appreciation for a job done well. The procedure for writing a thank-you letter follows.

Use a Business Letter Format. The format for a thank-you letter is the same as that of a business letter, which was presented in Chapter 5. Start the note with a heading that includes your address and the date. The inside address, which consists of the name and address of the recipient, follows the heading. The salutation, or greeting, comes after the inside address and is followed by a colon. The next segment of the thank-you letter is the body, which contains the main part of your message. The closing comes after the body and may contain words like *Sincerely*, *Respectfully*, or *With warm regard.* Capitalize the first letter and place a comma after the closing. Follow this with your signature and typed name.

Organize Your Ideas. Use the principles of outlining presented in Chapter 15. Cluster your thoughts and brainstorm about what you want to say. Begin by stating your reason for writing. Explain the details, facts, and ideas you want to cover in the body of the letter. In the last paragraph of the letter, mention something that will help to build and develop your professional relationship with the other person.

Personalize the Letter. Sometimes, it is necessary to write to several people at the same time. When you do this, it is important to personalize each thank-you letter. You can do this by acknowledging your last contact with the person. You can also personalize each thank-you letter by passing along a greeting to the person's family or co-workers, if you have met them.

Be Sincere. Reinforce the notion that you are honest and your reader can trust you. If you are insincere or deceitful, you may offend your audience.

Create a Good Impression. Check your letter for mistakes. Use correct grammar, and do not misspell any words, especially names. It is worth the extra time and effort to proofread all parts of your letter. This extra step shows that you care about what you do.

For additional information about business writing, see the *Guide to Business Communication* section of the Communication Survival Kit in the Appendix.

Communication Through Writing

Ms. Audrey Whitstone
Sunnyside Hospital
5514 Alameda Street
Los Angeles, CA 90036

October 30, 2002

Mrs. Walter Maier
3515 Welcome Street
Huntington Beach, CA 92647

Dear Mrs. Maier:

I am writing to thank you for your support of our fall fund-raiser. Your attendance and financial contribution will surely help with our efforts to build a new children's wing.

As you know, we are committed to providing quality health care for children in a pleasant, home-like environment. Your attendance at our fund-raiser will go a long way toward making this dream possible. With revenues from the fund-raiser, we are now three-fourths of the way toward our goal. The care and concern shown by people like you have made a considerable difference in funding this project.

Mrs. Maier, we are grateful for your ten years of faithful service to Sunnyside Hospital and hope to see you at our December luncheon to honor patrons like you.

Sincerely,
Audrey Whitstone
Audrey Whitstone
Director of Development

WRITING *Activity*

Assume that you are a member of a professional teaching organization. The organization has asked you to write a thank-you letter to a recent guest speaker. Write a thank-you letter using the following information. Use today's date and your own name and address. Make your letter as positive and personalized as possible.

- Your organization is called the National Teaching Association.
- Your group held its annual meeting last month in Washington, D.C.
- The name of the speaker was Wylie Butler. His address is 284 Connecticut Avenue, Washington, D.C. 20028.
- The topic of the speech was "Computers in the Classroom."
- The speaker appeared at a previous convention.
- A handbook summarizing the speaker's information was given to all of the teachers at the convention.
- Many teachers you have spoken to have already had great success using the speaker's suggestions.

CHAPTER 16 Assessment and Activities

Visit the *Glencoe Communication Applications* Web site at **communicationapplications.glencoe.com** and click on **Chapter 16 Activity** for additional practice in developing and supporting your ideas.

Reviewing Key Terms

On a separate sheet of paper, write whether each statement below is true or false. Rewrite each false statement, deleting the term that makes it false and underlining the term that you substitute.

1. A pathetic proof adds the strongest support to a point.
2. A testimony is a type of proof presented as a number.
3. Specific instances tend to relate information more personally than statistics.
4. A direct quote or summary of a quote is called a specific instance.
5. The most common ethical proof is personal experience.
6. A logical proof gives emotional appeal to a presentation.
7. A verbal description is a kind of audiovisual aid.
8. Oral style is the way a presenter uses objects.
9. Arranging sentences so phrases are similar in length and structure is called parallelism.
10. Alliteration involves pairing opposing words.

Reviewing Key Concepts

1. Why is the way a presenter develops and supports his or her main points important?
2. For what three purposes can statistics be used in a presentation?
3. When is expert testimony particularly effective for establishing credibility?
4. Why should a presenter avoid overusing pathetic proofs?
5. Name four kinds of amplification devices.
6. In what five ways do audiovisual aids enhance a presentation?
7. How can a presenter keep a model or live object from distracting the audience's attention from his or her message?
8. What kind of graph best illustrates the relationship between two or more trends?

Assessment and Activities

Reading and Critical Thinking Skill

1. **Making Comparisons** Compare the use of comparisons and contrasts as amplification devices.
2. **Classifying Information** In what category of audiovisual aids does a videotape belong?
3. **Summarization** Sum up the three ways to give your oral style clarity.
4. **Applying Information** Write a sentence that will give an audience a sense of urgency about preserving the environment.
5. **Synthesis** Create a passage for a presentation on how to preserve the environment by using two of the three rhetorical devices—rhetorical questions, parallelism, and antithesis.

Skill Practice Activity

Writing an Outline At the top of a separate sheet of paper, write the thesis statement "How can our environment be preserved?" Then, make an outline using phrases rather than sentences. List your main ideas six lines apart and number them with Roman numerals. Add supporting ideas, beginning with capital letters. Then, add details with numbers and more specific details with lowercase letters. Remember to indent each level of the outline.

Cooperative Learning Activity

Presenting Visual Aids As a class, organize into pairs. With your partner, pool the information in your outlines from the Skill Practice Activity. Next, brainstorm a list of the kinds of visuals that would support points in the outlines. Then, you and your partner each choose a way to present the visual aids from the following list: flip charts/poster boards, transparencies, slides, handouts, video/audio cassettes, and computerized displays. Create your visual aid and display it in the classroom beside your partner's work.

Chapter Project

Planning Find the words to a memorable speech, such as Abraham Lincoln's Gettysburg Address, Martin Luther King Jr.'s "I Have a Dream" Speech, or any other powerful speech. As you read the speech, look for the following language devices: similes, metaphors, personification, rhythm and rhyme, alliteration, rhetorical questions, parallelism, and antithesis.

Presenting On a poster, glue an enlarged copy of the speech you chose. Mark the examples of different language devices with different colored highlighters. Make a key at the bottom of the poster to show which color represents which device. Present your poster to the class, pointing out the various language devices. Display the poster in the classroom.

CHAPTER 17 Preparing for Presentations

"There are no secrets to success. It is the result of preparation, hard work, and learning from failure."
—Colin Powell, retired U.S. Army General

WHY IT'S IMPORTANT

Preparation is important for success in many arenas, including presentations. Working to plan your speeches before you make them will help you meet your presentation goals.

To better understand the final steps in preparing a presentation, view the **Communication in Action** Chapter 17 video lesson.

GLENCOE Online

Visit the *Glencoe Communication Applications* Web site at **communicationapplications.glencoe.com** and click on **Overview–Chapter 17** to preview information about preparing presentations.

Section 1

Preparing for Individual Presentations

GUIDE TO READING

Objectives

1. Describe when manuscript delivery is the best choice for a presentation.
2. Summarize the advantages and disadvantages of extemporaneous and impromptu deliveries.
3. Choose the best delivery method for a given situation.
4. Prepare notes and manuscripts for presentations.

Terms to Learn

method of delivery
manuscript presentation
extemporaneous presentation
impromptu presentation

Have you ever tried to repeat a funny story to some friends, only to discover that they failed to see the humor in it? That kind of thing can disappoint and bewilder you. The story was so funny when you first heard it. What happened?

Why didn't your friends laugh? The chances are good that the problem was the way you told the story. Much of the meaning of a message is in the way it is presented to an audience. If you want the audience to react in a certain way to a message, it's important to select the right way to present it.

SELECTING A METHOD OF DELIVERY

So far, you have worked to develop the message of your presentation. Now you need to select the best possible way of getting your idea across to your audience. In other words, it's time to select a method of

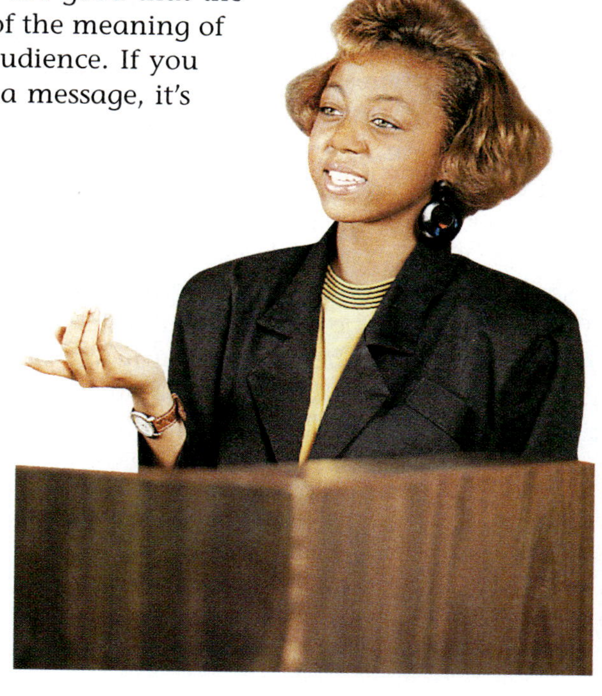

The success of a presentation can be determined by the preparation. **What determines how an audience receives a message?**

delivery for your presentation. The **method of delivery** is the way you orally send your message to your audience. You can use any of four different methods of delivery for a presentation:

- memorized
- manuscript
- extemporaneous
- impromptu

Memorized Presentations

When you memorize something, you learn it word for word. If you are apprehensive about your presentation, you may reasonably think your best plan is to memorize it.

Disadvantages Be cautious about using memorization as a delivery method. It can end up in disaster! If you forget even one word, you can lose your place and then lose the message of the entire presentation.

Another disadvantage to memorized presentations is that, very often, they sound memorized. The presenter forgets to think about the meaning of his or her presentation when it is in progress. The presenter concentrates on the words of the presentation instead of the message the words should relay to the audience. The result is a formal, boring recitation, rather than a lively interaction with an audience. When you deliver a memorized presentation, you must remember that, although the message is quite familiar to you, each audience member is hearing it for the first time. Adapt to audience feedback to bring a memorized presentation to life.

Advantages Despite the drawbacks of memorizing an entire presentation, there are times when a presenter may wish to memorize parts of a presentation. For example, when making a sales pitch to a client, a salesperson should have memorized the main features of his or her product or service. Having to flip through notes or ask someone else at a critical point in the presentation could damage the salesperson's credibility with his or her customer.

In addition, many presenters find it helpful to memorize just the introduction and conclusion of a presentation. This allows them to establish eye contact with audience members and be perceived with a positive image. Many presenters who use manuscript delivery, which you will learn about next, memorize the first and last sentence of each page so that they can maintain eye contact when turning the page. This helps the presenter keep the audience's attention focused on the message of the presentation instead of on the distraction of turning the page.

Manuscript Presentations

A **manuscript presentation** is delivered with the full text in front of the presenter. The presenter refers to the manuscript to be sure of his or her exact language during the presentation.

Advantages There are occasions when you may be asked to make a presentation on a very sensitive topic or when you will be held accountable for your exact words. Other times, the text of your presentation may be printed in a company newsletter or sent to local media. Perhaps the audiovisual aids in your presentation will make it necessary to use exact words to cue a technical assistant. In these cases, you will probably want to make a manuscript presentation.

Disadvantages Many beginning presenters are tempted to give manuscript presentations because they think it is the easiest type of presentation to give. Actually, unless you are very expressive when reading aloud, it can be difficult to keep an audience involved in a manuscript presentation. When you are tied to a manuscript, you do not have the flexibility to adapt your message to your audience. Audience members who do not understand your message will be left behind. Moreover, constantly looking down at the manuscript can keep you from developing eye contact and interacting well with your audience members. This can cause them to feel left out or, worse, to think that you don't know what you are talking about. Either impression damages your credibility.

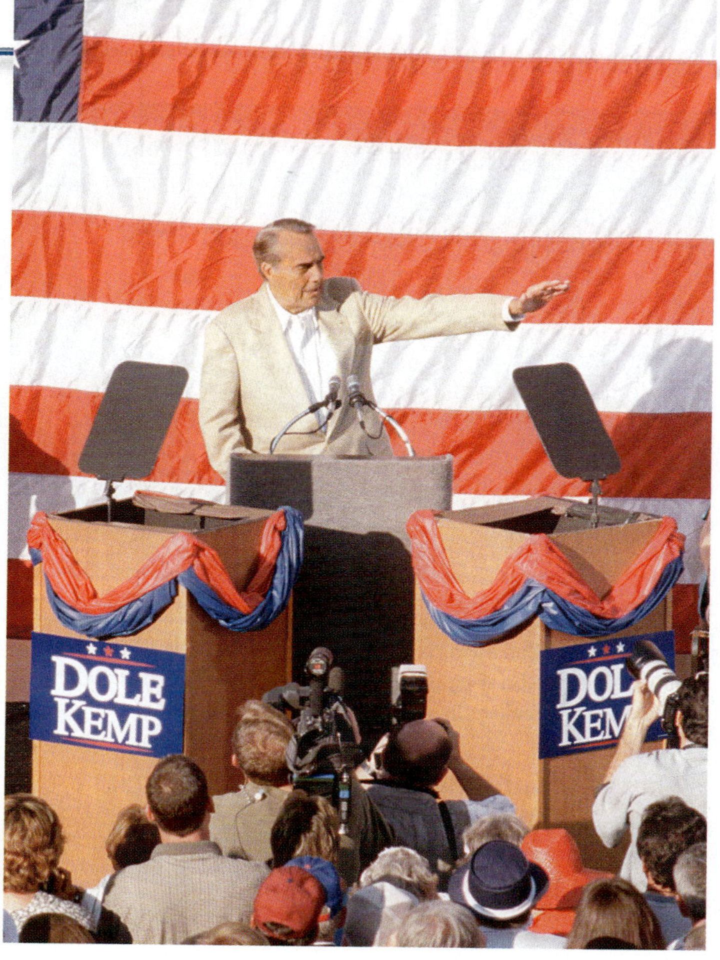

Presidential candidate Bob Dole uses a TelePrompTer® to deliver a manuscript presentation. What is a manuscript presentation?

Extemporaneous Presentations

An **extemporaneous presentation** is a presentation that is thoroughly prepared and rehearsed in advance and given with the use of notes. This is the type of presentation you might be asked to make to a group of new employees to explain your company's policies. Medical personnel sometimes make extemporaneous presentations to various support groups and special health-care interest groups. You may have a special cause or concern that motivates you to solicit funds or support. In any of these situations, an extemporaneous speech probably would be the best choice. In fact, *most* presentations you make are likely to be extemporaneous.

Advantages The first advantage is that you typically have plenty of time to prepare extemporaneous presentations. This preparation time allows you to adapt your presentation so that you can fully meet the needs of your specific audience, occasion, and task. An extemporaneous speech also encourages you to be more conversational in your presentation than you might be with a memorized or manuscript presentation.

Another advantage of an extemporaneous presentation is that it changes each time you give it. It is always fresh.

Disadvantages In some situations, being extemporaneous can be a disadvantage. For example, if you are required to say something in a specific way each time you present it, or if a record of your words is necessary, you probably would be better off using a manuscript. Another disadvantage of giving an effective extemporaneous presentation

The person called upon to answer the question Wolf Blitzer asked during a White House briefing gave an impromptu presentation. What is required of speakers in an impromptu presentation?

is that it usually takes more rehearsal time than other types of presentations. That's because you need to be sure of what you plan to say and how you plan to say it.

Impromptu Presentations

For many people, the most intimidating type of presentation is the impromptu presentation. An **impromptu presentation** is a presentation for which there is little or no time for advance preparation. Many of the informal presentations you will be required to make at work will be impromptu. For instance, your supervisor may stop by your desk and ask for a brief update on your project. A client may inquire about a charge on an invoice, and you will need to give a brief presentation on the spot. Even if you're not aware of it, you probably make a number of impromptu presentations at school each day. When a teacher calls on you in class, your answer is an impromptu presentation. You may use this type of presentation to voice your opinions during committee or club meetings.

An impromptu presentation requires you to "think on your feet" and speak accurately about something with no formal preparation. This can be unnerving to even the most experienced presenter. However, you can take comfort in the fact that most impromptu presentations are on topics you already know something about or that affect you personally. If you are asked to make an impromptu statement on a topic that you know very little about, it is best to decline politely or delay until you have time to learn more.

However, there are many times when declining would be impossible or unwise. If you must make an impromptu presentation, remember the Communication Strategies below.

Advantages The biggest advantage of learning how to make an effective impromptu

COMMUNICATION *Strategies*

Making an Effective Impromptu Presentation

- Take a moment to gather your thoughts on the topic.
- Run through the parts of a presentation and the presentation process in your mind.
- Make notes on a small piece of paper.
- State a point, support it, restate it, and relate it to the next point.
- Remember to include a brief conclusion.

presentation is that it gives you confidence to speak out on topics that concern you. Also, someone who makes good impromptu presentations at work often will be regarded as a leader or role model.

Disadvantages An obvious disadvantage of impromptu presentations is the lack of time to thoroughly prepare. Also, these presentations require you to think quickly and formulate ideas as you present them.

Memorized, manuscript, extemporaneous, and impromptu presentations make different demands on the presenter. However, no matter which method of delivery you use, your goal remains the same: to make the audience see your ideas and remember them.

Figure 17–2 Impromptu Presentation Notes

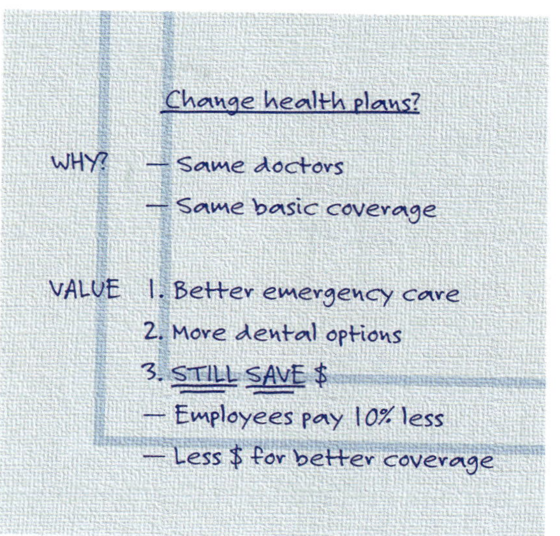

Change health plans?
WHY?
— Same doctors
— Same basic coverage
VALUE
1. Better emergency care
2. More dental options
3. STILL SAVE $
— Employees pay 10% less
— Less $ for better coverage

Preparing Notes and Manuscripts

With the exception of impromptu speeches, most of your presentations will allow you to follow the seventh step in the Presentation Preparation Process, as shown in Figure 17–1: Prepare your manuscript or notes or both for delivery. Once you have decided upon a method of delivery, you can then design the notes that will help you make a smooth presentation.

Figure 17–1 Steps of the Presentation Preparation Process

1. Determine a topic.
2. Limit the topic.
3. Determine the purpose.
4. Research the topic.
5. Organize and outline the presentation.
6. Select supporting information.
7. Prepare notes and manuscript for delivery.
8. Rehearse the presentation.

Notes for Impromptu Presentations

There really are no special techniques for developing notes for an impromptu presentation. You usually only have enough time to jot down the main ideas you want to cover in your talk. These notes can be written on any small piece of paper that you may have lying around—even if it is the back of an agenda or a napkin, such as the one in Figure 17–2.

As you think through what you want to say in your impromptu presentation, note the main ideas. If you know statistics or other types of support details, write them alongside or under the main idea. Try to keep your notes as brief as possible. You probably won't have time to rehearse, and you don't want to waste time during your presentation searching your notes for what to say next.

Figure 17–3 **Notes for Extemporaneous Presentations**

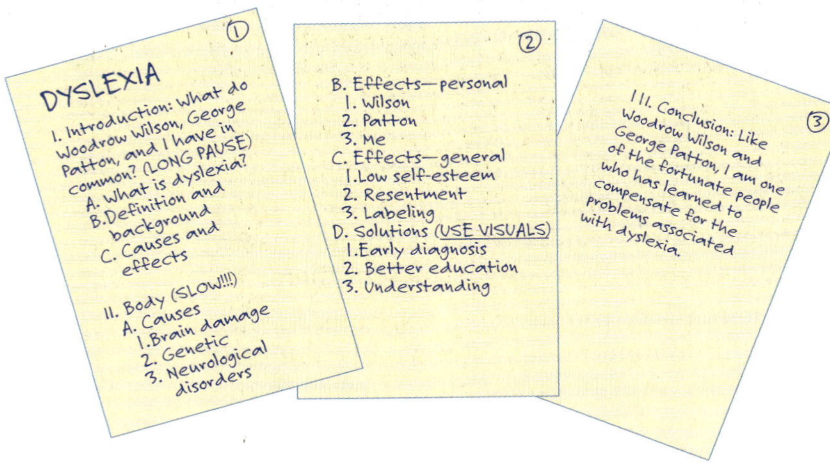

①
DYSLEXIA
I. Introduction: What do Woodrow Wilson, George Patton, and I have in common? (LONG PAUSE)
A. What is dyslexia?
B. Definition and background
C. Causes and effects
II. Body (SLOW!!!)
A. Causes
1. Brain damage
2. Genetic
3. Neurological disorders
②
B. Effects—personal
1. Wilson
2. Patton
3. Me
C. Effects—general
1. Low self-esteem
2. Resentment
3. Labeling
D. Solutions (USE VISUALS)
1. Early diagnosis
2. Better education
3. Understanding
③
III. Conclusion: Like Woodrow Wilson and George Patton, I am one of the fortunate people who has learned to compensate for the problems associated with dyslexia.

Delivery Methods

Delivery can make or break a presentation.

Methods of delivery: SMILE

1. memorized: risk losing place, no "illusion of the first time"
2. manuscript: still, distant, seem not to own the info
3. extemporaneous: thorough rehearsals, use notes, adapt to audience feedback
4. impromptu: think on your feet

Notes for Extemporaneous Presentations

The notes for an extemporaneous presentation should evolve as you rehearse your presentation so that your actual presentation is made using the fewest notes possible. Your notes should be as unnoticeable as possible so they won't be a distraction during your presentation. Many experienced extemporaneous presenters like to use one or two index cards like the ones in Figure 17–3. Some prepare their notes on these cards vertically rather than horizontally so that they will be easier to handle.

Most effective extemporaneous presenters also will memorize their introductions and conclusions in order to establish eye contact with the audience right from the beginning of

COMMUNICATION PRACTICE LAB

Preparing Notes for an Impromptu Presentation

To practice preparing notes for an impromptu presentation, follow these steps:

Step 1 Imagine that you have been asked to give an impromptu presentation on a chapter from this book.

Step 2 Choose a chapter on which you want to speak. Skim that chapter for several minutes.

Step 3 On a small piece of paper, take another minute to write brief notes for your presentation. Be sure to include the main ideas from the chapter.

Step 4 Discuss your notes as a class. What was most difficult about having to work within such a limited time frame? What strategies did you use to skim the chapter? How did you decide what to include in your notes?

a presentation. They will begin their notes with their thesis statement and then list the main ideas, leaving room to include the support materials.

It is a good idea to include in your notes a reminder about any visual aids you plan to use during your presentation. Also, it can be a good idea to write delivery reminders in your notes, even simple ones like "smile" or "slow down." Include whatever you feel will help you present your ideas effectively.

Manuscripts for Manuscript Presentations

Most presentation manuscripts are typed using a large font and double or triple line spacing. Words and ideas that are intended to be emphasized may be formatted in bold or in a larger font so that they will stand out on the page. In some cases, a presenter may remind himself or herself to stress a specific idea or statement by positioning that information by itself on a page of the manuscript. This can be

GLOBAL COMMUNICATION

What Do You Mean?

Have you ever heard the phrase, "That car is a lemon?" This statement doesn't mean that the car is a piece of sour fruit, it means that the car is poorly made. Translated literally, however, this statement could confuse audience members who are unfamiliar with it. Slang, or informal language, is commonly used in conversation between friends. In a speech presented to an audience from another culture, however, slang is not appropriate. List ten examples of slang words or phrases that should be avoided in formal language. Define each word or phrase. What are some ways that these words and phrases could confuse an audience from another culture?

Former President Ronald Reagan studies his notes for a manuscript presentation. **What kind of delivery reminders might presenters include in their notes?**

a very effective method, but it can cause a simple three-page manuscript to stretch into fifteen or twenty pages.

In addition to marking points of emphasis, you can also mark pauses, other delivery reminders, and cues for visual aids on the manuscript. The key to preparing your manuscript lies in making notations or markings that allow you to easily get back into your presentation if you lose your place. You may wish to use different colors of ink, different fonts or formatting, or even different types and colors of paper.

One way to make the pages of a presentation manuscript easier to handle is to put them into plastic page protectors. If you put the pages back-to-back in the protectors, you will have fewer pages to turn, which will be less distracting for your audience. The plastic covers will also keep the pages from getting ragged and torn as you rehearse your presentation.

Good notes can help you be an effective presenter, no matter what type of delivery you are using. Your notes will help you remember not only important content points but also important points about your delivery.

Section 1 Assessment

Visit the *Glencoe Communication Applications* Web site at **communicationapplications.glencoe.com** and click on **Self-Check and Study Guide 17.1** to review your understanding of preparing for individual presentations.

Review Key Terms

1. Define each term and write it in a sentence: method of delivery, manuscript presentation, extemporaneous presentation, impromptu presentation.

Check Understanding

2. Under what circumstances might a manuscript delivery be the best choice for a presentation?
3. Compare and contrast the advantages and disadvantages of extemporaneous delivery and impromptu delivery.
4. **Synthesize** Imagine that you are the public-relations representative of your company who must present to the media an official statement about a product recall. What type of delivery method will you use? Why?

APPLICATION *Activity*

Preparing Notes and Manuscripts As a class, brainstorm the main points for a persuasive presentation on the topic of e-mail security. Choose one of these main points and use it to develop notes for part of an extemporaneous presentation. Then, use your notes to write a manuscript for your chosen main idea. Compare your notes and manuscript with classmates who chose the same main point. What similarities and differences do you notice?

Technology Skill

Developing a Multimedia Presentation

Multimedia presentations use interactive CD-ROMs, computer-generated graphics, the Internet, slides, photographs, or video recordings. The following information explains how to develop a multimedia presentation.

Learning the Skill

When you're developing a multimedia presentation, there are several aspects to consider. First, consider how you will present your information in words. Think of the verbal portion of your presentation as the script. Your task is to choose visual media that will enhance the words. You can use any multimedia enhancement or any combination of enhancements to support your verbal information.

The next factor to consider is the setting of the presentation. The size and layout of the room should help you determine what multimedia enhancements you will be able to use effectively. If your presentation will be in a small room, for example, you may decide to show a videotape on a television monitor. This same strategy would not work as well in a large auditorium, however.

Another factor to consider is the cost in both time and money. For instance, overhead transparencies or slides will cost less and take less time to produce than video recordings or CD-ROMs. Make sure your schedule and budget will allow you to create the materials you want.

Before deciding on one or more multimedia enhancements, make sure the resources you will need are available to you. Don't decide to create an online presentation, for example, if you do not have access to the Internet for research, rehearsal, and performance.

Practicing the Skill

Follow the steps below to select multimedia enhancements that would strengthen a presentation on "How to Prepare and Use Notes and Text for Extemporaneous and Manuscript Deliveries." Describe how each enhancement would be used.

Step 1 Decide which multimedia enhancements will best support the verbal presentation of your subject.

Step 2 Decide whether the enhancements you have chosen are appropriate for the setting of the presentation.

Step 3 Consider the cost of the presentation in terms of both time and money.

Step 4 Make sure that the multimedia resources you need are available to you.

Step 5 Design your presentation.

Step 6 Review the results. Make any necessary improvements.

Develop a multimedia presentation using the theme "Safe Driving Habits." Address the topics of courtesy, defensive driving, traffic laws, and basic automobile maintenance. Choose the multimedia equipment that you will use in your presentation. Plan how each medium will be used, then produce your material after it has been approved by your teacher.

Section 2

Preparing for Group Presentations

GUIDE TO READING

Objectives

1. Identify and describe the four special types of group presentations.
2. Analyze the appropriateness of each type of group presentation in a given context.
3. Prepare, organize, and participate in a group presentation for an audience.

Terms to Learn

panel discussion
panel discussion-forum
symposium
symposium-forum

Imagine seeing banners around your school with the following advertisements: "Join us for our 15th annual Women's Symposium!" or "Today's Panel Discussion—The Virtual Classroom," or "The French Club Presents Studying Abroad in Paris.*" What might a listener find interesting about any of these events?*

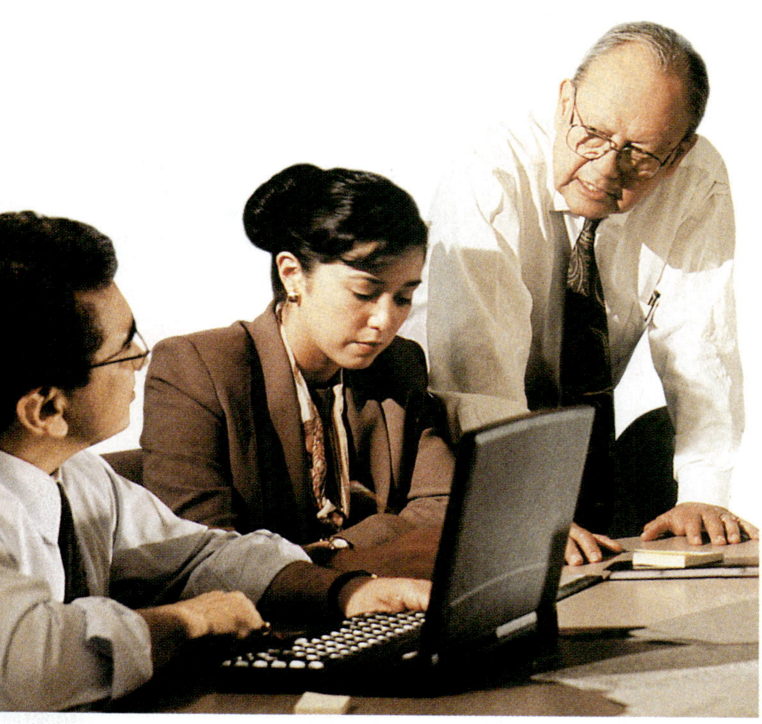

A group prepares for a formal presentation. What do group presentations offer?

Even if you weren't interested in the subject matter of any of these presentations, you still might be intrigued by their group formats. Group presentations allow a variety of speakers to connect with an audience. That variety can add a spark to a topic.

Group Presentations

Not all of the presentations that you make will be individual. The time may come when you are asked to participate with a group of coworkers, classmates, or community members in a formal group presentation. Formal group discussions often are the means by which companies share information—about new products and designs, trends, and innovations—or concerns about industry developments.

A group project at school may be delivered as an internal group presentation to your teacher or your classmates. In the workplace, group presentations may be given to an internal audience, such as a team of employees making proposals or status reports to others in their company. Other times, the audience for a group presentation may be external. Examples of external audiences include public officials explaining their plan to citizens or school officials informing parents of new policies.

Benefits of Group Presentations

Group presentations have a number of advantages over individual presentations. Because there is a variety of speakers, audience members have a greater opportunity to connect with at least one of them. This variety also helps keep the presentation from becoming boring or tedious for audience members.

Preparing a Group Presentation

It is important to remember that the people involved in a group presentation are all distinctive individuals. Therefore, when planning a presentation, group members should work together to determine a consistent overall approach and style. You don't want audience members to feel as if they are listening to several different speeches but rather to one cohesive speech presented by several speakers.

As a group, you might want to choose a leader or moderator. Alternatively, your group may instead choose to have a single spokesperson present the bulk of the information on each main idea. Other group members would then provide examples and extensions of each main idea.

Communication Strategies

Staging an Effective Group Presentation

- **Feel free to move around the room during your presentation.**
- **Remove any physical barriers (such as a podium or a table) between group members and the audience.**
- **Place group members around the room to increase interest and to involve as many audience members as possible.**

Finally, determine the timing and set the pace of your presentation. Since variety is the major advantage of a group presentation, try to balance everyone's speaking time equally.

Rehearsing together can be important to the success of your presentation. You will learn more about rehearsing presentations later in this chapter. However, it is important to remember that when working with a group, rehearsing cues and transitions will help you make the smoothest presentation possible.

Special Types of Group Presentations

Throughout your school and work career, you may participate in many group presentations. In professional and social contexts, there are four special types of group presentations. They are

- panel discussion
- panel discussion-forum
- symposium
- symposium-forum

Jesse Jackson is shown participating in a panel discussion. **What is the function of a panel discussion?**

Panel Discussion

A panel discussion is a formal presentation in which a group of people discusses an announced topic in front of an audience. The function of a panel usually is to provide expert analysis of a problem. The participants of the panel usually are selected because they have some special knowledge about the topic. Panel discussions provide the opportunity to present a variety of views to an audience in a short time frame.

If a panel group is made up of experts or celebrities from diverse locations, there is little likelihood that they will gather to rehearse before the panel. However, if you are involved in a local panel discussion group, you may wish to meet with other panel members prior to the discussion in order to prepare. This helps participants get to know each other, refine their topic, develop a plan for the presentation, agree to gather any additional information they need, and develop procedures for the discussion.

For maximum effectiveness, each panel member should be as prepared and informed as possible. Even one unprepared panel member can negatively influence the outcome of the presentation. The credibility of the overall group depends on the credibility of each individual group member. In addition, all members of the panel need to contribute on all aspects of the topic. This is because most of the information will be shared conversationally rather than as a formal presentation. Just as you wouldn't want one or two people to monopolize a conversation, audiences don't like to hear one or two speakers monopolize a panel discussion.

Format of a Panel Discussion

Even though the body of a panel discussion itself is informal, the format is highly organized, usually following the same organizational plan as an individual presentation. A predetermined leader or chairperson opens the discussion by introducing the members of the panel. The leader then goes on to introduce the topic and provide any audience orientation that may be needed. As you read in Chapter 15, an audience orientation may be necessary to give background information or to define unfamiliar terms.

The procedures that the group has decided upon also may be explained at this time. This may include how the discussion will flow from one topic to another or any other process the group will follow. The leader then may begin the discussion by previewing the main areas on which the discussion will focus. In other words, he or she will provide the introduction of the group presentation.

After the introduction, the entire group discusses the main ideas of the topic just as a presenter would cover the main points of a presentation. Some polite interruptions are allowed in order to keep a spirited discussion going. However, panel members should be courteous and respectful when other panel members are speaking.

The leader of the panel may enter the discussion and present information just like any other group member. However, his or her primary responsibility during this part of the discussion is to keep the panel focused on one topic at a time. It also is the leader's responsibility to provide helpful transitions from one main idea to the next.

At the end of the allotted time period, the leader should briefly summarize what the group has stated and conclude the discussion. If the audience will be allowed to comment or ask questions, the leader should establish the rules at this time. He or she will then act as the moderator of the audience interaction period.

Panel Discussion-Forum When post-discussion interaction with the audience is included as part of the presentation, it is called a **panel discussion-forum.** The audience and the panel members interact and continue the discussion following the panel's presentation.

COMMUNICATION PRACTICE LAB

Participating in a Panel Discussion

To prepare, organize, and participate in a panel discussion, follow these steps:

Step 1 As a class, brainstorm the five most important topics of interest to the students in your school.

Step 2 Divide into five groups according to topic. Choose a leader for your group.

Step 3 As a group, discuss your topic. Share or research enough information for a twenty- to thirty-minute panel discussion.

Step 4 Decide whether your presentation will be informative or persuasive.

Step 5 Prepare an introduction for your group leader to present.

Step 6 Hold your panel discussion with the other groups serving as your audience. Allow time for a question-and-answer session following your presentation.

Step 7 Discuss as a class the effectiveness of each presentation. Did group members all participate equally? Was enough information shared with audience members to adequately inform or persuade them?

Symposium

A symposium is a group presentation in which individual speakers give prepared presentations on aspects of a topic and have little or no interaction with the other presenters. Most often presenters for a symposium are selected because of their expertise on one specific aspect of a topic or for their differing points of view on a topic. Symposia usually are very formal events that do not include active audience participation.

During the actual presentation of a symposium, the leader or moderator has specific duties to perform to keep things flowing smoothly. He or she introduces the speakers and states the topic or topics of the symposium, once again shouldering the responsibility for the introduction. The leader or moderator then introduces each individual presentation, including summaries and transitions from one presentation to the next. Each of these individual presentations is a main point for the body of the group presentation.

Practice for the Workplace

It's a Team Effort Many companies have adopted a team approach in the workplace. It is not always obvious that a team has developed a workplace solution when only one team member presents the information. Sometimes, a group presentation is more powerful or convincing.

BUSINESS PRACTICE *Activity*

Imagine that you are an advocate for teens and suggest building a teen center in your neighborhood. Brainstorm a list of school and community leaders whom you would select to participate in a symposium for which you will be the moderator. What kind of information could each person present in support of the teen center?

These presenters are taking part in a symposium. What is a symposium?

One of the main duties of the leader or moderator is to keep the symposium moving and to prevent individual presentations from taking too long or getting off track. After all the presenters have spoken, the moderator also summarizes and concludes the total presentation.

Symposium-Forum When the audience is invited to ask questions or make comments after the individual presentations, the presentation is called a symposium-forum. As in a panel discussion-forum, in a symposium-forum the moderator is expected to control the forum part of the presentation. He or she should explain the rules for audience participation and then make sure the rules are followed. The moderator is usually the one who calls for each question and decides when a question has been sufficiently answered. When it is time to conclude the presentation, the moderator should thank the participants, summarize the presentation, and dismiss the audience and participants.

Group Presentation Choices

Each of these types of group presentations can be effective when it is presented with the audience and occasion in mind. Panel discussions are better for small audiences in comfortable surroundings. A symposium, with the speakers presenting from a podium or platform, can be overpowering for a small, casual group. On the other hand, it can be difficult for large audiences to understand a panel when each of the members is actively contributing to the discussion. A symposium is the better choice for a large audience and formal occasion.

Section 2 Assessment

Visit the *Glencoe Communication Applications* Web site at **communicationapplications.glencoe.com** and click on **Self-Check and Study Guide 17.2** to review your understanding of preparing for group presentations.

Review Key Terms

1. Define each term and write it in a sentence: panel discussion, panel discussion-forum, symposium, symposium-forum.

Check Understanding

2. Identify and describe the four special types of group presentations.
3. Imagine that a college audience is interested in hearing different professors' opinions on a controversial political issue. Which type of group presentation might be most appropriate? Why?
4. **Analyze** What do you think would be the most difficult part of preparing a group presentation?

APPLICATION *Activity*

Making a Group Presentation Use your notes from the Application Activity in Section 1 to prepare a group presentation. Form groups large enough to cover each main point in your presentation. Then, decide which type of presentation your group will give. Use what you have read in this section to prepare your presentation, and then present it to classmates. Finally, discuss the three formats. Which type was most effective for this topic? Which was easiest to prepare? Which was the most difficult?

Rehearsing Presentations

GUIDE TO READING

Objectives

1. Identify the factors that can contribute to communication apprehension.
2. Utilize strategies to manage communication apprehension, build self-confidence, and gain command of information.
3. Develop strategies to rehearse presentations.

Terms to Learn

communication apprehension
visualization
internalization

Can you imagine Tiger Woods playing in a championship match without ever having swung a golf club? What about a pilot landing a plane without ever having rehearsed landings in a simulator? Imagine a chef creating a seven-layer cake for someone's wedding without ever having baked even a batch of cupcakes.

Rehearsal is important in the development of most skills. Athletes, actors, musicians, surgeons, and many other professionals spend much of their time not in actual performances but behind the scenes, practicing and refining their skills. They realize the importance of practicing so that when they actually perform, they can do so competently.

To improve your presentation skills, it is important to rehearse effectively. In fact, the eighth and final step of the Presentation Preparation Process, shown in **Figure 17–4,** is to rehearse.

Rehearsal is an important step in the process for three reasons. First, it can help you manage any anxiety you are

Rehearsing is important to the development of an effective presentation. Why is rehearsing important?

Figure 17–4 Steps of the Presentation Preparation Process

1. Determine a topic.
2. Limit the topic.
3. Determine the purpose.
4. Research the topic.
5. Organize and outline the presentation.
6. Select supporting information.
7. Prepare notes and manuscript for delivery.
8. Rehearse the presentation.

feeling about your presentation. Second, it helps you gain command of your information. Third, it gives you an opportunity to develop your language and presentation skills, building the confidence you need for a successful presentation.

Managing Communication Apprehension

Your hands are sweaty. You feel perspiration on your brow. Your cheeks are flushed. Your heart is racing. You may even feel faint or sick to your stomach. No, you're not coming down with the flu! You're about to make a presentation. **Communication apprehension,** sometimes known as "stage fright," is fear or nervousness associated with making a presentation.

The physical symptoms described above are the body's way of responding to the surge of adrenaline that is released when you face a challenge. It is only natural to feel some apprehension; you have invested time and energy in preparing your presentation, and you care about the audience's acceptance of it. When you feel panicked, however, remember this: You are not alone. Many surveys show that people fear speaking in public more than anything else.

Causes of Communication Apprehension

There are many reasons for presenters to feel some anxiety before making a presentation. One reason is that doing so may be a new experience for you, and most of us have some fear of things we have not done before. Also, making a presentation focuses audience members' attention directly on you, which may make you uncomfortable. Some people thrive on being the center of attention, while others dread it. No matter which type of person you are, it is impossible to avoid the spotlight when you make a presentation. In fact, being the center of attention is really what you want. You want audience members to understand your message, and the only way for that to happen is for them to focus on you and what you are saying.

Previous bad experiences also can increase your anxiety level. If you have ever had a negative experience giving a presentation, the thought of giving another one may make your stomach feel as if it is full of fluttering butterflies. Remember, though, making a presentation is like falling off a bike. Learning from your mistakes can help you make better decisions next time.

The possible consequences of a presentation are another cause of apprehension for some people. Perhaps the presentation will influence your chances for a raise or promotion at work. Maybe it will affect your standing in your community. A large portion of your final grade in a course may be determined by a single presentation. Any of these situations is enough to make a presenter nervous. In cases such as these, it may be best to remember that the calmer you are, the smoother your presentation will be. Work at calming yourself down, just as you work on being prepared and speaking clearly.

Benefits of Communication Apprehension

Believe it or not, some apprehension is good. It means that you really do care about the outcome of your presentation. Also, the rush of adrenaline in your body increases your energy level so that you can look and sound enthusiastic. Finally, a little apprehension may help you to remain focused on the task of your presentation.

It may help to know that audiences rarely realize how nervous you are during a presentation unless you tell them. Many of the symptoms of nervousness are not visible to others. Even if your jitters are detectable, they probably won't detract from a good presentation. Most audiences want a presenter to succeed.

Communication Apprehension Strategies

There are a number of ways to manage your communication apprehension. Possibly the best way to overcome whatever apprehension you experience before making a professional presentation is to rehearse it. When you rehearse a presentation, you try to simulate the presentation. Rehearsing gives you an opportunity to get feedback about your presentation from someone whose opinion you trust. The more you rehearse a presentation, the more familiar you are with what you want to say and accomplish in the presentation. The more familiar you are with what you want to say and accomplish, the more confidence you have in the presentation and your ability to present it. Rehearsal strategies will be discussed later in this section.

In addition to rehearsing your presentation, there are three specific ways to effectively manage your stage fright. Remember to

- be prepared
- gain experience
- think positively

Be Prepared. One way to control communication apprehension is to be well prepared for your presentation. The better you know the information you want to deliver to the audience, the more confident you can be in presenting it. By following each of the steps in the presentation-preparation process, you can rest assured that your presentation will be well prepared.

Gain Experience. Another way to control communication apprehension is to give more presentations. This is a good way

*inter*NET ACTIVITY

Stage Fright! One of the most important things to remember about stage fright is that most people have it to some degree. For tips on how to prepare yourself mentally and physically for a presentation, search the Internet using the phrases *stage fright* and *performance anxiety.* What are some things that cause stage fright? What can be done to eliminate performance anxiety?

By permission of Mell Lazarus and Creators Syndicate.

to control the fear of the unknown. If you have a job that requires you to make occasional presentations with significant consequences, volunteer to make some smaller, less critical presentations to gain experience. Experience is vital for producing confidence, and confidence helps build credibility.

Think Positively. If you think that you can do something, you usually can. Presenters who face their presentations with a positive outlook tend to develop the confidence necessary to overcome apprehension. On the other hand, speakers who think that their presentations will fail are much more likely to be victims of communication apprehension.

The idea of each of these strategies is to learn to control communication apprehension and make it work for you instead of against you. An experienced presenter may have summed it up best by stating, "The butterflies never really go away; it's just that after a while you teach them to fly in formation."

Developing Rehearsal Strategies

There are a number of strategies to make your rehearsal time as effective as it can be. For maximum benefit from your rehearsals,

- visualize
- plan your rehearsals
- rehearse with an audience
- internalize
- rehearse with your audiovisual aids and notes

Visualize

Begin the process of rehearsing your presentation by visualizing it. Look at the picture in Figure 17–5 on page 552. Visualization is the process of mentally picturing yourself doing something successfully. Imagine making a successful presentation. Hear your name being announced and picture yourself walking confidently to the front of the room. Picture yourself making eye contact with the audience and starting the introduction with poise and self-assurance. Feel the sense of accomplishment you will have as you conclude your presentation knowing that you have done your very best.

Visualization is your mental rehearsal. It should focus only on the positive aspects of your presentation. Either ignore negative images or, better, turn them into positive images. For example, if a certain part of your presentation has been giving you problems, visualize getting through it without any trouble.

Figure 17–5 Visualization

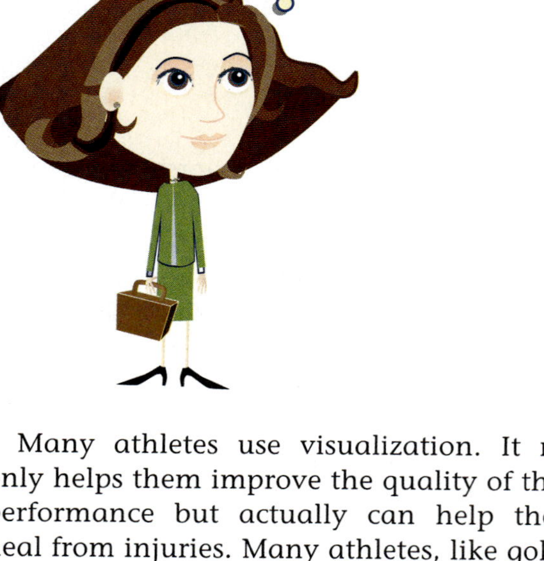

Many athletes use visualization. It not only helps them improve the quality of their performance but actually can help them heal from injuries. Many athletes, like golfer Greg Norman and Olympian Picabo Street, visualize the positive outcome of an ideal round, game, or run. This mental preparation has helped a number of athletes overcome great odds due to an injury or a formidable opponent.

As valuable as this mental rehearsal is, athletes, entertainers, surgeons, and experienced presenters know that they must also physically prepare for their competition or performance. For your presentation to succeed, you also need to take time to physically rehearse.

Plan Your Rehearsals

A rehearsal should be planned almost as carefully as the presentation itself. Try to rehearse in a place that is similar to where the actual presentation will occur. The more authentic the rehearsal surroundings, the more at ease you will be during the actual speech.

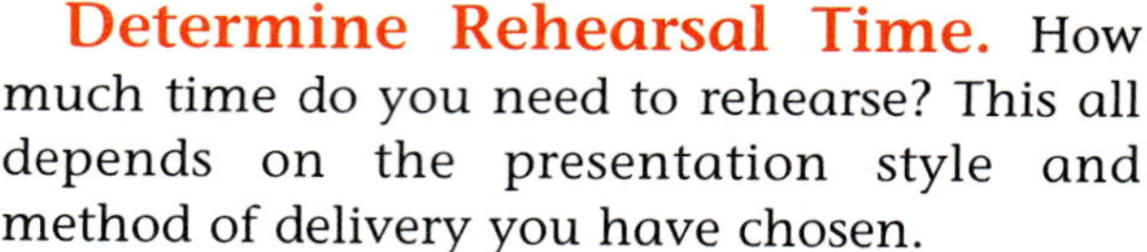

Determine Rehearsal Time. How much time do you need to rehearse? This all depends on the presentation style and method of delivery you have chosen.

In general, extemporaneous presentations require the least amount of rehearsal time. You probably will just need to review your notes aloud, getting used to the way your ideas sound. Your ideas always sound different when you speak them aloud for the first time. You will need to make adjustments in your notes as you familiarize yourself with the physical presentation of your ideas. Then, rehearse again to make sure that you have included enough information in your notes to get you through your presentation. Practice using your audiovisual aids at least three or four times before making the presentation. Remember that an extemporaneous presentation will be different each time you present it. You will need to spend enough time rehearsing so that you are sure you'll say what you want to communicate with your audience each time you make the presentation.

Manuscript presentations, on the other hand, require more rehearsal time for you to thoroughly internalize the information. You need enough practice time for you to master the information in your presentation without having to read it to the audience. This will help you develop enough confidence with your presentation so that during the real performance you can look away from your manuscript to develop eye contact with your audience.

A professional group rehearses together in preparation for a presentation. Which type of presentation requires the most rehearsal time?

Memorized presentations generally require the most rehearsal time of all. The exact amount of rehearsal time needed for a memorized presentation depends on how quickly you can memorize. Just as actors on a stage must memorize their lines and moves, you will have to spend a great deal of time memorizing a presentation.

The rehearsal of any type of presentation can be accomplished in bits and pieces at first. Then, as you develop longer concentration skills and get the individual parts of the presentation ironed out, you can rehearse larger portions of the presentation at one time. Always plan enough rehearsal time to practice your entire presentation several times from start to finish. This helps you develop a sense of the complete presentation.

COMMUNICATION PRACTICE LAB

Visualizing

To practice visualizing a difficult activity, follow these steps:

Step 1 Brainstorm as a class a list of difficult activities. These might include physical activities, such as climbing a mountain or running a marathon, or mental ones, such as taking a final exam.

Step 2 Choose one activity from the list. Think about the steps involved in completing the activity. In running a marathon, for example, you might imagine everything from lacing up your running shoes, to warming up, to walking up to the starting point, running, pacing yourself, and finally crossing the finish line.

Step 3 Close your eyes and visualize yourself completing the activity successfully.

Step 4 Discuss your visualizations as a class. Was positive visualization difficult for you? Did negative images come to mind often? How did you address these negative ones?

Decide How to Rehearse. There is no best way to rehearse a presentation. Select the rehearsal method that works best for you. Some presenters like to have a live audience to provide feedback during a rehearsal. Others prefer to rehearse facing a wall or corner so that they hear only their own voices with no distractions. Some like to watch themselves in a mirror or videotape their rehearsals in order to evaluate and make changes. Occasionally, a presenter will walk around a room, exaggerating his or her nonverbal strategies to get a feel for which ones work best. Experiment with each of these rehearsal methods or develop your own until you find the method that works for you.

TECHNOLOGY *Activity*

Variety is the Spice of Life The same is true in your presentations. One good way to hold your audience's attention is to use several media in presenting your information. With a group, brainstorm a list of ten speech topics that would be of interest to you. Identify how you could use music, slides, computer graphics, an overhead projector, a video recording, handouts, and posters in two of these presentations. Try to find a use for every medium with both speech topics.

Rehearse with an Audience

Try to rehearse with an audience, even if it is made up of only one or two people. An audience will help you practice interacting with and receiving feedback from listeners. During the rehearsal, try to develop eye contact with the audience as you present your ideas. Watch how listeners react to your presentation. Are there places where they seem confused or lost? If so, find a way to clarify the confusing information.

Following the rehearsed presentation, ask your listeners if they could understand your ideas, if they needed more details or description, and if your audiovisual aids could be clearly perceived and understood. That way, you have the time to make necessary changes or adjustments before your actual presentation.

It is a good idea to rehearse with an audience when possible. Why?

Internalize

Internalization is going over and over something until you absorb it. In communication, internalization falls just short of memorizing. When you internalize something, you learn what it means and the idea it conveys. The words may be different each time you relay it to an audience, but the message is the same.

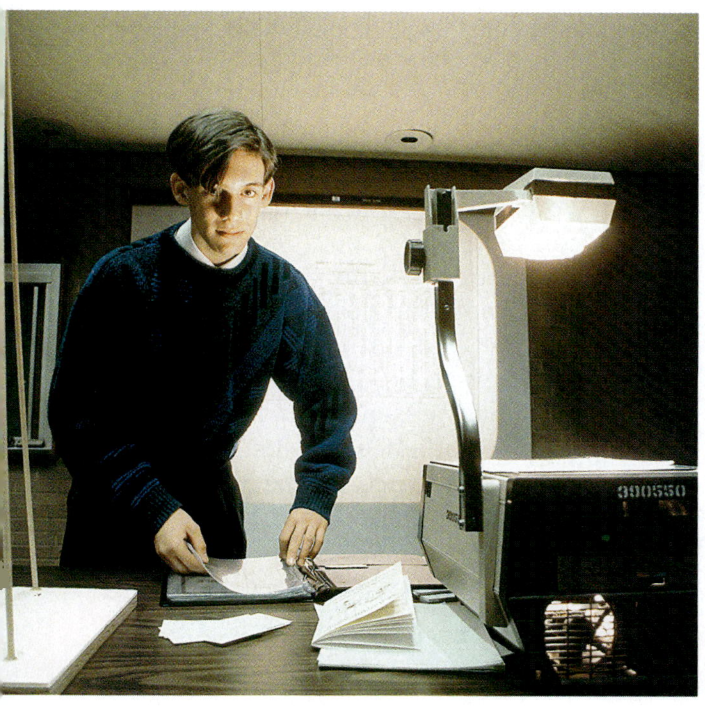

This young man prepares his visual aid equipment before a presentation. Why is it important to internalize an introduction and conclusion in rehearsal?

Since the introduction and the conclusion of a presentation make the greatest impact on an audience, spend extra time internalizing those parts of your presentation. If you internalize your introduction and conclusion in rehearsal, you won't need to look at your notes during the first or last parts of your presentation. Your introduction, then, can fully accomplish its tasks—getting your audience's attention, previewing your presentation, applying your presentation to the audience, and establishing your ethos. Your conclusion can leave your audience with a positive image of you and your presentation.

As you rehearse, you also internalize the other information in your presentation so that you won't need to constantly rely on your notes or your manuscript. Audiences generally do not respond well to a presenter who makes eye contact with only his or her notes or manuscipt. Even if you are using a manuscript delivery, you need to rehearse several times with the manuscript so that you don't have to read to the audience and communicate solely with the paper in front of you. It is helpful to internalize at least the introduction, the conclusion, and the beginning and ending of each page of the manuscript so that you can turn pages without looking down. Internalizing any type of presentation will free you from your notes so you can develop eye contact with your audience.

Rehearse with Audiovisual Aids and Notes

Rehearse using your audiovisual aids and notes as you practice your presentation. Flip charts need to be flipped; projectors need to

COMMUNICATION *Strategies*

HANDLING NOTES OR MANUSCRIPT

- Arrange your note cards or manuscript pages in a logical order.
- Practice turning pages or cards smoothly, with a minimum of shuffling and noise.
- If no table or podium is available, rehearse with your cards held in either hand but not in both hands. This gives you a free hand for gesturing and using your audio-visual aids.
- If you must hold your notes, write on only one side of the note card. Audiences may be distracted by any writing they can see on the backs of your cards.

be aimed and focused. These actions take time during a presentation and can present problems if you're not well prepared. Unfortunately, technical difficulties can destroy a presentation. Imagine, for example, that you have planned to use a number of overhead transparencies. However, at the last moment you discover that the only available overhead projector has a burned-out bulb. Audiences may lose interest while a presenter tries to fix an audiovisual aid that is not operating correctly. Rehearsal minimizes these inconveniences.

Also, make sure that your notes or manuscript will not detract from your message in the presentation. The rehearsal notes shown in the Communication Strategies checklist on the previous page can help you learn to handle your notes so they will not distract your audience members.

It is often said that the way to practice something is the way you will perform it. Making your rehearsal time as realistic as possible can help relieve your fears when the real presentation time rolls around. Moreover, the more fun you have rehearsing, the more lively and enthusiastic your presentation is likely to be. The more lively and enthusiastic your presentation is, the more interested your audience will be. The more interested your audience is, the more likely you are to accomplish the goals of your presentation.

Section 3 Assessment

Visit the *Glencoe Communication Applications* Web site at **communicationapplications.glencoe.com** and click on **Self-Check and Study Guide 17.3** to review your understanding of rehearsing presentations.

Review Key Terms

1. Define each term and write it in a sentence: communication apprehension, visualization, internalization.

Check Understanding

2. Name some of the causes of communication apprehension.
3. What is the most important strategy for managing communication apprehension? Name and describe three other management strategies.
4. **Hypothesize** How would you prepare thoroughly for a short extemporaneous presentation to your school board? Describe an ideal rehearsal session.

APPLICATION Activity

Managing Communication Apprehension What worries you most about giving a presentation? Write your main fears or concerns on the left side of a sheet of paper. Then, form groups of four to six students. As a group, discuss effective strategies for overcoming the most common presentation fears. Write any helpful pointers to the right of each fear you listed. Finally, discuss these tips as a class. Were you able to add pointers to your list? Write a brief plan for working these apprehension-management techniques into your rehearsals.

Communication Self-Assessment

Preparing for Presentations

How Do You Rate?

On a separate sheet of paper, respond to the following statements. Put a check mark at the end of each skill you would like to improve.

KEY: A Always **U** Usually **S** Sometimes **R** Rarely **N** Never

1. I have no difficulty remembering the ideas for presentations.
2. I use extemporaneous speaking as often as possible.
3. When asked to give an impromptu speech, I organize my ideas quickly and present them without difficulty.
4. To avoid being misunderstood, I present with a manuscript.
5. I work with other group members to develop a consistent approach and style for a group presentation.
6. I practice for a group presentation by paying attention to consistency, cues, and transitions.
7. When I am the leader of a panel discussion, I keep the panel focused on one topic at a time.
8. I choose a symposium to present several different points of view.
9. When worried about a presentation, I remind myself that a little apprehension may improve delivery.
10. I try to rehearse presentations with one or two people as an audience.

How Do You Score?

Review your responses. Give yourself 5 points for every A, 4 for every U, 3 for every S, 2 for every R, and 1 for every N. Total your points and evaluate your score.

41–50 Excellent You may be surprised to find out how much you can improve your skills.

31–40 Good In this course, you can learn ways to make your skills better.

21–30 Fair Practice applying the skills taught in this course.

1–20 Needs Improvement Carefully monitor your improvement as you work through this course.

Setting Communication Goals

If you scored Excellent or Good, complete Part A. If your score was Fair or Needs Improvement, complete Part B.

Part A

1. I plan to put the following ideas into practice:
2. I plan to share the following information about communication with the following people:

Part B

1. The behaviors I need to change most are:
2. To bring about these changes, I will take these steps:

Writing an Executive Summary

Busy managers don't always have time to read an entire report. For this reason, writers often include an executive summary at the beginning of a report. An executive summary is an abbreviated version of a long report. Use the following tips to write a useful executive summary.

- Introduce the Subject of the Report.
- Provide Background Information.
- Include Reference Points.
- Organize the Information.
- Highlight Key Information.

Introduce the Subject of the Report. Briefly describe the topic of the report at the beginning of your executive summary. If the report is written in a problem-solution format, explain this in your summary. If it is an investigative report, discuss the goal of the investigation. Prepare the reader for the information that comes next.

Provide Background Information. Give your reader enough information so that he or she can understand the main points of the report. You can use statistics or other data to clarify your ideas.

Include Reference Points. Provide page references in your executive summary. These features make it easy for readers to quickly locate more detailed information within the original report.

Organize the Information. Executive summaries are easier to read if they are organized. Although there are no specific rules for organizing an executive summary, the document should be designed in a way that makes it easy to read and understand. You can organize facts, ideas, and recommendations by separating them into paragraphs, numbering them, or using headings. Organization is an important consideration because most of the people who receive your report will read the summary.

Highlight Key Information. Headings and subheads are tools that aid readers. The main headings should appear in bold or italic type. Subheads can also be in bold or italic type. If so, they should be indented or underlined. Important recommendations and findings should also be clearly marked.

A model of an executive summary is shown on the next page. Notice how the main ideas and key points are set off by the use of numbers, italics, and boldface type.

For additional information about business writing, see the *Guide to Business Communication* section of the Communication Survival Kit in the Appendix.

EXECUTIVE SUMMARY

Subject: Steps that Flexible Steel Products can take to meet pollution regulations

Recommendations are listed in order of importance

1. By following all of these recommendations, Flexible Steel Products will exceed current industry pollution standards.

2. Upgrade Computer Systems: Newer computers increase efficiency.
Test Laboratory: A newer computer system can compute test results faster. This will help production run more smoothly (page 24).
Steel Production: A digital thermostat system can maintain an accurate constant temperature in the blast furnace. Avoiding temperature changes within the furnace will help conserve fuel (page 26).
Painted Products: Using computer programs that can calculate exact measurements of paint needed for each product will significantly reduce waste.

3. Reuse Materials:
Chemicals: Flexible Steel can clean and reuse the chemical blend used to treat steel.
Filters: Exhaust filters in the smokestacks are currently recycled after one use. A new process will allow them to be reused instead.

4. Replace Heating System: Flexible Steel Products can install a more efficient heating system for the building. A new natural gas system could cut pollution by up to 20 percent. For more information, see page 11 of the report.

WRITING *Activity*

Imagine that you are an advertising consultant. Stock Logic, a small investment firm, has hired you to determine the best way to spend its advertising budget. Write an executive summary for your report using the following information.

- 50 percent of the people who invest with large firms learn about those companies from national ads. The data is on page 7 of this report.
- Advertising nationally is extremely expensive. The rates appear on page 14 of the report.
- 30 percent of the people who invest learn about companies from local commercials. This information can be found on page 35 of the report.
- On page 40, the report shows that ads for television are the most expensive.
- The report states on page 45 that radio advertising is very beneficial for small firms.
- Stock Logic has lower fees than its competitors. 80 percent of the people who invest using the World Wide Web do so because the low fees. This is discussed on page 48.

CHAPTER 17 Assessment and Activities

Visit the *Glencoe Communication Applications* Web site at **communicationapplications.glencoe.com** and click on **Chapter 17 Activity** for additional practice in preparing presentations.

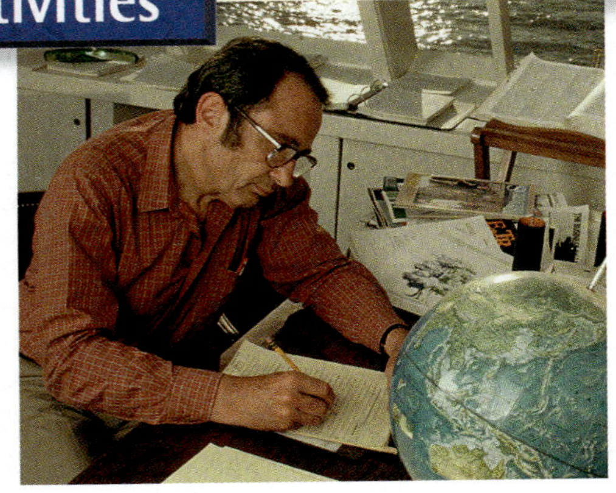

Reviewing Key Terms

Read each definition. On a separate sheet of paper, write the number of the definition and the letter of the term that fits the definition best.

1. Is given with little advance preparation
2. A group discussion in front of an audience where information is shared conversationally
3. Going over something until you absorb it
4. Is written out and read aloud to an audience
5. Individuals speak on aspects of the same topic but interact little with other speakers
6. Mentally picturing doing something well
7. Is rehearsed and given with the use of notes

a. manuscript presentation
b. extemporaneous presentation
c. impromptu presentation
d. panel discussion
e. symposium
f. visualization
g. internalization

Reviewing Key Concepts

1. What are four different methods of delivery for a presentation?
2. Explain two drawbacks of using memorization as a method of delivery.
3. Which method of delivery is best for a sensitive topic or for a presentation that will appear in print?
4. Why do many extemporaneous speakers use only one or two index cards for their notes?
5. How can a presenter use notes to help his or her delivery?
6. Why is preparing together important when group members plan a group presentation?
7. List three tips for staging an effective group presentation.
8. Why does each member of a panel need to contribute on all aspects of the topic?

Assessment and Activities

Reading and Critical Thinking Skill

1. **Compare and Contrast** How are extemporaneous and impromptu presentations alike and different?
2. **Summary** Summarize the methods for preparing a presentation manuscript.
3. **Classifying Information** You and three classmates are giving a presentation to the rest of the class. Is your audience internal or external?
4. **Synthesis** Make a list of a panel discussion leader's responsibilities.
5. **Predict** As a representative for a conservation organization, Jamar has given one presentation per week for the last six weeks. This experience has given him confidence. How will Jamar's confidence affect the next audience he addresses?

Skill Practice Activity

Writing an Executive Summary Recall the last time you felt communication apprehension. In an executive summary, describe the physical and emotional symptoms you felt. Then explain how you plan to apply the strategies in Section 3 of this chapter to effectively manage these stage fright symptoms during your next presentation. Include communication terms such as visualization and internalization in your summary.

Cooperative Learning Activity

Multimedia Presentation As a class, form groups of three. As a group, choose a historical period such as the Middle Ages or the Roaring Twenties. Have one member prepare a panel discussion-forum on the period. The other two members are responsible for collecting music and visuals—either slides or transparencies—that complement the presentation. Limit the presentation to five minutes. Include a question-and-answer session after the presentation.

Chapter Project

Planning Think of a career at which you would like to excel. What are some things that you can do in your everyday life that will contribute to your success in that field? If you would like to be a writer, for example, keeping a daily journal will help improve your language skills. Prepare a presentation that explains how regular daily activities can help you succeed professionally.

Presenting Conduct a symposium with the other students in your class. Choose another classmate to act as the moderator. Supply the moderator with a list of the group members' topics.

CHAPTER 18 Making and Evaluating Presentations

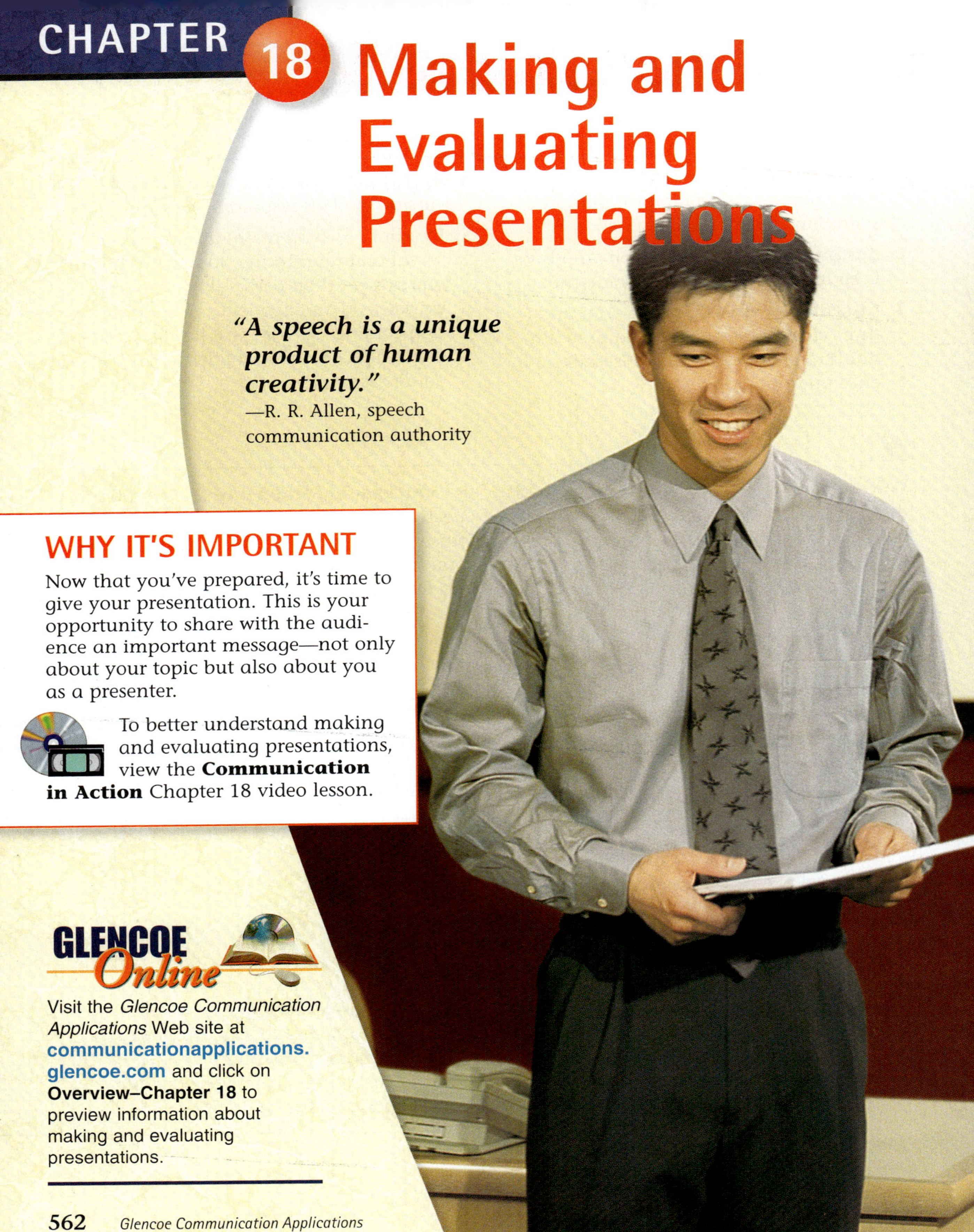

"A speech is a unique product of human creativity."
—R. R. Allen, speech communication authority

WHY IT'S IMPORTANT

Now that you've prepared, it's time to give your presentation. This is your opportunity to share with the audience an important message—not only about your topic but also about you as a presenter.

To better understand making and evaluating presentations, view the **Communication in Action** Chapter 18 video lesson.

GLENCOE Online

Visit the *Glencoe Communication Applications* Web site at **communicationapplications.glencoe.com** and click on **Overview–Chapter 18** to preview information about making and evaluating presentations.

Section 1

Making a Presentation

GUIDE TO READING

Objectives

1. Explain the importance of an effective delivery.
2. Explain how to achieve a positive stage presence.
3. Distinguish between emphatic and descriptive gestures.
4. Use effective verbal and nonverbal strategies in presentations.
5. Make individual presentations to inform, persuade, or motivate an audience.

Terms to Learn

delivery
projecting
stage presence
emphatic gesture
descriptive gesture

Imagine you arrive at school one morning and all your teachers are missing. Overnight, they were replaced with detailed guidebooks for each class. Your first reaction might be "All right! No teachers!" After a while, though, what do you think would happen to your interest level in class? Would a book meet all your communication needs? Do you think you would learn as much in class?

At one time or another, you probably have heard someone say, "It's not what you say but how you say it that counts." In the example above, certainly the basic information in the book would be similar to what your teacher might convey during the class. However, the book would be lacking that all-important human touch.

A guidebook cannot use facial expressions or body talk to help make messages clear. It cannot change its vocal characteristics to fit the situation and keep interest levels high. Most importantly, a book cannot check for understanding or adapt to feedback from its audience.

A speaker can offer information in a way that books can't. How does a speaker convey information differently from a book?

In your teacherless classroom, you soon would discover that the way a message is presented greatly affects the way it is received. Without an effective delivery method, the information in the guidebook probably would not have as much of an impact on you, the audience. **Delivery** is how a presenter uses his or her body and voice to communicate a message to an audience. In the pages that follow, you will examine the most effective strategies for delivering the message of your presentation.

Importance of Delivery

Just like most worthwhile efforts, developing a polished delivery takes practice. The payoff, however, is well worth it. A polished delivery not only gives you confidence for making presentations, but it also causes audiences to perceive you as more credible. With these two important factors on your side, it is much easier to accomplish the goals of your presentations. Without them, it can be very difficult to make a positive impact on your audience.

Consider, for example, that you have spent hours helping a friend prepare a presentation to the new-products division of her company. She wants to describe a new use for one of the company's existing products that is no longer selling well. The friend has thoroughly researched the marketing background of the product, has consulted with sales representatives, and even has developed a prototype for a modification of the product. In all, she has spent a great deal of time researching and developing her presentation.

Unfortunately, the morning of the presentation, your friend got soaked in the rain while running from her car to the building. Because she was running late, she didn't have time for her hair and clothes to fully dry before the meeting. She also was chatting when she was introduced to the group and did not hear until she was called a second time. To make matters worse, a minute or two into your friend's presentation, someone in the back asked her to speak up because she couldn't be heard. She mumbled that she was sorry, lost her place in her presentation, and ended up repeating herself.

When your friend finally unveiled her prototype, it was positioned poorly, causing her to speak with her back to the audience much of the time. In addition, she mispronounced several of the technical terms from her research.

Glad to finally finish with the presentation, your friend immediately bolted out of the room and went back to her office. She was notified that afternoon that the board had dismissed her idea and someone else would be researching other uses for the product. Of course, your friend was extremely disappointed. What went wrong?

Even though your friend put a lot of time and effort into preparing her presentation, she did not consider that the way she looked and sounded during her presentation would affect her credibility. In short, your friend forgot about the importance of an effective delivery.

TECHNOLOGY *Activity*

Using an Overhead Projector The best-prepared speakers consider all potential problems while getting ready for an upcoming presentation. Develop a list of problems you might encounter on the day you are to deliver a presentation. Next, provide a list of actions you might take to resolve or avoid these problems. Put your list of potential problems and solutions on a transparency and present them to the class using an overhead projector.

Some members of this audience appear to be having a hard time understanding the information. **Identify ways to utilize your voice effectively.**

Using Appropriate Vocal Characteristics

Two of the most important aspects of delivery are the quality and characteristics of your voice. Even a well-prepared presentation will be a failure if the audience cannot hear and understand your message. Remember to speak clearly and distinctly so that each person in the room can hear you. Also, remember what you read in Chapter 5 about developing a speaking voice that has a desirable, medium pitch and a broad enough range of inflection to convey emotion and interest.

Finally, pay special attention to the volume, tone, and rate of your voice. The following paragraphs provide some important tips for using these three characteristics effectively in your presentation.

Volume As you learned in Chapter 5, speaking too loudly or too softly can influence the way an audience perceives you and your message. In a presentation, the key to volume is to speak loudly enough so that the person farthest away can hear you clearly. This does not mean that you should shout if you are presenting to a large group. That can make the people closest to you very uncomfortable. Rather, you should be able to whisper and still be heard by the people in the back row. This is accomplished by projecting. **Projecting** means sending the sound of your voice to all areas of a room without shouting.

Projecting is a lot like throwing a ball to the person on the back row of your presentation. It takes only a certain amount of energy—no more, no less. You also must control the force or intensity of the throw. Finally, you have to consider the effects of outside factors, such as the other people in the room.

Your voice is very much like the ball in this example. You control its energy, force, and intensity through proper breathing. You also need to consider other existing factors. If some outside noise or the audience itself is creating a disturbance, you'll have to "toss" your voice a little harder to get it to that back row.

Tone Most presentations call for a relaxed, responsive, conversational tone of voice. Listeners tend to respond more favorably to voices that are conversational and friendly than to those that are harsh or overly formal. In general, audiences like to be talked "to" or "with" instead of "at." During your presentation, strive for a tone that reflects openness and friendliness. Think of how you would like to be talked to and imitate that tone.

Rate and Tempo In a presentation, remember to speak slowly enough so audience members can easily follow what you are saying but rapidly enough to hold their interest and attention. The rate and tempo of your presentation should reflect the mood and intensity of your message. It can be easily adapted for emphasis or clarity. For instance, you can emphasize an important statement by using a slow, deliberate rate of delivery. Increasing your rate can help you build emotion for a certain point in your presentation.

Your voice is an important tool of expression during a presentation. Volume, force, pitch, inflection, tone, and rate can all be adapted to provide emphasis and variety. However, any vocal techniques you use should be motivated by the content of your message and your sincere desire to communicate with your audience. When used appropriately, they can help you clearly convey meanings and feelings to make your presentation as effective as possible.

Improving Verbal Messages

An audience will judge how prepared you are as a presenter by the style of presentation you use during your presentation. If you want to convey an image to your audience that you are intelligent and competent, you will need to sound intelligent and informed. You do this in a presentation by using standard diction and correct grammar.

Diction In a presentation to a large group of people, you will want everyone in the room to understand what you are saying. You will want to use standard diction that is commonly understood by all members of your audience. You will want to use language that is clear and distinctly articulated and enunciated. You should also verify that you are pronouncing words correctly so that you don't confuse your audience. Many of the standards about clear and articulate speech that you learned in Chapter 4 will also apply to the way you use language in a formal presentation.

COMMUNICATION *Strategies*

Voicing Your Presentation Effectively

- Speak at a medium pitch with higher- and lower-pitched inflections.
- Use a broad range of inflection to convey emotion and make your presentation interesting.
- Choose a volume that is appropriate for the room size and audience size.
- Project your voice so that everyone in the room can hear you clearly.
- Use a friendly, conversational tone.
- Speak slowly enough to be understood but not so slowly that you're boring.
- Use standard diction and correct grammar.

Grammar In many of your daily communication interactions, a few grammatical slips will probably have no impact. However, when you are making a presentation, a grammatical error can greatly reduce your credibility with an audience. Even in an informal presentation, you may be able to get by with a grammatical violation here and there. In formal presentations, the rules for correct grammar apply. Subjects should agree with verbs, pronoun references should be clear, and modifiers should be correctly placed. If your language is a measure of the way an audience will perceive your preparedness, then you should use the most correct language you know how to use.

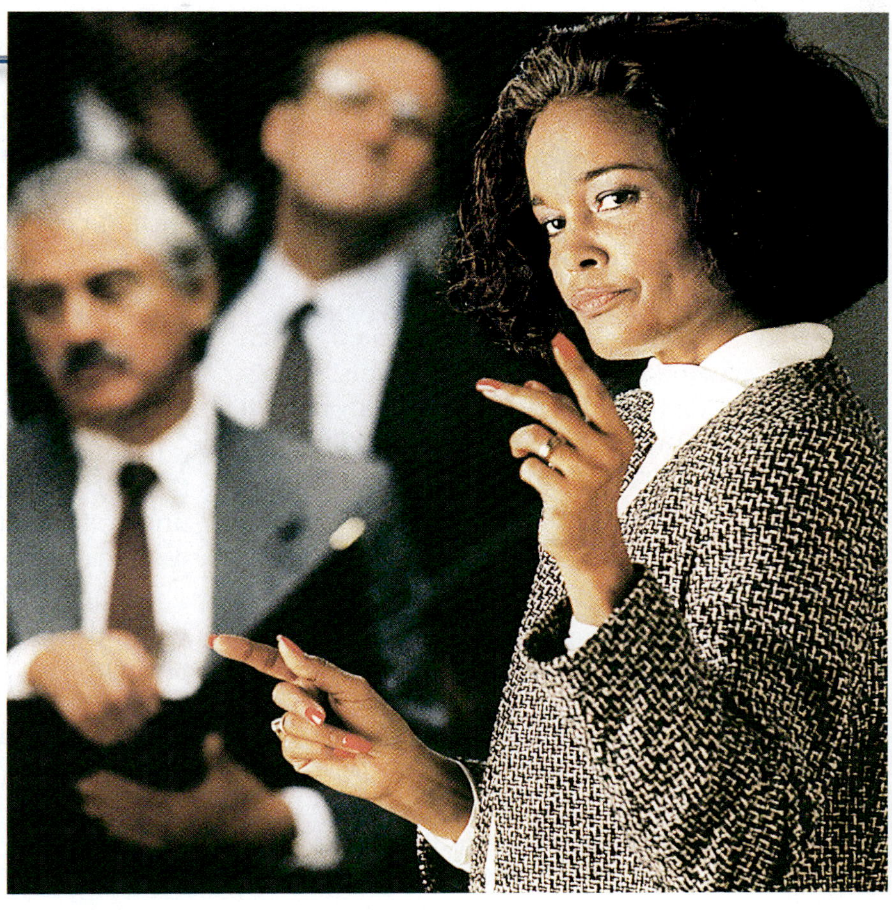

A professional appearance will send a message of competence to the audience. What type of clothing is appropriate when making a presentation?

Using Other Nonverbal Cues Appropriately

In the earlier example of the friend's presentation to her company, more consideration should have been given to her nonverbal messages. Your friend's hair and clothing were damp and probably a bit disheveled. She had to be introduced twice because she was talking instead of listening at the start of the meeting. These cues sent a message of unprofessionalism to her audience even before she began her presentation. They probably also planted seeds of doubt about her credibility.

Appearance What do you want your audience to perceive as you enter the room and approach the presentation area? Part of the presentation process is to consider clothing and grooming as valuable visual aids to your presentation.

As you read in Chapter 5, you typically will want to wear simple, tailored clothes that are appropriate for yourself, the audience, the occasion, and the task. Any accessories should be simple and tasteful, and neither clothing nor accessories should distract the audience from your presentation.

Remember, too, that your hair and shoes are part of your appearance. Hair should be neatly and conservatively styled so that it does not hang down in your eyes or hide much of your face. You may consider combing it quickly before your presentation. Shoes should be neat, clean, and comfortable.

It naturally follows that grooming and personal hygiene are important. You do not want any part of your appearance to distract your audience. If you want an audience to accept you as professional and well organized, make sure you project that visual image.

You may have heard the saying, "When you look good, you feel good." This simply means that taking a little extra effort with your appearance can help increase your confidence as a presenter. The more confident you are, the more you can concentrate on giving an effective presentation.

Your Entrance The way you approach the area where your presentation will be given is extremely important. Not only does it set the tone for your presentation, but it also can affect your own confidence. You begin to communicate a nonverbal message to the audience the moment you enter the room. From that point on, you establish what is known as "stage presence." **Stage presence** is an illusion created by the quality of the energy, poise, confidence, and control that a presenter conveys to an audience.

You will want the audience to perceive you as competent and sincere. Therefore, your gait and posture should convey confidence and enthusiasm. Ahead of time, watch yourself in a mirror as you practice entering the presentation area. Walk to the podium briskly, turn, and smile at your audience before you begin speaking. This gives the audience time to focus on you and what you are about to say. Don't rush the beginning of your presentation. Give yourself a minute to size up your audience and get settled before you begin.

A confident entrance not only projects a positive image to others, but it also is an effective strategy for battling communication apprehension. The more confident and informed you appear, the more self-assured you will be. Self-assurance can make it easier to remember all the information you wish to convey in your message.

Posture Good posture also communicates confidence and enthusiasm to your audience. It begins with well-balanced, firm footing. If you begin to speak with your body off balance, you may begin to sway or shuffle during your presentation. These actions can tell an audience that you are nervous or uncertain about what you are saying and can damage your credibility.

Remember from Chapter 5 the image of a string through your spine. Your head should be held up, your shoulders back, and your arms relaxed. This is considered good posture for speaking. A tense body communicates tension and anxiety that can create a negative audience perception.

This speaker projects a positive stage presence. What is stage presence?

When you use good posture during your presentation, you not only look more confident and credible, but you also sound better. When you stand up straight, you are better able to project your voice. This ultimately helps you communicate more effectively with everyone in your audience.

Movement Some amount of movement in a presentation is good. It keeps you from looking emotionless or overly tense. However, when you move from one position to another during your presentation, have a good reason. For instance, you may occasionally want to take a step to the left or to the right to emphasize a point or an idea. You may need to move closer to an audiovisual aid or field a question from a particular side of the audience. In a small or fairly informal presentation, you may wish to move out into your audience to make audience members feel more included.

Additionally, movement can be used to maintain control of an audience. If an audience is getting restless or unruly, simply stepping toward them or walking out into the room can bring their attention back to you and what you are saying. Try to be casual and conversational when you approach an audience. Walk at a slow or normal gait. A forceful or quick approach can be perceived as threatening and confrontational and can make an audience defensive. Becoming defensive will usually cause an audience to turn off what you have to say.

You will, however, want to watch carefully how much you move during a presentation. Constant movement can be distracting to an audience, because people may start watching you instead of listening to what you're saying. Therefore, have a reason for each movement.

Gestures Many presenters worry about what to do with their hands during a presentation. These people probably use their hands to reinforce their messages when talking with friends, but when they get in front of a group of people, their hands feel larger than life. Remember that the more natural you are as a presenter, the better you will be. Allow your hands to rest naturally at your side or on the podium when you are not using them for specific gestures.

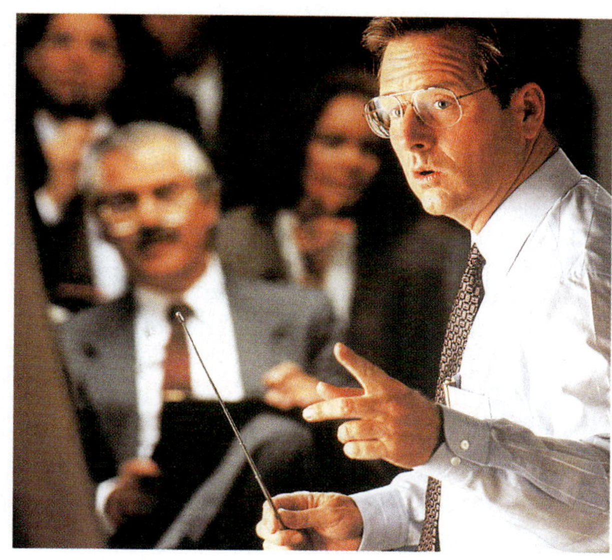

Speakers use movement and gestures as nonverbal cues during a presentation. What is the problem with constant movement?

Effectively using gestures in a presentation involves more than knowing what to do with your hands, however. When you communicate with an audience, you gesture with all parts of your body: You nod your head, you shrug your shoulders, or you lean toward your audience. In general, presenters use two types of gestures: emphatic gestures and descriptive gestures.

Emphatic Gestures An **emphatic gesture** stresses or places special attention on what a presenter is saying. It adds emphasis. Many popular presenters use emphatic gestures. They may slap their foreheads in disbelief or even bang their fists on the table. They may raise their eyebrows, roll their eyes, or gesture broadly to include the audience. This type of gesture shows that the presenter is excited about his or her topic and wants the audience to be as involved as he or she is. This type of gesture, when motivated, sincere, and done in moderation, can greatly increase your credibility as a presenter.

Descriptive Gestures A descriptive gesture allows a presenter to create a mental image to help his or her audience visualize what he or she is talking about. In a way, descriptive gestures are a form of visual aid. They can help a presenter convey the size or shape of an object, the position of two or more objects in relation to each other, or other spatial information.

You can make your presentations more effective if you learn how to use gestures to your advantage. First, gestures should be motivated by the text of your message. They also should enhance what you are saying without distracting your audience. Finally, gestures should be sincere and spontaneous, not overly planned or rehearsed.

Facial Communication

As you can see in Figure 18–1, facial expressions communicate a great deal to an audience. Have you ever watched the action on a television show when you couldn't hear the sound? If so, you probably were able to figure out the mood and attitude the actors were portraying without having to hear their words. Now, look around your classroom. You probably can tell who's interested and who's bored or daydreaming just by looking at your classmates' faces. Your facial expressions give an audience the same types of information when you make a presentation.

Figure 18–1 Facial Communication

interNET ACTIVITY

Famous Speeches The Internet provides access to complete speeches presented by leaders from around the world. Enter the words *famous speeches* into an Internet search engine to access three different speeches. Observe the tone, rate, and tempo of the presenters that you hear. If video is available, note each speaker's appearance, gestures, eye contact, and facial expressions as well. Which aspects are the most similar among the speakers? Which aspects do you think are most effective?

For the most part, use your facial expressions to tell audience members that you are interested in them and in the topic you are presenting. Try to look alert and focused. Also, allow yourself to convey emotions through your face. Remember, an important part of every message is its emotional content.

Smile! Finally, remember to smile whenever possible. When you smile at an audience, you communicate friendliness and sincerity. You also project an image of being comfortable with your subject and at ease with your audience. Such impressions increase your credibility and your personal appeal with the audience.

Eye Contact In many parts of the United States, we often think a person is more trustworthy if he or she looks us directly in the eye. A presenter who does not look at his or her audience loses its belief and trust as well as its attention. Therefore, the ability to develop eye contact with your audience is an important skill for an effective presenter to master.

The key to good eye contact is knowing your material. The better you know your material, the less you will have to rely on your notes, and the more you can look at your audience. The more you look at your audience, the more feedback you can receive. This allows you to adjust your message to make sure that everyone in your audience understands.

Eye contact also is an effective way to keep the audience involved in your presentation. By making eye contact with different members of your audience, you make people feel included and valued. Failure to make eye contact can have the opposite effect. For this reason, try to make eye contact with as many different audience members as possible. Not only will this make each person you look at feel special, but the farther away you are, the more people will think you have looked directly at them. With enough practice, you may be able to make an entire audience feel it has been personally included in your presentation.

Your Exit Once the spoken part of a presentation is over, some presenters are tempted to make the fastest getaway possible. However, just as you planned your entrance, you also should plan an orderly and controlled exit.

First, remain in position. Make sure that you smile and maintain eye contact with the audience for a few seconds after concluding your presentation. Sometimes, audience members will have questions about elements of your presentation. In other instances, they may want to come up and meet you. In any case, remember that you still are being evaluated by your audience—and your last impression may be almost as important as your first.

COMMUNICATION PRACTICE LAB

Using Nonverbal Cues Effectively

To practice using effective nonverbal cues in a presentation, follow these steps:

Step 1 Working in groups of four or five, choose a type of presentation: informative, persuasive, or motivational.

Step 2 Each member of the group should then create his or her own two-minute presentation of that type.

Step 3 Take turns making your presentations in front of the other group members. Use effective verbal strategies you learned in previous chapters and the effective nonverbal strategies you have just learned in this chapter.

Step 4 Have other group members take notes on your nonverbal behaviors in particular, pointing out which were effective, which were not, and why.

Step 5 Share your notes as a group. What conclusions can you draw about different types of nonverbal cues? Which were most or least effective for your specific type of presentation?

Step 6 After your group has discussed the notes, share your conclusions as a class.

Your actions at this point will influence the way people remember you as a presenter. You want to make sure that the audience focuses on what you have just presented to them, not on watching you make your exit.

Above all, don't damage the credibility that you have worked so hard to build. Hurrying back to your chair or rushing out of the room could make you seem insincere or unprofessional. Audience members may get the idea that you didn't really want to be there at all. Instead, take this opportunity to convey warmth and approachability. Allow your movements, gestures, and facial expressions to reflect the same confidence and enthusiasm you had at the beginning and throughout your presentation.

Finally, congratulate yourself mentally for a job well done. You have carefully prepared and presented your presentation. By delivering a successful presentation, you've taken another giant step toward becoming a competent and professional communicator.

Section 1 Assessment

Visit the *Glencoe Communication Applications* Web site at **communicationapplications.glencoe.com** and click on **Self-Check and Study Guide 18.1** to review your understanding of making a presentation.

Review Key Terms

1. Define each term and write it in a sentence: delivery, projecting, stage presence, emphatic gesture, descriptive gesture.

Check Understanding

2. Why is delivery an important aspect of a presentation?
3. Describe an entrance that projects a positive stage presence.
4. **Compare and Contrast** Give one example of an emphatic gesture and one example of a descriptive gesture. Explain how they are alike and how they are different.

APPLICATION *Activity*

Creating a Presentation Checklist Working with a partner, create a list of tips for using effective verbal and nonverbal strategies in presentations. Using your checklist, take turns giving a two-minute informative, persuasive, or motivational presentation. Check off each tip as you use it. Share your checklists with classmates and work together as a class to create a master presentation checklist.

Distinguishing Between Fact and Opinion

A fact is any piece of information that can be determined to be true without question. An opinion is a belief that cannot be supported by positive knowledge. Knowing the difference between the two will help you make decisions that are based on information rather than emotion.

Learning the Skill

When you are trying to tell the difference between a fact and an opinion, ask yourself if the statement is something that can be proved with your own senses. In other words, can you see, hear, taste, smell, or feel it for yourself? If someone says that ice is cold, you know it's true because you have touched ice before and it was cold. This is an observable fact. Next, check the statement for words that show comparison—words like *greatest*, *everyone*, *no one*, *better*, *worst*, *always*, or *never*. If you find any such words, the statement is probably based on opinion.

Some claims can be proved through research. These statements may involve past events or scientific claims. If you state that Neptune is farther away from the sun than Mars, you can prove it by finding information that supports your claim.

Finally, some claims are based on statistics. People tend to use only those statistics that are favorable to their position. The statistical information that is revealed is probably true, but it may not be entirely true. Therefore, claims that are based on statistical information should be carefully examined.

Practicing the Skill

Each statement below is based on fact or opinion. Decide which statements are facts and which are opinions and why.

1. Temperature is measured with a thermometer.
2. Dogs are the smartest animals.
3. Oranges are the best kind of fruit.
4. All spiders have eight legs.
5. Everyone supports the current tax laws.

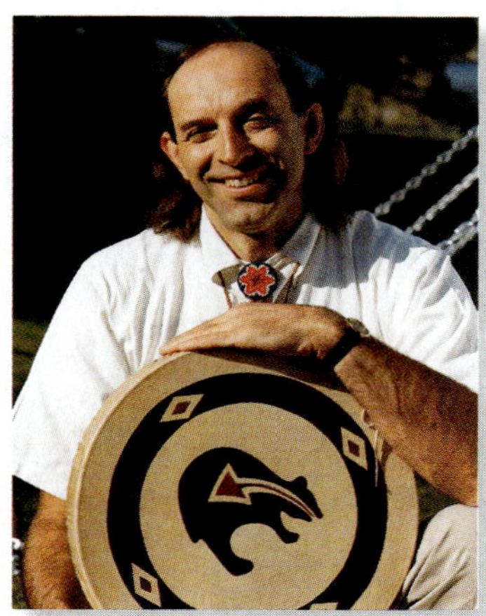

APPLICATION *Activity*

Joseph Bruchac is a Native American storyteller. Is this statement a fact or an opinion? From the photo, find three statements about Joseph Bruchac that are facts. Explain why each claim is true. Now find or develop three statements about Bruchac that are opinions. What makes these statements opinions?

Section 2

Evaluating Presentations

GUIDE TO READING

Objectives

1. Interpret audience feedback.
2. Respond empathically to audience interruptions.
3. Participate effectively in a question-and-answer session following a presentation.
4. Apply critical-listening strategies to evaluate a presentation.
5. Evaluate the effectiveness of one's own presentation.

Terms to Learn

critic
critical perspective
judgment by results
judgment by ethical standards
judgment by aesthetics
judgment by multiple standards

It's the big day—time to give your presentation in front of the whole class. You've practiced so much that you feel as though you could give this presentation in your sleep. As you begin your presentation, however, you notice that not everyone is behaving like a perfect audience member. Two students are whispering, while another keeps interrupting to ask you questions. How do you handle the unexpected?

Giving a presentation in front of an audience can be very different from practicing in front of a mirror. When real, live people are involved, you never know quite what to expect. Speaking to an audience doesn't have to be unpleasant or distracting, however. In fact, one of the most rewarding aspects of public speaking is interacting with your listeners. By evaluating their reactions—and listening closely to their evaluations of you—you will quickly learn which methods work, which don't, and which can help you build a reputation as an interesting and talented presenter.

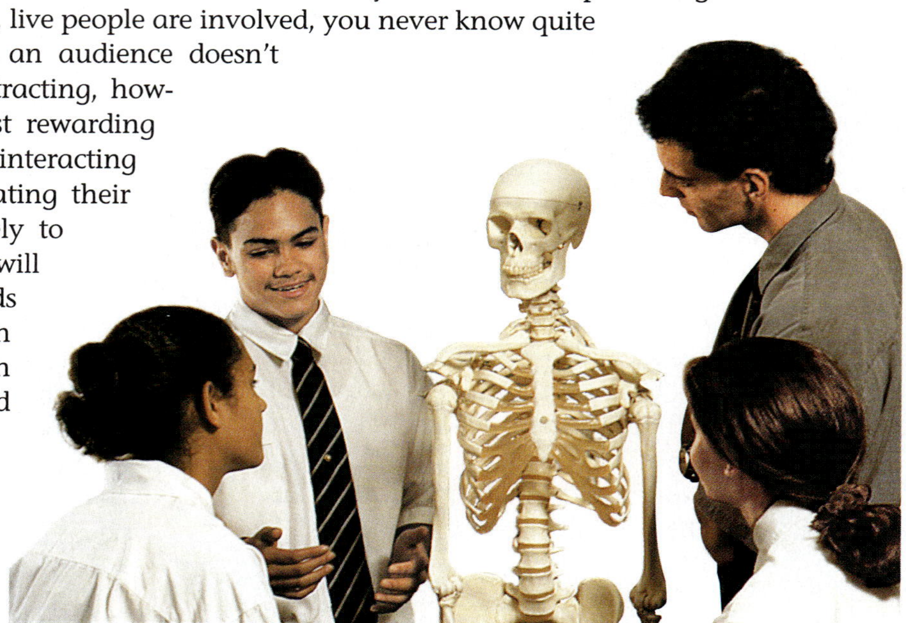

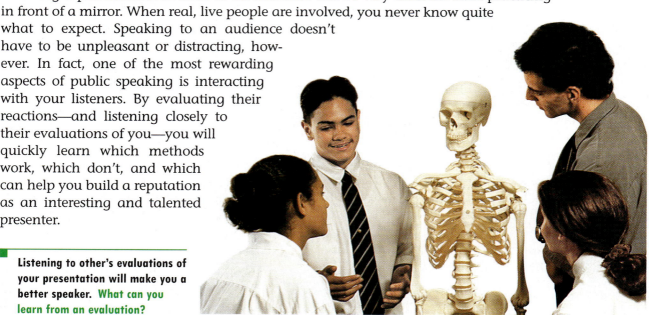

Listening to other's evaluations of your presentation will make you a better speaker. What can you learn from an evaluation?

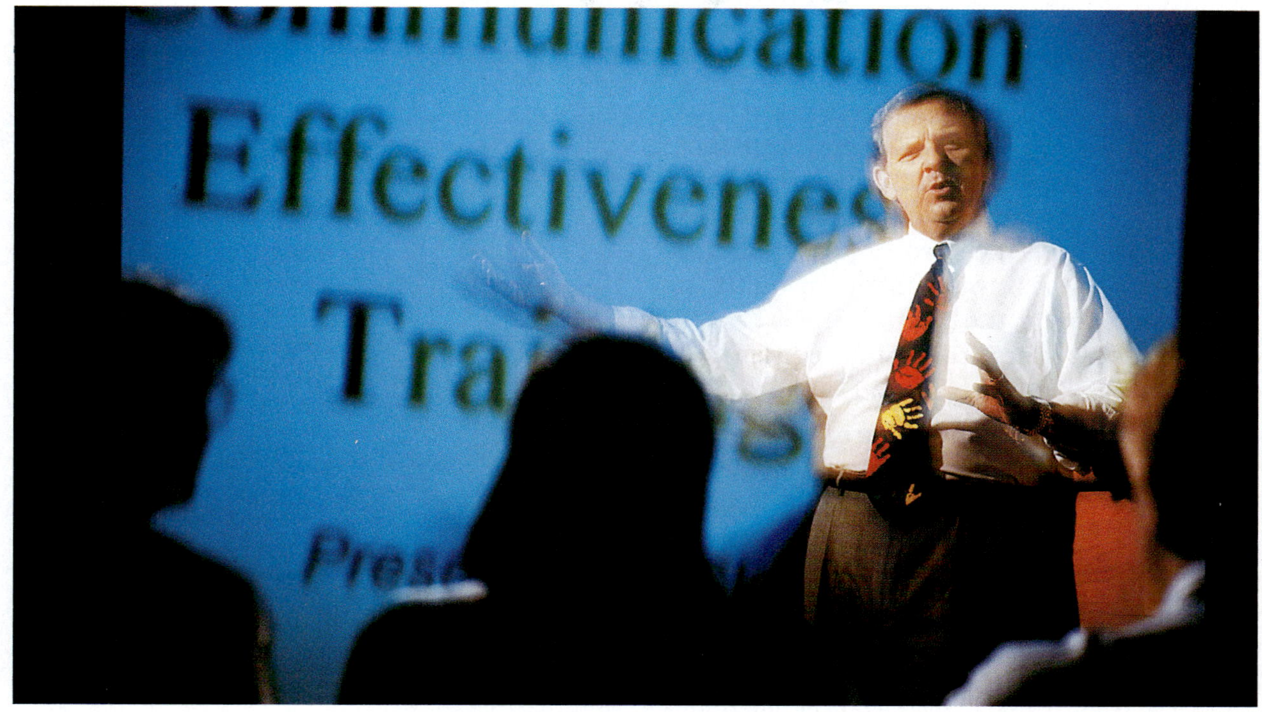

A presenter must always be aware of audience feedback. **Why?**

Interacting with the Audience

Audience members do not typically carry on conversations with the presenter during a presentation, but they always provide feedback. This feedback can range from facial expressions and other types of body talk to verbal outbursts. It is important to evaluate audience feedback carefully, regardless of its form. It most often is positive, sometimes is negative, and always is educational.

Sometimes, audiences will cheer, encourage, heckle, boo, or even hold up signs relating to highly controversial topics or presenters. On rare occasions, audience members who feel very emotional about an issue may interrupt a presenter and shout some comment or question during the middle of a presentation. Fortunately, however, these interactions do not occur in most presentations. Instead, most audience feedback is limited to nonverbal responses. As a presenter, you will want to watch for these responses so you can be sure your message is having the intended effect.

Adapting Messages to Audience Feedback

When you make a presentation, you have a lot of responsibility. Not only do you have to research, prepare, and present your information effectively, but you also are responsible for how it is received. Sometimes, a presenter will need to adjust his or her nonverbal behaviors to eliminate distractions and make the message easier to hear and understand. Other times, however, it is the message itself that needs adjusting.

Of course, the fact that someone doesn't agree with a message doesn't mean the message content automatically should be changed. Many times, presenters are responsible for delivering unpopular messages to listeners. However, if you anticipate a neutral or supportive response from your audience but get a negative reaction instead, you may need to adjust your message. Many times, this will mean adjusting your wording or the verbal style of your message rather than the actual content.

As a presenter, you can assess people's reaction to a message by monitoring their feedback. Do audience members look interested? Do they look puzzled? Are people actually leaving the room? Signals like these tell you whether or not it is necessary to adapt your message. For the most part, these signals take the form of audible feedback and body talk.

Audible Feedback Audible feedback is feedback you can hear. This may take the form of applause, vocalizations, and other nonverbal sounds. If not, it may be expressed as different types of verbal responses.

Nonverbal Sounds For instance, if audience members agree with what a presenter is saying or are pleased with a certain message, they may whistle or cheer. They may respond to a good joke by laughing or even applauding. These types of feedback help a presenter know that a message is coming through loud and clear and is generating the desired response.

If, on the other hand, a joke is followed by complete silence from the audience, the presenter may draw some different conclusions. Perhaps his or her attempt at humor seemed inappropriate or offensive to some audience members. Maybe the audience just didn't understand it. The presenter should note that the humor attempt failed and adapt his or her message to omit similar types of humor later on.

Some comedians have become enormously popular using outrageous or offensive humor. However, off-color humor and jokes that make fun of people generally are poor ethical choices for presenters in professional and social contexts. This includes humor about people of different ethnic groups, cultures, religions, ages, or gender. Also avoid making fun of people's choices of schools or clothing. You should also avoid other topics that may be related to socioeconomic status. This type of humor is sure to offend someone in your audience and generate negative—or even hostile—feedback.

In most public-speaking situations, the only person you can make fun of without any repercussions is yourself. In the right context, pointing out something funny about yourself can let others know you are approachable and not overly serious. Since everyone makes mistakes and has his or her own silly quirks, this type of humor often can help you bond with an audience. Be careful that you don't overdo it, though. Pointing out too many weaknesses may leave the impression that you really are weak.

COMMUNICATION Strategies

RESPONDING EMPATHICALLY TO INTERRUPTIONS

- Never respond rudely to an interruption, no matter how rude it is.
- Rephrase a rude or hostile comment in a neutral, non-insulting way.
- Look for the person's real, underlying concern and address that—not the inappropriateness of the interruption itself.
- Offer to field questions and comments at the end of the presentation.

Verbal Responses From time to time, audiences also use words to provide audible feedback. They may shout their agreement or disagreement with a presenter's comments. In some cases, they might offer a word or phrase to encourage a presenter or support or refute a point.

Verbal feedback typically does not happen as often as other forms of feedback. Seldom do audience members feel free to make verbal comments to the presenter while he or she is speaking. Still, it does happen. Verbal feedback is most likely to occur when either the message or the presenter taps into listeners' emotions.

For example, if a message is strongly opposed or supported by an audience, or if the presenters themselves are debating a topic, listeners may respond verbally. Sometimes, if a presenter has a great deal of notoriety, some audience members may attend a presentation for the sole purpose of protesting or otherwise getting the presenter's attention. These efforts often take the form of verbal interruptions of the message.

Nonverbal Feedback

A presenter has only the time he or she is at the podium to provide information, motivate, or make a persuasive appeal to an audience. That is why it is important to make sure the audience understands the message. Audible feedback such as applause or verbal comments makes it fairly easy to assess listeners' perceptions. However, feedback is not always this obvious. Most of the time, audience feedback will be nonverbal.

Approval and Disapproval If audience members are smiling, nodding, taking notes, and maintaining eye contact with the presenter, they probably are understanding the message and responding positively. They may express disagreement or disapproval by refusing to make eye contact, murmuring comments to their neighbors, sitting rigidly or shifting uncomfortably in their seats, frowning, or shaking their heads "no."

Feedback from an audience can be verbal and nonverbal. **What nonverbal signals generally indicate audience approval?**

Boredom If audience members feel a presenter is being ineffective and wasting their time, their nonverbal signals may be very similar to those for disapproval. They may begin side conversations, frown, shift in their chairs, or shake their heads "no." Restless or bored audience members also may tap their fingers or feet, yawn, check their watches repeatedly, or start looking around the room for something else to hold their interest. These audience members may just need the presenter to speed up the pace of the presentation or move on to new information or both.

Confusion When audience members are confused, they may send more subtle clues. They may look at one another in a questioning way, whisper questions back and forth, start searching through notes or handouts, or look around to see if others also are lost. It is especially important to pick up on this type of feedback because it signals that the message isn't coming through. Once the presenter is aware of audience confusion, he or she needs to take action and clarify his or her message.

Clarifying Information Once you notice signs of confusion in your audience, you can respond a number of ways. In a small, informal presentation, you might actually know the audience member or members who seem to be lost. If this is the case, you simply may wish to ask them where they stopped understanding. You can then go back to that point and explain your message more clearly.

A speaker responds to questions from an audience member. **Identify factors to keep in mind when responding to questions from the audience.**

Many times, however, you will not know the members of your audience. Even if you do, the potential for embarrassing someone may keep you from calling on him or her during the presentation. In these instances, it usually is better to stop, remark that some audience members look a little lost, and emphasize that you want everyone to understand the points you are making. Then, take the time to clarify your point before going on.

Restating the Message One effective method for clarifying information is to state it in a different way. Provide a brief summary of information up to that point, clarifying any areas that audience members might find particularly confusing. This may include stressing a specific order of events, grouping information into categories, pointing out important similarities or differences, or using visual aids. You also may wish to define additional terms or provide new examples to help your listeners understand.

Once the people who were looking puzzled begin nodding their heads or giving other nonverbal signals that they understand, you may move on with your presentation. In the meantime, be patient. Avoid looking frustrated with audience members who become confused. You might even put them at ease by commenting that this is a difficult concept or that it took you some time to understand it well yourself. This not only makes the audience feel better about not keeping up, but it also can help you build a bond with your listeners.

Responding to Questions

Many times, audience members will have questions about the information you are presenting. Although some presenters allow questions during a presentation, you may find it most effective to reserve questions until the end when they can be answered all at once. This prevents interruptions of your train of thought and keeps the audience from getting sidetracked by questions that have little to do with the content at hand. You cannot control what others will introduce into your presentation in

COMMUNICATION Strategies

HANDLING AUDIENCE QUESTIONS

- Ask for questions in a polite, inviting tone that indicates you genuinely want to help.
- Repeat each question before answering. This allows everyone to hear it and may eliminate duplicate questions later on.
- If a question is overly complicated or phrased in an insulting or accusatory manner, restate it more appropriately.
- Think through the question and respond simply and directly. Don't ramble or get sidetracked.
- Don't bluff—if you do not know the answer, say so. Offer to research the information and provide it later, if necessary.
- Keep your cool when faced with hostile questions. Resist the impulse to fight back.
- If someone tries to turn a question into a presentation, politely, but firmly, stop him or her. Interrupt the person and state his or her question as you understand it.
- Make a short statement to conclude the Q&A session, repeating key information and thanking audience members for their questions and interest.

the form of questions or comments. Therefore, you may wish to reserve them until your message is complete.

One way to prevent interruptions of this kind is to announce at the beginning of your presentation that there will be a question-and-answer period directly following your presentation. Even if you had not planned such a "Q&A" period, you may determine during the course of your presentation that one is necessary. In this case, you might make a statement such as "I see that some of you are going to want to discuss specific details or related issues. I'll be happy to address your questions at the conclusion of my presentation."

As audience members voice their questions, listen critically, deliberatively, and empathically. Make your responses as empathic and as clearly stated as possible. If someone asks a question about something you already said in your presentation, try to find a different way to state the answer. If the person didn't understand the first time, hearing your exact words again probably won't help. On the other hand, if a question has already been answered during the Q&A session, it's all right to say, "I believe that's already been covered." The checklist on page 579 provides additional tips for conducting Q&A sessions.

Setting Protocol for Q&A When beginning a Q&A session, it is important to set the protocol. Establishing a specific tone and expectations can keep discussions focused and productive.

Begin by setting a time limit. For example, you might say, "I'd like to open the floor to questions for the next fifteen minutes." Then, politely ask all participants to limit their questions to the topic of your presentation. This keeps participants on track and can help you avoid being stumped by an off-topic question.

For a Q&A session after a large presentation, you may wish to position a microphone in an aisle. Then, have audience members take turns asking their questions into the microphone. Explain that questioners should ask only one question at a time and remain standing at the microphone until that question has been answered. That way, if the presenter needs clarification or additional information, the person still has access to the microphone.

COMMUNICATION PRACTICE LAB

Participating in a Q&A Session

To practice conducting a question-and-answer session after a presentation, follow these steps:

Step 1 Read a short, informative article from a magazine, newspaper, or other resource available to you.

Step 2 When you have finished reading your article, choose a partner.

Step 3 Present a one-minute summary of the article to your partner.

Step 4 Conduct a question-and-answer session with your partner. Use the strategies you have learned in this chapter.

Step 5 Switch roles with your partner. Listen critically to his or her summary and then ask questions. Practice stating questions clearly and appropriately.

Step 6 As a class, discuss what you learned about fielding questions from an audience. Work together to solve any problems you experienced.

After a smaller presentation, a microphone probably will not be necessary. Simply ask audience members to stand while their questions are asked and answered. This helps others hear the question clearly and helps the presenter locate the person to whom he or she is directing the answer.

Finally, try to establish a positive tone for the Q&A session. Project an attitude of willingness to answer questions. Rephrase harsh or inappropriate questions to eliminate as much negativity as possible. Maintain open, nonjudgmental facial expressions and body language. Staying positive shows your listeners you are willing to do anything you can to help them understand your message. This not only puts the audience at ease but also may establish you as a trusted resource for future information.

Evaluating Presentations

In previous chapters, you have read that the listener ultimately determines the meaning of a message. This means that we all continually evaluate what we hear and apply it to ourselves. In other words, we all are amateur evaluators, to a certain extent.

Sometimes, however, a presenter needs a more in-depth evaluation of his or her presentation. Perhaps he or she isn't sure about the effectiveness of a certain rhetorical strategy. Perhaps you have noticed something about your own presentation style that you think needs further analysis. In these cases, it is important to know how to effectively evaluate a professional presentation.

Acting as a Critic

When you evaluate your own or someone else's presentation, you do more than simply express personal opinions. You take on the role of a critic. A **critic** is someone who, through training and experience, is qualified to analyze and make judgments about something. Critics use their critical listening skills to determine the strengths and weaknesses of a presentation or other performance.

Listening Critically Think about the listening skills that you learned in Chapter 6. To properly evaluate a presentation, it is crucial to make full use of your critical, deliberative, and empathic listening skills.

You use your critical listening skills to comprehend the ideas and information presented in the presentation. Critical listening is used to determine if the presentation is reasonable and understandable. Is the information given during the presentation appropriate to the purpose and the occasion?

You use your deliberative listening skills to analyze and evaluate the presenter's information as a basis for making immediate or future decisions. Deliberative listening is used by the critic for a persuasive presentation to determine if the presenter uses logic well, seems to have the listener's best interests at heart, and makes sense.

You use empathic listening to try to understand why the presenter has approached the topic in this way. What is the presenter's motivation for making this presentation? You also use empathic listening to determine if the presenter selected the best way for the topic to be presented to a particular audience.

As a critic, you will need to develop a specific set of criteria by which you can evaluate a presentation. Go back to the Communication Strategies for Critical, Deliberative, and Empathic Listening in Chapter 6. These tips should help you to develop appropriate criteria for evaluating a presentation. In addition to these criteria for evaluating a presentation, you will want to consider the perspective from which the presentation will be evaluated.

Figure 18–2 Critical Perspectives

- ☑ **Judgment by Results:** evaluates whether or not the presenter has accomplished the goal of his or her presentation
- ☑ **Judgment by Ethical Standards:** evaluates whether the presenter behaved ethically during the presentation
- ☑ **Judgment by Aesthetics:** evaluates the overall appearance or impact of the presentation
- ☑ **Judgment by Multiple Standards:** uses two or more critical perspectives to evaluate a presentation

Using Critical Perspectives

Critics use one or more critical perspectives when they evaluate a presentation. A critical perspective is a standard by which a presentation is judged to be successful or unsuccessful. Not all presentations are judged by the same standards. In fact, these perspectives may be combined or used alone to determine the success of any particular presentation. As Figure 18–2 shows, critics may evaluate a presentation based on any of the following perspectives:

- judgment by results
- judgment by ethical standards
- judgment by aesthetics
- judgment by multiple standards

Judgment by Results

A judgment by results evaluates whether or not a presenter accomplished the goal of his or her presentation. If it was an informative presentation, did the audience gain new insight into the topic? If it was a persuasive presentation, was the audience persuaded to believe or do what was asked? If it was a motivational presentation, did audience members leave feeling inspired and more optimistic about themselves or their abilities?

Judgment by results can be very straightforward. For instance, if a presenter is giving a persuasive sales presentation, he or she will probably be judged by how many products are sold as a result of that presentation.

Sometimes, however, this perspective can be more complicated. If you fail to be motivated by a motivational presentation, the presentation is not automatically a failure. Rather, you should judge how it affected the audience as a whole. If everyone else seemed to be motivated to some degree, it was probably effective.

Judgment by Ethical Standards

A second critical perspective is judgment by ethical standards, which determines whether a presenter behaved ethically in a presentation. With this perspective, it doesn't matter whether the goals of the presentation were accomplished. The most important point is whether the presenter violated any ethical standards during the presentation.

Global Communication

Cultural Appreciation

As you have learned, people from other places in the world may have had experiences that are quite different from yours. Many examples of regional and cultural differences have been examined in this course. Using what you have learned, develop five guidelines that would be important to keep in mind when you are evaluating a presentation made by someone from another region or culture.

When you use this perspective, you might say, "I told the truth about my company's product, used sound research to back up my main point, and used logical arguments." According to this perspective, it does not matter whether or not anyone bought the product as a result of your presentation. It only matters that you planned and presented an ethical persuasive presentation.

Judgment by ethical standards sometimes can be tricky for presenters because different standards may be set by any individual critic. Therefore, if a critic agrees to some degree with your point of view, he or she probably will declare the presentation effective. If the critic disagrees, he or she is likely to judge the presentation ineffective.

Judgment by Aesthetics Sometimes, the aesthetic, or artistic, form of a presentation is evaluated separately from its content. A **judgment by aesthetics** evaluates the overall appearance or impact of a presentation. A presentation is aesthetically effective if the presenter planned a proper introduction, body, and conclusion; used effective transitions, internal summaries, and audiovisual aids; dressed appropriately; and used other appropriate forms of nonverbal communication. Again, it doesn't matter whether the presenter actually accomplished the presentation's purpose. It is more important that he or she looked and sounded professional and well prepared.

Judgment by Multiple Standards Most often, presentations are subject to a **judgment by multiple standards,** which uses two or more critical perspectives to determine the success of a presentation. For instance, a critic may decide that it is important that a presenter accomplishes his or her goal (judgment by results) by giving a professional-looking presentation (judgment by aesthetics). Sometimes, all three critical

COMMUNICATION *Strategies*

Guidelines for Evaluating a Presentation

- Establish a set of criteria based on what you have learned about effective speaking and listening and the critical perspective you have chosen.
- Begin by pointing out the presenter's strengths.
- Keep an open mind.
- Be specific about both positive and negative points.
- Don't just point out a weakness. Suggest a specific way to fix it.
- Don't get personal. Remember, you're evaluating the presentation, not the person.
- If something is just your opinion, say so.
- Be reasonable. If something was out of the presenter's control or beyond his or her experience, take that into consideration.
- Show empathy for the presenter. Make your comments tactful and understanding.
- Phrase your criticism in a way that you would find helpful if you were the presenter.
- Realize that the presenter may not agree with you. Don't argue or try to force your ideas.
- Focus on the future. Help the presenter envision making a perfect presentation next time.
- Be brief.

Figure 18–3 Evaluation of Others

Evaluation Form
for Judgment by Multiple Standards

Presenter ______________________________ Evaluator ______________________

Score each element on a scale from 1 to 5 in which 1 = needs improvement, 2 = fair, 3 = average, 4 = good, and 5 = excellent. Write your comments in the extra space beside each question.

Presentation Elements
Introduction
______ Did the introduction capture listeners' attention?
______ Did the presenter state the thesis and preview the main points of the presentation?
______ Did the presenter apply the presentation to the audience?
______ Did the presenter establish his or her ethos?
Main Body
______ Was the information presented in a clear pattern of organization?
______ Did the presenter support the main points with details?
______ Did the presenter provide smooth transitions?
______ Did the presenter keep the audience interested while covering the main points?
Conclusion
______ Did the presenter summarize the main points and repeat the thesis?
______ Was there a clear, organized end to the presentation?

Performance Elements
Oral Style
______ Did the presenter make clear, effective word choices?
______ Did the presenter seem to follow ethical standards?
______ Was he or she interesting and/or creative?
______ Did the presenter effectively adapt to audience feedback?
Nonverbal Cues
______ Was the presenter's overall appearance professional and appropriate?
______ Did the presenter seem confident and well prepared?
______ Did he or she use appropriate vocal characteristics?
______ Did he or she use appropriate nonverbal strategies?
Audiovisual Aids
______ Was the presentation enhanced by the use of audiovisual aids?
______ If so, were the audiovisual aids professional and easy to see and understand?

Total Score: __________ of 100 possible points

perspectives may be required for the presentation to be judged effective. That is, the presenter must accomplish his or her goals, speak ethically, and give a polished performance for the presentation to be judged successful. As a critic, you probably will evaluate most presentations by all three perspectives.

Practice for the Workplace

Listen Carefully Some professional presenters have a way of finding out how each audience member feels about a presentation: They ask. By offering a simple evaluation form to your audience, you can gain valuable feedback. In some instances, you may be expected to provide evaluation forms, so it's a good idea to have them available.

BUSINESS PRACTICE *Activity*

Create an evaluation form that an audience could use to assess a presentation that you give. Develop five questions for the form. Your questions should determine whether the audience's needs were met by your performance. The form should also give audience members an opportunity to provide you with constructive criticism.

Forming Your Evaluation

Whether you are evaluating your own presentation or someone else's, the goal is to help the presenter build on his or her strengths as well as eliminate weaknesses. Focusing only on the negative aspects of a presentation does little to help a presenter. Instead, it may make that person feel like a failure or as if he or she is being picked on.

Therefore, it is important to be as positive as possible in your evaluation. Focus on what the presenter did right, as well as what needs improvement. Once you have prepared yourself with a positive attitude, follow the guidelines in the Communication Strategies checklist on page 583 for being an effective critic.

Providing Written Evaluations

Most of the time when you listen to a presentation in a professional or social context, you will not be asked to evaluate the presentation in writing. In this class, however, you may be asked to complete a form for every presentation you evaluate. The type of form you will complete depends on whether you are assessing someone else's or your own work.

Evaluating Others' Presentations

Sometimes, it can be difficult to evaluate the presentation skills of a friend or classmate. You may feel awkward about pointing out flaws in a friend's performance, and you may feel embarrassed about pointing out a classmate's strengths.

To make criticism easier, consider this: The person you are evaluating probably wants to be the best presenter possible. You are helping him or her achieve this goal. In addition, being a critic helps you learn to listen critically—a skill that will prove valuable throughout your life. Finally, evaluating others' presentations helps you know what to watch for in your own presentations. It also may give you ideas for adding special touches to your own presentations.

Another way to make evaluations easier is to use an evaluation form such as the sample form in Figure 18–3. Most evaluation forms provide a list of criteria for a successful presentation. These criteria often are listed as objective questions that help you focus on

Figure 18–4 Self-Evaluation

Self-Evaluation Form

Score each element on a scale from 1 to 4 in which 1 = needs improvement, 2 = fair, 3 = good, and 4 = excellent. Write your comments in the extra space beside each question.

Preparation Elements

Information

______ Did I choose an appropriate topic for self, listener, occasion, and task?
______ Did I limit the topic enough to cover it thoroughly in ______ minutes?
______ Did I conduct adequate research?
______ Is my outline well organized and complete?

Tools

______ Are my notes well organized, complete, and easy for me to use?
______ Is all necessary audiovisual equipment available and operating correctly?
______ Have I prepared interesting, easy-to-see, useful audiovisual aids?
______ Have I practiced using and explaining my audiovisual aids?

Self

______ Is the clothing for my presentation clean, pressed, and ready to wear?
______ Am I confident that I have full command of the information I'm presenting?
______ Have I practiced ways to manage performance apprehension and stage fright?

Content Elements

______ Did my introduction state the thesis and main points?
______ In the main body, did I support the main points with adequate information?
______ Did I conclude by summarizing the main points and repeating the thesis?
______ Did I provide a clear, organized end to the presentation?
______ Did I make the overall content relevant to my audience?

Performance Elements

Oral Style

______ Did I make my wording clear and my transitions smooth?
______ Did I make my presentation interesting and creative?

Nonverbal Cues

______ Was my overall appearance neat and professional?
______ Did I pay attention to vocal characteristics such as pitch, volume, and rate?
______ Did I stand up straight and use appropriate movements and gestures?
______ Did I use friendly and appropriate facial expressions?
______ Did I maintain eye contact with my audience and avoid staring at my notes?

Use of Audiovisual Aids

______ Did I face the audience as I used my audiovisual aids?
______ Were all my audiovisual aids easy for the audience to see and understand?

Total Score: __________ of 100 possible points

what is most important. To answer these questions effectively, you will need to use your best critical listening skills.

Evaluating Your Presentations Sometimes, you can be the most effective critic of your own presentations. After all, you know exactly how you want to appear to your audience, what your most important point or goal is, and what your main strengths and weaknesses are. Finally, you have unlimited opportunities to evaluate your own work and make improvements before the actual performance.

To evaluate the effectiveness of your own presentation, you will need to see or hear yourself in action. Videotape yourself giving the presentation, as shown in **Figure 18–5,** record your presentation using an audiocassette recorder, or watch in a mirror. Again, as you observe your performance, watch closely and use your critical listening skills to analyze what is most important.

One of the most important things to remember in self-evaluation is to remain objective. That is, try to judge yourself by the same standards someone else would use. Don't make excuses by saying, "I can't do any better than that," or "That's just my personality or style." An outside critic would point out any weak areas and suggest ways to improve them. Do the same for yourself.

To help you focus on the most important aspects of your presentation—and to help you stay objective—you may wish to use a self-evaluation form such as the one in **Figure 18–4.** This type of form is similar to the one you read previously, except it goes into a bit more detail and explores the preparation process.

Learning from Evaluations

Often, it can be difficult to accept others' evaluations of our efforts. After all, nobody enjoys having a weakness pointed out. However, constructive criticism is vital to becoming a competent and effective presenter. In fact, when it comes to making professional presentations, the more you can be evaluated, the better.

Try to think of evaluations as a team effort to help you reach your full potential as a presenter. No one expects you to be an expert presenter at first, but everyone wants to help you reach that goal eventually. With this in mind, ask others for tips and suggestions for improvement. Then, try these ideas out to see if they work for you.

Dealing with Errors From time to time, a critic's comment or suggestion may be off base. If you think this is the case, don't get defensive. Just weigh the advice against what you've learned and what other evaluators have said about your work. If the idea seems inconsistent or unjustified, check it with an objective party. Then, decide whether you think the comment has merit. If it doesn't, shrug it off and move on. Don't waste time getting angry over a difference of opinion.

Figure 18–5 Evaluating Your Presentation

Focusing on the Positive Finally, concentrate on the positive feedback you receive just as much as the negative. If you examine your evaluations carefully, you'll probably see that you have many of the valuable skills needed by professional presenters. By building on these skills and continuing to develop new ones, you'll quickly change your negatives to positives as you successfully achieve your presentation goals.

Section 2 Assessment

Visit the *Glencoe Communication Applications* Web site at **communicationapplications.glencoe.com** and click on **Self-Check and Study Guide 18.2** to review your understanding of evaluating presentations.

Review Key Terms

1. Define each term and write it in a sentence: critic, critical perspective, judgment by results, judgment by ethical standards, judgment by aesthetics, judgment by multiple standards.

Check Understanding

2. How might a bored audience member's nonverbal feedback differ from that of a confused audience member?
3. Imagine that while you are giving a motivational presentation, an audience member interrupts to ask if you will speak at his company meeting. Give an example of an empathic response.
4. **Hypothesize** Imagine that, during a question-and-answer session, someone asks you, "How can you possibly say this is the best plan for our group?" Give an appropriate response.

APPLICATION *Activity*

Evaluating a Presentation Choose one of the evaluation forms provided in this section and copy it onto a sheet of paper. Then, prepare a one- to two-minute presentation on a topic with which you are familiar. Use the form to evaluate your own presentation or the presentation of a partner (who, in turn, will evaluate your presentation). Discuss your evaluations as a class. Work together to devise a list of helpful hints for giving effective evaluations.

Communication Self-Assessment

Appraising Your Presentation and Evaluation Skills

How Do You Rate?

On a separate sheet of paper, use the key to respond to the following statements. Put a check mark at the end of each skill you would like to improve.

KEY: **A** Always **U** Usually **S** Sometimes **R** Rarely **N** Never

1. I practice my presentations to gain polish and confidence.
2. I project and pace my voice, using a conversational style of presentation.
3. I have mastered how to use nonverbal presentation strategies.
4. During a presentation, I make direct eye contact with my audience.
5. I use audience feedback to determine if I need to modify my presentation or repeat main ideas.
6. I answer questions and remain approachable to audience members.
7. I practice question-and-answer sessions.
8. When I evaluate presentations, I listen to find the main message and decide if it is worthwhile.
9. I include both strengths and needed improvements when I evaluate a presentation.
10. When I evaluate my own presentation skills, I try to be as objective as possible.

How Do You Score?

Review your responses. Give yourself 5 points for every A, 4 for every U, 3 for every S, 2 for every R, and 1 for every N. Total your points and evaluate your score.

41–50 Excellent You may be surprised to find out how much you can improve your skills.

31–40 Good In this course, you can learn ways to make your skills better.

21–30 Fair Practice applying the skills taught in this course.

1–20 Needs Improvement Carefully monitor your improvement as you work through this course.

Setting Communication Goals

If you scored Excellent or Good, complete Part A. If your score was Fair or Needs Improvement, complete Part B.

Part A

1. I plan to put the following ideas into practice:
2. I plan to share the following information about communication with the following people:

Part B

1. The behaviors I need to change most are:
2. To bring about these changes, I will take these steps:

Writing a Persuasive Sales Letter

Persuasive sales letters motivate people to buy goods and services. They are, very simply, product advertisements. These letters can be used to introduce or promote products, describe a product's advantages, convince consumers to take action, or make a sale. The basic format for a sales letter is the same as that of a standard business letter.

Spark Interest. To captivate your reader's attention, you will want to create interest in what you are selling. This can be accomplished by asking questions or making positive, factual statements about the quality of your product or service. You can also generate interest by appealing to emotion, comfort, or status.

Promote a Need. People do not question their need for food and water. However, a person might wonder why he or she would need an unfamiliar product or service. A good sales letter anticipates this response and explains how a product will meet the consumer's needs. For example, a sports magazine may be more appealing if it offers discounts on sports equipment to subscribers.

Why Buy Now? Give the reader a good reason to buy when he or she receives your letter. Some popular reasons are grand openings, free gifts, lower prices, or other incentives for buying before a given date. If a person is undecided about a product, the right promotion may convince him or her to take action.

State Your Product's Advantages. Part of creating demand for a product or service is describing it in some detail. Describe all of the positive points of your product or service in your sales letter. If your product has any unique features or capabilities, make them known to your readers. These points will attract the most attention if you mark them with arrows or bullets, as in the example on the next page.

Close the Sale. Give the reader an opportunity to purchase your product. Provide as many options as possible for consumers to take advantage of your product or service. Offer to set up a sales meeting, provide a telephone number, or encourage the reader to purchase the product by mail or on the Internet. If you make it easy for consumers to reach you, they will be more likely to accept your offer.

For additional information about business writing, see the *Guide to Business Communication* section of the Communication Survival Kit in the Appendix.

: Cable Connection
3 West Connecticut Boulevard
rrville, Texas 78029
ıgust 26, 2002

rs. William Holland
450 Grand Avenue
untley, Illinois 60142

)ear Mrs. Holland:

Are you familiar with The Cable Connection? We supply *affordable* cable television services to residents of the Huntley Community. For just pennies a day, we will install 20 new channels of entertainment, just for you.

Yes! Twenty channels of

- arts
- entertainment
- sports
- movies
- documentary films
- nature programming

all for only $19.95 per month!

For a limited time, we are installing The Cable Connection in your area FREE OF CHARGE. At the time of installation, you pay only $19.95 for your first month's service.

Please act soon by calling the telephone number on the enclosed brochure. The call is free. We hope to hear from you soon.

Sincerely,
Ravi Patel
Mr. Ravi Patel
President, The Cable Connection

WRITING *Activity*

Assume that you work for a store that sells electronic equipment and appliances. Your store holds a clearance sale each spring. You have been asked to write a persuasive sales letter that will be sent to the customers on the store's mailing list. The purpose of the letter is to make the customers aware of the sale. Use your address for the business, today's date, and your own name. Use the information that follows to compose the rest of your sales letter.

- Address the letter to "A Valued Customer." Use any street address for the recipient.
- The name of the store is The Arc Appliance Store.
- During the sale, your store will offer brand-name merchandise for one-fourth to one-third off.
- You will give customers a free, two-year warranty on all purchases.
- Customers may finance appliances with no interest for one year.
- You carry products that conserve energy and require minimal service.
- You offer convenient products, such as lightweight vacuum cleaners.
- All entertainment devices come with programmable remote controls.

CHAPTER 18 Assessment and Activities

Visit the *Glencoe Communication Applications* Web site at **communicationapplications.glencoe.com** and click on **Chapter 18 Activity** for additional practice in making and evaluating presentations.

Reviewing Key Terms

On a separate sheet of paper, write the communication term that completes each statement.

1. The image a presenter projects to an audience is called _______ .

2. A(n) _______ helps a presenter create a mental image for his or her audience.

3. _______ means sending your voice to all areas of a room without shouting.

4. Someone who is qualified to analyze and make judgments about something is a(n) _______ .

5. How a presenter uses his or her body and voice to communicate is called _______ .

6. Raising one's eyebrows or rolling one's eyes is an example of a(n) _______ .

7. A standard by which a presentation is judged successful or unsuccessful is called a(n) _______ .

8. A(n) _______ evaluates whether or not a speaker accomplished the goal of his or her presentation.

Reviewing Key Concepts

1. Name two ways a polished delivery helps a presenter when making a presentation.

2. Why do most presentations call for a relaxed, responsive, and conversational tone of voice?

3. How would a presenter use the rate of his or her delivery to emphasize an important statement?

4. List three guidelines for using gestures in presentations.

5. What should a presenter do immediately after his or her presentation?

6. When is an audience most likely to offer verbal feedback?

7. What message do audience members send by tapping their feet and checking their watches?

8. How should a presenter answer a question about something that he or she already covered in the presentation?

Assessment and Activities

Reading and Critical Thinking Skill

1. **Applying Information** Describe the hair and clothing of a successful presenter.
2. **Cause–Effect** How can a presenter make audience members feel included and valued during a presentation?
3. **Classifying Information** Which kind of audience feedback—body talk, nonverbal sound, or verbal response—is applause?
4. **Synthesis** Imagine you are speaking to an audience and commit a spoonerism, saying *ate of the start* instead of *state of the art*. Come up with a quip that will make fun of yourself and help you bond with the audience.
5. **Summary** Sum up strategies for presenters when responding empathically to interruptions.

Skill Practice Activity

Distinguishing Fact from Opinion Rewrite each of the following opinions as a fact.

Opinion: The salesperson's presentation was a complete failure.

Fact: No one ordered the salesperson's product.

1. The presentation was an artistic success.
2. The speaker's delivery was monotonous.
3. The conclusion to the presentation was excellent.
4. The presentation was boring.

Cooperative Learning Activity

Writing a Persuasive Sales Letter Imagine trying to persuade your principal to order this communication applications textbook. Write a sales letter and then exchange letters with a classmate. Use these questions to evaluate your partner's letter. Does the letter's introduction capture your attention? Will the letter appeal to the principal? Is the information clearly organized? Does the writer support the main points with details? Does the writer provide smooth transitions? Does the writer cover the main points in an interesting way? Does the letter end in a clear, organized manner?

Chapter Project

Planning Find a video that features a persuasive presentation. Watch the presenter and use the Evaluation Form for Judgments by Multiple Standards to evaluate him or her. Write a parody of the presentation from the video. Address a topic to which your classmates might relate. Practice using gestures and other techniques that the actor in the video used. Have someone tape the final version of your presentation. Watch yourself on video and evaluate yourself.

Presenting Give your presentation to the class and have the students evaluate you. Compare your scores to the score you gave the actor in the video.

Louis Armstrong—Father of Jazz

Singer and trumpeter Louis Armstrong was one of the most beloved performers of his time. A true jazz pioneer, he was able to captivate an audience with a combination of his sheer talent and endearing, larger-than-life persona. People who had the opportunity to hear him perform knew that they were in the presence of greatness. Armstrong's listeners were captivated by the emotion that he put into his playing and his genuine passion for music. Today, Louis Armstrong is remembered as one of the most influential musicians of the twentieth century. He has been widely imitated by almost everyone who has come after him, and his style formed the foundation for modern jazz music.

A Brilliant Soloist

Armstrong grew up in turn-of-the-century New Orleans, a musical city where he heard and absorbed a wide variety of musical styles. He learned to play the trumpet when he was still a teenager and developed his skill by playing in some of the city's brass bands and jazz outfits. Eventually, he was hired by King Oliver. Oliver's band, the Creole Jazz Band, was New Orleans' most popular jazz orchestra. At that time, jazz was mainly ensemble music. This meant that all musicians played at the same time and no one performer was featured over the others. However, Armstrong's playing was so skillful, so loud, and so energetic that it stood out from everyone else's. Soon, everyone in New Orleans had heard about King Oliver's new trumpeter. As Armstrong's fame grew, he started playing with other bands.

Armstrong's solos are among the greatest ever recorded. In many cases, he would play intricate passages created on the spot while the rest of the band supported him with simple chords. Just like a good public speaker knows how to improvise, Armstrong was able to develop a wide range of melodies and apply them as the music demanded it. Musical improvisation of that complexity had never been heard before. Sometimes with just a few notes, Armstrong was able to enhance the mood of a piece, deepen its emotion, or inject it with a newfound energy.

A Great Singer

Armstrong was also a great singer. His voice was not beautiful or smooth, but it was perfect for expressing his playful, rhythmic style. Armstrong had an ability to add texture and warmth to familiar songs, often improving upon the original recordings. His talent for conveying emotion through the intonation of his voice was itself a unique form of communication. Only a performer with a personality as joyous as Armstrong's could have succeeded. His singing style inspired many imitators.

Armstrong was also one of the first artists to record "scat" singing. When a singer "scats," he stops singing the lyrics to the song and instead makes up nonsense words to imitate the sound of a particular instrument. Singers had been "scatting" in New Orleans for years, but Armstrong was among the first to put it on record with a song called "Heebie Jeebies." He later said that when he was recording "Heebie Jeebies" the sheet music that he was reading fell off the stand, so he had to make up something quickly. Most people who bought the record were amazed because they had never heard anything like it before. This innovation was just another way Armstrong was able to mesmerize his audience.

A Musical Innovator

When Louis Armstrong's records started selling, jazz musicians all around the country began to mimic his style. His influence was so <u>pervasive</u> that most trumpet players who recorded between 1927 and 1940 sound like him. The great jazz musician Miles Davis recognized Armstrong's importance when he said, "There's nothing you can play on the horn that Louis didn't play first."

Armstrong's records also opened the door for a whole new type of singing, influencing

vocalists as diverse as Bing Crosby, Ella Fitzgerald, Frank Sinatra, and Billie Holiday. Today, jazz singers still scat and improvise, following Armstrong's lead.

In addition to influencing his fellow musicians, Armstrong played a huge role in popularizing the music he had helped to create. He spent his life playing concerts throughout the world, bringing jazz to millions of people who had never heard it before. His sound was so vibrant and uplifting that it appealed to audiences of nearly every social, economic, and cultural background. Relying on music instead of words to deliver his message, Armstrong created deep emotional responses in his listeners. His recordings remain inspiring to this day.

When Louis Armstrong started playing jazz, he brought a whole new style to the genre. This style was so popular that it eventually replaced what came before it. Armstrong reinvented jazz. Everything that makes up jazz today—improvisation, inventive melodies and rhythm, "scat" singing—can be traced back to him. For this reason, many people call him the "father of jazz."

1 Louis Armstrong is compared to a good public speaker because he —

A had a voice that was perfect for expressing his playful, rhythmic style

B was very skilled at complex musical improvisation

C played solos that are among the greatest ever recorded

D relied on music instead of words to deliver his message

2 The main idea of this passage is that Louis Armstrong —

F filled his music with emotion

G grew up in the musically rich city of New Orleans

H created a style that influenced all jazz music

J recorded a song called "Heebie Jeebies"

3 Louis Armstrong helped to popularize jazz music by —

A opening the door to a whole new type of singing

B appealing to people of many different backgrounds

C being hired by King Oliver to play in his band

D influencing his fellow musicians

4 Information in this passage implies that Armstrong's trumpet playing was —

F powerful

G lazy

H incoherent

J relaxed

5 Which of these is a FACT in the passage?

A Louis Armstrong invented "scat" singing.

B Louis Armstrong never played the piano.

C Louis Armstrong played concerts all over the world.

D King Oliver's band was better than any other band.

6 In this passage, <u>pervasive</u> means —

F limited

G subtle

H widespread

J destructive

Communication Survival Kit

Language Handbook

Guide to Business Communication

Troubleshooter

The Troubleshooter will help you recognize and correct errors that you might make in your writing.

Sentence Fragment

Problem: A fragment that lacks a subject

This new computer is fantastic. Is much faster than the old one. *frag*

Solution: Add a subject to the fragment to make it a complete sentence.

This new computer is fantastic. It is much faster than the old one.

Problem: A fragment that lacks a complete verb

The patrons poured from the theater. Theatergoers in excited groups. *frag*

The jet suddenly plunged. Passengers tumbling in the aisles. *frag*

Solution A: Add a complete verb or an auxiliary verb to make the sentence complete.

The patrons poured from the theater. The theatergoers chattered in excited groups.

The jet suddenly plunged. Passengers were tumbling in the aisles.

Solution B: Combine the fragment with another sentence. Add commas to set off a nonessential phrase, or add a comma and a conjunction to separate two main clauses in a compound sentence.

The theatergoers, chattering in excited groups, poured from the theater.

The jet suddenly plunged, and passengers were tumbling in the aisles.

Problem: A fragment that is a subordinate clause

Tim scored the goal. Although he was injured in the attempt. *frag*

My term paper is about Robert Frost. Who is my favorite poet. *frag*

Solution A: Combine the fragment with another sentence. Add a comma to set off nonessential clauses.

Tim scored the goal, although he was injured in the attempt.

My term paper is about Robert Frost, who is my favorite poet.

Solution B: Rewrite the fragment as a complete sentence, eliminating the subordinating conjunction or the relative pronoun and adding a subject or other words necessary to make a complete thought.

Tim scored the goal. He was, however, injured in the attempt.

My term paper is about Robert Frost. He is my favorite poet.

Problem: A fragment that lacks both a subject and a verb

Keisha recited the poem. From memory. *frag*

Solution: Combine the fragment with another sentence.

Keisha recited the poem from memory.

Rule of Thumb: Sentence fragments can make your writing hard to understand. Make sure that every sentence has a subject and a verb.

Run-on Sentence

Problem: Comma splice—two main clauses separated by only a comma

We went canoeing last weekend, my shoulders still ache. *run-on*

Solution A: Replace the comma with an end mark of punctuation, such as a period or a question mark, and begin the new sentence with a capital letter.

We went canoeing last weekend. My shoulders still ache.

Solution B: Place a semicolon between the two main clauses.

We went canoeing last weekend; my shoulders still ache.

Solution C: Add a coordinating conjunction after the comma.

We went canoeing last weekend, and my shoulders still ache.

Problem: Two main clauses with no punctuation between them

The museum has a new exhibit of modern art we haven't seen it yet. *run-on*

Solution A: Separate the main clauses with an end mark of punctuation, such as a period or a question mark, and begin the second sentence with a capital letter.

The museum has a new exhibit of modern art. We haven't seen it yet.

Solution B: Separate the main clauses with a semicolon.

The museum has a new exhibit of modern art; we haven't seen it yet.

Solution C: Add a comma and a coordinating conjunction between the main clauses.

The museum has a new exhibit of modern art, but we haven't seen it yet.

Problem: Two main clauses with no comma before the coordinating conjunction

We washed cars all day and then we went out for Chinese food. *run-on*

Solution: Add a comma before the coordinating conjunction to separate the two main clauses.

We washed cars all day, and then we went out for Chinese food.

Rule of Thumb: It often helps to have someone else read your writing to see if it is clear. Since you know what the sentences are supposed to mean, you might sometimes miss the need for punctuation.

Lack of Subject-Verb Agreement

Problem: A subject that is separated from the verb by an intervening prepositional phrase

The bus with the band members leave at noon. *agr*

The peaks of the mountain range glistens with snow. *agr*

Solution: Ignore a prepositional phrase that comes between a subject and a verb. Make the verb agree with the subject, which is never the object of a preposition.

The bus with the band members leaves at noon.

The peaks of the mountain range glisten with snow.

Problem: A predicate nominative that differs in number from the subject

Raisins (is) a delicious snack. *agr*

Solution: Ignore the predicate nominative and make the verb agree with the subject of the sentence.

Raisins are a delicious snack.

Problem: A subject that follows the verb

Outside the mall (stands) six men. *agr*

Over there (is) several more. *agr*

Solution: In an inverted sentence, look for the subject *after* the verb. Then make sure the verb agrees with the subject.

Outside the mall stand six men.

Over there are several more.

> **Rule of Thumb:** Reversing the order of an inverted sentence may help you decide on the correct verb form: "Several more are over there."

Problem: A collective noun as the subject

The committee (meet) at 3:30 every Wednesday afternoon. *agr*

The committee (casts) their votes for chairperson. *agr*

Solution A: If the collective noun refers to a group as a whole, use a singular verb.

The committee meets at 3:30 every Wednesday afternoon.

Solution B: If the collective noun refers to each member of a group individually, use a plural verb.

The committee cast their votes for chairperson.

Problem: A noun of amount as the subject

Thirty-five years are the average lifespan of a hippopotamus. *agr*

Fifty pennies fits into a coin roll. *agr*

Solution: Determine whether the noun of amount refers to one unit (and is therefore singular) or whether it refers to a number of individual units (and is therefore plural).

Thirty-five years is the average lifespan of a hippopotamus.

Fifty pennies fit into a coin roll.

Problem: A compound subject that is joined by *and*

Speakers and a joystick is plugged into my computer. *agr*

Cookies and cream are my favorite kind of ice cream. *agr*

Solution A: If the parts of the compound subject do not belong to one unit or if they refer to different people or things, use a plural verb.

Speakers and a joystick are plugged into my computer.

Solution B: If the parts of the compound subject belong to one unit or if both parts refer to the same person or thing, use a singular verb.

Cookies and cream is my favorite kind of ice cream.

Problem: A compound subject that is joined by *or* or *nor*

Neither the dictionaries nor the thesaurus are on the shelves. *agr*

Solution: Make the verb agree with the subject that is closer to it.

Neither the dictionaries nor the thesaurus is on the shelves.

Neither the thesaurus nor the dictionaries are on the shelves.

Problem: A compound subject that is preceded by *many a, every,* or *each*

Every student and teacher have passed through these halls. *agr*

Solution: Use a singular verb when *many a, each,* or *every* precedes a compound subject.

Every student and teacher has passed through these halls.

Problem: A subject that is separated from the verb by an intervening expression

My mother, as well as her brothers, were born in Sweden. *agr*

Solution: Certain expressions, such as *as well as, in addition to,* and *together with,* do not change the number of the subject. Ignore these expressions between a subject and its verb. Make the verb agree with the subject.

My mother, as well as her brothers, was born in Sweden.

Problem: An indefinite pronoun as the subject

Everyone enjoy mysteries. *agr*

Several of the top-seeded players is in the finals. *agr*

Solution: Determine whether the indefinite pronoun is singular or plural, and make the verb agree. Some indefinite pronouns are singular—*another, anyone, everyone, one, each, either, neither, anything, everything, something,* and *somebody.* Some are plural—*both, many, few, several,* and *others.* Some can be singular or plural—*some, all, any, more, most,* and *none*—depending on the noun to which they refer.

Everyone enjoys mysteries.

Several of the top-seeded players are in the finals.

Lack of Pronoun-Antecedent Agreement

Problem: A singular antecedent that can be either male or female

A lawyer often settles his clients' cases out of court. *ant*

Solution A: Traditionally, a masculine pronoun was used to refer to an antecedent that might be either male or female. This usage ignores or excludes females and is not acceptable in contemporary writing. Reword the sentence to use *he or she, him or her,* and so on.

A lawyer often settles his or her clients' cases out of court.

Solution B: Reword the sentence so that both the antecedent and the pronoun are plural.

Lawyers often settle their clients' cases out of court.

Solution C: Reword the sentence to eliminate the pronoun.

A lawyer often settles clients' cases out of court.

Problem: A second-person pronoun that refers to a third-person antecedent

Ms. Rivelli likes to travel to cities where you can get around by bus. *ant*

Solution A: Use the appropriate third-person pronoun.

Ms. Rivelli likes to travel to cities where she can get around by bus.

Solution B: Use an appropriate noun instead of a pronoun.

Ms. Rivelli likes to travel to cities where people can get around by bus.

Problem: A singular indefinite pronoun as an antecedent

Neither of the girls remembered to bring their gym clothes. *ant*

Solution: *Another, any, every, each, one, either, neither, anything, everything, something,* and *somebody* are singular and therefore require singular personal pronouns, even when followed by a prepositional phrase that contains a plural noun.

Neither of the girls remembered to bring her gym clothes.

Rule of Thumb: To help you remember that pronouns such as *each, either,* and *neither* are singular, think *each one, either one,* and *neither one.*

Lack of Clear Pronoun Reference

Problem: A pronoun reference that is weak or vague

The players were elated, which was long overdue. *ref*

The fire was nearing our camp, and that made us nervous. *ref*

Solution A: Rewrite the sentence, adding a clear antecedent for the pronoun.

The players were elated by their victory, which was long overdue.

Solution B: Rewrite the sentence, substituting a noun for the pronoun.

The fire was nearing our camp, and the situation made us nervous.

Problem: A pronoun that could refer to more than one antecedent

Dad and Uncle Mark started a company, and he is the president.

Now that the actors have agents, they are getting more work.

Solution A: Rewrite the sentence, substituting a noun for the pronoun.

Dad and Uncle Mark started a company, and Dad is the president.

Solution B: Rewrite the sentence, making the antecedent of the pronoun clear.

The actors are getting more work now that they have agents.

Problem: The indefinite use of *you* or *they*

When a loon utters its eerie cry, you get goosebumps.

In Boston they call a submarine sandwich a grinder.

Solution A: Rewrite the sentence, substituting a noun for the pronoun.

When a loon utters its eerie cry, listeners get goosebumps.

Solution B: Rewrite the sentence, eliminating the pronoun entirely.

In Boston a submarine sandwich is called a grinder.

Shift in Pronoun

Problem: An incorrect shift in person between two pronouns

They enjoy gliding, a sport in which you try to catch thermals to stay aloft.

I believe in telling the truth, even when you will be punished for it.

Once you have tasted this salsa, everyone will be amazed.

Solution A: Replace the incorrect pronoun with a pronoun that agrees with its antecedent.

They enjoy gliding, a sport in which they try to catch thermals to stay aloft.

I believe in telling the truth, even when I will be punished for it.

Once you have tasted this salsa, you will be amazed.

Solution B: Replace the incorrect pronoun with an appropriate noun.

They enjoy gliding, a sport in which pilots try to catch thermals to stay aloft.

Shift in Verb Tense

Problem: An unnecessary shift in tense

The astronomers focus on the comet and compared observations. *shift t*

Justine glided onto the ice as the audience bursts into applause. *shift t*

Solution: When two or more events occur at the same time, be sure to use the same verb tense to describe each event.

The astronomers focus on the comet and compare observations.

Justine glided onto the ice as the audience burst into applause.

Problem: A lack of correct shift in tenses to show that one event precedes or follows another

By the time help arrived, we were stranded on the ledge for hours. *shift t*

Solution: When two events have occurred at different times in the past, shift from the past tense to the past perfect tense to indicate that one action began and ended before another past action began.

By the time help arrived, we had been stranded on the ledge for hours.

Rule of Thumb: When you need to use more than one verb tense in a sentence, it may help to first jot down the sequence of events you're writing about. Be clear in your mind which action happened first.

Incorrect Verb Tense or Form

Problem: An incorrect or missing verb ending

Last year my sister work on a ranch for the summer. *tense*

Has she decide what she would like to do this year? *tense*

Solution: Add *-d* or *-ed* to a regular verb to form the past tense and the past participle.

Last year my sister worked on a ranch for the summer.

Has she decided what she would like to do this year?

Problem: An improperly formed irregular verb

We think our cat runned away last night. *tense*

I have teared an ad out of the "Lost Pets" section of the newspaper. *tense*

Solution: Irregular verbs form their past and past participle forms in some way other than by adding *-ed.* Memorize these forms, or look them up in a dictionary.

We think our cat ran away last night.

I have torn an ad out of the "Lost Pets" section of the newspaper.

Problem: Confusion between the past form and the past participle

We have occasionally beat their team. *tense*

Solution: Use the past participle form of an irregular verb, not the past form, when you use a form of the auxiliary verb *have.*

We have occasionally beaten their team.

Problem: Improper use of the past participle

Our glee club sung the national anthem at many games. *tense*

The thirsty picnickers drunk three cases of soda. *tense*

Solution A: The past participle of an irregular verb cannot stand alone as a verb. Add a form of the auxiliary verb *have* to the past participle to form a complete verb.

Our glee club has sung the national anthem at many games.

The thirsty picnickers have drunk three cases of soda.

Solution B: Replace the past participle with the past form of the verb.

Our glee club sang the national anthem at many games.

The thirsty picnickers drank three cases of soda.

Misplaced or Dangling Modifier

Problem: A misplaced modifier

Jenita got many compliments from her friends in her new outfit. *mod*

Dazed and terrified, we found the raccoon by the side of the road. *mod*

The birdwatchers spotted a yellow wagtail who had binoculars. *mod*

Solution: Modifiers that modify the wrong word or seem to modify more than one word in a sentence are called misplaced modifiers. Move the misplaced phrase as close as possible to the word or words it modifies.

In her new outfit, Jenita got many compliments from her friends.

We found the dazed and terrified raccoon by the side of the road.

The birdwatchers who had binoculars spotted a yellow wagtail.

Problem: Incorrect placement of the adverb *only*

Mustafa only collects stamps from island nations. *mod*

Solution: Place the adverb *only* immediately before the word or group of words it modifies.

Only Mustafa collects stamps from island nations.

Mustafa collects only stamps from island nations.

Mustafa collects stamps only from island nations.

Rule of Thumb: Note that each time *only* is moved, the meaning of the sentence changes. Check to be sure your sentence says what you mean.

Problem: A dangling modifier

After sandbagging for hours, the floodwaters finally began to recede. *mod*

Cutting the grass, a bee stung my arm. *mod*

Solution: Rewrite the sentence, adding a noun to which the dangling phrase clearly refers. Often you will have to add other words or change the form of the verb to complete the meaning of the sentence.

After sandbagging for hours, the residents watched the floodwaters finally begin to recede.

Cutting the grass, I was startled when a bee stung my arm.

Missing or Misplaced Possessive Apostrophe

Problem: Singular nouns

The duchess jewels were stolen by that airlines luggage handler. *poss*

Solution: Use an apostrophe and -*s* to form the possessive of a singular noun, even one that ends in *s.*

The duchess's jewels were stolen by that airline's luggage handler.

Problem: Plural nouns ending in *-s*

The veterans parade will be held next Monday. *poss*

Solution: Use an apostrophe alone to form the possessive of a plural noun that ends in -*s.*

The veterans' parade will be held next Monday.

Problem: Plural nouns not ending in *-s*

The womens department is located on the third floor. *poss*

Solution: Use an apostrophe and -*s* to form the possessive of a plural noun that does not end in -*s.*

The women's department is located on the third floor.

Problem: Pronouns

Please put everybodys potluck dishes on the table. *poss*

Their's is the biggest yacht I have ever seen. *poss*

Solution A: Use an apostrophe and -*s* to form the possessive of a singular indefinite pronoun.

Please put everybody's potluck dishes on the table.

Solution B: Do not use an apostrophe with any of the possessive personal pronouns.

Theirs is the biggest yacht I have ever seen.

Problem: Confusion between *its* and *it's*

One of the buffalo calves has wandered away from it's mother. *poss*

Its about time that someone spoke up about this problem. *cont*

Solution: Do not use an apostrophe to form the possessive of *it.* Use an apostrophe to form the contraction of *it is.*

One of the buffalo calves has wandered away from its mother.

It's about time that someone spoke up about this problem.

Missing Commas with Nonessential Elements

Problem: Missing commas with nonessential participles or participial phrases

The author smiling graciously signed copies of her books. com

Putting it bluntly I will not allow a potbellied pig in the house. com

Solution: Determine whether the participle or participial phrase is essential to the meaning of the sentence. If it is not essential, set off the element with commas.

The author, smiling graciously, signed copies of her books.

Putting it bluntly, I will not allow a potbellied pig in the house.

Problem: Missing commas with nonessential adjective clauses

Oklahoma which is rich in oil suffered a bad drought in the 1930s. com

Solution: Determine whether the clause is essential to the meaning of the sentence. If it is not essential, set off the clause with commas.

Oklahoma, which is rich in oil, suffered a bad drought in the 1930s.

Problem: Missing commas with nonessential appositives

Minstrels medieval singers entertained at royal banquets. com

Solution: Determine whether the appositive is essential to the meaning of the sentence. If it is not essential, set off the appositive with commas.

Minstrels, medieval singers, entertained at royal banquets.

Rule of Thumb: To determine whether a word, phrase, or clause is essential, try reading the sentence without it.

Problem: Missing commas with interjections and parenthetical expressions

Gee that was a beautiful ceremony. com

Your brother by the way has been waiting for you for an hour. com

Solution: Set off the interjection or parenthetical expression with commas.

Gee, that was a beautiful ceremony.

Your brother, by the way, has been waiting for you for an hour.

Missing Commas in a Series

Problem: Missing commas in a series of words, phrases, or clauses

The zoo's primate collection includes lemurs baboons and chimpanzees. com

Juan scowled turned on his heel and stomped off. com

The cat bounded out the window across the yard and over the fence. com

We videotaped the newlyweds walking down the aisle cutting the wedding cake and dancing. com

My sister is athletic my brother is musical and I am artistic. com

Solution: When there are three or more items in a series, use a comma after each item that precedes the conjunction.

The zoo's primate collection includes lemurs, baboons, and chimpanzees.

Juan scowled, turned on his heel, and stomped off.

The cat bounded out the window, across the yard, and over the fence.

We videotaped the newlyweds walking down the aisle, cutting the wedding cake, and dancing.

My sister is athletic, my brother is musical, and I am artistic.

> **Rule of Thumb:** When you're having difficulty with a rule of usage, try rewriting the rule in your own words. Then check with your teacher to be sure you have grasped the concept.

Troublesome Words

This section will help you choose between words that are often confusing. It will also alert you to avoid certain words and expressions in school or business writing.

a, an

Use the article *an* when the word that follows begins with a vowel sound. Use *a* when the word that follows begins with a consonant sound. Therefore, use *a* when the word that follows begins with a long *u* sound ("yew").

An elephant stomped through **a** field.

An aunt of mine has **a** unique house.

Use the article *a* when the word that follows begins with a sounded *h.* Use *an* when the word that follows begins with an unsounded *h.*

A helmet from an ancient Roman soldier is quite **an** heirloom!

a lot, alot

This expression is always written as two words and means "a large amount." Some authorities discourage its use in formal English.

When the truck swerved, **a lot** of sand spilled from it.

When the truck swerved, **a large amount** of sand spilled from it.

accept, except

Accept is a verb meaning "to receive" or "to agree to." *Except* is occasionally used as a verb, but more often it is used as a preposition meaning "but."

Please **accept** my apologies.

All of the officers, **except** one, attended the meeting.

affect, effect

Affect is a verb meaning "to cause a change in; to influence." *Effect* may be a noun or a verb. As a noun it means "result." As a verb it means "to bring about or accomplish."

Exercise will **affect** your fitness level.

Exercise will have a beneficial **effect** on your fitness level.

Exercise will **effect** an improvement in your fitness level.

ain't

Ain't is never used in formal speaking and writing unless you are quoting the exact words of a character or real person. Instead of using *ain't,* use *am not, is not,* or a contraction such as *he isn't* or *I'm not.*

Muriel **isn't** coming to the party.

all ready, already

All ready is an adjective phrase that means "completely ready." *Already* is an adverb that means "before" or "by this time."

The climbers were **all ready** for their final ascent, but the storm was **already** upon them.

all right, alright

The expression *all right* should be written as two words.

Were the children **all right** after their frightening experience?

> **Rule of Thumb:** Dictionaries are good guides to the usage of a word. Even though some dictionaries do list the single word *alright,* they indicate that it is not a preferred spelling.

all together, altogether

Use *all together* to mean "in a group." Use the adverb *altogether* to mean "completely" or "on the whole."

The scholarship winners stood **all together** on the stage.

They seemed **altogether** thrilled with their awards.

amount, number

Use *amount* to refer to things that cannot be counted. Use *number* to refer to things that can be counted.

This recipe calls for a large **amount** of pepper.

This recipe calls for a large **number** of eggs.

anxious, eager

Anxious means "uneasy or worried about some event or situation." *Eager* means "having a keen interest" or "feeling impatient for something expected."

I am **anxious** about my dog's reaction to her shots.

The children are **eager** to go to the amusement park.

a while, awhile

A while is made up of an article and a noun. *In* and *for* often come before *a while,* forming a prepositional phrase. *Awhile* is an adverb.

I'll practice in **a while.** I'll practice for **a while.**

I'll rest **awhile** before practicing.

being as, being that

The expressions *being as* and *being that* are sometimes used instead of *because* or *since* in informal conversation. In formal speaking and writing, always use *because* or *since.*

Because Kendra has the flu, we'll need to find another debater.

Since it's already three o'clock, we'd better get ready to leave.

beside, besides

Beside means "at the side of." *Besides* usually means "in addition to."

The prime minister sat **beside** the president on the plane.

Besides playing hockey, the boys compete on the track team.

between, among

Use *between* to compare one person or thing with one other person or thing or with an entire group. Use *among* to show a relationship in which more than two persons or things are considered as a group.

When the twins dress alike, I can't see any difference **between** them.

There is quite a difference **between** Monet's painting and the others in the exhibit.

The members will settle the issue **among** themselves.

bring, take

Use *bring* to mean "to carry from a distant place to a closer one." Use *take* to mean the opposite: "to carry from a nearby place to a more distant one."

Please **bring** those videotapes over here.

When you go to the store, don't forget to **take** money with you.

can, may

Can indicates the ability to do something. *May* indicates permission to do something or the possibility of doing it.

May I wear your sweater if I **can** fix the button?

Rule of Thumb: Although *can* is sometimes used in place of *may* in informal speech, you should distinguish between them when speaking and writing formally.

can't hardly, can't scarcely

These terms are considered double negatives because *hardly* and *scarcely* by themselves have a negative meaning. Therefore, avoid using *hardly* and *scarcely* with *not* or *-n't.*

Our entire class **can hardly** fit into the new classroom.

Without my glasses, I **can scarcely** see the movie screen.

capital, capitol

Use *capital* to refer to the city that is the center of government of a state or country, to money or other assets, or to a capital letter. Use *capitol* to refer to the building or group of buildings in which a state legislature meets.

Sacramento is the **capital** of California.

The **capitol** in Boston, Massachusetts, has a gold dome.

complement, compliment

A *complement* is something that fills up, completes, or makes perfect. A *compliment* is an expression of praise or admiration.

This sauce is a great **complement** for the fish.

He blushes whenever anyone pays him a **compliment.**

compose, comprise

Compose often means "to form by putting together." *Comprise* means "to contain; embrace."

The sauce was **composed** of tomatoes, fresh garlic, and chopped onions.

Our state **comprises** twelve counties.

continual, continuous

Continual describes repetitive action with pauses between occurrences. *Continuous* describes an action that continues with no interruption in space or time.

The jackhammer's **continual** bursts of noise were irritating.

The development of language is a **continuous** process.

could of, might of, must of, should of, would of

After the words *could, might, must, should,* or *would,* use the helping verb *have,* not the preposition *of.*

I don't know what **could have** gone wrong with that dishwasher.

We **must have** looked pretty silly covered with all those soapsuds!

different from, different than

The expression *different from* is generally preferred to *different than.*

John Coltrane's jazz is quite **different from** Charlie Parker's.

emigrate, immigrate

Use *emigrate* to mean "to leave one country to settle in another." Use *immigrate* to mean "to come to a country to live there permanently." Use *from* with *emigrate,* and *to* or *into* with *immigrate.*

My friend Zhu **emigrated** from China five years ago.

In the 1800s, many Irish **immigrated** to the United States.

Rule of Thumb: Remember that the *e-* in *emigrate* comes from *ex-* ("out of"); the *im-* in *immigrate* comes from *in-* ("into").

ensure, assure, insure

Ensure means "to make sure of something or to guarantee it." *Assure* means "to reassure someone or to remove doubt." *Insure* means "to cover something with insurance or to secure it."

Excellent grades should **ensure** your acceptance by a college.

I **assure** you that I will be there to meet you at 4:30.

Mortgage contracts require home buyers to **insure** the property.

farther, further

Farther refers to physical distance. *Further* refers to degree or time.

I think the monument is **farther** north.

Maybe we should stop to ask for **further** directions.

fewer, less

Use *fewer* when referring to nouns that can be counted. Use *less* when referring to nouns that cannot be counted. *Less* may also be used with figures that are seen as single amounts or single quantities.

There were **fewer** snowstorms this winter than last.

Could we have a bit **less** noise, please?

I paid **less** than $10.00 for these jeans. [The amount of money is treated as a single sum, not as individual dollars.]

good, well

Use *good* as an adjective. *Well* may be used as an adverb of manner telling how ably or adequately something is done. *Well* also may be used as an adjective meaning "in good health."

Your hair looks **good** that way. [adjective after a linking verb]

Josie did **well** on her final exam. [adverb of manner]

Grandpa says he doesn't feel **well** enough to travel. [adjective meaning "in good health."]

had of

Do not use *of* between *had* and a past participle.

I wish I **had ordered** the shrimp instead of the salmon.

hanged, hung

Use *hanged* as the past tense when you mean "put to death by hanging." Use *hung* in all other instances.

In many countries, people were once **hanged** for minor offenses.

We **hung** a flag outside our house on Flag Day.

in, into

Use *in* to mean "inside" or "within." Use *into* to indicate movement or direction from outside to a point within.

After work, Mom soaks her feet **in** warm water.

I stepped backward and fell **into** the pool.

irregardless, regardless

Use *regardless.* The prefix *ir-* and the suffix *-less* both have negative meanings. When used together, they produce a double negative, which is incorrect.

We'll go camping this weekend **regardless** of the weather.

lay, lie

Lay means "to put" or "to place"; it takes a direct object. *Lie* means "to recline" or "to be positioned"; it never takes an object.

Lay your towel under that beach umbrella.

The dog likes to **lie** on the sunny deck.

learn, teach

Learn means "to gain knowledge." *Teach* means "to give knowledge."

I was twelve before I **learned** how to swim.

Mrs. Murata **teaches** algebra at our high school.

leave, let

Leave means "to go away." *Let* means "to allow" or "to permit."

Do you think she will **leave** before the holidays?

Will you **let** me borrow your notes?

like, as

Like is a preposition and introduces a prepositional phrase. *As* is a subordinating conjunction and introduces a subordinate clause. (*As* can be a preposition in some cases, as in *He served as ambassador to Ireland.*) Many authorities say that it is incorrect to use *like* before a clause.

My two-year-old sister can swim **like** a fish.

The doctor is certain, **as** we all are, that you will recover.

loose, lose

The adjective *loose* (lo͞os) means "free," "not firmly attached," or "not fitting tightly." The verb *lose* (lo͞oz) means "to have no longer," "to misplace," or "to fail to win."

You're likely to **lose** your **loose** change if you have a hole in your pocket.

Remember, it's not who wins or **loses** that matters.

passed, past

Passed is the past form and the past participle of the verb *pass. Past* may be an adjective, a preposition, an adverb, or a noun.

A truck **passed** us at a high rate of speed. [verb]

Learn from your **past** mistakes. [adjective]

Turn left just after you have gone **past** the church. [preposition]

As we were walking **past,** we saw smoke coming from the roof. [adverb]

The man's **past** was a mystery. [noun]

precede, proceed

Precede means "to go before" or "to come before." *Proceed* means "to continue" or "to move along."

Kennedy's and Johnson's terms in office **preceded** Nixon's.

Graduates will please **proceed** directly to the auditorium.

principal, principle

As an adjective, *principal* means "most important." *Principal* can also be a noun that refers to the head of a school. The noun *principle* often refers to a fundamental truth or a rule.

Dad has been chosen to be the **principal** speaker at the convention.

That **principle** is stated in the Bill of Rights.

raise, rise

The verb *raise* means "to cause to move upward"; it always takes an object. The verb *rise* means "to go up"; it is intransitive and does not take an object.

I always **raise** the shades immediately after I wake up.

The price of swimsuits will **rise** just before summer begins.

reason . . . is that, because

Because means "for the reason that." Therefore, do not use *because* after *reason . . . is.* Use either *reason . . . is that* or *because* alone.

The **reason** I am not going **is that** I wasn't invited.

I am not going **because** I wasn't invited.

respectfully, respectively

Use *respectfully* to mean "with respect."
Use *respectively* to mean "in the order named."

Always speak **respectfully** to the principal.

Pines and maples are evergreen and deciduous, **respectively.**

says, said

Says is the present-tense, third-person singular form of the verb *say. Said* is the past tense of *say.* Be careful not to use *says* when you are referring to the past.

Marina now **says** her family is moving to Alaska.

Last week, she **said** her family was moving to Hawaii.

sit, set

Sit means "to place oneself in a sitting position." It rarely takes an object. *Set* means "to place" or "to put," and it usually takes an object. When *set* is used to mean "the sun is going down," it does not take an object.

Please **sit** in that chair.

Please **set** down that remote control.

What time will the sun **set** tonight?

than, then

Than is a conjunction. Use it in comparisons or to show exception. The adverb *then* usually refers to time and can mean "at that time," "soon afterward," "the time mentioned," "at another time," "for that reason," or "in that case."

I know that Rachel is a better swimmer **than** I am.

I would rather be anywhere else **than** here.

My parents didn't even know one another **then.**

I went home and **then** stopped by Dad's office.

I had almost finished my errands by **then.**

If you can solve the puzzle, **then** please speak up.

their, they're, there

Their is the possessive form of *they. They're* is the contraction of *they are. There* is an adverb that often means "in that place." *There* is also sometimes used as an interjection, expressing a sense of completion.

There! The packages are finally on **their** way!

Did the Jacksons say when **they're** going to China?

You'll find the book you want over **there** on that shelf.

toward, towards

These words are interchangeable. Both prepositions mean "in the direction of."

A meteor is heading **toward** the moon.

A meteor is heading **towards** the moon.

where . . . at

Do not use *at* after a question with *where.*

Can you tell me **where** the post office is?

whereas, while

Both *whereas* and *while* can be used as conjunctions meaning "although." *Whereas* can also mean "in view of the fact that." *While* can be used as a conjunction or noun indicating time.

Gil's favorite sport is rowing, **whereas** Dwyla's is tennis.

While I can read German well, I still can't speak it fluently.

Whereas all the tests are in, class is dismissed.

Mom worked nights **while** she went to school.

Rule of Thumb: The conjunction *whereas* is usually reserved for very formal occasions.

who, whom

Use the nominative pronoun *who* for subjects.

Who caught that line drive? [subject of the verb]

Did he mention **who** won first prize? [subject of the noun clause *who won first prize*]

Who did you say will be working at the refreshment stand? [subject of the verb *will be working*]

Rule of Thumb: When a question contains an interrupting expression such as *did you say* or *do you think,* it helps to omit the interrupting phrase to determine whether to use *who* or *whom.*

Use the objective pronoun *whom* for the direct or indirect object of a verb or verbal or for the object of a preposition.

Whom are you choosing as a partner? [direct object of the verb *are choosing*]

Whom did you hear Geoff tutored in math? [direct object of the verb *tutored*]

Naomi told **whom** my secret? [indirect object]

From **whom** did you borrow this book? [object of the preposition *from*]

Rule of Thumb: When speaking informally, people often use *who* instead of *whom* as the direct object in sentences like *Who should we call?* In writing and in formal speech, however, distinguish between *who* and *whom.*

Mechanics

Capitalization

This section will help you recognize and use correct capitalization.

Rule	Example
Capitalize the first word in any sentence, including the first word of a direct quotation that is a complete sentence. Capitalize a sentence in parentheses unless it is contained within another sentence.	The sign in the diner said, "Servers who are tipped don't spill." The answer (all answers were read aloud) surprised him. (He blushed.)
Always capitalize the pronoun no matter where it appears in a sentence.	I don't know if I can ever repay them for the kindnesses I've received.
Capitalize proper nouns, including **a.** names of individuals, titles used before a proper name, and titles used in direct address	King Hussein; Governor Jeanne Shaheen Thank you, General. [direct address]
b. names of ethnic groups, national groups, political parties and their members, and languages	Chinese Americans; Iraqis; the Republican Party; Democrats; Spanish
c. names of organizations, institutions, firms, monuments, bridges, buildings, and other structures	American Cancer Society; Field Museum; Hewlett-Packard Company; Statue of Liberty; Verrazano-Narrows Bridge; Chrysler Building; Wrigley Field
d. trade names and names of documents, awards, and laws	Levi's; Treaty of Versailles; Nobel Prize; Freedom of Information Act
e. geographical terms and regions or localities	Kenya; Tennessee; Lake Champlain; Fifth Avenue; Far East
f. names of planets and other heavenly bodies	Venus; Andromeda; Sirius; Io; Crab Nebula
g. names of ships, planes, trains, and spacecraft	HMS *Queen Elizabeth II;* the *Spruce Goose; Twentieth Century Limited; Challenger*

Rule of Thumb: Since people do not always speak in complete sentences, written dialogue may contain sentence fragments. In dialogue, capitalize the first word of each fragment, as well as of each complete sentence. For example: "Time to go home," Mom called.

Rule	Example
h. names of most historical events, eras, calendar terms, and religious terms	Civil War; Great Depression; Age of Reason; Tuesday; March; Thanksgiving Day; Allah; Mormon; Hinduism; Christmas; Talmud
i. titles of literary works and publications, works of art, and musical compositions	*Beloved; Seventeen; The Thinker; American Gothic; Schindler's List;* "Kiss from a Rose"
j. specific names of school courses	Philosophy II
Capitalize proper adjectives (adjectives formed from proper nouns).	Central American governments; Elizabethan collar; Indian spices; Jewish synagogue

Punctuation

This section will help you use punctuation marks correctly.

Rule	Example
Use a **period** at the end of a declarative sentence or an imperative sentence (a polite command or request).	These prices are higher than I expected. Please hand me that spatula.
Use an **exclamation point** to show strong feeling or after a forceful command.	Wow! What a fantastic play that was!
Use a **question mark** to indicate a direct question.	What kind of computer do you have?
Use a **colon:** **a.** to introduce a list (especially after a statement that uses such words as *these, the following,* or *as follows*) and to introduce material that explains, illustrates, or restates preceding material	Noted American aviators include these: Wiley Post, Charles Lindbergh, and Amelia Earhart. Nathan must be feeling better: he asked to borrow my tennis racket.
Rule of Thumb: Do not use a colon between a verb and its complement. To be used correctly, a colon must follow a complete sentence.	
b. to introduce a long or formal quotation	Winston Churchill said this about public speaking: "If you have an important point to make, don't try to be subtle or clever. Use a pile driver. . . ."

Rule	Example
c. in statements of precise time, in biblical chapter and verse references, and after business-letter salutations	2:34 A.M. 2 Kings 11:12 Dear Mr. Fleming: Ladies and Gentlemen:
Use a **semicolon:** **a.** to separate main clauses that are not joined by a coordinating conjunction	Hawaii's climate is mild all year round; many travelers choose to visit the islands in summer.
b. to separate main clauses joined by a conjunctive adverb or by an expression such as *for example* or *that is*	There are 132 Hawaiian islands; however, nearly all residents live on seven of the islands. Hawaiian muumuus and aloha shirts are often colorful; that is, they are brightly patterned.
c. to separate the items in a series when these items contain commas	Hawaiian words familiar to many mainlanders include *luau*, which means "feast"; *aloha*, which can mean "love," "welcome," or "farewell"; and *hula*, which means "dance."
d. to separate two main clauses joined by a coordinating conjunction when such clauses already contain several commas	Travel ads often focus on Oahu's attractions, such as Waikiki Beach, Pearl Harbor, and Diamond Head; but the state has many other interesting sites.
Use a **comma:** **a.** between the main clauses of a compound sentence	I recognize her, but I can't think of her name.
b. to separate three or more words, phrases, or clauses in a series	Ayala is a member of the Debaters' Club, the Glee Club, and the swimming team.
c. between coordinate modifiers	She is a smart, athletic student.
d. to set off interjections, parenthetical expressions, and conjunctive adverbs	Max is, in fact, a sports fanatic.
e. to set off long introductory prepositional phrases	After several days of constant exposure to the sun, your skin will be dry and leathery.

Rule of Thumb: Use a comma after a short introductory prepositional phrase only if the sentence would be misread without it.

Rule	Example
f. to set off nonessential words, clauses, and phrases	
–introductory adverb clauses	Although Petra can read English well, her spoken English is not very fluent.
–internal adverb clauses that interrupt a sentence's flow	Those orange and black birds, unless I am mistaken, are Baltimore orioles.
–adjective clauses	Some of Frank Stella's paintings, which hang in many museums, have oddly shaped canvases.
–participles and participial phrases	The prize winners, beaming, rushed to the stage.
	Chasing after squirrels, the dog injured her foot.
–infinitive phrases	To speak frankly, I don't care for that design.
–appositives and appositive phrases	Dolphins and bats, both mammals, can hear much higher frequencies than humans can hear.

Rule of Thumb: Nonessential elements can be removed without changing the meaning of the sentence.

Rule	Example	
g. to set off quotations in dialogue	"Yesterday," announced Kayla, "I won the debate."	
h. to set off an antithetical phrase	Dawna, unlike Theresa, enjoys playing chess.	
i. to set off a title after a person's name	Michael Todesca, M.S.W.; Delyna Smith, chair of the committee	
j. to separate the various parts of an address, a geographical term, or a date	St. Louis, Missouri	Saturday, July 4
	December 7, 1941	Cambridge, MA 02138
k. after the salutation of an informal letter and after the closing of all letters	Dear Mom and Dad,	Sincerely,
l. to set off parts of a reference that direct the reader to the exact source	This rule is found in *The Chicago Manual of Style*, chapter 10, paragraph 83.	
m. to set off words or names used in direct address and in tag questions	Keon, could you tutor me in algebra?	
	You've never had chicken pox, have you?	

Rule	Example
Use a **dash** to signal a change in thought or to set off and emphasize supplemental information or parenthetical comments. **Rule of Thumb:** A good test of the correct use of dashes is to delete the information that the dashes set off. If the remaining sentence retains its basic meaning, then the dashes were properly used. If the remaining sentence has lost crucial information, then the dashes were improperly used.	Mammoth Cave—its name is appropriate—has about 300 miles of tunnels. Hiroko went to college here—in the United States, I mean.
Use **parentheses** to set off supplemental material. A complete parenthetical sentence contained within another sentence is not capitalized and needs no period. If a parenthetical expression contained within another sentence requires a question mark or exclamation point, put the punctuation mark *inside* the parentheses.	Plain popcorn (lightly salted if desired) is a healthful and filling snack. Locusts form swarms (these insects are usually solitary) when their food supply is exhausted. I felt an incredible sense of relief (just think what might have happened!) when the plane landed.
Use **quotation marks:** **a.** to enclose a direct quotation, as follows:	Speaking of another writer's novel, Gore Vidal remarked, "This is not at all bad, except as prose."
When a quotation is interrupted, use two sets of quotation marks.	"All the really good ideas I ever had," said artist Grant Wood, "came to me while I was milking a cow."
Use single quotation marks around a quotation within a quotation.	Joe Namath, the legendary quarterback, said, "Till I was 13, I thought my name was 'Shut Up.'"
In writing dialogue, begin a new paragraph and use a new set of quotation marks every time the speaker changes.	"Dad, may I borrow five dollars?" I asked. "What for?" Dad replied. "Um, actually, it's for your Father's Day present," I answered sheepishly.
b. to enclose titles of short works, such as stories, poems, essays, articles, chapters, and songs	"Barometer Soup" is a song on that Jimmy Buffett CD.

Rule	Example
c. to enclose unfamiliar slang terms and unusual expressions	What does the slang word "dis" mean? Tom Wolfe coined the expression "radical chic."

Rule of Thumb: To tell whether question marks and exclamation points go inside or outside quotation marks, see how the quotation would be punctuated if it stood alone. If the quotation is a question or an exclamation, then the punctuation mark should go inside the quotation marks. If the quotation would end with a period, then the question mark or exclamation point should go outside the quotation marks.

Rule	Example
Use **italics:** a. for titles of books, lengthy poems, plays, films, television series, paintings and sculptures, long musical compositions, court cases, names of newspapers and magazines, ships, trains, airplanes, and spacecraft. Italicize and capitalize articles *(a, an, the)* at the beginning of a title only when they are part of the title.	*Beowulf* [long poem]; *Biography* [television series] *The Potato Eaters* [painting] *Appalachian Spring* [long musical composition] *Ebony* [magazine] *Eagle* [spacecraft] *Spirit of St. Louis* [airplane] *The Old Man and the Sea* [book] the *Boston Globe* [newspaper]
b. for foreign words and expressions that are not used frequently in English	The rider enjoyed the attention he got when he wore his *charro* costume.
c. for words, letters, and numerals used to represent themselves	The word *stationery*, with an *e*, refers to writing paper. I mistook your *3* for an *8*.
Use an **apostrophe:** a. to create a possessive form, as follows: Add an apostrophe and *-s* to all singular indefinite pronouns, singular nouns, plural nouns not ending in *-s,* and compound nouns. Add only an apostrophe to a plural noun that ends in *-s.*	nobody's fault — New Mexico's climate children's welfare — mass's density baby-sitter's duties — seat belt's buckle flowers' petals — Wongs' party
If two or more entities possess something jointly, use the possessive form for the last entity named. If they possess it individually, use the possessive form for each entity's name.	Aunt Ellie and Uncle Ed's house Newton's and Einstein's discoveries

Rule	Example
b. to express amounts of money or time that modify a noun	a twelve dollars' savings a two weeks' delay [You can use a hyphenated adjective instead: *a two-week delay.*]
c. in place of omitted letters or numerals	can't [cannot] the crash of '29
d. with *-s* to form the plural of letters, numerals, symbols, and words used as words.	7's *p*'s and *q*'s +'s Your speech contains too many *whosoever*'s and *nevertheless*'s.
Use a **hyphen:** **a.** after any prefix joined to a proper noun or proper adjective	mid-July pre-Raphaelite
b. after the prefixes *all-, ex-,* and *self-* joined to any noun or adjective; after the prefix *anti-* when it joins a word beginning with *i;* after the prefix *vice-* (except in *vice president*); and to avoid confusion between words that begin with *re-* and look like another word	ex-husband self-conscious anti-inflammatory vice-regent re-mark the sale tags make a snide remark re-sign the document resign from her job
c. in a compound adjective that precedes a noun	a thirty-year career his tear-stained face
d. in any spelled-out cardinal or ordinal numbers up to *ninety-nine* or *ninety-ninth* and with a fraction used as an adjective	forty-nine twenty-third two-thirds cup
e. to divide a word at the end of a line between syllables or pronounceable parts	sur-face en-hanced

Rule of Thumb: Remember that the prefix *anti-* requires a hyphen when followed by a word that begins with *i* in order to prevent spelling words with two successive *i*'s. Otherwise, *anti-* does not require a hyphen except before a capitalized word.

Abbreviations

Abbreviations are shortened forms of words. This section will help you learn how to use abbreviations correctly.

Rule	Example
Use only one period if an abbreviation occurs at the end of a sentence. If the sentence ends with a question mark or an exclamation point, use the period *and* the second mark of punctuation.	I addressed the letter to Jane Parsons, R.N. Do your friends live in the U.K.? It's already 11:00 P.M.!
Capitalize abbreviations of proper nouns and abbreviations related to dates and times.	George W. Bush Morrissey Blvd. 767 B.C. A.D. 1910 6:15 A.M.
Use all capital letters and no periods for abbreviations of organization names that are pronounced letter by letter or as words.	IBM SPCA NOAA AMA DOT NYPD NFL FBI GSA
When addressing mail, use the official ZIP-code abbreviations of state names (two capital letters, no periods).	AZ (Arizona) CA (California) IL (Illinois) OK (Oklahoma) SC (South Carolina) DC (District of Columbia)
Use abbreviations for some personal titles.	Arthur Ashe Jr. Dr. Caitlin Connor Maj. Jacob Stern Olivia DiMario, A.R.N.P. Mrs. Anita Brown Rev. Billy Graham
Abbreviate units of measure used with numerals in technical or scientific writing, but not in ordinary prose.	mi. (mile) oz. (ounce) tsp. (teaspoon) l (liter) kg (kilogram) cm (centimeter)

Rule of Thumb: In a letter it is appropriate to use a state abbreviation in the address. In other forms of writing, such as expository writing, spell out the name of a state.

Numbers and Numerals

This section will help you understand when to use numerals and when to spell out numbers.

Rule	Example
In general, spell out cardinal and ordinal numbers that can be written in one or two words.	I am one of twenty-nine students in Ms. Chung's algebra class. For the hundredth time, please turn the radio off.
Spell out any number that occurs at the beginning of a sentence.	Six thousand five hundred tickets were sold for the festival on Saturday.
In general, use numerals (numbers expressed in figures) to express numbers that would be written in more than two words. Extremely high numbers are often expressed as a numeral followed by the word *million* or *billion.*	There are 767 students in our high school. In 1977 a Soviet woman parachuted to the earth from an altitude of 48,556 feet. The federal deficit was about $350 billion that year.
If related numbers appear in the same sentence, use all numerals.	There are over 25,000 seats in the arena, but only about 1,000 have been reserved to date.
Use numerals to express amounts of money, decimals, and percentages.	$1.1 trillion 2.2 children per family 99.99 percent
Use numerals to express the year and day in a date and to express the precise time with the abbreviations *A.M.* and *P.M.*	Martin Luther King Jr. died on April 4, 1968. The carpenter said he'd be here by 8:30 A.M.
Spell out a number to express a century or when the word *century* is used, or to express a decade when the century is clear from the context. When a century and a decade are expressed as a single unit, use numerals followed by *-s.*	The United Kingdom of Great Britain—including England, Scotland, and Wales—was formed early in the eighteenth century. In the forties, however, England and Scotland were still fighting. American involvement in the Vietnam War in the 1960s and early 1970s became very controversial.
Use numerals for streets and avenues numbered above ten and for all house, apartment, and room numbers.	1422 West 31st Street 623 Third Avenue Room 273 Apartment 3B
Use numerals to express page and line numbers.	You'll find that reference on page 952, line 23.

Spelling

The following basic rules, examples, and exceptions will help you master the spellings of many words.

ie and *ei*

Many writers find the rules for certain combinations of letters, like *ie* and *ei,* difficult to remember. One helpful learning strategy is to develop a rhyme to remember a rule. Look at the following rhyme for the *ie* and *ei* rule.

Rule	Example
Put *i* before *e,*	pier, grief, shriek, yield
except after *c,*	deceive, conceit, conceive
or when sounded like *a,*	heiress, weight, skein
as in *neighbor* and *weigh.*	feint, unveiled, eighty

SOME EXCEPTIONS: seize, leisure, weird, height, either, forfeit, protein, efficient.

-cede, -ceed, and *-sede*

Because different combinations of letters in English are sometimes pronounced the same way, it is often easy to make slight spelling errors. Except for the exceptions below, spell the *sēd* sound at the end of a word as *cede:*

recede intercede secede

EXCEPTION: One word uses *-sede* to spell the final *sēd* sound: supersede.

EXCEPTION: Three words use *-ceed* to spell the final *sēd* sound: proceed, exceed, succeed.

Unstressed vowels

Notice the vowel sound in the second syllable of the word *or-i-gin.* This is the unstressed vowel sound; dictionary respellings use the *schwa* symbol (ə) to indicate it. Because any of several vowels can be used to spell this sound, writers are often uncertain about which vowel to use. To help spell words with unstressed vowels correctly, try thinking of a related word in which the syllable containing the vowel sound is stressed.

Unknown Spelling	Related Word	Correct Spelling
pos_tive	position	positive
ess_nce	essential	essence
insp_ration	inspire	inspiration
emph_sis	emphatic	emphasis

Adding prefixes

When adding a prefix to a word, keep the original spelling of the word. If the prefix forms a double letter, keep both letters.

dis + obey = disobey
ir + rational = irrational
mis + laid = mislaid

Suffixes and the silent *e*

Many English words end in a silent letter *e*. Sometimes the *e* is dropped when a suffix is added. When adding a suffix that begins with a consonant to a word that ends in silent *e*, keep the *e*.

idle + ness = idleness
live + ly = lively

COMMON EXCEPTIONS: awe + ful = awful; judge + ment = judgment

When adding the suffix *-y* or a suffix that begins with a vowel to a word that ends in silent *e*, usually drop the *e*.

grime + y = grimy
sense + ible = sensible

COMMON EXCEPTION: mile + age = mileage

When adding a suffix that begins with *a* or *o* to a word that ends in *ce* or *ge*, keep the *e* so the word will retain the soft *c* or *g* sound.

outrage + ous = outrageous
notice + able = noticeable
salvage + able = salvageable

When adding a suffix that begins with a vowel to a word that ends in *ee* or *oe*, keep the *e*.

free + ing = freeing
canoe + able = canoeable
decree + ing = decreeing

Suffixes and the final *y*

When adding a suffix to a word that ends in a consonant + *y*, change the *y* to *i* unless the suffix begins with *i*. Keep the *y* in a word that ends in a vowel + *y*.

pry + ed = pried
betray + ed = betrayed
essay + ist = essayist

defy + ing = defying
annoy + ing = annoying
gray + ish = grayish

Doubling the final consonant

When adding a suffix to a word that ends in a consonant, double the final consonant if it is preceded by a single vowel and the word is one syllable, if the accent is on the last syllable and remains there even after the suffix is added, or if the word is made up of a prefix and a one-syllable word.

plug + ing = plugging
propel + or = propellor
recap + ing = recapping
map + ed = mapped
deter + ent = deterrent
disbar + ed = disbarred

Do not double the final consonant if the accent is not on the last syllable or if the accent shifts when the suffix is added. Also do not double the final consonant if it is preceded by two vowels or by another consonant. If the word ends in a consonant and the suffix begins with a consonant, do not double the final consonant.

alter + ed = altered
contain + er = container
assess + ment = assessment
confer + ence = conference
descend + ant = descendant
pain + ful = painful

Adding *-ly* and *-ness*

When adding *-ly* to a word that ends in a single *l,* keep the *l.* If the word ends in a double *l,* drop one *l.* When the word ends in a consonant + *le,* drop the *le.* When adding *-ness* to a word that ends in *n,* keep the *n.*

usual + ly = usually
crumble + ly = crumbly
shrill + ly = shrilly
plain + ness = plainness

Forming compound words

When joining a word that ends in a consonant to a word that begins with a consonant, keep both consonants.

class + mate = classmate
book + store = bookstore
keep + sake = keepsake
fiber + glass = fiberglass

Forming plurals

English words form plurals in many ways. Most nouns simply add *-s.* The following chart shows other ways of forming plural nouns and some common exceptions to the pattern.

GENERAL RULES FOR FORMING PLURALS		
If a noun ends in	**Rule**	**Example**
ch, s, sh, x, z	add *-es*	lynx, lynxes
a consonant + *y*	change *y* to *i* and add *-es*	calamity, calamities
o or a vowel + *y*	add *-s*	barrio, barrios; array, arrays
a consonant + *o* common exceptions	generally add *-es* but sometimes add only *-s*	tomato, tomatoes silo, silos; halo, halos
f or *ff* common exceptions	add *-s* change *f* to *v* and add *-es*	chef, chefs; cuff, cuffs leaf, leaves; loaf, loaves
lf	change *f* to *v* and add *-es*	calf, calves
fe	change *f* to *v* and add *-s*	wife, wives

A few plurals are exceptions to the rules in the previous chart, but they are easy to remember. The following chart lists these plurals and some examples.

SPECIAL RULES FOR FORMING PLURALS	
Rule	**Example**
To form the plural of proper names and one-word compound nouns, follow the general rules for plurals.	Shabazz, Shabazzes Friedman, Friedmans overleaf, overleaves
To form the plural of hyphenated compound nouns or compound nouns of more than one word, make the most important word plural.	mother-in-law, mothers-in-law chief of staff, chiefs of staff solicitor general, solicitors general
Some nouns have unusual plural forms.	foot, feet goose, geese louse, lice
Some nouns have the same singular and plural forms.	moose deer series

Commonly Misspelled Words

When you exchange written communication with someone, spelling matters. To have your business communications taken seriously, you have to present your ideas professionally, which means logically, clearly, and conventionally. If words are misspelled in your writing, readers may fear that there are also other, even more important, mistakes in it.

Whenever you prepare a written communication, check all spellings of which you are not certain. You might also want to keep handy a list of vocabulary words often used in your business that you have trouble remembering how to spell. Some of the words on this list might appear there.

absence
abundant
accessible
accidentally
accommodate
achievement
acknowledgment
acquaintance
acquisition
administrative
advantageous
advertise
advisable
aggressive
analysis
analyze
apologize
applicable
appropriate
approximate
argument
assessment
assistance
attendance
attorney
average
bankruptcy
beginner
believe
beneficiary
benefited
bought
boundary
brochure
brought
budget
bulletin
business
calendar
campaign
canceled
cannot
cashier
catalog
ceiling
column
commission
committee
competitive
conceive
confidential
conscientious
conscious
continuous
convenience
coordinator
correspondence
courteous
deceive
decision
defendant
defense
definite
dependent
describe
desirable
development
difference
dilemma
disappoint
efficient
either
eligible
embarrass
emphasize
employee
environment
equipment
equipped
especially
essential
exaggerate
excellent
executive
existence
extraordinary
facsimile (fax)
familiar
feasible
financial
fiscal
foreign
forfeit
forty
fourth
freight
government
grammar
grateful
guarantee
handicapped
harass
height
illegal
immediately
implement
importance
initial
irrelevant
itinerary
judgment
knowledge
laboratory
leisure
liability
library
license
lieutenant
likelihood
maintenance
manageable
material
mileage
miscellaneous
mortgage
necessary
neighbor
neither
nineteen
ninety
ninth
noticeable
objective
occasion
occasionally
occur
occurrence
offered
omission
opinion
original
paid
pamphlet
parallel
particularly
permanent
persistent
persuade
pertinent
physician
possession
precede
precedent
preferred
preliminary
privilege
procedure
proceed
professor
programmed
quantity
questionnaire
receipt
receiving
recipient
recognize
recommend
reference
relevant
representative
requirement
resistance
responsibility
restaurant
resume
résumé
schedule
separate
sergeant
similar
sincerely
strength
subpoena
succeed
successive
sufficient
superintendent
supersede
supervisor
survey
technique
technology
tenant
thorough
through
transferred
truly
usable
vendor
volume
yield

Guide to Nonsexist Language

When you are writing about people and their professions in general, you know that the people may be either male or female. Traditionally, many professions had nouns for both males and females, such as *poet* and *poetess*. *Poetess* is no longer used, and *poet* can refer to both males and females. For other gender-neutral terms, refer to the following list.

Do Use	Don't Use
actor	actress
Briton	Englishman, Englishwoman
businessperson, businesspeople	businessman, businesswoman
chairperson, chair, moderator	chairman, chairwoman
a member of the clergy	clergyman, clergywoman
crafter, craftspeople	craftsmen
crewed space flight	manned space flight
fire fighter	fireman
fisher	fisherman
flight attendant	steward, stewardess
Framers, Founders	Founding Fathers
handmade, synthetic, manufactured	manmade
homemaker	housewife
humanity, human beings, people	mankind
it, its (in reference to ships, countries)	she, her, hers, he, his
land of origin, homeland	mother country, fatherland
letter carrier, mail carrier	mailman
police officer	policeman
representative	congressman, congresswoman
server	waiter, waitress
supervisor	foreman
watch, guard	watchman
worker	workman
workforce	manpower

Traditionally, masculine pronouns (*he*, *him*, *his*) were used to refer to mixed groups of people. It was understood that females were included. That is, a sentence such as *A surgeon must watch his patient's pulse* was understood to apply to both male and female surgeons. Now everyone is encouraged to use gender-neutral wording. Some possibilities for the sample sentence are *A surgeon must watch the patient's pulse*, *Surgeons must watch their patients' pulses*, and *A surgeon must watch his or her patient's pulse*.

Performance Appraisal Form

Annual Appraisal for Hourly Employees

Date ____________

Employee ______________________ Job Assignment ______________________

Supervisor ______________________ Department ______________________

Date Hired ______________________ Previous Appraisal Date ______________________

PERFORMANCE AREAS	Outstanding	Above Average	Average	Below Average	Unsatisfactory	Not Applicable
JOB KNOWLEDGE Comment:						
QUALITY OF WORK Ability to effectively use time and materials Ability to meet deadlines/production schedules Comment:						
SAFETY Result of work under safe/unsafe practices Comment:						
ATTENDANCE _____ Days not at work since previous appraisal: Personal: _____ Illness: _____ _____ Days late to work since previous appraisal Comment:						
PERSONAL QUALITIES						
INITIATIVE/LEADERSHIP Takes on new tools, skills, or projects Comment:						
FLEXIBILITY Adjusts to new situations Comment:						
COOPERATION Works well with assigned teams and supervisors Comment:						
DEPENDABILITY Completes the job reliably Comment:						

EMPLOYEE'S PRESENT JOB DESCRIPTION (Attach current job description and note any changes in job assignments here.)

____

____

____

EMPLOYEE'S STRENGTHS (What should the employee be commended for?)

1. ____

2. ____

3. ____

AREAS TO IMPROVE (What should the employee improve?)

1. ____

2. ____

3. ____

NOTE: What has been accomplished toward areas to improve set by the previous appraisal? If the employee has not taken any action, indicate why.

____

____

____

SUMMARY RATING:

______ Performance always exceeds job requirements.

______ Performance is above average in meeting job requirements.

______ Performance consistently meets job requirements.

______ Performance does not always meet job requirements.

______ Performance frequently does not meet job requirements.

SUMMARY COMMENTS ON RATING:

____

____

____

EMPLOYEE'S COMMENTS:

____

____

____

______________________ ______________________

Employee's signature/date Supervisor's signature/date

COMMENTS by next level of supervision:

____

____

____

Manager's signature/date

Writing a Business Letter

You will often write business letters to people you don't know. A business letter is a formal communication tool that you can adapt for many specific purposes. Your writing makes a first impression for you. A neat, brief, well-organized letter will encourage a prompt and positive response.

Here is an example of an application letter typed in the block style. Notice that the writer follows the tips suggested in the chart on the next page.

BLOCK STYLE

The letter is addressed to a specific person.

The writer names the job she wants.

She lists her qualifications.

She tells why she would be a good person to hire.

She asks for an application form.

23 Sagebrush Avenue
Las Cruces, New Mexico 88005
January 10, 2002

Ms. Sarah Grimes, Director
Camp Piney Woods
2630 Nature Trail Road
Piney Woods, Maine 04737

Dear Ms. Grimes:

I would like to apply for a job as a junior counselor at Camp Piney Woods for the coming summer.

I will be sixteen in May and have completed my lifeguard training. In addition, I have worked with children eight to ten years old for the past two summers in the Parks and Recreation Department here in Las Cruces. My duties included conducting nature hikes and teaching craft classes.

Because I am a responsible and enthusiastic person who loves children and the outdoor life, I believe I would be an asset to Camp Piney Woods. I will be happy to send you references of people who know me and my interests and abilities.

Please send me an application form and let me know if there is any other information you need from me.

Yours truly,

Rosalia Diaz

Rosalia Diaz

Types of Business Letters

A business letter is a formal letter written either to communicate information or to request action. Business letters provide a direct and effective means of communicating on a wide variety of topics. Knowing how to write a good business letter is a skill you'll find useful throughout your life.

Use the business letter format whenever you want to inquire, make a request, order a product, complain, express your views on a subject, or apply for a job, a scholarship, or a special academic or recreational program.

TYPES OF BUSINESS LETTERS

Request Letter	Complaint Letter	Opinion Letter	Application Letter
• Be brief. • State your request clearly. • Include all necessary information. • Make your request specific and reasonable. • Include your phone number or a self-addressed, stamped envelope.	• Identify the product or service clearly. • Describe the problem accurately. • Request a specific solution. • Be polite. • Keep a copy of your letter until your complaint has been resolved.	• Identify and summarize the issue. • State your opinion and support it with reasons, facts, and examples. • Summarize your main points and offer a solution, if possible.	• Write to a specific person. • Describe the job or program for which you're applying. • List your qualifications. • Tell why you're the best person for the position or award. • Request an application form or an interview.

When you write a business letter, keep your specific goal or purpose clearly in mind. Business letters are not necessarily about business, but they do mean business, so don't let them wander off the subject. Be brief. Include only what is essential. Confine your letter to a single page. The people you are writing are busy. The shorter and more attractive your letter looks, the more likely it is that someone will read it.

Because the tone of a business letter should be formal, don't use slang or worn-out expressions. Don't be wordy. "Thank you" is better than "I wish to express my gratitude." Remember to be courteous, regardless of your purpose.

Most business letters require some kind of persuasive writing. When you write a letter of inquiry, you want to persuade someone to fill your request or send you a product. When you write a letter of complaint, you want to persuade someone to do something to correct a problem. In an opinion letter, you want to persuade someone to agree with you or to take action. In a letter of application, your goal is to persuade someone to hire you or to accept your qualifications for a particular program or award.

Editing Tip

Always edit business letters carefully. Errors in spelling, grammar, or typing will seriously reduce the effectiveness of your message.

Style

Business letters are usually written in one of two forms: the block style or the modified block style.

Block Style

In the block style, all lines begin at the left margin. Paragraphs are not indented. The letter on page 637 is typed in the block style.

Modified Block Style

In the modified block style, the heading, the closing, your signature, and your typed name begin at the center of the paper. The paragraphs may be indented—five spaces on a typewriter or half an inch on a computer—or not indented. The letter below is in the modified block style with paragraphs indented.

Presenting Tip

If you use a word processor to prepare your letter, keep it simple by using just one style of type. Too many different type styles will make your letter look casual and informal. Choose a type that looks serious.

MODIFIED BLOCK STYLE

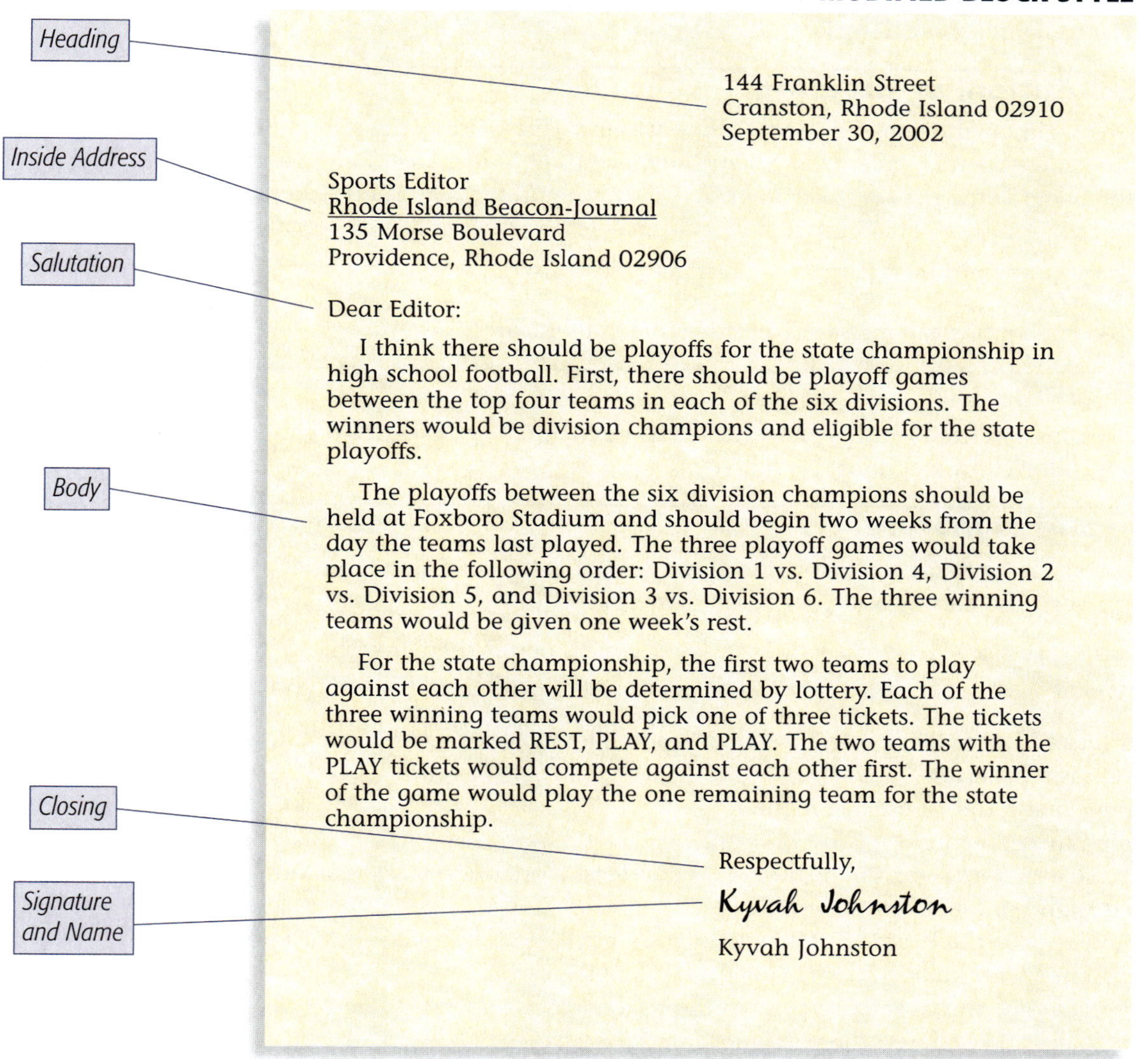

144 Franklin Street
Cranston, Rhode Island 02910
September 30, 2002

Sports Editor
Rhode Island Beacon-Journal
135 Morse Boulevard
Providence, Rhode Island 02906

Dear Editor:

I think there should be playoffs for the state championship in high school football. First, there should be playoff games between the top four teams in each of the six divisions. The winners would be division champions and eligible for the state playoffs.

The playoffs between the six division champions should be held at Foxboro Stadium and should begin two weeks from the day the teams last played. The three playoff games would take place in the following order: Division 1 vs. Division 4, Division 2 vs. Division 5, and Division 3 vs. Division 6. The three winning teams would be given one week's rest.

For the state championship, the first two teams to play against each other will be determined by lottery. Each of the three winning teams would pick one of three tickets. The tickets would be marked REST, PLAY, and PLAY. The two teams with the PLAY tickets would compete against each other first. The winner of the game would play the one remaining team for the state championship.

Respectfully,

Kyvah Johnston

Kyvah Johnston

The Parts of a Business Letter

A business letter has six parts.

> **Presenting Tip**
>
> If your letter is very short, you can increase the left and right margins and center the letter vertically on the page. Your word-processing software may have a feature that will automatically center the letter for you.

The Heading

There are three lines in the heading:

- your street address
- your city, state, and ZIP code
- the date

The Inside Address

The inside address has three or more lines:

- the name of the person to whom you're writing (with or without a courtesy title such as *Ms.*, *Mr.*, or *Dr.*)
- the title of the person to whom you're writing (A short title may be placed on the same line with the person's name. A long title requires a separate line.)
- the name of the business or organization
- the street address of the business or organization
- the city, state, and ZIP code

The Salutation, or Greeting

When you know the name of the person to whom you're writing, the salutation should include a courtesy title: *Dear Senator Gonzales* or *Dear Ms. Uchida*. If you don't know the name of the person, you can begin with *Dear* and the person's title: *Dear Editor* or *Dear Manager*. The salutation of a business letter is followed by a colon.

The Body

The body contains the message you want to communicate.

The Closing

The closing is a final word or phrase, such as *Respectfully* or *Yours truly*. The closing is followed by a comma.

Name and Signature

Type your name four lines below the closing. Then, sign your name in the space between the closing and your typed name.

Neatness Counts

Your letter is more likely to get a serious reading if you follow closely the formal rules for business letters.

- Type your letter or use a computer.
- Use unlined white 8 1/2" by 11" paper.
- Leave a two-inch margin at the top and at least a one-inch margin at the left, right, and bottom.
- Single-space the heading. Allow four to six blank lines between the heading and the inside address, depending on the length of your letter.
- Single-space the remaining parts of the letter, leaving an extra line between the parts and between the paragraphs in the body.

Address Abbreviations

United States (U.S.)

In most cases, state names and street addresses should be spelled out. The postal abbreviations in the following lists should be used with ZIP codes in addressing envelopes. They may also be used with ZIP codes for return addresses and inside addresses in business letters. The traditional state abbreviations are seldom used nowadays, but occasionally it's helpful to know them.

State	Traditional	Postal
Alabama	Ala.	AL
Alaska	(none)	AK
Arizona	Ariz.	AZ
Arkansas	Ark.	AR
California	Calif.	CA
Colorado	Colo.	CO
Connecticut	Conn.	CT
Delaware	Del.	DE
District of Columbia	D.C.	DC
Florida	Fla.	FL
Georgia	Ga.	GA
Hawaii	(none)	HI
Idaho	(none)	ID
Illinois	Ill.	IL
Indiana	Ind.	IN
Iowa	(none)	IA
Kansas	Kans.	KS
Kentucky	Ky.	KY
Louisiana	La.	LA
Maine	(none)	ME
Maryland	Md.	MD
Massachusetts	Mass.	MA
Michigan	Mich.	MI
Minnesota	Minn.	MN
Mississippi	Miss.	MS
Missouri	Mo.	MO
Montana	Mont.	MT
Nebraska	Nebr.	NE
Nevada	Nev.	NV
New Hampshire	N.H.	NH
New Jersey	N.J.	NJ
New Mexico	N. Mex.	NM
New York	N.Y.	NY
North Carolina	N.C.	NC
North Dakota	N. Dak.	ND
Ohio	(none)	OH
Oklahoma	Okla.	OK
Oregon	Oreg.	OR
Pennsylvania	Pa.	PA
Rhode Island	R.I.	RI
South Carolina	S.C.	SC
South Dakota	S. Dak.	SD
Tennessee	Tenn.	TN
Texas	Tex.	TX
Utah	(none)	UT
Vermont	Vt.	VT
Virginia	Va.	VA
Washington	Wash.	WA
West Virginia	W. Va.	WV
Wisconsin	Wis.	WI
Wyoming	Wyo.	WY

Postal Address Abbreviations

The following address abbreviations are recommended by the U.S. Postal Service for use on envelopes to speed mailing. In most other writing, these words should be spelled out.

Alley	ALY
Annex	ANX
Avenue	AVE
Boulevard	BLVD
Center	CTR
Circle	CIR
Court	CT
Drive	DR
East	E
Estates	EST
Expressway	EXPY
Heights	HTS
Highway	HWY
Island	IS
Lake	LK
Lane	LN
Lodge	LDG
Mount	MT
North	N
Parkway	PKY
Place	PL
Plaza	PLZ
River	RIV
Road	RD
South	S
Square	SQ
Station	STA
Street	ST
Terrace	TER
Trace	TRCE
Trail	TRL
Turnpike	TPKE
Viaduct	VIA
Village	VLG
West	W

Forms of Address

This chart shows the proper forms of address for writing letters to public officials, members of the armed services, and professional people. (To communicate with public officials by e-mail, see the feature on pages 645–646.) Shown here are the envelope's address, which is also the inside address, and an appropriate salutation. Where more than one salutation is supplied, the most formal is first.

The Person	The Address	The Salutation(s)
Public Officials		
President of the United States	The President The White House Washington, DC 20500	Mr./Madam President Dear Mr./Madam President
Vice President of the United States	The Vice President United States Senate Washington, DC 20510 *or* The Honorable *(full name)* Vice President of the United States Washington, DC 20501	Sir/Madam Dear Mr./Madam Vice President
Chief Justice of the United States	The Chief Justice of the United States Washington, DC 20543 *or* The Chief Justice The Supreme Court Washington, DC 20543	Sir/Madam Dear Mr./Madam Chief Justice
Cabinet Member	The Honorable *(full name)* Secretary *(department name)* Washington, DC *(ZIP code)* *or* The Secretary of *(department)* Washington, DC *(ZIP code)*	Sir/Madam Dear Mr./Madam Secretary
United States Senator	The Honorable *(full name)* United States Senator Washington, DC 20510 *or* The Honorable *(full name)* *(local address and ZIP code)*	Sir/Madam Dear Senator *(last name)*

The Person	The Address	The Salutation(s)
United States Representative	The Honorable *(full name)* House of Representatives Washington, DC 20515 *or* The Honorable *(full name)* Representative in Congress *(local address and ZIP code)*	Sir/Madam Dear Mr./Ms./Mrs./Miss *(last name)*
Governor	The Honorable *(full name)* Governor of *(name of state)* *(State Capital, State ZIP code)*	Sir/Madam Dear Governor *(last name)*
State Senator	The Honorable *(full name)* The *(name of state)* Senate *(State Capital, State ZIP code)*	Sir/Madam Dear Senator *(last name)*
State Representative or Assembly Member	The Honorable *(full name)* House of Representatives *or* The *(name of state)* State Assembly *(State Capital, State ZIP code)*	Sir/Madam Dear Mr./Ms./Mrs./Miss *(last name)*
Mayor	The Honorable *(full name)* Mayor of *(city)* *(City, State ZIP code)* *or* The Mayor of the City of *(city)* *(City, State ZIP code)*	Sir/Madam Dear Mr./Madam Mayor Dear Mayor *(last name)*
Members of the Armed Services		
Rank	*(full rank) (full name)* U.S. Coast Guard, U.S. Air Force, U.S. Army, U.S. Marine Corps, or U.S. Navy *(local address)*	Dear *(full rank) (full name)*
Professional People		
President of a College or University	*(full name, followed by comma and abbreviation for highest degree earned)* President, *(name of college)* *(address)* *or* Dr. *(full name)* President, *(name of college)* *(address)*	Dear President *(last name)* Dear Dr. *(last name)*

The Person	The Address	The Salutation(s)
Dean of a College or University	*(full name, followed by comma and abbreviation for highest degree earned)* Dean, *(name of college)* *(address)* *or* Dr. *(full name)* Dean, *(name of college)* *(address)*	Dear Dean *(last name)* Dear Dr. *(last name)*
Professor	Professor *(full name)* Department of *(subject)* *(name of college)* *(address)* *or* *(full name, followed by comma and abbreviation for highest degree earned)* Department of *(subject)* *(name of college)* *(address)* *or* Dr. *(full name)* Professor of *(subject)* *(name of college)* *(address)*	Dear Professor *(last name)* Dear Dr. *(last name)*
Member of Board of Education	Mr./Ms./Mrs./Miss *(full name)* Member, *(name of school district)* Board of Education *(address)*	Dear Mr./Ms./Mrs./Miss/Dr.
Principal	Mr./Ms./Mrs./Miss/Dr. *(full name)* Principal, *(name of school)* *(address of school)*	Dear Mr./Ms./Mrs./Miss/Dr.
Teacher	Mr./Ms./Mrs./Miss/Dr. *(full name)* *(name of school)* *(address of school)*	Dear Mr./Ms./Mrs./Miss/Dr.
Attorney	Mr./Ms./Mrs./Miss *(full name),* Attorney at Law *or* *(full name),* Esq. *(address)*	Dear Mr./Ms./Mrs./Miss *(last name)*
Dentist	(full name), D.D.S. (address)	Dear Dr. *(last name)*
Physician	(full name), M.D./D.O. (address)	Dear Dr. *(last name)*
Veterinarian	(full name), D.V.M. (address)	Dear Dr. *(last name)*

Sending E-Mail to Public Officials

E-mail provides a quick and easy way for you to get in touch with public officials, such as your city mayor, state governor, United States senator or representative, or the president. You can also contact a specific government task force or committee. You might use e-mail to ask for information or to express your opinions on an issue.

You can find the names and e-mail addresses of government officials, departments, and committees at a number of Web sites. For example, you might try sites such as www.senate.gov, www.vote-smart.org, or www.info.gov. Alternatively, do a search using the name of your state, followed by *AND government.* A menu of choices will lead you to the names and e-mail addresses you seek. After you click on the e-mail address of an official, some sites will take you directly to your own e-mail screen and enter the address of that official in the *To* field.

Then, it's time to compose your message. Keep in mind that some elected officials read e-mail from only the people they represent. Often, officials do not read e-mail themselves. Instead, a staff member will read your message and, perhaps, send you a form e-mail response.

The following tips will help ensure that your request or message is taken seriously. (Note that many of these tips apply to all e-mail.)

- Make sure that your request is reasonable and that you are sending it to the appropriate person.
- Be aware that your e-mail address may influence whether your message is given a careful reading. Compare dude@net.com with tthompson@net.com.
- In the subject field, clearly and briefly identify the main idea of your message.

Many e-mail messages omit the salutation or greeting because the intended reader's name is already listed in the heading. However, it would be a sign of respect to use the traditional forms of address for government officials. You can find them listed on pages 642–644 in this Guide to Business Communication.

- Begin your message by briefly identifying yourself. If appropriate, point out that you live in the area that the reader represents.
- State your concern or request at the beginning of your message, where it is most likely to be read. If you do not grab the reader's attention immediately, your e-mail might be deleted without being read completely. After explaining why you are writing, go into the reasons for your concern or your request.

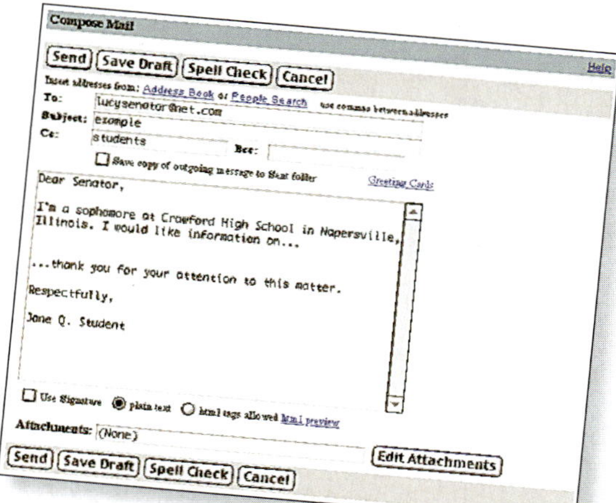

- If you are asking for information that cannot be e-mailed to you, include your street address or a fax number or both.
- You cannot sign your message, but do type your name at the end of it, especially if your name is not clear from your e-mail address.
- Be respectful, even if you feel that the official is misguided or misinformed about an issue.

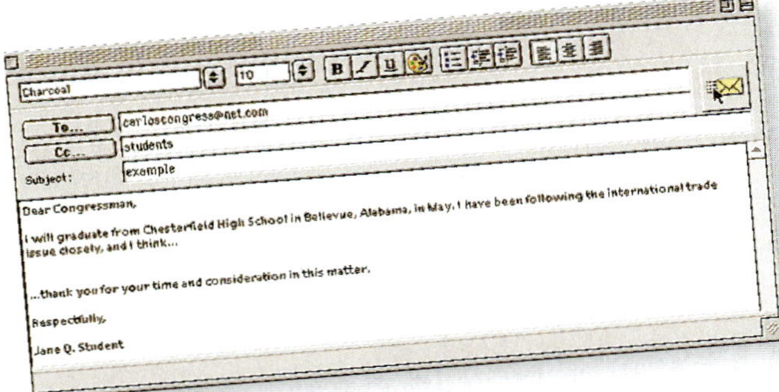

- Don't ever threaten a government official, even as a joke. You can say you will not vote for this person again, but do not say you would like to cause injury or harm to him or her. Depending on your reader, you could end up being investigated.
- Do not type your whole message in capital letters. This looks like shouting to most readers. It may make them feel defensive or annoyed.
- Do not write when you are angry. You will be more likely to insult your reader and less likely to get the response you want.
- Avoid emoticons, such as these: ;-) :-(. You can use these little symbols in informal e-mails to your friends but not in messages to government officials.
- Break your message into paragraphs, just as you would in a letter. Discuss only one main idea in each paragraph.
- Find and correct misspellings, grammatical errors, and typographical errors. If you do not, your message may not be read at all. This might not seem fair, but it is a serious issue.
- Proofread your message to make sure the ideas flow smoothly and are expressed clearly.

Let public officials know what you are thinking with well-thought-out and carefully organized e-mail messages.

Personal Style Profile

INSTRUCTIONS: Make a copy of this page and the next page. For each of the following groups of three adjectives, write **3** by the term that **best** describes you, **1** by the term that **least** describes you, and **2** by the remaining term.

1. a. _____ Adventurous
   b. _____ Polished
   c. _____ Stable

2. a. _____ Receptive
   b. _____ Determined
   c. _____ Enthusiastic

3. a. _____ Steady
   b. _____ Exacting
   c. _____ Original

4. a. _____ Poised
   b. _____ Patient
   c. _____ Orderly

5. a. _____ Forceful
   b. _____ Persuasive
   c. _____ Settled

6. a. _____ Cautious
   b. _____ Bold
   c. _____ Outgoing

7. a. _____ Persistent
   b. _____ Cooperative
   c. _____ Brave

8. a. _____ Attractive
   b. _____ Controlled
   c. _____ Correct

9. a. _____ Competitive
   b. _____ Diplomatic
   c. _____ Accommodating

10. a. _____ Careful
    b. _____ Decisive
    c. _____ Popular

11. a. _____ Dependable
    b. _____ Accurate
    c. _____ Inventive

12. a. _____ Convincing
    b. _____ Consistent
    c. _____ Open-minded

13. a. _____ Positive
    b. _____ Cordial
    c. _____ Even-tempered

14. a. _____ Conservative
    b. _____ Eager
    c. _____ Entertaining

15. a. _____ Amiable
    b. _____ Systematic
    c. _____ Self-reliant

16. a. _____ Sociable
    b. _____ Unhurried
    c. _____ Precise

Scoring Sheet

INSTRUCTIONS: Write your scores in the spaces below. Then, add the scores in each column and enter the total for each column in the space provided.

DOMINANCE	INTERACTION	STABILITY	CONTROL
1a ______	1b ______	1c ______	2a ______
2b ______	2c ______	3a ______	3b ______
3c ______	4a ______	4b ______	4c ______
5a ______	5b ______	5c ______	6a ______
6b ______	6c ______	7a ______	7b ______
7c ______	8a ______	8b ______	8c ______
9a ______	9b ______	9c ______	10a ______
10b ______	10c ______	11a ______	11b ______
11c ______	12a ______	12b ______	12c ______
13a ______	13b ______	13c ______	14a ______
14b ______	14c ______	15a ______	15b ______
15c ______	16a ______	16b ______	16c ______

Total ______ *Total* ______ *Total* ______ *Total* ______

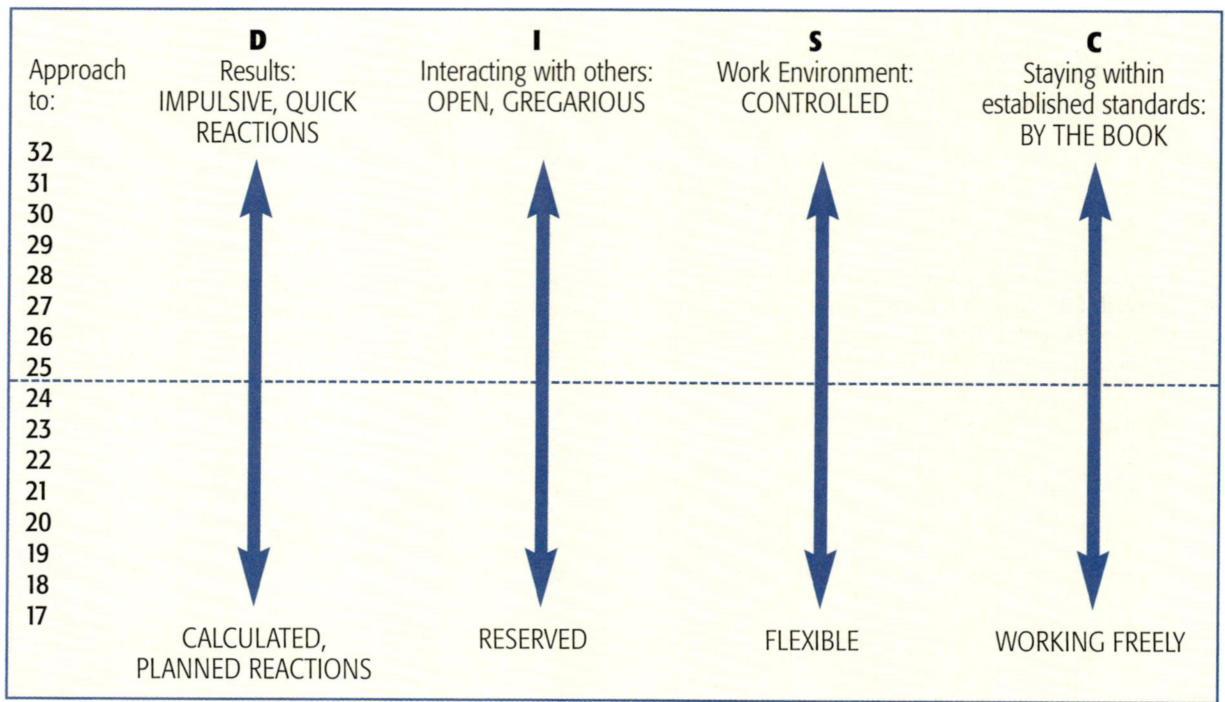

Informational Presentation

Mending the Body by Lending an Ear

THE HEALING POWER OF LISTENING; Address by CAROL KOEHLER, Ph.D., *Assistant Professor of Communication and Medicine; Delivered to the International Listening Association Business Conference, at the Ritz-Carlton Hotel, Kansas City, Missouri, March 19, 1998*

I would like to start this morning by telling you two different stories. Each story has the same two characters and happens in the same location. Both stories occur within a twenty-four hour period.

Over the Christmas holidays, my husband and I were invited to a formal black-tie wedding. This was to be an elegant event, so we put on our best evening clothes. Adding to that, I wore my mother's diamond jewelry and this fabulous mink coat that I inherited. Just before we left the house, I telephoned my 86-year-old mother-in-law for her daily check-up. When she answered, her voice sounded a little strange, so my husband and I decided to stop at her apartment to make sure she was all right before we went to the wedding.

When we arrived, she seemed slightly disoriented (she was 86 years old but wonderfully healthy, sharp-witted, and self-sufficient). We called her physician to ask his advice, and he said to bring her to the local Emergency Room and have her checked out. We did that. This was a Saturday night, so the Emergency Room was pretty active. When we arrived, I in my mink and my husband in his tux, we looked noticeably different from the general population in the waiting room. While my husband filled out forms, the doctors took my mother-in-law into a makeshift curtained room. When I noticed that the staff had removed both her glasses and her hearing aid, I realized she would experience some anxiety, so at that point I decided to stay with her to keep her from being frightened. As I went into the room, a young doctor said, "Ma'am, you can't go in there." Without missing a beat, I said, "Don't be ridiculous." With that, I went and found a chair in the waiting room, brought it into the examination room, and sat down. I remember thinking the staff looked a little bewildered, but no one challenged me at any time. When my mother-in-law's hands felt a little cool, I asked for a heated blanket, and one was brought immediately. So it went for the entire evening. We missed the wedding but finally got my mother-in-law in a permanent room about 2 a.m.

The next morning I went to the hospital about 10 o'clock in the morning, dressed in tennis shoes, a sweat suit, and no makeup. As I arrived at my mother-in-law's room, an unfamiliar doctor was just entering. I introduced myself and asked him to speak up so my mother-in-law would be aware of why he was there and what he was doing. I told him that she tends to be frightened by the unexpected, and without her glasses or hearing aid, she was already frightened enough. This thirty-something male doctor proceeded to examine my mother-in-law without raising his voice so that she could hear and without acknowledging me or my request in any way. Actually, he never really looked at either one of us.

In both these scenarios, I was listened to, not by ears alone, but by eyes, by gender, by age judgments, and by social status assessments. That started me thinking. . . .

Why did a recent article in the *Journal of the American Medical Association* indicate high dissatisfaction in traditional doctor-patient appointments? Why is it the *Wall Street*

Journal claims that perception of physician concern and not physician expertise is the deciding factor in the rising number of malpractice suits? Why did *The New England Journal of Medicine* report that the care and attention quotient is causing "alternative" medical practices to grow by leaps and bounds? Given this litany of events, what does it really mean to listen? And why, in the name of science, don't we produce better listeners in the medical profession?

The reasons are so obvious that they are sometimes overlooked. First, listening is mistakenly equated with hearing, and since most of us can hear, no academic priority is given to this subject in either college or med school. (This, by the way, flies in the face of those who measure daily time usage. Time experts say we spend 9 percent of our day writing, 16 percent reading, 30 percent speaking and 45 percent listening—just the opposite of our academic pursuits.) Second, we perceive power in speech. We put a value on those who have the gift of gab. How often have you heard the compliment, "He/she can talk to anyone?" Additionally, we equate speaking with controlling both the conversation and the situation. The third and last reason we don't listen is that we are in an era of information overload. We are bombarded with the relevant and the irrelevant, and it is easy to confuse them. Often, it's all just so much noise.

How can we address this depressing situation? Dan Callahan, a physician and teacher, argues that primacy in health care needs to be given to the notion of care over cure. Caring as well as curing humanizes our doctor-patient relationships.

Let's talk about what that might mean for health care. What comes to mind when someone is caring? (The audience responded with the words "warm," "giving," "interested," "genuine," and "sincere"). Now, what comes to mind when you think of the opposite of care? (The audience volunteered "cold," "uninterested," "egotistical," "busy," "distracted," and "selfish").

What might a caring doctor be like? If we take the word ***CARE*** and break it down, we find the qualities that are reflective of a therapeutic communicator—in other words, someone who listens not with ears alone.

C stands for concentrate. Physicians should hear with their eyes and ears. They should avoid the verbal and visual barriers that prevent real listening. It may be as simple as eye contact. (Some young doctors have told me they have a difficult time with looking people in the eye, and my advice is, "When you are uncomfortable, focus on the patient's mouth, and as the comfort level increases, move to the eyes.") In the placement of office furniture, try to keep the desk from being a barrier between you and the patient. Offer an alternative chair for consultations—one to the side of your desk and one in front of the desk. Let the patients have some control and power to decide their own comfort level.

A stands for acknowledge. Show them that you are listening by using facial expressions, giving vocal prompts, and listening between the lines for intent as well as content. Listen for their vocal intonation when responding to things like prescribed medication. If you hear some hesitation in their voice, say to them, "I hear you agreeing, but I'm getting the sound of some reservation in your voice. Can you tell me why?" And then acknowledge their response. Trust them and they will trust you.

R stands for response. Clarify issues by asking, "I'm not sure what you mean." Encourage continuing statements by saying "And then what?" or "Tell me more." The recurrent headache may mask other problems. Provide periodic recaps to focus information. Learn to take cryptic notes, and then return your attention to the patient. (Note taking is sometimes used as an avoidance tactic, and patients sense this.) Use body language by leaning toward the patient. Effective listening requires attention, patience, and the ability to resist the urge to control the conversation.

E stands for exercise emotional control. This means if your "hot buttons" are pushed by people who whine, and in walks someone who does that very thing, you are likely to fake interest in that patient. With your mind elsewhere, you will never really "hear" that person. Emotional blocks are based on previous experiences. They are sometimes activated by words, by tone of voice, by style of clothes or hair, or by ethnicity. It is not possible for us to be free of those emotional reactions, but the first step in controlling them is to recognize when you are losing control. One of the most useful techniques to combat emotional responses is to take a long deep breath when confronted with the urge to interrupt. Deep breathing redirects your response and, as a bonus, it is impossible to talk when you are deep breathing. Who of us would not choose the attentive, caring physician?

As it nears time for me to take that deep breath, I would just like to reiterate that listening is a learned skill, and learning to listen with CARE has valuable benefits for health care professionals and patients. As a wise man named J. Isham once said, "Listening is an attitude of the heart, a genuine desire to be with another, which both attracts and heals."

Thank you very much.

Persuasive Presentation

Managing the Privacy Revolution:
E-COMMERCE IS A GLOBAL ISSUE; Address by HAROLD McGRAW III, *President and Chief Executive Officer, The McGraw-Hill Companies; Delivered to the Privacy and American Business Conference, Arlington, Virginia, December 1, 1998*

I want to thank Privacy and American Business for hosting this conference—and for bringing together in one room so many key members of the business community, representatives of the U.S. Government, the European Union, and the government of Taiwan, as well as privacy advocates from academia and the think tanks—all of whom understand the challenges that accompany the many advantages of Electronic Commerce.

The international representation we see here today underscores the fact that E-Commerce is a global issue—one that transcends borders and barriers in a way few other issues have—and therefore presents challenges in terms of legislation and regulation that are qualitatively different than any we have faced in the past.

Without a doubt, E-Commerce is the kind of blink-of-an-electron event that has the potential to transform our economy, here at home and around the world—to the point that phrases like "here at home" and "around the world" are rendered electronically meaningless in terms of our old understanding of commerce, competition, and markets.

We're already seeing the impact of E-Commerce in the valuation of so-called "Internet stocks."

Case in point: EarthWeb, Inc., a provider of Internet-based IT services, went public last month. In its first week of trading, EarthWeb's shares soared from an offering price of $14 to more than $85 per share—a 600-percent increase in value!

And that's in spite of the fact that EarthWeb has yet to earn its first dollar in profit. Clearly, E-Commerce is a means of providing access to new markets on an unprecedented scale, a tool to reduce costs and to introduce efficiencies into the distribution process.

But in addition to that commercial promise, there's the promise of E-Commerce in expanding human potential: By erasing borders and making old barriers obsolete, E-Commerce provides people with a powerful tool in the ongoing effort to reach their full potential.

For all those reasons, understanding, utilizing, and embracing the electronic frontier may be the central issue challenging business today.

We at The McGraw-Hill Companies recognized early on that our future growth would be tied in significant ways to the growth of E-Commerce. Like other companies in this room, we have confidence in our products, and we naturally want to extend our reach to markets and consumers worldwide who—thanks to the marriage of modem, mouse, and Internet—now have even easier access to the products and services we offer.

All of that makes E-Commerce sound as if it's all "upside"—an easy way for companies to augment their revenues by connecting with consumers in markets they haven't been able to reach before.

But the fact is, E-Commerce remains a great unknown. It's possible to be website-rich and cash-poor—just as it's possible for undisciplined, unfocused investment in E-Commerce to become a black hole. Some of the "electronic unknowns" are tied to privacy issues, while others are entirely unrelated to it. At this point, neither customers nor companies fully understand what we're going to do with this technology—where the Internet will ultimately take us. That said, it's equally true we can't sit on the sidelines until things sort themselves out. Being ready to compete in the online world isn't optional—it is imperative.

Estimates about the potential for growth in E-Commerce are as easy to collect as they are hard to keep current. Here are a few of my own favorite "Leading Electronic Indicators":

In 1994, about 3 million people worldwide were connected to the Internet.
By 1996, the number had grown to 28 million.
By the end of 1998, Internet users will top 82 million.
In 1993—just 5 years ago—26,000 domain names were registered.
By the end of 1997, that number was 1.5 million.

Right now, the number of new websites is growing by 65,000 per day. At that rate, there will be more than 3,000 new websites between now and the time we're done eating lunch.

As for E-Commerce, total business-to-business sales will reach about $8 billion for 1998.

By 2002, estimates project total business-to-business sales at $327 billion for the U.S. and as much as $1.3 trillion globally.

It's hard for us to conceive of growth that rapid in a meaningful way. So look at it this way: What would be a good month for E-Commerce in 1998 will be a slow day in 2002.

Clearly, this is a medium—a virtual market—that is moving, as they say out in Silicon Valley, "at the speed of mind." But with all the well-deserved hype, it's easy to forget that the E-Commerce explosion is by no means inevitable.

Because there's one thing that can stop E-Commerce dead in its tracks. And any one of us has the power—literally—at our fingertips. All you need to do is sit down at your PC, use your mouse to slide the cursor over to the "Exit" icon—and click.

After all, that's how E-Commerce happens: One person at a time, one decision at a time, one click at a time—to the tune of $8 billion today, and as much as $327 billion in 2002.

As I see it, it's critical that we remember—as impressive as the prospects for E-Commerce are—this market is nothing more than the individual decision to purchase online, multiplied by millions of Internet users.

Consider this question: Why is it that some people will read their newspapers online, go online to do research for everything from the work they do to the vacation they take—but still won't buy something online?

It's a matter of trust.

That's one fact that technology doesn't change: Trust is the most precious asset any business has. It's the bedrock that business is built on—and in this era of new media, especially, trust becomes more critical than ever.

If people come to have trust that the system is secure, that private information remains private—they'll flock to E-Commerce in droves—and the predictions I cited a few minutes ago will be realized. Without trust, they won't. They'll move the cursor to Exit, and click, we're out of the game. That makes privacy policy imperative.

We know from surveys that two out of every three Internet users said that privacy matters so much that they'd leave a website if they were asked to provide private information.

Almost all consumers surveyed in the December 1998 Privacy and American Business/Harris Poll say it's important for them to know what information business are collecting about them.

Internet users understand better than most people that information is power. Information can be packaged and repackaged, assessed and analyzed, and used to individually tailor goods and services to a "market of one."

Now, none of that is nefarious—as long as the information has been obtained with the knowledge of the consumer.

Industry has made real progress in creating an awareness of the need for private-sector privacy policies—and many of the individuals and organizations who deserve the credit are represented this morning right here in this room.

Start with the Clinton Administration: Led by Vice President Gore, with his interest in all things Internet—and assisted by Ira Magaziner and Ambassador David Aaron, the "Virtual Secretaries of E-Commerce," this Administration has shown a real understanding of the private-sector potential to create a privacy protocol that gives consumers confidence.

The same can be said for the Department of Commerce's National Telecommunications and Information Administration and International Trade Administration, the FTC, and other agencies at work on this issue—each of which has given the private sector running room to craft a privacy policy that works for us all.

That's an effort that we at The McGraw-Hill Companies believe in. That's why we started work on our privacy policy in 1996. That's why we co-sponsored the first-ever multi-industry privacy conference back in March, with the American Business Press, the Association of American Publishers, the Information Industry Association, and the Magazine Publishers of America.

It's why we went to Cambridge, England, last July, to take part in the European Privacy Laws and Business Conference—to illustrate our understanding that privacy isn't just a U.S. issue, or an EU issue, but a global issue, just as the Internet is a global network. Privacy is an issue that spans countries and continents and cultures.

My aim today isn't to read a roll call and pass out the accolades, because for all the effort thus far, for all the progress the private sector has made, that would be premature.

Instead, my mission today is to underscore the sense of urgency that we must act. Because the fact of the matter is, our window of opportunity is closing. The chance for us to prove that the private sector can regulate itself is passing. And if the private sector does not act, government surely will.

A few minutes ago, I mentioned numbers like 65,000 per day and $327 billion dollars per year—numbers that float in the stratosphere of cyberspace. But the number that concerns me most today is far more modest by E-Commerce standards. The number is 80: the number of bills regulating privacy that were pending as the 105th Congress came to a close in October. In the 106th Congress, I have no doubt we'll see most if not all of those 80 bills reintroduced—and new bills added.

The message for us in the private sector is clear: The time has come for leadership. If we do not address the privacy issue—if we fail to do an effective job of regulating ourselves in terms of privacy protections—then the U.S. Government will do it for us. Or do it to us, as the case may be. And in a global network, so will the European Union, and any number of nations from Asia to Africa to Australia and Latin America, and everywhere else that the Internet can reach. And if that happens, not only will E-Commerce never be the same . . . E-Commerce may never be.

Now, I've heard that some companies are holding off on adopting a privacy policy because they think that if they don't have a stated policy, government entities that oversee the intersection of commerce and consumer interests won't be able to cite their policy against them. And in the early days of E-Commerce, I suspect it's been tempting to take that route. But I submit to you this morning that this "no-policy" policy's days are numbered.

We see signs that governments are beginning to act already. Case in point: the European Union, with its strict new Data Protection Directive, effective October 25. The clock is ticking. If we do not find a way to effectively regulate ourselves, government, and not just one government, but any number of governments, will do it for us.

And, despite the high level of mistrust among Internet users, the December poll results indicate that 69 percent would still prefer voluntary measures over government intervention.

This is our leadership moment—our time to take decisive action.

That's why I've come prepared today to share with all of you what works for us at The McGraw-Hill Companies.

It's a policy we post on our more than 80 company websites, built on four principles—expressed not in legalese that makes Internet users worry about loopholes, but in plain language people can understand. Together, they're the fruits of our extensive and intensive effort to create a privacy policy that's simple enough to understand and comprehensive enough to work.

The first principle is Notice: Tell prospective customers what information you're collecting—and what you're planning to do with it. When it comes to collecting information, uncertainty is the enemy: If you keep people in the dark about what's happening to their private information, they'll imagine the worst. Building Notice into your privacy policy builds confidence in customers.

The second principle is Choice: Adopt a policy with a procedure by which customers can choose not to have their information shared outside your company. It's a way of saying you recognize the information they've shared with you is—in important ways—still theirs.

The third principle is Security: Give the customers confidence that their information is safe from tampering, safe from theft, and safe from misappropriation and misuse.

The fourth and final principle is Review and Correction: Give customers a way to see what information has been collected from them—and a means to correct any errors in that data.

These four basics make a solid privacy policy—one that's understandable, defensible, and ultimately acceptable to most consumers. At least, that's what we're finding at The McGraw-Hill Companies.

There are Sensitive Data—such as specific financial data, certain medical data, and most information about children—that we believe merit additional protection. Having referred to children's privacy—and an important part of my organization focuses on the children's educational market—we have appointed what we call Personally-Identifiable Information Guardians, to help ensure that prior consent is obtained before data is collected from children under the age of 16, and to oversee the collection and security of children's data across all of our companies.

The fact of the matter is that smart privacy policy is smart business. We all profess to care about maintaining good customer relations—well, there's no better way to let customers know you take their concerns to heart than to respect and protect their privacy.

Certainly that's been our experience. Once people understand what we're doing—or more to the point, what we're not doing—with their personal information, their comfort level goes up. In fact, what we and other companies that have adopted privacy policies are finding is that once you inform the average consumer of your privacy policy, the opt-out rate is less than 5 percent.

But make no mistake: Privacy policy is only as good as the compliance component that gives it bite. To that end, I'm pleased to announce today our Compliance Mechanisms—procedures we've designed to be compatible and consistent with the "safe harbor" standards being negotiated this month by the U.S. Government and European Union.

Our compliance policy comprises five key components:

(One) Oversight: The McGraw-Hill Companies has established a Customer Privacy Steering Committee, comprising senior business and corporate executives, to make certain that privacy policy and privacy concerns are matters that merit the high-level attention they deserve and customers demand.

(Two) Review: Our corporate audit department in conjunction with our outside auditing firm and corporate staff have begun periodic random reviews of privacy policy compliance. Again, any evidence of failure to comply is pushed up to senior management, to ensure that changes are made to bring the business unit in question into compliance.

(Three) Ethics: At The McGraw-Hill Companies, integrity is the cornerstone of everything we do. That's why we have expanded our Code of Business Ethics to include a commitment to comply with our Privacy Policy—and to trigger disciplinary actions in cases where compliance is lacking.

(Four) A privacy point of contact: In each business unit, we have designated a Privacy Official—a person any customer can contact directly, by phone, fax, or e-mail, to raise their privacy concerns and make resolving their concerns our business.

(Five) Reporting: Beginning in 1999, after a full year's experience with our policy, we will post on our website and make available in print to our customers a business privacy report. It will tell customers about our commitment to our policy, our progress in implementing it across our corporation, and any changes in policy that we have made over the year.

We believe that this is an essential component of "self-certification"—letting stakeholders know you are doing in practice what your policy promises you'll do.

In essence, we have integrated our privacy policy and compliance mechanism into our business processes, and we as business leaders need to recognize that assuring internal compliance is critical but not easy. People get promoted, links get broken, accidents can happen. The key to success is having a process in place to quickly fix a problem and right the wrong.

If there's one thread that runs through all of this, it's that we've worked hard to instill a sense at The McGraw-Hill Companies that privacy is one area where we don't see a proprietary interest—although we do see a marketing advantage. And the fact of the matter is that no matter how much we or any other single company does to promote consumer privacy, if the rest of the Internet remains a kind of electronic version of the Old Wild West—where no one is safe and anything goes—we will suffer right along with everyone else.

Trust lost in the system is trust lost for everyone. That's one fundamental fact that technology doesn't change.

Of course, I don't pretend for a moment that our privacy policy constitutes the last word on this issue. There are ambitious, ongoing efforts in industry right now—efforts like:

the Direct Marketing Association's Privacy Promise,
the Information Industry Association's Fair Information Practices Principles,
and the work of the Online Privacy Alliance—
all efforts that we support and encourage.

These are great examples of the kind of benefits that flexibility brings when the private sector is given the freedom to take the initiative and innovate:

to adapt to changing circumstances,
to take advantage of next-generation technologies,
and to raise the bar, instead of settling for a "Floor's-the-Limit" approach.

There will be improvements in the future that will add to the level of protection afforded consumers—improvements we not only welcome but may well want to adopt, whether those changes are driven by the new EU Directive or by U.S. law or by new technology or changing consumer expectations.

Internet privacy is a "work in progress." As business leaders, we need to have the seriousness of purpose—and the steadiness of focus—to define a privacy policy that consumers find credible and that governments find adequate.

But the true test is whether our policy passes muster with the ultimate regulator of Internet use: the individual consumer.

And that really brings me full circle today.

Conferences like this one are enormously important—but only to the extent they recognize that the time to talk is over—and that the time to act is now.

I look forward to working with everyone in this room to take the lead—to put in place a privacy policy not only that we as citizens of the world's first Information Society can live with—but that we can grow and prosper with as the Information Economy unfolds. Thank you.

Motivational Presentation

Five Ways in Which Thinking Is Dangerous: Rebellion, Risks, and Outrageous Behavior; by Stephen Joel Trachtenberg; *Dr. Stephen Joel Trachtenberg, President of the University of Hartford, delivered his speech, "Five Ways in Which Thinking Is Dangerous: Rebellion, Risks, and Outrageous Behavior" at Newington High School Scholars' Breakfast, Newington, Connecticut, on June 3, 1986.*

It's an honor and a pleasure for me to be here today, and to have this opportunity to address this year's Newington High School Scholar's Breakfast.

I've been giving a lot of thought in recent weeks to what I ought to be saying to you this morning. The obvious thing would be to praise you for your hard work and your accomplishments and encourage you to continue achieving at this very high level.

But the more I thought about it, the less inclined I felt to do that. And when I asked myself why, a little voice inside my head replied as follows:

"Look, Steve, these kids are *teenagers*. And one thing we know about teenagers is that they are given to questioning the values handed them by adults. Sometimes they rebel in *not*-so-obvious ways. But if you go in there and praise them outright for their accomplishments, maybe one or two of them will reason that anything an adult tells them is good is probably bad."

Let me tell you, that voice inside my head really gave me pause. Basically it seemed to be suggesting that I use some reverse psychology. Instead of doing the obvious, I should do the *opposite* of the obvious.

In turn, that seemed to leave me only one course of action. I could come here today and *criticize* you for working so hard and accomplishing so much. I could urge you to relax a little, to lower your standards, and to try out the pleasures of poorer grades and a generally lower academic status. Then I imagined what the local newspapers would make of my remarks, and what the chances were that I would ever again be invited to address a group of students in any high school in Connecticut.

So I found myself back at Square One. Now I *really* had to get back to basics inside my head, and, drawing on all of the studying I did at Columbia, Yale, and Harvard, I reasoned as follows:

Those of us who have studied Western history of the 19th and 20th centuries know that the Romantic movement left us with a permanent bias in favor of rebellion, risk, and generally outrageous behavior. In other words, if you can pin an *"Establishment"* label on any particular set of behaviors . . . if you can make it sound as if everybody behaving in that particular way has a potbelly that is also bright yellow . . . then most folks in our culture will shy away from it, in favor of someone or something that is closer to Burt Reynolds or Humphrey Bogart.

Now I asked myself: Why is it that no one has considered the hypothesis that academic high achievement is actually as romantic, risky, and generally outrageous as being a pirate, or flying experimental jets, or doing any of the other things that most people are *afraid* to do? Maybe those who get high honors in a place like Newington High School are not just *smarter* than most of their contemporaries but braver too?

The more I considered this hypothesis the better I liked it, and I decided to entitle my talk today "The Five Major Risks of Academic High Achievement." An alternative and slightly broader title might be "Five Ways in Which Thinking is Dangerous."

Way Number One, it seems to me, is that thinking—analysis—the habit of probing deeply into things—can lead to depression.

Remember that people who are regarded as not being clever aren't necessarily lacking in brain-power. They just don't make use of the brain-power that they have available. And one of the reasons for that may be that when you inquire carefully into a lot of things that go on in our world, you find that many of them fall short of perfection. In fact, quite a few of them are positively lousy.

So you can't altogether blame folks who, rather than get upsetting answers, simply don't ask questions! They stay reasonably happy by not doing too much reasoning!

A second risk of academic high achievement is that there are those who will actually hold it against you—in other words, that it can sometimes lead to a lack of popularity where particular individuals are concerned. They're the ones who will label you a—quote—"brain," and imagine that this is a deadly blow, sort of like calling you a rat or a fink.

Though I imagine that some of you have had experiences like that, I wonder if you've considered the possibility that people like that are motivated by a good deal of fear and anxiety? Once you've established your reputation as having a lot of analytic capacity, *they* become nervous that you might turn that capacity in *their* direction. In other words, the person who fears your brain-power is probably a person with something to hide.

The third risk of academic high achievement lies, believe it or not, in your relationship to the adult world. I hope it won't come as a tremendous surprise when I tell you that many adults feel quite ambivalent where talented and high-achieving teenagers are concerned. On the one hand, they can't help but admire the energy and initiative teenagers like that are showing. At the same time, they can't altogether avoid the awareness that the young people they are admiring are also the—quote—"next generation" that is going to—quote—"take over the world."

In other words, a typical fear that adults have is that they are on the way to becoming obsolete. That's why dedicated teachers don't necessarily leap to their feet with enthusiasm when one of their students proves beyond a shadow of a doubt that they just made a mistake. *First* they wince. *Then* they manage to eke out a small smile. And *then,* having thought the whole thing over—then and *only* then—they leap enthusiastically to their feet!

A fourth risk of academic high achievement, in my opinion, is despair. Once you've set a high standard for yourself, there *have* to come moments when you ask yourself: "Can I keep this up?" At the age of 13 or 14 or 15, you ask whether you can keep going at this pace until you're *really old*—until you're 25, say, or 32. Then, when you've been doing it for 30 or 40 years, you wonder whether you can keep going at this pace until retirement. And after retirement, you look at the other vigorous senior citizens—every one of them playing championship gold or giving guest lectures at a nearby college—and you wonder whether you'll *ever* be able to take it easy! . . .

Finally, there is another risk of academic high achievement that bears some thinking about, which is that it often leads people to transform the world in which they are living, which in turn can cause a good deal of personal upset.

Let's say that you are in your teens or early twenties and you work really hard to develop a brand new concept and a brand new range of intellectual or scientific possibilities. Now the world begins to change because *you* dreamt up the microchip . . . or genetic engineering . . . or some altogether new way of looking at the human past. Well, by the time the revolution is peaking, you'll probably be 35 or 40 years of age—ready to settle down and be a little comfortable and complacent. At that point everything around you will get shaken up, and you'll find that your teenage son or daughter is criticizing you for being so completely out of it!

Now let me tote up the risks that I've set before you in the last few minutes:

Risk number one: You may find that you sometimes get depressed.
Risk number two: Some people won't like you.
Risk number three: Grown-ups may get a little nervous when they're near you.
Risk number four: You may feel an occasional twinge of despair over "keeping up the pace."
Risk number five: You may begin to have an impact on the world around you—and you will have to live with the changes you've helped to bring about.

Looking over those five risks of academic high achievement, I realize that they look very much like the risks of maturity. When you criticize someone for being too much of a kid, you usually mean that he or she is giggly even when that's not appropriate, that he or she tries to be universally popular, . . . that he or she expects life to be a nonending party, and that he or she can't imagine things being different from the way they are right now.

What that suggests to me is that academic high achievement—the kind represented here at Newington High School today—may also be a synonym for maturity. It carries some risks—which is *always* true of maturity. It means that life gets a little more complicated—which is what true adults take for granted as they try to get through an average day. It means that life is only *sometimes* a party, and that it is full of the unexpected.

Yes, there are some risks . . . but they are risks well taken. The benefits are worth the dangers. The eagle flying high always risks being shot at by some hare-brained human with a rifle. But eagles—and young eagles like *you*—still prefer the view from that risky height to what is available flying with the turkeys far, far below.

Personally, I admire eagles. That's because I am an unreconstructed romantic. And I admire *you* for what you've accomplished. Keep up the good work! My congratulations to you all!

Follow-up Letter After Job Interview

After a job interview, write a follow-up letter to the person who interviewed you. Your follow-up letter should be courteous and should show appreciation for the opportunity to interview for the job. You may also use the letter to mention highlights from your interview and show your interest in getting the job.

The following is an example of a follow-up letter typed in the block style. Notice that the writer follows the business letter format shown on pages 637–640.

Amanda Watson
1948 Durango Drive
Laramie, WY 82073

Ansellum Nasher
Nasher Food Service Staffing
717 South Third Street
Laramie, WY 82070

Dear Mr. Nasher:

Thank you for the opportunity to discuss the banquet coordinator position at The Ranch Restaurant. I appreciate the time you spent discussing the restaurant industry with me. Your company has an impressive reputation, and I would enjoy representing you and your staff.

I am still very interested in being The Ranch's banquet coordinator. I feel that my experience as a dining room manager, which we discussed during my interview, will help me excel at this job. I look forward to hearing from you soon.

Sincerely,

Amanda Watson

Amanda Watson

Glossary

This glossary lists the vocabulary words found in the selections in this book. The definition given is for the word as it is used in the selection; you may wish to consult a dictionary for other meanings of these words.

A

accommodation maintaining harmony with others by giving in to their wishes; p. 398

acquiring the physical process receiver-senders use to take in the sender's message; p. 49

action group a group appointed to plan and implement a specific course of action; p. 322

active listening participating fully in the communication process; p. 189

advocacy group a group set up specifically to support, protect, defend, or lobby for a cause or group; p. 315

agitator someone who injects negative energy into the group process; p. 350

ambiguous open to interpretation; confusing; p. 140

amplification device information that extends and/or clarifies an idea for an audience; p. 509

antithesis a rhetorical device that involves pairing opposing words or ideas; p. 524

appointed leader someone who is given his or her leadership position by a person in authority; p. 413

appreciative listening listening to enjoy a speaker's message or a performance on an artistic level; p. 194

appropriateness what is suitable for a specific situation; p. 4

articulation clearly and distinctly uttering the consonant sounds of a word; p. 108

artifacts articles of adornment used to decorate self or surroundings; p. 162

attending the act of choosing, consciously or subconsciously, to focus your attention on verbal or nonverbal stimuli; p. 177

attention device a tool used by speakers to grab the interest of an audience; p. 479

audience orientation providing audience members with information they likely do not already have but will need in order to understand a presentation; p. 481

authoritarian leader a leader who uses power to force followers to do what he or she wants them to do; p. 415

avoidance keeping away from or withdrawing from something; p. 397

B

balanced leader a leader who strives for an equal focus on both tasks and relationships; p. 416

barrier any obstacle that blocks communication; p. 45

body language the way people nonverbally express their feelings; p. 299

brainstorming the process of quickly listing all ideas that come to mind regarding a specific topic; p. 335

C

channel the space in which a message is transmitted; p. 44

chronological order arrangement according to the time in which events occur; p. 490

closed question a question that requires a very specific answer, often just one word; p. 239

coercion trying to force others to go along with your wishes; p. 399

coercive power the ability to force others to do something by punishing them if they do not comply; p. 424

collaboration working together to achieve a result; p. 401

colloquialism a term associated with a specific regional culture; p. 120

committee a group with a specialized task which is a part of the basic structure of an organization; p. 314

communication the process of creating and exchanging meaning through symbolic interaction; p. 3

communication apprehension fear or nervousness associated with making a presentation; p. 549

competent communicator someone who incorporates knowledge, attitude, and skills into his or her communication to communicate effectively and appropriately; p. 9

compromise settling differences by having each party give up something; p. 399

conflict a struggle between two or more parties who sense interference in achieving goals; p. 24

conflict over facts a disagreement over something that can be proven to be true or false; p. 388

conflict over policies a disagreement that deals with differences over how to best complete a task; p. 389

conflict over values a disagreement over priorities; p. 388

connotation emotions or feelings associated with a word; p. 125

conscientious style a style of communication that tends to be slow-paced and task-oriented; p. 226

constructive criticism a negative evaluation that brings about positive change; p. 259

context the situation in which communication occurs; p. 4

counseling interview an interview during which the interviewer helps the interviewee decide on a course of action; p. 279

criteria the standards or conditions that any solution must meet in order to be acceptable; p. 334

critic someone who, through training and experience, is qualified to analyze and make judgments about something; p. 581

critical listening listening to comprehend ideas and information in order to achieve a specific purpose or goal; p. 192

critical perspective the standard by which a speech is judged to be successful or unsuccessful; p. 582

culture the set of life patterns passed down from one generation to the next in a group of people; p. 16

culture shock confusion or anxiety that sometimes results when people come into contact with a culture different from their own; p. 17

D

data things that catch a communicator's attention, such as objects, people, sounds, thoughts, memories, and the messages sent by others; p. 48

decision making examining a set of alternatives and using reason and logic to select the best one; p. 336

decoding the mental process receiver-senders use to create meaning from language; p. 49

deliberative listening listening to understand, analyze, and evaluate messages to accept or reject a point of view, make a decision, or take action; p. 192

delivery the way a presenter uses his or her body and voice to communicate a message to an audience; p. 564

demeanor outward behavior; p. 298

democratic leader a leader who invites followers to participate in decision making in an effort to get the majority to agree with and commit to decisions; p. 416

demographics information about a group's age, gender, education, group affiliations, ethnicity, and sociocultural background; p. 445

denotation a word's objective description or meaning; p. 125

descriptive communication talk that paints a picture of the facts of a situation; p. 259

descriptive gesture a gesture used to create a mental image to help an audience visualize a message; p. 570

dialect a unique combination of speech sounds that identifies speech with a particular group of people; p. 110

diction the degree of clarity and distinctness in a person's speech; p. 107

direct question a question that is straightforward; asks exactly what the interviewer wants to know and leaves no room for ambiguity; p. 293

discriminate to treat differently based on reasons other than individual merit, or quality; p. 301

dominant style a style of communication that is fast-paced and more task-oriented than people-oriented; p. 224

E

emergent goal a goal set by the group itself; p. 316

emergent leader someone who is chosen by peers or members of a group because of his or her personality, power in the group, or the special circumstances of the group task; p. 414

emergent norm any group norm that develops from the group interaction and the mix of the group members' personalities; p. 347

empathic listening listening to understand, participate in, and enhance a relationship; p. 193

emphatic gesture a gesture used to stress or place special attention on what a presenter is saying; p. 569

employment interview a process for judging whether a job candidate is qualified and well-suited for a position; p. 280

encoding the mental process of assigning meaning and language to data; p. 49

enunciation clearly and distinctly uttering the vowel sounds of a word; p. 109

ethical proof the supporting information that builds a speaker's credibility on a topic; p. 508

ethos the image a presenter displays to an audience; p. 443

etiquette an established code of behavior or courtesy; p. 254

evaluative communication talk that tells how you interpret a behavior and how you feel about a situation; p. 259

exit interview an interview used to determine why a person has decided to leave an organization; p. 278

expert power the power held by the person who knows the most about the work that must be done; p. 425

extemporaneous presentation a presentation thoroughly prepared and rehearsed in advance and presented with the use of notes; p. 535

F

facilitator a group member who adds positive task energy to the group by helping group members follow through on tasks; p. 349

factual question a question that seeks information that can be proven; p. 293

feed-forward to offer an explanation that you want to make or a reason or explanation for a question, request, or offer; p. 80

feedback one person's observable response to another's message; p. 46

filler a word or phrase used to cover up a hesitancy in speech; p. 127

formal language language that conforms to a highly structured set of rules; p. 118

formal presentation a presentation scheduled in advance and usually involving individual or team research and audiovisual support; p. 442

formal social group a group whose members are chosen by an organization to participate in community activities; p. 323

functional approach the idea that leaders should both recognize and actively perform needed tasks; p. 417

G

grammar the basic understandings and rules that regulate the use of a language; p. 106

group a small number of people who identify and interact with one another because of a common interest, bond, or goal; p. 313

group discussion three or more people exchanging ideas on a specific topic for a specific purpose; p. 354

group dynamics the energy created as group members communicate and interact with each other in committees, teams, and other groups; p. 353

group goal the specific tasks and expected outcome of a group; p. 315

group norms informal, often unstated rules about what behavior is appropriate in a group; p. 345

groupthink poor decision-making in a group caused by members having a stronger desire to agree with one another than to solve the problem; p. 352

H

hearing the physical process of receiving sound; p. 176

highly closed question a question that not only seeks a specific answer but may even provide answers from which to choose; p. 293

hypothetical question a question that asks how a respondent might react in a given situation; p. 293

I

impatient listening short bursts of active listening that are interrupted by noise and other distractions; p. 190

impromptu presentation a presentation for which there is little or no time for advance preparation; p. 536

indirect question a question that seeks specific information without directly asking for it; p. 293

inflection the rising and falling of pitch that adds variety to speaking; p. 148

influencing style a style of communication that is fast-paced and more people-oriented than task-oriented; p. 225

informal language the language most often used in casual situations and with close interpersonal relationships; p. 120

informal presentation a presentation that may occur on a daily or ongoing basis, is usually shorter and more spontaneous than a formal presentation, and may involve a smaller audience; p. 442

informal social group a group in which membership may be encouraged, but not required, by an organization; p. 323

information-gathering group a group designed specifically to gather data; p. 320

information-gathering interview an interview in which an interviewer obtains information from an interviewee; p. 278

information-giving interview an interview in which an interviewer gives information to an interviewee; p. 279

informational power the power held by individuals who have access to needed information; p. 425

informative presentation a presentation that conveys ideas and information in a clear, accurate, and objective manner to gain the audience's interest; p. 454

initiator a group member who works to get the group started toward achieving the group goal; p. 348

integrating blending things so that they function together as a whole; p. 220

internalization going over and over something until you absorb it; p. 554

interpersonal communication communication between two people; p. 54

interpreting the process in which the receiver personalizes the sender's message to determine the meaning; p. 178

interview a formal two-party communication in which at least one of the participants has a set purpose; p. 274

interview process the sequence of actions that result in an effective interview; p. 283

interviewee someone who provides information to an interviewer; p. 274

interviewer someone who determines the purpose of an interview and ensures that the discussion remains focused on the purpose; p. 274

intrapersonal communication communication that occurs in one's own mind; p. 54

investigative interview an interview in which the interviewer uses questions to find out unknown information; p. 278

J

jargon technical language; p. 119

judgment by aesthetics evaluating the overall appearance or impact of a presentation; p. 583

judgment by ethical standards evaluating whether a speaker behaved ethically in a presentation; p. 582

judgment by multiple standards an evaluation using two or more critical perspectives to determine the success of a speech; p. 583

judgment by results evaluating whether or not a speaker accomplished the goal of his or her presentation; p. 582

K

kinesics the use of the body in communication; p. 153

L

laissez-faire leader a leader who gives up his or her power to the members of the group; p. 416

leader someone who influences or inspires others to act in specific ways to accomplish a common goal; p. 413

leading question a question that suggests the desired answer; p. 293

legitimate power power assigned to anyone who holds a particular position, office, or title; p. 424

listening a physical and psychological process that involves acquiring, assigning meaning, and responding to symbolic messages from others; p. 172

logical proof a specific piece of verifiable information that supports a statement; p. 506

M

maintenance need a need that relates to the feelings of group members and their relationships to one another; p. 361

manuscript presentation a presentation that is delivered with its full text in front of the presenter; p. 534

mass communication electronic or print transmission of messages to the general public; p. 56

mass media outlets of communication, such as radio, television, film, and print, that are designed to reach large audiences; p. 56

message information that is exchanged between communicators; p. 40

method of delivery a specific way of sending your message orally to your audience; p. 534

Monroe's Motivated Sequence a five-part organizational strategy designed for speeches that seek to persuade or motivate an audience to take immediate action; named after communication expert A. H. Monroe; p. 494

motivational presentation presentation that inspires or encourages an audience; p. 456

N

negotiation bargaining with others to gain what you want; p. 400

neutral question a question that implies no specific "right" or "wrong" answer; p. 293

noise anything that interferes with a message; usually temporary; p. 44

nonverbal communication a system of symbolic behaviors that includes all forms of communication except words; p. 136

norm a stated or implied expectation; p. 5

O

one-to-group communication communication that involves a speaker who seeks to inform, persuade, or motivate an audience; p. 55

open-ended question a question that is broad in scope, requiring more than a single-word answer such as "Yes" or "No"; p. 239

opinion question a question that asks for the respondent's judgment about something; p. 293

oral language language that is spoken and heard rather than written and read; p. 102

oral style the way a presenter uses language to express ideas; p. 519

organization a number of people with specific responsibilities who are united for some purpose; p. 15

organizational culture how an organization thinks, what it finds important, and how it conducts business; p. 17

P

panel discussion a formal presentation in which a group of people discusses an announced topic in front of an audience; p. 544

panel discussion-forum a panel discussion that includes post-discussion interaction with the audience; p. 545

parallelism arranging sentences so that words and phrases are similar in length and structure; p. 524

paraphrase repeating a message in your own words; p. 251

passive listening not actively participating in interactions; p. 190

pathetic proof support material that gives emotional appeal to a presentation; p. 508

perception check a question that helps you determine the accuracy and validity of your perceptions; p. 78

perception the process of assigning meaning to data about oneself or the surrounding world; p. 71

performance appraisal an evaluation of how well a person has achieved goals and objectives over a set period of time; p. 279

personal perception one's own understanding of reality; p. 75

personal style a pattern of clear and consistent communication choices that reflect a person's individuality and distinguish him or her from other individuals; p. 222

persuasive presentation a presentation that attempts to get an audience to voluntarily change its thoughts, beliefs, or actions on a topic; p. 454

pitch highness or lowness of sound on a musical scale; p. 147

policy-making group a group that has the task of creating procedural rules for all organizational members to follow; p. 321

power the ability to get others to behave in a particular way or to carry out certain actions; p. 423

prescribed goal a goal that is assigned by a person in authority; p. 315

prescribed norm a rule for appropriate behavior that is routinely taught to new group members; p. 346

primary question a question that begins a new topic; p. 293

primary source someone, including oneself, who has firsthand knowledge or experience regarding a topic; p. 462

problem difficulty or uncertainty—a difference between the way something should be and the way it is; p. 331

problem solving the act of understanding the nature of a dilemma, creating alternative solutions, determining which solution is best, and implementing that solution; p. 331

professional presentation an informed, organized oral statement made to a group of professional or social peers, supervisors, clients, or members of the general public; p. 442

projecting sending the sound of your voice to all areas of a room without shouting; p. 565

pronunciation the correct way to say a word; p. 108

protocol a code of etiquette that is written and prescribed by an organization; p. 254

R

range the span from the highest to the lowest pitch possible for a speaker to reach; p. 148

rate how fast or how slowly an individual speaks; p. 149

receiver-sender a person who receives, or believes he or she has received, a message; p. 39

referent power influence held by someone who is respected, liked, or otherwise admired by his or her followers; p. 427

relationship skill a communication skill needed to nurture and maintain goodwill with people; p. 11

resistance the force generated within a person that keeps him or her from accepting another's use of power; p. 423

responding reacting internally, emotionally, and intellectually to a message; p. 179

reward power the ability to repay others in exchange for complying with a given direction; p. 424

role a part played in a specific setting or situation; p. 5

S

sample the set of people one selects to respond to a survey or questionnaire; p. 464

secondary question a question that helps the interviewer better understand the answer to a primary question; p. 293

secondary source an information source such as a book, periodical, radio or television program, or Internet article that has been written by someone else about a particular topic; p. 460

selective perception the mental process of choosing which data or stimuli to focus on from all that are available to you at any given time; p. 72

self-concept the view one has of oneself; p. 83

self-disclosure the deliberate revelation of significant personal information that is not readily apparent to others; p. 90

self-fulfilling prophecy a prediction or expectation that shapes your behavior, making the outcome more likely to occur; p. 88

self-talk the inner speech or mental conversations that one carries on with oneself; p. 54

sender-receiver a person who sends a message to someone; p. 39

sensory perception the complex physical process of taking in data through the five senses; p. 48

sequential order arrangement according to the steps of a process; p. 491

slang a type of informal language that is typically used for only a brief period of time by a limited group of people; p. 121

small-group communication communication within formal or informal groups or teams; p. 55

social group a group that someone joins for purely personal reasons; p. 322

social responsibility an obligation or willingness to work toward the well-being of others; p. 20

social ritual a communication situation that is frequently repeated in daily social interaction; p. 123

spatial order arrangement according to how a topic is put together or by the physical location of its elements; p. 492

specific instance an account of an actual event or occurrence; p. 507

stage presence an illusion created by the quality of the energy, poise, confidence, and control that a presenter conveys to an audience; p. 568

standard an established level of requirement or excellence; p. 6

standard language language used by the majority of knowledgeable communicators within a specific language; p. 120

statistic an item of information that is presented as a number; p. 507

steady style a style of communication that tends to be slow-paced and both people- and task-oriented; p. 226

structure the way the different parts of a language are arranged; p. 105

style approach the idea that a leader's communication method and use of power determines his or her success; p. 415

survey interview an interview that gathers information from a number of people; p. 278

symposium a group presentation in which individual speakers give prepared presentations on aspects of a topic with little or no interaction with the other presenters; p. 546

symposium-forum a symposium that includes interaction with the audience; p. 546

T

tag a statement or question added to the end of a statement to invite approval or cooperation from others; p. 127

task group a group that is given a specific job, or a task, to complete; p. 318

task need a need that relates directly to the business and goals of the group; p. 361

task skill a communication skill needed to do a job, complete a task, or reach a goal effectively; p. 11

team a small group that usually is given the power to make and implement decisions; p. 314

technical language language associated with a particular profession, activity, or field of study; p. 119

tempo the rhythmic quality of a person's speech; p. 149

testimony a direct quote or summary of a quote; p. 507

thesis statement a clearly written, simple sentence or question that states the point you expect to make in your presentation; p. 480

tone a specific vocal quality; p. 149

topical order arrangement that groups ideas by some logical theme or division; p. 492

trait approach the idea that leaders share certain personality traits that help them lead successfully; p. 414

transactional involving an exchange; p. 35

transmitting the physical process of sending verbal and nonverbal messages; p. 49

U

understanding a complex mental process that involves decoding the symbolic message received from others and then interpreting and assigning a personal meaning to that message; p. 178

ungrammatical language language that does not use expected standards of grammar or mechanics; p. 122

V

visualization the process of mentally picturing yourself doing something successfully; p. 551

vocabulary all the word symbols that make up a particular code or language; p. 103

Spanish Glossary

A

acomodación (accommodation) mantener la armonía con los demás cediendo a sus deseos; p. 398

acuerdo de grupo (groupthink) decisiones ineficaces que toma un grupo debido a que sus miembros se preocupan más en lograr consenso que en solucionar el problema; p. 352

adornos (artifacts) artículos para decoración ambiental o arreglo personal; p. 162

adquisición (acquiring) proceso físico mediante el cual el receptor-emisor asimila el mensaje del emisor; p. 49

alcance de la voz (projecting) transmitir el sonido de la voz a todos los rincones de un recinto sin necesidad de elevarla demasiado; p. 565

ambiguo (ambiguous) que tiene más de una interpretación; causa confusión; p. 140

ansiedad comunicativa (communication apprehension) temor o nerviosismo que se siente al hacer una exposición; p. 549

antítesis (antithesis) recurso retórico que relaciona palabras o ideas opuestas; p. 524

apreciación estética (judgment by aesthetics) evaluación de la apariencia general o del impacto de una exposición; p. 583

apreciación por normas éticas (judgment by ethical standards) evaluación del comportamiento ético de un orador durante una exposición; p. 582

apreciación por normas múltiples (judgment by multiple standards) evaluación para determinar la eficacia de una exposición en la que se usan dos o más perspectivas críticas; p. 583

apreciación por resultados (judgement by results) evaluación para determinar si el orador cumplió con el objetivo de su exposición; p. 582

articulación (articulation) pronunciación clara de las consonantes de una palabra; p. 108

autoridad de experto (expert power) autoridad que ejerce una persona por ser la más calificada para realizar un trabajo; p. 425

B

barrera (barrier) todo obstáculo que dificulta la comunicación; p. 45

C

cadencia (tempo) manera proporcionada y grata de hablar que tiene una persona; p. 149

canal (channel) medio por el que se transmite un mensaje; p. 44

capacidad de relación (relationship skill) habilidad comunicativa requerida para cultivar y mantener buenas relaciones con los demás; p. 11

choque cultural (culture shock) confusión o ansiedad que ocasionalmente resulta del contacto que tiene una persona con una cultura diferente a la propia; p. 17

cinésica (kinesics) uso del cuerpo en relación con la comunicación; p. 153

circunstancia específica (specific instance) hecho o suceso verdadero; p. 507

clasificación temática (topical order) agrupación de ideas según una división o tema lógicos; p. 492

cláusula final interrogativa (tag) declaración o pregunta que se usa al terminar un enunciado para obtener la aprobación o cooperación de los demás; p. 127

codificar (encoding) proceso mental mediante el cual se asigna significado y lenguaje a la información; p. 49

coerción (coercion) someter a otros a la voluntad o los deseos de uno; p. 399

colaboración (collaboration) trabajo que se realiza en conjunto para alcanzar un objetivo; p. 401

comité (committee) grupo que forma parte de la estructura básica de una organización al cual se le encomienda una tarea especializada; p. 314

comprensión (understanding) proceso mental complejo mediante el cual se descrifra e interpreta un mensaje simbólico, al que luego se da un significado personal; p. 178

comunicación (communication) proceso mediante el cual se establece e intercambia significado a través de una interacción simbólica; p. 3

comunicación de individuo a grupo (one-to-group communication) comunicación en la que participa un orador con el fin de informar, persuadir o motivar al público; p. 55

comunicación de masas (mass communication) difusión electrónica o impresa de mensajes entre el público general; p. 56

comunicación en pequeños grupos (small-group communication) comunicación que se da dentro de grupos formales o informales, o equipos; p. 55

comunicación evaluadora (evaluative communication) conversación que ayuda a interpretar un comportamiento y lo que uno piensa sobre una situación; p. 259

comunicación expositiva (descriptive communication) exposición de los hechos de una situación; p. 259

comunicación interpersonal (interpersonal communication) comunicación entre dos personas; p. 54

comunicación intrapersonal (intrapersonal communication) comunicación que tiene lugar en la mente de una persona; p. 54

comunicación no verbal (nonverbal communication) sistema de comportamientos simbólicos que incluye todo tipo de comunicación, con excepción de palabras; p. 136

comunicador competente (competent communicator) persona que integra conocimientos, actitud y habilidades para comunicarse eficaz y adecuamente; p. 9

concepto personal (self-concept) opinión que uno tiene de sí mismo; p. 83

concesión mutua (compromise) cesiones recíprocas que hacen las partes para conciliar diferencias; p. 399

conducta (demeanor) comportamiento externo que exhibe una persona; p. 298

conflicto (conflict) problema entre dos o más partes cuando piensan que el otro obstaculiza el logro de sus metas; p. 24

conflicto sobre hechos (conflict over facts) desacuerdo sobre algo que al comprobarse podría resultar verdadero o falso; p. 388

conflicto sobre políticas (conflict over policies) desacuerdo o diferencias en cuanto a la mejor manera de llevar a cabo una tarea; p. 389

conflicto sobre valores (conflict over values) desacuerdo en cuanto a prioridades; p. 388

connotación (connotation) emociones o sentimientos relacionados con una palabra; p. 125

contexto (context) situación en la que se da la comunicación; p. 4

conveniencia (appropriateness) calidad de adecuado para una situación específica; p. 4

conversación interna (self-talk) conversaciones mentales que una persona sostiene con sí misma; p. 54

criterios (criteria) requisitos o condiciones que deben satisfacerse para que una solución sea aceptada; p. 334

crítica constructiva (constructive criticism) opinión negativa que genera un cambio positivo; p. 259

crítico (critic) persona que como resultado de su formación y experiencia está capacitada para analizar y emitir opiniones; p. 581

cultura (culture) conjunto de actividades humanas de un pueblo que se transmite de generación a eneración; p. 16

cultura de organización (organizational culture) manera de pensar, prioridades y operaciones de una organización; p. 17

D

dato estadístico (statistic) información representada en cifras; p. 507

datos (data) elementos que captan la atención del comunicador como objetos, personas, sonidos, ideas, recuerdos y mensajes transmitidos por otros; p. 48

datos demográficos (demographics) información referente a la edad, sexo, educación, afiliaciones, etnicidad y antecedentes socioculturales de un grupo; p. 445

denotación (denotation) significado o definición objetiva de una palabra; p. 125

descodificar (decoding) proceso mental mediante el cual el receptor y el emisor determinan el significado del lenguaje; p. 49

dialecto (dialect) conjunto de sonidos y expresiones que forman la lengua de un determinado grupo; p. 110

dicción (diction) grado de claridad y precisión con el que habla una persona; p. 107

dinámica de grupo (group dynamics) energía generada por la comunicación o interacción de los miembros de comités, equipos y otros grupos; p. 353

discriminar (discriminate) dar trato diferente a una persona por motivos no relacionados con su mérito o calidad personal; p. 301

discusión en grupo (group discussion) tres o más personas que intercambian ideas sobre un tema específico con un propósito determinado; p. 354

E

elocuencia (delivery) manera en que un presentador usa sus ademanes y voz para transmitir su mensaje al público; p. 564

emisor-receptor (sender-receiver) persona que envía un mensaje a otra; p. 39

entrevista (interview) comunicación formal entre dos partes en la cual uno de los participantes, por lo menos, tiene un propósito definido; p. 274

entrevista de asesoría (counseling interview) entrevista durante la cual el entrevistador ayuda al entrevistado a tomar una decisión sobre la línea de acción que seguirá; p. 279

entrevista de encuesta (survey interview) entrevista para recoger información de un grupo de personas; p. 278

entrevista de trabajo (employment interview) proceso mediante el cual se determina si un postulante está calificado y es apto para un cargo; p. 280

entrevista final (exit interview) entrevista para determinar la razón por la cual una persona deja una organización; p. 278

entrevista informativa (information-giving interview) entrevista durante la cual el entrevistador proporciona información al entrevistado; p. 279

entrevista investigadora (investigative interview) entrevista durante la cual el entrevistador formula preguntas para averiguar la información que necesita; p. 278

entrevista para obtener información (information-gathering interview) entrevista durante la cual el entrevistado proporciona información al entrevistador; p. 278

entrevistado (interviewee) persona que brinda información al entrevistador; p. 274

entrevistador (interviewer) persona que determina el propósito de la entrevista y mantiene la conversación centrada en dicho propósito; p. 274

enunciación (enunciation) pronunciación clara de las vocales de una palabra; p. 109

enunciación de tesis (thesis statement) oración o pregunta sencilla escrita con claridad, que establece la idea u opinión que uno desea transmitir; p. 480

equipo (team) pequeño grupo que cuenta generalmente con autoridad para adoptar e implementar decisiones; p. 314

escala (range) tiempo que le toma a un orador modular la voz desde el tono más elevado al más atenuado; p. 148

escucha (listening) proceso físico y psicológico mediante el cual uno adquiere, da significado y responde a los mensajes simbólicos de otros; p. 172

escucha activa (active listening) participación plena en el proceso de comunicación; p. 189

escucha con empatía (empathic listening) acción de escuchar para comprender, participar en una relación y fortalecer la misma; p. 193

escucha con sentido crítico (critical listening) acción de esuchar para captar ideas e información a fin de lograr un objetivo o meta; p. 192

escucha de apreciación (appreciative listening) acción de escuchar en la cual se disfruta del mensaje de un orador o una interpretación artística; p. 194

escucha deliberante (deliberative listening) acción de escuchar para comprender, analizar y evaluar mensajes a fin de aceptar o rechazar un punto de vista, tomar una decisión o hacer una acción; p. 192

escucha impaciente (impatient listening) intervalos cortos de escucha activa interrumpidos por ruidos y otras distracciones; p. 190

escucha pasiva (passive listening) participación no activa en el proceso de comunicación; p. 190

estándar (standard) norma o nivel de excelencia establecido; p. 6

estilo de influencia (influencing style) modo de comunicación acelerada que se concentra más en las relaciones humanas que en la tarea; p. 225

estilo dominante (dominant style) modo de comunicación acelerada que se concentra más en la meta que en las relaciones humanas; p. 224

estilo intencional (conscientious style) modo de comunicación pausado y orientado hacia una tarea específica; p. 226

estilo oral (oral style) manera en que el presentador usa el lenguaje para expresar sus ideas; p. 519

estilo personal (personal style) patrón de modelos de comunicación definidos y constantes que reflejan la individualidad de una persona distinguiéndola de los demás; p. 222

estilo uniforme (steady style) modo de comunicación pausado que se orienta tanto hacia una tarea específica como a las relaciones humanas; p. 226

estructura (structure) orden que siguen las diferentes partes del lenguaje; p. 105

ética (ethos) imagen que proyecta un presentador ante un público; p. 443

etiqueta (etiquette) código de conducta o cortesía establecido; p. 254

evaluación del rendimiento (performance appraisal) evaluación para determinar si una persona ha logrado eficazmente sus metas y objetivos en el transcurso de un tiempo dado; p. 279

evidencia conmovedora (pathetic proof) material complementario que da un toque emotivo a una exposición; p. 508

evidencia ética (ethical proof) información complementaria que ratifica el conocimiento que tiene el orador sobre un tema; p. 508

evidencia lógica (logical proof) pieza específica de información comprobable que apoya una declaración; p. 506

evitar (avoidance) manterse alejado o retirado de algo; p. 397

exposición con texto (manuscript presentation) exposición durante la cual el presentador sigue un texto en su totalidad; p. 534

exposición formal (formal presentation) exposición programada por anticipado que incluye investigación individual o colectiva y se complementa con material audiovisual; p. 442

exposición improvisada (impromptu presentation) exposición que no ha sido preparada anticipadamente por falta de tiempo; p. 536

exposición informal (informal presentation) exposición que puede darse a diario o en forma continua, que es generalmente breve y más espontánea que una exposición formal, y tiene un público menor; p. 442

exposición informativa (informative presentation) exposición durante la cual las ideas e información son transmitidas de manera clara, precisa y objetiva para capturar la atención del público; p. 454

exposición motivadora (motivational presentation) exposición para inspirar o animar al público; p. 456

exposición organizada extemporánea (extemporaneous presentation) exposición debidamente preparada y ensayada, y presentada mediante el uso de notas; p. 535

exposición persuasiva (persuasive presentation) exposición cuyo objetivo es convencer al público para que cambie sus conceptos, opiniones o tendencias sobre un tema; p. 454

exposición profesional (professional presentation) exposición oral informada y organizada hecha ante un grupo de colegas o relaciones sociales, supervisores, clientes o público en general; p. 442

F

facilitador (facilitator) miembro de un grupo que imparte energía positiva ayudando a sus miembros en la conclusión de las tareas; p. 349

fuente primaria (primary source) persona, incluido uno mismo, que tiene conocimientos o experiencia directa sobre un tema; p. 462

fuente secundaria (secondary source) fuente informativa, por ejemplo un libro, publicación periódica, programa de radio o televisión o artículo en Internet, sobre un tema específico escrito por otra persona; p. 460

G

gesto descriptivo (descriptive gesture) ademán que se usa para crear una imagen mental y ayudar a la concurrencia a visualizar un mensaje; p. 570

gesto enfático (emphatic gesture) ademán que se usa para destacar el mensaje del presentador o darle más énfasis; p. 569

gramática (grammar) conceptos y normas básicas que regulan el uso de un idioma; p. 106

grupo (group) número reducido de personas que se identifican e interactúan unidas por un interés, lazo u objetivo común; p. 313

grupo de acción (action group) grupo nombrado para planificar e implementar un plan de acción específico; p. 322

grupo de trabajo (task group) grupo al que se le asigna la realización de una tarea específica; p. 318

grupo defensor (advocacy group) grupo establecido con el objeto de respaldar, proteger, velar o cabildear por una determinada causa o sector; p. 315

grupo normativo (policy-making group) grupo cuya función es establecer las normas que deben seguir los miembros de una organización; p. 321

grupo para obtener información (information-gathering group) grupo constituido específicamente para recopilar datos; p. 320

grupo social (social group) grupo al que uno pertenece por razones meramente personales; p. 322

grupo social formal (formal social group) grupo cuyos miembros son elegidos por una organización para participar en actividades de la comunidad; p. 323

grupo social informal (informal social group) grupo dentro del cual se promueve la afiliación pero no es requerida por una organización; p. 323

H

habilidad funcional (task skill) habilidad de comunicación que se requiere para hacer un trabajo, completar una tarea o lograr una meta con eficacia; p. 11

I

incorporación (internalization) la acción de repetir o repasar algo hasta ser absorbido; p. 554

inflexión (inflection) elevación o atenuación de la voz que da variedad al discurso; p. 148

información voluntaria (feed-forward) la acción de dar una razón o explicación para una pregunta, petición u oferta; p. 80

iniciador (initiator) miembro de un grupo que motiva al resto para tomar el camino hacia la meta fijada; p. 348

instigador (agitator) persona que infunde energía negativa en el proceso de grupo; p. 350

integrar (integrating) unificar las partes para que funcionen como un todo; p. 220

interpretación (interpreting) proceso mediante el cual el receptor analiza el mensaje del emisor para determinar el sentido; p. 178

J

jerga (slang) tipo de lenguaje informal usado generalmente por un determinado grupo durante un período limitado; p. 121

jerga profesional (jargon) lenguaje técnico; p. 119

L

lenguaje corporal (body language) manera de transmitir sentimientos sin recurrir a la expresión verbal; p. 299

lenguaje estándar (standard language) lenguaje que usan la mayoría de los comunicadores experimentados dentro de un determinado idioma; p. 120

lenguaje formal (formal language) lenguaje regido por un conjunto de reglas sumamente estructuradas; p. 118

lenguaje informal (informal language) lenguaje que se usa generalmente en situaciones diarias y entre conocidos que mantienen una relación interpersonal; p. 120

lenguaje no gramatical (ungrammatical language) lenguaje que no aplica normas ni conceptos gramaticales establecidos; p. 122

lenguaje oral (oral language) lenguaje que se habla y escucha en vez de escribirse y leerse; p. 102

lenguaje técnico (technical language) lenguaje propio de una profesión, actividad o campo de estudio determinados; p. 119

líder (leader) persona que ejerce influencia en otros o los inspira a actuar de cierta manera para lograr una meta colectiva; p. 413

líder autoritario (authoritarian leader) líder que ejerce poder entre sus seguidores a fin de imponer su voluntad; p. 415

líder democrático (democratic leader) líder que incluye a sus partidiarios en el proceso de toma de decisiones para lograr el acuerdo de la mayoría y la adopción de decisiones; p. 416

líder emergente (emergent leader) persona elegida por sus compañeros o miembros de un grupo debido a su personalidad, autoridad dentro del grupo o circunstancias especiales de la meta; p. 414

líder equilibrado (balanced leader) líder que da importancia tanto a las tareas como a las relaciones humanas; p. 416

líder laissez-faire (laissez-faire leader) líder que cede su autoridad a los miembros del grupo; p. 416

líder nombrado (appointed leader) persona escogida por una autoridad competente para ocupar un cargo de liderazgo; p. 413

lluvia de ideas (brainstorming) actividad mediante la cual se generan rápidamente ideas sobre un tema específico; p. 335

M

mecanismo de atención (attention device) recurso empleado por los oradores para capturar el interés del público; p. 479

mecanismo de explicación (amplification device) información que amplía o clarifica una idea al público; p. 509

medios masivos de difusión (mass media) fuentes de comunicación, por ejemplo la radio, la televisión, el cine y materiales impresos, diseñados para llegar a un público extenso; p. 56

mensaje (message) información que intercambian dos comunicadores; p. 40

mesa redonda (panel discussion) exposición formal frente a un público, en la que participan varias personas que exponen e intercambian opiniones sobre un tema; p. 544

mesa redonda-foro (panel discussion-forum) mesa redonda que al finalizar incluye una sesión de preguntas y respuestas con participación del público; p. 545

meta colectiva (group goal) tareas específicas de un grupo y los resultados que espera obtener; p. 315

meta emergente (emergent goal) meta establecida por el grupo mismo; p. 316

meta establecida (prescribed goal) meta fijada por una autoridad competente; p. 315

método de elocuencia (method of delivery) manera personal de transmitir el mensaje al público; p. 534

método de estilo (style approach) opinión de que el método de comunicación y la autoridad que ejerce un líder determinan su éxito; p. 415

método funcional (functional approach) opinión de que los líderes deberían participar activamente en las tareas necesarias además de identificarlas; p. 417

muestra (sample) grupo específico de personas elegidas para participar en una encuesta o cuestionario; p. 464

N

necesidad de apoyo (maintenance need) necesidad asociada con los sentimientos de los miembros de un grupo y sus relaciones mutuas; p. 361

necesidad funcional (task need) necesidad que se relaciona directamente con las actividades y metas del grupo; p. 361

negociación (negotiation) la acción de transar con otros para conseguir lo que se desea; p. 400

norma (norm) expectativa establecida o implicada; p. 5

norma emergente (emergent norm) toda norma que surge de la interacción del grupo y la combinación de las personalidades de sus miembros; p. 347

norma establecida (prescribed norm) norma de comportamiento que se imparte a los nuevos miembros de un grupo; p. 346

O

oír (hearing) proceso físico de percibir los sonidos; p. 176

orden cronológico (chronological order) secuencia de eventos según la fecha en que ocurrieron; p. 490

orden espacial (spatial order) orden que se sigue en el desarrollo de un tema o según la ubicación física de sus elementos; p. 492

orden secuencial (sequential order) disposición de algo según los pasos de un proceso; p. 491

organización (organization) conjunto de personas que comparten un fin y cumplen responsabilidades específicas; p. 15

orientación para el público (audience orientation) información suministrada con la cual posiblemente no cuenta la concurrencia pero que necesitará para comprender una exposición; p. 481

P

parafrasear (paraphrase) repetir un mensaje usando palabras propias; p. 251

paralelismo (parallelism) la acción de colocar las oraciones de manera que las palabras y frases sean de tamaño y estructura similares; p. 524

percepción (perception) proceso mediante el cual se asigna significado a la información sobre uno mismo o el ambiente que lo rodea; p. 71

percepción personal (personal perception) interpretación que tiene una persona de la realidad; p. 75

percepción selectiva (selective perception) proceso mental que permite elegir la información o los estímulos deseados que están disponibles en un momento dado; p. 72

percepción sensorial (sensory perception) proceso físico y complejo de adquisición de conocimientos o información a través de los cinco sentidos; p. 48

perspectiva crítica (critical perspective) norma según la cual se evalúa la eficacia o ineficacia de un discurso; p. 582

poder (power) autoridad que ejerce una persona sobre otras para hacer que se comporten de cierta manera o lleven a cabo determinadas actividades; p. 423

poder coercitivo (coercive power) capacidad de forzar a otros a hacer algo, tomando represalias si sus órdenes no son cumplidas; p. 424

poder de retribución (reward power) capacidad de recompensar a alquien que sigue las instrucciones dadas; p. 424

poder informador (referent power) influencia que ejerce una persona que es respetada, considerada y admirada por sus seguidores; p. 427

poder informativo (informational power) autoridad que ejerce una persona que tiene acceso a información importante; p. 425

poder legítimo (legitimate power) poder otorgado a una persona que ocupa un puesto, función o cargo específicos; p. 424

postura característica (trait approach) opinión de que los líderes poseen ciertos rasgos comunes que los ayudan a ejercer su posición de liderazgo; p. 414

pregunta básica (primary question) pregunta que da inicio a un nuevo tema; p. 293

pregunta cerrada (closed question) pregunta que requiere una respuesta específica, a menudo de una palabra; p. 239

pregunta concreta (factual question) pregunta que requiere información que pueda comprobarse; p. 293

pregunta de interpretación abierta (open-ended question) pregunta de amplio alcance que no puede contestarse con una sola palabra como "Sí" o "No"; p. 239

pregunta de opinión (opinion question) pregunta para averiguar el punto de vista que tiene el entrevistado sobre un tema; p. 293

pregunta directa (direct question) pregunta clara y sencilla; pregunta que permite al entrevistador averiguar exactamente lo que desea saber sin dar lugar a dudas o confusión; p. 293

pregunta hipotética (hypothetical question) pregunta sobre cómo reaccionaría una persona en una situación determinada; p. 293

pregunta indirecta (indirect question) pregunta que busca información específica sin preguntar directamente por ella; p. 293

pregunta neutral (neutral question) pregunta que no implica específicamente una respuesta "correcta" o "equivocada"; p. 293

pregunta que sugiere la respuesta (leading question) pregunta que propone la contestación o reacción esperada; p. 293

pregunta secundaria (secondary question) pregunta que facilita al entrevistador la comprensión de una pregunta básica; p. 293

pregunta sumamente cerrada (highly closed question) pregunta que no solamente busca una respuesta específica sino que incluso podría ofrecer varias opciones de respuesta; p. 293

presencia de escena (stage presence) ilusión creada por la calidad de la energía, aplono, confidencia y control que proyecta un presentador ante un público; p. 568

prestar atención (attending) acción de concentrar la atención, consciente o subconscientemente, en un estímulo verbal o no verbal; p. 177

problema (problem) dificultad o incertidumbre; situación que se presenta de manera diferente a la esperada; p. 331

proceso de la entrevista (interview process) sucesión de pasos que se dan durante una entrevista eficaz; p. 283

profecía de realización personal (self-fulfilling prophecy) predicción o expectativa que modela el comportamiento, aumentando las posibilidades de obtener los resultados esperados; p. 88

pronunciación (pronunciation) manera correcta de decir una palabra; p. 108

protocolo (protocol) código de comportamiento establecido y prescripto por una organización; p. 254

R

receptor-emisor (receiver-sender) persona que recibe, o cree haber recibido, un mensaje; p. 39

regionalismo (colloquialism) término propio de una cultura regional específica; p. 120

reglas del grupo (group norms) normas de carácter informal, generalmente tácitas, sobre el comportamiento que debe observarse dentro de un grupo; p. 345

relleno (filler) palabra o frase que se usa para disimular algún titubeo al hablar; p. 127

resistencia (resistance) fuerza interna que impide a una persona aceptar la autoridad de otra; p. 423

resolución de problemas (problem solving) acción de entender la naturaleza de un dilema estableciendo alternativas de solución, identificando la mejor solución e implementándola; p. 331

responsabilidad social (social responsibility) obligación o interés en trabajar en beneficio de los demás; p. 20

respuesta (responding) reacción interna, emocional e intelectual a un mensaje; p. 179

retroinformación (feedback) manera cómo responde una persona ante el mensaje de otra; p. 46

revelación personal (self-disclosure) revelación deliberada de importante información personal que no es aparente a los demás; p. 90

ritmo (rate) rapidez o lentitud con la que habla una persona; p. 149

rito social (social ritual) situación comunicativa que se repite frecuentemente en la interacción social diaria; p. 123

rol (role) papel que asume una persona en una situación o circunstancia específica; p. 5

ruido (noise) todo lo que interfiere con un mensaje; generalmente de manera temporal; p. 44

S

Secuencia motivadora de Monroe (Monroe's Motivated Sequence) estrategia organizativa de cinco partes que se usa en discursos con el propósito de persuadir o motivar al público para que adopte una línea de acción inmediata; lleva el nombre del especialista en comunicaciones A.H. Monroe; p. 494

simposio (symposium) serie de exposiciones preparadas sobre un mismo tema y presentadas por diversos oradores con poca o ninguna interacción entre ellos; p. 546

simposio-foro (symposium-forum) simposio con la participación del público; p. 546

T

testimonio (testimony) cita directa o resumen de una cita; p. 507

tomar de decisiones (decision making) analizar en forma lógica y racional un conjunto de alternativas para elegir la más eficaz; p. 336

tono (pitch) elevación o atenuación de los sonidos en una escala musical; p. 147; (tone) cualidad vocal específica; p. 149

transaccional (transactional) que tiene que ver con un intercambio de algo; p. 35

transmisión (transmitting) proceso físico de transmitir mensajes verbales y no verbales; p. 49

V

verificación de la percepción (perception check) pregunta que ayuda a determinar la validez y precisión de las percepciones que tiene una persona; p. 78

visualización (visualization) representación mental que una persona hace de sí misma, en la cual realiza una tarea con éxito; p. 551

vocabulario (vocabulary) conjunto de palabras que forman parte de un código o lenguaje específico; p. 103

Index

Page numbers in *italics* indicate definitions.

A

B

Index

C

Index

D

E

F

Index

I

Index

N

P

T

Index

U

V

W

Acknowledgments

Ballpoint pen design element for Communication Through Writing pages: PhotoEssentials.

Collage of business memos design element for Communication Through Writing pages: First Image.

Cover (tl)Jon Feingersh/The Stock Market, (tr)Bryan Peterson/FPG, (c)Telegraph Colour Library/Masterfile, (bl)Graham French/Masterfile, (br)First Image; **v** Joe Sohm/Stock Boston; **vi** Jose L. Pelaez/The Stock Market; **viii** Bruce Ayres/Tony Stone Images; **xi** Fisher & Thatcher/Tony Stone Images; **2** Daryl Benson/Masterfile; **3** Aaron Haupt; **4** Doug Martin; **5** Michael Newman/PhotoEdit; **14** CORBIS; **17** ©The New Yorker Collection 1994, Mick Stevens from cartoonbank.com. All rights reserved; **19** Steve Woit/Stock Boston; **20** Courtesy City Year; **21** Melanie Carr/Uniphoto Picture Agency; **22** (l)©1998 DUOMO NBA/F. Medina, (c)Courtesy Mary Kay Inc., (r)Brooks Kraft/Corbis Sygma; **25** (t)Brent Turner/BLT Productions, (b)©The New Yorker Collection 1981, Mischa Richter from cartoonbank.com. All rights reserved; **32** Tony Freeman/PhotoEdit; **33** ©1998 DUOMO/Chris Trotman; **38** William Hart/PhotoEdit; **39** SuperStock; **41 43** Doug Martin; **44** Robin L. Sachs/PhotoEdit; **46** Steve Raymer/CORBIS; **53** Index Stock Photography; **55** Aaron Haupt; **56** David Young-Wolff/PhotoEdit; **59** Jeff Zaruba/The Stock Market; **61** Mary Kate Denny/PhotoEdit; **66** Tony Freeman/PhotoEdit; **68** Tom Able-Green/Allsport; **69** Ken Chernus/FPG; **70** Tim Defrisco/Allsport; **71** Reprinted with permission from *Modern Maturity.* Copyright, American Association of Retired Persons; **72** Aaron Haupt; **80** Reprinted by permission of John Jonik from *Psychology Today;* **83** David Young-Wolff/PhotoEdit; **87** Bruce Forster/Tony Stone Images; **88** Tony Freeman/PhotoEdit; **90** Ariel Skelley/The Stock Market; **98** Tom Able-Green/Allsport; **100** Joe Marquette/AP/Wide World Photos; **101** Dick Hemingway: Photographs; **103** Rafael Macia/Photo Researchers; **104** Robbie Jack/CORBIS; **106** Reprinted by permission of Sidney Harris; **109** Ron Chapple/FPG; **110** CORBIS; **111** Aaron Haupt; **113** North Wind Picture Archives; **116** The Gorilla Foundation/koko.org/Ronald H. Cohn; **118** Bob Daemmrich/Tony Stone Images; **119** Llewellyn/Uniphoto; **120** Richard Hamilton Smith/CORBIS; **123** Bonnie Kamin/PhotoEdit; **124** Timothy Shonnard/Tony Stone Images; **126** Steve Chenn/CORBIS; **132** Joe Marquette/AP/Wide World Photos; **134** James Goodwin/Tony Stone Images; **135** Walter Hodges/Tony Stone Images; **136** David Young-Wolff/PhotoEdit; **138** Sandy Felsenthal/CORBIS; **140** Tom McCarthy/The Stock Market; **144** Mark Peterson/Saba Press Photos; **145** Pablo Corral V/CORBIS; **148** Sergio Dorantes/CORBIS; **150** Fisher & Thatcher/Tony Stone Images; **151** Danny Lehman/CORBIS; **154** Dave Bartruff/CORBIS; **156** PhotoDisc, Inc.; **159** Mark Richards/PhotoEdit; **168** James Goodwin/Tony Stone Images; **170** Don Smetzer/Tony Stone Images; **171** Owen Franken/CORBIS; **174** Steve Chenn/CORBIS; **175** PhotoEdit; **179** Jim Cummins/FPG; **182** Anne Rippy/The Image Bank; **188** Ted Spiegel/CORBIS; **189** (b)PEANUTS reprinted by permission of United Feature Syndicate, Inc., (t)Jose L. Pelaez/The Stock Market; **190** W.B. Spunbarg/PhotoEdit; **191** Ronnen Eshel/CORBIS; **194** Myrleen Cate/PhotoEdit; **200** Don Smetzer/Tony Stone Images; **204–205** Jose L. Pelaez/The Stock Market; **206** R.W. Jones/CORBIS; **207** Jose L. Pelaez/The Stock Market; **208** Walter Hodges/Tony Stone Images; **210** DILBERT reprinted by permission of United Feature Syndicate, Inc.; **211** Jon Riley/Tony Stone Images; **212** Paul Barton/The Stock Market; **213** Roger Ressmeyer/CORBIS; **214** Lawrence Manning/CORBIS; **216** Jon Feingersh/The Stock Market; **217** Annie Griffiths Belt/CORBIS; **222** Chris Brown/Saba Press Photos; **223** Ariel Skelley/The Stock Market; **224** Robert Daly/Tony Stone Images; **228** Bill Luster/CORBIS; **234** R.W. Jones/CORBIS; **236** William Taufic/The Stock Market; **237** Zigy Kaluzny/Tony Stone Images; **238** Stewart Cohen/Tony Stone Images; **241** Bob Daemmrich/Stock Boston; **243** Bruce Ayres/Tony Stone Images; **245** Marc Romanelli/The Image Bank; **249** Gabe Palmer/The Stock Market; **250** Will Hart/PhotoEdit; **253** Michael Newman/PhotoEdit; **260** Jose L. Pelaez/The Stock Market; **261** Aaron Haupt; **263** Walter Hodges/Tony Stone Images; **264** Erik Lesser/Liaison Agency; **270** William Taufic/The Stock Market; **272** Michael A. Keller/The Stock Market; **273** Robert Maass/CORBIS; **274** David Young-Wolff/PhotoEdit; **276** Doug Martin; **278** Robert Brenner/PhotoEdit; **280** By permission of Mell Lazarus and Creators Syndicate; **283** Etena Rooraid/PhotoEdit; **285** Martin Simon/Saba Press Photos; **286** Paul Redman/Tony Stone Images; **287** Tony Freeman/PhotoEdit; **288** Jon Riley/Tony Stone Images; **291** Zigy Kaluzny/Tony Stone Images; **296** Michael Newman/PhotoEdit; **306** Michael A. Keller/The Stock Market; **310–311** Bruce Ayres/Tony Stone Images; **312** Sylvain Coffie/Tony Stone Images; **313** SuperStock; **316** Geoff Butler; **321** Aaron Haupt/Stock Boston; **322** Steve Hansen Photography/Stock Boston; **323** Tony Stone Images; **324** A. Ramey/PhotoEdit; **327** Geoff Butler; **328** Loren Santow/Tony Stone Images; **330** Icon Images; **331** Mark Richards/PhotoEdit; **333** Aaron Haupt; **335** Geoff Butler; **342** Sylvain Coffie/Tony Stone Images; **344** AFP/CORBIS; **345** Aaron Haupt; **346** Douglas Peebles/CORBIS; **349** Bob Daemmrich/Tony Stone Images; **354** The Far Side ©1993 FARWORKS, INC. Used by permission. All rights reserved; **356** Ron Chapple/FPG; **360** David Roth/Tony Stone Images; **361** Aaron Haupt; **362** First Image; **363 through 371** Aaron Haupt; **378** AFP/CORBIS; **380** NW Owen/Black Star; **381** David Young-Wolff/PhotoEdit; **382** Mug Shots/The Stock Market; **384** Jon Feingersh/The Stock Market; **386** THE BORN LOSER reprinted by permission of Newspaper Enterprise Association, Inc.; **388** Telegraph Colour Library/FPG; **390** GARFIELD ©1999 Paws, Inc. Reprinted with permission of UNIVERSAL PRESS SYNDICATE. All rights reserved; **394** Lonnie Duke/Tony Stone Images; **395** Michael Newman/PhotoEdit; **398** Bob Daemmrich/Stock Boston; **400** Richard Bloom/Saba Press Photos; **402** Tom & DeeAnn McCarthy/The Stock Market; **404** Fisher & Thatcher/Tony Stone Images; **410** NW Owen/Black Star; **412** Dirck Halstead/Liaison Agency; **413** Robert Kusel/Tony Stone Images; **414** Pablo Corral V/CORBIS; **419** Sam Sargent/Liaison Agency; **421** Michael Rosenfeld/Tony Stone Images; **423** Michael Rosenfeld/Tony Stone Images; **425** Andy Sacks/Tony Stone Images; **426** Darleen Rubin/Corbis Outline; **429** Walter Hodges/Tony Stone Images; **434** Dirck Halstead/Liaison Agency; **438–439** Fisher & Thatcher/Tony Stone Images; **440** Steve Niedorf/The Image Bank; **441** Ron Chapple/FPG; **443** John S. Stewart/AP/Wide World Photos; **448** Michael Newman/PhotoEdit; **450** Arthur Grace/Corbis Sygma; **452** Walter Hodges/Tony Stone Images; **454** Spencer Grant/Stock Boston; **456** Bruce Ayres/Tony Stone Images; **458** Benelux Press/The Stock Market; **462** Bob Daemmrich/Tony Stone Images; **467** Aaron Haupt; **474** Steve Niedorf/The Image Bank; **476** Bob Daemmrich/Stock Boston; **477** Tim Wright/CORBIS; **478** Kaluzny/Thatcher/Tony Stone Images; **480** Shaun Egan/Tony Stone Images; **481** Reuters/Mike Theiler/Archive Photos; **485** Tony Stone Images; **486** PEANUTS reprinted by permission of United Feature Syndicate, Inc.; **489** Walter Hodges/Tony Stone Images; **492** Bob Daemmrich/Stock Boston; **494** Jonathan Kirn/Liaison Agency; **496** Caroline Penn/CORBIS; **502** Bob Daemmrich/Stock Boston; **504** Jim Sugar Photography/CORBIS; **505** Fisher & Thatcher/Tony Stone Images; **507** Craig Lovell/CORBIS; **510** Andy Sacks/Tony Stone Images; **511** file photo; **512** Lonnie Duka/Tony Stone Images; **514** Doug Martin; **515** David Rubinger/CORBIS; **518** Thomas J. Croke/Liaison Agency; **522** Mark Lewis/Tony Stone Images; **532** Roger Ressmeyer/CORBIS; **533** Tim Cairns; **534** Joseph Sohm, Chromo Sohm Inc./CORBIS; **535** Simon Martin/Saba Press Photos; **539** CORBIS; **542** Kaluzny/Thatcher/Tony Stone Images; **544** Jacques M. Chenet/CORBIS; **546** file photo; **548** Layne Kennedy/CORBIS; **550** By permission of Mell Lazarus and Creators Syndicate; **553** Daniel Bosler/Tony Stone Images; **554** Gregg Mancuso/Stock Boston; **555** Layne Kennedy/CORBIS; **560** Roger Ressmeyer/CORBIS; **562** Ron Chapple/FPG; **563** Fisher & Thatcher/Tony Stone Images; **565** Nathan Benn/CORBIS; **567** Bruce Ayres/Tony Stone Images; **568** Fisher & Thatcher/Tony Stone Images; **569** Bruce Ayres/Tony Stone Images; **569** Rene Sheret/Tony Stone Images; **573** John Pflug; **574** Mug Shots/The Stock Market; **575** Stewart Cohen/Tony Stone Images; **577** Tim Brown/Tony Stone Images; **578** Tim Brown/Tony Stone Images; **592** Ron Chapple/FPG.

Acknowledgments

Grateful acknowledgment is given authors, publishers, photographers, and agents for permission to reprint the following copyrighted material. Every effort has been made to determine copyright owners. In case of any omissions, the Publisher will be pleased to make suitable acknowledgments in future editions.

"Children Learn What They Live" Copyright © 1972 by Dorothy Law Nolte, from the book CHILDREN LEARN WHAT THEY LIVE. Copyright © 1998 Dorothy Law Nolte and Rachel Harris. Used by permission of Workman Publishing Co., Inc., New York. All Rights Reserved.

"Are Students Ready for Work?" Copyright © 1997, *USA Today*. Reprinted with permission.

"Going Online in the United States" from the *Wall Street Journal Almanac,* 1999. Copyright © 1999, Dow Jones & Company, Inc. Reprinted by permission.

Excerpt from I'M OKAY, YOU'RE OKAY, by Thomas A. Harris. Copyright © 1967, 1968, 1969 by Thomas A. Harris, M.D. Used by permission of HarperCollins Publishers.

Johari window, from OF HUMAN INTERACTION by Joseph Luft. Copyright © 1969 by the National Press. Reprinted by permission.

Screen capture from the *New York Times* Web site. Copyright © The New York Times Company. Reprinted by permission.

Excerpts from www.Kent.edu/career/Job, reprinted by permission of The Career Services Center, Kent State University.

Behavior Profile, reprinted by permission of Performax Systems International.

From Schlesinger, Ann Wood (Stace), Ph.D., PUT YOUR MOUTH WHERE YOUR MONEY IS! EFFECTIVE COMMUNICATION ON THE JOB, Cincinnati, Exekuspeak, 1995. Information on DISC is adapted from the Personal Profile System®. ®1994 by Carlson Learning Company, Minneapolis, Minnesota. All rights reserved.

"Mending the Body by Lending an Ear" by Carol Koehler, reprinted by permission of the author.

"Managing the Privacy Revolution" by Harold McGraw III, reprinted by permission of the author.

"Five Ways in Which Thinking Is Dangerous" by Stephen Joel Trachtenberg, reprinted by permission of the author.